CW01123496

BANKS
MUSIC
YORK

NEW OXFORD HISTORY OF MUSIC
VOLUME VII

EDITORIAL BOARD

J. A. WESTRUP (*Chairman*)
GERALD ABRAHAM (*Secretary*)
DOM ANSELM HUGHES
EGON WELLESZ
MARTIN COOPER

THE VOLUMES OF THE NEW OXFORD HISTORY OF MUSIC

   I. Ancient and Oriental Music
  II. Early Medieval Music up to 1300
 III. Ars Nova and the Renaissance (1300–1540)
  IV. The Age of Humanism (1540–1630)
   V. Opera and Church Music (1630–1750)
  VI. The Growth of Instrumental Music (1630–1750)
 VII. The Age of Enlightenment (1745–1790)
VIII. The Age of Beethoven (1790–1830)
  IX. Romanticism (1830–1890)
   X. Modern Music (1890–1960)
  XI. Chronological Tables, Bibliographies, and Index

THE CLOSING SCENE OF HAYDN'S *L'INCONTRO IMPROVVISO*, 1775 (*see p. 178*)
A performance at Esterház under the composer's direction.

THE AGE OF
ENLIGHTENMENT
1745-1790

EDITED BY
EGON WELLESZ
AND
FREDERICK STERNFELD

LONDON
OXFORD UNIVERSITY PRESS
NEW YORK   TORONTO
1973

Oxford University Press, Ely House, London W.1
GLASGOW NEW YORK TORONTO MELBOURNE WELLINGTON
CAPE TOWN SALISBURY IBADAN NAIROBI LUSAKA ADDIS ABABA
BOMBAY CALCUTTA MADRAS KARACHI LAHORE DACCA
KUALA LUMPUR SINGAPORE HONG KONG TOKYO

© *Oxford University Press 1973*

PRINTED IN GREAT BRITAIN BY
RICHARD CLAY (THE CHAUCER PRESS) LTD
BUNGAY, SUFFOLK

GENERAL INTRODUCTION

THE *New Oxford History of Music* is not a revision of the older *Oxford History of Music*, first published in six volumes under the general editorship of Sir Henry Hadow between 1901 and 1905. It has been planned as an entirely new survey of music from the earliest times down to comparatively recent years, including not only the achievements of the Western world but also the contributions made by eastern civilizations and primitive societies. The examination of this immense field is the work of a large number of contributors, English and foreign. The attempt has been made to achieve uniformity without any loss of individuality. If this attempt has been successful, the result is due largely to the patience and co-operation shown by the contributors themselves. Overlapping has to some extent been avoided by the use of frequent cross-references; but we have not thought it proper to prevent different authors from expressing different views about the same subject, where it could legitimately be regarded as falling into more than one category.

The scope of the work is sufficiently indicated by the titles of the several volumes. Our object throughout has been to present music, not as an isolated phenomenon or the work of outstanding composers, but as an art developing in constant association with every form of human culture and activity. The biographies of individuals are therefore merely incidental to the main plan of the history, and those who want detailed information of this kind must seek it elsewhere. No hard and fast system of division into chapters has been attempted. The treatment is sometimes by forms, sometimes by periods, sometimes also by countries, according to the importance which one element or another may assume. The division into volumes has to some extent been determined by practical considerations; but pains have been taken to ensure that the breaks occur at points which are logically and historically justifiable. The result may be that the work of a single composer who lived to a ripe age is divided between two volumes. The later operas of Monteverdi, for example, belong to the history of Venetian opera and hence find their natural place in volume v, not with the discussion of his earlier operas to be found in volume iv. On the other hand, we have not insisted on a rigid chronological division where the result would be illogical or confusing. If a subject finds its natural conclusion some ten years after the date assigned for the end of a period, it is obviously preferable to complete it within the limits of one volume rather than to allow it to overflow into a second. An exception to the general scheme of continuous chronology is to be found in volumes v and vi, which deal with different aspects of the same period and so are complementary to each other.

The history as a whole is intended to be useful to the professed student of music, for whom the documentation of sources and the bibliographies are particularly designed. But the growing interest in the music of all periods shown by music-lovers in general has encouraged us to bear their interests also in mind. It is inevitable that a work of this kind should employ a large number of technical terms and deal with highly specialized matters. We have, however, tried to ensure that the technical terms are intelligible to the ordinary reader and that what is specialized is not necessarily wrapped in obscurity. Finally, since music must be heard to be fully appreciated, we have given references throughout to the records issued by His Master's Voice (R.C.A. Victor) under the general title *The History of Music in Sound*. These records are collected in a series of albums which correspond to the volumes of the present work, and have been designed to be used with it.

J. A. WESTRUP
GERALD ABRAHAM
ANSELM HUGHES
EGON WELLESZ
MARTIN COOPER

CONTENTS

GENERAL INTRODUCTION

INTRODUCTION TO VOLUME VII

I. OPERA IN ITALY AND THE HOLY ROMAN EMPIRE

(a) PROMOTION AND PATRONAGE. By ANNA AMALIE ABERT, *Professor of Musicology, University of Kiel* — 1
Court Opera — 1
Commercial Opera — 3
Travelling Companies — 5

(b) ITALIAN OPERA. By ANNA AMALIE ABERT — 7
Opera seria and the Metastasian Libretto — 8
The Music of *Opera seria* — 12
The Operas of Hasse — 25
Graun and Others — 31
Jommelli and Traetta — 33
Gluck — 42
Later *Opera seria* — 45
Opera buffa: its Styles and Forms — 47
The Composers of *Opera buffa* — 58
Cimarosa and Martin y Soler — 64

(c) GERMAN OPERA. By ANNA AMALIE ABERT — 65
Experiments in *Opera seria* — 66
Benda and Melodrama — 76
German *Singspiel* — 79
Viennese *Singspiel* — 89

(d) THE OPERAS OF MOZART. By ANNA AMALIE ABERT — 97
The Earliest Works — 97
Youthful Works in a Traditional Pattern — 102
The Supremacy of Music over Drama — 119
Idomeneo — 133
The Union of Music and Drama in *Die Entführung* — 141
Between *Entführung* and *Figaro* — 147
Le nozze di Figaro — 149
Don Giovanni — 154
Così fan tutte — 159
La clemenza di Tito — 163
Die Zauberflöte — 166

(e) THE OPERAS OF HAYDN. By H. C. ROBBINS LANDON
Introduction — 172
Composition of the Operas — 173
The Operas Assessed — 183

CONTENTS

II. OPERA IN FRANCE. *By* MARTIN COOPER	200
The 'Querelle des Bouffons'	201
J.-J. Rousseau and the New *Opéra comique*	202
Opéra comique outside France	204
Opéra comique at its Peak	206
Character of the New Genre	207
Monsigny and Philidor	209
Grétry	216
Tragédie lyrique	223
Gluck and French Operatic Principles	226
Iphigénie en Aulide	230
The Character of Gluck's Paris Operas	232
Iphigénie en Tauride	236
Echo et Narcisse	239
Piccinni	239
Salieri	241
Sacchini	243
Cherubini's appearance in Paris	244
Tarare and *Les Souliers mordorés*	244
Opéra comique in the 1780s	250
III. OPERA IN OTHER COUNTRIES	257
(*a*) ENGLISH OPERA. *By* ROGER FISKE	257
Ballad Opera and True Opera	257
Opera with Spoken Dialogue	260
The Work of Dibdin	261
Linley, Arnold, and Shield	263
Stephen Storace	265
Other aspects	268
(*b*) THE RISE OF RUSSIAN OPERA. *By* GERALD SEAMAN, Lecturer in Music, University of Auckland	270
Foreign Opera in Russia	270
The Beginnings of National Opera	271
The Miller-Magician	273
Matinsky, Pashkevich, and Others	274
Fomin	278
(*c*) OPERA IN SPAIN. *By* GERALD ABRAHAM, *formerly Professor of Music, University of Liverpool*	281
Italian Opera in Spain	281
The Later *Zarzuela*	282
The *Tonadilla escénica*	284
IV. CHURCH MUSIC AND ORATORIO. *By* EDWARD OLLESON, Lecturer in Music, University of Oxford	288
Stylistic Problems in Sacred Music	288
Church Music of the Neapolitan School	289

CONTENTS

Hasse's Church Music	291
Vienna and Salzburg	293
Symphonic Influences	298
Joseph Haydn	300
The Josephine Restrictions on Church Music	305
Mozart	306
Haydn's Late Masses	319
Church Music and Oratorio in England and France	323
The Oratorio in Catholic Europe	325
Choral Music in Protestant Germany	328
Haydn's *Creation* and *Seasons*	332
V. SOLO SONG. By ROSEMARY HUGHES	336
England	337
France	341
Germany	344
Austria	352
Haydn's German Songs	355
Haydn's English Songs	357
Mozart's Lieder	359
Mozart's Concert Arias	361
The Solo Cantata	363
VI. THE EARLY SYMPHONY. By EGON WELLESZ, Reader Emeritus, University of Oxford, and F. W. STERNFELD, Reader in the History of Music, University of Oxford	366
Italy: Galuppi and Jommelli	367
Later Italian Opera Overtures	371
Sammartini and the Symphony	374
Later Italian Symphonists	378
The Graun Brothers and Hasse	383
C. P. E. Bach	385
Form in C. P. E. Bach's Symphonies	389
Vienna	395
Monn and Wagenseil	395
Gassmann's Overtures and Symphonies	399
Ordoñez and Leopold Hoffmann	401
Dittersdorf and Vaňhal	402
Michael Haydn	405
Mannheim: the First Generation	407
The Younger Mannheim Composers	414
The Symphony in France	419
Parisian Cosmopolitanism	423
Symphonie concertante and *symphonie périodique*	425
German Symphonists in England	426
Native English Symphonists	429

CONTENTS

The Peripheries	431

VII. THE CONCERTO. By EGON WELLESZ and F. W. STERNFELD — 434

Evolution of the Concerto	434
Pattern and Clichés	437
Preference for the Solo Concerto	439
Performance	439
The Transitional Concerto in Italy	440
The Classical Concerto in Italy	443
North Germany	448
Friedemann and Emanuel Bach	452
Minor North Germans	455
Mannheim	456
The Later Mannheimers	460
The Concerto in Austria	465
Haydn and the Concerto	472
Paris and the Concerto	477
The *Symphonie concertante*	477
The Concerto in England	481
Johann Christian Bach	483
Other Foreigners in London	485
Native British Composers	486
Mozart	487
Mozart's Concertos with Violin	490
Mozart's Wind Concertos	492
Mozart's Piano Concertos	494

VIII. THE DIVERTIMENTO AND COGNATE FORMS.
By GÜNTER HAUSSWALD, *formerly Lecturer in Musicology, Friedrich Schiller University of Jena* — 503

Serenade, Cassation, and Notturno	504
French and Italian Divertimenti	506
Vienna and Mannheim	507
The Haydn Brothers	509
The Mozarts and the Divertimento	511

IX. THE RISE OF CHAMBER MUSIC. By KARL GEIRINGER, *Professor of Music, University of California at Santa Barbara* — 515

Introduction	515
The 'Solo' Sonata	517
The Trio Sonata	521
The Evolution to the Ensemble without Continuo	531
Mozart's Violin Sonatas	539
Mozart's Piano Trios	541
Mozart's Piano Quartets and Quintet	544
Duets for Strings or Wind	545

CONTENTS

String or Wind Trios	548
The String Quartet	552
Haydn's Earlier Quartets	553
Other String Quartets of the Period	555
String Quartets of the 1780s	560
Mozart's Mature Quartets	563
Haydn's Last Quartets	565
The String Quintet	566
Mozart's Quintets	569
Larger Ensembles	572

X. KEYBOARD MUSIC. *By* PHILIP RADCLIFFE, *Lecturer in Music, University of Cambridge*   574

Italy	574
France	578
Spain	579
England	579
Germany	581
C. P. E. Bach	583
Other German and Austrian Composers	593
Haydn	596
Mozart	602

XI. INSTRUMENTAL MASTERWORKS AND ASPECTS OF FORMAL DESIGN. *By* F. W. STERNFELD   611

Introduction	611
C. P. E. Bach and Other Influences on Haydn	613
Haydn's Early Symphonies and Quartets	615
Haydn's Last Symphonies	621
Mozart's Chamber Music	624
Mozart's Piano Concertos	627
Mozart's Symphonies	629

BIBLIOGRAPHY	637
CONTENTS OF *THE HISTORY OF MUSIC IN SOUND*, VOLUME VII	693
INDEX	695

Chapter I(*a*)–(*d*) has been translated by Charles Kessler and Chapter VIII by Peter Ward Jones.

ILLUSTRATIONS

THE CLOSING SCENE OF HAYDN'S *L'INCONTRO IMPROVVISO* (1775) (see p. 178)   *Frontispiece*
A performance at Esterház under the composer's direction. *By courtesy of the Theater-Museum, Munich.*

facing page

I. SCENE FROM JOMMELLI'S *CERERE PLACATA* (see p. 36)   36
A representation of the first performance of 15 September 1772 in Naples. *By courtesy of the Victoria and Albert Museum, London.*

II. A SCENE FROM UMLAUF'S *DIE BERGKNAPPEN* (1778) (see p. 91)   92
By courtesy of the Österreichische Nationalbibliothek, Vienna.

III. THE MAGIC PICTURE FROM GRÉTRY'S *ZÉMIRE ET AZOR* (1771) (see p. 222)   222
By courtesy of the Mander and Mitchenson Theatre Collection.

IV. TITLE-PAGE TO THE VOCAL SCORE OF STORACE'S *THE PIRATES* (1792) (see p. 267)   267
This shows the stage set for Act I, scene I. *By courtesy of the Victoria and Albert Museum, London.*

V. INTERIOR OF THE ABBEY CHURCH AT OTTOBEUREN (see p. xviii)   294
By Johann Michael Fischer (1748–66). *By courtesy of Hirmer Photoarchiv, Munich.*

VI. MOZART: PIANO CONCERTO IN C MINOR (K. 491)   500
First movement, beginning of the recapitulation (bars 361–77). The autograph shows that Mozart thought of the piano as not only solo but also continuo instrument, playing with the orchestra ('c B') through bars 362–5. *By courtesy of the Royal College of Music, London.*

VII. THE WIND PLAYERS OF THE WALLERSTEIN COURT ORCHESTRA.   572
A gold silhouette of *c.* 1785.

VIII. A PAGE FROM NO. 3 OF C. P. E. BACH'S *SONATEN MIT VERÄNDERTEN REPRISEN* (1760) (see p. 586)   586
The composer's own copy showing emendations and variants made by him probably not long before his death. *By courtesy of the Trustees of the British Museum, London.*

INTRODUCTION TO VOLUME VII

By Gerald Abraham

'It was the best of times, it was the worst of times, it was the age of wisdom, it was the age of foolishness . . .' And one might continue that famous exordium by saying 'it was the age of artificiality, it was the age of naturalism, it was the pre-classical era, it was the era of proto-romanticism'. No 'period of transition' has been marked by more dichotomies than the so-called Age of Enlightenment, for the term is a blanket covering very diverse tendencies.

The delicious elegance of Rococo, which embodied itself musically in the *style galant* as it did pictorially in *scènes galantes*, was the legacy of the Baroque age; it was still alive but its artificiality crumbled before Rousseau's naturalism and sentiment. Rousseau's assertion of the rights of the individual was the seed of that passionate revolt against convention which manifested itself in Germany in such works as Goethe's *Götz von Berlichingen* (1772) and Schiller's *Räuber* (1781), though it derived its label from a less distinguished drama, Maximilian Klinger's *Sturm und Drang* (1775). Taking into account that this was also the decade in which Herder began publishing and writing about the folk-poetry of the nations, we are amply justified in talking about 'proto-romanticism'.

On the other hand, 1781 was the year of publication not only of *Die Räuber* but of Kant's *Kritik der reinen Vernunft* which reinforced from a different angle Winckelmann's writings on the art of classical antiquity in helping to still the intellectual 'storm' and contain the emotional 'stress'. Both Kant and Herder had worshipped Rousseau, and nature and reason were also invoked by the other *Encyclopédistes*—the first volume of the *Encyclopédie* appeared in 1751—and by Voltaire: the standard-bearers of Enlightenment. Yet rationalistic Enlightenment cannot be equated with Rousseauism, though Rousseauism was a factor of it. It had a more aristocratic intellectual pedigree and its ideas could be adopted, at any rate in theory, not only by an intellectual élite but by such autocrats as Frederick the Great, Catherine II, and Joseph II; Rousseau was the champion of the common man. The radical thought of the *philosophes* was cool and unemotional; it would never have led to *Sturm und Drang*. The kind of artistic simplicity they admired was not that of Herder's 'voices of the peoples' but rather that of Greek and Roman sculpture, particularly after Winckelmann had written about it in his *Gedanken über die Nachahmung der griechischen Werke in der Malerei und Bildhauerkunst* (1755) and *Geschichte der Kunst des*

Alterthums (1764). Instead of proto-romanticism, they fathered a new classicism.

Music also was affected by the social and cultural ambience, though by no means all the changes it underwent in passing from the age of Bach and Handel to that of Haydn and Mozart can be linked with the ideas of Enlightenment. It is the most nearly autonomous of the arts and some of these changes—for instance, the displacement of harpsichord and clavichord by the pianoforte as the keyboard instrument *par excellence* or the unconscionably protracted demise of the redundant keyboard continuo, still catching its final gasps in Beethoven's C major Piano Concerto at the very end of the century—were no more than a part of the continuing process of exhaustion and renewal of techniques by which Western music always has evolved. But the popularity of the 'concert symphony', leading to the diffusion throughout Europe of printed sets of parts and consequently to the standardization of the orchestra, was the result of social change: the emergence of considerable middle-class audiences—who also flocked to the *opéra comique* in France, the *Singspiel* in Germany, the ballad opera in England, and the pasticcio opera everywhere. The same audiences, when they made music instead of passively listening to it, provided the principal market for the quantities of easy keyboard music, the keyboard sonatas with flute or violin accompaniment, the *Lieder* of the Berlin school, and the host of simple songs and *romances* with keyboard or harp accompaniment which came from the presses of London and Paris. Whether or not we can attribute directly to Rousseauism the vogue for folk-song which suggested to J. C. Fischer and J. C. Bach the introduction of folk-tunes in the finales of concertos, it belonged to the climate of Rousseauism.

The influence of the cultural environment went much deeper than this, however, for the *philosophes* were acutely aware of music, and leading musicians—Gluck, Quantz, C. P. E. Bach, Burney, Grétry—were acutely aware of the *philosophes*. It was not only Rousseau—composer of a great deal besides *Le Devin du village*, inventor of a system of notation, author of numerous writings on music including the famous *Dictionnaire* based to some extent on articles originally written for the *Encyclopédie*—who was deeply concerned with music, but also the leading spirits of the *Encyclopédie*, d'Alembert and Diderot. In his *Discours préliminaire* to the *Encyclopédie* d'Alembert talks about music 'imitating nature' but his *musique imitative* is really only that of the Baroque *Affektenlehre*, the stylized representation of codified *sentimens de l'âme*. Three years later, in his *Réflexions sur la musique*, he discovers a more directly, subtly, and versatilely emotional *musique naturelle* which 'aims not only to please but also to excite emotion':

Nous avons l'organe de l'ouie tellement conformée, que tous les sons harmonieux l'affectent d'une force agréable indépendamment des images qu'ils peuvent présenter à l'esprit ou des idées qu'ils sont capables de réveiller.

At almost exactly the same time C. P. E. Bach was telling the readers of his *Versuch über die wahre Art das Clavier zu spielen* (1753) that

Since a musician cannot move anyone else unless he is moved himself, he must necessarily be able to throw himself into all the emotions (*sich selbst in alle Affeckten setzen können*) which he wishes to arouse in his listeners; he makes his feelings clear to them and stirs them so as to make them feel with him. In languishing and mournful passages he becomes languishing and mournful, as one sees and hears. It is the same with vehement, merry and other ideas (*anderen Arten von Gedancken*) where he straightway throws himself into these feelings. He has scarcely stilled one than he excites another, constantly varying the passions.

Nothing could be further from the Baroque conception of the objective depiction of single emotions.

Diderot had already, in his *Lettre sur les aveugles* of 1749, proclaimed music to be the most intense of all the arts:

Vous pensiez juste ... quand vous assuriez de la musique que c'était le plus violent de tous les beaux-arts, sans en excepter ni la poésie ni l'éloquence; que Racine même ne s'exprimait pas avec la délicatesse d'une harpe; que sa mélodie était lourde et monotone en comparaison de celle d'un instrument, et que vous aviez souvent désiré de donner à votre style la force et la légéreté des tons de [C. P. E.] Bach. Pour moi, c'est la plus belle des langues que je connaisse. Dans les langues parlées, mieux on prononce, plus on articule ses syllabes; au lieu que dans la langue musicale, les sons les plus éloignés, du grave à l'aigu et de l'aigu au grave, sont filés et se suivent imperceptiblement; c'est pour ainsi dire une seule et longue syllabe, qui à chaque instant varie d'inflexion et d'expression. Tandis que la mélodie porte ses syllabes à mon oreille, l'harmonie en exécute sans confusion, sur une multitude d'instruments divers, deux, trois, quatre ou cinq, qui toutes concourent à fortifier l'expression de la première, et les parties chantantes sont autant d'interprètes dont je me passerais bien, lorsque le symphoniste est un homme de génie qui sait donner du caractère à son chant.

Thus did a cultivated, outstandingly intelligent amateur conceive the new music of the mid-century, a conception more sophisticated than Rousseau's with its axioms that music can 'ni toucher ni peindre avec ses beaux accords' and that 'sitôt que deux mélodies se font entendre à la fois, elles s'effacent l'une l'autre et demeurent de nul effet'. And we know from Diderot's edition (1771) of the *Leçons de clavecin* of Anton Bemetzrieder, who taught his talented daughter the harpsichord, that his favourite keyboard composers were Schobert, Honauer, Wagenseil, Eckardt, and C. P. E. Bach (to whom he wrote, asking for manuscript sonatas, when he passed through Hamburg in March 1774). This is confirmed by Burney who listened to the 'pretty and amiable' daughter for several hours and reports that 'not a single French composition was played by her the whole time, all was Italian and German; hence it will not be difficult to form a judgment of M. Diderot's taste in music'.

It was naturally in opera, through its involvement with the other arts, that the new aesthetics first manifested itself most obviously. Diderot, like the other *Encyclopédistes*, took the pro-Italian side in the 'Querelle des Bouffons' and in his *Avertissement* to the sixth volume of the *Encyclopédie* (1756) and the third *entretien* to his play *Le Fils naturel* (1757), like Algarotti in his *Saggio sopra l'opera in musica* (1755), he suggested operatic reforms that foreshadow Gluck. Gluck, or at any rate du Roullet, the librettist of *Iphigénie en Aulide*, must have known both Algarotti's writings and Diderot's. Algarotti appended to his *Saggio* a French libretto on that very subject and Diderot, in his *entretien*, has a dialogue in which his interlocutor quotes two passages from Racine's *Iphigénie* and describes how a composer could set them, one in the manner of *tragédie lyrique*, the other in a way that portends Gluck.

Both French *tragédie lyrique* and international *opera seria* were essentially aristocratic entertainments and, as Professor Abert points out in the opening chapter of this volume, 'breathed the spirit of the courtly convention from which it was born—elevated, spectacular, a portrayal of society in the *ancien régime*'. They were undermined by the Enlightenment, just as the *ancien régime* itself was undermined politically. And the undermining began when 'the Courts could not meet indefinitely the expenses involved in playing exclusively to an invited audience' and were obliged to admit a paying public who in turn favoured the newer, lighter, less rigidly stylized forms of *opera buffa* and *opéra comique*. Even *opera seria* itself became less rigid and more genuinely dramatic in the hands of Carl Heinrich Graun (composer at the 'enlightened' Court of Frederick the Great), Jommelli, and Traetta, while Rousseauism is stamped all over the *opéras comiques* and *Singspiele* with their realistic peasant or urban lower-class characters displaying simple virtue or cunning in the plots and singing melodies as naïve as folk-tunes and often more sentimental. Figaro was only the last and greatest of these triumphant lower-class heroes; *Die Zauberflöte*, greatest of *Singspiele*, glorifies Freemasonry—which was the Enlightenment's substitute for religion.

Religious music of the conventional kind could hardly flourish in this climate. It tended to be either florid and operatic, the equivalent of the Bavarian Rococo churches of Dominikus Zimmermann and J. M. Fischer[1]: or *empfindsam*, as Graun's *Der Tod Jesu* is; or in the contra-

[1] See Pl. V.

puntal *stile antico*; or sober and 'enlightened' like Michael Haydn's Graduals. The Age of Enlightenment was the very opposite of an Age of Faith, and even the faithful were not mystics; indeed eighteenth-century mysticism, so far as it exists, is apt to be nature mysticism rather than religious mysticism—though admittedly Kant thought Swedenborg 'very sublime'. The most vital element in religious music of the period was cross-fertilization from the area of symphonic music.

It is much less easy to define the intellectual, as distinct from the technical, nature of the new spirit in instrumental music. 'Sensibility' manifests itself as obviously in music as in *Pamela* or *The Man of Feeling*—in dynamics and melody, in the expressiveness of the new pianoforte, and even literally in the 'affettuoso', 'dolce', 'amoroso', and 'appassionato' markings which now appear. It is equally manifest in the heightened subjective pre-romanticism of C. P. E. Bach's keyboard fantasias, Mozart's B minor Adagio, K.540, and so many movements in Haydn, as well as mingled with calmer, more objective beauty in the truly classical balance of the final masterpieces of Haydn and Mozart. To isolate and describe the intellectual nature of the change of style is more difficult. An apt motto for the instrumental music of Enlightenment might have been Leibniz's famous definition, 'Musica est exercitium arithmeticae occultum nescientis se numerare animi', which one might translate as 'the hidden arithmetical exercise of a mind unconscious that it is calculating'. The intellect plays a part quite different from that employed in, say, the construction of a fugue; it is intelligence of the kind which Winckelmann said in his *Gedanken* 'the artist should dip his brush in' ('Der Pinsel, den der Künstler führt, soll in Verstand getunket sein'). The Baroque idea of the single emotion sustained through each movement is superseded by a conflict of emotional states within the movement, even within the theme, and this emotional flexibility is reflected in thematic flexibility: a concatenation of seemingly disparate but mysteriously related motives which not only the greatest masters of the period but often lesser ones string together with the surefootedness of sleep-walkers, *animi nescientes*. Tonality also is handled with a new flexibility to produce forms which seem to be 'organic', though they are not really so any more than the concatenation of motives is 'logical', and also excite and hold the interest of the listener. As Dr. Sternfeld puts it in the closing chapter of this volume: 'To recognize in the recapitulation the return of the primary group as well as the secondary and closing groups produced the kind of delight cherished by the Age of Enlightenment, for by this reprise one might understand more thoroughly the significance of the opening section.' This was music not for connoisseurs of singing or instrumental virtuosity nor for those who appreciated the intricacies of learned counterpoint, but for those—and there were now very many—who, like Diderot, were not musicians but loved music and very much wanted to understand it without learning it ('Comme je ne suis point musicien, que j'aime beaucoup la musique, et que je voudrais bien la savoir et ne la point apprendre . . .'). We do not know whether Diderot ever heard, say, one of Haydn's Op. 33 Quartets, with their all-through thematic texture (*durchbrochene Arbeit*) though he could have done. If so, he would almost certainly have listened to it as Goethe did: 'Man hört vier vernünftige Leute sich untereinander unterhalten, glaubt ihren Diskursen etwas abzugewinnen und die Eigentümlichkeiten der Instrumente kennenzulernen' ('You hear four intelligent people conversing, believe you get something out of their talk, and get to know the peculiarities of the instruments')—a remark on which Dr. Sternfeld also comments perceptively, 'The intelligent nature of the discourse and the improvement of the listener's mind were qualities dear to the Age of the Enlightenment.'

We do know that Diderot was aware of Burney's projected *History* and gave him a mass of materials he thought might be of use for it. The eighteenth century was a golden age of historical writing in every field, but Burney's *General History of Music* was in a sense an actual offshoot of the *Encyclopédie*, for he subscribed to the first edition—as Diderot and Rousseau did to his *History*—and he was originally stimulated to authorship by his visit to Paris in 1764. He first contemplated a translation of d'Alembert's *Élémens de musique théorique et practique*, then one of Rousseau's *Dictionnaire*, and only after abandoning that project arrived at his own great conception of a *General History of Music*. Musical historiography was not born in the eighteenth century, but until then there had been nothing comparable with 'Padre' Martini's projected *Storia della musica* (1757–81), the *General Histories* of Hawkins (1776) and Burney (1776–89), or the encyclopedic *Essai sur la musique ancienne et moderne* (1780) of Jean-Benjamin de La Borde. It remained (naturally) for a German, an alumnus of the famous 'Göttingische Geschichtsschule', Johann Nicolaus Forkel, to grapple with musical history scientifically and systematically in his *Allgemeine Geschichte der Musik*, of which the first volume appeared in 1788. Forkel has indeed, with some reason, been claimed as the initiator of *Musikwissenschaft*, although the word itself was not coined until more than seventy years later. People had begun not only to compose music in new ways and to listen to it in a new way; they were about to begin to think about it in a new way.

I

OPERA IN ITALY AND THE HOLY ROMAN EMPIRE

(a) PROMOTION AND PATRONAGE

By A. A. ABERT

IN the mainly German-speaking lands of the vast Holy Roman Empire, the period covered by this volume witnessed the transition from a stricter tradition to 'enlightened despotism'. The Imperial and other Courts still set the standard in every sphere of life, but to a growing degree the middle classes now claimed to play a part in cultural and other affairs.[1] In Italy the rulers of the small states regarded the fostering of the arts as their responsibility to a greater or lesser degree, but such sponsorship lay in fact with the local aristocracy or city fathers. Thus the promotion of opera, the most characteristic cultural activity of the time, was shared between official and private patrons, the latter largely middle-class.

COURT OPERA

Court opera represented a continuation of the oldest tradition of operatic presentation. Performances took place in front of an invited audience consisting normally of courtiers, members of the aristocracy, officers, and officials. Their princely sponsors expected no reward other than their own artistic gratification, the satisfaction of their guests, and some added lustre to their standing. They sought to outdo each other alike in the magnificence of their theatres and performances, the refinement of their stage machinery, and the virtuosity of their singers. Many a small ruler, like Duke Charles Eugene of Württemberg, impoverished his country and alienated the affections of his subjects by trying with insufficient means to compete with the productions of large Courts, particularly the French.[2] Artistic direction, moreover, generally lay in the hands of these rulers, from the Emperor down to the puniest German and Italian potentate. Many were themselves poets or composers, and consequently predisposed to a practical interest in theatrical affairs; but other rulers also were personally concerned. Thus such rulers as the

[1] Hans Engel, *Musik und Gesellschaft* (Berlin–Wunsiedel, 1960), pp. 39 ff.
[2] Rudolf Krauss, 'Das Theater', in *Herzog Karl Eugen von Württemberg und seine Zeit* (Esslingen, 1905), pp. 522 ff.

Empress Maria Theresa and Joseph II in Vienna, Frederick the Great in Berlin, the Electors Max Joseph and Charles Theodore of Bavaria and the Palatinate at Munich and Mannheim respectively, Duke Charles Eugene of Württemberg at Stuttgart, and countless German and other autocrats (for instance, Catherine II of Russia) also play a part in the history of opera.

They threw themselves wholeheartedly into the task of obtaining (for their Courts) the services, whether as guest artists or on longer engagements, of leading Italian singers, stage designers, and composers. They also obtained librettists, whom they appointed Court poets. Among these may be counted Claudio Pasquini at Mannheim and Dresden, Caterino Mazzolà, also at Dresden, Leopoldo de Villati and Giovanni Pietro Tagliazucchi at Berlin, and Mattia Verazi at Stuttgart. The Imperial Court, which had set the precedent in the seventeenth century, could boast the services a hundred years later of Pietro Metastasio, the most renowned Italian dramatist and librettist of his day. There was also much local talent among Court composers and conductors. Johann Adolf Hasse, conductor of the Dresden court orchestra from 1734 until 1763, was, despite his German origin, universally acknowledged during his lifetime to be the most eminent composer of operas. Carl Heinrich Graun, who held the same position in Berlin from 1740 until 1759, was almost his equal. Ignaz Holzbauer, Georg Christoph Wagenseil, Georg Reutter, and Florian Leopold Gassmann, the first at Stuttgart from 1751 to 1753, then at Mannheim, and the other three at Vienna, displayed a virtuosity that allowed them to face Italian competition with confidence. Of the Italian composers (including Giuseppe Bonno at Vienna and Giovanni Ferrandini, Giovanni Porta, and Andrea Bernasconi at Munich) outstanding distinction was achieved only by Niccolò Jommelli, who succeeded Holzbauer at Stuttgart and under whom the opera there experienced its most brilliant period (1753–69).

To begin with, the Courts favoured *opera seria*. The Berlin Opera opened in 1742 with *Cleopatra e Cesare*,[1] the Stuttgart Opera in 1750 with *Artaserse*,[2] both works by Graun, and the Munich Opera in 1753 with *Catone in Utica* by Giovanni Ferrandini. This genre breathed the spirit of the courtly convention from which it was born—elevated, spectacular, a portrayal of Society in the *ancien régime*. Hence an operatic production was always selected as the climax to festivities of all kinds: for birthdays and weddings in the ruling families as well as for State visits and coronations. But from the middle of the century onwards

---

[1] Albert Mayer-Reinach, 'Carl Heinrich Graun als Opernkomponist', *Sammelbände der internationalen Musikgesellschaft*, i (1899–1900), p. 459.
[2] Krauss, op. cit., p. 493.

attention was increasingly paid to the newer, gayer types of composition, such as *opera buffa*, *opéra comique*, and at a later stage the *Singspiel*. They heralded a fresh outlook, less rigidly traditional, which emphasized naturalness and expressed the feelings of the rising middle classes.

Court opera acknowledged the signs of the times by relaxing its social rules and admitting a wider, less aristocratic audience to its performances. Admittedly economic considerations played a prominent part in this conversion: the Courts could not meet indefinitely the expenses involved in playing exclusively to an invited audience. Sooner or later every Court opera began to pass on a part of its outlay to the general public, whether by charging its own admission fees (as happened from 1777 onwards at Stuttgart)[1] or by leasing to independent impresarios (the occasional practice from 1741 onwards at Vienna)[2] or by severely cutting the number of its own productions in favour of subsidies to private theatres (the case from the end of the Seven Years War in 1763 at Dresden).[3] In this way Court opera tended towards commercial opera.

COMMERCIAL OPERA

In its Italian homeland opera was promoted at innumerable centres. Apart from the principal operatic centres of Venice, Naples, Rome, Florence, and Milan, theatres (in some cases more than one) producing opera existed at Bologna, Genoa, Modena, Parma, Turin, and other cities. In Italy, more than in any other country, this art-form was a passion with everyone, from grandee to pauper. Thus, alongside the Court operas and private theatres of the upper classes, there were an immense number of public theatres. These were the property of private individuals or societies and were managed as commercial undertakings by impresarios, who were generally the lessees.

The theatrical year was divided into three seasons: Stagione di Carnovale (26 December until 30 March), Stagione di Ascensione (Easter Monday until 15 June), and Stagione di Autunno (1 September until 30 November). In each season the impresarios were expected to commission one or two new operas from reputable composers, engage the performers, and look after all details of production. Their public was well-informed and expertly critical of the treatment given to this favourite form of entertainment. For them opera was in the first place a matter of arias.

---

[1] Krauss, op. cit., p. 539.
[2] Harald Kunz, 'Höfisches Theater in Wien zur Zeit der Maria Theresia', *Jahrbuch der Gesellschaft für Wiener Theaterforschung 1953–54* (Vienna, 1958) pp. 21 ff.
[3] Richard Engländer, *Johann Gottlieb Naumann als Opernkomponist (1741–1801)* (Leipzig, 1922), pp. 52 ff.

They were ever ready to applaud the texts of Metastasio and his followers, and delighted particularly in the artistry of the singers. If expectations were fulfilled, the applause was generous, but when the performance disappointed, the public was at no pains to conceal its disfavour.[1]

Generally the composer was given the libretto at the same time as his commission (*scrittura*). In *opera seria* the dramatic scheme always adhered to the pattern set by Metastasio. Consequently the composer had merely to discover what singers were available and then furnish an attractive and effective line of melody to suit the generally familiar plot and the particular qualities of individual interpreters.

No less popular was comic opera, *opera buffa*. In cities where several opera houses were available it was frequently played in theatres different from those for *opera seria*. In Naples the latter took place in the old Teatro San Bartolomeo and, after 1737, its successor, the San Carlo, while *opera buffa* was seen at the theatres dei Fiorentini, della Pace, and Nuovo.[2] In Palermo it was the Teatro S. Cecilia which staged *opera seria*, while the S. Lucia (later S. Caterina) specialised in *opera buffa*.[3] The separation was explicable in terms of the very different requirements demanded by the two species of opera. All well-known composers wrote both serious and comic operas, but in the former their art was put principally at the service of individual vocal virtuosos, whereas in the latter it was attuned to the needs of an ensemble.

In *opera seria* it was the singers who ruled; above all, the adored castrati[4]—such as Francesco Bernardi (Senesino), Antonio Bernacchi, Gaetano Majorano (Caffarelli), Carlo Broschi (Farinelli), Gaetano Guadagni, and Giuseppe Millico—were regarded as the most exalted embodiments of a refined, lyrical kind of singing. The reputation of the great divas—such as Marianna Benti-Bulgarelli, Faustina Bordoni-Hasse, Francesca Cuzzoni, Regina Mingotti, and Catterina Gabrielli—stood no lower.[5] If, like Faustina Bordoni, they also possessed acting ability, this was singled out for special praise. But the lack of this ability in singers like Francesca Cuzzoni and Carlo Farinelli did not lessen their popularity. In *opera buffa*, on the other hand, the acting was the main interest; performers had also to be good singers, but virtuosity was from the start restricted by the urge towards simplicity and realism. For

---

[1] Cf. Percy A. Scholes, *Dr. Burney's Musical Tours in Europe*, ii (London, 1959), p. 82.
[2] Arnaldo Bonaventura, *Saggio storico sul teatro musicale italiano* (Leghorn, 1913), pp. 178 ff.
[3] Bonaventura, ibid., pp. 208 ff.
[4] Cf. Franz Haböck, *Die Gesangskunst der Kastraten* (Vienna, 1923); Angus Heriot, *The Castrati in Opera* (London, 1956).
[5] Cf. Margarete Högg, *Die Gesangskunst der Faustina Hasse und das Sängerinnenwesen ihrer Zeit in Deutschland* (Diss. Berlin, 1931).

castrati there was no room in *opera buffa* at all. An impresario had therefore to obtain entirely different sets of artists for comic and serious operas. For the second of these, which depended on individual virtuoso performances, the engagement of a leading castrato or famous female singer was a sufficient attraction. In *opera seria* the emphasis was on soprano and alto voices; tenors were required only for minor parts, basses not at all. In *opera buffa* a well-balanced ensemble and equally matched soloists in all four vocal registers were needed.

TRAVELLING COMPANIES

The popular character of *opera buffa* led to its incorporation into the repertoire of travelling companies of players. It was they who were mainly responsible for its introduction abroad. From 1747 onwards such a company performed in the Palace at Berlin; in 1752 a performance of Pergolesi's *La serva padrona* and other operas in Paris set off the 'War of the Comedians';[1] and in 1757 Giovanni Battista Locatelli's company brought this art-form to St. Petersburg.[2]

Locatelli's company specialized in, but was not limited to, *opera buffa*. It belonged to that category of travelling companies which, like those of Pietro and Angelo Mingotti, appeared wherever there was an unsatisfied demand for Italian opera performances of both kinds. In Germany, unlike Italy, relatively few cities had an organization for the production of opera. In such circumstances these travelling companies were really a counterpart to commercial opera in Italy. They were managed in Germany by impresarios who had to pay fees for permission to arrange performances as well as for the hall where they were to take place, and to recover their whole outlay from the takings. The impresarios in Italy were managers who engaged singers for established commercial undertakings. The directors of travelling companies, however, enjoyed no such support and brought together their ensemble—conductor, singers, musicians, dancers—solely on the credit of their own name. Locatelli, before going to Russia, performed at Prague;[3] the Mingottis travelled up and down Austria, Bohemia, and Hungary (Graz, Linz, Prague, Brünn (Brno), and Pressburg (Bratislava)), northern, central, and western Germany (Hamburg, Lübeck, Leipzig, Dresden, Frankfurt, and Bonn) as well as to Denmark (Copenhagen.)[4] The companies had first-class artists

[1] Cf. Chapter II, pp. 200–2.
[2] Robert-Aloys Mooser, *Annales de la musique et des musiciens en Russie au XVIIIme siècle*, i (Geneva, 1948), pp. 265 ff.
[3] Mooser, ibid.
[4] Cf., for following paragraph also, Erich H. Mueller, *Angelo und Pietro Mingotti: Ein Beitrag zur Geschichte der Oper im 18. Jahrhundert* (Dresden, 1917).

at their disposal: in 1740 Francesca Cuzzoni was a member of Angelo Mingotti's ensemble, and in 1748/9 Gluck was its conductor. Their repertoires and productions in no way lagged behind those of Court operas. They were popular with the audiences and generally enjoyed some additional donations from aristocratic or middle class, courtly or municipal patrons.

Admittedly they could never rely upon success. They might fail to meet the public taste, or they might arrive at an inopportune time, when they had to share attention with German or foreign dramatic companies, or when anticipated lucrative festivities were postponed. So it was no rare occurrence for the impresarios to become bankrupt and for the companies to disperse. Nevertheless these energetic managers always seemed to succeed in getting new companies together again.

The German travelling theatrical companies led a similarly insecure yet even more modest existence. They were at a severe disadvantage in competing with the more magnificent performances by Court operas and travelling Italian opera companies.[1] On their stages music was heard only as a minor part of the entertainment, in the form of interpolated songs or dances or, occasionally, where resources were available, as an overture or intermezzo. Nevertheless, after the middle of the century certain such companies began to pay more attention to the newly emerging *Singspiel*. The first to do this were the Schönemann and, above all, the Koch companies. They were followed by the Doebbelin ensemble, among others, and in Southern Germany and Austria by those of Marchand, Böhm, and Schikaneder. For a long time they were the only exponents of this new style, which did not enjoy any firm support until the foundation of the Vienna 'National Singspiel' by the Emperor Joseph II in 1778.[2] Classical German acting and the beginnings of German opera developed in these companies side by side. It depended upon the attitude of individual directors whether preference was given to plays or *Singspiele*. The members of these companies were always actors, and the earliest *Singspiele* were nothing but plays interspersed with songs. The quality of the acting was therefore much more important than that of the singing. As such pieces became increasingly popular with audiences and the part played by the music became more demanding, managers were obliged to consider more carefully the musical capacity of individual members when assembling their companies. Consequently, these German travelling companies came to consist of a highly versatile troupe in which singers and dancers knew how to act and almost every

---

[1] Cf. Wilhelm Stauder, 'Johann André. Ein Beitrag zur Geschichte des deutschen Singspiels', *Archiv für Musikforschung*, i (1936), pp. 318 ff.
[2] Robert Haas, Introduction to *Denkmäler der Tonkunst in Oesterreich*, xviii, 1.

actor could sing and dance as well (some of them could also play in the orchestra).

In the beginning these companies could afford neither an orchestra of their own nor a conductor. For the most part there was only a single musician available to arrange the scores for the singers and to rehearse them. The managers had to rely on finding instrumentalists in the towns where they performed, a most unsatisfactory system. But in time, and as the musical numbers became longer, more numerous, and more difficult, those companies which mainly produced *Singspiele* began to assemble their own orchestras. At first these were limited to the most essential instrumentalists, such as one or two violinists and one or two oboists who could also play the flute. Nevertheless their size grew rapidly, particularly once companies were able to concentrate more and more on certain places, and finally, to become resident.

The permanent theatres which resulted from these developments towards the end of the century were frequently subsidized by Courts or municipal authorities. They housed travelling and management companies as well as the occasional Court opera ensemble. On their stages all forms of opera were welcome, not only the *Singspiel*. Vienna was an exception, since certain houses there played only, or mainly, the local type of *Singspiel*. But the convergence of styles and the cultivation of various genres in the same theatre was on the whole one of the most important developments of the period. The strict social divisions of the *ancien régime* had disappeared so far as opera was concerned. Opera, once an exclusively courtly entertainment, was now not only open to all interested in it but was supported by all.

(b) ITALIAN OPERA

By A. A. ABERT

Around 1740 Italy stood at the height of its fame as the home of opera. There was continual coming and going between Italy and the countries to the north: northern musicians went to Italy as apprentices while Italians were summoned across the Alps to practise their art there as recognized masters. Among eighteenth-century Italian composers of standing there was hardly one who was not active abroad, whether as a Court conductor or on his own account. In the former capacity, in addition to those already mentioned, there were Davide Perez in Portugal,

Francesco Uttini in Sweden, Giuseppe Sarti in Denmark and later in Russia (where his predecessors and successors included Araja, Galuppi, Traetta, Paisiello, and Cimarosa), as well as Salieri and Cimarosa in Vienna. Of those who travelled on their own account a particularly large number went to Vienna, including Jommelli, Traetta, and Paisiello. Still more went to London (among them Hasse, Galuppi, Lampugnani, Gluck, Guglielmi, Sacchini, Anfossi, Traetta, and J. C. Bach who took up residence there).

Opera seria was regarded in 1740 as the typical Italian opera. It could look back upon a long, varied history and only recently the character of its libretto had been reformed by the poets Apostolo Zeno and Pietro Metastasio[1] to suit the genre aesthetically and dramatically to the period of Enlightenment. *Opera buffa* had just enjoyed its first successes in Italy. The paths taken by the two styles were to be basically different. *Opera seria* developed out of the conventionalized spirit of the courtly social order and was its special medium of expression, while *opera buffa*, in part a reaction against this, seized upon ordinary daily life with all its often trite naturalism. Yet, since the same composers often wrote for both categories, they inevitably shared many trends in common.

OPERA SERIA AND THE METASTASIAN LIBRETTO

Eighteenth-century operatic art is distinguished from the opera of the following period by its strict adherence to the rules. Everything in *opera seria*, starting with the number of acts, scenes, and dramatic personages, the characterizations, situations, and the twists and turns of the plot, even the classification and degree of difficulty of the arias, was laid down beforehand in an exactly defined and well-ordered scheme. A predetermined pattern was equally characteristic of *opera buffa*, which, after all, was also an offspring of Rationalism. But in *opera seria* this rationalism reached beyond a general reflection of the spirit of the times in becoming subservient to the social conventions in which that spirit had found its most marked, if not its most flexible expression.

During the second third of the eighteenth century the style of *opera seria* was profoundly influenced by the personality and work of Pietro

---

[1] Max Fehr, *Apostolo Zeno und seine Reform des Operntextes: Ein Beitrag zur Geschichte des Librettos* (Zürich, 1912); Remo Giazotto, 'Apostolo Zeno, Pietro Metastasio, e la critica del Settecento', *Rivista musicale italiana*, xlviii (1946), xlix (1947), 1 (1948), li (1949); Robert S. Freeman, *Opera without Drama; Currents of Change in Italian Opera, 1675 to 1725, and the Roles played therein by Zeno, Caldara and Others*, L.C. No Mic 67-13, 516 Ann Arbor University Microfilms (Princeton University Dissertation 1967); Sergio Martinotti, 'Un nuovo incontro con Apostolo Zeno, *Chigiana* 25 (nuova serie 5), 1968, pp. 81-98. On opera criticism of the eighteenth century generally, cf. Hugo Goldschmidt, *Die Musikästhetik des 18. Jahrhunderts und ihre Beziehungen zu seinem Kunstschaffen* (Zürich and Leipzig, 1915), pp. 263 ff.

Metastasio. He had passed the peak of his inspiration by the middle of the century, but his influence remained until its end; composers repeatedly re-used his material and librettists continued to follow his pattern faithfully. Whatever the description given to contemporary Italian opera (the old one of 'Neapolitan' is misleading and has recently been more or less rejected), 'Metastasian' is certainly appropriate to libretto-writing.[1]

The paramount significance of Metastasio derives from his unique capacity to identify himself utterly with the spirit of the music and yet to satisfy the inherent dictates of dramatic art.[2] The endless stream of less gifted librettists who followed him could not achieve either one or the other. But they adopted from him what was capable of being copied —which was a considerable amount in view of the highly stylized character of this art-form.

So far as content is concerned, the texts of *opera seria* are in the first place notable for their tendency to exalt a particular virtue which is required to prove itself through a series of difficult inner conflicts and external trials in order to blaze with greater glory in its final triumph over evil. This virtue, in the contemporary view, must be demonstrated at every turn in a moderate and well-bred way, i.e. sensibly and in accordance with the rules of Society. This applies equally whether the dramatic protagonists happen to be figures from classical mythology or from history, from established epics or more or less freely derived from their authors' imagination. The subject (patriotism, feudal loyalty, or claims of friendship, filial love, etc.), the plot and the personages were in fact simply variations upon a single rigid, lofty, and yet in its details highly variable theme. The noble hero and his counterpart, his beloved and her rival, together with the few additional figures moving on the periphery of the drama, always behave—leaving aside external differences in the plot's events—according to the same rules: the hero and his beloved, though obedient to the demands of virtue, invariably find themselves driven by opposing forces (who represent the mainspring of the action) into a conflict between this law of morality and their love. On the brink of despair and ruin a highly astonishing solution is usually arranged and they are rewarded for their steadfastness by being united. This 'lieto fine' (happy end) was in accord

[1] Rudolf Gerber, *Der Operntypus Johann Adolf Hasses und seine textlichen Grundlagen* (Leipzig, 1925); Helmuth Hucke and Edward O. D. Downes, 'The Neapolitan Tradition in Opera', in *Report of the Eighth Congress, New York, 1961*, ed. Jan LaRue (Kassel–Basle– London–New York, 1961), i, pp. 253 ff.

[2] Cf. Giazotto, op. cit. and *Poesia melodrammatica e pensiero critico nel Settecento* (Milan, 1952); Gerber, op. cit.; Andrea Della Corte, 'Appunti sull' estetica musicale di Pietro Metastasio', *Rivista musicale italiana*, xxviii (1921), pp. 94–119, and 'L'estetica musicale di P. Metastasio' in *Paisiello* (Turin, 1922).

with rationalistic morality, and Metastasio and his fellows seldom dared to avoid it. The second couple, whose fate is always interwoven with the first, are also united at the close. Even the villain is forgiven, so that the victory of virtue at once creates a state of perfect harmony.

This form of libretto seems to practise the art of variation not only in the choice and treatment of its themes but also in regard to overall form and details of phraseology. Since plots as a rule were limited to the overriding theme of the triumph of morality (i.e. good sense) and characters were continually repeated types, the dialogue too could not be other than typical. This is sufficiently evinced in the recitatives, which flow in a series of mainly unrhymed lines of changing metre, in many stereotyped turns of speech. The reflective monologues of the arias, usually consisting of two quatrains, are especially subject to these limitations. Their sentiments, whether joyous or melancholy, passionate or tender, martial or loving, find expression in a manner which hardly varies and which is in no way characteristic of the person delivering it. A love-song from Metastasio's *Alessandro nell'Indie*, Act I, scene vii illustrates the point:

Se mai turbo il tuo riposo,	If ever I disturb your rest
Se m'accendo ad altro lume,	If ever I kindle at another light
Pace mai non abbia il cor.	Never let my heart have peace again.
Fosti sempre il mio bel nume,	You were always my beautiful idol
Sei tu solo il mio diletto,	You alone are my delight
E sarai l'ultimo affetto,	And you will be my last affection
Come fosti il primo amor.	As you were my first love.

This could come just as well from a love scene in any other opera, just as any hero could part from his beloved with Alceste's words in Metastasio's *Demetrio*, II, xii:

Non so frenare il pianto,	I cannot stop my tears
Cara, nel dirti addio,	Beloved, in wishing you good-bye,
Ma questo pianto mio	But this is my weeping
Tutto non è dolor.	Is not wholly suffering.
È meraviglia, è amore,	It is wonder, it is love,
È pentimento, è speme,	It is remorse, it is hope,
Son mille affetti insieme	There are a thousand emotions together
Tutti raccolti al cor.	All collected in my heart.

Any hero of opera would be capable of expressing despair as it occurs in Metastasio's *Olimpiade*, II, xv:

Gemo in un punto, e fremo.	In one moment I groan and I shiver.
Fosco mi sembra il giorno,	Dark seems to me the day
Ho cento larve intorno,	I have a hundred spectres round me
Ho mille furie in sen.	And a thousand furies in my breast.

Con la sanguigna face	With blood-red torch
M'arde Megera il petto,	Megaera burns my heart,
M'empie ogni vena Aletto	Alecto fills every vein
Del freddo suo velen.	With her cold poison.

in the same way as every jealous lover could utter his wrath in the following terms (Metastasio, *Zenobia*, I, ii):

Cada l'indegno, e miri	May he fall, the worthless one and see
Fra gli ultimi respiri	During his last gasps
La man' che lo svenò.	The hand which kills him.

Mora, nè poi mi duole	May he die, nor do I grieve
Che a me tramonti il sole,	That for me the sun sets
Se il giorno a lui mancò.	If his day too has come to an end.

Each one of these sentiments could have been inserted into corresponding scenes of different operas. This is particularly true of the so-called simile arias, where the already schematic emotional conflicts seem to conform even more to a single pattern as they are compared to stereotyped conflicts in Nature or between Man and Nature. A special favourite was the parallel drawn between human fate and a ship at the mercy of waves and winds, as Metastasio, for instance, has it in *Ezio*, I, xiii:

Finchè un zeffiro soave	So long as a gentle wind
Tien del mar l'ira placata	Calms the wrath of the sea
Ogni nave è fortunata,	Every ship is fortunate
E felice ogni nocchier.	And happy every pilot.

È ben prova di coraggio	It is a great test of courage
Incontrar l'onde funeste,	To meet the deadly waves,
Navigar fra le tempeste,	To sail through tempests
E non perdere il sentier.	And not lose one's way.

Arias were in fact during the eighteenth century frequently interchanged between operas,[1] while the interpolation of verses from Metastasio into the texts of insignificant librettists was very popular.

The number and distribution of arias within the three acts was another point largely settled beforehand. After Apostolo Zeno's reform of the structure of the libretto only one aria was allowed to each scene and that was, almost without exception, placed at the end, as the singers' final flourish before their exit.[2] The leading parts, being more important, had more arias allotted to them than the secondary ones—a point on which ambitious principal singers of both sexes set the greatest store. Hence the arrangement of the plot depended in large measure on the number and

[1] Gerber, op. cit., pp. 40 ff.
[2] Fehr, op. cit.

importance of the characters, and the satisfactory construction of a libretto resembled the solution of a mathematical problem. The librettist's sole concern, within the framework of a variation upon a given theme, was therefore to achieve a reasonably graceful solution of this task in reasonably singable verses. No one, it was freely admitted, could compete with Metastasio, who himself invented this minutely worked out and polished form of artistry. And yet it was just this strict adherence to rules which tempted so many minor versifiers to try their hands, thus producing a generous supply of thoroughly mediocre librettos. Nevertheless so long as they adhered in form and content to the established rules, there was a composer for them, and also an audience.

THE MUSIC OF *OPERA SERIA*

The main point of interest in *opera seria* was, however, the music. Metastasio was indeed the idol of his time as a poet. But though he was proud of the literary quality of his dramas, and received the critics' praise for this,[1] he owed his popularity with opera audiences to his talent, derived from a combination of musical sensibility and acute artistic understanding, for writing genuine 'poesia per musica'.

Libretto-writing for *opera seria* observed a strict division between the action itself and the reflection of this action in the observations of the various characters. The reflections of the protagonists furnished the composers with their sole opportunities to demonstrate the subtleties of their art. (It must be remembered that composers as well as poets, as true children of their age, were restricted to certain types of form and expression.) The speedy action, which in any case was unsuited to a well-balanced musical shaping, was at the time not thought a matter for composition. It was, therefore, declaimed in a deliberately inexpressive, dry (*secco*) style, the *recitativo secco*.[2] Nor did the composers usually take much trouble over it, since audiences attached no importance to these musically slight portions, not hesitating to chatter or play chess at the back of their boxes during its duration,[3] and giving their attention to the stage again only when an aria was sung. Generally the singers, irrespective of character or situation, were made to recite in a quick *parlando*, much of it held on one note—a monotonous delivery that was broken only by the endings of clauses and sentences, and even then always using stereotyped formulae. The accompaniment confined itself to a few sup-

[1] Goldschmidt, op. cit.; Giazotto, 'Apostolo Zeno'.
[2] Edward Downes, '*Secco* Recitative in Early Classical *Opera Seria* (1720–80)', *Journal of the American Musicological Society*, xiv (1961), p. 50.
[3] Charles de Brosses, *Lettres familières sur l'Italie* (Paris, 1931), ii, p. 36.

porting chords, a limited number of conventional harmonic progressions on the harpsichord:[1]

Ex. 1

Vi - vi e l'og-get - to cam - bia del - le ven - det - te tu - e! Se cerchi un fi - ne, che lo tol - gan gli Dei a cos - to de' miei dì, sia lu - mi - no - so; al - trui non si nas - con - da, e al chia - ro vi - ver tuo fa che ris - pon - da!

(Live, and change the object of your vengeance! If you seek a goal, may the gods forbid at the cost of my life, let it be shining bright; let it not be hidden from others and may it reflect the brightness of your life.)

Busy composers frequently left the providing of this *recitativo secco* to their pupils as hack work.

At first composers rarely used the orchestra in addition to the harpsichord to accompany passages of special emotional intensity in the recitative, but the practice became more common after the middle of the century. In this *recitativo accompagnato*, which often linked *recitativo secco* and aria, singers progressed from dry *parlando* to musically expressive declamation. The orchestra underlined the mood created by the singing and in between vocal passages interpreted the meaning of the text by embellishments of its own:

[1] Exx. 1, 2, 4, 6, 7, and 8 are taken from Hasse's *Arminio* (1745), ed. Gerber, *Das Erbe deutscher Musik*, xxvii.

Ex. 2

Ma che tardo? Ma che tardo a ferirmi... Al fin da forte si vibri il fatal colpo, Disperata...

(Why do I delay? Why do I delay in wounding myself. At last let the fatal blow strike.)

At such points the composer's work disregarded all extra-dramatic purposes, and confined itself to the drama. Indeed, every effort to breathe new dramatic life into *opera seria* during the eighteenth century began by giving more latitude and depth to the *accompagnato*.

The composer's main responsibility, however, lay in the writing of arias. Even here his scope was limited by stringent rules. Since the end of the seventeenth century the earlier formal diversity in song had been abandoned in favour of a single musical form. This was the *da capo* aria in three sections, where the composer set the first and second stanzas differently and at the end repeated the first (I–II–I). By 1740 this formula had for some time been extended to five sections by dividing section I into two parts, thus arriving at the pattern Ia–Ib–II–Ia–Ib. Ia begins with an instrumental ritornello[1] which usually anticipates the actual start of the vocal portion, and ends on the dominant; Ib, after another ritornello, embellishes the same material (including the whole initial quatrain) rather more richly with coloratura, then returns to its original key, and ends with a ritornello. Section II may be related thematically to section I or be independent of it, but is in any case always shorter and simpler, and moves to a related key. The repetition of I, which

[1] Uwe Baur, 'Studien zur Arieneinleitung in der Oper des 18. Jahrhunderts', *Studien zur Musikwissenschaft*, xxvii (1966), pp. 125 ff.

follows after an interlude that is frequently identical with the introductory ritornello, was generally not written out but indicated simply by 'da capo' or 'dal segno' (the latter generally referred to the beginning of the singing, omitting the introduction). This repetition revealed the singer's capacity for finding fresh and ingenious ways of enhancing what had already been heard, particularly where the song had been ornamented with coloratura flourishes by the composer (especially in Ib), and where the final cadences of I and II had already given plenty of scope for the display of his or her gift for improvisation. Shortly after the middle of the century two modifications of the five-sectional aria made their appearance, which had the effect of compressing its content. In one the *da capo* was shortened by half, in the other (recalling the original three-sectional character of the aria) there was an undivided opening section and a fully written out, usually diversified, repetition. These modifications served to give greater variety to the composition, but in their application were just as strict as the original framework had been.

These musical structures illuminate the spirit which animated this art-form. It was dominated by the desire for clarity and symmetry. The composer was from the outset kept from employing modes of expression which were too subjective or too strongly contrasted, while the singer was challenged to deploy all the virtuosity at his disposal.

For it was the singer, or, more accurately, the extremely refined artistry which singers could display, that was the pivot of *opera seria* of the time. The inexhaustible resilience of audiences in facing again and again the same operatic plots and texts, even in the works of second-rate musicians, can be explained only in terms of a primary delight in singing, which was able entirely to disregard the words and accompaniment. It mattered, of course, whether a composer had a natural bent for lyricism and could adapt himself to the idiosyncracies of a singer. He had to know the latter's capabilities precisely and judge to a nicety what he could demand of him by way of nimble arpeggios, vaulting intervals, long-held notes, and other vocalists' tricks, but it was the art of improvisation that was considered the highest achievement of a singer. What could be achieved in this direction may be exemplified in the case of the soprano castrato Carlo Broschi, called Farinelli:[1]

Ex. 3

[1] From Haböck, op. cit., p. 141.

(That nightingale who amorous sings alone.)

Contemporary satirists[1] delighted in attacking the public adoration in which such virtuosos basked and the outrageous vanity and arrogance which led them to become sheer tyrants of the operatic stage.

In an entertainment which concentrated so much upon vocal effects, the orchestra naturally played a secondary part, as a rule merely accompanying the singer and taking care not to drown him. In essence the orchestra consisted of a string quartet: first violin (normally playing the melody in unison with the voice); second violin and viola (in subordinate accompanying and harmonizing roles); and violoncello (supported by a double bass and, at times, the harpsichord, and providing the foundation of the texture). Often enough composers contented themselves (especially in the middle section of arias) with orchestration in three parts:

[1] Cf. above all Benedetto Marcello, *Il teatro alla moda* (Venice, undated, probably 1720; English translation by Reinhard G. Pauly, *Musical Quarterly*, xxxiv (1948), p. 371, and xxxv (1949), p. 85), whose description also holds good for the period after 1740.

either the second violin being in unison with the first (see Ex. 6 below) or the viola in octaves with the bass, as for instance in the following bars from the middle section of the aria quoted as Ex. 8:

Ex. 4

qual sia t'ap-pren-de-rà il pro-prio tuo des-ti-no qual via,

(What it may be, your own destiny will teach you, what path)

Only rarely—when the text was especially descriptive or its emotional content invited such a course—did composers allow the orchestra any greater individuality, by releasing the first violin from its association with the vocal line, or by allowing the middle parts to enjoy a musical function of their own. In the opening aria of *Il re pastore* by Hasse[1], for example, the viola imitates the murmuring of the brook:

Ex. 5

(quel)bas-so mor-mo-ri-o, quel bas-so mor-mo-

[1] Dresden, Sächsische Landesbibl. 2477/F 81.

(That low murmur)

By way of wind instruments there were often flutes and/or oboes, which followed the lead of the violins, and horns to add volume (see Ex. 8 below). For symphonies, marches, festive choruses, and suitable arias, composers also occasionally employed trumpets. If the specific character of the aria required it, all the instruments could be used in concerto fashion, vying either with the violins or with the voice.

The age demanded balance and smoothness, to which was added the Italians' insistence on vocal virtuosity. But everything was subject to the needs of an emotional content already precisely established. The challenge so crucial to Romantic and post-Romantic composers, to come to personal terms with a libretto and to provide an individual interpretation, was unknown to composers of *opera seria*. For them, children of the Enlightenment, natural behaviour and good sense were identical, the latter being represented by moderation and orderliness. These were limits which at all times had to be strictly respected even though violent emotions might be involved. Only by obedience to these laws could a composer fulfil his own hopes and the expectations of his contemporaries: by creating a 'pleasing', at the most 'affecting', certainly never a stirring impression. This also was the way in which it was possible to produce types of aria which were musically predetermined though differentiated in expression.

It was a matter of course that composers of the Age of Sensibility should be particularly successful in the expression of gentle and delicate sentiments of joy and sorrow. This gave the singers opportunity to revel in soft, lyrical, yet wonderfully balanced, truly 'cantabile' melodies, often in triple rhythms, which the orchestra supported with suitable discretion. This type is clearly shown in Ex. 6:

Ex. 6

(If my idol is dear to me, Love knows, the gods know.)

The opposite emotions, fear and dismay, found their musical expression in impetuously dashing arias, phrased in a short, abrupt, and breathless manner (*quasi parlando*), frequently driven forward on a syncopated rhythm which would be only sparingly accompanied by the orchestra:

Ex. 7

(You promise me the glory of a brave spirit, it is true, but you take from me meanwhile the freedom to love.)

Should these outbursts become charged with fury and despair, bellicosity and the flush of victory, then the composers seized the chance, so far as was consistent with the opera and the singing, to introduce bravura arias with fanfare-like progressions in triads, large leaps, and a profusion of coloratura virtuosity, often accompanied by solo instruments:

Ex. 8

(Go, proud one, daring one, go, go, you shall have war; the peace you have refused will cost you dear.)

These three types of aria, entirely different musically and in the demands made upon the singer, were at that time classified as *aria cantabile, aria parlante, aria di bravura*,[1] and were distributed through the opera according to the requirements of the text, which determined their character. The more solemn *aria di portamento* and the less dramatic *aria di mezzo carattere* still displayed kinship with the first; they were mostly sung by the second-line male and female singers, as Ottone's aria in Hasse's *Ruggiero*, II, i exemplifies:[2]

---

[1] John Brown, *Letters on the Italian Opera* (London, 2nd edn., 1791). pp. 36 ff.
[2] Dresden, Sächsische Landesbibl. 2477/F 97.

Ex. 9

[musical notation with text: "E dal cor so al - te - ro fiu - me l'ar - re - star dif - fi - cil me - no l'ar - re - star dif - fi - cil me - no"]

(Less difficult to stop a proud river from its course.)

The conventional texts of the metaphor-laden arias presented the composers with a welcome opportunity to ring the changes on the different types of aria without foregoing the number wanted by the singers. Descriptions of storms at sea, tempests, and battles of all kinds were the favourite subjects, for instance, for the *aria di bravura*, whereas the *aria cantabile* was suited to the idyllic cooing of turtledoves, murmuring brooks, and whispering breezes. A magnificent reproduction of a tempest, where the instruments play an independent part, is represented by Alessandro's aria in Hasse's *Il re pastore*, I, iii, of which some bars are reproduced here:

Ex. 10

(co)-sì___ e fol - go - ra e mi - nac - cia sull'
a - - - - - ri - do ter - ren e
(+ Oboes)
fol - - - go - ra e mi - nac - cia

(and flashes and threatens on the barren earth.)

The whole art of *opera seria* was directed so exclusively towards development of the individual vocal line that ensembles were completely thrust into the background—the different voices would, especially in the case of anything more than a duet, have only impeded each other. For this reason trios and more numerous combinations were distinct exceptions after 1740. Even duets were rare. They would occur occasionally as expressions of lamentation on the part of a pair of lovers, when they would generally be sung in the three-sectional *da capo* aria form with the voices usually starting after each other on the same line of melody and then proceeding together at intervals of thirds and sixths. So here too it was primarily a matter of bringing out a fine vocal tone, for which no special technical ability was required of the composer.

It is obvious that the choral and purely instrumental musical portions were bound in these circumstances to play an even more insignificant part. The chorus habitually made its appearance at the end of the third act to provide a close to the opera that was conventional, composed in chordal homophony, and festive. Even when it appeared in magnificent crowd scenes during the course of a performance, it lacked proper musical function and was merely there to add to the richness of sound. The same applied to instrumental movements when these were sparingly interspersed as processional or march music.

In the overture[1] the composer was free from the fetters of stage action, but still not from the rigidities of contemporary conventions. It too followed a set pattern and broadly reflected in its three movements characteristics of the various types of aria. Often the festive and spirited opening movements with their use of triad themes, runs of scales, dotted rhythms, and large leaps, preferably over drumming basses, are reminiscent of arias which express triumph, wrath, or vengeance. The idyllic slow second movements corresponded to the tender love-songs, and the manner of the final movements, quick, cheerful, and not infrequently dance-like, was echoed now and again in the gay style of the secondary vocal parts.

Between the acts of *opera seria* were played either short, comic scenes —so-called intermezzi—which had a high standard of comedy; or, following French fashion, ballets. The latter were particularly designed to satisfy the desire of Court audiences for splendour of décor. It was rare for a composer to write the ballet music himself, as Mozart did for *Idomeneo*. Usually this was left to some member of the orchestra who frequently remained anonymous. The practices of Stuttgart (under Jommelli) and Vienna differed in this respect. At Stuttgart Florian Deller and Johann Joseph Rudolph were inspired to outstanding achievements by the French choreographic reformer Noverre;[2] and in Vienna respected composers like Franz Aspelmayr and Josef Starzer were employed especially for ballet.

Courtly splendour was also to the fore in the case of the *serenata* or *festa teatrale*, an entertainment not basically different from *opera seria*. These occasional pieces, in one or two acts, intended for festivities in princely houses, were generally based on vacuous, conventional texts paying homage to the patrons under mythological guise, and were accompanied by music of a rather colourless kind.

Nothing reveals more clearly the lack of major dramatic themes in *opera seria* than the popularity of *pasticcio* (literally, 'pie'). This was the

---

[1] Cf. Helmut Hell, *Die neapolitanische Opernsinfonie in der ersten Hälfte des 18. Jahrhunderts* (Tutzing, 1971).
[2] Hermann Abert, *Niccolò Jommelli als Opernkomponist* (Halle, 1908).

name given to operas where the music was by different composers, either because from the start each of the three acts had been separately commissioned or because when an opera was repeated in a different theatre managers or singers inserted new arias by other composers, or had the old texts set to new tunes.

THE OPERAS OF HASSE

The style of *opera seria* remained established for as long as the outlook reflected by the libretti continued. The works of Johann Adolf Hasse (1699–1783) showed it in its purest form and were for his contemporaries the ideal accomplishments of their kind. Though German-born, he dedicated himself wholeheartedly to the spirit of Italian opera[1] during his residence in Italy and remained faithful to it for the rest of his life. This spirit he had acquired in Naples from the aged Alessandro Scarlatti, Nicola Porpora, and above all Metastasio, who was of his own age and towards whom he felt a particularly close affinity throughout his creative life. He set nearly all Metastasio's dramas to music. His last opera, *Ruggiero*, was also the poet's last work. Hasse lived in Italy from 1722 until 1733, first in Naples, then in Venice. He soon became a popular favourite and was given the complimentary appellation 'il caro Sassone'. Even when he became Court conductor at Dresden, he still remained the leading *opera seria* composer and made extensive journeys, sometimes alone, sometimes with his wife Faustina Bordoni, one of the most celebrated singers of her time. These visits took him to Italy, his adopted homeland, and to other European countries, including England.

What was so much admired in Hasse's operas was the combination of musical invention with deep insight into the purpose and character of *bel canto* and a highly developed sense of drama. Charles Burney, who was thoroughly familiar with the master and his works, expressed current opinion when he said that Hasse was of all living musicians 'the most natural, elegant, and judicious composer of vocal music'.[2] He called Hasse 'natural' because of the latter's ability to achieve the greatest effects by the most economic means; 'elegant' because of his masterly command of composition and vocal techniques; and 'judicious' because of the balance instinctively maintained between the preserves of poet, singer, and composer.

In these circumstances it is not surprising that Hasse enjoyed the trust

[1] Cf. Carl Mennicke, *Hasse und die Brüder Graun als Symphoniker* (Leipzig, 1906); Gerber, *Der Operntypus*.
[2] *The Present State of Music in Germany* . . . 1st edn. 1773, 2nd edn. 1775; reprinted and ed. Scholes, op. cit., ii, p. 82. Cf. also facsimile edition of German translation (Hamburg, 1773), ed. R. Schaal (Kassel, 1959), ii, p. 173.

and esteem of his intellectual *alter ego*, Metastasio.[1] Like him, he understood perfectly the art of moderation and in his operas displayed emotion only so far as would be tolerated by the taste of his time, which was primarily concerned with maintaining balance, clarity, and elegance. As with the poems of Metastasio, there is virtually no creative progress to be observed in his fifty-six or so dramatic works, *opere serie* and *feste teatrali*, composed over a period of half a century (from 1721 to 1771). Development is only to be seen in the arias in so far as the two curtailments in the rigid five-part scheme (see p. 14) are made more and more frequently in the operas after the fifties.[2] *Accompagnato* recitative is also used more often and for longer stretches in the later works. In *Ruggiero*, for instance, it plays a prominent part not only in the monologues but in the dialogue between leading personalities, as shown in the excerpt here from Act II, scene ix:

Ex. 11

[1] Metastasio was particularly complimentary in his detailed letter of 20 October 1749 on *Attilio Regolo*. Cf. Mennicke, op. cit., pp. 405 ff.
[2] Gerber, *Der Operntypus*, pp. 173 ff.

vo . . . se res - to . . .
LEONE
Er - mi - nio? A - mi - co, ah qua - le in - du - gio è
RUGG.
que - sto! Ec - co - mi a te! Vie - ni, t'af - fret - ta!
OTTONE
E sen - za ri - spon - der - mi tu par - ti?
RUGG.
Ah, per pie - tà non tor - men - tar - mi!

(Ruggiero: I feel my heart break into a hundred parts.

Ottone: Come, make up your mind, Ruggiero!

Rugg.: If I abandon the one ... if I thus forget the other ... if I go ... if I stay ...

Leone: Erminio? Friend, ah what delay is this!

Rugg.: Here I am (ready) for you! Come, hurry!

Ottone: Do you leave without answering me?

Rugg.: Ah for pity's sake do not torment me!)

This forward-looking technique in Hasse's late creations was overshadowed, however, by the rigid conventions governing the types of aria which, in early and late works alike, retained their importance and traditional style. Yet, though the kinds of melody and rhythm remained as before, within these narrow limits Hasse's richness of invention was admirable. This is especially evident in those arias where the middle section stands in contrast to the first. In Act I, scene i of *Il re pastore* (1755) the shepherdess Elisa sings the following charming song:

Ex. 12

(I shall go with my beloved flock to the wood, to the meadow, to the fountain.)

The introduction of the F minor key and the unison of orchestra and voice in the middle part are marked departures from the caressing tone of the beginning:

Ex. 13

Tu ___ quel roz - zo an - gu - sto tet - to che ___ ri - cet - to a noi ___ da - ra

(You, that rough and narrow roof which will give us shelter.)

The contrast becomes even stronger when both parts of an aria belong to distinctly different types of music. In Leone's aria 'Quell' ira stessa' in *Ruggiero*, II, iii, the first part is driven forward on a syncopated beat whereas the middle portion flows gently along in 3/8 time:

Ex. 14

Quell' i - ra i - stes - sa che in te ___ fa - vel - la, che in te ___ fa - vel - la di -

(That same anger which speaks in you, becomes so beautiful.)

(If your scorn is so beautiful, what would your pity be?)

In scenes iv and v of Act III of the same opera the lovers Bradamante and Ruggiero sing two laments which Hasse clearly meant to be related to one another, since both are written in C minor and combine sensitive

(with musical notation)

se — mi — re - si - ste il   cor

(I shall obey you, beloved, if my heart endures.)

(ii) Pur mi - se - ra qual so - no al mio do - lor per - do - no se da — si du - ro pas - so sa — li - be - rar mi al - men

(Yet, wretched as I am, I overlook my suffering if from such hard straits it can at least free me.)

singability with vigorous rhetoric. In the first, Ex. 15, the cantabile part is at the beginning, in the second, Ex. 16, it stands in the middle.

GRAUN AND OTHERS

Hasse brought Metastasian opera to its highest musical–dramatic pitch and thus expressed the spirit of his age to a finer degree than any

Ex. 16
(i) Ho per - du - to il mi - o te - so - ro o - gni

spe - me ho già smar - ri - ta

(I have lost my treasure, I have already lost all hope.)

(ii) M'ha ra - pi - to il fa - to a - va - ro quan - to al mon - do a me fu ca - ro

(Covetous fate has stolen from me all that was dear to me in this world.)

other contemporary composer of *opera seria*. How far these other composers, especially younger ones, were directly influenced by Hasse is an open question, for the operatic pattern was laid down for them by tradition. In principle they were all his disciples—those from the North of Italy, Giovanni Battista Lampugnani (1706–84), Baldassare Galuppi (1706–85), Giuseppe Sarti (1729–1802); as well as those from the South, Davide Perez (1711–82), Niccolò Jommelli (1714–74), Tommaso Traetta (1727–79), Pasquale Anfossi (1727–97), Nicola Piccinni (1728–1800), Pietro Guglielmi (1728–1804), Francesco di Majo (1732–70), Antonio Sacchini (1734–86), Giovanni Paisiello (1740–1816), even Domenico Cimarosa (1749–1801) and Antonio Salieri (1750–1825) at the outset of their careers; also the Spaniard Domenico Terradellas (1713–51) and the Germans Carl Heinrich Graun (1703/04–59), Johann Christian Bach

(1735–82), and Johann Gottlieb Naumann (1741–1801), to mention only the most important names. Gluck and the much younger Mozart also began their composition of operas with works falling into the *seria* category. Naturally each brought to the form his individual interpretation, derived from his background and talent and the generation to which he belonged.

The operas of Graun were remarkably close in style to those of his compatriot, Hasse. Frederick the Great admired Hasse but was also greatly interested in the operas of his Court conductor, for whom he sometimes wrote libretti. Influenced by the King's taste, Graun in his last works favoured the simpler pattern of the two-part cavatina over the traditional *da capo* aria. The cavatina had previously been used sporadically but came to be employed more frequently as composers sought to achieve greater flexibility within the rigid scheme. Graun's first consistent application occurred in *Montezuma* (1755), an opera well above the contemporary average, the text of which had been written in French by the King himself and then translated into Italian by the Court poet Tagliazucchi.[1]

JOMMELLI AND TRAETTA

One section of the young school of composers was inclined (usually after some initial efforts in Hasse's well-balanced manner) to deviate from the traditional style by a more intensive treatment of the dramatic elements; while another group tended to upset the balance by giving unbridled rein to purely musical considerations.

To the first belonged, above all, Niccolò Jommelli and Tommaso Traetta. In contrast to their contemporaries they did not confine their activities to a display of their native art to an admiring public that was exclusively Italian. Both were for a short period in Vienna for performances of their works, Jommelli in 1749/50, Traetta in the early sixties. They also found engagements at courts under strong French cultural influence: Jommelli from 1753 to 1769 as Court conductor at Stuttgart, and Traetta from 1758 to 1765 at Parma. They took advantage of the opportunity to acquire fresh knowledge and extend their powers of expression.[2] They turned to their own purposes the achievements of the Viennese opera tradition and of French opera to bring plot and music closer into line, so far as the framework of traditional *opera seria* permitted. The sharp contrast between *secco* recitative and arias was

[1] Ed. Mayer-Reinach, *Denkmäler deutscher Tonkunst*, xv; the cavatina 'Godi l'amabile' is reprinted in Archibald T. Davison and Willi Apel, *Historical Anthology of Music*, ii (London, 1950), p. 214. Cf. Mayer-Reinach 'Carl Heinrich Graun' and Mennicke, op. cit.
[2] Cf. Donald Grout, *A Short History of Opera* (New York and London, 2nd. edn., 1965), p. 221.

softened by replacing the former, to a considerable extent, with expressive *accompagnati*, occasionally interspersing the arias with recitative passages, and introducing many formal modifications into the arias themselves. In addition, their operas contained dramatic choruses and ensembles as well as full-scale instrumental movements to underline the drama. These diverse elements were no longer linked by *secco* recitative as the traditional agglomeration was replaced by extensive scenes, the component parts of which were blended into unity by stirring *accompagnati*. The growing independence and refinement of the orchestra in arias, *accompagnati*, and purely instrumental movements reflected the influence of the flourishing state of German instrumental music of the time. The introductory symphony, hitherto an independent and interchangeable piece, was drawn into a relationship with the work either thematically or by being continued into the first scene.

Jommelli regarded Hasse as his mentor (though he was not his pupil) and is said to have held him always in high esteem, above all for his artistry in avoiding excess of any kind.[1] For a long time he also enjoyed the especial goodwill of Metastasio[2]—a clear sign that to begin with he adhered fully to tradition. Nevertheless his efforts to give recitative and arias dramatic flexibility and to achieve independence for the orchestral parts are noticeable very early on, even before his sojourns abroad. This is shown in the growing number and greater length of the *accompagnati* just as it is also evident from the orchestra's independence of vocal line in general:[3]

Ex. 17
SEMIRAMIDE (1742)

(The waves are stilled.)

[1] Abert, op. cit., p. 105. [2] Ibid., pp. 50 ff. [3] Ibid., p. 164.

and the independence of the middle parts, particularly of the wind instruments:[1]

Ex. 18 (i)
ACHILLE IN SCIRO (1749)

[musical notation with text: Quell' on - da ri - stret - ta in va - no si ren - de]

(That wave when dammed turns in vain . . .)

(ii)
DEMOFOONTE

[musical notation with text: Se tut - ti i ma - li mie - i, se tut - ti i ma - li mie - i io___ ti po - tes - si dir]

(If I could tell you all my woes.)

One may observe, in his Vienna period, a certain partiality towards the insertion of independent instrumental movements, while in operas

[1] Ibid., pp. 240 and 184.

composed for Italy later on there were to be found carefully worked out ensembles rather than the more traditional duets.

Prior to the operas composed for Stuttgart Jommelli had in more than twenty pieces prepared for the stage of his artistic development already described, which may properly be called 'musical–dramatic'. At Stuttgart he had the stimulus of French opera, which was dramatically more lively and rich in great orchestral and choral movements. This is shown particularly in his operas *L'Olimpiade* (1761), *Vologeso* (1766), and *Fetonte* (1768). Although he still adhered to the Metastasian style, Metastasio himself warned him in 1765 against neglecting the power of song to stir the heart in favour of an all too artistic orchestral treatment.[1] This shows that Jommelli had in those years abandoned Hasse's ideal of the primacy of song in opera in favour of a dramatization of all the facets of musical sonority. Passages like the following from Act I, scene vi of *Fetonte*, the last *opera seria* written for Stuttgart,[2] where the vocal part intermingles with orchestral phrasing instead of dominating it

Ex. 19

(Ah, pardon!)

[1] ibid., p. 352. [2] Ed. Abert, *Denkmäler deutscher Tonkunst*, xxxii–xxxiii. His last stage-work was a dramatic cantata *Cerere placata* (1772) for the Neapolitan court (see pl. I).

PLATE I

SCENE FROM JOMMELLI'S *CERERE PLACATA* (see p. 36)
A representation of the first performance of 15 September 1772 in Naples.

are no rare occurrence, especially at emotional points. The same basic principle of equality between voices and instruments prevails in numerous extended and finely worked out *accompagnati*, as for example in *Fetonte*, II, iii:

Ex. 20

(Adagio)

tu qui res - ti, o Fe - ton - te?

E qual t'in - gom - bra in - do - len - te stu - po - re?

Ir - re - so - lu - to chi ti re - se co -

(Do you stay here, Phaethon? What indolent stupor weighs you down? Who has made you so irresolute? Perhaps you don't believe it? Perhaps? But what?)

and also in those sections of major scenes where voices and instruments, soloists, chorus, and orchestra are interwoven according to dramatic requirements.

Traetta[1] started with the same operatic conventions as Jommelli, but was readier to experiment. He was younger than the latter when, at Parma, he came into contact with endeavours to unite Italian and French opera styles on the lines of Jommelli's at Stuttgart. His work did not display quite such consistent progress as did that of the older composer. Nevertheless his principal operas (above all, *Sofonisba* (Mannheim, 1762), *Ifigenia in Tauride* (Vienna, 1763), and *Antigona* (St. Petersburg, 1772))[2] attain at least the same level in daring of musical and dramatic

[1] Henry Bloch, 'Tommaso Traetta's Reform of Italian Opera', *Collectanea Historiae Musicae*, iii (1963), p. 5.
[2] Specimens from these works, ed. Goldschmidt, in *Denkmäler der Tonkunst in Bayern*, xiv (1) and xvii. Cf. also Goldschmidt's introduction to xiv (1), and, on Traetta's stay in Russia, Mooser, op. cit., ii. Also Antonio Nuovo, *Tommaso Traetta* (Bitonto, 1938); Adelmo Damerini, 'Un precursore italiano di Gluck: Tommaso Traetta', *Il pianoforte* (July 1927).

conception. His treatment of the orchestra in the case of *accompagnati* and arias is just as independent and expressive:

Ex. 21 (i)
LA SOFONISBA (1762)

(Everything yields to your valour, O unconquered companions, and everything yields to the destiny of Rome; now that Syphax is conquered Africa is conquered. Already emulous Carthage at the sad news . . .)

(ii)
IFIGENIA IN TAURIDE (1758-9)

(Like a murderous right hand, death approaches me.)

and indeed in the dramatic employment of the chorus Traetta goes far beyond Jommelli. The Furies scene of *Ifigenia*, II, iv:

Ex. 22

(The sad neglected mournful shade)

interspersed as it is by Orestes' solos, and the mourning for the dead in *Antigona*, II, i:

Ex. 23

A-scol-ta il nostro pianto, a-scol-ta il nostro pianto, i gemiti, i sospiri, i gemiti, i sospiri

(Listen to our tears, our moans, our sighs.)

are close to Gluck. Significantly enough, the texts for these two operas were based on texts by the Vienna Court poet Marco Coltellini, who was himself familiar with the reforming ideas of Gluck's librettist, Ranieri Calzabigi.

GLUCK

Gluck's *Orfeo* (1762)[1] originated not only as a birthday celebration for the Emperor Francis, a fact which determined its character, but also as an implicit demonstration against the court poet Metastasio. The anti-Metastasio faction was led by two other Italians: the Genoese Count Durazzo, Intendant of the Court Theatre and part librettist of Traetta's *Armida* (Vienna, 1761), and the Livornese Ranieri Calzabigi, who had

[1] *Denkmäler der Tonkunst in Österreich*, xxi (2), ed. H. Abert, and *Gesammelte Werke*, ed. Gerber *et al.*, i.

spent a number of years in Paris. Another Italian member of the clique was Gasparo Angiolini, the dancer for whom Gluck had written in 1761 the dramatic ballet *Don Juan*, which may be regarded as the first practical implementation of J. G. Noverre's *Lettre sur la danse et sur les ballets* (1760). In fact Gluck's final effecting of the reforms which had been mooted in Italy for at least a generation was the direct result of French influence at German and Italian courts (Jommelli at Stuttgart and Traetta at Parma) mediated through Italian artists and achieving its natural consummation at the truly cosmopolitan court of Vienna.

Although Gluck himself, in a letter to the *Mercure de France* published in 1781, named Calzabigi as the true architect of the reform, it was the unique quality of his own music that made *Orfeo ed Euridice* a turning-point in the history of opera. The positive innovations in the score are all French in origin: the greatly increased importance given to the chorus, the *corps de ballet*, and the orchestra, the use of a double orchestra facilitating the baroque echo-effects in Act I, and the inclusion in Act II of the predominantly orchestral tone-picture 'Che puro ciel', in which Orfeo's rapture in the Elysian Fields recalls the scene of Renaud's enchantment in Lully's *Armide* (1686). Negatively Gluck's innovations were no less striking, for he abandoned two of the fundamental forms of the *opera seria*: the *secco* recitative and (with a single exception) the *da capo* aria. On the other hand he gave the role of Orfeo to a *castrato* singer, opened the work with a purely conventional overture unconnected with the drama, and still felt bound by the convention of the *lieto fine*. The musical interest of the last act is in any case noticeably lower than that of the first two, where the choruses reach a degree of purely musical expressiveness unknown in opera since the death of Monteverdi, and the music for the ballets (choreographed by Angiolini) possessed a concentrated dramatic power and rhythmic vigour unequalled even by Rameau.

The greatest of all Gluck's innovations, however, lay in the uniquely simple character of his melodies. Although on many occasions in the future he was to revert to the florid vocal style of the *opera seria* when it suited either the dramatic situation or the nature of his commission, it was by the completely unadorned, speaking simplicity of his vocal lines, whether these were French or Italian in general character and configuration, that his music earned a just comparison to the 'antique' sculpture newly revealed to the German-speaking world by Johann Winckelmann, whom Gluck had almost certainly met in Rome early in 1756. In asking his singers to display not simply their technical achievements but their faculties of empathy and their mastery of true *espressivo* Gluck was of course taking a great risk. He even referred to this in the dedication of

Paride ed Elena (1770),[1] where he observes of Orfeo's 'Che faró senza Euridice?' that 'with the slightest change of expression this may become a *saltarello di burattini*' or, as we should say, a barrel-organ tune.

The theory of operatic reform was not codified by Gluck until the dedication of his next opera, *Alceste*, performed in Vienna in 1767 and printed in 1769. In this manifesto Gluck enunciated the principle underlying all music-drama and therefore common to both Monteverdi in the past and Wagner in the future: the subordination of musical detail to dramatic propriety (hence the suppression of florid vocal passages designed simply to display the singer's art, instrumental ritornellos that are non-functional, and all purely formal repetition):

> I have striven to restrict music to its true office of serving poetry by means of expression and by following the situations of the story, without interrupting the action or stifling it with useless superfluity of ornaments. . . . Furthermore, I believed that my greatest labour should be devoted to seeking a beautiful simplicity, and I have avoided making displays of difficulty at the expense of clearness . . . and there is no rule that I have not thought right to set aside willingly for the sake of an intended effect.[2]

Even the overture, he thought, 'ought to apprise the spectators of the nature of the action to be represented and to form, so to speak, its argument. . . .'

The overture to *Alceste* represents a major vindication of this principle, an *intrada* directly foreshadowing the drama and leading logically and naturally into the opening scene; so too are the march and the Oracle in Act I, whose simple solemnity has no trace of *opera seria* pomposity and was to inspire Mozart both at the beginning and at the end of his career. Calzabigi's libretto contains two Metastasian confidants and Alceste's two children, all parts destined to be pruned from the Paris version of the work,[3] though the equally inorganic part of Hercules was then added. As in *Orfeo*, the musical and dramatic interest of *Alceste* declines steeply in the later scenes, where the protraction in Act II of the contest of nobility, and in Act III of Admetus' repining, defers to the contemporary taste for such emotional displays.

With *Paride ed Elena* (1770) Gluck, in answer to the terms of his commission, attempted a society-piece within the terms of his new principles. In his dedication he refers to his concern with making a clear musical distinction between Spartans and Phrygians, and this was plainly intensified by the choreography, which was designed by Noverre himself. Calzabigi's libretto, indebted to Ovid rather than to Homer, is less remarkable for its dramatic qualities than for the strong erotic note,

[1] *Gesammelte Werke*, iv.
[2] Quoted in Strunk, op. cit, p. 674.
[3] See p. 228.

which Gluck did not fail to capture in his music, as in Paris's 'O del mio dolce ardor' and Erasto's description of Paris's appearance in an urgently sensuous *recitativo accompagnato*, both in Act I. Paris was sung by the same *castrato*, Millico, who had created the role of Orfeo; and much of the dialogue is conducted in a recitative so thinly accompanied as to be hardly distinguishable from *secco*.

LATER *OPERA SERIA*

Gluck's reforms, and the regenerative efforts of Jommelli and Traetta, found little response in Italy, the home of *opera seria*. Jommelli's last works written for Italian houses were nearly all badly received. Of the younger opera composers, only the later Dresden Court conductor Johann Gottlieb Naumann followed in Gluck's footsteps after starting along traditional lines. His inspiration derived from the Swedish cultivation of Gluck within the framework of the 'Gustavian opera', a programme to which he contributed decisively with his operas *Amphion* (1778), *Cora och Alonzo* (1782), and *Gustaf Wasa* (1786).[1] Among the leading Italian composers grouped around Jommelli and Traetta, Davide Perez (*Alessandro nelle Indie* 1749, *Solimano* 1757), Giuseppe Sarti (*Giulio Sabino* 1781) and Francesco di Majo—the first two in individual operas or scenes, Majo throughout his work—sought to write compositions imbued with dramatic spirit. Antonio Sacchini was influenced by Gluck's music drama only towards the end of his life, in Paris.[2]

All these composers, beginning with Hasse, who felt some responsibility towards the text and its plot, had one characteristic in common: the main effort of their operatic composition was directed towards *opera seria*. To the best of their ability they applied to heroic (and at times stilted) librettos music that was dramatically more expressive and formally less restricted than had been the case with their predecessors.

The case was different with such composers as Galuppi, Anfossi, Piccinni, Guglielmi, Paisiello, and Cimarosa, whose talents led them rather along the path of *opera buffa*. With the exception of the older Galuppi, they belonged to a generation whose creative activities did not begin until *opera seria* was being, or had already been, passed over in favour of comic opera. In *opera seria* they were now solely concerned with writing beautiful, lively music, regardless of the text, albeit they made liberal use for that purpose of the advances that had been made in *opera buffa*. These included the use of small independent orchestral themes in arias and *accompagnati*, aria forms like the rondo

[1] Engländer, op. cit. (see p. 3, n. 3), *Joseph Martin Kraus und die Gustavianische Oper* (Uppsala and Leipzig, 1943), 'Gluck und der Norden', *Acta Musicologica*, xxiv (1952) p. 62 and 'Gluck-Pflege und Nachfolge Glucks im Schweden Gustavs III', *Musa-Mens-Musica* ed. E. H. Meyer (Leipzig, 1969), p. 215. [2] Cf. Mooser, op. cit., on Sarti in Russia.

independent of *da capo* arias, popular melody-forms, ensemble finales, and single-movement symphonies.

Between the two groups stands Johann Christian Bach, Johann Sebastian's youngest son, who was completely devoted to *opera seria*, without paying any particular attention to its dramatic aspects. For him opera was 'a refined musical treat', a world 'which plays with dramatic illusion without taking it seriously'.[1] The fame of his works rested in the first place upon their captivating euphony in which his copious gift of melodic invention together with colourful instrumentation and finely worked orchestral phrasing all had equal part:

Ex. 24(i)
CATONE IN UTICA (1761)

E di pre-miar-ti po-i la - - - - - scia la cu - ra a me.

(And leave to me the task of rewarding you afterwards.)

(ii)
ALESSANDRO NELL' INDIE (1762)

Se ___ mai tur - - bo il tuo ___ ri - po. - so,

[1] Abert, 'Johann Christian Bachs italienische Opern und ihr Einfluss auf Mozart', *Zeitschrift für Musikwissenschaft*, i (1918–19), p. 313; Charles Sanford Terry, *John Christian Bach* (London, 2nd edn., 1967).

se_____ m'ac-cen - do ad al - - tro lu - me

(If ever I disturb your rest, if I kindle at another light)

J. C. Bach and the masters of *opera buffa* brought the old species of *opera seria* to the threshold of the nineteenth century without affecting its basic features and its truly operatic character.

OPERA BUFFA: ITS STYLES AND FORMS

Comic opera offered audiences of every nationality in the eighteenth century a desirable contrast to the rigid solemnity of *opera seria*. By 1740 Italian comic opera, *opera buffa*, had passed the first stage of its development. It had left behind coarse dialect comedy, and had achieved with Giovanni Battista Pergolesi's intermezzo *La serva padrona* (1733) its first peak. Whether in the form of *intermezzo* or *commedia musicale*, it lacked as yet the international recognition given to *opera seria*. This recognition came about half-way through the century, thanks not least to Pergolesi's piece. In Italy, however, it enjoyed an earlier popularity,[1] attracting composers and audiences alike by its light-heartedness and naturalness. True, its texts too followed certain set patterns, but the types of character and situation it presented were taken from life and not designed to embody a code of social conduct. Characters found in everyday Italian life played the principal parts in *opera buffa*, as in the *commedia dell'arte* from which it derived its inspiration. The plot always ended with a victory for good sense over wealth and bourgeois status, a glorification of natural gifts over conventional attainments. Thus the maid Serpina (in *La serva padrona*) succeeds finally in winning the rich, confirmed bachelor Uberto despite his strong resistance; the merchant's son Lindoro (in *La contessina* by Florian Gassmann, 1770) outwits the class-conscious Count with the help of valet and lady's maid; and the wily barber Figaro (in *Il barbiere di Siviglia* by Giovanni Paisiello, 1782) snatches the rich Dr. Bartolo's ward Rosina from him and unites her with Count Almaviva.

[1] See Vol. V. On the development of the libretto in *opera buffa*, see Michele Scherillo, *Storia letteraria dell'opera buffa napolitana dalle origini al principio del secolo XIX* (Naples. 1883).

Parallel to this ancient comic theme of the superiority of mother-wit over worldly endowments, which was presented in endless variations throughout the century, was the equally popular theme of parodied *opera seria*. Librettists, composers, and players delighted in the freedom from the bonds of convention which these comic plots provided: they ridiculed *opera seria* to their hearts' content. Above all, they made fun of the managements and the whole operatic production machine. Practically every eighteenth-century composer of standing contributed something to this aspect of *opera buffa*, including Galuppi in *La cantarina* (1756), Piccinni in *La bella verità* (1762)—both of these with texts by Goldoni—Jommelli in *La critica* (1766; text by Martinelli), Gassmann in *L'opera seria* (1769; text by Calzabigi), and Salieri in *Prima la musica e poi le parole* (1782; text by Giambattista Casti). Whenever the libretto permitted, they also inserted parodies of well-known characters, arias, and types of scene from *opera seria*.

The more *opera buffa* spread and the greater the demand for texts, the more the librettists were forced to extend the narrow limits of their material and to widen their scope. The need was met, from the middle of the century onwards, in two ways. First and above all, the plays of Carlo Goldoni introduced fresh, serious characters (*parti serie*). Thus Goldoni introduced into comedy the moralizing 'comédie larmoyante bourgeoise', sentimental rather than comic, bringing his efforts in this direction to a climax with his *Cecchina ossia La buona figliuola*, set to music first by Duni (1756) and then by Piccinni (1760), the plot being taken from Richardson's novel *Pamela, or Virtue Rewarded* which he had already turned into a comedy.[1] Secondly, the libretti of the Neapolitan Francesco Cerlone opened up the realm of the marvellous, the fabulous, or the exotic. Cerlone's innovations pointed the way towards the unconventional and the adventurous, an approach that rendered possible, for example, the absorption of the Don Giovanni theme. Both of these new ways enriched the original crude character of the genre. In their novel surroundings the individuality of its figures was confirmed, but at the same time stripped of too farcical elements. As harmless and coarse comedies of the old sort and parodies of *opera seria* persisted alongside such new libretti, in the second half of the eighteenth century *opera buffa* came to avail itself of a variety of material (with possibilities for dramatic conflict) and types of character with which *opera seria* could not hope to compete. Admittedly the librettists generally made use of this store of wealth with an eye to broad popular success, mixing up its components without discretion or good taste. They had among them no writer of the

---

[1] See William C. Holmes, 'Pamela Transformed', *Musical Quarterly*, xxxviii (1952), p. 581.

standing and range of Metastasio, who could put the composition of dramas and opera texts on the same level and respect them equally. Even Goldoni, famous as the author of spoken comedies, openly regarded the writing of opera texts as a subordinate activity. He stated in the preface to one of his libretti that in scribbling *per musica* he lacked all creative ambition, having in mind mainly the performers, the composer, and the audience's pleasure; indeed, he would prefer these works simply to be performed and not read at all.[1]

Innumerable minor text-writers produced hack imitations of Goldoni, the leading librettist of Venice, and of Cerlone and Giambattista Lorenzi of Naples. But as the century took its course, librettists resident outside Italy, like Giambattista Casti and Lorenzo da Ponte in Vienna,[2] turned their attention to *opera buffa*—a sure sign that the genre had grown from being an Italian—often dialect—popular entertainment to the status of an internationally acknowledged type of comedy.

Like *opere serie*, *opere buffe* were of course planned to accommodate a regular alternation of recitative and arias. But the element of comic drama in them was much more important than the quality of singing, while a sharp division between action and reflection was not appropriate to the solid everyday characters. Thus the nature and style of recitatives and arias were much less sharply differentiated than in *opera seria*. The arias generally form an integral part of the action and develop in their content from the recitative itself, instead of interrupting it.

To composers who had previously dealt with *opera seria* only, these texts offered a welcome opportunity to extend their musical range of expression. *Recitativo secco* was taken over, but underwent several kinds of adaptation. Sometimes composers continued to employ *parlando*, even increasing repetition of notes. At other times the recitative was split into still shorter phrases akin to the quick speech of the common people, as may be seen from the following excerpt from Piccinni's *La buona figliuola*, I, vi:

Ex. 25

[1] *La Statira*, libretto from 1756, quoted from Ulderico Rolandi, *Il libretto per musica attraverso i tempi* (Rome, 1951), pp. 93–4. Cf. also Goldoni, *Mémoires*, 3 vols. (Paris, 1787).

[2] Cf. *Memorie di Lorenzo da Ponte da Ceneda scritte da esso*, 4 vols. (New York, 1823, 1826, 1827). English translations by L. A. Sheppard (Boston, 1929) and Elisabeth Abbott (ed. Arthur Livingstone) (Philadelphia, 1929).

(Cav.: Sweet country-girl! San.: Greetings, good sir. Cav.: Do you belong here? San.: Yes, sir. Cav.: I should like to know if your mistress has risen. San.: I don't know; I've just returned from a distance to bring the Signora this fruit. Cav.: Can I see her? San.: Who are you? Cav.: I am the Cavaliero Armidoro.)

Moreover, even these comparatively unexciting passages gave opportunities for caricature and characterization, so that here too the music affected the drama. The more solemn *recitativo accompagnato* played no significant part in these comedies, except for purposes of ridicule in mock-*seria* scenes, as in the one with the servant Mengotto in the same opera, II, vi:

Ex. 26

(and my Master takes her away from me. Yes, I want to kill myself, poor and unfortunate as I am.)

Recitativo secco and aria were closely integrated in the libretto; as a consequence *accompagnato* was not required as a transition from *secco* to aria, a function it often served in *opera seria*. At appropriate points arias could even embody recitative passages or approach *recitativo secco* with the speedy, syllabically accentuated recitation of the words:[1]

Ex. 27

Per il bu - co del - la chia - ve hò ve - du - to la ra - gaz - za che pa - re - va mez - za paz - za, che pa - re - va mez - za paz - za

(Through the keyhole I've seen the girl who seemed half mad.)

It was out of the question to apply a formal pattern, in the *opera seria* manner, to arias whose dramatic presentation had become so elastic. In any case, the virtuoso singing which had been the primary end of *opera seria*, and to the display of which the *da capo* aria had been more and more devoted, was of no importance in *opera buffa*. The castrato and the dominating prima donna were both absent. Instead, as was appropriate since the *buffo* characters were taken from life, the four natural types of voice, i.e. soprano, alto, tenor, and bass, came into their own again, particular significance often being given to the 'basso buffo'. Everyone was provided with different types of song, from the simple strophic song, the aria in one single section, and the two-part cavatina, to the three- and four-part sectional series and rondo forms—whatever happened to be appropriate to their character and the particular situation. In the course of time the double-section aria, consisting of a slow

[1] All examples from *La buona figliuola* (Exx. 25–30) are taken from Dresden, Sächsische Landesbibl., Musica 3264/F 8. There is an edition by Giacomo Benvenuti, *I classici musicali italiani*, vii (Milan, 1942).

and a quick part, became especially popular. The *da capo* form also made its appearance, but as a display of virtuosity—as in *opera seria*—it was used only for purposes of parody.

While the formal organization of the aria in *opera buffa* avoided becoming too stylized, the aria also retained its musical freshness. Herein the influence of folk music, whether in its comic or its lyrical aspect, was of outstanding importance. It provided composers with an unending source of material which they could leave unaltered or adapt in the most varied manner as character and situation demanded:

Ex. 28 (i)

(Family affection does not suit the lover.)

(ii)

[musical notation]

tut - to, mi__ fa tut - to, tut - to, tut - to, tut - to giu - - bi - lar

(And only the beautiful Cecchina makes me rejoice.)

(iii)

[musical notation]

Po - - ve - ri - na, po - - ve - ri - na, tut - to il dì fa - ti - car__ deg - gio__ co - sì, fa - ti - car__ deg - gio__ co - sì

(Poor girl, poor girl, I must work so hard all day long.)

Besides this, since they all wrote *opera seria* as well, its modes of expression were available to them for use in *opera buffa* where suitable. The more the 'parti serie' came to the fore, the more they made use of this facility. *Arie di bravura* continued to make their appearance only as explicit or implied parodies, as would seem to be the case in the Marchesa's revenge aria in *La buona figliuola*, I, xiv:

Ex. 29

[musical notation]

Fu - rie di don - na i - ra - ta in mio soc - cor - so in-

(I call the fury of an angry woman to my aid. Ah! my fire grows.)

Expressive songs of the *aria cantabile* type, on the other hand, were just as much in keeping with the serious characters of comic opera as with the pair of lovers in *opera seria*:

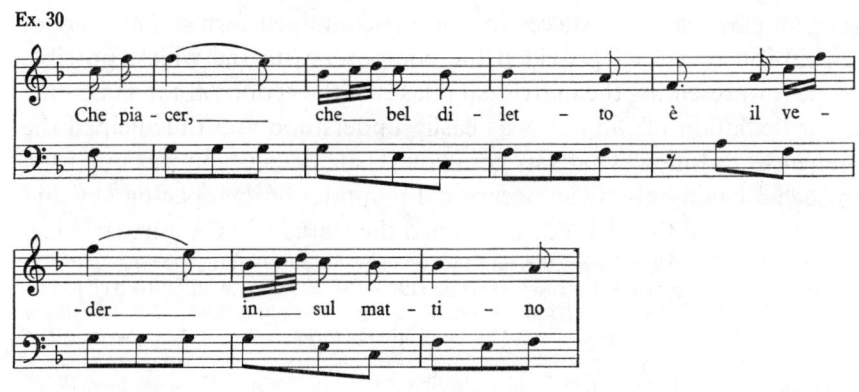

Ex. 30

(What a pleasure, what a delight it is to see in the morning ...)

In *opera seria* arias were strung together in a row on the thread of the *recitativo*. In *opera buffa*, however, where drama was of primary importance, skill in combining parts—the ensembles—showed itself from the outset to be essential for success. Since the four voices were given equal emphasis, musically and dramatically, composers were increasingly led to introduce ensembles, which served at times to intensify and support dramatic situations, at other times to act as a respite from an exclusive diet of solo arias and their rigid formal patterns.[1] Ensembles gave as many opportunities for formal and musical contrasts as did arias. In dramatic versatility they far surpassed them since, by the 1740s, composers were at pains to achieve simultaneous musical characterization, distinguishing individuals, or at least groups, from one another.

The tendency towards greater unity of plot and music in finales was especially promising for future developments. To begin with, ensembles like the *arie finali* in *opera seria*, of a purely reflective content and with no relation to the plot, were often thought enough. But from the 1740s onwards composers were more and more concerned to evoke, at the end of the act, the action itself in music; and to place the dramatic situation within a musical frame that would be appropriate and at the same time provide a musically satisfactory form of close to the action. Thus it was that the complex structure of the finale came into being.[2] Its existence set composers new and difficult problems which in the second half of the century they tried to solve by the most various means. The most radical solution, from the dramatic point of view, was that of the through-composed finale where situation and characters, i.e. the dramatic interest, were the determining factors, and attention to musical form of any kind receded into the background.[3]

The so-called 'chain finale' represented a compromise between mirroring the course of the action and an endeavour to make the structure musically more comprehensive. Here the music followed the flow of the plot, but by way of a succession of self-contained forms. This sort of conclusion to an act provided the composer with the widest possible scope for presenting the individual phases of the action; at the same time the articulation of the plot was easily understood and thus helped the audiences to follow what was going on. Usually cohesion was imparted to such a chain only by an occasional reminder of the opening key and a return to it at the end. But it attained the status of a complete musical

[1] Cf. Edward J. Dent, 'Ensembles and Finales in 18th Century Italian Opera', *Sammelbände der internationalen Musikgesellschaft*, xi (1909–10), p. 543, and xii (1910–11), p. 112.

[2] Cf. ibid. Cf. also Hermann Kretzschmar, 'Zwei Opern Nicolo Logroscinos', *Jahrbücher der Musikbibliothek Peters* (1908), pp. 47 ff., reprinted in *Gesammelte Aufsätze über Musik*, ii (Leipzig 1911).

[3] An example is the vocal trio finale to the first act of Logroscino's *Il governatore* (1747), printed in Kretzschmar, op. cit., appendix.

form when the practice was introduced of relating the parts to one another according to the principle of a free rondo. This allowed a passage that was particularly characteristic of a situation to return in ritornello fashion and to alternate with various episodes. Thus for the first time a preconceived musical form was brought into harmony with the course of the plot.[1] In the second half of the century the different forms of the finale underwent the most manifold combinations. The desire to consolidate the finale in an intellectually and musically compact unity became steadily more important—witness the saying of da Ponte that the finale was 'una specie di commediola o di picciol dramma da sè'.[2]

These 'miniature dramas', when soloists and ensembles were brought together in set-pieces, at first occurred only at the end of the first two acts. But they gradually supplanted the simple concluding ensemble or chorus of the third act, and finally infiltrated the course of the action in the guise of 'intermediate finales'. In order to counterbalance the finales an 'introduzione' was added at the beginning of the first act; this also developed from a simple ensemble to a dramatically lively scene.

In achieving greater dramatic flexibility in the arias and ensembles of *opera buffa*, the orchestra played an important part. Without covering the voices, it frequently took an independent line in its treatment of the themes. Moreover, it also contributed to the dramatization of individual scenes, particularly where the voices were most laconic and declamatory. Here sparkling and imaginative motifs, usually brief, could knit together whole sections or bridge separate ones, as in Figaro's aria in Act I of Paisiello's *Il barbiere di Siviglia* (1782)[3]:

Ex. 31

The overtures to *opera buffa* did not at first differ fundamentally from those for *opera seria*. They too were in three movements with the normal quick–slow–quick sequence. In time, however, they displayed increasingly more refined orchestral treatment, and used melodies more instrumental than vocal in character. In the last quarter of the century single-movement overtures made their appearance; but their tripartite structure and prolonged contrasting middle section betrayed their debt to the old three-movement pattern.[4]

[1] Especially characteristic for the rondo finale form are, for example, the first and second finales to Piccinni's *La buona figliuola*.
[2] Op. cit.
[3] Dresden, Sächsische Landesbibl., Musica 3481/F 13.
[4] Cf. Fritz Tutenberg, 'Die Opera-buffa-Sinfonie und ihre Beziehungen zur klassischen Sinfonie', *Archiv für Musikwissenschaft*, viii (1926), pp. 452 ff.

THE COMPOSERS OF *OPERA BUFFA*

For a long time *opera buffa* had its own authors and performers, appropriately, since it was derived from folk comedy. Its composers were, however, from the start identical with those concerned in *opera seria*, for basically both types made the same musical-technical demands. The only difference lay in the proportion of a composer's output devoted to one or other form. Hasse, Perez, Jommelli, and Traetta, for example, wrote comparatively few *opere buffe*. Nicola Logroscino (1698–1765) and Gaetano Latilla (1711–88), however, though almost the same ages respectively as Hasse and Perez, concentrated on this genre. Their Venetian contemporary Galuppi wrote more *opere serie* than comic operas; but while in the former he remained completely within the traditional frame-work, in the latter he played a decisive part in the development of *opera buffa*.[1] Among eminent *buffo* composers of the second half of the eighteenth century he was the only Venetian. His fame rests principally upon his collaboration with Goldoni, begun in 1749, though he was not alone therein since Goldoni's star as a libretto writer was just then rising throughout Italy.

Galuppi's aim as a *buffo* composer was in principle the same as that of his junior contemporaries from Southern Italy, Piccinni, Guglielmi, and Anfossi, whose works appeared a little later than his (the middle to the end of the fifties). All of them were exponents of the new developments already described, particularly in ensembles and finales, orchestral technique and characterizing melodies. These embodied a musical and dramatic refinement of the genre, irrespective of whether the librettos were coarse or subtle or even sentimental in character. Indeed, the attraction of their compositions lay in the mixture of these elements, where extremes might collide in sharp contrast or imperceptibly lead into one another. The outstanding common factor between them was their indebtedness in numerous and varied ways to folk music, which itself ranges in expression from the violent to the sentimental.[2] In contrast to the tradition-bound *opera seria*, *opera buffa* appeared more and more as the medium for progressive experiments. Nevertheless, its dramatic character as a whole remained unaltered until the end of the century and for much longer; many later composers, such as Paisiello, Giuseppe Gazzaniga (1743–1818), and even Cimarosa and Vicente Martín y Soler, whose earliest *opere buffe* did not appear until the 1770s, still adhered to its rules.

---

[1] Cf. Werner Bollert, *Die Buffoopern Baldassare Galuppis* (Diss. Berlin, 1935). An aria from Galuppi's *Il filosofo di campagna* (1750) is printed in Davison and Apel, op. cit., p. 221, and a *buffa* aria by Logroscino is recorded in *The History of Music in Sound*, v.

[2] A study of the influence of folk music upon *opera buffa* has not yet been undertaken.

Shades of difference between the personal manners of individual composers are hidden to a considerable extent by the resemblance between their works necessarily arising from the genre itself. Piccinni had a particular partiality for the rendering of delicate, elegiac sentiments, and was inexhaustible in the invention of ever fresh musical nuances in this range of feeling.[1] It is not a matter of chance that the naïve, rapturous Cecchina—Richardson's Pamela—should be one of his most famous creations; the following lament, from *La buona figliuola*, I, xii clearly delineates her character as a typical Piccinni figure:

Ex. 32

---

[1] On Piccinni, cf. Abert, 'Piccinni als Buffokomponist', *Jahrbücher der Musikbibliothek Peters*, (1913), p. 29, reprinted in *Gesammelte Schriften und Vorträge* (Halle, 1929); Della Corte, *Piccinni (settecento italiano)* (Bari, 1928). On Paisiello, cf. Abert 'Paisiellos Buffokunst und ihre Beziehungen zu Mozart', *Archiv für Musikwissenschaft*, i (1918), p. 402, reprinted in *Gesammelte Schriften und Vorträge*; Della Corte, *Paisiello*, op. cit.

[Musical notation]

(A poor girl who has no father and mother is maltreated, is ill-used; this is too much cruelty.)

Yet he would not have achieved such a reputation as a *buffo* composer had he not had a gift for the musical representation of comic characters, as in this aria sung by the German soldier Tagliaferro in the same work, II, vi:

Ex. 33

[Musical notation with text: Star trom-bet-ti, star tam-bur-ri, star chi-tar-re, e ciu-fo-let-ti, star stru-men-ti in quan-ti-tà, star stru-men-ti in quan-ti-]

(There are trumpets, there are drums, there are guitars and flageolets, there are lots of instruments, charming little girls to dance with.)

In Paisiello's case the emphasis was reversed. His 'parti serie' by no means lack tones of expressive sentiment—the opening of Rosina's aria from I, iii of *Il barbiere di Siviglia* (1782) may serve as an example:

Ex. 34

(Praise be to heaven who at last released my many-eyed jealousy.)

and his Nina, in the opera of the same name (1789), is a direct successor to Piccinni's Cecchina. But the characterization of coarsely comic figures was more in his line, as were also adaptable, crafty plebeian characters like Figaro, who in his duet with the Count (*Barbiere*, Act I, no. 8) first adapts himself to the latter's aristocratic line of melody only to diverge into rude, *buffo* patter:

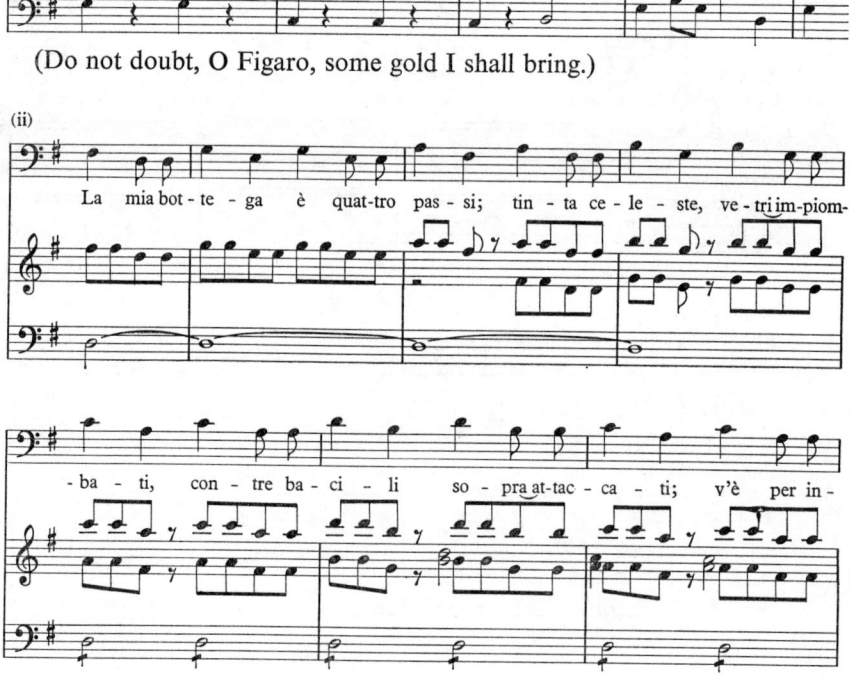

Ex. 35
(i)

Non du - bi - tar, o Fi - ga - ro, non du - bi - tar, o Fi - ga - ro, dell' o - ro, io por - te - rò, dell' o - ro io por - te - rò.

(Do not doubt, O Figaro, some gold I shall bring.)

(ii)

La mia bot - te - ga è quat - tro pas - si; tin - ta ce - le - ste, ve - tri im-piom- -ba - ti, con - tre ba - ci - li so - pra at-tac - ca - ti; v'è per in-

(My shop is a couple of steps away, painted blue with leaded windows, with three basins overhead; there is as a sign an eye in a hand: *consilio manuque*.)

Anfossi was a pupil of Piccinni and adhered closely to his ways of composition; Guglielmi inclined more to the carefree gaiety of Paisiello. Yet it would be an exaggeration to speak of an antithesis between them.[1]

Florian Leopold Gassmann (1729–74), a Bohemian by birth, began his operatic composition in Venice and later moved to Vienna. Generally speaking he remained firmly within the conventions of the genre. The influence of the extraordinarily complex Viennese atmosphere is shown in his particularly careful orchestral writing and in the echoes of Viennese *Lied* and French *air* which Gassman frequently employs besides the typically Italian *buffo* idiom for the purpose of dramatic characterization. The servant Gazzetta in his *drama giocoso La contessina* (1770) (2) is an example; disguised as a marquis he mimics the musical style of *opéra comique* in III, iv:

Ex. 36

(To your feet, charming queen, tender love leads my steps.)

---

[1] For both composers, cf. the appropriate articles in *Die Musik in Geschichte und Gegenwart*, i and v respectively; on Guglielmi also Francesco Piovano, 'Elenco cronologico delle opere (1757–1802) di Pietro Guglielmi', *Rivista musicale italiana*, xii (1905), p. 407.

[2] Ed. Haas, *Denkmäler der Tonkunst in Oesterreich*, xxi. Cf. also Gustav Donath, 'Florian Gassmann als Opernkomponist', *Studien zur Musikwissenschaft*, ii (1914), p. 34.

CIMAROSA AND MARTÍN Y SOLER

The operas of Mozart and Joseph Haydn will be examined later. Mozart's supremacy in the field of *opera buffa* is now taken for granted but in his own day two contemporaries, Domenico Cimarosa (1749–1801) and Vicente Martín y Soler (1754–1806), won greater acclaim. Most of Cimarosa's operas were composed for Naples or Rome, two—both *opere serie*—for St. Petersburg in 1788–9, though his earliest notable success, *Giannina e Bernardone* (1781), was produced in Venice and his last, *Il matrimonio segreto* (1792), based on Colman and Garrick's comedy *The Clandestine Marriage*, was first performed in Vienna. Influenced by Sacchini, who was one of his teachers, by Piccinni, and latterly by Mozart, his music is informed by a real comic spirit and by characterization that is by no means merely superficial, while his treatment of finales and his dramatically and picturesquely imaginative employment of the orchestra were unusual. All these qualities appear in *Giannina e Bernardone*, but his wit and charm may be illustrated by this excerpt from Demofoonte's canzonetta in the First Act of *I due baroni di Rocca Azzura* (Rome, 1783):[1]

Ex. 37

(Don't be proud, girls, for you'll be getting older . . .)

They reach their fullest development in Cimarosa's masterpiece, the *Matrimonio segreto*.[2]

[1] Modena, Bibl. Estense, MSS. Mus. F.258. Quoted complete in Gino Roncaglia, *Il melodioso settecento italiano* (Milan, 1935), p. 364.

[2] From which the duet, 'Io ti lascio', in Act I, is recorded in *The History of Music in Sound*, vii.

Martín y Soler was a Spaniard by birth and spent the last seventeen years of his life in Russia.[1] Before then, he had been persuaded by Nancy Storace to settle for a time in Vienna where he brought out his masterpiece, *Una cosa rara, o sia Bellezza ed onestà*, in 1786. *Una cosa rara* ('A rare thing') deserves to be remembered by much more than Mozart's witty quotation from the First Act finale in the supper-scene of *Don Giovanni* or the waltz in the Second Act finale[2] which is said to have done much to popularize that dance-form. Da Ponte, the librettist of both operas, based both on Spanish subjects—in this case on Luis Vélez de Guevara's *La luna de la sierra*—and Martín took the opportunity to introduce a suggestion of national colouring, particularly in the part of the peasant-girl Ghita:

Ex. 38

(So long as you're mine, I always want your love only. If I'm a bit angry with you, I mean it—as you can suppose.)

(c) GERMAN OPERA
By A. A. Abert

In the years around 1740 it was Italian opera that set the fashion for German-speaking lands. By that time the last opera houses which had sought to foster German opera had closed their doors. So-called 'early

[1] See p. 277.
[2] Quoted by Mosco Carner, *The Waltz* (London, 1948), p. 17.

German opera', heterogeneous in style and heavily dependent on foreign example, had shown itself inferior to Italian and French opera. Hence these latter carried the day, especially Italian opera, which was strongly represented at the major Courts throughout the Empire and was also powerful through its itinerant companies. Nevertheless, public opinion still occupied itself with the problem of native opera at two levels, that of theory and that of straightforward practice.

GERMAN *OPERA SERIA*

Johann Christoph Gottsched's absolute rejection of opera as in any way a separate species[1] provoked a lively discussion among theorists and critics as to whether there existed an aesthetic justification for opera at all. Most of them recognized opera's claim to be an art-form and regarded Gottsched's condemnation as applying only to certain of its excesses—a view, incidentally, that Gottsched himself adopted at a later stage.[2] Johann Adolf Scheibe, the only musician to participate in this literary dispute, took this line. In his *Der Critische Musicus*[3] he dealt with the problems in great detail. He ascribed the downfall of early German opera to the incompetence of its librettists and the lack of taste of its composers in choosing their texts. The rules he proposed for improving this sorry state of affairs amounted to compressing and simplifying the florid form of the baroque libretto—rules which were substantially the same as those to which Metastasian drama adhered. Scheibe went a step farther by providing a demonstration of his ideas in a text of his own. In 1749 he published the libretto of *Thusnelde, ein Singspiel in vier Aufzügen, mit einem Vorbericht von der Möglichkeit und Beschaffenheit guter Singspiele* ('Thusnelde, a *Singspiel* in four Acts, with a Preface on the Possibilities for and Conditions of good *Singspiele*'). Even though no composer set the libretto to music, it remains important because Scheibe was the first literary author to move towards a national German opera, free from baroque pomposity.

Scheibe's endeavours were continued by some of the greatest of German classical poets. All of them were concerned with the theory and aesthetics of opera,[4] which they considered a matter of high creative artistry. They acknowledged Gluck's great part as a reformer and would have been delighted to bring into being a classical German opera under

---

[1] Especially in his *Versuch einer critischen Dichtkunst für die Deutschen* (Leipzig, 1730) For this and the following, cf. Goldschmidt, *Die Musikästhetik des 18. Jahrhunderts*, particularly Section B, 'Die Oper des 18. Jahrhunderts in der Beurteilung der Zeitgenossen und der Ästhetiker insbesondere'.

[2] Goldschmidt, p. 82.

[3] New, augmented, and revised edition, Leipzig, 1745.

[4] Cf. Wilhelm Bernard Schwan, *Die Stellung der deutschen klassischen Dichter zur Oper* (Bonn dissertation, 1926).

his aegis. But Gluck, a true cosmopolitan, was not interested in these problems. What mattered to him was the creation of a work of art that transcended national boundaries; the question of language was of no importance. He declined to set to music Herder's *Brutus*, conceived by the poet in 1774 as a 'drama for music', and, two years later, ignored proposals for an opera by Wieland. Nor did his collaboration with Klopstock bear any permanent fruit in the field of dramatic music.[1]

Wieland and the composer Anton Schweitzer had already sought to realize the ideal of German opera. Though the textual form and style of their *Alceste*[2] were clearly on the Metastasian pattern, the contents conformed to Gluck's ideals of unity, simplicity, and naturalness. Indeed Wieland, admiring Gluck as he did, embodied these ideals with an austere simplicity that brought the already sparse action of the legend to the verge of monotony. Schweitzer was an excellent musician. As conductor in a travelling company he was thoroughly conversant with the German *Singspiel* (see infra, pp. 79–97). He had also spent some time in Italy, like many other German composers of the eighteenth century, though he wrote no Italian operas. He was familiar with the typical components of an *opera seria* and could handle them skilfully in isolation, but he lacked the experience necessary to smooth out general mistakes in dramatic construction. Carried away by the enthusiastic poet's exuberance, he threw himself with ardour into every situation presented by the drama. His *recitativo secco* was not merely carefully worked out, it allowed for appropriate emotional declamation and, in contrast to traditional Italian recitative, was distinguished by frequent, widely sweeping melodic lines:

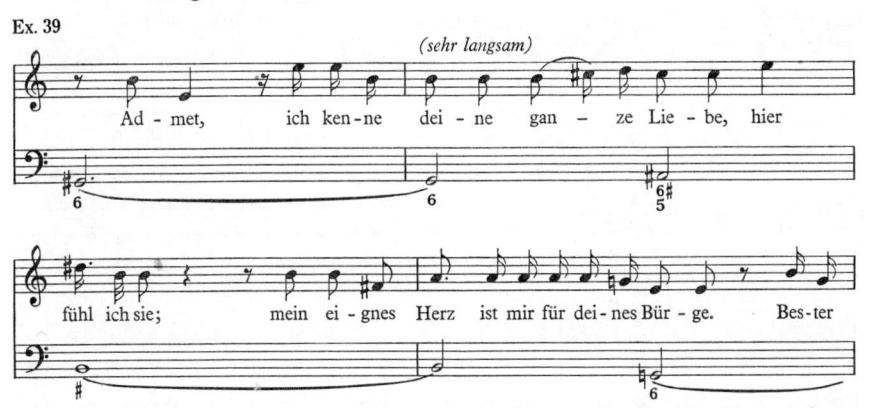

Ex. 39

[1] Herder's *Brutus*, the score of which has disappeared, was set to music by Johann Christoph Friedrich Bach, the so-called 'Bückeburger Bach', as Herder was working in Bückeburg at that time. Cf. F. E. Kirby, 'Herder and Opera', *Journal of the American Musicological Society*, xv (1962), p. 316.

[2] The score was published by the Schwickertsche Verlag (Leipzig, 1774). (There is a copy in the Musikwissenschaftliches Institut of the University of Kiel.)

(Admetus, I know how great your love is. I feel it here; my own heart answers for yours. Dearest husband, I know the goodness of your soul: it is great and noble and this should decide our difference.)

The same expression of grandeur produced by large, and indeed bizarre, leaps can also be seen in the arias, particularly those of the heroine Alceste. With the very independent treatment given to the instruments and a harmony rich in suspensions and dissonances, an unusual and sombre effect is achieved. The beginning of the aria in the first act, where Alceste consecrates herself to the divinities of death, may serve as an example:

Höl - le, ihr furcht - ba - ren Schat - ten!

(You Gods of Hell, you terrible shades!)

If this vehement expression sometimes seems exaggerated in the arias, it is highly suitable in the numerous *recitativi accompagnati*. Admetus's solo in the fourth act, where the king recalls with yearning the happiness of the past and then, in spirit, follows Alceste's shadow on its way to the underworld, 'O Jugendzeit, o gold'ne Wonnetage der Liebe', is outstanding among them because of the variety of ways in which the pictorial allusions and emotions of the text are interpreted, as the following bars show:

Ex. 41

(Maestoso, ma ben sostenuto)

Fl. in 8ves with V. I

Wo bist du? wo bist du?

irrst du schon,

70 OPERA IN ITALY AND THE HOLY ROMAN EMPIRE

(Where are you? Dearest shade, do you roam even now on Lethe's bank? Ah, I see her walk! In sad majesty she walks alone on the darkening strand.)

The regular 'French' overture, which introduces the work and consists of a solemn grave and a fugal allegro, is likely to have been composed at the librettist's suggestion. In his 'Essay on the German *Singspiel*'[1] Wieland had been most disapproving of the harmlessly festive Italian opera symphonies.

The opera was performed at Weimar on 28 May 1773. As the first sign of a renaissance of German opera it was very successful there, and later elsewhere. But sharp criticism, both literary and musical, was not lacking. Wieland himself had provoked his fellow-poets by his remarks in *Briefe an einen Freund über das deutsche Singspiel Alceste* ('Letters to a Friend respecting the German *Singspiel Alceste*').[2] The reaction culminated in Goethe's wittily mordant satire *Götter, Helden und Wieland* ('Gods, Heroes, and Wieland'). The most important of the musical critics was Mozart, who dubbed the opera 'Sorrowful Alceste'[3] because of its unvarying melancholy. On 11 September 1778, after attending the rehearsals at Mannheim for Wieland and Schweitzer's second opera, *Rosemunde*,[4] he wrote to his father about the unsingable character of the vocal line: 'unfortunate is the singer who falls into Schweitzer's hands, for he will never learn to write music that can be sung'.

Wieland had received the commission to write another opera for the Mannheim Court Theatre as the result of a performance of *Alceste* at Schwetzingen in 1775. For the libretto he chose *Rosemunde*, a story from medieval England for which, unlike *Alceste*, he furnished abundant chorus and ballet scenes. Schweitzer followed his lead and was particularly concerned to insert suitably important orchestral movements for the famous Mannheim orchestra. Nevertheless the opera failed utterly, because the author, and even more the composer, lacked true dramatic power.

A more important result of the Schwetzingen *Alceste* performance of 1775 was the stimulus it gave the Mannheim artistic circle. Mannheim was highly receptive of such influences: the foundation of a Palatinate Society for the fostering of the German language, and the building of a German national theatre (where Schiller's *Räuber* was produced in 1782) was making it into a stronghold of German literary and dramatic effort.[5] Thus it came about that Anton Klein, man of letters and critic, wrote the text of *Günther von Schwarzburg* for the Court Conductor Ignaz

---

[1] 'Versuch über das Deutsche *Singspiel* und einige dahin einschlagende Gegenstände', published in the *Teutsche Merkur* (1775).
[2] Published in the *Teutsche Merkur* (1773).
[3] Letter to his father, 18 December 1778.
[4] Performed at Mannheim on 20 January 1780.
[5] Friedrich Walter, *Geschichte des Theaters und der Musik am kurpfälzischen Hofe* (Leipzig, 1898).

Holzbauer. In contrast to Wieland, he chose a theme from German history with patriotic implications. In the handling of its intrigue-loaded action, however, its black-and-white painting of the characters and its structure, Klein was simply a disciple of Metastasio.

Holzbauer had, like Schweitzer, studied in Italy. But, unlike Schweitzer, his experience of opera derived from decades of activity, first in Vienna, the city which was his home, and then as chief conductor at such culturally prominent Courts as Stuttgart and Mannheim. He had already appeared as a composer of Italian operas. He could therefore face this new task more easily than Schweitzer, who was a novice in operatic forms and modes of expression. *Günther von Schwarzburg*[1] was a genuine *opera seria* composed of *secco* and *accompagnato* recitatives, arias, and a few ensembles and choruses; yet it gives an impression of unusual originality because of the freedom with which the composer has treated and brought together these formal elements. Stereotyped separate scenes of recitative and arias are abandoned in favour of large dramatic complexes. The *accompagnato*, sometimes in the middle of the recitative portions, sometimes linking recitative and aria, seems almost the work's most important component. In it Holzbauer cleverly varies theme, tempo, or instrumentation to suit the drama's passionate sway of emotions. A few bars will illustrate the point. They are taken from the solo scene I, iv, of the fiendish schemer Asberta:

Ex. 42

[1] Ed. Kretzschmar, *Denkmäler deutscher Tonkunst*, viii–ix.

(Then I shall scatter them like dust, the princes! But how to destroy this mountain that stands before me? All voices were united in electing Rudolf. I shall speak to Günther himself and Günther must give way.)

74 OPERA IN ITALY AND THE HOLY ROMAN EMPIRE

In this way Holzbauer improved the frequently bombastic recitative texts and often transformed textual poverty into musical riches. In arias he kept more closely to tradition. There are some *arie di bravura* with solo instruments and extended coloraturas unconnected with the content. Most arias, however, resemble the *accompagnati* in displaying a concern with the meaning of the text, and reflect, if not the character of the individual, at least the dramatic situation. In them the composer commands sometimes a dignified, almost lyrical simplicity—as in the E flat major aria of the Palatine Count Rudolf in II, v:

Ex. 43

Wenn das Sil - ber dei - ner Haa - re Helm und Stir - ne, Helm und Stir - ne schmückt,

(When the silver of your hair adorns helmet and forehead.)

prophetic of Sarastro—sometimes an exaggerated vehemence reminiscent of Schweitzer—as in the middle portion of Asberta's aria I, v:

Ex. 44

nein! Durch nichts wird er ge - bo -

(No, nothing can bend him! I make a sign: You are Empress of the Germans.)

Holzbauer, however, never completely loses sight of singability.

Having also become known as a composer of symphonies, and being in charge of the Mannheim orchestra, one of the most famous of its time, Holzbauer would clearly not neglect the part given to the orchestra. But because of the layout of *opera seria*, independent instrumental movements were of only minor importance, apart from the single-movement overture. To compensate for that, he introduced many extended and colourfully scored introductions to the arias in a solid symphonic idiom and in addition, as the above examples have shown, repeatedly provided the instruments with work of their own during the accompaniments to arias.

Günther von Schwarzburg was enthusiastically received when its first performance took place at Mannheim on 5 January 1777 and it appeared on many German stages during the course of the following years. Professional critics took strong exception to the libretto which was marred by clumsy effects and lack of originality, but the music was highly praised. Mozart expressed the contemporary attitude precisely when he wrote to his father on 14 November 1777, 'Holzbauer's music is very beautiful. The poetry is unworthy of such music. . . . It is unbelievable what fire there is in the music.'

And yet Schweitzer's and Holzbauer's operas, in spite of the excitement they caused, remained for some time isolated experiments. Evidently they were felt to be stylistically too closely tied to the foreign, Metastasian type of opera, which by then no longer represented the spirit of the period. By contrast the German *Singspiel*, which was then gaining in favour (see pp. 79 ff.), relied heavily upon the native song tradition. With its realistic texts it was much closer to the taste of composers and audiences, who demanded naturalism and were tired of the old conventions. The Dresden circle around Johann Gottlieb Naumann showed itself sympathetic to the desire for German opera, and his *Cora*, composed to a Swedish text, was published in 1780 with a German translation even before its performance in Sweden.[1] Yet the Dresden circle did not succeed in producing a genuine German opera, nor did Johann Friedrich Reichardt with his *Singspiele* and operas at Berlin.[2]

BENDA AND MELODRAMA

On the other hand German composers, so ready at this time to experiment, gave a particular welcome to the new type of melodrama which derived from Rousseau's 'scène lyrique' *Pygmalion*.[3] Here Rousseau had tried to relate music and drama without making use of song. The action was entrusted to the spoken word or mime, while music interpreted and supplied the background. Georg Benda was the first to follow this example in Germany.[4] In his *Ariadne auf Naxos* and *Medea* (both 1775) the spoken word and orchestral music intermingled closely and sometimes even overlapped, in imitation of the major *accompagnato* scenes of Italian operas. The more polished orchestral idiom employed in the new *Tanzdrama* was used to give background effect to the mimed action, whereby the heroine's emotions, ranging from gentle plaint to passionate frenzy, were faithfully reflected in the music:[5]

[1] Engländer, 'Dresden und die deutsche Oper im letzten Drittel des 18. Jahrhunderts', *Zeitschrift für Musikwissenschaft*, iii (1920–1).
[2] Rolf Pröpper, *Die Bühnenwerke Johann Friedrich Reichardts* (Bonn, 1965).
[3] Cf. Edgar Istel, *J.-J. Rousseau als Komponist seiner lyrischen Szene 'Pygmalion'*, (Leipzig, 1901); J. van der Veen, *Le Mélodrame musical de Rousseau au Romantisme* (The Hague, 1955).
[4] Fritz Brückner, 'Georg Benda und das deutsche Singspiel', *Sammelbände der internationalen Musikgesellschaft*, v (1903–4), particularly pp. 580–6; Istel, *Die Entstehung des deutschen Melodrams* (Berlin, 1906).
[5] Illustrations taken from the 'more complete and improved' (undated) score of Benda's duodrama *Ariadne auf Naxos*, published by the Schwickertsche Verlag, Leipzig. (There is a copy in the Musikwissenschaftliches Institut, University of Kiel.) Modern edition, ed. Alfred Einstein (Leipzig, 1920).

Ex. 45 (i)
(Adagio)

Einst war ich schuldlos. Ohne Kummer, ohne Tränen, heiter und froh blühte mein Frühling, noch unbekannt der Liebe.

An meiner Mutter Busen ruhend, ihr Stolz, ihr süsses Mädchen, von ihren Küssen bedeckt, von ihren Armen umschlungen, so, so entfloh sie mir, die beste goldne Zeit!

Kann nichts sie zurück erflehen?

Bin ich ohne Rettung verloren?

(Once I was free from guilt. Without grief or tears, my spring blossomed full of gladness and gaiety, and love was as yet a stranger. Resting on my mother's bosom, her pride, her sweet girl, covered with her kisses, clasped in her arms, thus, thus did I pass the best, the golden time. Can nothing persuade it to return? Am I lost without help? Lost through a single false step?)

(Here am I now, deserted, deserted for ever! Gods, just, offended gods! How can you tolerate the evil-doer? You heard his vows, you know his perjury, his crime, and you do not punish him? Why does the thunder of your vengeance fall on me and not on him?)

These pieces caused a great sensation and immediately found imitators among opera and *Singspiel* composers, including Christian Gottlob Neefe, Reichardt, and Johann Rudolf Zumsteeg. Though they continued to be widely imitated, however, the first rapture soon died away. Goethe's attitude is evidence of this: his *Proserpina* of 1777 was an excellent contribution to the genre, but a decade later in his *Triumph der Empfindsamkeit* he unequivocally turned his back on it. At the same time the principle that lay behind melodrama, intensive delineation of the spoken word through music, was adopted by the *Singspiel* (in France by the *opéra comique*) and played an outstanding part at important stages of the action far into the nineteenth century.

GERMAN *SINGSPIEL*

While theorists and critics were expressing their views on opera in general and German opera in particular without any very tangible results, practical men of the theatre were actually laying the foundation of German opera by turning their attention to simple drama with musical numbers. The demise of early German opera and the consequent disappearance of the personnel which had performed it had left a vacuum which the German travelling companies of common players now endeavoured to fill. In the first place music was included in their baroque dramas and extempore comedies solely as an accessory, just like dances, scenic effects, and mechanical devices, for the sake of the impression produced on audiences. But at least by this means it was kept alive on German-speaking stages. Operatic arias and ensembles were used as well as popular lyrics and other forms of song. This development, starting in Vienna (see pp. 89 ff.), soon spread to Southern Germany.[1] In Central and Northern Germany it had to combat attempts at literary purity by Gottsched and the theatrical manager Karoline Neuber, and took root less easily. Nevertheless, audiences there too wanted to hear popular melodies which, being simple and well known, or of a familiar type, were easy to remember and take home. The players did their best to meet this taste.

The production, as a part of these efforts, by the Schönemann company of Charles Coffey's ballad opera *The Devil to Pay, or The Wives Metamorphos'd* (1743) in a German translation proved epoch-making. The simple song interpolations—probably the original English ballad tunes—were unassuming and catchy, exactly suited to their audience's fancy.[2] Dramatic managements were not slow to recognize that modest pieces of this kind gave them the best chance to enjoy full halls with comparatively small outlay. Schönemann performed the ballad opera in the following years at Hamburg and Leipzig. At the latter town the poet Christian Felix Weisse revised it, while the theatre musician of the newly assembled Koch company, J. C. Standfuss, provided it with new tunes. Then the company performed it there in 1752 with great success. In 1759 the same company produced at Lübeck the second part of the opera, *The Merry Cobbler* (*Der lustige Schuster*), after it had been revised by the same team. Gottsched might bluster against the farcical *Singspiele* as he had done against opera, but they continued to enjoy the utmost popularity, not least on account of Standfuss's fresh melodies, akin to folk tunes:[3]

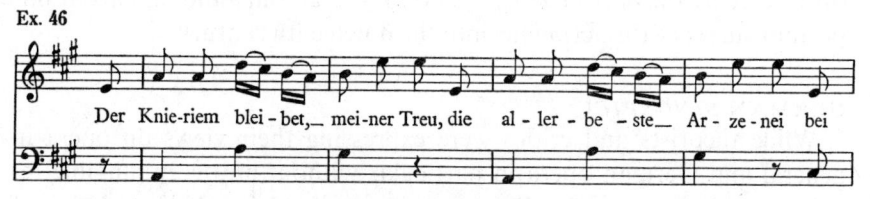

Ex. 46

Der Knie-riem blei-bet, mei-ner Treu, die al-ler-be-ste Ar-ze-nei bei

[1] Otto Bacher, 'Frankfurts musikalische Bühnengeschichte im 18. Jahrhundert. Teil I: Die Zeit der Wandertruppen (1700–1786)', in *Archiv für Frankfurts Geschichte und Kunst*, Fourth Series, i (Frankfurt, 1925), pp. 133 ff.

[2] Cf. Georgy Calmus, *Die ersten deutschen Singpiele von Standfuss und Hiller* (Leipzig, 1908) and Walter H. Rubsamen, 'Mr. Seedo, Ballad Opera, and the *Singspiel*', in *Miscelánea en homenaje a Mons. Higinio Anglés*, ii (Barcelona, 1958–61), p. 775.

[3] Calmus, ibid., p. 7. Another example is printed in Arnold Schering, *Geschichte der Musik in Beispielen* (Leipzig, 1931), p. 467.

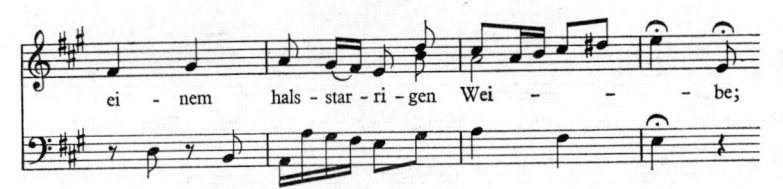

(By my faith, the strap's the best medicine for a stubborn wife.)

The progress of this rather primitive genre was at first impeded by the Seven Years War, so damaging to the activities of the travelling companies in Central Germany. When, however, the Koch company resumed its performances at Leipzig after the conclusion of peace, Weisse recast the two comedies after the French manner—he had been in Paris and seen the development of *opéra comique*. He extended the number of acts to three, polished the coarse language of farce, and above all considerably increased the number of songs, retaining of course the spoken dialogue. Thus the pieces were transformed from farces with interpolated songs into proper *Singspiele*. With the death of Standfuss, their musical setting was taken over by the immensely versatile Johann Adam Hiller, a man equally competent as composer, author, and organizer.[1] In this way the genre was saved from becoming simply a vulgarly comic box-office attraction.

Hiller was a well-educated man of good taste who knew all the styles of his day. He particularly liked the Italianate opera of Hasse, whom he idolized, but he was well aware that in *Singspiel* simple, tuneful songs were all-important. In his first attempt, *Die verwandelten Weiber oder Der Teufel ist los* (1766), he was accordingly careful to follow in Standfuss's footsteps. Indeed, he incorporated a large number of Standfuss's own melodies, as he did in the *Singspiel* performed in the same year, *Der lustige Schuster*. Even in these early works, however, he was so successful in striking the sentimental tone agreeable to German taste of the time that soon songs such as the following were on everybody's lips:[2]

Ex. 47

[1] Cf. article 'Hiller' in *Die Musik in Geschichte und Gegenwart*, vi.
[2] Max Friedlænder, *Das deutsche Lied im 18. Jahrhundert* (Stuttgart and Berlin, 1902), i (2), p. 137.

(Without love and wine what would our life be worth! All that gives us pleasure is due to them. When the great enjoy themselves what is it they enjoy? Pretty girls, good wine—just these alone.)

In his three most important and most popular *Singspiele*, *Lottchen am Hofe* (1767), *Die Liebe auf dem Lande* (1768), and *Die Jagd* (1770), he succeeded in blending the flowing line of *bel canto*, the chatter of *buffo* style, and the attractively pointed manner of speech in *opéra comique*—all within the framework of German tunefulness. Now one, now another of these characteristics was brought to the fore in the context of the dramatic action and yet without breaching the homogeneity of the *Singspiel*. A love-song of Prince Astolph:

Ex. 48

(Come, sweet hope, sink into my loving breast, fill me wholly, intoxicate me.)

and two lyrics sung by Lottchen:[1]

[1] Vocal score (Leipzig, 1769). Hiller brought out all his *Singspiele* in vocal scores with an eye to amateur performance. For the same reason he printed all the voice-parts in the treble clef.

Ex. 49

Ha ha ha ha ha ha ha ha ha ha ha ha ha ha ha, wie schnack-isch steh ich da, wie schnack-isch steh ich da! Das gros-se Ding zu tra - gen muss ich als wie ein Wa - gen von bei-den Sei - ten gehn

(How funny I look! To wear that great thing I've got to waddle from side to side like a cart.)

Ex 50

O macht mir doch von ew' - ger Treu nur nicht so viel Ge - schrei; be - ständ' - ge Lie - be macht nur Schmerz

(Oh don't make such a to-do about being eternally true; constancy in love only causes pain.)

from *Lottchen am Hofe* will serve as examples of Hiller's stylistic diversity. The orchestral score was kept as modest as possible in view of the limited resources of a travelling company,[1] although Hiller insisted upon a Neapolitan-style overture in three movements in all his works.

Simple strophic songs predominated in all Hiller's *Singspiele*. The success of these plays was in the first place based upon them. Of the following song from *Die Jagd*:

Ex. 51

Als ich auf mei-ner Blei - che ein Stück-chen Garn be - goss,
da kam aus dem Ge - sträu - che ein Mäd-chen a - tem - los,

das sprach: Ach, ach, Er - bar - men, steht mein-em Va - ter bei

(While I was bleaching a bit of yarn, there came from the bushes a breathless girl who cried, Oh mercy, help my father.)

Reichardt wrote in his essay 'On German Comic Opera':[2] 'the whole German nation is agreed that it is as perfect as songs of the kind can be. For everybody, from the highest to the lowest, sings and plays and whistles it—I might almost say, dins it into our ears—to such a degree is it being pressed into service all over Germany.' In the same essay Reichardt set up Hiller as a model to all *Singspiel* composers, defending him against the criticism that his works lacked variety. Hiller, he argued, produced unity which must not be confused with monotony.

Hiller's great importance does in truth rest upon the consistency with which he transferred contemporary German song to the stage. By doing so, he presented the German-speaking world with a 'German operetta'[3] even before Schweitzer and Holzbauer, and more obviously than they did. The recognition he received was accordingly widespread and great. Admittedly the reproach of monotony was not wholly unjustified: the predominance of sometimes flirtatious, sometimes sentimental, but always homespun songs, the absence of major musical forms, the very

---
[1] Cf. supra, p. 7.
[2] *Ueber die deutsche comische Oper, nebst einem Anhange eines freundschaftlichen Briefes über die musikalische Poesie* (Hamburg, 1774), p. 60.
[3] Ernst Ludwig Gerber, *Historisch-biographisches Lexikon der Tonkünstler* (Leipzig, 1790).

sparing use of ensembles, of small choruses, and of unintegrated instrumental contributions—all this, taken together, had a distinctly cramping effect and created a petit-bourgeois impression.

To the musical unity was added the unity between text and music, a requirement to be expected when travelling companies performed before audiences that were mainly middle-class and demanded a modicum of dramatic logic. *Opéra comique*, on which *Singspiel* was now modelled, embodied an ideal of naturalism derived from Rousseau. The plain, tuneful songs were the appropriate mode of expression for the peasants and craftsmen among whom the plots were laid. Four of Weisse's texts— *Der Dorfbalbier* (1771) in addition to those already mentioned—were adaptations of French pieces,[1] while others such as *Der Aerndtekranz* (1771) and *Die Jubelhochzeit* (1773) are slavish imitations. But the tendency of *opéra comique* to criticize society and praise the virtue of the lower classes at the expense of aristocrats, faded into the background of Weisse's worthy world of Lottchens, Röschens, Gürges, and Töffels. Hiller's music, deliberately undemanding, also helped to eliminate the element of social criticism.

For these reasons the *Singspiel* soon ran the risk of stagnation. As far as its texts were concerned, no one recognized this more clearly than Goethe.[2] He tried to give the genre greater variety of theme and better literary quality with products of his own, including *Erwin und Elmire* (1773-74), *Claudine von Villabella* (1774), *Lila* (1776), *Jery und Bätely* (1779), *Die Fischerin* (1782), and *Scherz, List und Rache* (1784). Goethe was able to do this because his work was produced in the highly cultivated atmosphere of the Court of Weimar, where he had no need to take into account the financial considerations of a travelling company, for instance the need to appeal to a wide range of tastes.

Most of his *Singspiele* were in the first place set to music by members of his Weimar circle, Grand Duchess Anna Amalie, Freiherr von Seckendorff, the singer Corona Schröter, and the musician Philipp Christoph Kayser. In addition, many of them were also set by Reichardt and later still by numerous other composers. Nevertheless, though Goethe provided every opportunity in these pieces for the use of more extended musical forms and distinctively operatic features, his musical collaborators mainly wrote the unpretentious type of German song

---

[1] The text of Hiller's first independent *Singspiel* subsequent to the adaptation of the two Standfuss compositions, the 'romantic' opera *Lisuart und Dariolette* (1766-7) by Daniel Schiebeler, was also taken from a previous *opéra comique* and, following its pattern, presents the first example of the German fairy-tale *Singspiel*. Songs from *Lisuart* and *Der Aerndtekranz* are printed in Davison and Apel, op. cit., p. 259, and Schering, op. cit., p. 468, respectively.

[2] Cf. Abert, *Goethe und die Musik* (Stuttgart, 1922); Friedrich Blume, *Goethe und die Musik* (Kassel, 1948).

favoured by adherents of the so-called 'Zweite Berliner Liederschule' ('second Berlin song school'), to which Reichardt also belonged.

Further progress in the *Singspiel* came not in the text but in the music. The petit-bourgeois background of Weisse's librettos continued to set the tone, despite Goethe's efforts, while at the same time, likewise under French influence, plays about magic and with exotic settings (Turkish especially) gained in importance. Those composers whose creative period began subsequent to Hiller—such as his contemporary Georg Benda, the younger Anton Schweitzer, Johann André, and Christian Gottlob Neefe—at first based their compositions on his type of *Singspiel*, but interspersed the short tuneful songs with true operatic arias of the most varied kinds, as well as extended ensembles. Finally they took to joining individual numbers to form entire scenes. In addition, as the companies acquired their own orchestras, the orchestration became more varied and colourful.

Even though the spoken dialogue stayed fundamentally unaltered, all these measures gave the *Singspiel* a larger scale and more operatic character, while at the same time forfeiting the unity Hiller had provided. Many composers regarded it as an experimental field for the evolution of German opera. Benda's earliest *Singspiel*, *Der Dorfjahrmarkt* (1775)[1] contained, for instance, such heterogeneous components as the brisk popular introductory chorus:

Ex. 52

(Drink! Since a drop still sparkles in your flask.)

[1] Ed. Theodor W. Werner, *Denkmäler deutscher Tonkunst*, lxiv. On Benda, cf. also Fritz Brückner, op. cit., p. 571.

GERMAN *SINGSPIEL*

a sentimental *da capo* aria:

Ex. 53

Hier steh ich vom Ge- fühl durch- drun- gen, ge- grüsst, ge- grüsst seid mir Er- in- ne- run- gen

(Here I stand filled with emotion, and salute my memories.)

and Bärbchen's unmistakable *opera seria* aria:

Ex. 54

Mich willst du, o Ge- lieb- ter, mich willst du, mich ver-

(You want to leave me, beloved, desert me! I will not let you go from my arms; only death shall separate me from you.)

Benda's later *Singspiele* (including *Walder* and *Julie und Romeo*, both 1776; and *Der Holzhauer*, 1778) comprised dramatically varied ensembles after the manner of *opera buffa*, *accompagnati* on the pattern of *opera seria*, and musical compounds in which the most heterogeneous forms were mingled. In providing a continuous musical setting for dramatically stirring scenes André and Neefe, who were much younger than Benda, went substantially farther and produced for the end of their acts finale-like movements or actual finales (André in *Der Barbier von Bagdad*, 1783, and *Die Entführung aus dem Serail*, 1781; and Neefe in *Adelheit von Veltheim*, 1780).[1] Besides this they extended the *Singspiel's* range of expression

[1] On André, see Stauder, 'Johann André'.

by absorbing melodrama into it André being the first to do so in *Laura Rosetti* (1778). In this respect, as in all their efforts to permeate the drama of the *Singspiel* with music, they were forerunners of Mozart. The latter's *Entführung* (1782) is largely identical textually with André's work of the same title, and Neefe's *Adelheit von Veltheim* is related to it at least so far as material is concerned.[1]

Besides the composers already mentioned, the composers of the Stuttgart Court gave *Singspiel* a specially enthusiastic welcome. Christian Ludwig Dieter and Johann Rudolf Zumsteeg in particular took part in the operatic elaboration of the form.[2] Both, being pupils of Jommelli, sought a fusion between the style of *Singspiel* and the elements of *opera seria*. Dieter, who in 1784 set the same text by Christoph Friedrich Bretzner that André had used for his *Entführung*, inclined by temperament rather more to the unpretentious tunefulness of Hiller's *Singspiele*. Zumsteeg preferred more demanding material (*Armida*, 1785; *Zalaor*, 1787) as well as dramatically live forms on a larger scale; he frequently introduced melodrama.

VIENNESE *SINGSPIEL*

In Central Germany the musical character of the *Singspiel* had been based on the *Lied* of the middle-classes of the time. These lyrics were popular indeed and appealed to more than one layer of society. But to make them part and parcel of a dramatic whole had required stimulation from the outside and this had first come through English ballad opera and then from French *opéra comique*. In contrast the Viennese *Singspiel* grew both musically and dramatically out of an indigenous tradition, namely, local presentations of improvised comedy which was couched, needless to say, in the native German.[3] Much of this has survived in oral tradition and in print, largely because of the popularity of Josef Felix von Kurz, who first appeared in the comic part of Bernardon in 1737. Sorcery and spectres and stage-machinery were prominent in these pieces, frequently for purposes of parody, as were cues calling for strong musical support. The oldest surviving music for the Viennese *Singspiel* are fragments from the fifties,[4] and these early specimens already displayed a variety of styles that went far beyond the German *Singspiel*.

[1] Cf. Walter Preibisch, 'Quellenstudien zu Mozarts "Entführung aus dem Serail": ein Beitrag zur Geschichte der Türkenoper', *Sammelbände der internationalen Musikgesellschaft*, x (1908–9), p. 430.
[2] Cf. Abert, 'Die dramatische Musik', in *Herzog Karl Eugen von Württemberg und seine Zeit*, vii (Esslingen, 1905), pp. 588 ff.
[3] Haas, 'Die Musik in der Wiener deutschen Stegreifkomödie', *Studien zur Musikwissenschaft*, xii (1925); Vladimir Helfert, 'Zur Geschichte des Wiener Singspiels', *Zeitschrift für Musikwissenschaft*, v (1922–3), p. 194.
[4] *Deutsche Komödienarien, 1754–1758*, ed. Haas, Denkmäler der Tonkunst in Oesterreich, xxxiii (1).

On the one hand, folk-songs, well-known songs of the day, and arias from Italian *opere serie* and *buffe* were taken over while, on the other, every current musical fashion was cleverly copied, since Vienna was one of the centres of European music at the time. Echoes from the Austrian folk music tradition, as in this *Ländler*-like song from *Der aufs neue begeisterte und belebte Bernardon* (1754):

Ex. 55

O je-gerl, potz-tau-send wie bin ich voll Freud,
ich bin ganz da-kem-ma, ich bin nim-mer

gscheit, gelt ja mei liebs Bu-berl, die I-sa-bel-la, die

hat dich recht lie-berl, von Her-zen ey ja.

(Goodness gracious, how happy I am, I hardly know what to do with myself. Tell me, dear laddie, Isabella loves you with all her heart, doesn't she?)

together with imitations, which often border on parody, of Italian arias, as in this extract from the same work:

Ex. 56

la Sor-te mia_____ cru-

[Musical notation with lyrics: "-de - le, la Sor - te mia cru - de - le lässt mir das bon-heur nicht, lässt mir das bon - heur nicht"]

(My cruel fate does not allow me to be happy.)

with appropriate texts for these different categories, played the most important part. The composers of the musical numbers,[1] often very witty, remained for long unknown. One of the first to be identified was Joseph Haydn, but the music to his *Der krumme Teufel* has been lost.[2] The pieces, with texts largely by Kurz—called Kurz-Bernardon and later simply Bernardon[3]—were enormously popular in Vienna despite the fact that after the sixties they could not compete with the musically more accomplished *opera buffa* or the stylistically coherent *opéra comique*, both of which also enjoyed Viennese encouragement. Nevertheless, as in Germany, *Singspiel* composers in the course of time sought more and more to give their work an operatic dimension.

In 1778 the Viennese *Singspiel* acquired in the new Burgtheater, opened by Joseph II as a 'national theatre', a new and, for the first time, a permanent home. Operatic performances in German began successfully on 17 February 1778 with Ignaz Umlauf's *Original-Singspiel* '*Die Bergknappen*'[4] which with its miscellany of musical styles was certainly faithful to Viennese tradition. There are unpretentious popular songs:

---

[1] Cf., for example, the crude parody lament and *ombra* scene in *Denkmäler der Tonkunst in Oesterreich*, xxxiii (1), p. 8, and the connection with an elegiac main aria section in G minor and a G major middle section wherein a series of gay national dances follow one another, ibid., p. 15.

[2] See infra, p. 174.

[3] Besides Haydn, who seems to have composed more than the *Teufel* for Kurz, the 'Bernardon' composers included Josef Starzer (1727–87), Franz Aspelmayr (1728–86), and Adalbert Fauner (d. 1769).

[4] Ed. Haas, *Denkmäler der Tonkunst in Oesterreich*, xviii (1). See pl. II.

Ex. 57

(Nothing is more cunning than love, it makes even the stupid crafty; follow your instincts and Sophie will be your wife.)

Italianate coloratura arias with solo instruments:

Ex. 58

PLATE II

A SCENE FROM UMLAUF'S *DIE BERGKNAPPEN*, 1778 (*see p. 91*)

(If Heaven smiles on me and makes me happy too, new life will be given me this day.)

genuine *opera seria* adjurations:

Ex. 59

Him - mel hör jetzt mei - - ne Bit - te,

raub mir mei - ne Ju - gend-blü - te.

(Heaven, now hear my prayer, rob me of the flower of youth.)

parlando-like *opera buffa* arias:

Ex. 60

[Musical notation with text: "Mein Herz fängt an zu za-gen, die Furcht ver-zeh-ret mich, es sind der Höl-le Pla-gen, die Lie-be rä-chet sich."]

(My heart begins to quail, fear consumes me, these are the tortures of hell, love has her revenge.)

simple music for wind instruments only, for the miners, alternating with chorus and succeeded by a highly emotional *accompagnato* in which the chorus joins; and finally a vaudeville finale on the model of *opéra comique*.

The same evidence of stylistic as well as formal richness, of a colourful interchange between solos, ensembles, and chorus, of carefully worked and varied instrumentation, is displayed in Umlauf's other *Singspiele* and in those of other Viennese composers such as Franz Aspelmayr, Maximilian Ulbrich, Johann Schenk, Joseph Ruprecht, Franz Teyber, Johann Mederitsch, and Joseph Weigl.[1] They differ from the earlier *Singspiel*-like comedies above all in the preponderance of music over spoken dialogue, just as the demands made upon singers and instrumentalists were greater. The aim was to engage for German opera in Vienna 'none but true musical virtuosos and no songsters'.[2] This last point contrasted sharply with the conditions under which composers for the *Singspiel* in Germany proper, such as Hiller in Leipzig, had to operate. In their texts the pieces followed partly the pattern of *opera buffa*, partly that of *opéra comique* but with the difference that the revolutionary trend of French libretti, which Weisse formally adopted, was completely ignored.

[1] See Haas, ibid, xviii (1).   Ibid., xviii (1), p. x.

Nevertheless, regardless of the zeal with which all concerned, from the Emperor down, nurtured this 'German opera', it was unable to prevail against the foreign variety. From the first season translations of French *opéras comiques* and Italian *opere buffe* began to appear on the boards of the national *Singspiel* theatre, and in succeeding years they became more and more popular. By contrast, specimens of the *Singspiel* imported from Germany, were generally rejected.[1] The Viennese were proudly aware of their own musical abundance and great tradition and were unsympathetic to the restraint of the Hiller school. In the spring of 1783 the German opera ensemble was disbanded. Italian opera had once more carried the day, and it remained predominant in Vienna's theatrical life even after regular German opera performances were resumed in the Kärntnertortheater in the autumn of 1785.

Those were the years when Karl von Dittersdorf's outstanding works (*Doktor und Apotheker* and *Betrug durch Aberglauben*, both 1786; and *Die Liebe im Narrenhaus*, 1787) roused the enthusiasm of audiences, including the Emperor himself. Dittersdorf, who had composed a series of *opere buffe*,[2] had an exact knowledge of how to write lively ensembles, particularly finales. During the eighties he introduced these features into the *Singspiel*—see, for instance, the following excerpt from *Doktor und Apotheker*:[3]

Ex. 61

[1] Ibid., xviii (1), *passim*.

[2] Some of them are available in German translation in the form of *Singspiele* with spoken dialogue in the place of recitative. Cf. Lothar Riedinger, 'Karl von Dittersdorf als Opernkomponist', in *Studien zur Musikwissenschaft*, ii (1914), p. 212.

[3] Vocal score, ed. Richard Kleinmichel (Leipzig, 1890). An aria from *Doktor und Apotheker* is recorded in *The History of Music in Sound*, vii; another is printed in Davison and Apel, op. cit., p. 267.

[Musical notation with vocal lines:]

wär auch schon ge-sche-hen, doch hab ichs nicht ge-wagt. Wa-rum nicht,

CLAUDIA

sprich, wes-we-gen?

ROSALIE

Sie woll-te sich just le-gen.

(LEONORE: Ah dearest mother, yes dearest mother! CLAUDIA: I've already told you. You should have gone to bed. LEONORE: I would have already, but I didn't dare. CLAUDIA: Why not, tell me? ROSALIE: She wanted to lie down just now.)

He thereby strengthened the operatic element and generally his lightness of touch enabled him to manipulate the various styles so skilfully that they no longer seemed simply heterogeneous components strung together but formed a fresh unity. How far the influence of Mozart, whose *Figaro* had been performed shortly before, played a part in this development must remain an open question.

When in the spring of 1788 the German opera company once more closed its doors, the *Singspiel* was again handed over to the suburban stages, especially those of the Theater in der Leopoldstadt and the Theater auf der Wieden. With their dependence on the box-office, these theatres frequently relied upon scenic tricks, and the resultant form was rightly called a *Maschinen–Komödie* (comedy involving stage machinery). Within this tradition two genres became prominent: the fairy-tale opera, which retained some of the grander operatic features within the style of the *Singspiel* (for example, *Oberon* by Paul Wranitzky, and *Das Sonnenfest der Brahminen* by Wenzel Müller: both 1790), and the musical fairy-tale farce with its greater emphasis on coarse and comic elements (for example, *Kaspar der Fagottist, oder Die Zauberzither* by Wenzel Müller, 1791). It was from components such as these that Mozart created his *Zauberflöte* and thereby made the Viennese *Singspiel* the most important point of departure for the development of German opera.

(d) THE OPERAS OF MOZART
By A. A. ABERT

THE EARLIEST WORKS

From the outset of his career as a composer of operas Mozart displayed his genius in his choice of texts.[1] Their selection was not a matter of chance but of intuition. After the commission to write a Latin school opera, *Apollo et Hyacinthus*, which he received at the age of eleven—a work which tended in the direction of *opera seria*—there followed three commissions which clearly prefigured the categories within which Mozart's operatic genius was to find its expression: the *opera buffa La finta semplice*, the German *Singspiel Bastien und Bastienne*, and the *opera seria Mitridate*. It is a striking fact that Mozart, though so versatile an artist and susceptible to all impressions, made no contribution to the two categories of French opera, *tragédie lyrique* and *opéra comique*. In the realm of instrumental music, too, it will be recalled, Mozart seemed to select his models with an unerring instinct when he was only eight years of age, as was shown by the manner in which he absorbed the styles of Johann Schobert in Paris and Johann Christian Bach in London.[2]

Indeed, the influence of the 'London' Bach, whose work and vivid personality he came to know in 1764, was considerable. At the same time, some basic instruction in the Italian art of singing, indispensable to an incipient opera composer, was provided by the castrato Giovanni Manzuoli. How deeply he had already penetrated the world of *opera seria* is shown in two aria improvisations which, according to a contemporary critic, were wholly correct in construction and expression, and 'showed most extraordinary readiness of invention'.[3] The first fruits

---

[1] All the operas are contained in the old complete edition (Leipzig, 1876–1907), Series V. Those which have already appeared in the *Neue Mozart-Ausgabe* will be indicated as such.

[2] See Otto Jahn–Hermann Abert, *W. A. Mozart*, 2 vols. (Leipzig, 7th edn., 1955), i, p. 62. The present account owes much to the foregoing work, but acknowledgement is made only in special instances. It will hereafter be cited as Abert, *Mozart*. See also Dent, *Mozart's Operas: A Critical Study* (London, 2nd edn., 1947).

[3] Daines Barrington's report is printed in *Mozart. Die Dokumente seines Lebens*, ed. Otto Erich Deutsch (Kassel, 1961), p. 86.

of the inspiration received in London were the arias 'Va dal furor portata' (K. 21 = 19c[1]) and 'Conservati fedele' (K. 23); the recitative and aria 'Or che il dover' and 'Tali e cotanti sono' (K. 36 = 33i), cast in the form of a *licenza* (song of homage at the close of an opera); and, finally, the recitative and aria 'A Berenice' and 'Sol nascente' (K. 70 = 61c), set down immediately after his return to Salzburg in December 1766.[2]

Almost eleven now, he was faced with commissions of a larger and more difficult sort. He had to provide the music to the first half of Ignaz Anton Weiser's oratorio, *Die Schuldigkeit des Ersten Gebots* (K. 35; first performance Salzburg, 12 March 1767) and was then invited to compose the intermezzi for the performance of a Latin play by the pupils of the university-school. Since the city's best musicians were called upon to compose the interludes,[3] Mozart's selection for this task showed that university circles recognized his claim to be taken seriously. The performance of the Latin play *Clementia Croesi* took place on 13 May 1767, together with an untitled operatic intermezzo. The play deals with the vacillations of King Croesus between wrath and love for his favourite Adrastes, who had killed his son. The story of the intermezzo closely resembles that of the play. Oebalus, whose son Hyacinthus has been killed, rages against his reputed murderer, the god Apollo, though in fact it was Zephyrus who did the deed. Apollo transforms Zephyrus into a breeze while his victim is metamorphosed into a flower. The god, reconciled with Oebalus, then marries Melia, his daughter. The title *Apollo et Hyacinthus* was an insertion, made as late as 1799, in the handwritten list of Mozart's early works originally compiled by his father.[4]

Mozart, at this early age, confronted this dull Latin text without preconceived dramatic ideas and set it to music, perhaps understandably, as if it had been an Italian libretto. The intermezzo was composed in three parts, of which the 'Prologus' followed the play's prologue. 'Chorus I' and 'Chorus II' followed the play's second and fourth acts respectively. The difficulties of Latin metre in the recitative portions Mozart evaded by treating the verse as prose; the self-contained pieces—a chorus, a trio,

---

[1] Each work by Mozart is referred to by the standard abbreviation K (Köchel) and also given the revised number assigned to it in Ludwig von Köchel, *Verzeichnis sämtlicher Tonwerke Wolfgang Amadé Mozarts* (Wiesbaden, 6th edn., 1964), ed. Franz Giegling, Alexander Weinmann and Gerd Sievers.

[2] See Herbert Klein, 'Unbekannte Mozartiana von 1766–67', *Mozart–Jahrbuch 1957* (Salzburg, 1958), p. 182, n. 34.

[3] See Robert Haas, 'Eberlins Schuldramen und Oratorien', *Studien zur Musikwissenschaft*, viii (1921), and Constantin Schneider, 'Die Oratorien und Schuldramen Anton Cajetan Adlgassers', *ibid.*, xviii (1931).

[4] Further details in Alfred Orel's preface (1959) in the *Neue Mozart–Ausgabe*. Leopold Mozart's list is reprinted in *Mozart: Briefe und Aufzeichnungen*, ed. Wilhelm A. Bauer and Otto Erich Deutsch, 4 vols. (Kassel, 1962–3), i, pp. 287–9.

some arias, and duets—though on a larger scale, were composed with the same skill in the manipulation of form and means of expression as the earlier single arias had been. By and large the various pieces successfully express the meaning and feeling of the text. In Apollo's aria (No. 3), 'Jam pastor Apollo', wherein the god reveals himself as the shepherd and helper of all living beings, the gently moving melody aptly underlines the words in the first part:

Ex. 62

musical notation with text: Iam pa-stor A-pol-lo cu-sto-di-o gre-ges, ni-xus et ba-cu-lo vi-gi-lans sto:

(Now I, Apollo the shepherd, guard the flocks, and stand on watch leaning on my staff.)

On the other hand, the changes of key and of signature in the second part seem entirely arbitrary:

Ex. 63

Moestos levare, aegros juvare est sola tangens Apollinem res:

(To cheer the sad, to help the sick alone concerns Apollo.)

The recitative is generally conventional and schematic, but at two important junctures of the action, the death of Hyacinthus and his metamorphosis, it becomes an expressive *accompagnato*. The two duets were among Mozart's best. In the first he sought to bring out a descriptive contrast between the wrathful Melia and the innocent Apollo. The second, an elegiac duet between Melia and Oebalus,[1] is distinguished by subtle instrumentation (first violins *con sordini*, second violins and bass pizzicato, divided violas, and two horns) and a line of melody appropriate to the situation, both dignified and graceful:

[1] See Roland Tenschert, 'Das Duett Nr. 8 aus Mozarts "Apollo et Hyacinthus" und das Andante aus der Sinfonie K. 43. Vergleichende Studie', *Mozart–Jahrbuch 1958* (Salzburg, 1959), p. 59.

Ex. 64

(My son falls, and the injured god departs, without my wish or knowledge.)

Noteworthy in both the vocal numbers and in the overture are the use of divided violas and the independent lines of the orchestral parts, both features deriving from the traditions of Salzburg.

YOUTHFUL WORKS IN A TRADITIONAL PATTERN

Having tested his talents on the home ground of Salzburg University, Mozart proceeded to put to use the experience thus acquired by composing for the stage. During a visit to Vienna in 1768, in company with his father, the Emperor Joseph invited him to write an opera for the Court theatre. Leopold Mozart felt that Wolfgang's hour had struck and decided in favour of an *opera buffa*, since this genre was enjoying a growing popularity and the ensemble of singers available was likely to be good. The selection of the text, however (probably Leopold's choice), was not propitious: *La finta semplice* by Goldoni, as adapted for the Viennese theatre by the Court poet Marco Coltellini.[1] The theme was that of the old miser, hoodwinked by a young pair. The wily heroine, the 'finta semplice', with the aid of two light-hearted servants, in fact defies two old bachelors in order to further the cause of her brother, who is in love with the young sister of the two old men. This crude plot was made worse by the clumsiness of the libretto. Apart from the introduction, the three finales and a single duet, the self-contained pieces of the opera consisted exclusively of arias that expressed the usual uncomplimentary feelings of one sex towards the other. This method was quite contrary to *opera buffa's* principal attraction which lay in the abundance of ensembles.

Mozart probably did not notice these flaws as such. Without any preconceived plan he eagerly set one aria after another, restricting his attention to the text of a single number, and endeavouring to express its meaning. For instance, the song of Rosina, 'finta semplice', addressed to the Amoretti (no. 15), is an appealing love lyric in the spirit of Johann Christian Bach:

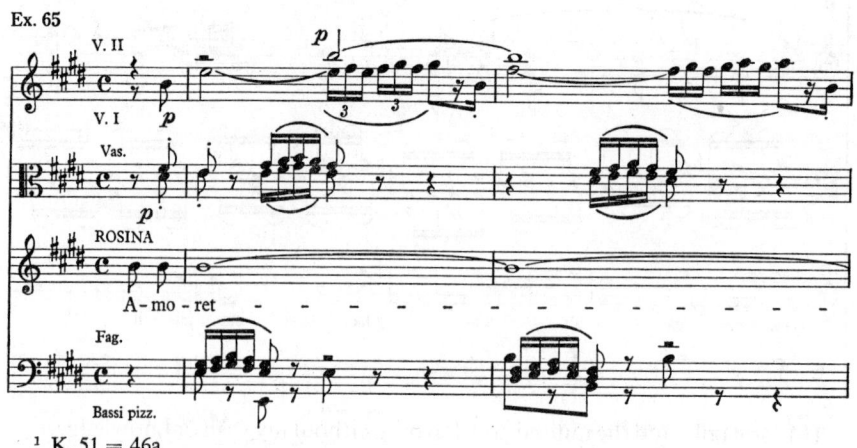

Ex. 65

[1] K. 51 = 46a

(Little cupids who are hidden here and wound as you fly around)

In old Cassandro's aria (no. 16) he made delightful use of the orchestral instruments to depict the drunkard's staggering:

Ex. 66

(I am not drunk, no, I am not drunk, I am a little merry, I am a little merry.)

In duet No. 12 he gets palpable enjoyment from the portrayal of a duel. He was not, however, yet equal to a more penetrating interpretation, with the result that in the majority of arias the music is not closely tied to the words. In aria No. 7, 'Cosa ha mai la donna', Mozart borrowed heavily, to the extent of actual passages, from the aria, 'Manches Übel will zuweilen' in his own oratorio *Die Schuldigkeit des Ersten Gebots*, though there is not the slightest connection between the two texts.

Nevertheless this opera showed a great step forward in the young composer's creative achievement. He would seem to have made good use of his time in Vienna and especially to have listened with understanding to the works of the contemporary leading Viennese *opera buffa* composer, Florian Gassmann. In *La finta semplice* the arias were predominantly bipartite in accordance with current *opera buffa* practice, either as simple cavatinas or in two parts, each of which were divided into two further sub-sections differentiated by pace and time-signature. Mozart adhered to the *da capo* form in two arias only, sung by the lover Fracasso. His careful treatment of the orchestra, which often interpreted the action instead of merely accompanying the voices (cf. Exx. 65 and 66), revealed the influence of Gassmann and the Viennese *buffa* school. Though Mozart had made a beginning with his little school opera, he profited now from the richer instrumentation of his models. In aria No. 9, 'Senti l'eco', for instance, in addition to the usual string quartet, he used a solo oboe and a pair each of cors anglais and hunting horns, with the oboe playing the role of the echo. To the Viennese tradition, too, belongs the admixture of popular elements reminiscent of the *Lied* as seen, for example, in the following passage from the third finale:

Ex. 67

[musical example: Andante grazioso, with parts for Vns., Vas., ROSINA/POLIDORO, and bass, with text "Al-me bel-le in-na-mo-ra-te, u-na man che voi bac-cia-te, vi può"]

(Beautiful enamoured spirits, a hand which you kiss.)

The finales are in the usual 'chain' or rondo pattern and lack any particular dramatic distinction. For his overture he fell back on his D major symphony of January 1768 (K. 45), simply altering the instrumentation and omitting the minuet.

To the great disappointment of father and son, a performance of the opera did not take place in Vienna;[1] instead, it occurred at Salzburg on

[1] See Leopold Mozart's letters to Hagenauer, 30 July and 21 September 1768 in Emily Anderson, *The Letters of Mozart and His Family*, 3 vols. (London, 1938), i, pp. 132 and 138.

1 May 1769.[1] *La finta semplice* was followed by an invitation by the magnetist Dr. Franz Anton Mesmer of Vienna to set the *Singspiel Bastien und Bastienne* to music.[2] This commission called for a new approach. The previously caricatured Italian *buffo* types were replaced by a pair of unsophisticated pastoral lovers whose fate takes a fortunate turn thanks to the intervention of the wise village soothsayer. The text originated from Rousseau's famous *intermède Le Devin du village* of 1752[3], which not only furthered the development of French comic opera in the spirit of the author's naturalism, but, like all successful French operas, forthwith inspired a parody, *Les Amours de Bastien et Bastienne* by Favart, his wife, and Harny. Mozart used the German translation of Friedrich Wilhelm Weiskern with no more than minor emendations.

This unpretentious one-act German text made small demands in comparison with the Italian opera in three acts which he had just completed. Yet in the latter case he had simply to imitate the general style of numerous predecessors, whereas no clearly established pattern existed for the *Singspiel*. Mozart neatly solved the problem by blending the familiar German song style with the *buffo* manner, employing the one or the other according to the demands of character portrayal or dramatic situation.

The overture, entitled 'Intrada', consists of a single movement, and with the modesty of its solitary, often quoted theme it serves from the start to outline a charmingly pastoral atmosphere. The rustic character is sustained by Bastienne, the innocent country girl, in her first aria:

Ex. 68
Andante, un poco adagio
BASTIENNE

Mein lieb-ster Freund hat mich ver-las-sen, mit ihm ist Schlaf_ und
Str. & Ob.
p

[1] Alfred Loewenberg, *Annals of Opera* (Geneva, 2nd edn., 1955), cols. 306–7. But Deutsch, *Dokumente*, p. 82, questions the date.
[2] K. 50 = 46b. Leopold Mozart in his list of Mozart's early works dates *Bastien und Bastienne* before *La finta semplice*, whereas Georg Nissen (*Mozart*, Leipzig, 1828) puts it later. There exists also a hypothesis, not as yet proven, that Mozart began the composition of *Bastien* at Salzburg in 1767, interrupted it when he left for Vienna, and resumed work on it only at Mesmer's encouragement. See Loewenberg, 'Bastien and Bastienne Once More', *Music and Letters*, xxv (1944), p. 176; Orel, 'Die Legende um Mozarts "Bastien und Bastienne"', *Schweizerische Musikzeitung*, xci (1951), p. 137.
[3] See infra, pp. 202–3.

(My dearest friend has left me, and sleep and peace have gone with him.)

The irresponsible Bastien, who is something of a braggart, is given arias more in the nature of a *buffo* hero:

Ex. 69

(To render profound thanks to you, Mr. Colas, is my duty.)

And the invocation of the spirits by the village soothsayer Colas (no. 11) adds to the unpretentious rural frame a parody of *opera seria*, the ever-popular ingredient in *opera buffa*. This element of parody is present in the gibberish of the text as well as in the music, which is unrealistically serious in both tonality and vocal line:

Ex. 70

Andante maestoso
COLAS

Dig - gi, dag - gi, schur - ry, mur - ry, ho - rum, ha - rum,

The young Mozart merged a variety of styles into a homogeneous product, and he successfully achieved a harmonious work in keeping with the text. The formal patterns and the orchestration are distinctly simpler than in *La finta semplice*. The scoring is modest: to the quartet of strings are added two oboes (on one occasion two flutes) or two horns, and it is only in the two closing ensembles that oboes *and* horns are called on to amplify without ever becoming obbligato. Only once (no. 14) does Mozart substitute for the spoken dialogue typical of the *Singspiel* a recitative leading to an arioso.

Bastien und Bastienne was probably first performed in the autumn of 1768 in Dr. Mesmer's house.[1] Like its predecessors, *Apollo et Hyacinthus* and *La finta semplice*, it was an experiment which was enjoyed by the narrow circle for which it was intended and then was heard no more: the indubitable gain in artistry was thus not coupled with a gain in reputation. Leopold was more than ever eager to take his son to Italy, where young German-speaking composers were still accustomed to win their spurs.

Complete success awaited Mozart there. In the space of three years, 1770–2, he received three commissions for performance at important opera houses, only two of which, for Milan, he was able to execute.[2] In

[1] Not, as formerly supposed, in Mesmer's garden theatre, which had not yet been built. For this reason Orel, op. cit., doubts whether the performance took place at all.

[2] The contract for the third commission, with the Teatro S. Benedetto at Venice, is reproduced in Deutsch, *Dokumente*, p. 121.

addition, he was entrusted by the Viennese Court with the composition of a festive serenata for the Archduke Ferdinand's wedding celebrations in Milan. These years also witnessed the installation of a new archbishop at Salzburg in whose honour another solemn serenata had to be composed.

With the performance of four stage works—*Mitridate, re di Ponto* (K. 87=74a), Milan, 26 December 1770; *Ascanio in Alba* (K. 111), Milan, 17 October 1771; *Il sogno di Scipione* (K. 126), Salzburg, probably at the beginning of May 1772; *Lucio Silla* (K. 135), Milan, 26 December 1772—this period formed the peak of the young opera composer's career, a series of successes which was not to be repeated for the rest of his life.

Mozart first busied himself with *opera seria*, the customary practice-ground for young opera composers. The arias produced during the preceding years in London, The Hague, and Salzburg, not to mention his Viennese commissions, showed his familiarity with the genre. No opportunity was missed to visit the opera houses in Italy, and his letters to his sister displayed genuinely professional judgement on the works and especially on the performances to be seen there. Equally professional was the range of newly composed arias which he presented to Italian audiences in the spring of 1770, including three each from Metastasio's *Artaserse* (K. 78, 88, 79 = 73b, c, d) and *Demofoonte* (K. 77, 82, 83 = 73e, o, p) and one from *Demetrio* which has not been preserved (K. 72a). They were influential in shortly procuring for him his first commission for the Milanese Teatro Regio Ducale.

There is no doubt that for a youthful composer with ideas and in command of his craft, *opera seria* was textually and musically far less flexible in its patterns and formulae than *opera buffa* and therefore based on a technique which was more easily employed. Only within the framework of such a tradition could Mozart have succeeded in the enormous task of composing, rehearsing, and directing four stage-works as well as innumerable other pieces during his three Italian journeys.

Of the four works mentioned, the first, *Mitridate, re di Ponto*[1], opened the door to further commissions and the last, *Lucio Silla*, finally closed it. Both were genuine specimens of *opera seria*, with standard types of action, stock personages, and the whole following faithfully in Metastasio's footsteps. In both cases the hero of the title is a ruler who, as a powerful rival, threatens the happiness of a young couple, and at the last brings himself to noble renunciation. Mozart behaved like a true *compositore scritturato*: he accepted the librettos without a murmur and set them to music in conformity with the tradition exemplified by J. C.

[1] Ed. Luigi F. Tagliavini in *Neue Mozart-Ausgabe* (Series II, Group 5, iv, 1966).

Bach and Hasse. He paid attention to his singers' capabilities and—to a considerable extent—their wishes. By these methods he caught the public taste. At its first performance in Milan on 26 December 1770, *Mitridate* was received with warm approbation. There were twenty-two subsequent presentations[1]—a noteworthy success for a work by a foreigner barely fifteen years old. This success was repeated two years later with *Lucio Silla*, which enjoyed twenty-six performances.

Despite the many characteristics which linked the two operas, there were far-reaching differences: in the interpretation of action and emotions; and in the overall structure and individual patterns of the music itself, in regard to the techniques of both composition and instrumentation. The earlier opera, with its stereotyped alternation of *secco* recitative and aria (only rarely interrupted by brief *accompagnati*), with only two ensembles and no chorus, was by far the more regular and conservative. The two customary contemporary abridgements of the *da capo* form predominated among the arias;[2] besides them there were a few songs in two sections, whose second part was a variant of the first.

In *Lucio Silla* the rigid uniformity of the genre underwent considerable relaxation. The *accompagnato* recitatives are more numerous and of a higher quality. There are five ensembles and choruses, and towards the close of the first and second acts the composer's wish to link these various dramatic components into a dramatic relationship becomes clear. This is particularly the case with the concluding scenes of the first act which take place in the burial vault and which include such varied components as Cecilio's extended *accompagnato*, an invocatory chorus on the lines of Gluck, a further *accompagnato* and a duet by the pair of lovers. The chorus, as in so many works of Gluck, offers a diversity of sonority and texture by incorporating a solo by the heroine. Whereas in *Mitridate* Mozart had used a limited number of formal patterns, however freely he may have handled them, in *Lucio Silla* he uses an abundance of structural shapes. Both conventional and novel constructions make their appearances: the old *da capo* form in five sections (no. 1) as well as bipartite forms where the second part offers a sharp and piquant contrast, in the manner of *opera buffa* (nos. 13 and 22).

The instrumentation is also richer. In *Mitridate* Mozart used a string orchestra, plus two oboes and two horns (occasionally only one of these groups). This was normal in Italian opera, Trumpets were brought in for a single aria (no. 1). In *Lucio Silla* there are oboes, horns, and trumpets, reinforced here and there by kettle-drums and once by bassoons. Moreover, all the parts are allowed greater

[1] Deutsch, *Dokumente*, p. 116.
[2] See above, p. 15.

independence, though it goes without saying that Mozart was always mindful of the resultant ensemble. Cecilio's aria (no. 14) is a rare example, at this stage of Italian opera, of the use of obbligato wind instruments:

Ex. 71

The main sign of progress in *Lucio Silla* was that the music frequently expressed the feelings of the characters. To be sure, even in *Mitridate* the young composer had aimed in this direction, but only rarely did he succeed, as in the G minor lament of Aspasia (no. 4). Here purely musical effects, such as prolonged ritornellos and coloratura features, were set aside. Instead the heroine's sensations were depicted by the choice of key, the chromatic progressions, and the faltering declamation of the voice to the discreet accompaniment of the orchestra:

YOUTHFUL WORKS IN A TRADITIONAL PATTERN

Ex. 72

(In my breast beats my suffering heart, my sorrow calls me to weep.)

But despite this effort to reflect emotions, the meaning of the words in *Mitridate* was seldom so persuasively underlined. The majority of the arias do not extend beyond a conventional, though fresh, musical style. Indeed, this opera contains some astonishing infelicities of expression. The entrance aria (no. 1) of Aspasia, a prayer, is scored as an *aria di bravura* and unsuitable melismas adorn the vanquished Mitridate's proud proclamation (no. 7) that in spite of disaster his heart remains steadfast.

Lucio Silla has no such errors. The arias show that far more than in previous works Mozart dismissed convention and put his mind to the text. Significantly, these arias are in two contrasting parts, a form which *opera seria* had lately taken over from *opera buffa*. The arias are

Ex. 73

(Amid most gloomy thoughts of death)

mainly allotted to the heroine Giunia, whose numbers differ from those of the traditional type of leading lady in several ways: the avoidance of the *da capo* form, the careful integration between the emotions, as suggested by the libretto, and the expressive character of the music. The taut introduction to aria no. 22 (Ex. 73), in which Giunia thinks her lover has invited her to join him in death, is devoted entirely to a reflection of the mood, and points to the Mozart of the future.

As in *Mitridate*, however, he had to allow for the deployment of purely vocal virtuosity, always working closely with the singers. Hence, in deference to the prima donna and the primo uomo *Lucio Silla* has the customary *arie di bravura* (for instance, nos. 2 and 11) which are noticeably different from those arias in which one finds personal and individual expression. About half the arias are preceded by prolonged *accompagnato* recitatives distinguished by particularly detailed interpretation of the words. A passage from Cecilio's recitative prefacing aria no. 9 may be taken as an example:

Ex. 74

(O gods, and in the meantime does my bride remain beside my enemy? Alas, who defends her? But what if he comes here?)

The thematic homogeneity of this movement, which hints once more at the later Mozart, is exceptional in *Lucio Silla*. Obbligato wind instruments were added to the strings in the *accompagnati* preceding nos. 6 and 22. The *recitativo secco* is carefully set in both operas, though in *Lucio Silla* it is, at times, more varied in harmony than in the earlier piece. The overtures to *Mitridate* and *Lucio Silla* betray the influence of their Italian models: the succession of the three component movements as well as the structure and character of these movements are more unmistakably Italian than Mozart's concert symphonies composed during these years.

In accordance with Mozart's desire for greater flexibility *Lucio Silla* was an attempt to inject more life into the rigid form of *opera seria*, so far as his talents then allowed. This may have been one of the reasons why, in spite of the opera's success, no further commissions were forthcoming. On the other hand, Mozart was probably no longer considered an infant prodigy. Fortunately, his departure from Italy and return to Salzburg did not impede his progress as an opera composer. Instead he was led to concern himself once more with other operatic genres, the techniques of which he had already mastered as a boy.

The two festive serenatas which were written between *Mitridate* and *Lucio Silla*, *Ascanio in Alba* and *Il sogno di Scipione*, contained no developments of importance not already observed in the operas. Both have the sub-title 'azione teatrale', customary at the time for such occasional works. The text of *Ascanio in Alba* was especially written by the Milanese poet Giuseppe Parini for the wedding of the Archduke Ferdinand and Maria Ricciarda Beatrice of Modena. *Il sogno di Scipione*, originally intended for the Emperor Charles VI's birthday on 1 October 1735, was an already existing poem by Pietro Metastasio in which only the names in the *licenza* (epilogue) had been altered. The action simply formed an excuse for compliments to the bride and bridegroom or the celebrant, and the composer had no responsibility except to provide an inspired flow of music.

Ascanio, celebrating a marriage in the Austrian Imperial family, aptly proved that Mozart was master of the art not only of Neapolitan opera, which was composed mainly for soloists, but of Viennese opera as well, which made lavish use of choral music. Nearly half its numbers consist of choruses distributed throughout the two acts and repeated in a variety of ways. (Chorus no. 2, 'Di te più amabile', reappears as nos. 4 and 18; no. 6, 'Venga de' sommi Eroi', is repeated in nos. 7, 10, 11, 15, and 26.) The choruses are all homophonic, written partly in a simple chordal style—as in the initial and final choruses—and partly embellished by a certain amount of imitation. Indeed, the three-part chorus of the shepherdesses, no. 24, begins like a canon:

Ex. 75
Allegro

(What strange event disturbs the virgin this day! No, let us not leave her.)

As well as composing the ballet music[1] for the entr'acte of this serenata Mozart also worked on the overtures of both *Ascanio* and *Scipione* in order to make them suitable for instrumental performance in their own right. Both these overtures had been closely connected with the initial scenes of the respective operas, but now he added finales, thereby making them independent concert symphonies. The wedding festivities for the Archduke Ferdinand (October 1771) included the presentation of Mozart's youthful *Ascanio* as well as of *Il Ruggiero* by the aged Hasse.[2] The coincidence was noteworthy, for Hasse's career was now finished, and Mozart appeared to be taking over from him where he had left off. Yet it was soon evident that this was not to be.

In the spring of 1773, following the première of *Lucio Silla*, Mozart's appointment as Konzertmeister (leader) to the Prince Archbishop necessitated his return to Salzburg. Major operatic performances at Salzburg were reserved for special festive occasions, and Mozart's Italian success had apparently not been great enough to earn him commissions from German-speaking theatres elsewhere. Thus Mozart's first operatic period, in which he skilfully imitated established styles was, perforce, separated from the second period by some years of highly fruitful activity in the fields of ecclesiastical and instrumental music. The compositions of that time—principally the String Quartets K. 168–73, the Piano Concerto K. 175, the 'little' G minor Symphony K. 183, and the A major Symphony (K. 201 = 186a)—showed him fully engaged in making his mark as a musician of individual stamp.

[1] Leopold Mozart to his wife, 7 September 1771; Anderson, *Letters*, i, p. 286. Only the vocal bass part survives in a copyist's version. The ballet *Le gelosie del serraglio*, K. App. 109 = 135a, belongs to *Lucio Silla*, not *Ascanio*; moreover, its authenticity is dubious, see Walter Senn, 'Mozarts Skizze der Ballettmusik zu "Le gelosie del serraglio"', *Acta Musicologica*, xxxiii (1961), p. 169.

[2] See the edition by Tagliavini in the *Neue Mozart–Ausgabe* (1956), p. ix; also Hans Engel, 'Hasses Ruggiero und Mozarts Festspiel Ascanio', *Mozart–Jahrbuch 1960–61* (Salzburg, 1961), p. 29.

THE SUPREMACY OF MUSIC OVER DRAMA

This period claims a composition which, though no opera, was written for the stage and was in Mozart's thoughts for a long time. It consisted of the choruses and the entr'acte music to the 'heroic drama' *Thamos, König in Ägypten* by Tobias Philipp, Freiherr von Gebler (K. 345=336a). He probably received the commission when he stayed in Vienna from July to September 1773, and the performance took place in Vienna on 4 April 1774.[1] The two choruses from the first and fifth acts were hymns in honour of the divinity. These choruses were composed on a far more majestic scale than those of *Ascanio in Alba*. Their structure and character was determined by the alternation between the lively flowing duets of female or male voices and solemn, compact choral ritornellos in which all four parts were united. Mozart later recast the two choruses and added a third whose text did not form part of Gebler's drama.

Just when the entr'acte music was conceived is uncertain; there is no mention of it in connection with the Vienna performance of 1774, although stylistically it would fit into this period,[2] and only the melodrama after the third act might suggest a later date. In any case the music of *Thamos* forms a bridge between the early operas and Mozart's second operatic period, which began in 1774 and ended with his move to Vienna in 1781. This period produced four operas: *La finta giardiniera* (K. 196), Munich, 13 January 1775; *Il re pastore* (K. 208), Salzburg, 23 April 1775; *Zaide* (K. 344=336b), composed Salzburg 1779/80; and *Idomeneo, re di Creta* (K. 366—367), Munich, 29 January 1781. Their dramatic structure remained traditional, but from the very start they showed not only Mozart's characteristic musical originality but also marks of the masterpieces to come.[3] So far as the texts for these operas were concerned, the old procedure was unaltered: they arrived along with the commissions. This practice inevitably restricted the composer's scope. *Il re pastore*, the second of the group, which Mozart was commissioned to set for the elaborate reception of the Archduke Maximilian at Salzburg, was a particularly striking example. The adaptation produced a truncated version of Metastasio's drama in two acts and concluded with a fresh text which related to the honoured guest, turning an opera, as it were, into a festive serenata.

---

[1] Deutsch, *Dokumente*, pp. 131 and 133.

[2] See Théodore de Wyzewa and Georges de Saint-Foix, *W. A. Mozart*, 5 vols. (Paris, 1912–46), ii, pp. 116 ff.; iii, pp. 186 ff.

[3] See Alfred Heuss, 'Mozarts "Idomeneo" als Quelle für "Don Giovanni" und "Die Zauberflöte"', *Zeitschrift für Musikwissenschaft*, xiii (1930–1), p. 177; Alexander Hyatt King, 'The Melodic Sources and Affinities of "Die Zauberflöte"', *Musical Quarterly*, xxxvi (1950), p. 241; A. A. Abert, '"La finta giardiniera" und "Zaide" als Quellen für spätere Opern Mozarts', *Musik und Verlag* (Kassel, 1968), p. 113.

The fable of the shepherd who, unknown to himself, is heir to a vast kingdom, with its constant reflections upon the qualities of a good shepherd and a good ruler, was highly suitable to the occasion. Mozart's music remained within the framework of the genre, and he attempted no individual delineation of character or scenes. Nevertheless, the balance between voices and orchestra, the skill in orchestral writing, and the supple and original melodic material, were signs of a mastery far surpassing the level of his more youthful works. A passage from the rondo no. 10 of the hero Aminta, 'L'amerò, sarò costante', with its splendid group of instruments—flutes, English horns, bassoons, horns, and solo violin alongside the strings—gives the impression of being more appropriate to concert platforms than the stage, as indeed, does the entire movement.

Ex. 76

so - spi - re - rò.

(I shall sigh only for her.)

The overture, a single movement leading into the first scene, was later expanded into a concert symphony by an additional movement, a procedure also followed with the introductions to *Ascanio in Alba*, *Il sogno di Scipione*, and *La finta giardiniera*.[1]

Mozart may have felt the Salzburg commission had resulted merely from his appointment and was therefore one to be got out of the way quickly. The invitation of the Munich Court, however, to compose an *opera buffa* for the carnival season 1774–5 heralded his long-awaited return to the great world of opera. Seven years, during which he had developed into a self-reliant musician, as well as a practised operatic composer, had passed since *La finta semplice*, his initial essay in the comic vein. It is not known exactly when Mozart wrote *La finta giardiniera*. What is known is that he travelled to Munich on 6 December 1774[2] and that the première did not take place until 13 January 1775. The text is thought to have been derived from Ranieri Calzabigi and arranged by Marco Coltellini.[3] The plot concerns Violante who enters the service of old Anchise disguised as the gardener Sandrina to search for her lover Belfiore, only to discover that he is unfaithful. At the same time she herself has to fend off her master's advances. Not so coarse as the story of *La finta semplice*, it was just as clumsily executed. Its 'parti serie' put it into the category of sentimental comedy, but these serious parts were confusingly intermingled with farcical elements. This

---

[1] It is probable that the *sinfonia* movement K. 120 = 111a was used as finale to the overture to *Ascanio in Alba* while the overture to *Il sogno di Scipione* was turned into the symphony K. 161 = 141a by addition of the movement K. 163. Mozart probably intended that the single movements K. 102 = 213c and K. 121 = 207a should be added to the overtures of *Il re pastore* and *La finta giardiniera* respectively.

[2] See Deutsch, *Dokumente*, p. 134.

[3] Loewenberg, *Annals*, col. 341. *La finta giardiniera* does not, however, appear in the 1774 or 1793 editions of Calzabigi's works. The quality of the text, too, seems to render his authorship dubious.

was especially so in regard to the completely unprepared fits of madness suddenly experienced by Sandrina and Belfiore, of which they are just as unexpectedly cured—in *opera buffa* a popular occasion for buffoon-like parody.

C. F. D. Schubart's *Deutsche Chronik* pronounced the following judgement:[1] 'Flames of genius flickered here and there; but this is not yet the quiet, steady altar fire that rises to heaven in clouds of incense—an aroma pleasing to the gods. If Mozart is no hot-house plant, then he must become one of the greatest composers that has ever lived.'

La finta giardiniera is the first opera where Mozart's language is for long stretches his own. Melody, harmony, and rhythm have a wholly individual stamp, with anticipations of the melodic style of later compositions. It was, moreover, the last time that he allowed the libretto to force him to follow traditional conventions too closely.

In a conventional Italian *opera buffa* the juxtaposition of burlesque and non-comic numbers did not necessarily cause lack of homogeneity: so long as the serious element was not exaggerated the two components were complementary. In a few instances, it is true, Mozart prevents serious situations from becoming ponderous by the use of parody bordering on satire. Belfiore's mad scene, no. 19, with its excessive musical response to every image, in the *accompagnato* as well as in the aria, is an example. But as a general rule, fully aware of his resources, he gives the *parti serie* passionate outbursts inappropriate to *opera buffa*. Sandrina's C minor aria no. 21 is an outstanding instance. It is connected with the following *accompagnato* by an instrumental passage full of emotion, thereby giving the impression of a larger dramatic complex rather than of a single aria.

Ex. 77

[1] Reproduced in Deutsch, *Dokumente*, p. 138.

[Musical example]

-ma - te cru - de - li, oh Dio!

(Cruel ones, stop, oh God!)

The contrast is provided in an E flat section whose élan, based on syncopated movement and wide sweep, directly foreshadows Mozart's latest manner:

Ex. 78

[Musical example — Allegro agitato]

SANDRINA: Ah Nu - mi son per - du - ta, son per - du - ta, muo - ve - te-via pie - tà, muo - ve - te-via pie - tà

(Ah gods, I am lost, have mercy.)

Further examples of excited utterances of horror or fury are represented by the arias nos. 13 and 26, in G minor and C minor respectively. Parody was emphatically not Mozart's intent, but all the same the possible effect upon an audience expecting genuine *opera buffa* was, in part, responsible for the mixed opinion of the work quoted above.

Belfiore, in the main, is shown as a lyrical lover, a forerunner of Belmonte in *Die Entführung aus dem Serail,* as in these bars[1] from aria no. 6:

Ex. 79

Che bel - tà,—— che leg - gia - dri - a, Che splen - do - re e - ter - ni De - i, che splen - do - re e - ter - ni Dei

(What beauty, what grace, what splendour, eternal gods.)

In aria no. 8, however, he behaves without warning like an oafish *buffo* hero, boasting extravagantly of his noble lineage:

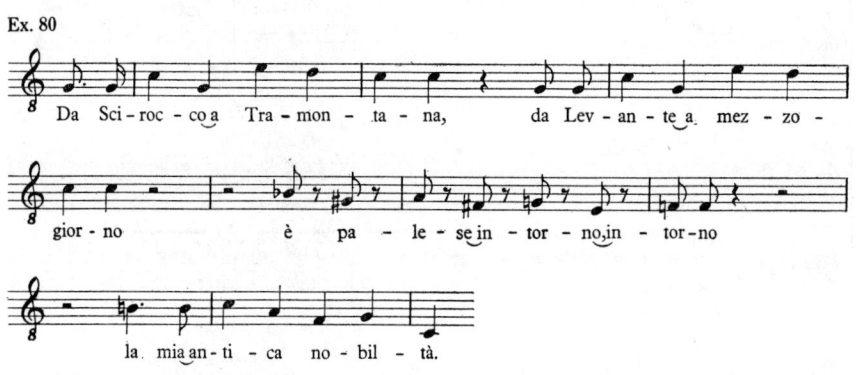

Ex. 80

Da Sci - roc - co a Tra - mon - ta - na, da Lev - an - te a mez - zo - gior - no è pa - le - se in - tor - no in - tor - no la mia an - ti - ca no - bil - tà.

(From South-East, to North, from East to South my ancient nobility is everywhere renowned.)

In the same way Arminda, who in the G minor aria no. 13 shows herself a heroine eager for vengeance, in no. 7 strikes quite a different note, that of a sly lady's maid. Here, as elsewhere in this work, Mozart paid attention only to the immediate situation and not to consistency of characterization.

[1] The beginning of the aria may have been intended as parody; but clearly from the second theme onwards (here quoted) there can be no question of this.

In the finales of the first two acts, where the characters are brought together in a mad whirl, Mozart's skill in characterization within the limits of *opera buffa* came to the fore for the first time. The various sections do indeed end in homophonic ensembles, but prior to this the participants are suitably contrasted or attuned to each other. At the beginning of both finales, this is done by letting everyone successively sing the same melody, and then very soon varying it with an individual twist:

Ex. 81

Later in the finales, the individual pairs are often identified by musical similarities and set off against the other characters.

La finta giardiniera was received at its première with great enthusiasm. All the same it was repeated at Munich only twice, and no further opera commission resulted. On 1 May 1780 the Böhm troupe performed at Augsburg a *Singspiel* version, *Die verstellte Gärtnerin* in a German translation by Franz Xaver Stierle, a member of the company. Perhaps Böhm, who played at Salzburg during the 1779–80 season, persuaded Mozart to make this revision. Subsequently, it formed part of his repertoire, and he staged it at Nuremberg, Frankfurt-on-Main, and other places.[1]

After the Munich performance Mozart returned to Salzburg and busied himself, as was expected of him, with writing music for society and the Church. By way of secular vocal music he composed six arias (K. 209, 210, 217, 255, 256, 272) before proceeding on his important journey to Mannheim and Paris in September 1777. They were meant for various singers, generally as interpolations in other operas; and the recitative and aria for soprano, 'Ah lo previdi! Ah t'invola agl' occhi miei' (K. 272) was one by which he still set store much later. But that he was not content with this sort of operatic activity, and in fact longed for fresh commissions, can be seen in many of his letters during his travels in September 1777 and the months that followed.

The journey did not, however, see his wish fulfilled. In spite of his numerous works for the stage he had not gained fame as a composer of opera, and the reputation that preceded him to Munich and Mannheim related to his virtuosity as a pianist and his good musicianship. Indeed, the Bavarian Elector urged him first 'to travel to Italy, and make a name for himself'. The same situation obtained in Paris, though here Mozart himself was less keen on receiving a commission. His letters mention one or two plans, though without enthusiasm. Had these projects materialized, it is more than likely that his personal feelings would have stood in the way. From the letters of 5 April, 14 May, and 3 July 1778, one gathers that the proposals made by Noverre related to a two-act play, *Alexandre et Roxane*, and a French translation of Metastasio's *Demofoonte*. Evidently Mozart was reluctant to take sides in the battle between the adherents of Gluck and Piccinni which was then exciting the whole Parisian intellectual world. His pragmatic nature was unmoved by polemics about the greater or lesser aesthetic justification for this or that style of opera, which was the source of all the argument. He wrote: 'I do not seek the acquaintance of either him [Piccinni] or any other composer. I understand my job—and so do they—and that is enough.'[2] He paid no further regard to the controversy in his letters. His attitude was also affected by his repugnance for the French language, which he frequently

---

[1] Bacher, op. cit.; Loewenberg, *Annals*, col. 341; R. Münster, '"Die verstellte Gärtnerin". Neue Quellen zur authentischen Singspielfassung von W. A. Mozarts "La finta giardiniera"', *Die Musikforschung* xviii (1965), p. 138.

[2] 9 July 1778; Anderson, *Letters*, ii, p. 835.

mentioned. But in the light of his apathetic reaction to all operatic projects this was not a decisive attitude.

In practical terms, then, the result of the Mannheim–Paris journey for Mozart's operatic career was a fiasco, particularly when compared with his Italian journeys. In February 1778, at Mannheim, he wrote for Aloysia Weber, Anton Raaff, and Dorothea Wendling the arias K. 294, 295, and 295a. In July, in Paris, he composed for Aloysia the recitative and aria 'Popoli di Tessaglia' and 'Io non chiedo, eterni dei' (K. 300b), taking the text from the *Alceste* of Calzabigi and Gluck. It was intended to display the singer's virtuosity and made considerable demands in every way. In August there followed a scena with an accompaniment that was unusually full in the wind section, for the castrato Tenducci which, however, has not been preserved (K. App. 3 = 315b). Mozart's sole work for the Parisian stage was the music for Noverre's ballet, *Les petits riens* (K. App. 10 = 299b). Like the arias of this period, it is distinguished by the delight in colourful instrumentation which the playing of Parisian orchestras roused in him.

Meagre as the harvest was, the stimulation that he drew from French art and his experiences at Mannheim deserves recognition. His correspondence does not contain any remarks on Paris opera performances, but he could scarcely have stayed away from them altogether. From Mannheim he reported in detail on the staging of Holzbauer's *Günther von Schwarzburg* and Wieland and Schweitzer's *Alceste* and *Rosemunde*. He was enthusiastic, too, about Georg Benda's melodrama *Medea*, which he heard there, and it was his intention to write one himself for Mannheim, *Semiramis*. The idea for the work was proposed by the local theatre manager, Heribert von Dalberg, and the text written by Otto Freiherr von Gemmingen; neither text nor score has, however, been preserved. Dalberg urged him to compose an opera, but he declined because there was little likelihood of a production.[1] Nevertheless, the many and various impressions served to broaden Mozart's horizon which had hitherto been effectually restricted to that of an Italian opera composer.

Still, subsequent to his return, Mozart's compositions betrayed little of this change and remained within the genre expressed in *La finta giardiniera*, although enriched by a few single features due to the Mannheim–Paris journey. Chief among these compositions were two which were written for some unknown occasion and for which no record of performance exists: the revision of *König Thamos* and a fragmentary, untitled *Singspiel* now known as *Zaide*.

[1] See letters of 12 and 24 November, 3 and 18 December 1778; Anderson, *Letters*, ii, pp. 936–40, 945–7, 947–9, 951–6.

In *König Thamos* the melodrama at the close of the third act was clearly written *after* the Paris and Mannheim visit, i.e. after acquaintance with Benda's melodramas. The larger scale, the forceful contrasts, the independence of the orchestra and the more colourful instrumentation of the revisions of the 1773 choruses, as well as the additional closing chorus,[1] indicate the effects of Paris. Very possibly the reworking had to do with the engagement of Böhm's troupe at Salzburg in 1779.[2] The choruses were later given religious texts, perhaps at Mozart's own instance.

The second work inspired by an unchronicled occasion is important in relation to Mozart's later *Singspiele*. It was never completed and was later named *Zaide* (probably by the publisher André) after its principal figure.[3] It showed Mozart's fine musical mastery, though his dramatic skill was still not nearly so well developed. The text was by Andreas Schachtner, probably modelled on a previous libretto, *Das Serail oder die unvermuthete Zusammenkunft in der Sclaverey zwischen Vater, Tochter und Sohn*, by Franz Joseph Sebastiani.[4] The plot had one of those Turkish backgrounds so popular in the eighteenth century and especially favoured by the *Singspiel*. The slave, Zaide, is wooed by the Sultan Soliman but prefers her Christian fellow-slave Gomatz. She seeks, unsuccessfully, to flee with him, and in consequence both are at the mercy of the Sultan. There the score came to a stop, and it remains an open question whether Schachtner needed only a few more numbers to finish off the act or an entire third act for the usual happy ending. The affinity with *Die Entführung aus dem Serail* is obvious, and the difference between the two works is the more noticeable. Each employed the variety

[1] See above, p. 119. The text of the final chorus is attributed to Andreas Schachtner. Heckmann has shown in the preface (1956) to the *Neue Mozart–Ausgabe*, pp. vii–viii, that this chorus was intended to replace a final instrumental movement.

[2] As early as 1785, if not before, Böhm's troupe used the *Thamos* music for the play *Lanassa* by K. M. Plümicke which formed part of its repertory. See Heckmann, op. cit. Orel, 'Mozarts Beitrag zum deutschen Sprechtheater. Die Musik zu Geblers "Thamos"', *Acta Mozartiana*, iv (1957), pp. 45–53 and 74–81, ascribes the reworking to a performance of *Thamos* in 1776 at Salzburg. A factor that militates against the earlier date of composition, apart from its style, is that neither the *Theaterwochenblatt für Salzburg* nor the diary of Joachim Ferdinand von Schiedenhofen, friend of the Mozart family, mentions Mozart as composer in connection with the performance of *Thamos* (Deutsch, *Dokumente*, p. 139).

[3] The dating of *Zaide* between Mozart's return to Salzburg in 1779 and his departure for Munich in 1780 can be regarded as certain. But Senn, in 'Mozarts "Zaide" und der Verfasser der vermutlichen Textvorlage', *Festschrift Alfred Orel zum 70. Geburtstag* (Vienna, 1960), p. 173, suggests that it was Mozart's first effort to establish himself in the Viennese *National-Singspiel*, a plan that would not, however, exclude its having been intended earlier for performance by Böhm or Schikaneder at Salzburg; see F. H. Neumann's remarks, in 1963, in the *Kritische Bericht* of the *Neue Mozart–Ausgabe* (Series II, Group 5, x), p. 22. In 1838 André published a score with the title *Zaide* to which, according to the preface, he himself contributed an overture and a final chorus (see Neumann, ibid., p. 25).

[4] See Alfred Einstein, 'Die Textvorlage zu Mozarts "Zaide"', *Acta Musicologica*, viii (1936), p. 30; Senn, 'Mozarts "Zaide"'; as a summary of the question Neumann, op. cit., p. 13.

THE SUPREMACY OF MUSIC OVER DRAMA

of styles characteristic of the Viennese *Singspiel*. The patchwork character of the later *Entführung* was modified by Mozart's effort to delineate each character appropriately and to achieve homogeneity by harmonizing them with one another. In *Zaide* the incongruity is all too apparent. Secondary personages—the slaves with their simple folk-song-like chorus:

Ex. 82

[Musical example with text: Brü-der, laßt uns lu-stig sein, trot-zet wak-ker den Be-schwer-den; denkt, es ist der Fluch der Er-den: je-der Mensch hat sei-ne Pein.]

(Brothers let us be gay, bravely defy your troubles; consider it the curse of the earth that every man must suffer pain.)

and the servant Osmin with his *buffo*-type aria no. 10:

Ex. 83

[Musical example with text: Wer soll nicht drü-ber la-chen? Ha ha ha ha ha ha ha ha ha ha ha ha ha ha ha ha ha ha ha!]

(Who can fail to laugh at it? Ha ha ha!)

were, for no particular reason, set in juxtaposition to each other as well as the principals. In his two arias in the second act, the Sultan Soliman behaves much like the standard villain in *opera seria*. In aria no. 9, his 'proud lion's' fury is vividly illuminated by the orchestra, while the vocal part begins with a melody reminiscent of *Le nozze di Figaro* and is followed by the characteristic leaps of 'rage'-arias:

Ex. 84.

[Musical example with text: "Trüm-mern, in Trüm-mern zur Erd', die Ket-ten in Trüm-mern zur Erd'."]

(He roars with a terrible voice and in furious anger flings the broken chains to the ground.)

Allazim, the lovers' noble protector, also utters his thoughts in the conventional form of *da capo* arias, in the manner of *opera seria*.

These songs show Mozart at the peak of his ability at the time, particularly in their orchestral treatment, but the banality of the text obstructs any dramatic expression. Later on he would probably have declined to provide music for arias of this sort. The lovers' numbers are fairly evenly divided between dramatically lively and more conventional ones. For instance, in the second act, the heroine sings a song that may be described as a conventional 'image' aria, in the *opera seria* tradition, beautiful in its music but lacking in character portrayal. This is followed by a second *da capo* aria (no. 13), which paints a well-defined image of her mental state, contrasting flaming anger and bitter pain.

A similar contrast exists between the two arias of Gomatz in the first act: the first aria is conventional but the second (no. 6) gives a highly individual expression of the text:

Ex. 85

[Musical example, Allegretto, GOMATZ: "Lass' mich dei-ne Knie um-fas-sen,"]

(Let me clasp your knees, yet I must leave you quickly for I burn with desire. Let me kiss you, let me hold you.)

At the beginning of each act Mozart employed melodrama in place of *accompagnato* recitatives to set contemplative monologues to music. He was concerned in both instances to find a suitable interpretation for the abundance of sentiment portrayed. In *Zaide* the ensembles rather than the solos anticipate *Die Entführung*. The duet no. 5 and the quartet no. 15 both offer a foretaste of 1782: the first points to the love duet in the third act of the later opera, while the quartet looks forward to Konstanze's aria no. 10 in the second act of *Die Entführung*. Moreover, both numbers come close to the quiet intensity and lyrical fairy-tale atmosphere of the Viennese opera. In the quartet where the vengeful Sultan confronts the lovers and their protector, the characters are clearly differentiated, both when they sing successively and in ensemble. This again is reminiscent of *La finta giardiniera*.

In its form *Zaide* had little to offer by way of variety. Although it contained a strophic song and several bipartite and rondo forms, the simple tripartite *da capo* form predominated among the vocal solos. The colourful instrumentation contrasted with this formal uniformity. One can no longer talk of a standard orchestration, varied in the case of one or two numbers. Flutes, oboes, bassoons, horns, trumpets, and kettle-drums in all sorts of combinations were added to the strings; only three songs had a simple string accompaniment. The wind instruments were often used in obbligato fashion—the quartet, for example, was introduced by a ritornello for wind instruments only. Mozart's skill in handling the wind instruments was, together with the use of melodrama, the most tangible development arising from his journey to Mannheim and Paris.

IDOMENEO

Whatever prospects of performance Mozart had in mind for the *Singspiel Zaide* proved deceptive. Perhaps that was why he never finished it, or perhaps the new commission received in the autumn of 1780 was responsible. Once more the Munich Court approached him and invited him to compose an *opera seria*, the subject, as usual, accompanying the invitation. It was the French drama *Idoménée* by Antoine Danchet, set to music in 1712 by Campra and now translated into Italian as a three-act *opera seria* by the Salzburg Court chaplain Abbate Giambattista Varesco[1]. For Mozart there was a twofold attraction. On the one hand the invitation fulfilled his longing, which had had no expression since *La finta giardiniera*, to create an Italian opera. 'My one burning ambition now is to write operas,' he had written from Mannheim, 'but they must be French rather than German and Italian rather than either'.[2] On the other hand, the French element in the libretto at last provided him with the opportunity to use choruses and instrumental movements

---
[1] See Daniel Heartz, 'The Genesis of Mozart's "Idomeneo"', *Mozart-Jahrbuch 1967* (Salzburg, 1968), p. 150 and *Musical Quarterly*, lv (1969), p. 1, and preface to the *Neue Mozart-Ausgabe* score (1972).
[2] 7 February 1778; Anderson, *Letters*, ii, p. 692.

which would allow him to realize the ideas born of his Mannheim and Paris visits on a major operatic stage with first-class resources.

Idomeneo holds a key position in Mozart's operatic career. As a Court commission it still belonged firmly to the world of convention and tradition; at the same time it released the composer, if only temporarily, from a thraldom at Salzburg that became ever more oppressive with the passing of years. Though the work was begun at Salzburg he completed it in close conjunction with the singers at Munich whither he went in November 1780. There he was away from his family, and *Idomeneo* is thus the first opera about which he made significant comments in writing. His letters contained detailed reports on progress in composition, rehearsals, the singers' performances and their demands, as well as the reactions of others to the various numbers and acts. They show for the first time his close preoccupation with his text and foreshadow the important passages in his later letters relating to *Die Entführung*. His remarks about the quartet in the third act are especially interesting for their surprising combination of attitudes: the old complaisance towards the singers and a new sense of dramatic responsibility.[1]

Apart from the exceptional case of the late *Clemenza di Tito*, *Idomeneo* was the last opera for which Mozart meekly submitted to an imposed text. Varesco's handling of his French model followed the more condensed style of Metastasio's librettos and restricted the number of characters to a minimum: Idomeneo, the titular hero, the lovers Idamante and Ilia, the latter's jealous rival Elettra, and the confidant Arbace. The central theme is not, as in most Italian contemporary opera texts, the conflict between lovers and a rival, but the consequences of the vow made by King Idomeneo during a storm at sea, that upon his return home he would sacrifice to Neptune the first mortal he encountered. This unhappily proves to be his son Idamante. The subsequent complications reach a climax when Ilia offers to die in her beloved Idamante's place. The ensuing conflict of magnanimity between the pair is ended when Neptune renounces the sacrifice, raises Idamante to the throne in his father's stead, and unites him to Ilia.

This libretto, with the development of its plot dictated by supernatural powers, still in baroque fashion, and its characters conforming to contemporary convention, Mozart accepted as the basis for an *opera seria*. In his reports to his father he writes continually of the singers' varied capacities and the need to adapt himself to them. He was particularly considerate of Anton Raaff, the Idomeneo, whom he held in high respect but whose age, clumsy acting, and exclusive reliance upon certain vocal effects resulted in arias that were dramatically not at all in keeping

[1] 27 December 1780; Anderson, *Letters*, ii, p. 1037.

with the rest of the work, though at a purely musical level they display complete mastery. In contrast, Arbace's two arias (nos. 10a and 22) are of an absolutely orthodox character.

A source of much annoyance was the young castrato Vincenzo del Prato, who sang Idamante and in Mozart's view was inadequate both as singer and actor. In fact, his incompetence as a singer proved beneficial, since all virtuoso glitter was omitted from his arias (nos. 2, 7, and 27a). As a lover's utterances these movements fall into the category of *arie cantabili*, and in nos. 2 and 7 Mozart was at pains to reflect the emotions of the verse, probing far deeper than the conventional pattern.

Ilia's first aria is a passionate *aria parlante* whose forward surge depends largely on its string syncopation:

Ex. 86

(Father, brothers, farewell! You are no more, I have lost you.)

In her second aria, the conflict being past, the Princess gives free rein to her sentiments of lyrical love and childlike security. Here Mozart's intention[1] was to write an aria of purely musical quality with four obbligato wind instruments. He was most successful where he took least

---

[1] 8 November 1780; Anderson, *Letters*, ii, pp. 978–80.

notice of the emotional content of individual words but concentrated instead on the spirit of the text, irrespective of whether the vocal part, accompanied by the strings, mingled or contrasted with the wind quartet:

Ex. 87

(You are father to me, welcoming abode.)

Mozart was fortunate in having to pay little heed to the demands of the singers of Ilia's and Elettra's arias, for from the outset Dorothea and Elisabeth Wendling[1] accommodated themselves to his ideas.

The passionate Elettra, like the lyrical Ilia, is a standard *opera seria* figure, whose conventional character Mozart nevertheless mitigated and rendered more flexible as far as the text and situations permitted. The D minor revenge aria no. 4, 'Tutto nel cor vi sento', combines breathless

[1] Deutsch, *Dokumente*, p. 170. 15 November 1780; Anderson, *Letters*, ii, p. 985.

ejaculations and intense chromaticism. Prolonged coloraturas are altogether absent and sparing use is made of the large leaps so characteristic of revenge arias. These features are equally absent in the third act when, after the oracle's pronouncement Elettra's agitation in the despair aria 'D'Oreste, d'Ajace ho in seno i tormenti' (no. 29a) pulsates in the continuous quaver movement of the divided violas and the trills of the violins.

Ex. 88

(I have in my breast the torments of Orestes, of Ajax.)

Bipartite form prevails in the arias and ensembles of *Idomeneo*. The second half is generally a variation upon the first and there is rarely any contrast between the two. But Mozart made use also of the three-part *da capo* form, the hall-mark of *opera seria*, employing it always when the text was of a conventional nature. Such is the case in Arbace's two arias, Idomeneo's *bravura* aria in the second act, and Ilia's and Idamante's arias in the third act.

Of the opera's three ensembles one, the lovers' lyrical duet (no. 20a), still keeps to traditional lines. On the other hand, the trio (no. 16) between Elettra, Idamante, and Idomeneo shows at its inception a decided effort to delineate the characters individually. The quartet no. 21, which brings together the four principals at the moment of greatest confusion, Mozart regarded as outstandingly successful. It is, indeed, a piece in which the participants 'talk more than they sing'.[1] First they give in rapid alternation their various reactions to the turn of events, then unite in bewailing the hopelessness of the situation that presses on them. Here, immediately before the moment of catastrophe, Mozart wrote a passage that, in both composition and dramatic technique, can be placed alongside the ensembles of his later operas.

Mozart did not comment on his writing of the *Idomeneo* choruses, but at Mannheim in 1778 he had described choruses as his 'favourite type of composition'[2] and in the same connection mentioned appreciatively 'the choruses of Gluck'. These, and their forerunners, the French opera choruses that Mozart had got to know in Paris, were of course his models. Some of the choruses in *Idomeneo* merely enhance the brilliance of the festive scenes. In others, the populace comments on the happenings and becomes associated with the main personages. Here the role of the chorus demands more than merely conveying the prevailing mood (for instance, nos. 17, 18 and 24). Particularly characteristic is the magnificent chorus of the shipwrecked company (no. 5). Mozart himself was responsible for its division: a distant chorus with four voices and a nearer one with two ('coro lontano' and 'coro vicino'). The two groups are sharply contrasted, except at the beginning and end where fearful cries of 'Pietà, Numi, pietà' ring out antiphonally. Those at sea confine themselves, on the whole, to declamation in repeated crotchets on a single note, with the quaver runs of the wind instruments gliding across like waves, while those on shore utter short imitative phrases supported by agitated playing of the strings. Mozart has not treated this chorus as a separate block of music but has connected it, by way of orchestral transitions, with the preceding aria of Elettra and the succeeding entrance of the rescued Idomeneo. These transitions utilize motives from the chorus proper. The result supersedes the traditional, neatly divided numbers and creates a great musical web in which the storms of the soul echo those of the sea.

Apart from its choruses, *Idomeneo* surpasses Mozart's earlier contributions to *opera seria* in two respects, the large number and the shaping of the *accompagnati*, and the masterly treatment of the instrumentation. Frequently, following Gluck's example, the *accompagnati* introduce a significant reference to a theme previously used, in place of the traditional fashion of continual novelty. Indeed, on occasion an *accompagnato* is linked to the succeeding aria by anticipating its

[1] 27 December 1780; Anderson, *Letters*, ii, p. 1037.
[2] 28 February 1778; Anderson, *Letters*, ii, p. 737.

theme. The work has scarcely an aria or ensemble that does not either arise out of or proceed into an *accompagnato*. In addition, there are *accompagnato* interpolations in *secco* recitative and, above all, especially in the third act, entire *accompagnato* scenes. In all of them the orchestra is responsible more than ever before for setting the tone and interpreting subtle emotions, whether it alternates with the voice or supports it or, at climactic points, holds its own as an equal. (Such and other expressive passages overshadow the *secco* recitative, but the declamation of the text in the *secco* is always careful, and sometimes a lively bass line brings the *secco* closer to the *accompagnato*.)

In Munich Mozart had at his disposal for the first time an orchestra of world-wide reputation.[1] At last he was able to turn the lessons of his Mannheim and Paris journey to full account, although they had been applied to some extent in *Zaide*. The evidence of his new orchestral mastery is to be seen both in separate instrumental movements and in concerted movements for orchestra and voices. Three of the marches are notable: no. 8 for the prominence given to the woodwind instruments; no. 14 for the employment of muted horns and trumpets;[2] and no. 25 for its anticipation of the march of the priests in *Die Zauberflöte*. The single-movement overture is no longer a festive prelude applicable to a variety of operas, but, as with Gluck, an introduction to the heroic tragedy of *this* opera. The colourfulness of the instrumentation goes beyond that found in *Zaide*, especially since the Munich orchestra contained the clarinets Mozart had so long wanted. Not that he in fact made use of them other than for songs of a tender, elegiac nature. In general, indeed, his instrumentation is attractive precisely for the discriminating care with which in practically every number he selected from the rich choice of instruments at his disposal. The complete orchestra never comes into play. There is constant alternation among the woodwind instruments, trombones are the prerogative of the oracle, trumpets and kettle-drums serve only to emphasize solemn splendour or represent the sway of supernatural powers.

With so brilliant an orchestra to hand, Mozart accepted with alacrity the commission to compose the ballet. This would not normally have been his task, since according to the convention of the time the ballet did not form part of an opera. 'I am glad of it, for now all the music will be by the same composer,' he wrote to his father on 30 December, and he composed the ballet's five long, richly varied, and inventive movements[3] as an integral part of the work, not as entr'acte entertainment. At what

[1] In 1778 the famous Mannheim orchestra transferred, for the most part, to Munich, along with the Elector.
[2] 29 November 1780; Anderson, *Letters*, ii, p. 1001.
[3] K. 367, published in *Neue Mozart–Ausgabe*, series II, group 2.

point the ballet was introduced in the original performance is unknown, but the correspondence between the beginning of the chorus no. 32 and the chaconne no. 1 suggests an association with the close of the third act.

Like *La finta giardiniera* the opera was only infrequently staged after its première on 29 January 1781; nevertheless it did not cease to preoccupy its composer. In the autumn of 1781 Mozart thought of having a new German version made, recasting the music for a production at the Vienna opera, but this plan was never fulfilled. In March 1786 an amateur performance in the palace of Prince Karl Auersperg at Vienna caused him to alter and shorten a good deal of the opera. The duet No. 20 between Ilia and Idamante was replaced by the far less conventional 'Spiegarti non poss'io' (K. 489), the music of which is more tautly drawn. In addition, Idamante was given the extended rondo 'Non temer, amato bene' (K. 490) with solo violin accompaniment that opens the second act.

This reappearance of *Idomeneo* even in the later Viennese period points clearly to its key position in the evolution of Mozart's operatic style. It represents the peak of the second phase, where the traditional forms of opera become infiltrated, indeed sometimes submerged, by the composer's musical individuality. Obviously, he was still stronger as a musician than as a dramatist. He was avid for commissions, because opera provided him with the fullest outlet for the profusion of music within him. As yet, he did not select or alter a libretto as carefully as in later years, but the occasional appearance of a link between score and text which goes beyond conventional interpretation demonstrates the growth of the portraitist alongside the musician, and suggests what is to come. The music of *Idomeneo*, moreover, is not only beautiful and full of Mozartian touches of all kinds but also to no small degree characteristic and worthy to associate with *Die Entführung*, which it preceded by a bare eighteen months.

The year of the first performance of *Idomeneo*, 1781, was the decisive year in Mozart's life. The breach with the Archbishop released him from the shackles of the Salzburg Court's service. Simultaneously it showed that he was already far on the way to having attained intellectual freedom from the bonds of convention. *Die Entführung aus dem Serail*, the first opera he wrote as a 'free' man and the first that saw his trenchant intervention in its dramatic structure, was the manifestation of this. With it begins the third phase of his operatic creativity, when musician and dramatist are equals.

THE UNION OF MUSIC AND DRAMA IN *DIE ENTFÜHRUNG*

Mozart's efforts to obtain a fresh operatic commission were an important aspect of his endeavours to establish himself in Vienna, and he achieved success with relative speed. He had arrived at Vienna on 16 March 1781, and already in April there was talk of a piece which 'young Stephanie' was proposing to put at his disposal, a project that was brought to fruition at the close of July. In the circumstances prevailing in the Austrian capital, this could only be a German-language opera, i.e. a *Singspiel*, for the 'National Theatre'. In the first instance Mozart seems to have thought of employing the incomplete *Zaide* to this end, but the plan was dropped when the director-producer, Gottlieb Stephanie the younger, demurred.[1] The libretto which Stephanie then delivered to him, *Belmont und Constanze oder Die Entführung aus dem Serail*, was strikingly similar to *Zaide*, but in its constant alternation between gravity and merriment was theatrically far more effective. Written by the Leipzig author Christoph Friedrich Bretzner for Johann André, it had already been performed at Berlin on 25 May 1781, to the latter's music.

In accordance with his usual practice, Mozart ascertained who the performers were to be and then at once proceeded to the composition of individual numbers. On 1 August he wrote: 'I am so delighted at having to compose this opera that I have already finished Cavalieri's first aria, Adamberger's, and the trio which closes Act I.' But a few weeks later he was reporting to his father one change after another that Stephanie had had to make at his bidding—that, indeed, at the end of the second act 'the whole affair is being turned upside down' at his own demand. These were no longer the words of the 'commissioned' composer but of the master who felt responsible for the drama as well as the opera. His remarks about Stephanie culminate in the sentence, 'He is, after all, arranging the libretto for me—and what is more, as I want it—exactly—and, by Heaven, I do not ask anything more of him.'[2] The conclusion he drew from this collaboration with his librettist is contained a little later in the famous letter of 13 October 1781: 'In opera the poetry must be altogether the obedient daughter of the music.' Above all, on the basis of his recent experience with Stephanie, he claims for the composer a decisive role in the shaping of the text. He was himself, in fact, 'the good composer who understands the theatre and is capable of making a contribution to it', but he had only now become such after the discovery of his own musical language and after the widening and deepening of

---

[1] 18 April 1781; Anderson, *Letters*, iii, p. 1078.
[2] 26 September 1781; Anderson, *Letters*, iii, p. 1146.

his dramatic knowledge which experience of Vienna's variegated stage life had given him.

There was nothing original about Bretzner's text, which contained elements of various older 'Turkish' operas. There was a close affinity with various libretti, particularly Gaetano Martinelli's *La schiava liberata* (1768), Isaac Bickerstaffe's *The Sultan, or A peep into the Seraglio* (1776), and G. F. W. Grossmann's *Adelheit von Veltheim* (1780). Of the last of these Bretzner said that he had been astonished to find that Grossmann and he 'had, without having the slightest idea of one another, practically taken the same path'.[1] Clearly, the contents of the *Entführung* accorded with public taste.

The individuality it now displayed was due to Mozart. The major change mentioned in his letter of 26 September, the shift of the elopement scene to the end of the second act and the introduction of a completely fresh intrigue in the third act, was not in fact made. But the embellishment of the part of Osmin far beyond anything found in Bretzner's text was of particular importance. The librettist's version had allowed this 'overseer at the Pasha's country villa' no more than a single song (no. 2). At Mozart's request he was given aria no. 3, the duet with Belmonte which follows his song no. 2, and probably also the aria no. 19 and the duet no. 9 with Blonde.[2] Undoubtedly Mozart had in mind the qualities of his singer, the excellent bass Fischer. Nevertheless his remarks reveal that the figure of Osmin as such interested him. In his letter, so important to operatic criticism,[3] he wrote:

As we have given the part of Osmin to Herr Fischer, who certainly has an excellent bass voice . . ., we must take advantage of it, particularly as he has the whole Viennese public on his side. But in the original libretto Osmin has only this short song and nothing else to sing, except in the trio and the finale; so he has been given an aria in Act I, and he is to have another in Act II. I have explained to Stephanie the words I require for this aria—indeed I had finished composing most of the music for it before Stephanie knew anything about it . . . Osmin's rage is rendered comical by the accompaniment of the Turkish music. In working out the aria I have given full scope now and then to Fischer's beautiful deep notes . . . The passage 'Drum beim Barte des Propheten' is indeed in the same tempo, but with quick notes; but as Osmin's rage gradually increases, there comes (just when the aria seems to be at an end) the allegro assai, which is in a totally different measure and in a different key; this is bound to be very effective. For just as a man in such a towering rage oversteps all the bounds of order, moderation and propriety and completely forgets himself, so must the music too forget itself. But as passions, whether vio-

---

[1] Deutsch, *Dokumente*, p. 167. See also Preibisch, 'Quellenstudien zu Mozarts "Entführung aus dem Serail": ein Beitrag zur Geschichte der Türkenoper', *Sammelbände der internationalen Musikgesellschaft*, x (1908/9), p. 430, where Turkish operas of all categories are cited.

[2] For this and kindred matters, see Preibisch, op. cit.

[3] 26 September 1781; Anderson, *Letters*, iii, p. 1143.

lent or not, must never be expressed in such a way as to excite disgust, and as music, even in the most terrible situations, must never offend the ear, but must please the hearer, or in other words must never cease to be *music*, I have gone from F (the key in which the aria is written) not into a remote key, but into a related one, not, however, into its nearest relative D minor, but into the more remote A minor.

Mozart left Pasha Selim as a mere speaking part,[1] while Osmin was raised musically to be the sole counterpoise to the two pairs of lovers. Mozart thus created from a secondary figure, whose role had been to personify the Turkish background, a principal character having, indeed, more individual features than the still strongly stereotyped *Singspiel* couples. Admittedly, the part of Belmonte underwent considerable expansion. Three of his four arias (nos. 1, 15, and 17) were additions by Stephanie, the first demonstrably at Mozart's request.[2] It may be said that Osmin's songs introduce the composer as musical portrait-painter, while those of Belmonte, as the lyrical lover, are more likely to have been an outlet for Mozart to express his love for Konstanze Weber.

Hence, the shape of the libretto carries to a considerable degree the Mozartian stamp. Apart from Belmonte's final aria (no. 17) which gives the impression of dramatic irrelevance for the sake of operatic convention, and Konstanze's *bravura* aria no. 11, seemingly inserted to display vocal virtuosity, the additions and alterations were well planned and dramatically apposite. The music made use of the proliferation of styles assembled in the *Singspiel* genre, namely *opera seria*, *opera buffa*, *opéra comique*, and *Lied*, but the individual elements served the composer as no more than the thread from which he then sought to weave his own fabric.

The musical characterization of Osmin was especially successful. The words themselves, 'Wer ein Liebchen hat gefunden', represent a strophic song of utmost simplicity. But Mozart's choice of key, G minor, and his orchestration indicate that Osmin is portrayed as an individual, not as a type. In this connection the orchestral accompaniment, varied from stanza to stanza, and in particular the semiquaver figures in the woodwind at the beginning of the third stanza, are highly suggestive. By contrast, in C. L. Dieter's *Belmont und Konstanze*[3] the same lyric is set as a modish *Singspiel* ditty that could just as well have been sung by Blonde or Pedrillo:[4]

---

[1] Initially, as emerges from the enumeration of *four* male singers, 1 August 1781 (Anderson, *Letters*, iii, p. 1123), Mozart had planned the part as a singing one. But in a list of characters which must be dated subsequent to 19 September he already notes 'has nothing to sing': *Mozart: Briefe und Aufzeichnungen*, iii, p. 161.
[2] 26 September 1781; Anderson, *Letters*, iii, p. 1143.
[3] For further details, see Preibisch, op. cit.
[4] The song is printed in the appendix to Abert, 'Die dramatische Musik'.

Ex. 89

Wer ein Liebchen hat ge - fun - den, die es treu und red - lich meint, lohn es ihr durch tau - send Küs - se, mach ihr all das Le - ben süs - se, sei ihr Trö - ster, sei ihr Freund

(He who has found a sweetheart who has a true and loyal heart, let him reward her with a thousand kisses, let him sweeten her whole life and be her solace and her friend.)

But with Mozart it leads into the Osmin–Belmonte duet which, in turn, is followed by the aria 'Solche hergelauf'ne Laffen', both numbers added at Mozart's instigation. A prime example of the composer's powers of musical characterization occurs in the vaudeville at the close where, in accordance with *opéra comique* standards, the characters, one after another, pronounce the final moral to the same melody, with the entire group joining in the refrain. Osmin, whose turn is last, comes in so abruptly after Blonde's stanza that the refrain is dropped altogether at this point. A few bars later he proceeds to the coda, 'Erst geköpft, dann gehangen', of his aria no. 3, and to its strains dashes off the stage. Thus, in contrast with the Pasha who, in the end, acquits himself with high magnanimity, he remains to the last, musically and dramatically, within the narrow confines of his seething hate. This emotion is 'rendered comical'[1] by the employment of mock-Turkish music with all its trimmings—tumultuous movement and strident instrumentation, together with crude melody and harmony.

Of the pair of lovers Belmonte is musically more of a piece than Konstanze. He is the proper fairy-tale prince, predecessor to Tamino though lacking the latter's strongly ethical outlook. His aria no. 4, 'O wie ängstlich, o wie feurig', most clearly expresses his character. Mozart's description suggests that he was here concerned only with the kind of tone-painting associated with the traditional metaphor aria: 'this is the favourite aria of all who have heard it, and it is mine also. I wrote it expressly to suit Adamberger's voice. You feel the trembling, the faltering, you see how his throbbing breast begins to swell; this I have expressed by a crescendo. You hear the whispering, the sighing, which I have indicated by the first violins with mutes and a flute playing

---

[1] 26 September 1781; Anderson, *Letters*, iii, p. 1144.

in unison.'[1] Nevertheless, in addition to such illustrations there are melodic and harmonic turns that seem to be the direct expression of genuine emotion. The rapturous tone that pervades this aria also distinguishes Belmonte's other songs.

The part of Konstanze evidently interested Mozart far less. About aria no. 6, 'Ach ich liebte', his letter of 26 September was perfectly frank: 'I have sacrificed Konstanze's aria a little to the flexible throat of Mlle Cavalieri. I have tried to express her feelings, "Trennung war mein banges Los, und nun schwimmt mein Aug' in Thränen" as far as any Italian *bravura* aria will allow.' In fact, apart from the displays of coloratura at cadential points it does not bear many of the marks of an 'aria di bravura'. The description fits much better aria no. 11, 'Martern aller Arten', which is a masterly concertato between four solo instruments and voice and was surely fashioned for the singer's sake. It begins with a ritornello of sixty bars like the movement of a *sinfonia concertante*, after which the voice predominates. The coloratura increases in virtuosity during the course of each of the three sections. Such a concession to vocal dexterity would not have been made by Mozart at a later stage, least of all at such an inappropriate moment when it is directly preceded by another aria of Konstanze, totally at variance with it. 'Traurigkeit ward mir zum Lose' (no. 10, G minor), is not at all in a heroic mould but seeks to depict her as truly womanly and Belmonte's beloved. The aria is developed organically from the chromatic 'sighing' motive of the *accompagnato*. Several elements in this number point directly to Pamina's G minor aria, 'Ach ich fühl's': its tonality, its character, which is both declamatory and akin to a *Lied*, and the discreet interplay of voice and orchestra.

The songs of the servant pair Pedrillo–Blonde are more homogeneous than those of their aristocratic masters. The tone is principally that of the *Singspiel* with an occasional bow to *opera buffa* or *opéra comique*, and the result is remarkably flexible, suiting situations as they arise. Blonde's interpretation of her boisterousness in aria no. 12 is persuasive; only the remembrance of Konstanze's 'schwaches, feiges Herz' for a few bars here and there interrupts her cheerful chatter with more tender moments.

Pedrillo's aria no. 13 shows the internal struggle between his natural timidity and his longing for gallant action. The movement consists of a fourfold alternation between joyous boldness ('Frisch zum Kampfe—

[1] Same letter as footnote 1, p. 144; Mozart writes 'mit Sordinen' (with mutes). There are however, no mutes in the first edition (Leipzig, c. 1813, p. 64) or the complete edition, Series 5, xv (Leipzig, 1882, p. 61). The whereabouts of the autograph of the first act, formerly in the possession of Ernst von Mendelssohn–Bartholdy, later in the Staatsbibliothek, Berlin, are not known at present, cf. Köchel, *Verzeichnis* . . . 6th edn. (1964), p. 410.

nein, es sei gewagt') and faint-hearted discouragement ('Nur ein feiger Tropf verzagt'), clearly echoed in motives of the brass section on the one hand and hesitant string figures on the other. Pedrillo's divided nature is even more subtly illuminated by the *romanza* no. 18, which expresses both temporizing and daring: at this juncture the music is also expressive of the general air of uncertainty which precedes the attempted escape. *Romanze* at critical points of the action, a borrowing from *opéra comique*, were no novelty in the *Singspiel*, and Mozart was simply following established practice. But he improves upon that practice by hovering between major and minor and by raising the piece to a level where it helps logically to enhance character and plot. Johann André, for example, had at this turn introduced a simple lyric reminiscent of a folk-song, which merely served as a signal to the two waiting girls[1] but did not in itself express uncertainty and fear:

Ex. 90

Im Moh-ren-land ge - fan - gen ward ein Mä-del hübsch und fein

(Held captive in the land of the Moors was a maiden fair and fine.)

The plainest proof that in the *Entführung* Mozart the dramatist had caught up with Mozart the musician is furnished by his predilection for characterizing the personages, above all Belmonte and Osmin, through ensembles. In three out of the four duets Osmin is confronted successively with Belmonte (no. 2), Blonde (no. 9), and Pedrillo (no. 14), and in the trio at the end of the first act with both Belmonte and Pedrillo. All constitute *opera buffa* ensembles of the most various sorts.

These four comic ensembles, of which nos. 9 and 14 can certainly be designated character duets, are balanced by predominantly serious numbers: the love duet (no. 20) and the quartet (no. 16) at the close of the second act. The love duet starts with an *accompagnato*—a rarity in the *Entführung*—which, like its counterpart, the *accompagnato* before Konstanze's G minor aria no. 10, is held together by an orchestral motive. In the introduction to no. 20 this motive is characterized by violin sforzatos and a syncopated accompaniment. In the bipartite duet proper the blending of *bel canto* and lyricism finds its culmination in the quiet and dedicated intensity of Mozart's *Singspiel* tone ('Mit dem Geliebten sterben', bars 134 ff.).

The quartet finale to the second act[2] may well be called the first truly

[1] Preibisch, op. cit., p. 473.
[2] Recorded in *The History of Music in Sound*, vii.

Mozartian ensemble scene, and it is not surprising that in content it originated mainly with the composer. Its essence lies firstly in the confrontation of the two pairs, where each of the four persons retains his or her individuality *vis-à-vis* the others, and secondly in the kaleidoscopic alternation of emotions, punctuated by magical moments when confusion and suspicions dissolve suddenly into pure harmony. This occurs when the A major andante in 6/8 time is unexpectedly introduced after the preceding G minor passage, a succession which takes the listener by surprise and has the effect of a release. Formally, this seven-part movement constitutes a 'chain finale'.

In the overture to *Die Entführung* the Oriental atmosphere predominates. The middle section brings in the melody of Belmonte's entrance song, transformed from major to minor, a clever effect which produces a doubly pleasing impression when the fairy prince actually enters in a major key. The instrumentation of the opera is full of colour and in no way lags behind *Idomeneo*. The treatment of the individual instrumental lines is often of dramatic significance and quite on a par with the later masterpieces. An instance is the middle section of the duet No. 9 where the oboe (to the words, 'O Engländer, seid ihr nicht Thoren') anticipates Blonde's answer.

BETWEEN *ENTFÜHRUNG* AND *FIGARO*

Accustomed as they were to the more primitive *Singspiel* and to Italian opera, Mozart's contemporaries were as yet unable to appreciate these refinements. The work had a great success at its première on 16 July 1782, and experienced numerous repeat performances. In fact, it was retained in the repertory of the 'Nationalsingspiel' when its programme was curtailed.[1] But in spite of this success no further *Singspiel* commission was forthcoming. Nor did the composer profit from Gluck's 'very complimentary' remarks or the popularity of the opera outside Vienna. For the next few years the Vienna opera houses took no notice of Mozart and so, once more, as in the period before *Idomeneo*, he began making plans of his own. As Viennese operatic taste shifted, these revolved around now an Italian, now a German opera. On 21 December 1782 he told his father that the Court theatre director, Count Rosenberg, had suggested writing an Italian opera and mentioned efforts to obtain a *buffo* libretto. A month later he asked that the Salzburg operatic composer Luigi Gatti should be reminded of the 'operatic books' he had promised to forward. On 5 February there was also talk of a German opera: 'I have chosen Goldoni's comedy, *Il*

---

[1] The German-language troupe ended its activity with a performance of *Die Entführung* on 4 February 1788.

servitore di due padroni, and the whole of the first act has now been translated.' But apart from the draft score for two arias, the idea was not put into execution.[1] On the other hand, Mozart continued to pursue the project of an Italian opera. He read (as he wrote on 7 May 1783) 'a hundred or more texts' without finding an appropriate one, and finally accepted the libretto, *L'oca del Cairo*, which the Salzburg Abbate Varesco, author of *Idomeneo*, had submitted to him. He knew how ponderous a poet Varesco was and had intended to adjust the details of the text to his own taste. But since he and his author could not see eye to eye from the outset,[2] and the commission by the director of the Court theatre was not definite, he soon lost interest in the undertaking.[3] There remains only an incomplete summary of the libretto with no more than the first act fully set down. Of the music three arias, two duets, one quartet, the finale, a recitative scene, and various sketches have survived in draft score. The majority of these numbers would have been allotted to subsidiary persons; they were of a *buffo* character and intimate that *Figaro*[4] was hovering in the wings:

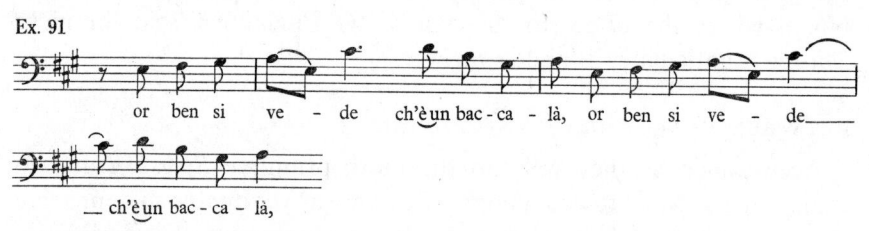

Ex. 91

or ben si ve - de ch'è un bac-ca - là, or ben si ve - de

— ch'è un bac-ca - là,

(Now we see clearly that he is a blockhead.)

The sprightly finale can, properly, be described as the first really successful Mozartian *buffo* finale.[5]

More or less simultaneously with *L'oca del Cairo* Mozart's attention was focused on another Italian libretto which he mentioned in a letter to his father of 5 July 1783. This was presumably *Lo sposo deluso ossia La rivalità di tre donne per un solo amante* by Lorenzo Da Ponte,[6] of

---

[1] Einstein (Köchel, *Verzeichnis* . . ., 3rd edn., 1937, p. 517) conjectures that the arias K. 435=416b, 'Müsst ich auch durch tausend Drachen', and 433=416c, 'Männer suchen stets zu naschen', formed part of the projected German-language opera.

[2] 21 June, 6 and 24 December 1783, and 10 February 1784; Anderson, *Letters*, iii, pp. 1271, 1286, 1288, and 1292.

[3] The fragments, K. 422, were published in 1960 in the *Neue Mozart-Ausgabe*, series II, group 5, xiii.

[4] See *Le nozze di Figaro*, Act III, duet no. 16, bar 29 ff.

[5] A version of the work by Titus Charles Constantin, with a French text by Victor Wilder, *L'Oie du Caire*, also containing numbers from *Lo sposo deluso* and other Mozartian compositions, was performed on 6 June 1867 in Paris and subsequently in a German translation in Germany and Austria (see Loewenberg, *Annals*, col. 992).

[6] Köchel, *Verzeichnis* . . ., 6th edn. (1964), p. 462.

which there remain the overture, a quartet, a trio, and two arias (both in draft score only). The overture leads straight into the quartet, namely, the 'introduzione' and is thematically close to it as well as being completely attuned to its dramatic situation. The short trio between the three principals is distinguished by a characteristic interlacing of pithy orchestral themes and vocal parts, again significantly forecasting *Figaro*. The lofty coloratura aria for the heroine Eugenia strikes notes that are almost duplicated in *Don Giovanni*.[1]

Ex. 92

Both these Italian designs failed to progress beyond their earliest stages. Though the reasons are not firmly established, the absence of an official commission in both cases seems likely. Nor is it improbable that these experiences induced Mozart to turn down, on 21 May 1785, the libretto for a German opera offered him by Professor Anton Klein of Mannheim. It was his misfortune that at this time the Viennese *Singspiel* was dominated by translations from French and Italian works and that opera was under the sway of Italian composers. He devoted his attention mainly to chamber music and piano concertos, here and there writing an aria to please this or that singer.[2] On 7 February 1786, on the occasion of festivities in the orangery of Schönbrunn Palace, Mozart's occasional piece, *Der Schauspieldirektor* was performed along with Abbate Giovanni Battista Casti's *opera buffa*, *Prima la musica e poi le parole* (with music by Antonio Salieri). It was one of those skits on theatrical life so popular in the eighteenth century, Mozart having been given the commission to compose the music for the text by Stephanie who had adapted the libretto of the *Entführung*. It had been a fairly thankless task. The musical numbers, apart from the overture, consisted of only two arias, a trio, and the vaudeville. The trio, 'Ich bin die erste Sängerin'—a quarrel between the two rival female singers which the tenor tries to mitigate—was the only piece which allowed the composer any chance to show his mature artistry as musician and dramatist.

LE NOZZE DI FIGARO

In any case he was now already plunged into work upon something destined to prove rich compensation for past disappointments. As early

---

[1] See *Don Giovanni*, trio no. 16 in the second act.
[2] The scena and rondo for soprano K. 416 and the soprano arias K. 418 and 419 for his sister-in-law Aloysia Lange and the tenor aria K. 420 for Valentin Adamberger, the last three as insertions to Pasquale Anfossi's opera *Il curioso indiscreto*; the tenor aria K. 431 = 425b, probably for Adamberger too, the bass aria K. 432 = 421a, probably for Ludwig Fischer, and the ensembles K. 479 and 480 as insertions to Francesco Bianchi's *La villanella rapita*.

as 7 May 1783, Mozart had written to his father that, although he did not view the matter very hopefully, a 'certain Abbate Da Ponte' was willing, when time allowed, to prepare a libretto for him. Apparently *Lo sposo deluso*, for which no stage could be found, represented the fulfilment of this promise. Nevertheless, librettist and composer must have resumed their co-operation no later than the autumn of 1785, for Leopold Mozart wrote to his daughter on 11 November that Wolfgang had reported at the beginning of the month that he must, 'precipitately complete the opera *Le nozze di Figaro*'. As a result of the growing estrangement between father and son no letters are extant regarding Mozart's share of the work. His librettist, on the other hand, has given some account in his vivid, though not always entirely reliable, memoirs.[1] According to these, the proposal to adapt *Le Mariage de Figaro* by Caron de Beaumarchais emanated from Mozart. The piece had been performed at Paris in 1784, but forbidden in Vienna by the Emperor Joseph. Da Ponte maintains that it required all his diplomacy to overcome the Imperial misgivings, alleging that his assurance that all objectionable portions had been omitted from the necessarily shorter libretto version, and his praise of the 'quite exceptional beauty' of the music, undermined all scruples. The Emperor agreed to Mozart's playing portions of the opera to him, and he could readily see that Da Ponte had divested Beaumarchais's text of all its revolutionary character and made a genuine *opera buffa* out of it. The omission of the political observations towards the end of *Le Mariage* and the substitution in *Le nozze* of Figaro's outburst against women, 'Aprite un pò quegl'occhi' delivered in the traditional *buffo* manner, is a case in point. The change was all the easier since the characters in the original comedy resembled *buffo* prototypes.[2] Beaumarchais had in the first instance planned *Le Barbier de Séville*, the drama which precedes *Figaro*, as *opéra comique*, and only subsequently transposed it into straight comedy.

The political slant of the play had probably never been of any consequence to Mozart.[3] What he sensed was the presence of established types and the possibility of transforming these into individuals. He had, moreover, consciously or not, hit upon the right subject by proposing this skilfully manipulated *comédie d'intrigue* to Da Ponte, whose gift was more for deft adaptation and preparation than original inspiration. At the same time it speaks for Da Ponte's instinct that he should so

[1] Lorenzo Da Ponte, *Memorie*, op. cit.; English translation by Elisabeth Abbott (New York, 1967).
[2] See Eric Blom, 'The Literary Ancestry of Figaro', *Musical Quarterly*, xiii (1927), p. 258.
[3] See, however, Frits Noske, 'Social Tensions in "Le nozze di Figaro"', *Music and Letters*, l (1969), p. 45.

staunchly have taken up the cudgels on behalf of Mozart, who was definitely an outsider in the Viennese operatic world. Thus an operatic career seemed once more to be opening to the composer. The co-operation between these two can, indeed, be considered fortunate, especially since Mozart was himself quite clear that he had at last met with the 'able poet' whom he had sought for so long. Nothing is known of Mozart's share in the shaping of the text, but in the light of his detailed observations on *Entführung*, his painstaking quest for another libretto, and his eventually judicious selection, considerable participation can be assumed.

The basic novelty of the piece lay in the figures of Figaro and his bride Susanna. The stock types of the artful manservant and the resourceful lady's maid were familiar from *opera buffa*, and in *Le Barbier de Séville* Figaro is still wholly devoted to the service of his noble lord. But in *Le Mariage de Figaro* the two are engaged in fighting him on behalf of their own happiness, and Figaro, as Beaumarchais presents him, assumes the character of a revolutionary representative of the downtrodden Third Estate—an attribute that Da Ponte and Mozart expanded into a quality of pure humanity. In the opera Figaro faces the Count as man to man, and the latter has no choice but to accept the situation, more especially since his wife and Susanna pursue their affairs in common and as between equals. The page, Cherubino, scarcely more than a boy, must also have appealed to Da Ponte and particularly to Mozart, on grounds of sheer humanity. The remaining cast, with Marcellina, Bartolo, and Basilio in the lead, were unqualified *parti buffe*, simply serving to develop the intrigues and to provide a background for the principals.

The chief musical characteristic of the opera[1] is its wealth of ensembles and the colourful alternation between these and the arias. This interchange, corresponding with the comings and goings of the stage characters, in itself furnishes proof of the way in which music *per se* penetrates the plot. The duets and trios no longer constitute contemplative 'arie a due' or 'a tre' but comprise short dramatic scenes. Action may still proceed in *secco recitativo*, but its flow is not impeded by the ensembles or, in the main, by the arias.

The initiative rests not with Figaro but with his bride Susanna. She it is who first realizes what is at stake, devises the schemes, and sees that their momentum is maintained. Accordingly, she has the principal musical part in so far as she is the only character to participate in all of the ensembles (six duets, two trios, one sextet, and three finales) and so is involved with every one of the opera's figures. Figaro is given one

[1] See Siegmund Levarie, *Mozart's 'Le Nozze di Figaro'. A Critical Analysis* (Chicago, 1952).

more aria than his bride, but the last of these (his polemic against women, no. 26) is, as we have seen, of a *buffo* sort, whereas not one of Susanna's arias approaches any stereotype. In particular, her garden aria no. 27, 'Deh vieni, non tardar', demonstrates Mozart's avoidance of clichés with its subtle changes of emphasis, at one moment expressing Susanna's rapturous sentiments, and at another the peace of nature which the quiet evening promises.

The lively scenes of his first arias involve Figaro in partnership, though a silent one, with two different principals. In the cavatina no. 3, 'Se vuol ballare, signor contino', the Count is, indeed, only before his mind's eye and, consequently, the fiction of his address to him is upheld solely during the opening and closing sections of the cavatina. In between Figaro moves ever farther from the original 'dance' concept with mounting agitation. By contrast, during the aria no. 9, 'Non più andrai farfallone amoroso' which Figaro directs at Cherubino, the latter is not only present but is also the figure of the young fop that Figaro depicts in the first portion of his song. This air, one of the most popular in the opera, is slightly reminiscent of the military songs popular alike in *opera buffa* and *opéra comique*, but far transcends its prototypes.

What applies to Figaro and Susanna holds good as well for the Count and Countess: both have their models in *opera buffa* but are more subtle than the stock *buffo* figures. The utterances of the Count as a man of his class possess an aristocratic brio that, according to situation, may be of bewitching charm or tempestuous passion. The first is reflected in his duet no. 16 with Susanna, the second in his sole aria, no. 17, in the third act, whose vengeful second half points towards Pizzaro's aria in Beethoven's *Fidelio*. The fundamental character of the Countess's two solo pieces, the cavatina no. 10, 'Porgi amor', and aria no. 19, 'Dove sono', is that of a nobility and dignity that is not a quality of class but springs from the core of her being. This finds expression in the strangely solemn bearing of the beginning of the two arias, whereas the turbulent continuations, once in the second portion of the cavatina and later in the third portion of the aria, have a passionate character, revealing the true partnership between Countess and Count.

Her youthful admirer, Cherubino, is also a unique and musically homogeneous personality. His aria no. 6, 'Non so più', and his canzone no. 11, 'Voi che sapete', with sentimental interspersions by the wind section, are manifestations of a vague yearning that motivates the boy and brings about his involvement in the intrigues of the adults.

Where the secondary characters are concerned, librettist and composer adhered closer to the typical figures of *opera buffa*. Their arias are largely of a reflective kind without any bearing on the action and were fashioned by Mozart into autonomous musical miniatures.

Many of the characters are introduced by means not of an aria but of an ensemble, the significance of this being that in such a musical scene the idiosyncracy of each is displayed in contrast with that of the others. Figaro and Susanna, for instance, open the first act with two duets, separated by no more than a brief recitative dialogue; the Count and Basilio have their introduction in the trio no. 7. Mozart's great artistry lay in his ability to achieve a rapprochement between dramatic requirements and musical shape: the longest and dramatically most complex finale appears perfect in form and the briefest, formally most lucid duet as a scene full of motion.

In the ensembles of the finales the composer's talent for portraying individual figures simultaneously achieves its greatest triumph. Admittedly, his collaborator, Da Ponte, possessed great dramatic and aesthetic acumen and had devoted much thought to the nature and function of the *buffo* finale. He defined it, in his memoirs, as 'a kind of comedy or minor drama in itself, requiring fresh complications of plot and a special interest of its own. This is the great occasion for showing off the genius of the composer and the ability of the singers in order to conduct the opera towards its climax'.

In the finale to the second act eight sections are fitted together in a manner where each succeeding section throws doubt upon its predecessor by introducing additional characters or adducing fresh evidence. Musically, each section has its own characteristic motives which recur in judiciously chosen places in the orchestra or the voices, and thus create both dramatic and musical coherence.

The role of the *accompagnato* is reduced, as one would expect from the vivacity of the *secco*, let alone of the arias and ensembles. The opera has only four *accompagnati*, each of which prepares for the atmosphere and character of the aria to follow, achieving this aim by concise, forward-driving orchestral motives. Sometimes the portrayal of mood involves several changes of tempo, sometimes it is the character of the vocal line which gradually proceeds to a cantabile anticipating the aria itself.

Similarly, choral and purely instrumental numbers, though purposefully employed, play a comparatively subservient role. The choruses of the country folk, nos. 8 and 21, and the duet with chorus refrain by the peasant girls in the third finale are simple and homespun, the very antithesis of the sophisticated movements which surround them. Their function is to impede plot and counter-plot and to embarrass the characters involved. The same applies to the wedding march and the fandango at the close of the third act, to whose harmless strains further webs of intrigue are spun. The overture is based on its own motives and thus provides an independent introduction into the mad whirl of the drama.

In 1789 Mozart composed two additional arias for the singer Adriana Ferrarese del Bene. 'Al desio di chi l'adora' (K. 577) was a substitute for the garden aria no. 27; 'Un moto di gioja mi sento nel petto' (K. 579) for Susanna's disguise aria no. 12.[1] Dramatically, neither could compete with the original arias.

Figaro as *opera buffa* was something new, but despite this novelty the audience at the première on 1 May 1786 was greatly impressed. At Vienna there were eight repeat performances in the same year, although the work then disappeared completely from the stage for two years, during which popular favour was bestowed on Vicente Martín y Soler's *opera buffa*, *Una cosa rara*, its text also by Da Ponte. During this interlude, however, *Figaro* won wholehearted approval at Prague, which gave rise to a further commission, thereby smoothing the path for the *dramma giocoso*, *Don Giovanni*.

DON GIOVANNI

The actual genesis of this opera and the details of the collaboration between librettist and composer are as little known as in the case of *Figaro*. Da Ponte, in his memoirs, states that it was he who proposed the idea to Mozart in answer to his request for a further libretto and that the composer 'liked it very much'. The story had enjoyed an international popularity[2] for a hundred and fifty years. Dramatists like Tirso da Molina, Shadwell, and Goldoni had treated it, quite apart from the improvisations of German travelling troupes. Musical versions of the story were not slow to follow, both as ballet (among these Gluck's *Le Festin de pierre*, Vienna, 1761) and as opera. Naturally, operatic versions predominated in Italy, where since the seventies a flood of pieces on the subject had appeared.[3] One of these was the one-act opera, *Don Giovanni o sia Il convitato di pietra*, by Giovanni Bertati with music by Giuseppe Gazzaniga. It was performed at Venice on 5 February 1787. Whether or not this piece was directly responsible for Da Ponte's and Mozart's choice of the subject remains uncertain. But without doubt Da Ponte made considerable use of the libretto, including some actual turns of speech. In his adaptation Da Ponte's two aims were to extend

---

[1] Köchel, *Verzeichnis...*, 6th edn. (1964), p. 652.
[2] Ann Livermore, 'The Origins of Don Juan', *Music and Letters*, xliv (1963), p. 257; János Liebner, 'Don Giovanni et ses ancêtres ou la métamorphose d'une légende', *Schweizerische Musikzeitung*, civ (1964), p. 237.
[3] Abert, *Mozart*, ii, pp. 363-73.

the action to make it fill an entire evening and at the same time to achieve a tighter dramatic construction. In the second aim he was quite successful. By eliminating some of Bertati's figures and distributing their characteristics among the remainder of the cast the main figures gained in individuality and became more than mere conventional roles. There are still suggestions of *buffo* types in *Don Giovanni*, but such stereotypes as Bartolo, Marcellina, and Basilio in *Figaro* are absent. To achieve his first aim, of transferring Bertati's one-act piece into a full evening's opera, he followed his model[1] closely. The second act largely consists of situations analogous to the first act, until the cemetery scene, where he caught up with Bertati. This results in the libretto's two acts running a parallel course. Each contains two attacks on the hero by his enemies, the second more vehement than the first.

The original title, 'Il dissoluto punito ossia Il Don Giovanni', focused on the tale's moral. Grouped about the protagonist as he moves from one misdeed to another are his deserted love, his wily manservant, and two pairs of lovers, one aristocratic, the other rustic—*opera buffa* types fundamentally, of whom the hero makes sport, and who finally accompany his downfall with moralizing comments. Only Don Giovanni himself and his adversary, the Commendatore, do not fit into the *buffo* scheme. They are the morality's antagonists: the Commendatore as the protector and avenger of virtue, Don Giovanni as the cynic whose ruin points the moral.

The plot of *Don Giovanni*, in contrast with *Figaro*, does not pivot around a series of intrigues but concentrates on the misdeeds of its hero. Thus the introduction and the second finale, when Don Giovanni and the Commendatore meet, constitute the cardinal points of the drama between which there extends a chain of colourful, *buffo*-like scenes. The first half of the first act shows all the characters facing the hero. He is given the opportunity to display the force of his seductive personality without singing a single aria. Only gradually do his victims and enemies unite forces, notably in the first finale, when his hopes are dashed, and in the *buffo* echo of this débâcle during the sextet (no. 19) when Don Giovanni's pursuers trap his manservant, disguised as the master.

Throughout the opera the interest of its characters depends solely on the hero. This feature of the plot, whose dramatic flow is far more continuous than that of *Figaro*, seems likely to have been the prime attraction for Mozart, if indeed he did not himself have a hand in the shaping of the material. Apart from Don Ottavio's and Donna Anna's

[1] Or, rather, models. Da Ponte is sure to have known the pieces by Tirso da Molina, Molière, and Goldoni as well. Cf. *Neue Mozart-Ausgabe*, series II, group 5, xvii (1968).

arias, nos. 21 and 23, there are no contemplative pauses. On the contrary, every aria and ensemble, irrespective of its participants, offered the composer an occasion for the illustration of Don Giovanni's unflagging vitality.

Don Giovanni, dominant from the moment he steps upon the stage, in the course of no. 1, does not sing his first aria until much later (no. 11). It reveals a sinister force of nature, driving the hero to his inevitable ruin. If the significance of this song lies in the irresistible way in which Don Giovanni shows the very essence of his being, then his two solos in the second act, the canzonetta no. 16 and the aria no. 17 are remarkable for their ambiguity: disguised as his servant Leporello, he sings them as a simple serenade with mandolin accompaniment and as a *buffo* aria. Nevertheless, the aristocratic verve of the first, and the now imperious, now garrulous, tone of the second never leave any doubt of the identity behind the menial mask.

Leporello is represented by Mozart, in deliberate contrast to the exceptional character of his master, as a commonplace *opera buffa* figure who serves as a continual foil to Don Giovanni. The more his master shows himself to be an unscrupulous miscreant the more patently the servant discloses his partly frivolous, partly faint-hearted *buffo* nature. An exception is the duet in the second act where Don Giovanni, seeking to win him over, attunes himself to Leporello. The latter is best revealed in his two arias, the famous 'catalogue aria', no. 4, and the aria no. 20, 'Ah! pietà.' The first displays his impudence, his love of adventure, and above all, his admiration for the master whose captivating personality scintillates through the concluding portion; the second reveals his slyness and adaptability to any person from whom he can expect help.

Except for the Commendatore, all the other figures simply mark stations on Don Giovanni's road to ruin. The failure of the Don's assaults on Donna Anna and Zerlina show that his career is drawing to its end. These attempts arouse vengeance, though no human avenger proves a match for the evil-doer. Donna Anna, bravely as she resists him in the introduction (no. 1), withdraws after the death of her father into the circle of his passive enemies. This attitude makes her an appropriate bride for the impractical Don Ottavio—whom the murder of the Commendatore provokes to meditation, but not to action. His bearing remains consistent throughout the ensembles and is well shown in his aria 'Il mio tesoro' (no. 21) as well as in the later composed 'Dalla sua pace' (no. 10b). Thus, as the only gentle character among Don Giovanni's enemies, he presents an absolute antithesis to the Don; a greater contrast than that between his arias and Don Giovanni's 'Fin ch'han dal vino' is inconceivable.

There is, on the other hand, a certain affinity between this forceful song and Donna Elvira's 'Ah fuggi il traditor' (no. 8), in which she warns Zerlina against the Don. Her wild, seemingly breathless utterances paint a picture of the betrayer and at the same time of herself, a passionate woman who continues to love her faithless lover. The same holds good for the subsequently written aria, 'Mi tradì quell'alma ingrata' (no. 19c). This theme of disappointed love forms the subject of all her songs and makes Donna Elvira more than any other mortal Don Giovanni's direct adversary. He, in fact, sings more frequently with her than with any of the other characters opposing him—in the finales as well as in nos. 3, 9, and 15. In these pieces, too, he seems musically linked to or subtly attuned to her.

Zerlina and Masetto, the rustic bridal pair, are no less important to the plot than the pair of noble lovers. They make an effective contrast to the main stream of events and also provide an occasion to show Don Giovanni as seducer and, at the same time, his arrogant behaviour towards Masetto. Their encounter characterizes the two. Masetto's aria, 'Ho capito, Signor, si' (no. 6), reveals him as a plain, impulsive fellow, capable of recognizing the danger to his happiness, yet incapable of withstanding Don Giovanni's imperious personality. With the cheerful tunefulness of her arias, 'Batti, batti o bel Masetto' and 'Vedrai, carino', Zerlina is the simple country girl. All the same her duettino with Don Giovanni, 'La ci darem la mano', betrays her willingness to adapt herself to the deftly flattering tone of the aristocrat, just as the latter, in the second part of the duet, adapts himself to her. Along with the trio no. 15 and the duet no. 22 it is a masterpiece of Mozart's mature skill in the simultaneous characterization of personalities.

The first finale is an extended structure of over six hundred bars. Much of it is characterized by noisy gaiety and by unmistakable ballroom music. In the midst of this the quiet prayer of the masked trio (bars 251–72) introduces one of those moments of introspection by which Mozart puts the main action into perspective: it loses some of its surface importance, yet gains in psychological interest. This trio follows upon the minuet in F major. The return of the minuet in G major (bars 406–67) gives Mozart the opportunity to make three orchestras play three different dances simultaneously: the minuet in its customary 3/4 time, with a 'contradanza' (2/4) and a 'Teitsch' (a waltz, 3/8). The technique of having dance music played on the stage to bring the plot to a point of high tension was often copied in the nineteenth century, notably in *Rigoletto*, but the musical excellence of the first *Don Giovanni* finale has never been equalled. The second finale embodies the two extremes between which the opera oscillates: earthly pleasure and divine retribution. The first is vividly illustrated by a group of wind instruments on the stage playing excerpts from well-known contemporary operas including *Una cosa rara* and *Figaro*. The second is symbolized by the key of D minor, heavily emphasized dotted rhythms, and the use of trombones which occur only twice in the opera, namely, here and as accompaniment to the Commendatore's words in the graveyard scene.[1] The octave-runs in the bass, before the close of the scene with the Statue, are a vivid reminder of the duel in the 'introduzione', while the scene itself furnishes the opening bars for the overture.

The concluding portion of the finale, after Don Giovanni's descent to Hell, is thoroughly appropriate to a 'dramma giocoso'. It has given rise to much controversy, strengthened by the supposition that Mozart eliminated it for the Vienna revival of 1788, for which he wrote a series of additional numbers. A recently recovered score prepared for this revival tends to disprove this notion.[2]

The *buffo* ending formed an essential part of the structure of the opera. Both dramatically and musically we have here the satyr play which follows the tragedy and retrospectively enhances what has preceded it. After the catastrophe, the surviving characters seem unreal. This sense of unreality, if not of dehumanization, is apparent in Mozart's progress from *Figaro* to *Così fan tutte*, and the treatment of *Don Giovanni* is an important stage on the way.[3]

The overture to the opera, necessarily changed in the concert version, leads straight into the opening number and condenses and reflects the drama in mirror form, as it were. It starts with the solemn andante from the statue scene in the second finale and follows it with a light-hearted allegro, which in compactness and agitation anticipates the opening scene. Unlike the andante, the allegro has no major thematic links with the opera, but it distils into music the essence of the hero and the turbulence of the world upon which he impinges.

The première of *Don Giovanni* at Prague on 29 October 1787 was received with enormous applause. But the composer's hopes of having it quickly followed by a performance in Vienna were not fulfilled. The first performance in the Austrian capital did not take place until six months later, and then it proved a failure. Da Ponte reports the Emperor Joseph

---

[1] Köchel, *Verzeichnis*. . ., 6th edn. (1964), p. 595; Einstein, 'Concerning some Recitatives in "Don Giovanni"', *Music and Letters*, xix (1938), p. 417.

[2] Christof Bitter, 'Don Giovanni in Wien, 1788', *Mozart–Jahrbuch 1959* (Salzburg, 1960), p. 146.

[3] It should also be noted that Tirso da Molina's *El burlador de Sevilla* was a morality play performed in Spain on All Souls' Day. The last scene which sums up what happens to a profligate and blasphemous villain contains the moral of the play, and its excision would violate the integrity of the drama.

as saying, 'It is a divine opera, perhaps even more lovely than *Figaro*, but no dish to set before my Viennese.' The reactions to performances in other cities during the succeeding years were also mixed,[1] a sign that Mozart was more and more leaving behind the style of his contemporaries.

COSÌ FAN TUTTE

The revival of *Figaro*, staged at Vienna in August 1789, was successful and probably induced the Court to offer Mozart another operatic commission. Following the old procedure, the choice of the libretto was not left to the composer but prescribed: it was another *buffo* text, *Così fan tutte ossia La scuola degli amanti*. Fortunately, its author was none other than the librettist of *Figaro* and *Don Giovanni*, the Court poet Da Ponte. With *Così fan tutte* (K. 588) began the last phase of Mozart's operatic activity. Once again he wrote, as he had done earlier in his career, specimens of the major genres of opera, namely, in addition to *opera buffa*, an *opera seria*, *La clemenza di Tito*, and a *Singspiel*, *Die Zauberflöte*. In these last years of penury and privation Mozart seemed to leave the practicalities of daily existence behind him. It is symptomatic that we know so little about the occasions for which his last works were written or about the reception which they received: the last piano concerto, the last string quintets, the clarinet concerto seem intended not so much for the approval of the large and fickle public as for the 'quiet approval' which he treasured when he experienced it in the response to *Die Zauberflöte*.[2]

Not that the balance between musician and dramatist was tipped completely in favour of the former. The dramatist continued to retain his hold on the overall concept while under his watchful eye there was infused into characters and situations an abundance of pure music. This attitude probably explains why, after texts like *Figaro* and *Don Giovanni*, Mozart was prepared to accept, apparently without resistance, a flimsy frivolity like *Così fan tutte*, to assume the thankless task of setting to music an outdated libretto like *La clemenza di Tito* at lightning speed and acquit himself of it in a style worthy of his fame, and, in the end, to reach towards an artistic creation of abstract ideas like *Die Zauberflöte*.

In the interval between *Don Giovanni* and *Così fan tutte*, during which he wrote so much instrumental music, including the three great symphonies, Mozart had no operatic commissions except occasional arias for insertion into rival composers' works (K. 541 for Francesco Albertarelli; K. 578, 582, and 583 for Louise Villeneuve, and K. 580

[1] Abert, *Mozart*, ii, pp. 356 ff.
[2] See letter of 7-8 October 1791; Anderson, *Letters*, No. 614, iii, p. 1437.

for Josefa Hofer). In addition, he composed two concert arias (K. 528 and 538) for Josepha Duschek and Aloysia Lange. When he began work on *Così fan tutte* is unknown and the details of its progress are as obscure as those of the two preceding operas. Da Ponte merely mentions the title in his memoirs; Mozart, in a letter of December 1789 invites a friend, Michael Puchberg, to attend 'a small opera rehearsal' and in another note states that the first instrumental rehearsal at the theatre has been fixed for 21 January. The first performance took place on 26 January 1790, but was no more than a passing success, even though Count Zinzendorf thought the music 'charmante', and the subject 'assez amusant', while the reporter of the *Journal des Luxus und der Moden* described it as 'a first-class work by Mozart'.[1]

The plot had its model in a comedy by Tirso da Molina.[2] But *Così* differs significantly in several respects from *Figaro* and *Don Giovanni*. The playfulness of the action suited Mozart's growing tendency towards the unreal and precluded the *parti serie* so characteristic of the two previous operas. The story of lovers who test the constancy of their fiancées by an elaborate pantomime is typical of *opera buffa*. Alfonso, who moves his four puppets with complete assurance, and Despina, the artful maid who acts as his assistant, are also stock figures of the genre; Despina's two disguises, as doctor and later as notary, are another commonplace of Italian comic opera.

Mozart entered into the foolery of the libretto with great zest. Obviously the confusion inherent in the *buffo* ensemble intrigued him, and here the abundance of ensembles—eighteen including the finales— is significant when compared with a total of twelve solo numbers. Mozart's treatment of these ensembles further emphasized the *buffo* tone. In the finales of *Figaro* and *Don Giovanni* he had often found different musical facets for the characters. In *Così fan tutte* there is little evidence of this technique. The duets are like all the ensembles of the opera, pieces of beguiling euphony, but the emotions expressed by the singers are identical or at least similar, and the melodic lines behave accordingly. The individual singers are not characterized by setting one voice against the other, except in the duet no. 29, which is closer to a dramatic scene than to a conventional duet; its subdivision into several sections and its abundance of contrast tend in that direction.

In the trios of the three male principals (of which there are no less than three at the beginning of the opera) the two lovers are opposed to Alfonso, but, again, they and he are not differentiated and thereby

---

[1] Deutsch. *Dokumente*, p. 318.
[2] See Livermore, '"Così fan tutte"; a Well-kept Secret', *Music and Letters*, xlvi (1965), p. 316.

characterized. The *terzettino* (no. 10) between the two ladies and the philosopher serves to create an atmosphere (as well as an exquisite sound) but does not distinguish between the characters that make up the ensemble; the same might be said of the serenade duet of the two lovers with chorus (no. 21). In the larger ensembles, on the other hand, there is a greater degree of characterization, particularly in the sextet, no. 13, and in the two finales. Within the individual pairs, whether of lovers or brides, the partners sing very similar music and are attuned to each other, as in the duets; yet the pairs are in some degree set off against each other, even more so when Alfonso or Despina intervenes. For these two, without abandoning the *buffo* character common to both, support now the one, now the other group and act as catalysts between the pairs. In a few exceptional instances even the solidarity within the pairs gives way to individual characterization. Examples are the quintet, no. 6, where at one point ('il destin così defrauda le speranze') Ferrando parts company with Guglielmo and follows the impassioned tune of the ladies; and, in the second finale, the canon in A flat major ('E nel tuo, nel mio bicchiero') where Guglielmo goes his own way in text as well as music.

But the prevailing technique obliges the lovers to act and sing in pairs. This quasi-duplication, by comparison with the earlier operas, has the effect of increasing the proportion of ensembles as well as the number of participants (1 sextet, 2 quintets, 1 quartet, 5 trios). In view of the many consecutive thirds, pure sound for its own sake plays a much larger role, and the interplay of groups of singers produces a dense texture, carefully and artfully controlled. Moreover, the make-believe of the plot allowed Mozart to devote his attention to purely musical subtleties without disregarding the text. This is especially true of the finales which are full of vigorous action, more so than any previous finale of Mozart's, and yet command that magic sonority which is Mozart's alone. In the A flat major canon in the second finale Mozart elevates the characters in this extravagant comedy of disguises above themselves and above the jest in which they are engaged.

It is noteworthy that when either of the two lovers or the two ladies sings an aria there is a greater amount of characterization. In her two arias nos. 14 and 25 Fiordiligi tends towards the grandiloquent, which Mozart portrays by an ironical *seria* style with wide leaps and coloratura. True, Dorabella adopts a similarly pathetic tone in no. 11, but she never ventures as far as an actual *aria di bravura*. Her frivolous nature finds more spontaneous expression in her next solo piece, no. 28, a lovely rondo in 6/8 time. The behaviour of the two male lovers is, however, the very opposite of their respective objects of devotion.

Unlike his bride Fiordiligi, Guglielmo moves wholly within the *buffo* tradition (nos. 15 and 26). Ferrando, on the other hand, is the impassioned lover *par excellence*, a heightened version, as it were, of Belmonte in *Die Entführung*. In his songs, as in the ensembles, one loses sight of the irony of the stage game because of the purely musical beauty. This is true whether he engages in lyrical observations (no. 17) or is carried away to the point where he forgets the masquerade and makes a fervent protestation of love (no. 24) or hopelessly and passionately confesses his old love (no. 27).

Despina is the typical chambermaid of *opera buffa*, whether she pronounces an impudent sermon to the male establishment (no. 12) or teaches an amusing, dance-like lesson on how to treat men (no. 19). As the moving spirit of the entire comedy Alfonso participates in all ensembles (except the duets) and this incessant activity in trios, quartet, quintets, sextet, and finales explains why he has no contemplative arias. Even so, he is given two pieces of solo singing. At the end of the terzettino no. 10 he sings of the capriciousness of women, and his similes of wind and waves are ironically illustrated in the strings. His only separate number is the F minor aria, no. 5, which grows without break out of the preceding *secco*. In a way this is more of an *accompagnato* than an aria; the almost breathless declamation and syncopated violin accompaniment are tokens of the game of deception which the philosopher starts at this point.

A comparatively large number of *accompagnati* are interspersed throughout the work: they manage to be unobtrusive but are remarkable for the motivic unity of each piece. This is particularly impressive in Ferrando's 'In qual fiero contrasto' (preceding his no. 27) where a chromatic motive in the strings holds together the entire fabric and constitutes the perfect expression of the wavering lover. That the arias of this opera are not inferior to the ensembles so far as the magic of sound goes is largely due to the instrumentation, which shows the utmost refinement, particularly in the wind section. Whether the prevalent tone is *buffo* as in the aria no. 12 and the trio no. 3, or serious as in the aria no. 17 and the terzettino no. 10, Mozart always manages to obtain a variety of highlights by changing combinations of wind instruments, sometimes alternating with strings and voices, sometimes proceeding parallel to them. In more than half of the numbers, with the notable exception of those ensembles which are exclusively *buffo*, the luxuriant sonority of the clarinet plays a major role.

Mozart's first concern in this opera was, obviously, with purely musical effects, particularly of sonority and melody. The dramatic effects to be obtained from the music were inevitably a by-product in the case of a composer with so much theatrical experience. In the nineteenth century, which found the action altogether improbable as well as improper, various attempts were made to improve the libretto, but these efforts must be rejected. Only the original text could permit Mozart to create a new primacy of music in his operatic output without interfering with the drama. True, he did not choose the libretto, but once he had accepted it he welded text and music into a singular unity which must not be tampered with.

LA CLEMENZA DI TITO

Così fan tutte, Mozart's last *opera buffa*, was also his last operatic commission for the Imperial Court in Vienna. In 1791, the year of his death, he reintroduced himself to the public as a dramatic composer with two further works, offered within the same month: on 6 September there was the première of *La clemenza di Tito* at Prague; on 30 September, *Die Zauberflöte* in the Theater auf der Wieden at Vienna. The first commission came from the impresario Domenico Guardasoni, known to Mozart from the time of the Prague performances of *Figaro* and *Don Giovanni*. Guardasoni was responsible for arranging, on behalf of the Prague Estates, the festival opera on the occasion of the Emperor Leopold II's coronation as King of Bohemia. Mozart probably received the libretto in mid-July;[1] whether negotiations had been proceeding since the composer's passage through the city in April 1789, as Volek surmises, remains uncertain.[2]

Metastasio's *La clemenza di Tito*, with its glorification of the Emperor Titus as the prototype of magnanimity, was particularly suited to enhance the festivities of the reigning houses of Europe and had already been set to music by a great number of composers. The current adaptation by the Dresden Court poet Caterino Mazzolà had reduced it from three acts to two without removing the overall conventionality characteristic of *opera seria*. All of the characters remain pale and schematic. The noble, wise Titus who 'knows not vengeance' is as far removed from Sarastro in *Die Zauberflöte* as is Vitellia with her love–hate from Donna Elvira in *Don Giovanni*; frosty aphorisms take the place of outbursts of genuine passion. The same is true of the subsidiary figures as well as of the hero Sextus, the friend of Titus, who is inspired by his love for Vitellia to murder the Emperor. Despite this typical

[1] Not mid-August, as hitherto assumed; see Abert, *Mozart*, ii, p. 586, and Dent, *Mozart's Operas*, 2nd edn. (London, 1947), p. 212, and on the other hand Bernhard Paumgartner, 'Zur Dramaturgie der "Clemenza di Tito"', *Österreichische Musikzeitung*, iv (1949), p. 172, and preface to *Neue Mozart-Ausgabe*, series II, group 5, xx (1970).
[2] Tomislav Volek, 'Über den Ursprung von Mozarts Oper "La Clemenza di Tito"' *Mozart-Jahrbuch 1959* (Salzburg, 1960), p. 274.

Metastasian conflict between love and friendship Sextus never gets beyond anaemic observations.

The task of setting this libretto to music meant for Mozart a return to a world whose assumptions had crumbled with those of the *ancien régime* in France two years before. A decade earlier he had himself liberalized the conventions of the genre in *Idomeneo* and had abandoned them entirely in the masterpieces composed since. That he should accept a commission of this kind while engaged on *Die Zauberflöte* is to be explained solely by dire financial necessities. Still, to the modern student it seems almost macabre to see the composer of Sarastro's creed caught in the toils of dated conventions, whether courtly or operatic or both. Fortunately, he was now able to accommodate these conventions with greater freedom and to inject into the several types of arias the musicality of his final period, which in a variety of guises reveals the tone of *Die Zauberflöte*, encompassing, as it were, both hymn and ditty, as in the hero's aria in Act I:

Ex. 93

(This is the only gain of the loftiest throne, all the rest is torment and all is servitude.)

It is true that at times this nobility and conciseness yield to another style allowing for more extended forms and greater virtuosity; examples are nos. 9 and 23, where obbligatos for clarinet and basset-horn are employed. At the first performance both these instruments were played by the excellent clarinettist Anton Stadler. And in spite of the acknowledgement of the virtuoso quality of the singers, the primo uomo[1] and the prima donna, these arias are so beautiful in themselves that they must be reckoned among Mozart's finest contributions to the repertory of clarinet and basset-horn. There is a variety of formal patterns among the arias of the two principals, often containing contrasting strains within the same number.[2] The text, of course, permits such contrasts, but only in the case of no. 23, a freely shaped rondo, is this feature demanded. Accordingly, this aria of Vitellia is the only one we may consider a dramatic as well as a musical masterpiece, to be set alongside the first finale.

Apart from a limited number of festive choruses, Metastasio's *Titus*, according to well-established custom, allowed only for solos. Hence Mazzolà's most forward-looking innovation lay in the introduction of numerous ensembles (three duets and three trios). Of these the little friendship duet, no. 3, akin to a folk-song, gives the impression of having strayed by accident from *Singspiel* into *opera seria*. The lyrical love duet of the secondary pair, no. 7, is a straight *aria a due*. The trio no. 10 between Vitellia, Annius, and Publius is more like an expression of the heroine's despair, to which the other two voices supply a background, than a dialogue between three equals. In the duet no. 1 and the trios nos. 14 and 18, however, the composer turned the first part into a colloquy between sharply differentiated personalities and the second into a musically co-ordinated ensemble, a happy compromise between dramatic and musical requirements, even though not comparable with the ensembles in *Figaro* and *Don Giovanni*.

Mozart was careful, in general, to keep well within the dramatically even and restrained style of *opera seria*, in which *opera buffa* ways of full-blooded characterization would have been out of place. Only once, in the finale of the first act, did Mozart breach the convention. This occurs in the tumultuous scene of the burning of the Capitol, a scene which consisted of related yet individual solos, ensembles, and choral

---

[1] In this case the castrato Domenico Bedini. The part of Annius was also soprano; in the absence of a suitable male performer, it was given to a female singer. In the sketches the part of Sextus was planned for a tenor. See Jack A. Westrup, 'Two First Performances: Monteverdi's "Orfeo" and Mozart's "Clemenza di Tito"', *Music and Letters*, xxxix (1958), p. 333; Christopher Raeburn, 'Mozarts Opern in Prag', *Musica*, xiii (1959), p. 158; Paul Nettl, 'Prager Mozartiana', *Mitteilungen der Internationalen Stiftung Mozarteum*, ix (1960), Nos. 3-4, p. 4.

[2] As in no. 20, recorded in *The History of Music in Sound*, vii.

interpolations and which was preceded by a passionate *accompagnato*, strikingly homogeneous in its thematic material. The instrumental underlining of the catastrophe, in severe contrast with the neatly ordered world of the other numbers, was vivid and graphic, and it was probably this overall effect that the Empress, an Italian princess, had in mind when, as is alleged, she described the opera as a 'porcheria tedesca'. In comparison, the second finale, introduced by a festive march with chorus and an *accompagnato*, is simply a solemn termination in which solos, ensembles, and chorus are brought together in a rousing climax.

Apart from these finales the function of the chorus is confined to panegyrics on Titus in two homophonic movements (nos. 5 and 15), the first again introduced by a march. In view of the general development of *opera seria*, and particularly the precedent set by *Idomeneo*, it is surprising that there are only three *accompagnato* recitatives, a sign that Mozart regarded the work as a festive serenata, rather than a drama. They occur at climactic moments of the action, before the two finales and Vitellia's great aria no. 23, and are marked by typical orchestral interpolations, economic accompaniment, and colourful harmonization. The *secco* recitatives have not come down to us in Mozart's hand, and so far their authorship has not been established.[1]

The overture to *Titus* is a piece of solemn music with no inherent connection with the main body of the opera. Its contrapuntal development section, strange in a movement of this sort, is clearly late Mozart, and yet the varied instrumentation of the earlier works is missing, as, indeed, it is in the whole of the opera. In this respect the composer adhered punctiliously to the prime rule of *opera seria*, that the vocal part should, in all circumstances, dominate the orchestra.

DIE ZAUBERFLÖTE

The success of *Titus* was slight. Critics and audience were probably too much aware of the constraint Mozart had put on himself.[2] Soon after its performance Mozart returned to Vienna and put the finishing touches to *Die Zauberflöte* (K. 620),[3] the score of which had been nearly completed in July, when the commission for *Titus* was received. The begetter of this last opera was Emanuel Schikaneder, manager since 1789 of the Freihaus-Theater auf der Wieden and a long-standing acquaintance from Salzburg, where he had been on tour with his company in 1780–1. The proposal by the versatile theatre manager to

---

[1] See Franz Giegling, 'Zu den Rezitativen von Mozarts Oper "Titus"', *Mozart-Jahrbuch 1967* (Salzburg, 1968), p. 121.

[2] Erich H. Müller von Asow, 'Mozarts "La Clemenza di Tito" im Spiegel des zeitgenössischen Schrifttums', *Wiener Figaro*, xi (1941), p. 1.

[3] *Neue Mozart-Ausgabe*, series II, group 5, xix (1970).

offer the public yet another magic opera was in line with contemporary popular Viennese taste. It would be difficult to establish where the responsibility lies for the transformation of this magic opera into a work of ideas of the noblest sort. It was probably Mozart who felt the urge to raise the naïve *Singspiel* to a higher sphere. Schikaneder, whether as manager or author, was a man of the theatre with his eye firmly fixed on the box-office and for this reason more concerned with external than with intellectual effects. Mozart and he were much together during the time *Die Zauberflöte* was written, and closest co-operation may be assumed even in the absence of actual reports. Design and execution were undoubtedly those of Schikaneder, whilst Mozart is likely to have had his say in regard to the high ethical interpretation of the plot.[1] It has been argued that the final result is the reinterpretation of an originally harmless fairy-tale. Most listeners sense that the plot takes a turn with the first finale and the entry of Prince Tamino into the world of the initiates. Up to this point Tamino moves through a realm ruled, as it seems, by a fairy queen (surrounded by good spirits) who has suffered injustice by the abduction of her daughter Pamina. The first finale makes it clear that Tamino has been deceived: the reputed villain is lord of the Realm of Light and Pamina has been abducted only so that, together with Tamino, she may be initiated into the mysteries of the Covenant of Light. Whether at this stage there was a change of plan, or whether from the outset the drama was envisaged as a compromise between a magic fairy opera and work of a high ethical cast, must remain an open question.[2] Suffice it to say that Mozart's music for the first act is stylistically unified without any suggestion of break.

The works that may be accounted sources of *Die Zauberflöte* are numerous. *Oberon, König der Elfen* by Carl Ludwig Giesecke, performed to the music of Paul Wranitzky at the Theater auf der Wieden in 1789, probably played an important part in suggesting the lines of the plot.[3]

[1] Abert, *Mozart*, ii, pp. 626 ff.; Engländer, 'The Sketches for "The Magic Flute" at Upsala', *Musical Quarterly*, xxvii (1941), pp. 345 ff.

[2] See J. N. A. Armitage-Smith, 'The Plot of "The Magic Flute"' *Music and Letters*, xxxv (1954), p. 36; Dent, 'The Plot of "The Magic Flute"' ibid., p. 175; Liebner, 'Encore Shakespeare et Mozart. La Tempête. La théorie de la "cassure" de "La Flûte Enchantée"', *Schweizerische Musikzeitung*, cii (1962), p. 292; Alfons Rosenberg, *Die Zauberflöte, Geschichte und Deutung von Mozarts Oper* (Munich, 1964); E. M. Batley, 'Textual Unity in Die Zauberflöte', *Music Review* xxvii (1966), p. 81; Jacques Chailley, *La Flûte Enchantée. Opéra Maçonnique* (Paris, 1968).

[3] Giesecke's reputed claim to have been the actual librettist of *Die Zauberflöte* probably derives from this work which was based on the *Singspiel* libretto *Hüon und Amanda* by Friederike Sophie Seyler, published in the same year, which in turn was an offshoot of Wieland's *Oberon*. Concerning Giesecke's claim, see Dent, *Mozart's Operas*, p. 234; Deutsch, 'Der rätselhafte Giesecke', *Die Musikforschung*, v (1952), p. 152, and *Das Wiener Freihaustheater auf der Wieden, 1787–1801* (Vienna and Leipzig, 1937).

Many individual traits, such as the title, the three boys, the Queen of the Night, the rascally Moor, the test by fire and water, and love inspired by a portrait, were taken from Wieland's collection of fairy-tales, *Dschinnistan oder auserlesene Feen- und Geistermärchen* (1786–9). The glorification of liberal ideas in the garb of freemasonry was derived from such various models as the novel *Sethos, histoire ou vie tirée des monuments anecdotes de l'ancienne Egypte* by the Abbé Terrasson,[1] the *Singspiel Das Sonnenfest der Brahminen* by Karl Friedrich Hensler (performed at Vienna in 1790 to the music of Wenzel Müller), and Gebler's *König Thamos*, for which Mozart himself had written incidental music years before.[2]

All of these sources contain passages that have been incorporated almost verbatim into the libretto of *Die Zauberflöte* and, even more important, the background is remarkably similar: a company of priestly initiates, a sun temple, and a final feast of victory at the temple, apostrophizing goodness and universal brotherhood. It was not difficult to link the world of fairy-tale and that of freemasonry. This had already been done by Wieland, whose *Dschinnistan* was derived from the same masonic spirit as Terrasson's *Sethos*. Schikaneder and Mozart, freemasons both, could easily extend the conjunction between fairy magic and rites of initiation. Certainly, the fact that so many related sources exist suggests the popularity of the central theme of *Die Zauberflöte* (the conflict between Light and Darkness) on two levels: as a simple fairy-tale for the groundlings and as an ethical parable for an intellectual élite where freemasonry counted for much. That despite these different levels of appeal the libretto should have proved so homogeneous and dramatically effective speaks for the combined skills of Schikaneder and Mozart. Here, indeed, was the union between the 'good composer who understands the stage' and the 'able poet' which Mozart had claimed as the prerequisite of good opera.

In *Così fan tutte* Mozart had turned to a world of jest; in *La clemenza di Tito* to one of convention; now, in *Die Zauberflöte* he moved in a world of ideas where each figure had its fixed status within its group.

---

[1] Published at Paris in 1731 and in German translation by Matthias Claudius at Breslau in 1777–8. See Nettl, 'Sethos und die freimaurerische Grundlage der "Zauberflöte"', *Bericht über die musikwissenschaftliche Tagung der Internationalen Stiftung Mozarteum in Salzburg 1931*, ed. Schenk (Leipzig, 1932), p. 142. Nettl cites as another possible model for Schikaneder *Osiris*, an opera by J. G. Naumann (Dresden, 1781), whose plot presents an exact parallel to the Sethos novel.

[2] For the various textual sources, see also Egon Komorzynski, *Emanuel Schikaneder* (Vienna, 1951). In addition Livermore, '"The Magic Flute" and Calderón', *Music and Letters*, xxxvi (1955), p. 7, points to Calderón's *El purgatorio de San Patricio* as a source of *Die Zauberflöte*. Liebner, 'Le chant du cygne de Shakespeare et de Mozart', *Schweizerische Musikzeitung*, cii (1962), p. 28, has underlined the similarity of content between *Die Zauberflöte* and *The Tempest*.

The hierarchical gradations from Sarastro to Tamino and even Papageno, from the Queen of the Night to Monostatos, were, of course, reflected in the immense stylistic variety which the Viennese *Singspiel* permitted. Beyond that, the dichotomy between the realms of Light and of Darkness found its manifestation in opposing musical styles, that of the German *Lied* versus that of Italian opera. The simple pair of lovers sing in folk strains which progress to arioso style in the mouths of the noble pair, and receive a hymn-like intensity in the songs of Sarastro. The world of Darkness is expressed either by the splendid but cold style of *opera seria* (Queen of the Night) or the light babbling of *opera buffa* (Monostatos, the three ladies).

All numbers show the characteristics of Mozart's last style: conciseness, and a pregnancy of expression which often appears even in the orchestral introductions. In the accompaniment of the arias, too, the instrumentation is more varied than it would be traditionally on such occasions, and the texture is more reminiscent of chamber music than of the standard opera orchestra.

Papageno's songs (nos. 2 and 20) are childlike, strophic ditties of popular origin. The second of these, 'Ein Mädchen oder Weibchen' is related to many tunes, some secular, some sacred.[1] Mozart's melody ultimately became a folk-song itself, adapted to the text 'Üb' immer Treu und Redlichkeit'.

Tamino's aria, no. 3, is distinguished by the close relationship between voice and instruments, and in Pamina's G minor aria, no. 17, the strings convey the troubled mood in a fairly continuous figuration against which the vocal line depicts the heroine's despair by wide leaps and chromatic intervals. The solemn and lofty tone of Sarastro (nos. 10 and 15) stands half-way between the simple and natural tone of Papageno and the elegiac raptures of the pair of lovers. This is yet another indication that the world of the guardians has understanding for both spheres.

The first aria of the Queen of the Night (no. 4) is, perhaps, the only musical number that may be said to reflect the reinterpretation of the plot, discussed earlier. Its first section, an *accompagnato*, displays a mighty queen; the succeeding larghetto conveys grievous longing of the kind associated with Tamino and Pamina, and the final allegro-moderato, with its *bravura*, is more festive than threatening. Only in the second act (no. 14) does the Queen sing a genuine 'revenge aria', though Mozart manages to remove it from convention by means of dynamics and modulation.

[1] Abert, *Mozart*, ii, p. 584, n. 5; Komorzynski, 'Ein Mädchen oder Weibchen wünscht Papageno sich', *Wiener Figaro*, x (August, 1940), p. 10; Frederick Sternfeld, 'The Melodic Sources of Mozart's Most Popular *Lied*', *Musical Quarterly*, xlii (1956), p. 213.

Monostatos, of the Queen's party, and traitor to the realm of Light, is allocated a midway position between the contending parties. His song, No. 13, is melodically simple and approaches the tone of the *Lied*; but an impression of villainy and an atmosphere of doom are conveyed by restless motion, doubling of first violins and piccolo, and Mozart's rubric 'sempre pianissimo'.

The ensembles, too, are on the whole attuned to the opposed worlds of the protagonists. When characters from both parties are involved, the tone is a hybrid of *buffo* and popular song, as in the quintets nos. 5 and 12. But the trio of the three boys (no. 16) has, unmistakably, the lyrical hymn-like tone of Sarastro, and the duet between Pamina and Papageno (no. 7) clearly demonstrates how cognate the two pairs of lovers are, different as their social and intellectual stations may be. The two finales show certain affinities in their construction. Both have at the outset a solemn trio by the boys, and both close with a chorus by the initiates. Between these terminal points the plot concerning the two couples (and Monostatos) develops. In the first finale the vicissitudes of the two pairs of lovers are interwoven, but in the second the high and low worlds of Tamino and Papageno are sharply separated, involving several changes of scene. Whereas the *buffo* finale, especially in the hands of Da Ponte and Mozart, involves a logical chain of events, the alternation of varied tableaux in *Die Zauberflöte* is rather loosely motivated, though held together by the harmonic relationship of the tonalities involved.

The first finale falls into three major sections: Tamino and the Speaker; Pamina, Papageno, and Monostatos; Sarastro and the characters of the preceding sections. Although externally the final chorus represents a climax of sorts, nothing, in text or music, surpasses the initial scene between Tamino and the Speaker, where the hero for the first time meets the world of the initiates. The orchestra, strings and woodwind, with sparing interjections and modulations to remote keys, impels the parley steadily forward to its climax where the Speaker solemnly intones the gospel of friendship (Andante a tempo).

The second finale is related to the first as a fulfilment is to a promise. Here all the characters, differentiated according to their proper spheres, receive their final rewards. In the first finale it was Tamino whom the three boys led to the portals of the temple. Now it is Pamina whom they bring to the terrifying threshold where she is to be united with Tamino. Mozart made this trial scene—a magnified and at the same time a heightened refinement of the Speaker's scene from the first finale—the climax of the second finale and of the opera. This he achieved by treating the song of the men in armour as the subject of a grand chorale variation, lifting it above the variety of styles encountered in the opera heretofore, and creating an atmosphere of dedication surpassing human frailty and reaching to the beyond. Scholars have argued whether the chorale functions generally as a symbol of the metaphysical or whether its specific text, 'Ach Gott vom Himmel, sieh darein', is a sermon on the sinfulness of man.[1] What is beyond argument is the impressiveness of the chorale, both in its statement and in the counterpoints which surround it. The melody itself is doubled in four octaves in the vocal lines of the two men in armour, woodwind, and trombones; against this the strings, in rapid figuration, employ a 'sighing' and a 'stepping' or 'marching' motive. In the succeeding andante the realms of fairy-story and ideas are radiantly merged in the hymn of the lovers. The adagio of the trial scene proper takes no notice whatever of fire or water; the world of ideas triumphs over the elements. This triumph is symbolized by the sound of the 'magic' flute, softly accompanied by sparse chords of the brass section and by kettle drums. The ensuing scenes of Papageno and Papagena, and of the Powers of Darkness give the popular component of the magic opera its due and enable Mozart to accompany the change of scene from the site of the destruction of the enemies to the Temple of the Sun by a necessarily short, but magnificent, modulation from C minor to B flat major and E flat major. Thus, the opera ends, dramatically, with the apotheosis of the humanitarian ideal and, musically, in the key of the overture.

The overture itself, like that of *Don Giovanni*, prepares the audience for the two worlds in which the opera moves. The opening adagio and the second adagio which precedes the development section represent the world of the initiates, while the allegro in fugal style characterizes the many-coloured, fantastic fairy-tale world from which the other figures derive.

The opera as a whole is characterized by a variety of styles necessitated by the several planes of action; nevertheless, it displays great musical homogeneity in a web of rhythmic, melodic, and harmonic formulas which encloses and unifies all its component parts. It is this unity which is the essence of *Die Zauberflöte*, establishing the mood of the whole and pervading the strains of Sarastro as well as those of the Queen of the Night, the songs of lowly and simple children of nature as well as the hymns of the initiates. In this way the magic plays of the Viennese tradition, the world of fairy-tales, and the drama of ideas, with their miscellany of concepts and mutual contradictions, find their

[1] For the first view, see Reinhold Hammerstein, 'Der Gesang der geharnischten Männer. Eine Studie zu Mozarts Bachbild', *Archiv für Musikwissenschaft*, xiii (1956), p. 1; for the latter, Abert, *Mozart*, ii, p. 676, and Wilhelm Fischer, 'Der welcher wandelt diese Strasse voll Beschwerden', *Mozart–Jahrbuch 1950* (Salzburg, 1951), p. 41.

musical fusion. The ancestry of many of the melodies goes back as far as *Idomeneo*, yet these tunes seem to find their fulfilment only in the world of *Die Zauberflöte*.[1] As such, Mozart's last opera is a synthesis of all his previous operatic activities. It was no coincidence that the speedy success of *Die Zauberflöte* eased the way for the triumph of his operas and, ultimately, of all his works.

(e) THE OPERAS OF HAYDN
By H. C. ROBBINS LANDON

INTRODUCTION

In 1776 Haydn was asked to supply an autobiographical sketch for an Austrian literary magazine[2] and, speaking of his compositions, he wrote that the 'following have received the most approbation: the operas *Le pescatrici, L'incontro improviso* [sic], *L'infedeltà delusa*, performed in the presence of Her Imperial and Royal Majesty [Maria Theresa], the oratorio *Il ritorno di Tobia*, performed in Vienna; the *Stabat Mater* . . .'. Later in the article he mentions works 'in the chamber-musical style', but there is no word about his symphonies, sonatas, and other instrumental works. Musical history has reversed the emphasis.

There is, in fact, considerable evidence, apart from the document quoted above, that Haydn considered his most important works the big operas composed for and lavishly produced by his patron, Prince Nicolaus Esterházy. His symphonies, brilliant though they sounded, and carefully written as they were—the autographs themselves are models of calligraphy and precision—were undoubtedly composed and presented as *pièces d'occasion*, just as were, for example, Bach's Brandenburg Concertos. If Burney had been among the brilliant audience for the first performance of *L'infedeltà delusa* at the Schlosstheater in Esterház that September evening in 1773, and had asked Haydn what he considered his greatest and most important work, the modest composer would certainly have pointed to the tall folio manuscript of the opera.

Several years later, in 1781,[3] Haydn received a letter from Le Gros, Director of the Concert Spirituel in Paris, and wrote about it to the Viennese publishers Artaria:

---

[1] Heuss, 'Mozarts "Idomeneo" als Quelle für "Don Giovanni" und "Die Zauberflöte"', *Zeitschrift für Musikwissenschaft*, xiii (1930–1), p. 177; Eric Werner, 'Leading or Symbolic Formulas in the "Magic Flute": a hermeneutic examination', *Music Review*, xviii (1957), p. 286; Hyatt King, 'The Melodic Sources and Affinities of "Die Zauberflöte"', *Musical Quarterly*, xxxvi (1950), p. 241.

[2] *Das gelehrte Österreich*. See H. C. R. Landon, *The Collected Correspondence and Notebooks of Joseph Haydn* (London, 1959), p. 19.

[3] Ibid., p. 28.

INTRODUCTION

The gentlemen asked permission to have [the *Stabat Mater*] engraved. They made me an offer to engrave all my future works on the most favourable terms for myself, and were most surprised that I was so singularly successful in my vocal compositions; but I wasn't at all surprised, for they have not yet heard anything. If they only could hear ... my most recent opera, *La fedeltà premiata*, I assure you that no such work has been heard in Paris up to now, nor perhaps in Vienna either; my misfortune is that I live in the country.

Nevertheless, 'in the country' though he was, Haydn was an industrious conductor, as well as composer, of opera.

During the years 1776-90, Esterház rivalled Naples, Milan, Vienna, and Paris as one of the leading opera houses in Europe, not only as to what may be presumed to have been the quality of performance but, even more surprising, the quantity as well.[1] Between the years 1776 and 1790 Haydn conducted over one hundred operas by himself and other composers. During these years he not only rehearsed the cast, prepared the scores (with the usual cuts and transpositions), supervised the acquisition of new scores and a staff of copyists who worked day after day to produce the thousands of pages of parts needed; he also wrote two dozen new arias as substitutes for those he found wanting,[2] reorchestrated the meagre scoring of a Gazzaniga or Traetta, and actually conducted all the performances. Between 1780 and 1790 there were no less than 1,038 actual operatic performances at the castle. In the year 1786 alone Haydn introduced eight new operas and revived nine others; that year they gave 125 performances on the stage. It is a mystery how Haydn found any time to compose at all in these years. Apart from the regular opera house, there were frequent performances of puppet operas in the German language in a theatre especially constructed for that purpose. Haydn himself wrote some half a dozen marionette operas, of which two have survived.[3]

COMPOSITION OF THE OPERAS

On 5 October 1762 Gluck's *Orfeo ed Euridice* was performed for the first time at the Burgtheater in Vienna. Thirty miles away, in Eisenstadt, the Esterházy Court was preparing the first 'operatic festival' under its new reigning prince, Nicolaus 'the Magnificent', who had succeeded to the title upon the death of his elder brother, Paul Anton, on 18 March

---

[1] Dénes Bartha and László Somfai, *Joseph Haydn als Opernkapellmeister* (Budapest 1960); János Harich, 'Das Repetoire des Opernkapellmeisters Joseph Haydn in Eszterháza (1780–1790)', *Haydn-Jahrbuch*, i (Vienna, 1962), p. 9.

[2] Landon (ed.), *13 Arien für Sopran*, (Salzburg, 1961); *4 Arien für Tenor* (Salzburg, 1964); *3 Arien für Bariton* (Salzburg, 1964).

[3] Landon, 'Haydn's Marionette Operas and the Repertoire of the Marionette Theatre at Esterház Castle', *Haydn-Jahrbuch*, i (1962), p. 111.

1762. Nicolaus, who had lived surrounded by music and theatre (in the form of strolling players) in a hunting lodge at Süttör, moved to Eisenstadt and at once commissioned Haydn to write a series of short Italian comedies (of which all but a fragment of one, *La Marchesa Nespola*, have disappeared) and a large-scale *opera seria* or 'festa teatrale', entitled *Acide e Galatea*.

This was by no means Haydn's first personal encounter with the world of opera. Some ten years before, when a penniless student in Vienna, in his own words 'eking out a wretched existence', he had been 'discovered' by the famous comedian, Felix Kurz-Bernardon,[1] and engaged to write a comic opera in German entitled *Der krumme Teufel*. It has been suggested that Haydn continued to write some of the music for Kurz's *Singspiele*, and the few extant arias in score from Kurz's plays could well be by Haydn.[2] Unfortunately no complete copy of *Der krumme Teufel* has survived, although it was played all over Europe; nor do we know for certain the exact date of the opera's first performance, though a recently discovered document records a single performance on 29 May 1753. A copy of the original libretto—one of two known copies—is in the Vienna City Museum. It is clear, at any rate, that Haydn must have gained much valuable experience writing for the Kurz troupe; and, as we shall see, he preserved a warm affection for the earthy, often drastically realistic humour of this genre, which was to flower in his marionette opera, *Das abgebrannte Haus*. This explains, at least in part, the professional sureness with which he tossed off the score to *Acide e Galatea*.[3]

The new work, with a libretto by Giovanni Battista Migliavacca, was performed on a temporary stage at Eisenstadt in January 1763; the singers were recruited partly from Vienna and partly from the troupe at Haydn's disposal at Eisenstadt, while the decorations were made by Girolamo Bon. A repetition of the opera was considered in 1773 in connection with a visit of the Empress Maria Theresa to Esterház. Either there was not time to complete the revision, or it was dropped for other reasons, and *L'infeldeltà delusa* was performed.

In the years following the production of *Acide* and the little Italian comedies, music and opera were given in all the beautiful Esterházy

---

[1] See pp. 89–91.
[2] Robert Haas, 'Die Musik in der Wiener deutschen Stegreifkomödie', *Studien zur Musikwissenschaft*, xii (1925), p. 3; also Landon, 'Haydn's Marionette Operas', in *Haydn Yearbook*, i (1962), p. 145.
[3] An incomplete autograph of the original version of *Acide* is in Budapest Nat. Széch. Lib., Ms. mus. I. 8. 16. The overture is in Paris, Bibl. Nat. du Conservatoire Prés. 138 (2). Paris, Bib. et Musée de l'Opéra, and in Budapest Nat. Széch. Lib., Ms. mus. I. 8. 16. The work has never been printed in its entirety. Overture, ed. Landon (Vienna, 1959); 'Aria di Nettuno', from the revised version, in *3 Arien für Bariton*.

palaces. On 6 February 1767 the Esterházy *Operntruppe* gave a guest performance in the garden of the Prince Archbishop at Pressburg (Bratislava), at which the Archduchess Maria Christine, her husband Duke Albert von Sachsen-Teschen, with members of the Viennese Court, were present. The opera was a new intermezzo by Haydn entitled *La canterina*; he had written it the year before, and it had been tried out at Eisenstadt (the costume bills are extant for this trial run). The work was a short comedy on the lines of Pergolesi's *La serva padrona*.[1]

In these years Prince Esterházy regularly engaged *Wandertruppen*, strolling players who took up residence at Eisenstadt or Esterház. Foremost among them was the famous Karl Wahr troupe, who brought Shakespeare to Esterház in new translations and played the newest works of German playwrights (including Goethe's *Stella*). The Prince began to enlarge his hunting lodge at Süttör into a magnificent rococo palace. Still standing today, Esterháza (or Esterház) is one of the most splendid architectural achievements of the period. The celebrated gardens, which no longer exist, rivalled those of Versailles. Here Prince Nicolaus built comfortable quarters for the musicians and strolling players. By 1766 this building was completed, while the opera theatre was not ready until 1768, the marionette theatre not before 1773. Haydn also provided and conducted the music to these plays: that to *Hamlet*, of which a report is given in the *Pressburger Zeitung* of 1774, seems to be lost, but in Symphony No. 60 we have the incidental music to the German translation of Regnard's *Le Distrait*, while in Symphony No. 63 we have the *Bühnenmusik* to Favart's *Solimann II*.[2]

The splendid new opera house was opened in the autumn of 1768 with Haydn's *Lo speziale*, based on the textbook of Carlo Goldoni. It was the first of three Goldoni subjects which Haydn was to set to music, and the first of his operas to be revived in modern times.[3]

Gradually the fabulous productions at Esterház Castle must have reached the ears of the Viennese, for on 22 March 1770 the whole Esterházy troupe gave a guest performance of *Lo speziale* at the house of Freiherr von Sumerau. 'It was such a success,' reported the *Wiener Diarium* No. 24 shortly afterwards, 'that by special request it was

---

[1] The autograph, complete except for a few pages, is in the Budapest, Nat. Széch. Lib., Ms. mus. I. 1. A copy of the original libretto is in the Budapest University Library. Full score (ed. Bartha) in *J. Haydn: Werke* (Munich and Duisburg), series 25, ii.

[2] Landon, *The Symphonies of Joseph Haydn* (London, 1955), pp. 349 and 359; also *Supplement* (London, 1961), p. 38.

[3] A copy of the original libretto is in the Gesellschaft der Musikfreunde, Vienna. The opera has not survived in its entirety: a good deal of the third act is missing. The only contemporary source is Haydn's autograph, Budapest, Nat. Széch. Lib., Ms. mus. I. 2. Full score (ed. Helmut Wirth), *Werke*, series 25, iii. Reconstruction of the missing music in the practical edition ed. Landon (Salzburg, 1970).

repeated the next Thursday as a musical Academy [concert], something which is a flattering mark of approbation to Herr Kapellmeister Haydn, whose great talents are well known to all amateurs of music . . .' There is no doubt that with *Lo speziale* Haydn's talents as a dramatic composer are fully revealed for the first time.

That same year, 1770, saw one of the first of Prince Nicolaus's lavish festivals in which music, theatre, fireworks, succulent banquets, balls, and hunting parties combined to make a display of Medici-like grandeur. The occasion was the marriage of the Prince's niece (Countess Lamberg) on 16 September 1770. Haydn had begun work on the new opera for this occasion, *Le pescatrici*, the year before, as we know from the incomplete autograph in the Esterházy Archives at Budapest. Again, the text was by Goldoni, no doubt because of the success of *Lo speziale*. The *Wiener Diarium* reported on the events at Esterház and noted that Haydn's new opera was, if anything, an even greater success than *Lo speziale*. In fact, the musical structure is considerably more complicated, with large-scale ensembles, including a brilliant septet in the first act, several choruses, and three finales.[1]

The year 1773 marks a climax in the production of Haydn's operas at Esterház, both quantitatively and qualitatively. For the birthday of the Dowager Princess Maria Anna Louise Esterházy (widow of Paul Anton) it was planned to resuscitate Haydn's *Acide*. Meanwhile, Haydn had become a master and no doubt found his first Italian opera too old-fashioned and conventional: he began to rewrite it (see p. 174). No doubt the choice of the old opera was connected with the Dowager Princess, who may have had sentimental feelings about it. In the end, however, the plan was dropped and Haydn wrote instead his greatest stage work so far, *L'infedeltà delusa*,[2] which was first performed on the Dowager Princess's name day, 26 July 1773. The author of the libretto was none other than Marco Coltellini, the friend of Gluck and the first reformer of *opera seria*. (Coltellini also wrote or adapted two librettos for Mozart.) The Italian had shortly before left Vienna for Russia, and we do not know if the revisions, as against the only other extant setting of the libretto, in Florence, were made especially for Esterház.

In September of that year Prince Esterházy staged (the only appropriate word) his most famous and lavish festival, for the Empress Maria Theresa and the Court. Descriptions of this veritable orgy of music, art, and 'spectacle' may be found elsewhere.[3] In particular, *L'infedeltà delusa* was performed with great success on 1 September. The Empress went

---

[1] Vocal score, (ed. Landon), (Vienna, 1965).
[2] Full score (ed. Bartha and Jenö Vecsey), *Werke*, series 25, v.
[3] e.g. Karl Geiringer, *Haydn* (New York, 1946), pp. 63–4.

back to Vienna and told everybody, 'If I want to hear a good opera, I go to Esterház,' a remark which was not calculated to increase Haydn's popularity among his Viennese (or rather Italian) colleagues at the Court opera. Indeed, it may be that the malicious intrigues against Haydn at the Vienna opera were launched by this oft-quoted remark.

The Empress's visit also marked the inauguration of the new marionette theatre, the puppets and machinery of which the Prince had purchased from Karl Joseph von Pauersbach, who had achieved some celebrity as a playwright in Vienna. (One of his plays was given at Esterház in 1774.) We do not know if Pauersbach himself managed the puppet operas for this season, but by 1776 he was an integral part of the Esterház theatrical life. At any rate, on 2 September the new marionette theatre—opposite the opera house behind the palace—opened with *Der Götterrath*, a prologue, followed by *Philemon und Baucis*, both German *Singspiele* with music by Haydn. Presumably the Prince's librarian, Philipp Georg Bader (who later wrote other marionette operas for Haydn, including *Dido* and *Die bestrafte Rachbegierde*) adapted the libretti. The puppet operas created a sensation: the Empress was enchanted by the lightning swift changes of scene (a speciality at Esterház of which everyone was proud) and the deft manipulation of enormous numbers of beautifully carved puppets. The costumes were especially, and we may be sure lovingly, made by the garderobière, Madame Handl, and other ladies of the Court. The sons of the Prince's grenadiers arranged for special effects such as gunpowder, storms, and complex crowd scenes. The 'extras' were not only paid: they and the cast also received free tea and coffee in the intervals. The *Pressburger Zeitung* was beside itself when describing the new theatre and the music of Kapellmeister Haydn, and soon the fame of this brilliant little marionette theatre spread all over Europe. Incidentally, no admission was charged, either at the theatre or at the marionettes and anyone, if properly dressed, was free to attend.[1]

Later in the year, Haydn produced still another puppet opera, entitled *Hexen-Schabbas*, of which not only is the music lost, but not even a copy of the printed libretto has survived. In the following years Haydn wrote the music for *Dido* (text by Bader, first performance March 1776; music lost, libretto in Vienna City Library), *Das abgebrannte Haus, oder Die Feuersbrunst* (first performance probably in 1776),[2] and *Die bestrafte Rachbegierde*[3] (text by Bader, first

[1] See *Beschreibung des hochfürstlichen Schlosses Esterhass im Königreiche Ungern* [sic] (Pressburg, 1784).
[2] Vocal score ed. Landon (London, 1963).
[3] Libretto in the University of California Library (Berkeley).

performance autumn 1779, music lost). Haydn also compiled music for several other marionette operas, probably including an occasional aria or ensemble of his own. It is interesting to note that whereas the Italian operas were given without sizeable employment of chorus, all the German marionette operas had choruses, sometimes dozens in one work (e.g. *Dido*). There was, no doubt, a simple explanation: whereas all sorts of local people could be found to form a good German-speaking chorus, not enough of them could speak Italian well enough and memorize their parts in this language to make an Italian chorus possible. Since singers and orchestra were behind the stage in the marionette theatre, it was not necessary to learn parts by heart, so that much rehearsal time was saved.

On 28 August 1775 the Archduke Ferdinand and his wife paid a state visit to Esterház. The marionette theatre gave Ordoñez's *Alceste*, while on 29 August Haydn presented a new opera, *L'incontro improvviso*.[1]

Beginning with the following year (1776), an unbroken season of regular opera and marionette operas ensued in the two castle theatres, in addition to the usual visits of strolling players. Up to this time, opera at Esterház had been principally a special occasion, for Esterházy's 'festivals'; with a few exceptions, most of these operas were composed by Haydn. From 1776 to 1790, when Prince Nicolaus died, there were regular seasons of operas by other composers. At the beginning, Haydn staged quite a few works of his friend and contemporary, Carl Ditters (later von Dittersdorf); gradually, however, Italian opera began to dominate the repertoire and, again, with only a few exceptions, it consisted mostly of *opera buffa*, a genre which Prince Nicolaus evidently preferred to *opera seria*.

By 1776 Haydn's fame was of sufficient proportions for the Court opera in Vienna to ask him for a work to open the new Italian opera company's season in January 1777. The composer was given *La vera costanza* as a subject. The jealousy of his colleagues in Vienna, however, was of such proportions that Haydn actually went to the Emperor Joseph II, who promised to see that the intrigues ceased. The Court opera, despite this royal intervention, made the production of the new opera so difficult that Haydn withdrew the score and went back to Esterház. 'I told my Prince the whole tale,' related Haydn to his biographer Dies, 'and the Prince did not criticize my action but performed the work in 1779.' The libretto of *La vera costanza* was written by Francesco Puttini and Pietro Travaglia, who was

---

[1] See frontispiece. Libretto after Dancourt by Karl Friberth, first tenor of the Esterházy troupe; full score (ed. Wirth), *Werke*, series 25, vi.

soon to become the principal designer for opera sets at Esterház.[1]

On 3 August 1777 Count Nicolaus, second son of the Prince' celebrated his marriage to Countess Maria Anna Franziska von Weissenwolf. For this occasion Haydn performed his third Goldoni subject, *Il mondo della luna*.[2]

The reputation of the marionette theatre at Esterház was bruited abroad. The *Gothaer Theater-Kalendar* of 1778 reports that the Empress had heard of a fantastic 'spectacle' at a reputed astronomical cost of 6,000 gulden. This report was probably induced by Haydn's *Dido* which required six separate choruses, countless changes of scenery, and ended with Carthage in flames. 'The Empress herself asked to see it, a theatre was constructed at Schönbrunn', continues the chronicle. Actually, *Dido* proved unmanageable for a guest performance. Instead, the troupe performed at Schönbrunn in July 1777 *Alceste* by Ordoñez, libretto by Pauersbach, and *Hexen-Schabbas* by Haydn.[3] The performances were conducted by Pauersbach, the director of the marionette troupe, since Haydn himself was busily preparing for *Mondo della luna* at Esterház.

In November 1779 the opera theatre burned down, and performances were held either in the marionette theatre or in the big dining-hall of the palace. On Prince Nicolaus's name-day, 6 December, Haydn's new opera, *L'isola disabitata*[4] (text by Metastasio) was performed in these reduced circumstances. It was the only *opera seria* Haydn ever wrote at Esterház after *Acide* of 1762, but despite the interesting new method of recitative the work was not successful and was performed, the next year, only once.[5]

The marionette theatre was rapidly changed to accommodate the opera troupe, while for the marionettes a small building in the garden served. Since Pauersbach had left Esterház for Russia in December 1778 everyone gradually lost interest in the marionette theatre; in 1779 Haydn wrote his last work in this genre, *Die bestrafte Rachbegierde*, with a delightful text by Bader (in which Haydn himself appears for a moment).[6] One more gigantic marionette spectacle, the most difficult ever staged at Esterház, was given in 1783, *The Siege of Gibraltar*, for which months

---

[1] A partly autograph full score is in Paris, Bibl. Nat. du Conservatoire, Ms. 1383. A copy of the original libretto is in the Gesellschaft der Musikfreunde, Vienna. Modern edition, German text only, entitled *List und Liebe* (vocal score, ed. G. Schwalbe and W. Zimmer) (Berlin, 1959).

[2] Vocal scores, ed. Mark Lothar (Berlin, 1932), and Landon, as *Die Welt auf dem Monde* (Kassel, 1958), text in Italian and German.

[3] See Landon, 'Haydn's Marionette Operas', p. 115.

[4] Vocal score (ed. Welleminsky), (Vienna and Leipzig, 1909).

[5] Harich, op. cit., p. 25. Haydn composed an entirely new finale for the second act in 1802 (autograph in a Swiss private library).

[6] Landon, 'Haydn's Marionette Operas', p. 189.

of rehearsal and barrels of gunpowder were necessary. But with Pauersbach's departure, the opera itself became even more important.

Prince Nicolaus lost no time in rebuilding the opera house, which was supposed to be finished by the autumn of 1780. It was not until 25 February 1781,[1] however, that Haydn's new opera, *La fedeltà premiata* (original title, *L'infedeltà fedele*, text by G. B. Lorenzi, originally set to music by Cimarosa) officially opened the new theatre, which seated no less than five hundred. The Prince, as many reports confirm, was not only a musician himself but also a real connoisseur. He seems to have thought *L'isola disabitata* stiff and dull which, apart from a glorious moment or two, it is. *La fedeltà premiata*, on the other hand, was at once a huge success. It was repeated twice in February, eight times in March, once in April, and five times in September. It remained in the repertoire year after year, and was thus the greatest operatic success of Haydn's career to date.[2]

The penultimate opera that Haydn was to compose for Prince Nicolaus was *Orlando Paladino*,[3] 'dramma eroi-comico in tre atti, musica del celebre Sign. Giuseppe Haydn', which was intended to grace the visit of a Russian Grand Ducal pair in 1782. It was performed on Prince Nicolaus's name-day and became almost as popular as *La fedeltà premiata*. The text was by the Esterházy 'poet in residence', Nunziato Porta. In the years following, *Orlando Paladino* achieved no less than thirty performances (six less than *Fedeltà*). Both operas were translated into German and widely performed. *Orlando* as 'Ritter Roland', in the translation of Giržik (or Giržick), was performed by Schikaneder's troupe in Vienna, also in Prague, Munich, Frankfurt, Dresden, Leipzig, and Hamburg among many other cities. Obviously, when Haydn's operas escaped from the boundaries of Esterház they were most successful.[4]

In 1785 Giržik translated into German, among other Haydn operas, *La vera costanza* and performed it as *Die wahre Beständigkeit* at the Erdödy theatre at Pressburg. There, too, the opera was so successful that Prince Esterházy decided to put it back into repertory at Esterház. It was revived in April and repeated sixteen times that year. The Prince liked marionette operas in German, but he seems otherwise to have preferred opera in Italian, and thus *La vera costanza* was revived in that language. Haydn made some changes in the score for this new series of performances.

Haydn's last opera for Esterház was the 'dramma eroico' *Armida*,

[1] Harich, op. cit., pp. 53 f.
[2] Full score (ed. Günter Thomas), *Werke*, ser. 25, x.
[3] Vocal score (ed. E. Latzko), (Leipzig, 1935).
[4] Ludwig Wendschuh, *Über Joseph Haydns Opern* (Rostock, 1896), pp. 101 ff.

based on Tasso's *Gerusalemme liberata*, which was the most complicated to stage. Six singers and the full orchestra were aided by six 'Bandisten' ('supers'), four girls, twenty-four grenadiers in Roman and Turkish costumes, and a further eight grenadiers for changing the scenery. The opera was first performed on 26 February 1784, after four full rehearsals and a dress rehearsal. *Armida* was the most successful of Haydn's operas and in the following years (1785–8) it achieved no less than fifty-four performances. Haydn wrote, after the second performance, to his Viennese publishers Artaria, that it was received with 'general approbation. I am told it is my best work up to the present.'[1] This is the end of the chronicle at Esterház, as far as Haydn's operas are concerned. In 1790 Prince Nicolaus died, and the theatre closed down.

The history of Haydn's last opera, *L'anima del filosofo* (*Orfeo ed Euridice*) is a curious one indeed. When Johann Peter Salomon came to Vienna late in 1790 to fetch Haydn to London, he carried with him an offer from Sir John Gallini, with whom Haydn had been in correspondence for some years. Haydn was to write a new opera for Gallini's company which would include the famous tenor, Giacomo Davidde (or Davide), who was also engaged to sing at the Haydn–Salomon concerts. Naturally, Haydn must have been eager to accept, for Salomon would have told him that the London opera had at its disposal a large choir and full orchestra, in addition to the soloists.

Haydn arrived in London on 2 January 1791, and six days later wrote to a friend in Vienna:[2] 'I am working on symphonies, because the libretto of the opera is not yet decided on . . .' The same day, however, Gallini and Haydn seem to have made up their minds, for the composer writes in another letter, to Prince Anton Esterházy, who succeeded Nicolaus:

> The new opera libretto which I am to compose is entitled *Orfeo*, in five acts, but I shall not receive it for a few days. It is supposed to be entirely different from that of Gluck. The *prima donna* is called Madam Lops [Rosa Lops] from Munich—she is a pupil of the famous [Regina] Mingotti. *Seconda donna* is Madam [Theresa Poggi] Capelletti [*sc.* Cappelletti—she also sang at the Haydn–Salomon concerts]. *Primo homo* is the celebrated Davidde. The opera contains only three persons, *viz.* Madam Lops, Davidde, and a castrato, who is not supposed to be very special. Incidentally, the opera is supposed to contain many choruses, ballets and a lot of big changes of scenery . . .

[1] Full score (ed. Willhelm Pfannkuch), *Werke*, series 25, xii. The greater part of the autograph is in the Royal College of Music, London, other parts in Harvard University Library. The original libretto is with the Gesellschaft der Musikfreunde, Vienna, who also possess a fine copy of the full score, ref. Q1485 (IV 33853), in the handwriting of Johann Elssler, Haydn's factotum and copyist. Another copy of the score, with corrections by Haydn, is in the Sándor Wolf Museum, Eisenstadt. In 1785 the Erdödy Theatre at Pressburg commissioned Giržik to translate *Armida* into German (first performance 16 October 1785).
[2] Landon, *The Collected Correspondence*, pp. 113 ff.

By the middle of March we find him writing to his mistress, Luigia Polzelli:

> Up to now our opera has not yet opened, since the King won't give the licence. Signor Gallini intends to open it as if it were a subscription concert, for if he doesn't, he stands to lose twenty thousand pounds Sterling. I shan't lose anything, because the bankers Fries in Vienna have already received my money. My opera, entitled *L'anima del filosofo*, will be staged at the end of May; I have already completed the Second Act, but there are five acts, of which the last are very short ... [At the dress rehearsal of *Pirro* by Paisiello] the ballet was simply magnificent ...

As indicated, there were two rival companies, one backed by the Prince of Wales (Haydn–Gallini) and one by the King, and Gallini's company was not allowed to open. Haydn completed the opera which turned out to have four principal characters and to comprise four, not five, acts. There is a report that Haydn actually began the first rehearsal and had played through forty bars when the King's officials appeared and forbade the composer to rehearse further.[1]

When Haydn returned to Vienna there was some talk of *L'anima del filosofo* being given in the Schönbrunn Schlosstheater, but nothing seems to have come of this plan. There is evidence that Haydn played some of the arias in the Salomon concerts; and Breitkopf and Härtel published, in full score, eleven numbers, which were often sung in concerts.

It was generally believed that the work had been left unfinished. Hugo Botstiber was the first to point out that *Orfeo* was 'nearly complete' and Karl Geiringer, who studied the autograph score in the Berlin State Library, rightly maintained that Haydn's last opera was, to all intents and purposes, complete.[2] During the two decades 1950–70 our knowledge of the original sources has been considerably enlarged. It is now clear that the Berlin autograph is not complete, since it lacks certain numbers published in the contemporary Breitkopf score. Also, the autograph does not present the numbers in the order of appearance in the opera. Happily these defects are in large part compensated for in a copy made by Haydn's English copyists and now in Budapest.[3] Even more recently than the Budapest manuscript a third source turned up in the Paris Conservatoire. It is the most complete copy of the opera and contains one recitative (a *secco* in Act II between Euridice's death aria and Orfeo's entrance) which is omitted in the Budapest manuscript.[4]

[1] Albert C. Dies, *Biographische Nachrichten von Joseph Haydn*, 2nd edn. (Berlin, 1962), p. 97.
[2] Carl F. Pohl–Hugo Botstiber, *Haydn* iii (Leipzig, 1927, p. 341); Geiringer, *Haydn* op. cit., p. 299.
[3] Nat. Széch. Lib. Ms. mus. I. 7.
[4] A vocal score of *Orfeo* was edited by Wirth (Vienna, 1951).

In 1796, when Haydn had returned from London to be once again Kapellmeister for Prince Nicolaus II at Esterházy, he wrote incidental music to a German play, *Alfred*, translated from Alexander Bicknell's English tragedy, *The Patriot King*. It is not certain whether Haydn wrote the music for a performance at the Schikaneder theatre in Vienna or for a group of strolling players at Eisenstadt; but one aria, for soprano with wind band accompaniment, interrupted most dramatically by speaking voice, is among his finest operatic creations *en miniature*.

THE OPERAS ASSESSED

In discussing Haydn's position in the history of opera the first question is: were Haydn's operas part of the operatic mainstream? The answer is, at first glance, negative. The relative, and to Haydn it must have seemed at times painfully complete, isolation in which most of his operas were produced is one of the most curious phenomena and undeniable. It is true that a few works in translation made the rounds of German opera houses but by the time *Ritter Roland* (*Orlando Paladino*) was in circulation in the early nineteenth century it was, stylistically, ancient music. But the isolation of Esterház operated in one direction only: Haydn's operas did not get out, but those of everyone else came in, and Haydn was able to follow the developments and progress of Italian opera directly under his own sharp conductor's eye.

Among the influences bearing on Haydn one of the most interesting and vexing is that of Gluck. In this context it must be remembered that Gluck's famous reform concerned *opera seria*, but that the reform of *opera buffa* was carried out by such composers as Piccinni, Paisiello, Gazzaniga, Cimarosa, and of course Mozart. It is true that Haydn's *opere serie*, *Acide*, *L'isola disabitata*, and *Orfeo* make direct and obvious use of Gluck's ideas (as do Mozart's *Idomeneo* and *Tito*). But not even composers of the stature of Haydn and Mozart could succeed in establishing such works as *Orfeo* or *Idomeneo* for any length of time in the repertoire, in spite of the magnificent music they contained. It was clearly in *opera buffa* that the crucial developments of the period took place, and here Haydn's contribution to the genre is noteworthy, though it did escape general notice at the time.

Thus the greatest influence of Gluck appears in one of Haydn's least important operas, *Philemon und Baucis*, composed in 1773 for marionettes. And here, as in all of his operas, we have a typically Haydnesque situation, derived from his consistent view that the music should come first. A great many Gluckian musical ideas are used (indeed, one number subsequently turned out actually to be by Gluck)[1] while Gluck's

[1] See Landon, *Supplement*, p. 37.

principle that the words must come first is rejected. This was not a philosophy to which Haydn subscribed, nor one in which his genius could thrive; and it is no surprise that Gluck's influence was of no help in breathing life into the world of Jupiter, Mercury, and a cowering Phrygian population.

After his initial *opera seria*, *Acide e Galatea*, of 1762, Haydn turned his back on this moribund form and, with the little intermezzo, *La canterina* (1766), we are plunged into the gay, farcical world of Italian comic opera and, if we may use a misused word, the ordinary bourgeois. Naturally, these 'ordinary' people are at first figures, the standard and well-loved symbols of the *commedia dell'arte*—the spoiled singer, the jealous lover, the thwarted ward. Yet, even in *La canterina* Haydn raises the level of the whole from the standardized humour of *La serva padrona* to something quite different. Haydn was essentially a witty composer: he told his biographers, 'I prefer to see the humorous side of life'; but he was also possessed of a trenchant realism, and in *La canterina* everything is treated sardonically. The Neapolitan 'vengeance aria' becomes, in Gasparina's C minor aria in Act II, so violent a piece of *Sturm und Drang* that in the ritornello we are reminded of the stormy and impassioned symphonies of the coming years, such as nos. 26 in D minor and 49 in F minor. (The scoring includes two cors anglais, instruments to which Haydn was partial, and which he used in almost all his large-scale religious and operatic works of the period.)

Ex. 94

Is the expression of this aria a parody, or is it truth cloaked within the protective armour of a standard 'vengeance aria', i.e. a play within a play? Throughout *La canterina* it will be seen that Haydn's entire attention is devoted to the music; the characters, in other words, remain static; they do what we expect them to do (the *commedia dell'arte* was in many ways as self-circumscribed as the *opera seria*), and the whole interest is centred on the musical development. The finest piece in the opera is the first quartet (there are only four singers in *La canterina*), and even at this early stage we are struck by Haydn's fascination with ensembles; unlike the thinly orchestrated *intermezzi* of its Italian prototype, *La canterina* is brilliantly scored with that lean, biting, instrumental efficiency for which Haydn's symphonies of 1764–7 are justly famous; the entrance of the two oboes can be an orchestral wash of colour.

Haydn remains within the bourgeois world in the choice of his next subject, the *dramma giocoso* by Goldoni, *Lo speziale* (1768). In his cast, it will be noted that, like *La canterina*, which has two soprano and two tenor parts, Haydn's vocal balance is uneven in that there are only soprano (Grilletta, Volpino) and tenor (Sempronio, the old apothecary, and the Leporello-like Mengone) roles, of which Volpino is a *Hosenrolle* (a boy's part played by a woman). *La canterina* was in two short acts, *Lo speziale* is in three; most of the third act is missing (*recitativo secco*, an aria of Sempronio, a duet between Grilletta and Mengone).

Roughly, the work is constructed as follows: Act I aria (Mengone), leading into *recitativo accompagnato*, and then into *secco*; recitative; aria (Sempronio); recitative; aria (Mengone); recitative; aria

(Grilletta); recitative; aria (Volpino); recitative; finale. Act II is similar, a series of arias leading to the finale. Act III has the (lost) duet. It is a typical feature of Haydn's libretti, and we shall see in *Il mondo della luna* that the duet between the lovers is one of the dramatic highpoints of the opera. Musically, the most original piece in *Lo speziale* is a 'Turkish' aria (Volpino) in Act III, with two oboes, a bassoon, two horns, two violin parts, a third 'violino pizzicato', viola, cello, and 'violone' (bass). The characteristic repeated thirds, such as occur in the overture to *Entführung*, and the bizarre harmonies (Ex. 95) make this brief excursion into the fascinating world of the East a musical delight.

Ex. 95

On the whole, however, *Lo speziale* has been overrated. Despite the tightness of the action and the real characterization of the four 'personaggi', despite the expert construction of the finales (which move forward dramatically and literally, i.e. by increased tempi and quicker metres), and even despite the wit of Goldoni's text, *Lo speziale* cannot compare with Haydn's mature operas. Haydn hardly goes beyond the musical, dramatic, and overall structural level of his Italian prototypes except, as always, in the orchestration and in the Turkish aria mentioned above.

The only extant musical source of *Le pescatrici* is incomplete, but this *dramma giocoso* has now been reconstructed. Haydn's second setting of a text by Goldoni is infinitely superior to his first. Unlike the two previous operas, which had only *buffo* characters, the new book shows traces of the reform of *opera buffa* which was occurring in Italy, whereby figures were incorporated from the *opera seria*. The typical *opera buffa* or *intermezzo* was content with four principals; the new 'reformed' *opera buffa* required more: *Le pescatrici* has no less than seven. Goldoni has cleverly mixed the fairy-tale world of the *opera seria* with the down-to-earth atmosphere of *opera buffa*; and by eliminating middle-class figures the contrast between the aristocratic figure of Prince Lindoro and the peasant world of the fishing village is sharply drawn.

Within the bounds of a simple but attractive plot, Haydn's musical imagination was obviously stimulated, and the whole score has a light, airy originality. He breaks away from the soprano-tenor dominated texture, and in *Le pescatrici* we have two sopranos, one alto, two tenors, and two bass parts, which at once lend to the big ensembles a textural solidity and massiveness that four vocal parts could hardly hope to achieve. The orchestra is much larger and more varied, too: flutes, oboes, two cors anglais, bassoons, horns, and strings.

The great glory of *Le pescatrici*, however, is its ensembles. In the typical *opera buffa*, and in Haydn's previous works, the ensemble was generally reserved for the finales. Here, the first and third acts each begin with a chorus; and in the first act we also have another 'coro' of six soloists, a septet, and a finale, in addition to the usual arias. The third act, likewise, is dominated by ensembles: of the five numbers, only one is an aria. These trends are magnificently summed up in Haydn's next Italian opera: *L'infedeltà delusa* (1773). In many respects the libretto sums up the reform taking place in Italian *opera buffa* at the time. As if in violent revolt against the *opera seria*, only peasants take part in the action, while the only aristocrat who appears in the work is, in fact, the clever Vespina (the leading role), disguised as the servant of the Marquis of Rippafratta, a caricature of an aristocrat.

In this opera the book calls for only five soloists (two sopranos, two tenors, one bass). For the first time the orchestra includes Haydn's favourite C alto horns, piercing and brilliant instruments which figure largely in C major symphonies of the period, and kettledrums, which actually have a crashing solo in the last finale. Everything in *Infedeltà* is tighter, swifter, more sharply etched; formally it is the most beautifully balanced of all Haydn's operas. Part of this is due to the libretto's structure, for in two acts Haydn finds it easier to achieve this kind of rounded formal symmetry than in three. (A weakness of some Italian libretti is that the third act often seems superfluous.) Tonally, the work begins with the overture in C; the first act starts in F and lands in G, while at the end of Act II we are securely brought back to the key of C. Haydn has taken great pains to achieve a unified whole by even more subtle means, however. In the finale of Act II, when Vespina reveals herself as having been 'la vecchia col "dice il proverbio"' and 'il servo tedesco', the music quotes her F major aria from Act I and actually swerves into the key of F to do so:

Ex. 96

Aria Presto ... *Finale*

Trin - che vai - ne al - le - gra - men - te   Il ser - vo te -
- de - sco, 'der tai - fle star rausch'

(Drink wine merrily. *Finale:* The German servant, 'the devil of a tipsy fit')

Musically, *Infedeltà* already achieved that marriage between Italian opera and Viennese symphonic thought which was so greatly to affect the future history of opera. Haydn entirely emancipated himself from the clichés of Italian opera; he made use of their formal patterns, but the music with which he filled to overflowing these time-honoured and often sterile moulds was wholly his own. The beginning of the opera is typical: it is a large, 400-bar ensemble in two basic sections (an alla breve moderato moving to an allegro in 3/8), of which the first is a vast rondo-like structure for four soli. Here the mood is set—'Bella sera ed aure grate, che del giorno cancellate'—and the curtain rises on what might be called the greatest single operatic 'piece' Haydn ever wrote, a glorious unfolding of his lyric warmth. And in the middle of this 'set piece' the characters begin to arrange themselves in their dramatic roles, and the real opera begins. How far Haydn has progressed from the Italian forms can be seen in two typical examples: in Act I, Nencio sings a warm, E flat serenade of the classical Neapolitan cast, with lilting 6/8 rhythms. At the end, there is a half-cadence and a double pause, followed by a searing dissonance on the word 'guai' (woe) which must have come like a physical shock in 1773, as, indeed, it still does:

Ex. 97

[musical example with parts: Ob., Hns., V. I, V. II, Va., NENCIO singing "per-chè guai per chi ci cas-ca, per chi ci cas-ca"]

Why this woe? Why fall into this state?

Filippo's aria in Act II is a major achievement. In its vivid description of the text (Ex. 98i), and with the typically Haydnesque melody to mirror 'love and charity' (Ex. 98ii) it is of a startling poignance. This lyrical warmth returns often in Haydn's operatic writing and has been termed his *Liebesphrase*; this sort of tensely emotional lyricism was by no means the exclusive property of Paisiello and Mozart, it is equally typical of great Haydn.

Ex. 98 (i)

[musical example with parts: Ob. II, Ob. I, V. I, V. II, Va., FILIPPO singing "pien di vi-zie, e di pec-ca-ti, pien di", Va. col Basso]

[musical notation]

vi zie, e di pec - ca - ti,

(Full of vices and full of sins)

(ii) V. I, II
dolce
FILIPPO
sen - zaa - mor — nè ca - ri - tà, — sen - za a-
Va. Vc. B.

- mor nè — ca - ri - tà,

(Without love or charity)

L'infedeltà delusa rounds off what may be described as the first period of Haydn's operatic style. It is also the end of a great period in Haydn's symphonies and string quartets (Op. 20, 1772), as well as in his church music (*Missa Sanctae Caeciliae*, written, as it would now seem, side by side with *Infedeltà*). If one wanted to characterize this period by any one quality, it would be the terseness, the fierce concentration of the music. Beginning with *L'incontro improvviso* (1775), Haydn takes another course, that of profusion, in his operatic writing; and this tendency continues and reaches its high point in *Armida* (1784), the last stage work written for Esterház. It can be cogently argued that this profusion is the most important single feature of Haydn's operatic writing in the next decade.

When talking about his operas to his biographer Dies, Haydn once said that they were all rather long. 'Nothing was too lengthy for my Prince,' he added. This is, indeed, a typical feature of the operas written during the next ten years; in the quiet evenings at Esterház there was time to sing long, beautifully worked-out *adagio* arias, delicately orchestrated with intricate string writing and soft woodwind colour. There was time for many arias, which succeeded one another in profusion. Yet this prodigious length could bring the action to a standstill dramatically. Still, one of the loveliest pieces of music Haydn ever wrote is the *terzetto* for three women, 'Mi sembra un sogno che diletta', in *L'incontro improvviso* (1775), where the other-worldly sound of the two cors anglais in a slow movement in E flat major transports us into the world of dreams and timeless fantasy—so timeless that the action simply stops for the near quarter of an hour that this exquisite music requires.

Naturally, not all the music is of this astonishing length and luxuriance: in *La vera costanza* there is an accompanied recitative and aria which even surpasses *L'infedeltà delusa* in dramatic pithiness: the Count's scene in Act I before the finale. Here Haydn tries out an entirely new formal scheme: a furious recitative (with biting C alto horns and kettledrums) leads to a fanfare-dominated aria; there is a stop, and a slow movement sets in. It appears to be a typical tripartite Italian form. But Haydn has other plans. He breaks off the slow movement and lurches into the most grim and unexpected continuation. To carry this break-away from tradition to its fullest extent he plunges into C minor and remains there for the rest of the aria. The finale to Act I is also one of Haydn's most dramatic. Notice how agitation (Ex. 99i) is calmed (Ex. 99ii). This succession of tension and relaxation, which is so characteristic of the Viennese classical school is demonstrated here in a nutshell.

Ex. 99 (i)
[Allegro]

Most of Haydn's protagonists have also become less stereotyped. He had progressed, in *La vera costanza*, a long way from *La canterina*. In fact, *La vera costanza* is scarcely a *buffa* opera in the conventional sense. We deal no longer with the primitive emotions of a spoiled Italian soprano, for Rosina, in *La vera costanza*, is just as much a real person as the Countess in *Le nozze di Figaro*. This concern with the dramatic reality of the persons of the libretto is apparent even in the gay Goldoni farce, *Il mondo della luna*, written in the same year as *La vera costanza*. In *Il mondo* Haydn is, for the last time, content to use typical figures of the *commedia dell'arte*. But he is careful that the music shall, if possible, remedy any superficialities or defect of the libretto, if one may speak of defects in connection with Goldoni. The third act of *Il mondo* is a good example of how Haydn saves a precarious dramatic situation.

It is a fact that the third acts of many Italian opera libretti are anticlimactic, even anti-dramatic. *La vera costanza*, *Il mondo della luna*, and *La fedeltà premiata* all suffer from this basic weakness. The third act of *Il mondo* was not originally part of the Goldoni libretto: it would seem to have been added for Astaritta's setting of the text in Venice (1775), but whether Goldoni wrote it or not cannot at present be determined: probably not. Since Haydn's task was to compose the Astaritta version he set to work to remedy the weakness of the third act by purely musical means. It was not an easy task. The finale of Act II ended with a large-scale ensemble in which the foolish Buonafede, who thinks he has been transported to the moon, is informed that he has been cruelly, even sadistically, duped. (It would be revealing to have a study of cruelty in *commedia dell'arte*.) Buonafede has lost his daughters as well as his mistress, and the action may be considered completed. At this point the third act begins, and to make us forget that it is superfluous, Haydn writes, for the young lovers, a most exquisite love duet, a shadowy Largo of infinite wistfulness in which the two lovers lose themselves in the soft Mediterranean night and in which, for the first time in the gay Venetian farce, the action becomes real, serious, and almost frighteningly intense:

Ex. 100

(O God! Lift this weight from my shoulders or I shall die on the spot.)

It is clearly the high point, musically speaking, of the entire opera.

Haydn finally turned away from *opera buffa*. He made one more excursion into the lost world of *opera seria*, but the failure of *L'isola disabitata* was decisive. In *Orlando Paladino*, it is true, Haydn created a farce, but not the farce of the *commedia dell'arte*; rather of the more sardonic, Falstaffian kind. The Knight Roland is treated as a chivalric joke, and all manner of subjects are hurled into the whirlpool of Haydn's sarcasm: *opera seria*, the Elysian fields (an ironical reference to Gluck's *Orfeo*), and the new type of 'heroic' opera satirized in the sabre-rattling Rodomonte who, mounted on a prancing horse, growls empty threats—it is the end of *opera buffa*.

Before he finally renounced comic opera Haydn indulged in one full-length work devoted to the old Hanswurst, that downtrodden, misunderstood, lovable figure of Viennese 'Volkstheater' descended from the Venetian *commedia dell'arte* and taken to Vienna at an early age. *Das abgebrannte Haus*, also known as *Die Feuersbrunst*, seems to have been written for puppets about 1776. It is in certain respects a direct precursor of *Zauberflöte*—the enchanted world of dragons makes a brief appearance in Haydn's work—but unlike Mozart, Haydn remains, except for the dragon's entrance (and this is clearly a parody of serious operatic dragons), within the world of the Austria he knew. The aristocracy is mercilessly lampooned, and the underdog Hanswurst eventually wins his Colombine away from the clutches of the upper-class scoundrel. *Das abgebrannte Haus* is a piece for the coachmen and servant-girls at Esterház, and it may actually have been produced by Haydn in his own puppet theatre, which we know to have existed as early as 1774. Whatever the origins of the work (and they are probably lost to us for ever), *Das abgebrannte Haus* remains one of the most important examples of the German *Singspiel* before *Die Zauberflöte*.

In Haydn's last opera for Prince Nicolaus, *Armida*, the text is partly based on one of Coltellini's 'reform' libretti. In the story of Rinaldo the Crusader and Armida the sorceress, the libretto eschews the usual happy ending. The work ends as Rinaldo sorrowfully leaves Armida to join his Christian brothers, while the sorceress faints into the arms of her lady-in-waiting.

Of all Haydn's operas for Esterház, this one has the fewest ensembles. Except for the final duet there are none in Act I; in the second act there is only the final *terzetto*, which Helmut Wirth rightly calls 'the peak of the opera'[1] while the third act contains 'a short piece in which everyone appears'. So, in a sense, Haydn has renounced the principles which created the earlier masterpieces, *Le pescatrici* and *L'infedeltà delusa*. The sacrifice has its good and bad points: we miss the rich and varied sound of the large-scale ensembles, as well as the variety that they lend in breaking the chain of arias and recitatives. On the other hand, Haydn was able to achieve an increased concentration on the individual characters. As the plot unfolds, the character of Rinaldo develops, both in musical and in dramatic terms; the violent struggle within himself between fulfilling his Christian duty and yielding to Armida's charms is admirably set off by the simple, military 'right and wrong'-ness of Ubaldo, who sees through Armida long before Rinaldo does. Incidentally, it has been said, with considerable justification, that the central figure in the opera is not Armida but Armida's *selva incantata*, the enchanted forest which colours the action much as the city of Nuremberg does in *Die Meistersinger*. In *Armida* this all-pervading atmosphere is announced quite clearly in the overture which, like that to *L'isola disabitata*, gives us the whole sweep of the drama *in nuce*. In the *sinfonia*

[1] 'The Operas of Joseph Haydn before "Orfeo"', in *Orfeo ed Euridice: analytical notes* (Boston, 1951), p. 47.

to *Armida*, Haydn even goes so far as to imitate a *recitativo accompagnato*, an effective lead-back to the last part of the overture.

There seems little doubt that Haydn's decision to stop writing operas after *Armida* was in part caused by the emergence of Mozart as the supreme operatic composer of the time: a supremacy which Haydn not only acknowledged but also, on every occasion, selflessly confirmed. It is symbolic, one feels, that Mozart's *Figaro* was the last opera Haydn conducted at Esterház, and this fact does, perhaps, more to illuminate Haydn's attitude towards Mozart than many a document, though there is certainly something touching in Haydn's letter to Marianne von Genzinger, of 1789, in which he tells his friend how he woke up on a bitter, lonely night at Esterház, dreaming of *Figaro*. And what a pleasant picture it is to think of Mozart walking to the Burgtheater with Haydn and Puchberg to hear the rehearsals of *Così fan tutte*: the only people, as Mozart said, that he had invited to hear his newest work.

Just as it can be maintained that Mozart's *Idomeneo* is a magnificent failure as a music drama, it may be said of Haydn's last opera, *L'anima del filosofo* (*Orfeo ed Euridice*), that it was doomed, dramatically, before Haydn set a note of it on paper. By 1791 there was indeed no hope for *opera seria*, not even for Mozart's, whose *Clemenza di Tito* was written in the same year. Yet, musically, Haydn's *Orfeo* contains some of his grandest thoughts, for within the rigid framework of the form the composer managed to write a beautiful farewell to an ancient and honourable form of art. Two numbers stand out particularly: the beautiful death-aria of Euridice in the second act (preceded by a poignant slow recitative) and the powerful conclusion of the opera, a shattering D minor chorus which dwindles away to nothing except a lonely timpani roll. In the frantic inspiration with which he committed this piece to paper, the notes themselves seem to surge forward (much as they do in the second act of *Tristan*); and not satisfied with the large orchestral apparatus, which even includes trombones, Haydn seems to have thought of an organ continuo (there suddenly appear figures under the bass part) to increase the doom-ridden fury of the drowning *baccanti*.

As in *Armida*, Haydn and his librettist, Carlo Francesco Badini, did away with the *lieto fine*, the happy ending which disfigures Gluck's opera on the subject. Returning to the original legend, Orfeo is poisoned by the *baccanti* who shriek with delight as they prepare to tear into pieces the body of the Thracian prince, until the river Lethe rises up in anger and drowns the frenzied women. At the end, the storm gradually sinks away, leaving the stage empty and dark while the remains of Orfeo are carried away by the waters, to find rest on the isle of Lesbos.

Ex. 101

sen - to man - car la vi - ta

Il ciel s'o-scu-ra   fi - ni - rà con la mor-te·   o - gni scia-gú-ra

CORO

Mor(-to è il Tracio cantore.)

(I feel life slipping from me. The heavens darken, and death will bring an end to every calamity. CHORUS: Dead is the Thracian singer.)

Haydn uses the chorus in this opera in the manner of a Greek tragedy: to comment on the action and, occasionally, to take part in it as *amorini* or *baccanti*. The chorus plays a decisive role in *Orfeo*, and many of the finest pieces are choral. A striking effect is obtained at the beginning of the opera when Euridice sings, in company with the chorus, in a furious C minor Vivace. She interrupts, crying, 'Deh, per pietà! Lasciatemi!', but the chorus cuts her off, warning her, 'Ferma il piede, o Principessa!' It is noteworthy that at Esterház no operatic chorus was available to Haydn.

Throughout the work one trait is conspicuous, which does not appear in Haydn's earlier operas: the composer's uncanny ability to create a doom-ridden atmosphere. The music tells us again and again how this drama will end; in the beautiful E major aria of Creonte in Act I ('Il pensier sta negli oggetti'), there is a sudden and sinister pianissimo hush and the double basses enter to cloud the peaceful arabesques of flute and strings. In Orfeo's first *scena* in Act I (with solo harp by the way), there is the same interruption before the end of the aria proper. And even in the happy love duet between Orfeo and Euridice at the end of Act I, Haydn stops to introduce this chilling presentiment of the outcome. Technically, this feeling of doom is often achieved by the same means: the music stops, and the double basses then enter on the dominant with soft repeated quavers (or whatever the basic quick pulse may be) while the upper parts slide across the texture with diminished seventh chords which do, indeed, have a peculiarly ominous effect.

In summing up, it is obvious that *L'anima del filosofo* is one of Haydn's most impressive works and likewise one of the great monuments of *opera seria*. Despite its inability to succeed as a stage piece, it rounds off, in a curious way, Haydn's activities as an operatic composer. Any true chronicle of Haydn's achievements in London would be impossible without consideration of *L'anima del filosofo*.

It remains briefly to consider the many arias which Haydn inserted in the operas of other composers at Esterház. The music is now available in a critical edition, and the background has been admirably treated by Bartha and Somfai.[1] Most of these delightful 'insertion arias' are for comic operas, and many were written for roles sung by Haydn's beloved Italian mistress, Luigia Polzelli. One characteristic stands out: most of the arias are for Despina-like characters, light and pert figures whom Haydn obviously felt he could describe in musical terms more deftly than did the original composers. These arias start off, by and large, with an Andante or Adagio and then shift into a rapid, 6/8 *parlando* kind of Presto of great formal conciseness and bubbling humour. There

---
[1] op. cit.

are striking exceptions, such as the big tenor *scena* for Traetta's *Ifigenia* and the *Aria di Beatrice*, 'Infelice sventurata' of 1789, for dramatic soprano.

Haydn seems to have composed dramatic scenes for soprano solo, to be sung in the concert hall, on two different occasions. The texts were generally from *opere serie*. The first is a cantata, 'Misera noi, misera patria',[1] and the second the greatest single operatic scene in all Haydn, the *Scena di Berenice* (from Metastasio's *Antigono*), written in London in 1795 for the famous dramatic soprano, Brigitta Banti.[2] *Berenice* must rank with Beethoven's 'Ah, perfido' (written a year later) as among the finest dramatic pieces for soprano of the period. Apart from a piano score published in Vienna in Haydn's lifetime, the work remained completely unknown during the nineteenth and early twentieth centuries. What impresses one particularly in this work is the bold harmonic sweep and the contrast between the beauty of the central, slow aria and the tempestuousness of the quick conclusion in the minor mode. If we end this survey of Haydn's activities as an opera composer with this single *scena*, it is because it shows Haydn the dramatist at his most striking and persuasive.

[1] Full and vocal scores, ed. Landon (Vienna, 1959); miniature score (Vienna, 1966).
[2] Ed. Orel (Leipzig and Vienna, 1937), and Landon (Vienna, 1965); miniature score (Vienna, 1966).

II

OPERA IN FRANCE

By Martin Cooper

Despite the enthusiasm aroused by Rameau's masterpieces of the 1730s, French interest in lyrical tragedy continued to wane as the century approached its middle point. It was not merely that musical connoisseurs, wits, and journalists became tired of comparing Rameau's merits with Lully's. The whole world of the opera with its mythological heroes and personified virtues and vices, its formal nobility and tenderness and its rhetorical declamation, was beginning to seem hopelessly remote from reality, a relic of the *grand siècle* surviving into an age whose interests and passions were quite different from those of Louis XIV and his courtiers. The glory of Rameau's operas lay in their music, and only a very small proportion of French society was interested enough in music as a self-sufficient art to accept an opera on its musical merits alone. The large majority had always looked to the opera house for entertainment, for dramatic excitement and spectacular magnificence, and Rameau provided them with little that was novel in any of these departments. The intellectual world which was eager for the iconoclastic wit of Voltaire, the new humanism of Rousseau, and the scientific materialism of the Encyclopedists was only very moderately interested in lyrical tragedy. The Court was different. There the taste for the old forms of spectacle and for the formal graces and sentiments of the mythological opera persisted in a backwater comparatively untroubled by the new currents of intellectual speculation and emotional unrest; and it is significant that a majority of Rameau's works after *Platée* (1745) were intended for Versailles or Fontainebleau rather than for Paris.

Four years before *Platée* was produced at Versailles—a single performance not repeated in Paris until four years later—a very different work, and one much more in accordance with the taste of the day, reached no less than two hundred performances. This was *La Chercheuse d'esprit* (1741), an *opéra comique* by Charles Simon Favart, a witty and rather indecent treatment of the Daphnis and Chloe theme. Favart was the son of a pastry-cook who used to set his kitchen recipes to the current *timbres, fredons, vaudevilles* and popular operatic arias of the day, and it was from this familiar material that young Favart drew the music of *La Chercheuse d'esprit*. Julien Tiersot mentions the following ingredients: an air from Lully's *Amadis*, a musette of Rameau's, the *chansons* 'Quand la bergère vient des champs' and 'Rossignolet du vert bocage' and onomatopoeic refrains such as 'O riguingué, o lon lan la' or 'Tarare ponpon'[1] in which we can easily recognize the ancestors of the Victorian 'tarara-boom-de-ay' or the more recent 'vo-di-o-do'. Such was the traditional musical specification of the *opéra comique*, which had as yet attracted hack musical 'compilers' rather than composers; and the charm of Favart's piece lay not in any musical originality but in its lively wit, in the comic aptness of its musical adaptations and its shrewd allusions to everyday human experience, thinly veiled beneath transparent pastoral allegory. It was very much the same charm that, just over a hundred years later, was to captivate Paris in the works of Offenbach, with this difference—that Offenbach composed his own music instead of relying on the flotsam and jetsam already familiar to his listeners.

THE 'QUERELLE DES BOUFFONS'

When, only five years after *La Chercheuse d'esprit* appeared, an Italian company came to Paris and gave Pergolesi's *La serva padrona*, it made little impression. This is strange, for here were the same kind of wit, the same verve and popular appeal, wedded to delightful and original music. Possibly the barrier of language and the unfamiliarity of the music proved too formidable obstacles, possibly *La Chercheuse d'esprit* was still too popular. Whatever the explanation, it was not until the same work was given six years later by the Italian comedians, or *bouffons*, (August 1752) that Paris suddenly discovered that this was the music for which it had been waiting, the embodiment of all that was natural, charming, and lively, and the antithesis of the dusty, creaking splendours of the old *tragédie lyrique*.

The 'Querelle des Bouffons' has been called a journalists' campaign, and there is no doubt that this sudden craze for Italian *opera buffa* was cleverly exploited by publicists anxious to make their names, and in some cases to pay off old scores. Melchior Grimm, a young German secretary who had arrived in Paris in 1749, had already in his *Lettre sur Omphale*[2] entered the musical lists as a champion of Rameau and stirred Rousseau, a disappointed amateur composer himself, to a reply. Now both these very opinionated foreigners launched broadside attacks on French music in general, Grimm in his amusing *Le Petit Prophète de Boehmisch-Broda*[3] and Rousseau in his *Lettre sur la musique*

[1] *Histoire de la chanson populaire en France*, (Paris, 1889), pp. 516–17.
[2] *Lettre de M. Grimm sur Omphale de Destouches* (Paris, 1752).
[3] Lengthy excerpts translated in Oliver Strunk, *Source Readings in Music History* (London, 1952), p. 619. The 'prophet' promised the Parisians 'Je leur . . . apprendrai à être simple sans être plat et ils n'appelleront plus le beau simple ce qui est monotone. Et je créerai le récitatif, et je leur apprendrai à faire de la musique qui ait un caractère et un mouvement exact et marqué qui ne soit pas vide d'expression.'

française. Rousseau's essay, more trenchantly written, was characteristically intemperate. He compared counterpoint and polyphony to 'the porches of our Gothic churches, subsisting only to reflect disgrace on those who had the patience to construct them'[1] and he was properly dismissed by Rameau as an ignorant, musically half-trained littérateur, while the musicians of the Opéra hanged and burned him in effigy. Nevertheless, the craze for the Italian *bouffons* swept Paris and extended to the Court, where the party of the new Italian music enjoyed the patronage of the Queen and the conservative partisans of French music that of the King. The Italians had the whole fashionable world and the powerful intellectuals on their side, and their season lasted for nineteen months, during which they played thirty different works by contemporary Italian composers including Pergolesi, Ciampi, Latilla, and Rinaldo di Capua. The plots of these little works were not unlike those of the French *opéra comique*. Their superiority lay in the quality of their music, composed instead of compiled; in the swiftly moving, much inflected, musical dialogue to which the Italian language lends itself so well; in the naturalism of Italian acting and the sensuous charm of Italian singing. It was the perfect music for the amateur. 'Italian music,' Grimm had written in the *Lettre sur Omphale*, 'promises and furnishes pleasure to everyone with ears, no further preparation is necessary. Since it is the function of music to excite agreeable sensations by means of harmonious and well-ordered sounds, every man who is not deaf has a right to decide whether or not it fulfils its function.' Such a definition, with its superficial logic and purely hedonistic standard, could hardly satisfy Rameau or indeed any serious-minded musician; but the commercially astute purveyors of the *opéra comique* soon saw where their interests lay in the matter and acted accordingly. It was not for nothing that parody had been the earliest, and for a long time the staple, ingredient of the *opéra comique*. This tradition could now be turned to account, and the five years following the arrival of the *bouffons*, from 1752 to 1757, are starred with native French imitations and parodies of the fashionable Italian style.

J.-J. ROUSSEAU AND THE NEW *OPÉRA COMIQUE*

Rousseau himself led the way with *Le Devin du village* given, less than three months after the initial success of *La serva padrona*, on 18 October 1752 at Fontainebleau. Described as 'an intermezzo in the Italian style', the original version had a *pasticcio* overture and recitatives by Francoeur and the singer Jélyotte. A second version, for which Rousseau

[1] *Lettre sur la musique française* (Paris, 1753), p. 44. Excerpts translated in Strunk, op. cit., p. 636.

himself furnished the recitatives and possibly the overture, was given five months later at the Opéra in Paris and the fame of the author, coupled with the fashionable nature of the little piece, led to countless private performances, including one at Choisy where Madame de Pompadour took the part of Colette and sang 'rather out of tune'. It is difficult for the modern ear to discern anything particularly Italian in this work, whose musical naïveté is even more remarkable than its consciously unsophisticated story. Rousseau's strongest point lay in a thin vein of melodic invention very much in the traditional French manner, of which Colette's 'Si des galans de la ville' is a good example.[1]

Ex. 102

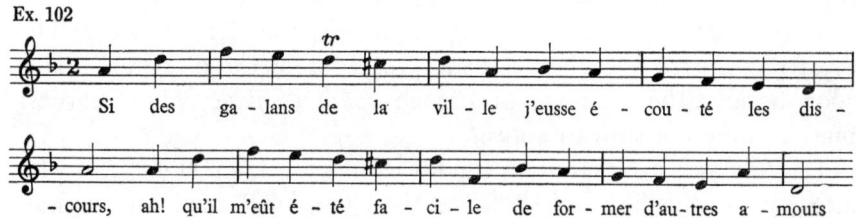

Si des ga - lans de la vil - le j'eusse é - cou - té les dis - cours, ah! qu'il m'eût é - té fa - ci - le de for - mer d'au - tres a - mours

(If I had listened to the gallants of the town, ah! how easy it would have been for me to form other attachments.)

It served him well in the pantomime of the wicked courtier who tries to seduce a village girl but is finally won over by the distress of his victim and her rustic sweetheart; and in a set of dances including a French *pastorelle* as well as an Italian *forlane*. He attempts a four-part chorus with very modest success and his recitatives, by which he laid great store like all partisans of the *bouffons*, are much below the standard soon to be reached by French *opéra-comique* composers. For the truth is that the popularity of the *bouffons* provided just the stimulus needed to convert the *opéra comique* from a play with songs adapted from a variety of already existing music, into a genuine musical genre capable of interesting professional composers, however modest, instead of musically minded theatrical hacks; and Rousseau's humble effort led the way. It was followed immediately not only by Favart's parody, *Les Amours de Bastien et Bastienne* (Weiskern's German version of which was set by Mozart in 1768[2]) but also by a far more professional imitation of the Italian *opera buffa* which was to have far-reaching effects. This was *Les Troqueurs* (1753) by Antoine Dauvergne (1713–97), a violinist and composer of instrumental works soon to hold important official appointments. Dauvergne and his librettist Vadé, knowing that only Italian works had any chance of popular success, gave out that

[1] Another example is in Davison and Apel, *Historical Anthology of Music*, ii (London, 1950), p. 235.
[2] See p. 107.

their joint work was translated from the Italian; and *Les Troqueurs*, thus insured, was immediately acclaimed. The story of two yokels who agree to exchange sweethearts and then have difficulty in persuading them to return to their original lovers is based on La Fontaine, and obviously foreshadows Mozart's *Così fan tutte*. There is a short, suite-like overture (Presto 2/4 F major; Andante 2/4 F minor; Presto 3/8 F major) and the orchestra consists of two each of oboes, flutes, and horns with the strings. The characterization of the two girls, one a vixen and the other phlegmatic, is thoroughly Italian, with instrumental touches pointing and illustrating airs and dialogues. The use of musical instead of spoken recitative was not generally followed by Dauvergne's successors who, however much influenced by Italian models, found that their public greatly preferred the characteristic 'comédie mêlée d'ariettes'. This soon became the set form of French *opéra comique*, whose earliest masters were not slow to appear.

The first was a Neapolitan, Egidio Romoaldo Duni (1709–75), who after much travelling had settled at the Court of Parma. This was an outpost of French culture under the Bourbon dukes, and the performances of Rameau's music at Parma exercised an indirect influence on Gluck and his Viennese collaborators. In 1755 Duni's parody or imitation of one of the *bouffons*' most admired works—Ciampi's *Bertoldo in corte* (imitated by the librettist Favart as *Ninette à la cour*)—was so successful in Parma that he decided to move to Paris, where in 1757 he scored an immediate success with his *Le Peintre amoureux de son modèle*. This was praised not only for its music but also for its excellent French prosody, though the music is thoroughly Italian in style.[1] Almost simultaneously the first French masters of the new genre appeared before the public—André Danican Philidor (1726–95) with an 'arrangement' *Le Diable à quatre* (1756) and an original work *Blaise le Savetier* (1759); and Pierre Alexandre Monsigny (1729–1817) with *Les Aveux indiscrets* (1759).

OPÉRA COMIQUE OUTSIDE FRANCE

So powerful and far-reaching was the influence of French taste on the Courts of Europe in the middle of the eighteenth century, that Vienna was almost before Paris in establishing the *opéra comique* as a truly musical genre. This was owing to the fact that Gluck, musical director to the Habsburg Court since 1754, was engaged to write new airs for many of the fashionable little pieces dispatched post-haste from Paris to

[1] 'One of M. Duni's lesser merits lies in the fact that, although a foreigner who speaks French with great difficulty, he never does violence to French prosody in his music, whereas all our French composers—from the great Rameau to the little Boismortier—have mangled it mercilessly.' *Correspondance littéraire* iv (Paris 1813), pp. 456–7.

Vienna by the Austrian ambassador, Count Starhemberg, and performed before the Court at Schönbrunn or Laxenburg. The first of these was *Les Amours champêtres* (1755), in which the extent of Gluck's contribution is not certain; but during the next six years he contributed probably the majority of new airs for *L'Isle de Merlin*[1] and *La fausse Esclave* (1758), *L'Arbre enchanté* and *Le Diable à quatre* (1759), *L'Ivrogne corrigé* (1760),[2] and *Le Cadi dupé* (1761). On the very eve of producing his first masterpiece *Orfeo ed Euridice* (1762),[3] Gluck revealed the astonishing pliability of his musico-dramatic sense by conforming perfectly to the half-French, half-Italian style required by these pieces, many of whose texts were the work of Favart.

Gluck is concerned here [wrote Alfred Einstein] with stupid, mean or grumbling old men, shy pairs of lovers, roguish girls, merry lads, beatific drunkards—all of whom are characterised in a masterly way by delicate strokes, and from among many conventionalities emerge little melodic blossoms, tiny melodic piquancies of the utmost charm. The spirit which Rousseau called 'the return to nature' is to be perceived everywhere; in the orchestra nature's ways are painted by means of figuration and tone-colour.[4]

An air such as the following, from *Le Diable à quatre*—probably by Gluck himself, but possibly by the Italian Vincenzo Ciampi (1719–62)—is a good example of simple but effective delineation of character and suggestion of movement. It is sung by the distraught wife of a drunkard.

Ex. 103

---

[1] *Gluck: Sämtliche Werke* (ed. Rudolf Gerber *et al.*), (Kassel, 1951–1969), ser. IV, i.
[2] Ibid., IV, v. [3] Ibid., I, i; also ed. Hermann Abert, *Denkmäler der Tonkunst in Oesterreich*, Jg. 21 (Bd. xliv *a*). [4] *Gluck* (London, 1936), p. 55–6.

Oui, oui, c'est trop long-temps souff-rir, c'est trop long-temps souff-rir, à moi des coups! je ne puis le souff-rir.

(Yes, yes. I want to escape. I swear that the insult is intolerable, I cannot bear it. Yes, yes I have suffered too long—strike me! I cannot bear it.)

Gluck may even have drawn on his early memories of touring the countryside of Bohemia with his viola da gamba when he introduced rhythms foreshadowing the polka into *L'Isle de Merlin* and *L'Arbre enchanté*. It was only a few years later, in 1764, that Catherine the Great, following the preferences of her friends among the Parisian Encyclopedists, introduced French *opéra comique* to the Russian Court, where it remained steadily popular for the rest of her reign. Thus in hardly more than a single decade French *opéra comique* was established on a new footing not only in France itself but also wherever French taste was paramount—from Parma and Vienna in the South, through the princely courts of Germany, to the German–Russian Court of St. Petersburg.

OPÉRA COMIQUE AT ITS PEAK

In Paris the new status of the *opéra comique* received practical confirmation in 1762, when the Théâtre de la Foire St. Germain amalgamated with the Comédie Italienne. Closed in 1745 at the jealous instigation of the Comédie Italienne and the Comédie Française, the Théâtre de la Foire St. Germain had been reopened in 1751 by Monnet; but although the title 'Opéra Comique' was not adopted by the new theatre until 1790, from 1762 onwards there was no question of either the repertory or the majority of the performers being anything but French. This was not true of the composers who turned their attention to this new and fashionable genre. Gluck was still in Vienna at this time, and when he came to France it was not to write *opéras comiques*; but we have already seen J.-J. Rousseau, a Swiss, initiating the new genre and he was followed by the Italian Duni, the German Martini (whose real name was Schwarzendorf), the Italian Fridzeri, the Bohemian Kohout, and the Belgian Grétry, all of whom obtained great success with the Parisian public. The appeal of the *opéra comique* was not only international; it also transcended the social barriers which, in these last years before the Revolution, were already beginning to waver in France. Rousseau and Grimm, champions of the *opéra comique*, were noblemen's secretaries, and Monsigny, the most admired of all *opéra-comique* composers in the 1760s, was *maître d'hotel* to the Duke of Orléans. At the other end of the social scale we have seen Madame de Pompadour performing in *Le Devin du village*, and thirty years later royalty, in the person of the Comte de Provence, was to take a hand in the libretto of Grétry's *La Caravane du Caire*. The identity of one of the most successful composers of this genre, known as Nicolas Dezède, has never been fully established and his pseudonym ('de Z') was said to conceal illustrious but illegitimate birth. Another favourite, Fridzeri—whose best-known piece *Les Souliers mordorés* (Versailles, 1776) shows close affinity with the Mannheim symphonists and a remarkable anticipation of Leporello in the comic valet Michel—was advertised as 'blind from the age of one'. In fact, the *opéra comique* found its patrons and practitioners in those social, intellectual, and musical demi-mondes which attract men of talent as well as adventurers and often achieve great power and influence during the last years of a society, when traditional beliefs are questioned, conventions relaxed and pleasure is pursued with the same fanaticism—and often by the same men—as revolutionary politics.

The troupe at the Comédie Italienne contained many of the most famous actors and actresses of the day; and although as a body they seem to have inherited the original Italian company's improbable reputation for fervid piety, this did not prevent individuals among them from pursuing some of the most highly advertised *carrières amoureuses* of the day. This was particularly true of the men, who included Jélyotte, Clairval, and Michu (for whose favours two society hostesses fought a famous duel). Most famous among the women were Marie Fel and Justine Favart, wife of the librettist, the first actress to play a shepherdess (Bastienne in her husband's parody of *Le Devin du village*) in realistic woollen frock and clogs and with simply dressed, unpowdered hair.

CHARACTER OF THE NEW GENRE

The thirty-seven years between the arrival of the Italian *bouffons* and the outbreak of the Revolution formed the golden age of the *opéra comique*. If the scurrility and crude indecency of the old parodies is replaced by a wit graceful even when salacious, it was largely owing to Favart. Voltaire wrote to him in 1775, 'You are the first to have made a decent and ingenious amusement out of a form of production which before you did not concern polite society. Thanks to you it has become the delight of all decent folk.' To Favart we owe especially the pastoral idylls such as *Rose et Colas* (set by Monsigny), in which Rousseau's rustic sentimentalities and Boucher's artificial shepherds and shepherdesses find their perfect musical and dramatic counterparts. In his fairy pieces such as *La Fée Urgèle* (set by Duni) Favart continued an old tradition of the *opéra comique* and found a rival and successor in Marmontel, the librettist of Grétry, for whom he prepared *Zémire et Azor*—as Favart had taken *La Fée Urgèle*—from a *conte* by Voltaire. But this allegorical style, in which social criticism is veiled under an oriental or fairy exterior, was to go out of fashion as the unrest and discontent which were eventually to issue in the Revolution became more and more open, until it was in its turn parodied, as in Champein's *Le Nouveau Don Quichotte* (1789). Pastoral pieces soon took on an openly social colouring in Philidor's *Blaise le Savetier* and *Le Jardinier et son seigneur*, or Blaise's *Annette et Lubin*, all dating from the 1760s. The librettist of the first two was Michel Jean Sedaine, an inelegant but serious-minded playwright who had made a career for himself in spite of his very humble origins. *Annette et Lubin*, which travelled all over Europe during the next twenty years, was the work of a syndicate of authors, including Favart and his wife, and was based on one of Marmontel's *Contes moraux*. The composer, Blaise, was a bassoon player at the Comédie Italienne, and the contrast between country ignorance and virtue and the evils of sophistication and education is represented musically by a rustic 6/8 melody with bagpipe, or musette, drone-accompaniment on the one hand, and on the other 'l'air qu'on chante au château' with its ornamented line and long roulades on the word *enchaîne*. In Philidor's *Le Jardinier et son seigneur*, the squire visiting Maître Simon arrives with two mistresses, drives his carriage through the hedge and across the garden, and tries to seduce his host's daughter, whose mother comments bitterly: 'Ces seigneurs-là n'ont qu'un doigt pour faire du bien; ils en ont neuf pour faire du mal.' Dramas of innocent rustic love disturbed by scheming village authorities (generally the *bailli*, or notary) or of unscrupulous young noblemen in search of amusement, remained very popular, and the dialogue is often extraordinarily frank, as in this passage from *Le Jardinier et son seigneur*. The *bailli* in *Annette et Lubin*, who accuses his peasant rival of anarchic behaviour, is met with a proud response worthy of Rousseau himself. 'Vous vivez sans lois,' he says. 'Tant mieux,' replies the youth. And Rousseau would have appreciated the high-flown sentiment of Annette when she complains to Lubin, 'Je t'ai cru mon ami, tu n'es que mon amant.' Not that this noble diction is characteristic of the *opéra comique* as a whole, where the language is often as realistically rustic as Madame Favart had made the costumes.

As late as 1783, when the *opéra comique* was taking on a different complexion, a piece such as Dezède's *Blaise et Babet* was written largely in countrified dialogue. 'On a ben raison d'dire que l'amour est un bon réveille-matin,' muses Babet. 'Et c'est ben pis quand à st'amour-là i' se mêle un p'tit brin d'jalousie.' Countrified oaths ('morguenne', 'jarnigué') and bad grammar ('j'avons') are freely used to heighten the effect of rustic realism.

MONSIGNY AND PHILIDOR

Among the librettists of the *opéra comique* Sedaine has the honour of having carried the sentimental *comédie bourgeoise*—the *pièce à mouchoirs*, or 'tear-jerker'—into the lyric theatre. Sentiment in one form or another had already become the distinguishing note of the genre by the middle 1760s. With Philidor's *Tom Jones* (1765), founded on Fielding, and Grétry's *Lucile* (1769), the purveyors of sentiment were no longer peasants but bourgeois, and their dramas belonged not to some idealized rural paradise but to eighteenth-century middle-class life, the world depicted by Diderot in his plays and by Greuze in his pictures. The famous air from *Lucile*, 'Où peut-on être mieux qu'au sein de la famille?', which became a household tag, is both in sentiment and in musical character an interesting foreshadowing of what Beethoven was to universalize in his *Fidelio* more than a generation later:

Ex. 104

Où peut-on ê- tre, où peut-on ê- tre mieux qu'au sein de la fa- mi- lle?

(Where can one be happier than in the bosom of the family?)

Neither *Tom Jones* nor *Lucile* had a libretto by Sedaine, but he was responsible for the first major success of the new genre, Monsigny's *Le Déserteur* (1769). Since this opera is in many ways characteristic and maintained its popularity in France for more than a hundred years, it may be as well to describe it in some detail. Sedaine's story concerns a young soldier, Alexis Spinaski, whose love for his village sweetheart is cruelly tested by the whim of the local châtelaine. The first of the three acts takes place outside a village on the Flanders frontier, where the French army is encamped. Louise's father explains the scheme by which Alexis is to be told that Louise is marrying another admirer. Louise protests in an A major ariette ('Peut-on affliger ce qu'on aime?') but the ingénue

Jeannette is instructed to explain the situation to Alexis. After Jeannette's 6/8 D major chansonette ('J'avais égaré mon fuseau') Alexis, a high baritone, enters to a heroic D major, and expresses his joy at the prospect of seeing his sweetheart. His air is a formal *recitativo accompagnato*, depicting his passionate excitement. When a marriage procession appears and Jeannette's answers to his questions destroy his illusions, the F minor duet which follows is succeeded by an explosion of grief and indignation, tenderness and despair in another *recitativo accompagnato*. Alexis decides to emigrate, but is captured making his escape and arrested as a deserter. The entr'acte separating the first from the second set skilfully returns to the music of Louise's 'Peut-on affliger'. The second act shows Alexis in prison. His warder, Montauciel, is drunk and his comic air (dotted 3/4) is interrupted by Louise's arrival, The lovers make up their quarrel (G minor duet) and after a *fugato prestissimo* trio with Alexis and her father, Louise leaves to beg Alexis's pardon from the King, who is inspecting the nearby camp. Montauciel and the yokel Bertrand indulge in a somewhat drunken musical diversion.

Ex. 105

(*Bertrand.* All men are good, one finds nothing but open-hearted fellows, so long as their interests are observed.
Montauciel. Long live wine, long live love! loving and drinking in turn, I snap my fingers at melancholy.)

In the third act, Montauciel, after vainly attempting to decipher a letter, asks Alexis to teach him to read and is so insulted by his deciphering 'Vous êtes un blanc bec' that he challenges Alexis to a duel. Alexis, now in despair, sings 'Il m'eût été si doux de t'embrasser' with many affecting pauses and stammers and the characteristic appoggiaturas which suggest the emotional style of performance associated with the *opéra comique*.

Ex. 106 ALEXIS

Il m'eût é-té si doux de t'em-bras-ser!

(It would have been so sweet to kiss you!)

A messenger enters and describes Louise's errand in a long narrative air ('Le Roi passait et le tambour battait aux champs') and she herself arrives with the pardon but faints before she can speak. Alexis, now prepared to face the firing-squad, takes a last farewell in 'Adieu! chère Louise', when cries of 'Vive le Roi!' are heard off-stage and these lead to the final vaudeville, as the lovers are reunited. Monsigny's overture to *Le Déserteur* is a primitive and miniature symphonic poem in which the forthcoming drama is musically foreshadowed. The opening allegretto, with its D major military fanfares, is suddenly interrupted by D minor tremolo and tragic unison passages presto. A pastoral (6/8) interlude alternates with this, and after the final reappearance of the presto, a slow chromatic descent reintroduces the military fanfares with which the overture began.

Monsigny was less ambitious in his musical illustrations than many other composers. Philidor's *Le Maréchal ferrant* (1761), for instance, contains a number of illustrative touches which ensured the popularity of the work and were to be often copied by later composers. First the blacksmith accompanies himself with blows on his anvil:

Ex. 107

Chan-tant à plei-ne gor-ge dès que je vois le

(Singing at the top of my voice as soon as day breaks, I keep sleep and love far from my forge. In good heart from early morn, I keep up my spirits unvexed.)

In La Bride's 'Quand pour le grand voyage Margot plia bagage', the village bells are suggested by pizzicato scales in the strings against ding-dong octaves in the voice part. In another air La Bride, a coachman, clacks his tongue and his musical miming of a breakneck run lands him on a long-held top C. (The soprano and tenor parts in many of these operas lie very high, with B flats occurring comparatively frequently in the normal line, not only at climaxes.) In the final vaudeville the original anvil rhythm reappears against . In a duet in which a bill is dictated the second singer repeats the last phrase of the first, just as in the letter scene between Susanna and the Countess in Mozart's *Marriage of Figaro*. More curiously, Colin's 'Mon cœur s'en va', sung after taking the blacksmith's drug for an operation, is couched in a tragic style yet marked 'Andante con spirito'.

Ex. 108

(My heart sinks, my eyes cloud. What can I have drunk? My sickness increases.)

Besides a gift for musical illustration Philidor showed on occasion an unusually developed sense of character. This is well marked in the concerted numbers of his *Tom Jones* (1765). In the first act there is a duet for Sophie and Honora, in which their characters are distinguished both rhythmically and melodically. 'Philidor', wrote Grétry, 'is, so far as I know, the inventor of these concerted numbers with contrasting rhythms. I certainly heard none in Italy, before I came to France.'

Ex. 109

-voirs que tu m'im - po - ses
Qu'un jeu - ne dril - le, qu'un jeu - ne
tri - ste rai - son
dril - le lui par - le l'a - mou - reux jar -
ont de ri - gueurs tu gé -
-gon
-mis, So - phie, et tu n'o - ses t'in - ter - ro-

(Sophie. Oh! how the duties that you impose on me, dull reason, irk me with their rigours! You lament, Sophie, and dare not question your own heart on its grief.

Honora. Evening and morning the silly young thing sits sad and lonely, yielding to her grief. If a young spark speaks of love to her, her heart leaps and she prattles away.)

The finale of the second act of *Tom Jones* is a skilfully conducted septet, in which Sophie and Tom plead together and the other five singers (Honora, Mrs. Western, Blifil, Alworthy, and Western) make their separate comments or objections to the match. Squire Western's hunting ariette ('D'un cerf dix cors') uses harmonics in the lower strings as well as the horn-calls that were plainly demanded by the context. *Tom Jones* also contains what is said to be the first unaccompanied vocal quartet to appear in any opera.

Philidor's professional skill as a chess-player had taken him abroad between 1745 and 1754, eventually to London, where he became acquainted with Handel's music; and in 1777 he returned to England, where he stayed two years. If his later works never enjoyed a popularity comparable to that of his earlier pieces, this was because first Grétry and then Gluck had engaged the attention of Parisian music-lovers. The same reason accounts for the disappearance of Monsigny's name after 1777, when his setting of Sedaine's *Félix ou l'Enfant trouvé* brought him his last great success.

GRÉTRY

André Ernest Modeste Grétry (1742–1813), a native of Liège, had studied five years in Rome when he arrived in Paris in the autumn of 1767, armed with recommendations from Voltaire himself. In the following year he scored a notable success with his setting of Marmontel's *Le Huron*,[1] based on one of Voltaire's *contes*; but it was the two operas which he produced in 1769—*Lucile* and *Le Tableau parlant*[2]—that carried him immediately to the front rank of popular favour, where he remained for the next fifteen years. In his *Memoirs* Grétry described himself as 'having received from Nature the gift of appropriate melody', but as lacking that of 'strict and complicated harmony'.[3] His harmonies are thin, he very seldom writes for more than two voices in concert and his orchestration is in water-colour tints at a time when the range of orchestral colour and power was being greatly increased. The passage from *Le Tableau parlant* in Ex. 110 is typical.

Grétry was no more than just when he prided himself on the appropriateness—or, as we should say, the psychological truth—of his melody. He catches the expression, the tone, the pace, and the weight of a character to perfection, whether it be a country *ingénue*, a scheming bailiff, an amorous old man, or a vain widower. He was a conscious and persistent observer of human nature and his aim was dramatic truth, to which musical charm was for him quite secondary. Possessed of a natural fund of melody, he used it as a means rather than as an end, and if most of his music is forgotten today, it is because the characters and

---

[1] *Collection complète des œuvres de Grétry* (ed. François Fétis, François A. Gevaert et al.), (Leipzig and Brussels, 1883–1936), xiv.
[2] Ibid., ii and ix.
[3] *Mémoires ou Essai sur la musique* (Paris, 1789), p. 516.

Ex. 110

(*Cassandre*: We must part, oh! terrible torture ... My pretty child, dry your eyes.
  Colombine: Can one leave one's heart's delight—dear Isabelle?
  Isabelle: Alas! what am I doing here alone?)

situations in his operas have to a great extent lost their interest for the general public. The two pairs of lovers who dupe old Cassandre in *Le Tableau parlant*, the village lovers and their persecutor in *La Rosière de Salency*,[1] the contrast between court and cottage in *Colinette à la Cour*,[2] and the rustic comedy of *L'Épreuve villageoise*[3] have few counterparts in the modern world, and Grétry's music, though perfectly adapted in each case to the characters and the drama, has not enough intrinsic interest to hold the attention when the characters have lost theirs.

When he attempts a larger canvas, his music loses its character, and his operas on *Pierre le Grand* (1790) and *Guillaume Tell* (1791)[4] have only incidental interest, such as the use of the *ranz des vaches* and the young Tell's ariette 'Noisette, noisette, je ne veux point te cueillir', with its hypnotic pedal bass. This is a direct foreshadowing of that use of popular ballad or folk-song that we find in Weber's *Der Freischütz*. A rhythmic parallel can be found in Pedrillo's 'In Mohrenland gefangen war', in Mozart's *Die Entführung aus dem Serail*, which in its turn suggests a parallel with Blondel's song in Grétry's *Richard Cœur de Lion*.[5]

Ex. 111

---

[1] *Collection complète*, xxx.
[2] Ibid., xv.
[3] Ibid., vi.
[4] Ibid., xl and xxiv.
[5] Ibid., i. Richard's aria in Act II is recorded in *The History of Music in Sound*, vii; the wedding *couplets* in Act III are given in Davison and Apel, op. cit., p. 268.

(Nut, little nut, I do not want to pick you in the copse. I have no time, I am still too young to try to pick you in the copse.)

These, however, were much later attempts to recapture popular favour in the historical genre which Grétry himself virtually created with his *Richard Cœur de Lion* (1784), a celebration of loyalty to the monarchy in the very last years before the Revolution. *Richard* is an early example of the 'rescue' opera, and Sedaine's libretto, well constructed and closely knit dramatically, so that the composer was not tempted to divagate, played an important part in the work's success. Blondel feigning blindness in order to have access to his imprisoned master and the jailer Williams with his daughter Laurette suggest close parallels with Bouilly's *Léonore ou l'Amour conjugal* which Beethoven was to use for *Fidelio* twenty years later. That Beethoven knew Grétry's *Richard* is suggested by the pianoforte variations that he wrote on Blondel's 'Une fièvre brulante' in 1797-8; this air was consciously employed by Grétry as a reminiscence theme and appears nine times, serving to identify Blondel to his invisible master and to the Countess Marguerite when he plays it on his viol. On this occasion it is taken up by horns, oboes, piccolo, and lower strings, while the violins provide an accompanying embroidery. In the last act the castle in which Richard is imprisoned is taken by assault to the accompaniment of lively military music; but nothing so ambitious as that to be found in the isolated instance of an earlier historical (and also distinctly royalist) opera, Martini's *Henri IV* (1774). Jean Paul Martini (1741-1816) was a German musician in the household of the exiled Polish King Stanislas at Lunéville from 1761 to 1766, and an assiduous composer of military music. *Henri IV* is a drama of love and politics and shows the disguised Henry IV entertained on the eve of the battle of Ivry by a family in which political loyalties are divided. Both harmonically and instrumentally Martini's music is adventurous for its day, belonging to the school of Philidor rather than that of Monsigny; but nothing in the opera is so remarkable as the battle music played between the second and third acts. This is orchestrated for fifes, clarinets, oboes, horns, cymbals, drums, and cannon, to which the composer suggests adding musketry fire (cues marked) and a primitive form of wind-machine.

Grétry was considerably less crude in his ideas of orchestral propriety. His own battle music in *Guillaume Tell* (1791)—written, that is to say, less than twenty years before Beethoven's incidental music to Goethe's *Egmont*—is worth quoting for a passage remarkably similar to Beethoven's *Siegessymphonie*:

Ex. 112

He compared the relationship between voice and orchestra to that of a statue and its pedestal; for music to him and all the Encyclopedists was the art of human expression and the human voice the perfect, because the only 'natural', instrument. But this did not prevent Grétry from occasional excursions into comparative elaboration when the dramatic situation seemed to demand it. A typical instance is to be found in the third act of his *Zémire et Azor*[1] (1771), where a 'magic' orchestra in the wings (clarinets, horns, and bassoons) accompanies the vision of Zémire's lamenting father and sisters, conjured up by Azor.[2] In *La Rosière de Salency* (1773)[3] the entr'acte separating the second and third acts consists of a miniature set of variations (for solo oboe, bassoon, violin, and viola respectively, with string accompaniments) and the theme reappears with words in the final vaudeville. A more primitive entr'acte is found in *L'Épreuve villageoise*[4] (1784) where a sixteen-bar 2/4 melody is repeated twice, each time faster than the last. Grétry's later, more ambitious, operas show a natural but unfortunate desire to follow the fashion, set by Gluck, for a more robust kind of music suited

[1] *Collection complète*, xiii.
[2] See pl. III.
[3] Ibid., xxx.
[4] Ibid., vi.

PLATE III

THE MAGIC PICTURE FROM GRÉTRY'S *ZÉMIRE ET AZOR*, 1771
(see p. 222)

to tragic themes, but as long as he kept within the limits of the *opéra comique* Grétry had nothing to fear except a change in public taste. This, of course, took place after the outbreak of the revolution in 1789, a year in which he produced a curious combination of fairy-story and rescue-opera, *Raoul Barbe-Bleue*.[1] Until then his primacy in his own field had been unchallenged since 1769, though it is perhaps significant that none of his best works were written during the five years between 1774 and 1779, when Gluck was in Paris. During those years 'lyrical tragedy' engaged the attention of both public and musicians after an interval of twenty years.

TRAGÉDIE LYRIQUE

Between Rameau's *Dardanus* (1739) and Gluck's *Iphigénie en Aulide* (1774) lyrical tragedy had been kept alive only by desperate measures, and before we examine in detail Gluck's achievement it will be as well to glance at the state of the patient that he was called in to revive.

Although Rameau did not die until 1764, his last *tragédie lyrique* to be performed was *Zoroastre* (1749) and his last masterpiece in the genre, *Dardanus*, dates from ten years before that. The titles of Rameau's works written during the fifties make it clear that while the Italian *bouffons* were capturing Paris and the French *opéra comique* was emerging as a virtually new musical form, the old national taste was maintained not so much in mythological tragedies, as in pastoral scenes and ballets or *opéra-ballets*. Rameau's own essays in this style have already been discussed in Volume V, but he was not, of course, alone in the field. There were other composers working at this time who, like Rameau, had been born when Lully was still alive, although in fact the movement away from high tragedy towards a lighter, more varied style of spectacle became recognizable during the last years of Louis XIV's reign and most clearly under the Regency. Many of the best-known composers of those various kinds of *divertissements*, such as Campra and Mouret, were dead; but Joseph Boismortier (1689–1755) was a practitioner whose pastoral opera *Daphnis et Chloé* (1747) earned the honour of a parody (*Les Bergers de qualité*). Boismortier was a voluminous composer of instrumental music and the best of *Daphnis et Chloé* is to be found in the *fugato* chorus of the Prologue and the powerful final chaconne. The contrasting orchestration of two *tambourins* and the delicate illustration of Chloé's air 'Ornemens de ma bergerie', in Act III, scene 6, show a characteristically French sense of colour and decoration, but Boismortier had little sense of words and could happily mangle his own language.

[1] Ibid., xviii.

Jean Joseph de Mondonville (1711–72) was of a younger generation than Rameau and Boismortier, but his appointment as 'Surintendant de la Chapelle du Roi' in 1744 gave him a privileged position, which was further enhanced by the favour of Madame de Pompadour. It was natural that he should be chosen by the King's party, the 'Coin du Roi', as champion of the pro-French faction in the Guerre des Bouffons. This circumstance gave an added importance to his *Titon et l'Aurore* which was given at the Opéra on 9 January 1753. It is significant that this work, 'the French party's counter-blast to the *bouffons*', was not a *tragédie lyrique* but a *pastorale héroïque*. The influence of Rameau is often plain in the storm scenes, in an air such as Aeolus's 'Fiers aquilons', and in the overture, which departs from Lully's scheme and approaches the Italian *sinfonia* in homophonic texture and dynamic brilliance. Like Boismortier, Mondonville was a composer of church and instrumental music rather than for the theatre, and *Titon et l'Aurore* enjoyed a *succès d'estime* which did nothing to stem the flood of popular enthusiasm aroused by the *bouffons*. Seen in historical perspective, however, the score shows occasional prophetic signs announcing the 'pathetic' style which was to be developed during the next twenty years by the composers of the *opéra comique*. Here, for instance, Tithonus revisits his native village:

Ex. 113

Mondonville, like Mouret, Campra, and Boismortier, was a southerner and he turned this circumstance to account in the following year by producing at Fontainebleau a *pastorale languedocienne*, *Daphnis et Alcimadaure*, with a Provençal text. This opens with a Prologue containing *jeux floraux* and an *air gai* in which strings and three-part woodwind answer each other antiphonally. There is a characteristic coloratura imitation of bird-song in 'Gazouillats, auzetas, à l'oumbre del feuillatage', and in the second act a page of recitative with the unusual key signature of five flats. Horns are introduced not only for the hunting scene but also in the big gigue. (We know that Johann Stamitz, in a letter written from Mannheim in 1748, advised Rameau's patron, the banker Le Riche de La Pouplinière, to add horns to his private orchestra.)[1]

Neither Boismortier nor Mondonville had in effect done anything to save or revive the moribund *tragédie lyrique*, and even before Rameau's death a list of operas produced at the Académie Royale de Musique—the Paris Opéra—provides eloquent proof of the shifts to which the directors were put in order to renew the repertory. One device was to produce favourite extracts from works in the existing repertory and we read of 'fragments héroïques' performed in 1759 and 'fragments nouveaux' or 'lyriques' in 1767. In 1758 Dauvergne (author of *Les Troqueurs*, see pp. 203–4) was successful in resetting the libretto adapted from Fontenelle's *Enée et Lavinie*, originally set by Colasse in 1690; and Pierre Berton, conductor at the Opéra from 1756 to 1778 and director during the 1770s, went further and undertook additions to and 'arrangements' (*racommodages*) of works by Lully: *Amadis* (1771) and *Bellérophon* (1773). To inaugurate the new opera house built to replace that burnt down in 1763 he even broached Rameau's works: *Castor et Pollux* (1764)—the year of Rameau's death—*Dardanus* (1768), and *Zoroastre* (1770). Berton's own *Adèle de Ponthieu* (1772) was one of the last original works produced at the Opéra before Gluck's arrival in Paris.

When Dr. Burney went to the Opéra in Paris on 15 June 1770, he heard a *ballet-héroïque* by Joseph Royer, *Zaïde*, dating from 1739.

> It is somewhat wonderful [he wrote] that nothing better, or of a more modern taste, has been composed since. The style of composition is totally changed throughout the rest of Europe; yet the French, commonly accused of more levity and caprice, than their neighbours, have stood still in music for more than thirty or forty years. Nay, one may go still further and assert boldly that it has undergone few changes at the great opera since Lulli's time, that is to say, in one hundred years ... It must be allowed that the theatre is elegant and noble; that the dresses and decorations are fine; the machinery ingenious; and the dancing excellent. But alas! these are all objects for the *eye*, and an opera elsewhere is intended to flatter the *ear*.[2]

Burney admired Grétry's *Le Huron*, on the other hand, and he speaks of another *opéra comique* that he heard, apparently Saint-Aman's *Alvar et Mincia*, which he describes as 'extremely serious', 'a comic opera in the modern French manner, with airs in the Italian style, set to French words, but without recitative, all the dialogue and narrative part being spoken'. The truth was that not even composers such as Gossec and Philidor, whose instrumental music showed that they were masters of the art and capable of a broad imaginative sweep, could breathe new

---

[1] Georges Cucuel, *La Pouplinière et la musique de chambre au XVIIIe siècle* (Paris, 1913), p. 324.
[2] *The Present State of Music in France and Italy* (London, 1771), pp. 30–1.

life into an obsolete form which implied an aesthetic intimately bound up with the Court and society of Louis XIV. This could only be done by a genius who, like Gluck, approached the subject from an entirely fresh point of view and did not feel overwhelmed by the burden of a century-old French tradition. Moreover, as we shall see, if Gluck's Paris operas were successful works of art, it was in spite of the limitations imposed upon the composer by the traditions of the *tragédie lyrique*. Moreover, their success did not lead to any revivification of the form, which died in 1779 with his *Iphigénie en Tauride*, just as decisively as Italian *opera seria* died with Mozart's *La clemenza di Tito* twelve years later. The works of Cherubini, Spontini, and the young Rossini, in which both traditions seemed to linger on, were in fact prompted by a quite different spirit. They reflect unmistakably conceptions of human personality popularized, though not initiated, by the French Revolution and expressed in musical forms freer and more individualized. Gluck's were still, basically, Court operas, and their psychology was borrowed from the Encyclopedists, just as their visions of 'Nature' and 'Antiquity' were borrowed from Rousseau and Winckelmann.

GLUCK AND FRENCH OPERATIC PRINCIPLES

Gluck was, in fact, an eighteenth-century musical radical working for a closed, still largely autocratic, society, rather than a nineteenth-century prophet addressing a middle-class public. His 'reform' of Italian opera should properly be seen as part of the same movement which had carried Handel from the aristocratic opera to the middle-class oratorio and set Haydn causing a sensation, by the 'extraordinary naïveté and liveliness' of his first quartets, and provoking talk of the 'degradation of music for the sake of tomfoolery'.[1] What offended good musical society was the plebeian accent of Haydn's music, and the same complaint was made, with equal justification, against the Italian *recitativo secco*, when it was introduced into France by the *bouffons*. Caux de Cappeval states unambiguously:[2]

> Le plat récitatif des Romains adopté
> Est le simple discours du bas peuple emprunté.

When Gluck was writing his Paris operas, he was not thinking primarily of their effect on the Court, or even his one-time pupil Marie Antoinette, but of Rousseau, Grimm, d'Holbach, d'Alembert, and the small, but enormously influential set of middle-class publicists, *littérateurs*, and *philosophes* who could make or destroy a reputation.

[1] E. L. Gerber, *Historisch-biographisches Lexikon der Tonkünstler* (Leipzig, 1790–2).
[2] *Apologie du goût français relativement à l'opéra* (Paris, 1754).

These men were without exception enthusiasts for Italian music and if aware, then more than tolerant, of its plebeian character.

There was little need in France for Gluck to insist on the principles which he had laid down in the preface to *Alceste*, for in almost every case they were part of existing French operatic theory, even if sometimes neglected in practice. In French opera, music was already subservient to poetry, the *da capo* aria was rare, the overture was already linked to the main body of the work in character and often in material, and such roulades as were permitted to the singers had in most cases at least a show of dramatic justification. In a sense, then, Gluck's reform of Italian opera was simply a demand that French principles should be applied to the Italian *opera seria*, where music (or rather singers) had ruled undisputed. There was never any questioning the superiority of Italian dramatic music or singers as such. What the Parisian intellectuals wanted was 'an art in which the bulk of French traditions should be preserved, but where the *chant* should be Italian.... Italian wine in French bottles.'[1]

What Gluck encountered in French opera was an art-form which suffered from an excess of rationalization just as Italian opera suffered from an excess of undifferentiated music. The apologists of the Lully era were quite clear in their assertion that opera was not a fusion of several arts—what Wagner was later to preach as the *Gesamtkunstwerk* —but quite simply 'sung tragedy'. According to Lecerf de la Viéville[2] the role of the composer in an opera was to illustrate the poetic text ('repeindre la poésie') and nothing more. Music was, in fact, allowed no independent existence of its own in the main body of the *tragédie lyrique* but took refuge in the accessory scenes—ballets, *divertissements* of all kinds, storms, pastoral or martial interludes, and the like. Those accustomed to the spontaneous melodic charm of Italian opera, in which the words were merely so many pegs on which to hang notes, found the *tragédie lyrique* disappointingly devoid of purely musical interest and excitement; and the popular conversational tone of Italian *recitativo secco* made the formal, courtly style of French recitative seem unbearably pompous, modelled as it had been on the speech of the Court as transplanted to the theatre by Corneille and Racine. J.-J. Rousseau, attacking French operatic recitative, declared that Lully and Rameau did not even succeed in capturing the true character of French speech in their recitatives; and his claim that this could only be done by maintaining a severe simplicity of line and avoiding all large intervals

---

[1] Cuthbert Girdlestone, *Jean Philippe Rameau* (London, 1957), p. 555.

[2] 'Dissertation sur le bon goût de la Musique d'Italie, de la Musique Française, et sur les Opéras' in *Histoire de la Musique et de ses effets* (Amsterdam, 1725), p. 292.

was indeed eventually vindicated, though only a hundred and fifty years later, by Debussy. Concerned simply with music's power to touch the heart and to paint emotional states or moods, Rousseau believed exclusively in 'melody' of the simplest kind. 'La musique ne saurait aller au coeur que par le charme de la mélodie,'[1] he wrote; and it was this narrow doctrinaire attitude that led him to condemn polyphony and all elaboration of purely musical thought as 'unnatural'. Rousseau's neglect of characterization in opera, or his confusion of it with mere mood-painting, placed him in fact among the extreme champions of Italian opera. Neither these nor the die-hard supporters of the traditional *tragédie lyrique* of Lully and Rameau could logically accept Gluck, who drew his admirers from among the moderates of both parties, French and Italian, and even more from among those music-lovers who instinctively recognized his genius and were not handicapped by the conflicting theories of the doctrinaires.[2]

A good key to the difference between the Viennese (that is to say, Italian) and the French conceptions of opera is to be found in the alterations that Gluck made in the original *Orfeo ed Euridice* and *Alceste* when he wished to produce them in Paris in 1774 and 1776. In *Orfeo* the castrato voice was replaced by a tenor, the orchestration was enriched (especially by an increased use of the trumpet), the scene at the gates of Hades and in Elysium was expanded, and Cupid and Eurydice were given new arias. In *Alceste* he was chiefly concerned to give more movement and verisimilitude to the story, and this he did by altering the order of several scenes, cutting out Alceste's two confidantes and adding the new figure of Hercules. All these alterations can be explained by Gluck's awareness of the French interest in the drama and in dramatic spectacle, and of the greater importance of the orchestra in Paris. This may well have been explained to him by the librettist of *Iphigénie en Aulide*, du Roullet, whose Paris patron, Le Riche de La Pouplinière, was one of the main agents in introducing the music of the Mannheim symphonists into France.

Gluck's name had become known in Paris very soon after his appointment as musical director to the Viennese Court in 1754, for we have seen him arranging and recomposing Favart's pieces for performance at Schönbrunn or Laxenburg during the years between 1755 and 1760. In 1760 Count Durazzo, the director of the imperial theatres and the man to whom Gluck owed his appointment, sent to Favart two of Gluck's French pieces, *La Cythère assiégée* and *L'Isle de Merlin*, and

[1] Op. cit., p. 4.
[2] For a full account and discussion of these theories, see Hugo Goldschmidt, *Die Musikästhetik des 18. Jahrhunderts* (Zürich, 1915).

Favart replied complimenting the composer on his French prosody. Two years later Durazzo had a score of *Orfeo ed Euridice* published in Paris, and although only nine copies were sold during the next three years, Philidor and Mondonville were among the composers who bought them; and in 1765 Blaise interpolated airs from *Orfeo* and *La Rencontre imprévue*[1] into his *Isabelle et Gertrude*. The fact that one of Gluck's royal pupils, the Princess Marie Antoinette, had become *dauphine* of France and ascended the throne as queen in 1774 was only the last link in a chain of events which made Gluck's appearance in Paris increasingly probable. On his side there were many inducements—the attraction of making his name in the cultural capital of Europe and of recouping himself for the severe financial losses which he had incurred in 1769 as part-contractor of the Viennese Burgtheater, as well as the prospect of developing his operatic ideals in a new and sympathetic milieu. The French opera had probably interested him ever since 1745, when he had passed through Paris on his way to London and may have heard one of Rameau's operas. Ranieri Calzabigi, his librettist for *Orfeo*, had spent some seven years in Paris before arriving in Vienna in 1761, and he must certainly have described to Gluck at considerable length the state of French opera, the chances of reviving interest in lyrical tragedy and thereby making a fortune—a subject on which Calzabigi was something of an authority, having established a lottery under the protection of Madame de Pompadour in 1757. More indirectly, Gluck had come into contact with French operatic ideals and practice in the works of Tommaso Traetta (1727–79), *maestro di cappella* at the Bourbon Court of Parma. Traetta twice visited Vienna to conduct his own operas. It would hardly be an exaggeration to say that by 1758, when Traetta was appointed, Parma was one of the last strongholds of French *tragédie lyrique*. The Intendant was a Frenchman, du Tillet, and he not only had Rameau's music performed in the court theatre but had the libretti of *Hippolyte et Aricie* and *Castor et Pollux* translated into Italian and set in 1759 and 1760 by Traetta. Parma's reputation among Italian music-lovers can be gathered from a letter written in 1758 by Count Agostino Paradisi to Algarotti, whose *Saggio sopra l'opera in musica* (1755) is one of the earliest pleas for operatic reform. 'I went to the opera in Parma,' he writes, 'where I found many things entirely to my satisfaction . . . the way seemed to me open for a renewal of the miracles of that art which the Greeks so much prized.'[2] Traetta's two operas for Vienna have revealing titles—*Armida* (1761), with a libretto based on Quinault,

[1] *Sämtliche Werke*, ser. IV, vii.
[2] Three of Count Agostino Paradisi's letters to Algarotti are to be found in *Raccolta di prose e lettre scritte nel secolo xviii*, Vol. 2, tomo I (Milan, 1804), pp. 292–7. These unfortunately deal with literary criticism only.

and *Ifigenia in Tauride* (1763), with a libretto by Marco Coltellini.[1]

IPHIGÉNIE EN AULIDE

Gluck's immediate introduction to a practical scheme for reviving French lyrical tragedy in France itself was through an attaché at the French Embassy in Vienna, François du Roullet. A contemporary of Gluck's, du Roullet had spent much time during the 1750s at the house of Le Riche de La Pouplinière, a *fermier-général* who spent much of his enormous wealth on music and the arts. Rameau, and later Gossec, were members of his household, where Voltaire, Rousseau, and Marmontel were intimates; and the Mannheim composer Johann Stamitz was the banker's guest during his visit to Paris in 1755. Du Roullet had therefore been at the centre of Parisian musical life and well acquainted with both the tradition of the *tragédie lyrique* and its determined opponents among the Encyclopedists. He was aware that Algarotti and Diderot had recommended Racine's *Iphigénie en Aulide* as an ideal opera subject, and he set about shaping a libretto with the object of disproving Rousseau's claim that French was a language unsuited to singing. This was the chief point made by du Roullet in the letter which appeared in the *Mercure de France* on 1 October, 1772, canvassing interest in Gluck's opera; and it was taken up by Gluck himself in his letter to the same paper four months later.[2] In this Gluck refuses to favour any one language—'that which will always suit me best will be the one in which the poet offers me the most varied means of expressing the passions'; and he sought to disarm Rousseau by pleading for his collaboration in the production of 'a music fit for all the nations' and free of 'the ridiculous distinctions of national music'. Dauvergne, now director of the Opéra, consented to examine the score of the first act of *Iphigénie en Aulide*, and was so impressed that he insisted on Gluck entering into an engagement to produce six operas of the kind, 'since this one alone would be sure to drive all the French operas off the stage'.

It was not until April 1774 that *Iphigénie en Aulide*[3] had its first performance, and this would never have taken place had not Gluck been able to enlist the interest and influence of Marie Antoinette. On his arrival he had found conditions of performance at the Opéra disastrous. The singers only knew how to 'shout or intone', the chorus was a herd of automatons in white gloves and the orchestra sunk

---

[1] For further information on Traetta's music and its influence upon Gluck, see pp. 38–42.
[2] Both letters are translated in full in Strunk, op. cit., pp. 676 and 681.
[3] Full score (ed. F. Pelletan and B. Damcke), (Paris, 1873).

in routine. The violins played with their gloves on in winter; flutes doubled recorders, although tuned a quarter-tone apart; hunting horns and a regimental trumpet made up the brass section; and one of the violin section played the drums. Nuances of any kind seem to have been unknown. The forces normally employed were twenty-four violins, five violas, seventeen basses (cellos and double basses), six each of flutes and oboes, two clarinets, eight bassoons, two horns, one trumpet, and one harpsichord. The fact of Gluck's presence at the rehearsals, which lasted six months, doubtless ensured the quality of the performance, but it led to ambiguities in the written score which have puzzled subsequent editors—*col basso* markings whose extent and application are uncertain, wind solos in which the instrument intended is not specified, and exchanges of parts confused by using the same stave for two different instruments.

Before examining in detail the character of Gluck's Paris operas it will be as well to establish the chronology of his five-year association with the French capital. *Iphigénie en Aulide* had its first performance at the Opéra (Académie Royale de Musique) on 19 April 1774. At the beginning of the following August *Orphée et Eurydice*,[1] the new French version of *Orfeo*, was given and in the early autumn Gluck returned to Vienna. At the end of 1774 Louis XV died, and in the following February *Iphigénie en Aulide* was revived in a revised version, with a new *dénouement* introducing Diana. Gluck came from Vienna to direct both this and the performances of his *L'Arbre enchanté* and *La Cythère assiégée*, both revised. He worked on a French version of *Alceste*[2] and returned to Vienna with two Quinault librettos, *Roland* and *Armide*. In March 1776 he was in Paris again for the first performance of *Alceste*, but returned to Vienna early in June, deeply affected by the death of his adopted daughter. During this time the Italian faction, headed by Marmontel and La Harpe, had commissioned the Neapolitan Niccolò Piccinni to set Quinault's *Roland*, meaning to confront the two composers on the same ground. Gluck got wind of this and wrote an indignant letter to du Roullet, who published it, without Gluck's consent, in the *Année littéraire*; and this incident unofficially inagurated the quarrel of *Gluckistes* and *Piccinnistes*. Gluck destroyed his sketches for *Roland* but returned to Paris in May 1777, and was present at the first performance of his *Armide* in September of that year. He stayed in Paris for Piccinni's *Roland*,[3] given in January 1778, returning to Vienna in March. He was back in Paris in November, bringing his *Iphigénie en*

---

[1] *Sämtliche Werke*, I, vi.
[2] Ibid., I, vii.
[3] Vocal score in *Chefs-d'œuvre de l'opéra français* (Paris, c. 1880).

Tauride,[1] which was given the following May. After the failure of his *Echo et Narcisse*[2] in September of the same year (1779), he left for Vienna, where he remained until his death in 1787.

THE CHARACTER OF GLUCK'S PARIS OPERAS

What were the characteristics which made Gluck's Paris operas so successful? We must try to discount the social and journalistic cliques and cabals, the publicity agents and the personalities which cast a smoke-screen round the works themselves. When Romain Rolland declared[3] that Gluck was a man, while his rivals were merely musicians, he put his finger on the right spot. Gluck won his Parisian audiences by the bold simplicity of his music, a quality which has been given other, harsher names by many musicians who find his scores rhythmically unenterprising and instrumentally stolid, but one which captivated his first listeners, with their literary and rationalistic rather than purely musical tastes. He wound up the debate between the champions of French and Italian music by combining the strong points of both schools and writing Italian music in French forms. The 'reform' of Italian opera that he had carried out some fifteen years earlier was, as we have seen, very largely the application of principles drawn from existing French practice; but Gluck's own formation and all his early works had been exclusively Italian, and it was unthinkable that he should ever abandon what was in fact the foundation of his whole musical character. Like many geniuses, he felt no obligation to be consistent in the practice of his own theories. In his Paris operas he often uses 'closed' forms, including the *da capo* aria; words are repeated for purely musical reasons; the recitative is often hardly distinguishable from Italian *recitativo secco*;[4] and in the case of *Armide* (as in the earlier *Orfeo*) the overture shows no organic connection whatever with the drama that follows. These were not so much conscious concessions (though Gluck was ready to make these, too, as is shown by Achilles's *aria di bravura* 'J'obtiens Iphigénie') as reversions to type, and they worry only historians or theorists of opera. The Italian *Orfeo* and *Alceste* had the static qualities of a frieze or a series of dramatic tableaux, but Gluck knew that the French public demanded (and his French librettists

[1] *Sämtliche Werke*, I, xi; miniature score (ed. Hermann Abert and Walther Vetter), Leipzig, n.d.).
[2] *Sämtliche Werke*, I, x.
[3] *Musiciens d'autrefois* (Paris, 1908), p. 246.
[4] Rousseau, op. cit., p. 74: 'Le meilleur récitatif français doit rester entre de fort petits intervalles, n'élever ni n'abaisser beaucoup la voix, peu de sons soutenus, jamais d'éclats, encore moins de cris... peu d'inégalité dans la durée ou valeur des notes, ainsi que dans leurs degrés.' This is, as Rousseau goes on to point out, the exact opposite of Lully's practice; it was an ideal never realized until Debussy's *Pelléas et Mélisande* (1902).

THE CHARACTER OF GLUCK'S PARIS OPERAS 233

furnished) a dynamic drama of events. Du Roullet was not above introducing irrelevancies that spoil the chaste economy of Racine's tragedy—the figure of Patroclus (to gain a bass voice for a quartet) and the intrigue by which Agamemnon attempts to discredit Achilles in the eyes of Clytemnestra and Iphigénie. The *divertissements*, too, though by no means an imposition of French taste only (as can be seen from *Orfeo*) weaken the work for the modern listener when he finds them taking the place of a true dramatic *dénouement*. When all these blemishes have been acknowledged, *Iphigénie en Aulide* still remains in the history of opera one of the great human tragedies. The tragic strain is heard with the first phrase of the overture, borrowed from Gluck's earlier *Telemacco* (and, possibly, from a Mass by Feo, though in fact similar contrapuntally workable phrases are common throughout the church music of the eighteenth century). When it reappears as the music of Agamemnon's 'Diane impitoyable', we are aware that the suspensions in the music are used as a symbol of the tragic suspense in the mind of a man whose public duty appears to conflict beyond hope of remedy with his human feelings as a father.

Ex. 114.

(Pitiless Diana, in vain you ordain this hideous sacrifice.)

Compare with this the parallel passage in *Telemacco*:

Ex. 115

[Musical example with text: di-ce il pa-dre mio dov' è? Dov' è? Bass: B♭ A B♭ A B♭ Dov' è? A]

(Ah! which of you will point him out, who will tell me where my father is?)

The passage later in the same scene where the oboe echoes 'le cri plaintif de la nature' was something entirely new in opera, an instrument added, as it were, to the *dramatis personae*. Nothing quite so fine as this scene[1] appears again until the third act, where Clytemnestra's 'Quels tristes chants se font entendre!' against the chorus off-stage, looks forward to many scenes in nineteenth-century opera—Cherubini's *Médée*, Wagner's *Lohengrin*, Berlioz's *Les Troyens*, and Verdi's *Aida*. Iphigénie herself is the most markedly French of the protagonists. Her music is always hovering between recitative and aria or arioso, and there are two occasions on which Gluck gives her a French *petit air* (or *air de mouvement*, from its more regular rhythm) embedded in a passage of recitative. Nothing could be more French, in form and sentiment, than this:

Ex. 116

[Musical example with text: Il faut de mon des-tin su-bir la loi su-prê-me jus-qu'au tom-beau je bra-ver-ai ses coups]

(I must submit to the supreme law of my destiny, I shall brave its blows unto death.)

Other purely French features of *Iphigénie en Aulide* are the passacaglia in Act II and the final chaconne; the *ballet de caractère* (where the 'Air pour les esclaves', with pizzicato and drone bass, was described as 'tirolais ou cosaque'); and the ornamentation of the vocal line with 'affective' appoggiaturas. This was a regular feature, as we have seen, of the *comédie larmoyante* in the *opéra comique* and we have only to compare four bars from Monsigny's *On ne s'avise jamais de tout* (1761) (Ex. 118) with Clytemnestra's 'Par un père cruel à la mort condamnée' (Ex. 117) to be aware of the similarity:

[1] Recorded in *The History of Music in Sound*, vii.

Ex. 117

Par un pè - re cru - el à la mort con - dam - né - e, Et par les dieux a - ban - don - né - - e

(Condemned by a cruel father to die and abandoned by the gods.)

Ex. 118

Pour moi tout est son i - ma - ge! Mon cœur en a sou - pi - ré

(I find her image everywhere! My heart has sighed for it.)

For the 1775 revival, when Gluck added the figure of Diana to the *dénouement*, there were considerable additions to the score, all taken from previous works—the chorus 'Que d'attraits' in Act II is from *La clemenza di Tito*; and *Cythère assiégée, Don Juan, Telemacco,* and *Paride ed Elena* (twice) were all pillaged to provide dances or choruses in Act II.

After the pruning and adaptation of *Orfeo ed Euridice* to French taste Gluck, as we have seen, retired to Vienna with two opera-books, *Roland* and *Armide*. *Roland* he never completed, but *Armide* was heard on 23 September, 1777. Here Gluck was transported forcibly by Quinault's libretto (written for Lully in 1686) into the baroque age, with its personifications, its symbolism, and its passion for the grandiosely spectacular. Gluck was nothing if not a professional and a good businessman, and he would have accepted any libretto within reason if he had thought it to his advantage to do so. But it is significant that he used more borrowed material here than in any other of his mature operas. The overture was lifted almost bodily from *Telemacco* which also supplied the music for 'Esprits de haine et de rage' (Act II) and for 'Plus on connaît l'amour' in Act III, though here he was borrowing from even earlier works, *Ippolito* (1745), and also *Le Feste d'Apollo* (1769). This recourse to his own past, not (as in *Iphigénie en Aulide*) to fill out a formal scene with dances and choruses but to supply music for some of the most crucial moments of the opera, suggests that Gluck's heart was not wholly in *Armide* and that he was more concerned to hasten the completion of a work which he knew must be ready to meet the challenge of Piccinni in the contest planned by the Parisian publicists.

The great, and prophetic, moments in *Armide* are the double chorus demanding vengeance, at the end of Act I, with its dotted, hammering rhythms, a tableau such as Meyerbeer was to develop sixty years later; the oboe solo with divided violas, pizzicato basses, and staccato triplets in the violins, which foreshadow those of Berlioz's sylphs; the chaconne and the final discomfiture of Armide in the fifth act. Wagner remembered Armide when he created Kundry and the scene in Klingsor's magic garden. Indeed, it is as a quarry for operatic builders of the future that *Armide* is most important.

IPHIGÉNIE EN TAURIDE

With *Iphigénie en Tauride*, coming at the end of Gluck's career and perhaps his greatest opera, we move into an entirely different world; still that of the French classical tragedy but penetrated with psychological understanding and presented with an economy of means much nearer to Euripides' original than du Roullet's *Iphigénie en Aulide*.

Gluck's librettist was Nicolas-François Guillard, who is said to have written his drama under the influence of *Iphigénie en Aulide* and sent it to du Roullet, who forwarded it with a strong recommendation to Gluck. Guillard adds none of the *confidantes* or counter-plots, the additional motivation or decoration with which the eighteenth century normally 'modernized' their Greek models; and Gluck seized with delight on a poem whose directness of utterance and clear, simple structure demanded exactly the music that he alone could give. The result is unquestionably a masterpiece and the last great 'classicist' opera, for when Cherubini wrote his *Médée* only eighteen years later the French Revolution had hastened and intensified the growth of that Romanticism which had already begun to pervade the *opéra comique*, although it hardly touched Gluck.

From the opening storm, which leads straight into the first scene, to the end of the first act, there is no hesitation, not a superfluous bar. Iphigenia's dream of horror leads naturally to the priestesses' chorus of sympathy and her own sublime prayer ('O toi qui prolongeas mes jours') in which the oboe again plays its familar role. Thoas is shown as a superstitious barbarian king, and his 'De noirs pressentiments' presents the greatest possible tonal and rhythmic contrast to the transfigured world of Iphigenia's Hellenic, ethically coloured religion. The arrival of Orestes and Pylades is hailed in a series of bloodthirsty choruses and dances which conclude the act with brutal suddenness, in the relative minor of the original tonic (D major–B minor).

The second act, which shows Orestes and Pylades in prison, opens with a quotation from Gluck's ballet *Semiramide* (1765).[1] This also puts on the stage a parricide, and it is significant that Gluck quotes again from this same work immediately before the sacrifice of Orestes is interrupted by Iphigenia's recognition of him as her brother. The contest between Orestes and Pylades as to which shall die may seem to modern taste unduly prolonged, though it was a situation much relished by the eighteenth-century public, whose appetite for such exhibitions of fine feeling was insatiable. Orestes' 'Dieux, qui me poursuivez', which lies high and is heavily orchestrated (horns, trumpets, timpani) immediately suggests the hypertension of a psychopath, and the following scene is a masterly psychological representation of a nervous crisis. Left alone, Orestes deliberately invokes the gods' punishment, falls to the ground, and apparently loses consciousness. Returning to himself, he seems for a moment relieved, though the wild beating of his heart suggested by the syncopated viola figure (♫ ♩. ♫♫ | ♫ ♩ ♫♫) contradicts the words with which he seeks to reassure himself. He sinks into an uneasy sleep of exhaustion and is at once assailed by the Furies. Their chorus, with its inexorable trombone scale rising in unison with the voices, is another borrowing from *Semiramide*, where the passage appears soon after the opening of the first scene. Orestes begs for mercy, but each time (five altogether) the Furies reiterate their accusation 'il a tué sa mère'. For a dreadful moment Clytemnestra herself appears, and when Iphigenia enters Orestes starts up and mistakes his living sister for his dead mother, a wonderfully true touch. Iphigenia questions him and learns the truth about their family, except in one point on which he deceives her, telling her that Orestes is dead. The elegiac choruses of priestesses and Iphigenia's own despairing lament 'O malheureuse Iphigénie'—the more despairing for its G major tonality, which breathes a kind of relief that there can be no more horror to learn—bring the act to a peaceful end. In the aria Gluck returns to his favourite alternation of solo oboe and voice, though the music is borrowed from his own *La clemenza di Tito*, just as the final chorus of the act is an arrangement of 'Que d'attraits, que de majesté', from *Iphigénie en Aulide*.

The third act is the weakest in the opera, perhaps because Gluck himself could not maintain his interest in the quarrel between Orestes and Pylades over the right to self-sacrifice. But there is an interesting example of his continued indebtedness to French *opéra comique* models in the lilting trio 'Je pourrais du tyran'; and in Pylades' 'Divinités des grandes âmes', with its very unadventurous harmonic character and repeated cadences, in which Gluck seems to be aiming at the same

[1] *Sämtliche Werke*, II, i.

noble, static, oratorio-like effect that Beethoven was to use in the last act of *Fidelio*. The last act opens with a 'brilliant' aria for Iphigenia, 'Je t'implore et je tremble', which Gluck had used in both *Telemacco* and *Antigone*. But the final version of the *dénouement*, which gave the composer so much trouble and only reached its final form at rehearsal, after two previous versions had been scrapped, shows Gluck's dramatic art at its finest, simplest, most concise. It is only as Iphigenia raises the sacrificial knife to strike him that Orestes, in a touching aside, reveals his identity.

Ex. 119

[musical score]

(*Iphigénie*: Ye gods! all my blood freezes in my veins... I tremble... and my faltering arm... *Chorus*: Strike! *Oreste*: 'Twas thus you perished in Aulis, Iphigénia, my sister!)

In the scene that follows, it was originally Orestes, not Pylades, who killed Thoas.

The final chorus is borrowed from *Paride ed Elena,* and Gluck gave permission for music from the Gossec–Noverre ballet *Les Scythes enchaînés* to be used for the final *divertissements.*

ECHO ET NARCISSE

Iphigénie en Tauride is the last and in many ways the most distinguished opera in the Racine–Lully tradition which enjoyed, thanks to its stimulus, one further final decade of popularity before the revolution of 1789 swept it away with the society which had created it. Gluck himself wrote only one more work before he returned finally to Vienna. *Echo et Narcisse* was written for the dancers Vestris and La Guimard, to Noverre's choreography, but Gluck insisted indignantly that it was not a return to the pastoral style of the old *opéra-ballet.* He conceived the myth as a 'true tragedy', and although he was not assisted by the weak libretto provided by another diplomat, the Baron de Tschudi (a Lorrainer of Swiss origin), there are signs of a nostalgic desire to re-create the transfigured, static, frieze-like style of *Orfeo.* Seldom very imaginative in his handling of the orchestra, Gluck here seems more than usually concerned with the purely sonorous quality of his music; his handling of the double orchestra in the overture, and the echo effects throughout suggest a relationship with the baroque *festa teatrale.* If, despite its incidental felicities, *Echo et Narcisse* was a failure, Gluck had only himself to blame. He had accustomed his listeners to sterner, more full-blooded musical and dramatic delights, and they were no longer content with anything less immediately striking.

PICCINNI

Gluck's shadow falls heavily over all the lyrical tragedies produced in Paris during the 1780s, when the most successful composers were all Italians, though the style of their works is without exception cosmopolitan. The most important of these was the unhappy Piccinni. When he was brought to Paris in 1776 by the leaders of the anti-Gluck faction, Piccinni was already famous in his own country as the composer of more than a dozen *opere buffe* and almost a score of Metastasio settings (*opere serie*). Marmontel, one of his chief sponsors, provided him with the librettos for his chief Paris productions, rewriting Quinault's *Roland* (1778) and *Atys* (1780), and providing an original poem for *Didon* (1783). Piccinni himself was incurably naïve and could not be made to understand the purpose for which he had been summoned to Paris. It was as though some friendly and inoffensive local champion were pitted against an international 'star' of the boxing world, with whom he only asked to fraternize, conscious of his own immeasurable inferiority. 'Transplanted, isolated, in a country where all was new to me,' he wrote in his preface to *Roland,* 'intimidated by a thousand difficulties, I needed all my courage, and my courage forsook me.' Such frank lack of spirit cannot have endeared him to the promoters of the contest with Gluck; and Gluck's own strategic amiability, which fell little short of patronage, finally spoiled all the chances of a serious contest. Yet Piccinni's music is by no means contemptible. Conscientiously determined to satisfy his backers' demand for French music, he planned large and well-developed choruses for *Roland,* included a considerable number of *divertissements* in the French style and restricted his florid vocal writing to such words as *naufrage* or *enchaîné,* where French use permitted them. The flexibility of his vocal line, the variety of his rhythms and forms, and his freer use of decorated instrumental figures betray the Italian behind the French mask. It was cruel to ask such a composer to challenge Gluck in another *Iphigénie en Tauride* (1781), and Dubreuil's libretto was inferior to Guillard's; and yet this is one of Piccinni's best scores. The overture is more symphonic than any of Gluck's, and the inclusion of the storm within the narrative of Iphigénie's dream and its return when the arrival of Orestes and Pylades is announced, give the first act a unity which Piccinni cleverly exploits. The act ends dramatically in the dominant of F (minor) and the second act follows without interruption, in F major. Of the concerted numbers the double chorus in Act I and the trio ('Si mon cœur ressent leurs alarmes') equal any but the best of Gluck. In *Atys,* too, the final chorus of Act I, with its regular canonic entries, has an almost Handelian grandeur, and Piccinni showed originality when he gave the accompaniment of a crucial recitative in Act II to two solo violas. The subject of *Didon*[1] was in its favour, and here Piccinni never sinks below, though he seldom rises above, the new level of dramatic truth, the interest and invention to which Gluck had accustomed his audiences. Dido's dream of her dead husband, interrupted by the hunting chorus of the Trojan visitors, is a particularly happy idea, and Antoinette de Saint-Huberty's performance in the title-role seems to have been one of the earliest instances of the romantic, personal identification of an individual singer with a tragic role, which came to depend entirely on her for its success. Despite his adoration of Gluck and his partisan temperament, Berlioz was to admit that there was very little difference between the 'systems' of Gluck and Piccinni, and it would be strange if he had not examined the score of *Didon* when he was engaged on his own Vergilian opera. He may well have

[1] Vocal score in *Chefs-d'œuvre.*

learned something from Piccinni's strong musical handling of Iarbas and from the manner in which the older composer contrives to keep Dido the mistress of every situation, however humiliating, and to present her always in an emotionally favourable light without reducing the other characters to puppets.

SALIERI

Didon achieved a popular success only when Madame de St. Huberty took over the title-role in January 1784, and Piccinni's work was soon ousted from its place in the public attention. Beaumarchais's *Le Mariage de Figaro* after much intrigue finally evaded the censor and reached the stage on 23 April. Three days later this was followed by an opera whose mysterious origin and scandalous nature strongly appealed to all sections of the Parisian musical public. *Les Danaïdes* was announced as a work of Gluck's in which he had been 'assisted by his pupil Antonio Salieri'. After the twelfth performance Gluck announced from Vienna that Salieri was sole author of the music, and Calzabigi published a letter in the *Mercure de France* protesting strongly against the misappropriation of his libretto. In fact he had supplied Gluck with an Italian *Ipermestra* in 1778, and Gluck had eventually given this to du Roullet and Tschudi to adapt and translate into French, at the same time ceding his rights as a composer to Salieri. Gluck's action was morally (and would be today, of course, legally) indefensible, but *Les Danaïdes*[1] is both musically and dramatically a strong, well-knit work, and a by no means contemptible treatment of a singularly gruesome subject. The Greek myth tells of Danaus, who from motives of revenge pretends to end a feud by giving his fifty daughters in marriage to the fifty sons of his old enemy. In reality, however, he orders his daughters to murder their husbands on their wedding-night, and all but one agree. Hypermestra refuses, and the opera shows the predicament of a woman who has a homicidal maniac for a father and is torn between her duty as a daughter and her natural instinct to protect the man she loves. The audience is spared nothing, neither the death-cries of the murdered husbands nor the final scene of retribution in which Danaus and his forty-nine daughters are shown writhing in the torments of hell. No wonder it was described as a 'tableau d'horreurs dégoûtantes et incroyables, amas d'atrocités froides',[2] and achieved much the same *succès de scandale* as Strauss's *Salome* a hundred and twenty years later. Yet Hypermestra is a live, deeply touching woman and her terrible predicament, resisting her insane father and hiding the true horror of

[1] Vocal score, ibid.
[2] Vocal score, p. 236.

the situation from her lover Lynceus, is fully worked out in Salieri's music. The mounting tension during the marriage festivities and the alternation between tender love scenes and tragic despair sustain the interest throughout five acts. The situation is already prefigured in the overture, where the 'chants d'allégresse' of the nuptial feast are rudely interrupted.

Ex. 120

In Act V the signal for the murder is a single B flat in horns, trombones, timpani, bassoons, and strings, held over three bars and rising from *pp* to *ff* (a device to be used later by Berg in *Wozzeck*), followed by the hysterical, bloodstained women crying 'quel palais faut-il mettre en cendre?'.

The music of the final scene could not match the horror of the spectacle on the stage. Danaus's palace is struck by lightning and disappears to reveal Hell—the Tartarus (apparently mistaken for a river) flowing blood and Danaus chained to a rock, his bleeding entrails devoured by a vulture (actually the fate of Prometheus), while his head is repeatedly struck by lightning. The Danaids, in groups, are tortured by demons and devoured by serpents or chased, shrieking, by Furies under a never-ending hail of fire (borrowed no doubt from Dante). Nothing less grandiose than the music of the final scene of *Die Götterdämmerung* would have sufficed here, and no eighteenth-century composer possessed the language equal to such a scene. Salieri inevitably resorts to diminished sevenths, rocketing semiquaver figures, syncopated and tremolando chordal passages, and strong *sforzato* accents.

SACCHINI

After 1777, when the tenor Legros took over the direction of the Concert Spirituel from Gossec and Gaviniès, and Piccinni had started giving Marie Antoinette two singing lessons a week, Italian singers and Italian music became increasingly fashionable in Paris. Even in 1770 the *concert spirituel* attended by Dr. Burney contained two Italian concertos to one motet by Lalande and another by Philidor, whom Burney praises 'for being among the first to betray the French into a toleration of Italian music'. Gluck, it should never be forgotten, came to Paris as an Italian composer, and it cannot have surprised the French to find Italians carrying on the work done by Gluck in creating a cosmopolitan style. After Piccinni and Salieri it was the turn of Antonio Sacchini, a Florentine composer who won an international reputation during the early 1770s, settling in London in 1772 and producing nearly a score of operas there during the next ten years. The Emperor, Joseph II, gave him a warm letter of recommendation to his sister Marie Antoinette, and by 1783 Sacchini had moved to Paris, where he started by adapting two of his earlier operas (*Rinaldo* and *Il Cidde*) and went on to produce a new French work *Dardanus* (1784), for which he used La Bruère's libretto set by Rameau in 1739. None of these works had more than a limited success and it was only in 1786, a year after the composer's death, that his *Oedipe à Colone* revealed him as a full-blooded and legitimate successor to the Gluck tradition. His conscious desire to imitate Gluck appears on every page of the score, though like Piccinni he never lost his Italian fluency or his taste for purely musical elaboration, even when the dramatic situation does not demand it.

His librettist was Guillard, the author of Gluck's *Iphigénie en Tauride*, who makes Oedipus, haunted by the Furies, mistake Antigone for Jocasta, just as Orestes had mistaken Iphigenia for Clyemnestra in the earlier work. Sacchini's choruses show that he had not been deaf to Handel's music during his stay in England and the heroic unisons of Polynices' 'Le fils des dieux, le successeur d'Alcide' and the chorus of priests and soldiers in Act I make the same very powerful yet still basically

Italian impression as similar passages in Gluck or even Mozart. Sacchini, however, reveals a fatal Italian mildness or relaxation of temperament in the scene where Oedipus curses his son in a string of diminished sevenths, and his old-fashioned bow to the throne ('Les pères et les rois, arbitres souverains Sont votre image sur la terre') must have sounded little less than servile in 1786. Even so, *Oedipe à Colone* remained in the French repertory until 1844, a period when Berlioz was lamenting the neglect of Gluck.

CHERUBINI'S APPEARANCE IN PARIS

We have already seen how England, with no native school of opera, yet exerted an influence on many of those composers who were engaged there and heard during their stay performances of Handel's music. Gluck was the first, then Philidor; and in a later generation two Italians who did their latest and best work in France. In the year of Sacchini's death (1786) there came to Paris, also from London, another Florentine, who was to play a major role in French musical history for almost half a century. This was Luigi Cherubini, who eventually settled in Paris in 1788, when he produced his *Démophoon* at the Opéra. Apart from a C minor overture strikingly foreshadowing the dramatic style of the young Beethoven, and rather richer harmonic and contrapuntal choruses, this classical tragedy closely resembles others by these followers of Gluck.

TARARE AND *LES SOULIERS MORDORÉS*

A considerably more interesting and original work that enjoyed a great success in Paris this same year (1787) was Salieri's *Tarare*,[1] with a libretto by Beaumarchais. (With an Italian libretto arranged by da Ponte and a new title, *Axur, re d'Ormus*, this work was given six months later in Vienna. During the next thirty years it was heard all over Europe and translated into German, Russian, Polish, and English.) *Tarare* is the drama of a noble commoner pursued by the jealousy of a sadistically vindictive king, yet finally triumphant by virtue alone. This was not an unusual subject for the period, but the drama is preceded by a Prologue in which Nature and Genius are seen creating the characters from 'atomes perdus dans l'espace'. Salieri's overture represents the winds raging over primeval chaos (a breeze starts from nothing in C major and rises to a conventional C minor storm, on which the curtain rises). An E flat major chorus is followed by a dialogue between Nature and Genius, and as the spirits of the yet unborn emerge they express their aspiration to human existence.

[1] Vocal score in *Chefs-d'œuvre*.

Ex. 121

(sheet music: CHOEUR DES OMBRES — "Quel charme inconnu nous attire! Nos cœurs en sont épanouis d'un plaisir vague! Je soupire je veux l'exprimer Je ne puis, Je ne puis")

(What strange charm draws us on! Our hearts are expanded by an indefinable pleasure! I sigh and long to express it . . . I cannot.)

It is surely inconceivable that Mozart, who must have heard *Axur, re d'Ormus* in Vienna, had not this passage somewhere in his memory when he wrote the Three Boys' 'Bald prangt, den Morgen zu verkünden' and the music accompanying Pamina's and Tamino's trials in Act II of

Die Zauberflöte. Salieri attempted to distinguish in *Tarare* between singing and *parlando* styles of performance (*parlé* and *chanté* appear in the score) and marks several passages to be sung 'd'un ton dogmatique' —especially those of the villainous high priest Arthenée, who adjures his colleagues in terms which reflect Beaumarchais's troubles with ecclesiastical and other censorship—'Pontifes, pontifes adroits, remuez le cœur de vos rois!' Unlike Sacchini, Salieri found himself committed to the expression of strongly anti-monarchical sentiments. When Nature and Genius are allotting their roles in life to the newly created beings, this dialogue takes place:

> Un de vous deux est roi. Lequel veut l'être?
> Roi! je ne m'y sens aucun empressement.
> Égaux par la nature, que vous en serez loin dans la société!

(One of you will be a king. Which of you wishes to be? King! I feel no eagerness. Equal by nature, how far from equal you will be in society!)

The place and character of the Italian Spinette at the Turkish court, where the action of *Tarare* is set, repeatedly recall those of Blonde in *Die Entführung aus dem Serail*. The curtain of Act III, where Tarare is left for a moment alone and removes his mask, foreshadows Beethoven:

Ex. 122

[musical notation]

-né   qui croit à   tes bien-faits

(All-powerful God, you never disappoint the unhappy man who believes in your mercies.)

Mozart's work has already been mentioned[1] in connection with Fridzeri's *opéra comique Les Souliers mordorés*, which was given in 1776 and was so successful that it may well have been still performed two years later while Mozart was in Paris. There the comic valet Michel, complaining of being kept up at night by his master's escapades, opens the work in the full Mannheim–Italian manner:

Ex. 123

[musical notation]

[1] See p. 207.

MICHEL
Quel - le fu-reur.....
quel - le fu-reur D'al - ler dan - ser... la nuit ent - ièr - e se
tré - mous - ser se ha - ras - ser, se
tré - mous - ser....... dans la pous - siè - re, se

(What madness to go dancing the whole night long, frisking and tiring oneself out, while I'm ready to drop, waiting in the street, with my teeth chattering from the cold.)

Later in the opera (Act II, Scene iii) the same Michel dances a contredanse, an anglaise, and an allemande, which clearly recall the dance movements in *Figaro* and *Don Giovanni*. Mozart may well have known

Umlauf's setting of the same libretto, *Die schöne Schusterin*,[1] given in Vienna, first in 1779 and then again in 1785.

OPÉRA COMIQUE IN THE 1780s

Meanwhile during the 1780s, while Gluck's successors were supreme in the field of serious opera, new names were appearing in the field of the *opéra comique*. Grétry, the acknowledged master of the seventies, was still producing a work almost every year, but only *Richard Cœur de Lion* and *La Caravane du Caire*[2] (both 1784) can be counted among his major successes, and the latter owed its popularity partly to its character as a kind of oriental revue, and partly to the fact that the Comte de Provence (the future Louis XVIII) was reputedly concerned in the libretto. Monsigny had retired from active musical life, and Philidor, after devoting himself to serious opera for ten years, had small success with his last *opéras comiques*, produced between 1785 and 1788. Like all forms of popular entertainment, the *opéra comique* throve on novelty—new ideas and new composers—and it was two Provençal musicians who made their names in the last decade before the revolution. Nicolas Dalayrac (1753–1809) had already had seven works performed in Paris when his *Nina ou La Folle par amour* made his reputation in 1786. This work represents a new departure from the conventional sentimentality which was by now the most marked feature of the whole genre. Psychological disturbance had a new interest for a public already accustomed to the restless and angry mood of society and to the violence and scandals that marked the last years of the old régime. Dalayrac was a musical nullity and had no idea of matching the psychological complexities of Marsollier's story (amnesia caused by shock and cured by forcing the patient to relive the painful experience). In the first act of *Nina* the heroine enters— 'her hair unpowdered and loose, dressed in a white frock, with a bunch of flowers in her hand, her gait unsteady'—but Dalayrac matches this with a commonplace 6/8 D major, in which the muted horns provide the only mild note of eccentricity. *Les deux petits Savoyards* (1789) exploits the old situation in which a charitable nobleman finally recognizes in the two beggars whom he assists the children of a long-lost brother. The theme of the benevolent nobleman was popular in the eighties, as can be seen from Floquet's *Le Seigneur bienfaisant* (1780)—which caused Gluck to reflect bitterly on the incorrigible triviality of French taste—and Martini's *Le Droit de Seigneur* (1783). The Martini opera shows in a more sentimental light the situation treated by Beaumarchais in *Les Noces de Figaro*. It opens with a striking pastoral overture:

[1] Mentioned in Mozart's letter to his father of 24 December 1783 (*Letters*, ed. Anderson, iii, 1290).
[2] *Collection complète*, xxii.

OPÉRA COMIQUE IN THE 1780s

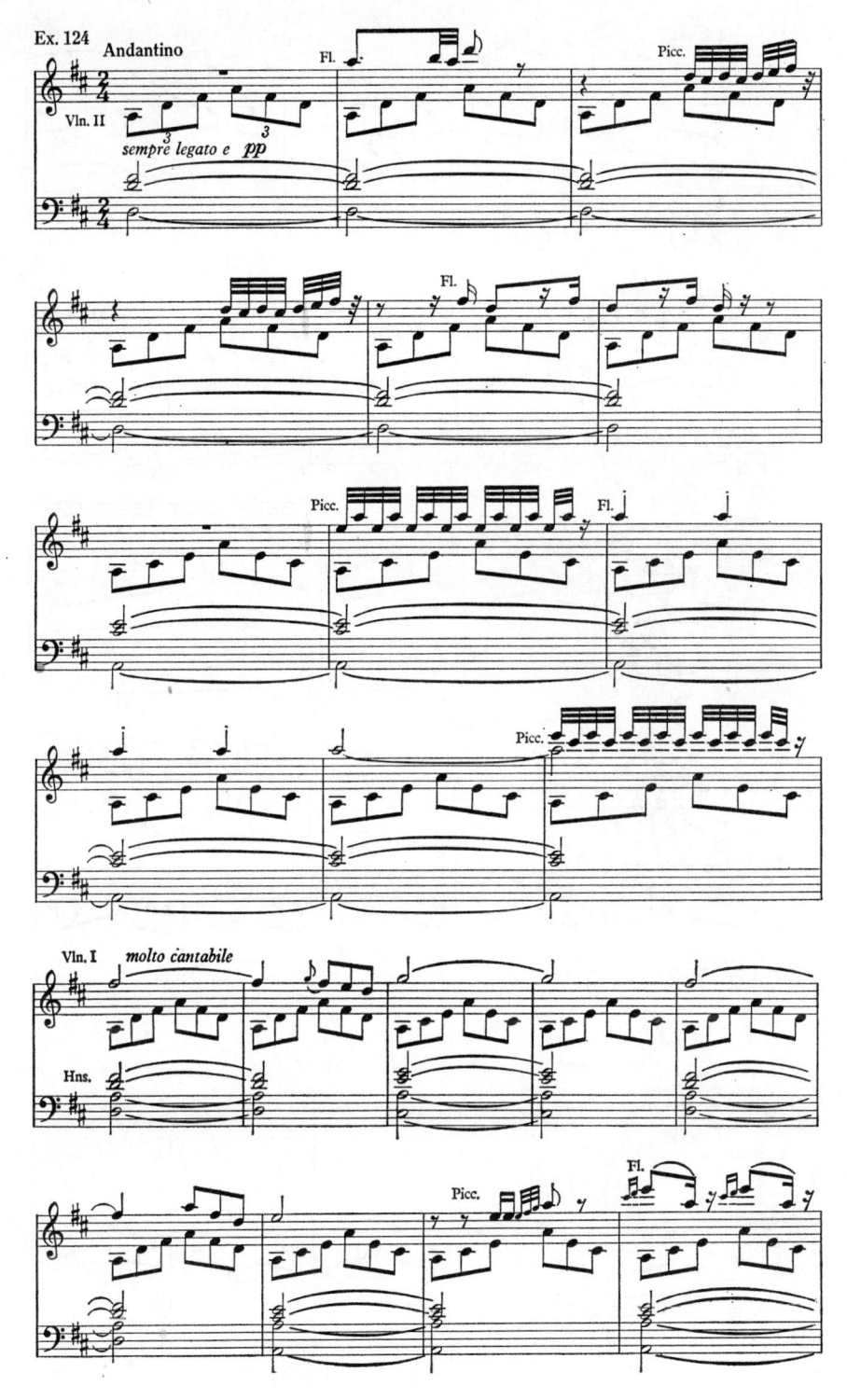

Ex. 124

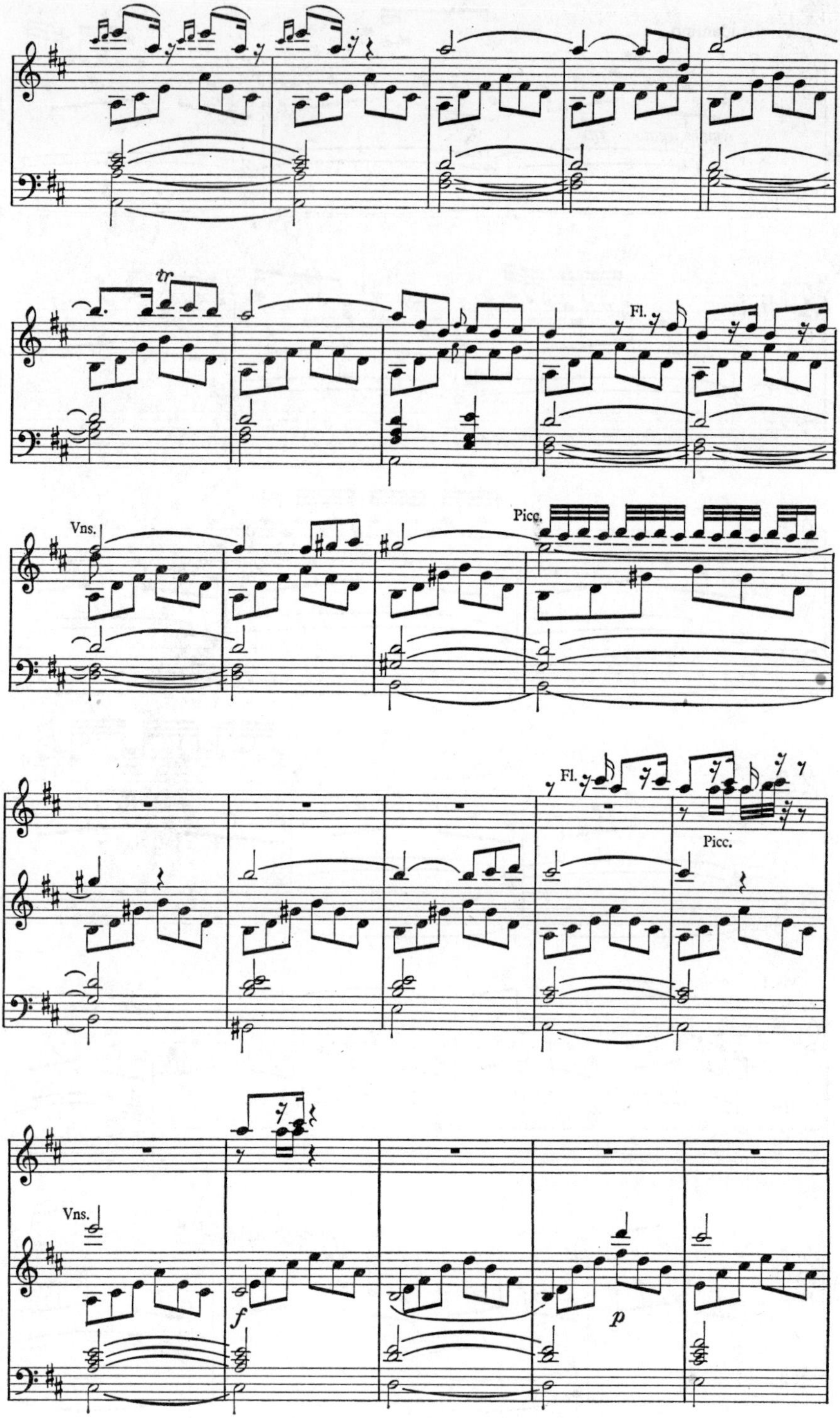
tr
Fl.
Vns.
Picc.
Fl.
Picc.
Vns.
f
p

[musical example]

and later the bird chorus opens thus:

There are details in J. B. Marsollier's libretto for *Les deux petits Savoyards* which even seem to foreshadow Dickens's sentimental handling of his child characters—one of the children, Joset, climbs a chimney, and a doll, Bébé, and a dog, Brusquet, are introduced for the sake of pathos. In one air, 'Une petite fillette', the singer is instructed to imitate the harsh, loud voice characteristic of Savoyards. Dalayrac quotes from Grétry's popular *Richard Cœur de Lion* in this work, and he himself set one of the fashionable medieval stories in his *Raoul, Sire de Créqui* (1789). Grétry had written an *Aucassin et Nicolette*, in which he attempted archaic effect, as early as 1779:

Ex. 125

[musical example]

Another of Dalayrac's pieces, *Renaud d'Ast* (1787), soon achieved a European popularity, but today it is chiefly memorable for a passage from Céphise's air 'Viens, viens à ma voix, douce espérance'. *Renaud* was given at the Theater auf der Wieden in Vienna on 27 August, 1791 (in German, as *Georg von Asten*) and on 30 September *Die Zauberflöte* had its first performance, in the same theatre. Dalayrac, it seems, may have contributed his humble mite to Mozart's music for the Queen of the Night in whose aria 'Zum Leiden bin ich auserkoren' the last two bars of Céphise's aria appear note for note:

The other Provençal who made his name in the *opéra comique* during the decade before the revolution was Stanilas Champein (1753–1830), who successfully exploited an old genre long favoured by the *opéra comique*—that of the satire on musical life—in his *La Mélomanie* (1781). *Il maestro di musica*, with music by Pietro Auletta and a number of other unnamed composers, had been one of the pieces brought to Paris by the Italian players for their historic season in the summer of 1752. The quarrel between the partisans of French and Italian music, both then and later when Piccinni was pitted against Gluck, had regularly provided material for the *opéra comique*. Champein's one-act piece shows Géronte, an elderly enthusiast for Italian music, who wishes to marry his daughter Lisette to Fugantini, an Italian musician whom he has never seen. Crispin, a resourceful valet of the traditional type, arranges for Lisette's lover to impersonate Fugantini, with the usual happy result. Champein writes much amusing parody of Italian instrumental music—busy triplets, repeated notes, semiquaver passages, and tremolandos—and Lisette has a comic *recitativo accompagnato* which pokes good-natured fun at the high tragic manner. Mozart's *Der Schauspieldirektor* was written five years after *La Mélomanie*, but there is no reason to suppose that he knew Champein's work, which appears not to have been given in Vienna. The subject was in any case popular throughout the second half of the eighteenth century, and in 1790 Martín y Soler set a Russian version of the libretto of *La Mélomanie, Pesnolyubie*, in St. Petersburg.

Champein's second triumph was with another form of parody, *Le Nouveau Don Quichotte*. This was given in May 1789, and was dedicated to 'Citoyen Duveyrier, Tribune of the People.' It opens with the conventional 'storm' overture and shows a comically cowardly Crispin assisting his master Dorlès to rescue his lady-love Claire from her guardian, Manquinados, who believes himself to be Don Quixote's grandson. Dorlès disguises himself as a giant to frighten Manquinados, who fights in his sleep and then executes a comic dance for Claire. In the chorus of chevaliers who come to the rescue Champein plainly parodies Gluck. In fact, this irreverent treatment of Cervantes, like Grétry's handling of the Bluebeard story in *Raoul Barbe-Bleue* (also 1789), was sixty years later to provide Offenbach with a precedent when he shocked the equally frivolous society of the Second Empire by using the august myths of the Greeks as a vehicle for contemporary satire. Champein, however, was no Offenbach, and his music hardly rises above the decent average achieved in the *opéra comique* thanks to the work of Monsigny, Philidor, and Grétry.

The effects of the revolution of 1789 were felt, as we should expect, sooner in the *opéra comique* than in any other department of French musical life. As early as April 1790 Berton's *Les Rigueurs du cloître* combined the favourite rescue theme with strong anti-clerical sentiments which were echoed in Devienne's *Les Visitandines* (1792). In fact, the *opéra comique* quickly adopted the high moral tone and the strong social and political colours of the new régime. It was a far cry from the elegant indecencies, the pastoral sentiments, the parodies and fairy-stories of earlier days to the speech delivered by the officer of the Republic who rescues Berton's Lucile from her convent. 'The most perfect being in the eyes of the Divinity,' he tells the assembled community, 'is he who worthily fulfils his duties as a man, a citizen, a husband, a father and a friend.'

III

OPERA IN OTHER COUNTRIES

(a) ENGLISH OPERA

By ROGER FISKE

BALLAD OPERA AND TRUE OPERA

Throughout the latter half of the eighteenth century there were only two winter playhouses in London, and each presented from September to the following June a mixed repertoire that was in varying degrees operatic. In 1750 David Garrick had just started managing Drury Lane, while at Covent Garden John Rich was nearing the end of his long reign. In 1767 they were joined, though not in rivalry, by the Little Theatre in the Haymarket, which was licensed to stage a similar repertoire in the summer months when the playhouses were closed. Outside London successful plays and operas were quickly presented by permanent companies in such places as Dublin, Bath and York, and by travelling companies in almost all towns.

An evening's entertainment consisted of one full-length piece and one half-length 'afterpiece', and in three categories music predominated in the 1750s. Pantomimes were the most popular items and at Covent Garden could be seen throughout the season on about one night in three. Invariably they were afterpieces, with no speaking, a number of songs and ensembles, and a continuous orchestral accompaniment in the mimed scenes. The music for miming was known as 'The Comic Tunes', and a number of sets of these little pieces were published in keyboard arrangements. Some pantomimes ended with masques on classical themes, the music fully operatic in style. Covent Garden pantomimes consisted almost entirely of survivals from the 1720s when Rich himself had danced Harlequin and Galliard had written most of the music. At Drury Lane Garrick, much against his will, had to create a new repertoire because the theatre had no big successes in this field to fall back on, and without pantomime he could not make his theatre pay. Burney and Boyce were among those who wrote pantomime music for him.

The next popular category in the 1750s was the ballad opera, and the term should be used only for such spoken comedies as were decorated with numerous short song-tunes already familiar to most of the audience, and mainly of a 'traditional' nature. The prototype was *The Beggar's*

Opera (1728), the only full-length example still popular in the second half of the century. No season went by without performances at both playhouses, and in 1759 a new Polly, Charlotte Brent, filled Covent Garden for weeks on end. In 1777 the piece was refurbished for Drury Lane by Thomas Linley the elder (1733–95) with more elaborate accompaniments in the *galant* style; though never printed, they were in use well into Victoria's reign.[1] The handful of afterpiece ballad operas that were popular in the latter half of the century all originated in the 1730s; on the few occasions when new examples were staged, they failed.

The third main category most nearly accorded with modern ideas on what is an opera, though many examples at the time were described as masques. Often they were occasional pieces prompted by a state wedding or funeral; usually they were sung throughout, but it is significant that the only lastingly successful example, Arne's *Comus* (1738), had most of Milton's words spoken. The same composer's *Eliza* (1754), though musically superior, was doomed to failure by its boring and wholly uneventful libretto about English shepherds at the time of the Armada. This was the most recent event that had been treated in an all-sung English opera, for it was still thought that only cardboard figures from the distant past were tolerable when singing their way through a story. Two full-length, all-sung Shakespearean operas were written for Garrick by John Christopher Smith, the son of Handel's amanuensis, but the music of *The Fairies* (1755; based on *A Midsummer Night's Dream*) and *The Tempest* (1756) is not better than worthy. Throughout this decade the proportion of opera in the repertoire was small, and Arne's abilities were little used largely because he was both quarrelsome and unreliable in his dealings with Garrick.

In 1759 John Beard, for long Drury Lane's best tenor, married Rich's daughter and defected to the rival theatre. When Rich died two years later Beard found himself in charge of Covent Garden and its policy. The straight play continued to provide the greater part of the repertoire, but Beard very considerably raised the proportion of opera and reduced the proportion of pantomime, and against all expectation the theatre prospered. This was due in part to the remarkable singing of Miss Brent (later she became Mrs. Pinto), and rather more to the fact that in 1762 Beard extracted two highly successful operas from Arne. For twenty years Arne's musical pieces had failed consistently in both playhouses; Beard was alone in being able to draw the best out of him. *Artaxerxes*, which was entirely sung, and *Love in a Village*, which had spoken dialogue, were to remain popular all over Britain for fifty years and more, and their success led to the proportion of opera in the playhouse reper-

[1] Addison's edition of *c.* 1827 is based on Linley's version and has an interesting preface.

toires being increased tenfold and staying at this higher level for the rest of the century.

Artaxerxes was an Italian opera in both form and theme, the libretto a translation by Arne himself of one by Metastasio that had often been set by others. Some of the songs have an English flavour, and in places there is *galant* influence; the big coloratura arias seem wholly Italianate. Much of the scoring is surprisingly lavish; for instance the first of the sung items, a duet in which the string band is held back until the middle:

Ex. 127

Elsewhere, as in most English operas of the 1760s, there are parts for clarinets. Like *Eliza*, *Artaxerxes* was published in full score but without recitatives and final chorus; the latter does not survive. It was the only all-sung, full-length English opera of the century that was an undoubted success. Garrick, searching for a counterblast, staged three precisely similar operas at Drury Lane in 1764–5: *The Royal Shepherd* by George Rush, *Almena* by Arne's natural son Michael and Jonathan Battishill, and *Pharnaces* by William Bates. Like their model, all were based on translations of outmoded Italian libretti and, their music much inferior, they all failed. The only other full-length, all-sung English opera before 1800 was by Storace, and that failed too. Counting Smith's operas and *Eliza* there were only eight examples in fifty years, a pitifully short list.

OPERA WITH SPOKEN DIALOGUE

On the other hand operas with spoken dialogue abound. *Love in a Village*, a success in itself, was successfully imitated. Isaac Bickerstaffe's libretto was freely adapted from *The Village Opera* of 1730, but the lyrics, instead of being sung to the short simple melodies of ballad opera, were mostly fitted to fully orchestrated English songs and contemporary Italian opera arias. Arne wrote new settings for seven songs and helped to adapt a selection of his old ones to the new words; he could claim about half the score as his, and arguably the better half. Apart from the 'Servants' Medley' that ends Act I, only four songs out of forty have traditional tunes in the old style, and these relics of the past were expunged altogether from the pastiche operas that imitated *Love in a*

Village. For the first time English comedies of intrigue set in modern times were being sung in fully operatic style, and quite soon younger and more go-ahead composers than Arne were writing Italianate ensembles as finales for each act—for instance, in *The Maid of the Mill* (Covent Garden, 1765) and *Lionel and Clarissa* (Covent Garden, 1768). These operas also had libretti by Bickerstaffe, who collaborated in the first-named with Samuel Arnold (1740–1802) and in the second with Charles Dibdin (1745–1814). Much the best of these pastiche operas was *The Duenna* (Covent Garden, 1775), which had a splendid libretto by Sheridan and music mainly selected and composed by Thomas Linley the younger (1756–78), who had been trained in Italy. About a quarter of the music was new, and of excellent quality, for the younger Linley was the most promising English composer of the century. (He was drowned when only twenty-two.) To save time in the composing Sheridan had written some of his lyrics to fit 'Scotch Song' tunes he knew. When such songs had been drawn on for ballad operas, the tunes had been doubled by violins and the accompaniments played only by continuo instruments. In 1775 such treatment was out of date. Linley managed to devise more elaborate accompaniments in the new *galant* idiom, and thereby gave these old tunes a new lease of life; for the rest of the century one or two are to be found in almost every opera as a result of Linley's innovation. *The Duenna* also made use of arias by Sacchini, Giordani, and Rauzzini. It was the last successful pastiche opera, and in Sheridan's lifetime more popular than any of his plays.

THE WORK OF DIBDIN

Charles Dibdin was too much of an individualist to be happy in the pastiche field, and usually wrote every note of his operas himself. In 1768 he moved to Drury Lane, and immediately composed the best of his afterpieces, *The Padlock*, to another Bickerstaffe libretto. He also revised *Lionel and Clarissa*, writing new arias to replace some that had previously been borrowed, and in this new form the opera is mostly his own work and also his masterpiece.[1] Though he had scarcely any musical training and knew much less than Arne about the technique of composing, he was much more a man of the theatre, being himself a good actor, singer, and lyric-writer. His music, though often thin and poorly developed, shows at its best an ebullient sense of situation and characterization. Alone among English composers except for Storace, he wrote effective Italianate ensembles in several sections, full of bustling and amusing

[1] Vocal score of the original version (London, 1768); vocal score of the revised version (London, 1770).

stage action. There are good examples in *Lionel and Clarissa*, in *The Wedding Ring* (Drury Lane 1773; the plot but not the music from *Il filosofo di campagna* by Galuppi) and in *Poor Vulcan*, an all-sung burletta making fun of the classical deities (Covent Garden 1778). He also wrote two all-sung, half-length operas for Ranelagh Gardens, much the better being *The Ephesian Matron* (1769), though *The Recruiting Sergeant* (1770) has the added interest for us today of having been published, alone of Dibdin's operas, in full score.[1] Also sung throughout were the short 'Dialogues' he wrote for the variety programmes at Sadler's Wells. Each was based on a contemporary cockney situation of low life, and four survive in short score: *The Brickdust Man*, *The Grenadier*, *The Ladle*, and *The Mischance* (1772–5). In these, as in almost all Dibdin's operas, the music makes up in spirit what in lacks in depth, and it 'sings' much better than might be expected from the look of it.

As an example of Dibdin's style a passage may be quoted from the ensemble that opens *The Ephesian Matron*. Bickerstaffe got the plot from Petronius, and it reappears in Christopher Fry's *A Phoenix too Frequent*. The 'Matron' is in her husband's tomb bewailing his recent death, though not perhaps with total sincerity. The music expresses her gulping hysteria with delightful humour, and it will be noticed that her father and her maid are distinguished by quite different rhythms. The indications of accompaniment figures are almost meaningless in the contemporary

Ex. 128

[1] London, *c.* 1770.

vocal score, the only source, yet in performance it leaps to life and 'sings itself'; it is real theatre music, deft and professional.

Dibdin suffered from one defect more damaging than his lack of training. He was incapable of getting on with other people. In his quarrel with Garrick he was wholly in the wrong; with Covent Garden he managed to quarrel twice. By 1781 both playhouses regarded him as unemployable.[1] With enough ability to have had English comic opera at his feet, he frittered away the rest of his long life giving one-man shows at his own little 'theatre', where his flair for sea-songs, accents, and comic patter brought him some measure of self-adjustment. Equally damaging to English opera was Bickerstaffe's flight from the country in 1772 after a crime described as 'unmentionable'. The next generation of composers found no librettist with nearly as much wit and ability; indeed, Dibdin himself seemed to need Bickerstaffe's collaboration as Sullivan needed Gilbert's.

LINLEY, ARNOLD, AND SHIELD

In the last quarter of the century the three theatres settled down to a pattern that scarcely varied. Each had its own 'house' composer, the elder Linley and then Storace (from 1789) working for Drury Lane, Shield for Covent Garden, and Arnold for the Little Theatre in the Haymarket.

[1] For his own ill-tempered views on theatrical personages, see his entertaining *Musical Tour* (London, 1788). He did, however, feel undying respect and admiration for Arne. Cf. Elizabeth M. Lockwood, 'Charles Dibdin's Musical Tour', *Music and Letters*, xiii (1932), p. 207, and Edward R. Dibdin, 'Charles Dibdin as a Writer', ibid., xix (1938), p. 149.

All wrote a handful of full-length 'dialogue' operas and a much larger number of afterpiece examples, and all but Storace wrote pantomime music as well, Shield a great deal of it.

In these twenty-five years nearly a hundred vocal scores of theatre music were published and only one full score—of William Jackson's afterpiece opera, *The Lord of the Manor* (1780).[1] Before *Artaxerxes* complete vocal scores were virtually unknown, and all operas were published in full score; afterwards the reverse was the case. In these vocal scores arias were printed in the main on only two staves, one for the voice and one for the bass, with instrumental cues in small notes added to the top stave where practicable. A few songs might be given in short score on three or even four staves in order to show more of the orchestral detail, but it is often hard or even impossible to judge the effect and substance of the accompaniments. Until about 1790 wind solos are usually indicated, but later vocal scores do not even show which are the borrowed items. In the operas of Shield and Arnold, and in some of those by Storace, borrowings amounted to about a quarter of the whole. There was nothing underhand about the practice, which was a relic of ballad opera. Storace was praised for the skill with which he appropriated suitable music from French, Italian, and Viennese operas.[2] Scotch songs were also drawn on, as already mentioned, while Shield, a Durham man, occasionally introduced north country folk-tunes, and Arnold English examples that we would associate with Cecil Sharp; for instance, *The Castle of Andalusia* (1782) has a version of 'The Keeper', and *The Children of the Wood* (1793) a version of 'The Truth sent from above'. Irish tunes were being freely used for the first time in the early 1780s, partly perhaps as a result of the publication of *A Favourite Collection of the so much admired old Irish Tunes* (Dublin, *c.* 1780) by Turlough Carolan, the Irish harpist, and even more because Shield began collaborating with an Irish librettist, John O'Keeffe, who sometimes wrote lyrics to fit tunes he remembered from his youth. It might be thought that such operas must be pastiches of the same kind as *Love in a Village* and *The Duenna*, but there is a clearly marked difference of degree. In *Love in a Village* and its imitators, the amount of new music never exceeds a quarter of the whole, it is not a major attraction (being forced on the compilers by exigencies of the libretto), and sometimes there is no new music at all. But in the operas of Shield, Arnold, and Storace the new music is the main attraction, almost always exceeding a half of the whole and usually amounting to about three-quarters.

Little need be said about the operas of the elder Linley and Arnold.

---

[1] London, *c.* 1782, in Glasgow University Library, Euing Music Collection.
[2] See Michael Kelly's *Reminiscences* (London, 1826) ii, p. 36.

Sheridan, the manager of Drury Lane from 1776 onwards, had eloped with and then married Linley's eldest daughter Elizabeth, and though the families were soon reconciled Linley never wrote for Drury Lane with much heart, partly because his life was clouded by the early deaths of so many of his children. Almost alone in his day, he did not use borrowed items in his operas. None of them had much success. Samuel Arnold was much more prolific, writing at great speed and with little thought, though his melodies sometimes show charm and individuality, as for instance in *The Siege of Curzola* (1786). Today he is better remembered for his ambitious edition of Handel than for his innumerable operas.

William Shield (1748–1829) was a more interesting figure, and equally prolific, for his published vocal scores number over thirty. For some years he played the viola in the Italian operas at the King's Theatre, and this experience gave him sufficient knowledge both to borrow sensibly and to write big Italianate *coloratura* arias for such singers as Mrs. Billington, who joined the Covent Garden company in 1788. Shield also wrote many concertante parts for the better instrumentalists in the Covent Garden orchestra, notably for Parke the oboist[1] and Sarjent the trumpeter. In *Robin Hood* (1784) there is a coloratura aria with a complete concerto exposition for oboe and orchestra before the voice comes in. But Shield's success rested more firmly on his short English-style airs such as 'The Plough Boy' in *The Farmer* (1787). Besides *Robin Hood*, his full-length operas included *Fontainbleau* (1784), *The Woodman* (1791) and *The Travellers in Switzerland* (1794), and such was Shield's popularity that for *The Woodman* his publishers paid him a thousand guineas. But his afterpieces were more performed and better loved. *Rosina* (1782) and *The Poor Soldier* (1783) each received over a hundred performances in the first six years, and remained in the repertoire for half a century. The hero's role in the latter was a travesty part for an actress (later it was often played by Mrs. Jordan), and it was in this opera that Londoners acquired a taste for Irish songs. All these pieces are marred by Shield's unwillingness to attempt any sort of ensemble other than a glee. He had little of Dibdin's dramatic sense or Storace's professionalism, and he chose, or was compelled to choose, librettos whose insipidity and 'staginess' would make revival today almost impossible.

STEPHEN STORACE

Stephen Storace (1762–96) was the son of an Italian double-bass player, Stefano Sorace or Storace, resident in Britain since about 1748; his

[1] W. T. Parke's *Musical Memoirs* (London, 1830) are a useful source of gossipy information about English operas.

mother was English. The father had run the music at Marylebone Gardens, and the Storace family had long been friendly with both the Linleys and the Sheridans. Like the elder Linley, the elder Storace had the sense to send his son abroad to study; it was then almost impossible to acquire professional technique in Britain. Stephen was trained at the San Onofrio Conservatoire in Naples (where his uncle was a bishop), and probably had a few lessons from Mozart during the time his sister, the original Susanna in *Figaro*, was Vienna's prima donna (1783–7). He even had two operas produced in Vienna, presumably through the good offices of his sister who was a close favourite of the Emperor; he had had no stage experience in England and so far no success anywhere. *Gli sposi malcontenti* (1785) and *Gli equivoci* (1786) were given in several European opera houses for some twenty years, but they have never been performed in England. *Gli equivoci* has an excellent libretto by da Ponte based on Shakespeare's *The Comedy of Errors*, and would merit revival; at least two manuscript full scores survive abroad.[1]

In 1787 the Storace family and the tenor Michael Kelly returned to London expecting that their wide continental experience would give them an entrée into the King's Theatre in the Haymarket, but they soon found that the Italian clique in charge was very averse to anyone born in England having any hand in the performances.[2] By 1789 the two Storaces and Kelly were established at Sheridan's Drury Lane, where they soon raised musical standards out of all recognition. Storace's first big success was *The Haunted Tower* (1789), whose Gothic mysteries preceded Mrs. Radcliffe's. His masterpiece, *The Pirates* (1792), is remarkable for its action ensembles and long finales in several sections; also for the Viennese warmth and lyricism of its music. The work is on the same scale as *Die Entführung aus dem Serail*. In places there are verbal echoes of *Figaro*:

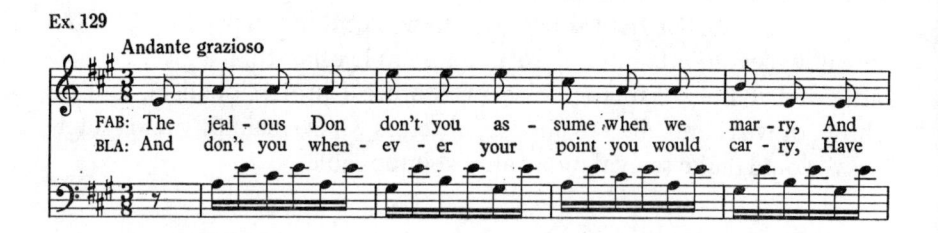

Ex. 129

Andante grazioso

FAB: The jeal - ous Don don't you as - sume when we mar - ry, And
BLA: And don't you when - ev - er your point you would car - ry, Have

---

[1] Manuscript copies in Vienna, Österreichische Nat. Bibl., K.T. 133, and Dresden, Sächsisches Landeshauptarchiv, Mus. 4109/F/1.

[2] See the letter from Stephen Storace to the English Ambassador in Vienna (London, Brit. Mus. Add. 35538).

PLATE IV

TITLE-PAGE TO THE VOCAL SCORE OF STORACE'S *THE PIRATES*, 1792 *(see p. 267)*
This shows the stage set for Act I, scene I.

The libretto was never published because Sheridan hoped thereby to prevent Covent Garden's staging it—for long he refused to publish his own successful comedies for the same reason—but some items from the score survive in manuscript.[1] The setting is Naples, and many of the details must have come from Storace himself, as also, in all probability, did the back-cloth picture of the Bay of Naples given on the title-page of the vocal score;[2] for a brief period Storace had been trained as an artist. His only serious, as also his only all-sung opera with English words, *Dido, Queen of Carthage* (1792), was a failure, and the music does not survive. The libretto, like that of *Artaxerxes*, was based on Metastasio, and critics found the recitatives wearisome. Also full-length were *The Siege of Belgrade* (1791; the plot and half the music from Martín y Soler's *Una cosa rara*) and *The Cherokee* (1794). Storace's afterpieces were musically much inferior to his full-length operas. By far the best was *No Song No Supper* (1790),[3] an intentionally naïve imitation of Shield's short countrified afterpieces.

[1] E.g., two songs borrowed from Storace's first Italian opera, *Gli sposi malcontenti*, of which a manuscript survives in Dresden, Sächsisches Landeshauptarchiv, Mus. 4109/F/2.
[2] See pl. IV.
[3] Full score (ed. Roger Fiske), *Musica Britannica*, xvi (London, 1959).

Part of the long introduction to an aria in *The Siege of Belgrade* will serve as an example of Viennese influence on Storace's more serious music. This was the last of his vocal scores to indicate the instrumentation, and by standards of the day it was a conscientious publication, yet it is obvious that much has been omitted under the clarinet solo.

Ex. 130

OTHER ASPECTS

Storace's early death was but one of several disasters that beset English opera in the eighteenth century. Another was the disappearance of almost all the manuscript full scores and orchestral parts that must at one time have been in use up and down the country. Most no doubt were burnt in the fires that destroyed both playhouses early in the nineteenth century, but some must have disintegrated with use and been thrown away by Victorian librarians intent on finding space for more fashionable music. The British Museum has a set of orchestral parts of Shield's

Rosina,[1] and the Royal College of Music has manuscript full scores of *Love in a Village* and Storace's *No Song No Supper*.[2] In the Guildhall Library there is a manuscript full score of a pantomime, *Harlequin Captive or The Magic Fire* (Drury Lane 1796), with music mostly by Linley's youngest son, William. Between *Artaxerxes* and the end of the century no other theatrical scores of any substance have survived in complete manuscript.

English operas were sung in part by actors and actresses with musical leanings like Mrs. Jordan and in part by professional singers such as Beard, Mrs. Billington and Nancy Storace. All operas were tailor-made for a particular company. Until Michael Kelly went to Drury Lane in 1789 all male singers sang their top notes falsetto, changing around E or F. Shield took baritones up to a' and tenors up to d". Contralto soloists were almost unknown in opera. All singers, especially sopranos, decorated the vocal line, and about 1801 the decorations Mrs. Billington had sung in *Artaxerxes*, *Love in a Village*, and *The Duenna* were published at the instance of Thomas Busby. About 1780 Domenico Corri in Edinburgh published his lavish three-volume *Select Collection* of songs mainly from English and Italian operas, all of them lightly decorated. Airs by Arne, Dibdin, Shield, and Arnold are included; there is plenty of evidence as to how such songs were sung.

All through the century there was argument as to whether or not the English language was a proper vehicle for recitative. The usual verdict was that its hard consonants and slow gait made it unsuitable, and that opera with spoken dialogue was preferable to the all-sung sort. Other reasons for this view are well put by General John Burgoyne in the preface to the libretto he wrote for Jackson's *The Lord of the Manor:*

> In a representation which is 'to hold a mirror up to nature', and which ought to draw its chief applause from reason, vocal music should be confined to express the feelings and the passions, but never to express the exercising of them. Song, in any action in which reason tells us it would be unnatural to sing, must be preposterous . . . Music, if employed to express action, must be confined to dumb show (as in pantomime) . . . It must not only be restrained from having part in the exercise or action of the passions; care must be also taken, that it does not interrupt or delay events for the issue of which the mind has become eager. It should always be the *accessory*, and not the *principal*, subject of the drama.[3]

Shield and Arnold would have agreed with every word of this. Gilbert, and perhaps Sullivan, would have seen much sense in it. But not Dibdin

[1] Ms. Add. 33815.
[2] RCM 342 and 597.
[3] See also John Brown, *A Dissertation on the rise, union and power, the progressions, separations and corruptions of poetry and music. To which is prefixed, The cure of Saul, a sacred ode*. (London, 1763).

or Storace, who, with longer careers in the theatre and a little luck, might well have upset Burgoyne's widely-held view and given England a repertoire of all-sung classical comic opera of enduring worth.

(b) THE RISE OF RUSSIAN OPERA

By GERALD SEAMAN

FOREIGN OPERA IN RUSSIA

In the reigns of the three Empresses, Anna, Elizabeth, and Catherine II, Russia made the acquaintance of west European opera and some of its leading exponents and in a relatively short period, under the inspiration of their foreign mentors, a school of Russian composers arose, many of whom turned to folk-song for their material.

Russia's acquaintance with European opera began in 1731, when Moscow was visited by two foreign opera companies—one headed by Giovanni Ristori, the other by Johann Kayser—and *Calandro*,[1] Ristoris' three-act *commedia per musica* was given in Moscow on 30 November 1731 (old style); this must be considered the first opera to be performed in Russia.[2] In 1733 Russia was visited by an Italian company, which performed several comedies and intermezzi in St. Petersburg, and these were translated into Russian or German where appropriate. This company stayed till 1735. In the summer of 1735, however, St. Petersburg was visited by a brilliant company of performers, headed by the composer Francesco Araja (1700– c. 67). An opera by Araja, *La forza dell'amore e dell'odio*, was given in Italian at the Winter Palace Theatre on 29 January 1736, translations being made into Russian and German by the poet Trediakovsky and Jakob von Stählin respectively. Between the acts of the opera were inserted ballets. In the succeeding years two further operas by Araja were performed, *Il finto Nino overo la Semiramide riconosciuta* (1737) and *Artaserse* (1738), the libretti of which were by Metastasio. After *Artaserse* the opera company left Russia and no operas were staged during the last two years of Anna's reign, though Araja's services were retained. The coronation of the Empress Elizabeth was celebrated by a performance of Hasse's *La Clemenza di Tito* with additional numbers by Luigi Madonis and Domenico dall'Oglio. It is possible that the Court audiences made the acquaintance of *Singspiel* during the visit of Neuber's German dramatic company in 1740.

[1] Robert Aloys Mooser, *Annales de la musique et des musiciens en Russie au XVIII siècle*, i (Geneva, 1948), pp. 50–1, 80–1.

[2] All dates are according to the Russian calendar which in the eighteenth century was eleven days behind that of the Western Gregorian calendar.

It was not till 1755, however, that an opera was given in the Russian language and played by Russian artists. This was *Tsefal i Prokris* (Cephalus and Procris) a typical Italian *opera seria*, with music by Araja and words by Sumarokov. Its première took place at the St. Petersburg Court Theatre on 27 February 1755.

During the following decades Russia was visited by a whole stream of foreign opera composers, among them Galuppi, Traetta, Cimarosa, Sarti, Manfredini, and Paisiello, whose celebrated comic opera *Il Barbiere di Siviglia* was written specially for the Imperial Court in 1782. The activities of these and others served to familiarize the future school of Russian composers with the principal forms of European opera—*opera seria, opera buffa, Singspiel, intermezzo, opéra comique*, and the *comédie mêlée d'ariettes*. Such works were performed not only at the Court theatres but at the Petersburg Smolny Institute for Daughters of the Nobility, in the private theatres of the great landowners such as Sheremetev, and at the public theatres of Locatelli, Maddox, and Knipper.[1]

THE BEGINNINGS OF NATIONAL OPERA

Russian opera, in the strict sense, began in the last third of the eighteenth century and from its inception showed strong links with Russian folk-lore and folk music. About one hundred operas were written in the course of the last years of the eighteenth century, but of these the music of only about thirty (consisting mostly of manuscript scores and orchestral parts) has survived.[2] Of thirty operas examined, fifteen appeared to make use of Russian or Ukrainian folk music, including at least fifty-five identifiable folk-songs. Although several of the composers of these operas were foreigners, it is remarkable that they too utilized folk material in order to give their music national colouring. At first folk-song was employed mostly in the form of simple quotations, but by the end of the century composers were able to write freely in the folk idiom. In the early period composers sometimes exercised little judgement in the choice of song. Melodies were distorted in order to make the words fit, and harmonies alien to the spirit of the original tune were employed in the accompaniment. In the works of the better composers the selection of folk-songs is more careful and in some cases the melodies appear to have been collected by the composer himself. At

---

[1] A comprehensive list of operas and other large-scale vocal works performed in Russia in the eighteenth century will be found in Mooser, *Opéras, intermezzos, ballets, cantates, oratorios joués en Russie durant le XVIII siècle* (3rd edn., Basle, 1964).

[2] The majority of these are preserved in the Gos.-Tsentral'naya muzïkal'naya biblioteka pri teatre im. S. M. Kirova, Leningrad.

least two composers attempted to suggest folk polyphony (a characteristic feature of Russian folk music), while others wrote successfully in the folk idiom. A common device in early Russian opera is the inclusion of genre scenes such as the peasant wedding ritual, examples of which occur in *Mel'nik-koldun, obmanshchik i svat* (The Miller-magician, Deceiver and Match-maker), and *Sanktpeterburgskïy gostinïy dvor* (The St. Petersburg Bazaar).

The underlying principle of all Russian opera in the eighteenth century is simplicity, the reason being that the operas were for the most part sung by actors, who were incapable of singing anything complex. It is understandable, therefore, that the model followed by the early Russian opera composers was not Italian *opera buffa* with its brilliant vocal writing and sparkling recitative but French *opéra comique* with its greater economy and simplicity and its employment of spoken dialogue. In early Russian opera the overture and the solo aria are the chief forms, though ensemble numbers and choruses are also encountered. The orchestral writing is likewise of the simplest construction, though an essentially Russian feature is the occasional employment of pizzicato strings to suggest the sounds of balalaikas.[1] As regards the libretti, often the subject is of a satirical nature. In *Neschastie ot karetï* (The Misfortune of having a Carriage), for instance, the theme is that of a landowner who is quite willing to sell two of his serfs in order to purchase a new French carriage, till he suddenly discovers that they can speak a few words of French, a factor which will give him added distinction in the eyes of his neighbours. The *St. Petersburg Bazaar* is conceived in the spirit of Molière and satirizes the mendacity of the times. Other operas take the form of folk comedy or are concerned with the world of fantasy. In a number of cases the language is not a literary one but employs folk idioms and peasant dialect.[2]

The first Russian opera almost certainly by a native composer appeared in the year 1772. This was *Anyuta* with libretto by M. V. Popov, which was performed in Russian by the Court Singers at Tsarskoe Selo on 26 August 1772. The name of the composer is not known and the music has not survived. However, the libretto suggests that folk elements

[1] Four vocal scores of Russian operas were published during the eighteenth century—fragments of Kerzelli's *Derevenskoy vorozheya* (Moscow, 1778), Pashkevich's *Fevey* (St. Petersburg, 1789), Martín y Soler's *Gore–bogatïr' Kosometovich* (St. Petersburg, 1789), and *Pesnolyubie* (St. Petersburg, 1790). An orchestral score of the opera *Nachal'noe upravlenie Olega* by Pashkevich, Canobbio, and Sarti was published at St. Petersburg (1791). A piano score of Martín y Soler's ballet, *Didon abandonnée*, was issued at St. Petersburg in 1792.

[2] For some excerpts from Russian opera libretti of the period, see S. L. Ginzburg, *Russkiy muzïkal'nïy teatr 1700–1835* (Moscow–Leningrad, 1940). For precise details and sources of the libretti, see Grigoriy Bernandt, *Slovar' oper vervïe postavlennïkh ili izdannïkh v dorevolyutsionnoy Rossii i v SSSR/1736–1959* (Moscow, 1962), and Mooser, *Opéras, intermezzos, ballets*.

may have been employed.¹ The year 1777 saw the appearance of an opera *Lyubovnik-koldun* (The Lover-magician) with words by N. P. Nikolev and music by M. F. Kerzelli. Again the music is lost, but as fourteen out of a total of twenty-four songs are specifically marked 'golosa'—i.e. are intended to be sung to folk tunes or popular melodies —the presence of a folk element is beyond question.

The first Russian opera to be preserved in its entirety is Zorin's *Pererozhdenie* (The Rebirth), which was first performed on 8 January 1777 in Moscow.² Of the composer we know practically nothing, though most probably, like Sokolovsky, he was an orchestral player at the Maddox or Locatelli Theatre in Moscow. The surviving score is of special interest in that it is the first extant example of a Russian opera partly based on folk melodies, melodies which later appeared in Prač's well-known collection. As a composer Zorin was not without powers of invention but he was handicapped by a poor technique.

THE MILLER-MAGICIAN

The most important year in early Russian opera, however, is 1779, since it possibly saw the appearance of the three operas, *The Miller-magician*, *The St. Petersburg Bazaar*, and *The Misfortune of having a Carriage*, referred to above.

The Miller-magician, the first Russian opera to achieve real success, was performed for the first time in Moscow on 20 January 1779. The libretto was by Aleksandr Ablesimov, a gifted playwright, who himself stipulated the employment of a number of well-known folk-songs, which were sung to words of his own. The subject of the opera is very simple and clearly owes something to Rousseau's *Le Devin du village*, which had perhaps been performed at the Moscow orphanage in 1778.³ It consists of three short acts and employs spoken dialogue. The music is made up of short songs and was arranged in the first instance (in accordance with Ablesimov's directions) by Sokolovsky, a violinist at the Moscow Russian Theatre. It appears, however, that Sokolovsky's music was later revised by Fomin and it was under Fomin's name that a vocal score of the opera, prepared by Konstantin Albrekht, the result of further nineteenth-century revision, was published by

[1] Aleksandr S. Rabinovich, *Russkaya opera do Glinki* (Moscow, 1948), and Tamara Livanova, *Russkaya muzïkal'naya kul'tura XVIII veka*, 2 vols. (Moscow, 1952 and 1953). These should be checked with Mooser, since they contain inaccuracies.
[2] Score in Leningrad Gos.-Tsen. bibl., Ms. IIZ 3862. Excerpts in S. L. Ginzburg, *Istoriya russkoy muzïki v notnïkh obraztsakh*, i (Moscow–Leningrad, rev. ed., 1968), pp. 60–4.
[3] See Mooser, *Opéras, intermezzos, ballets*, p. 42.

Jurgenson in 1884.¹ The greater part of the music of *The Miller-magician*² is based on folk-songs, most of which appeared later in the collections of Prač, Trutovsky, and Gerstenberg. In some cases (as in Anyuta's song 'Kaby ya, mlada, uverena bïla') the folk melody is used unaltered in the first part of an aria, and is then followed by a second section, perhaps related to the first by means of similar musical figures. *The Miller-magician*, like several other operas of the eighteenth century, includes a *devichnik* scene (a farewell party given by the bride-to-be to her girl-friends on the night preceding the wedding) at the beginning of the third act. This consists of three wedding songs arranged for two-part female chorus, but whether they are authentic melodies it is impossible to tell. The remaining numbers are written either in imitation of urban folk-songs or in a general light-hearted manner typical of the period. Of a different character is the overture, long ascribed to Fomin but now proved almost certainly to have been composed by Ernest Vančura as the first movement of a 'Russian symphony'. The overture is unique among Russian music of the time in being based on two folk-songs.³

MATINSKY, PASHKEVICH, AND OTHERS

Another opera which perhaps appeared in 1779—generally known as *Sanktpeterburgskïy gostinïy dvor* (The St. Petersburg Bazaar)—is of such interest that it deserves to be examined in greater detail. The first version is generally supposed to have been first performed in the capital on 26 December 1779 at Knipper's Free Theatre. However, this date is questioned by Yury Keldïsh, who adduces evidence to suggest that it took place three years later—in 1782.⁴ At any rate the opera reappeared in a second version under its proper title, *Kak pozhivesh, tak i proslïvesh* (As you live, so are you judged), and was performed at Court on 2 February 1792.⁵ The music and libretto were written probably in both cases by Mikhail Matinsky (1750–182?), serf and illegitimate son of Count Yaguzhinsky and a man of exceptional talents as translator, teacher, and author.⁶ *The St. Petersburg Bazaar* is outstanding from

---
¹ The earliest surviving materials are a set of orchestral parts preserved in Leningrad Gos.-Tsen. bibl. MS. I 1 762, dating from 1806, though even these are incomplete.
² The excerpts in the first edition of Ginzburg, *Istoriya* (1940), pp. 161 ff., are based on the Jurgenson edition and should be neglected; those in the revised edition, pp. 113 ff., are based on the 1806 set of parts.
³ Revised edition of Ginzburg, *Istoriya*, p. 477.
⁴ *Russkaya muzïka XVIII veka* (Moscow, 1965), pp. 315–16.
⁵ The score of this second version is in Leningrad Gos.-Tsen. bibl., Ms. I l. M 343. Excerpts in Ginzburg, *Istoriya*, pp. 139 ff., and Rabinovich, op. cit., pp. 187 ff.
⁶ See Mooser, *Annales*, ii, p. 269, and V. A. Prokofyev, 'Mikhail Matinskiy i evo opera "Sanktpeterburgskïy gostinïy dvor"' in *Muzïka i muzïkal'nïy bït staroy Rossii*, ed. A. Finagin (Leningrad, 1927), p. 58.

both the literary and musical points of view, since it presents a vivid picture of contemporary life in which the everyday language of the merchants is used. Like *The Miller-magician* the opera employs folk melodies. The melodies of the seven wedding choruses, heard at the beginning of Act II, are remarkable in that they are not to be found in any collection and seem to have been written down by the composer exactly as they were performed, though some of the words are found later in Prač. The overture, which is conceivably the work of Pashkevich who played some part in the writing of the second version of the opera, is one of the best examples of its kind in early Russian music; and at one point fragments of the two folk tunes forming the overture's principal thematic material are heard simultaneously on the basses and clarinets:

Ex. 131

Of a total of twenty-seven numbers at least twelve make use of folk music, and folk-songs are introduced into the two big numbers (Nos. 25 and 27, a sextet and final chorus) heard at the end of the work. The orchestra consists of two flutes, two clarinets, two horns, two trumpets, timpani, and strings, and the orchestration is not without a certain picturesqueness. In keeping with the fashion of the times the names of the characters also provide an insight into their personalities. Thus, Skvalygin means 'miser', 'grasp-all'; Kryuchkodey, 'caviller', 'pettifogger'; Khavronya, 'a sow'; while Pryamikov means 'an upright man'.

The third opera to appear in the year 1779, *Neschastie ot kareti*, was written to a libretto by Knyazhnin with music by the serf composer Pashkevich (*c.* 1742–1800) and was given its première at the Hermitage

Theatre on 7 November 1779.[1] It is of lesser stature than *The Miller-magician* or *The St. Petersburg Bazaar* and makes little use of the folk element.

Before turning to the works of Fomin, one of the most gifted Russian operatic composers of the eighteenth century, brief mention must also be made of certain other operas of interest.

In *Sbitenshchik* (The *Sbiten*-seller)[2] by the Czech composer A. Bullandt, which was first performed in 1783 or 1784, one comic aria appears to be based on the traditional cries of the *sbiten*-seller.[3] In *Fevey*,[4] written to a libretto by Catherine II with music by Pashkevich and first performed in 1786, of particular interest is the use of a 'changing background' accompaniment to Ledmer's song in Act II ('Kak u nashevo soseda'), a device which anticipates Glinka. A special place is occupied in Act IV of the same opera by the so-called 'Kalmïk chorus', in which Pashkevich has made a deliberate attempt to imitate oriental colouring. *Khrabrïy i smelïy vityaz' Akhrideich* (The Brave and Bold Knight Akhrideich), or, as it was later called, *Ivan Tsarevich*, was also written to a libretto by Catherine, the music being by the same Vančura who was probably responsible for the overture to *The Miller-magician*. This opera[5] (which was first performed in 1787) makes use of a number of folk-songs,

Ex. 132

Po - slu - shay - te me - nya lest - ny go - spo - da,

---

[1] Score in Leningrad, Gos.–Tsen. bibl. Ms. I 1 п 222. Excerpts in Ginzburg, *Istoriya*, pp. 65 ff.

[2] *Sbiten*—a Russian drink of hot water, spices, and honey.

[3] Score in Leningrad, Gos.–Tsen. bibl. Ms. I 1 Б907. The aria is printed in Ginzburg, op. cit., pp. 461 ff.

[4] Score in Leningrad, Gos.–Tsen. bibl. Ms. I 1 п 222. Excerpts including Ledmer's Song and the Kalmïk chorus, in Ginzburg, op. cit., pp. 99 ff.

[5] Score of *Ivan Tsarevich* in Leningrad, Gos.–Tsen. bibl. Ms. I 1 B171-5.

[musical notation with lyrics: "de - lit mne vas do - sta - los che - re - da, de - lit vas." and "Mne do - sta - los che - re - da."]

(Listen to me, flattering ladies and gentlemen, it is my turn to share [something] among you.)

including a setting of the well-known 'Vo pole berëza stoyala', subsequently employed by Tchaikovsky in his Fourth Symphony. Compared with Prač's accompaniment to the song as it appears in his collection, Vančura's is fuller and more detailed (Ex. 132).

Of the remaining operas (both to libretti by Catherine), *Gore-bogatïr' Kosometovich* (Kosometovich, the Woeful Knight) was written to music by the Spaniard Martín y Soler immediately on his arrival in Russia in 1789.[1] The overture employs three folk tunes, all of which appeared later in Prač.[2] The foreign composers Sarti and Canobbio were also partly responsible for the music to the monumental opera *Nachal'noe upravlenie Olega, podrazhanie Shakespiru bez sokkhraneniya featral'nïkh obïknovennïkh pravil* (The First Government of Oleg, in imitation of Shakespeare without preservation of the customary theatrical laws) (1790). This was a large-scale work in five acts in the form not so much of an opera as of a play with musical episodes.[3] Folk music is employed throughout the work, folk-songs (occurring in Prač) being introduced

[1] Score in Leningrad, Gos.–Tsen. bibl. Ms. I 1 M 292.
[2] A piano duet arrangement of the overture is given in Ginzburg, op. cit., original edition, p. 383, though not in the 1968 edition.
[3] Full score (St. Petersburg, 1791); there is a copy in the British Museum.

by Canobbio into the overture and the entr'actes to the second and third acts. Canobbio's treatment of the folk-song 'Pri dolinushke' in the entr'acte to Act III is quite imaginative, the tune being used as a kind of ritornello.[1] The only Russian composer to provide material for *Oleg* was Pashkevich, whose three wedding choruses appear in the second act. These are for three-part female chorus and make highly original use of folk-material.[2] The second contains typical folk features, notably the occasional octaves between the extreme voices, the shape of the melodic phrases, the cadence, and, of course, the words:

Ex. 133

Presto

Po - se - ne -chkam, se - ne -chkam tut kho - di - la, gu -

(accompaniment omitted.)

- lya - la mo - lo - da - ya bo - ya - ri - nya

(A noble young lady was walking up and down the porch.)

As Keldish points out, the opening is almost identical with that of the well-known 'Slava' introduced by Beethoven in the second 'Razumovsky' quartet and Mussorgsky in *Boris Godunov*. Sarti's music is of interest in that, in attempting to underline the classical nature of the verse (part of Pindar's *Odes* and Euripides' *Alcestis* are used in the course of the action), he employed music written in what he considered to be the ancient modes. The march in the third act (also written by Sarti), scored for four trumpets, two trombones, two serpents, and triangle is a rare example of a march for wind instruments in Russian music of the eighteenth century surviving in score.

FOMIN

The most gifted composer of early Russian opera was Evstigney Ipatevich Fomin (1761–1800), who, like Matinsky, Berezovsky, and

---

[1] The entr'acte to Act III in Ginzburg, op. cit. (original edition only), p. 373. A chorus by Sarti from the same opera, pp. 375 ff.
[2] Yury Keldïsh, *Russkaya muzïka XVIII veka* (Moscow, 1965), pp. 311 ff.

Bortnyansky, received his musical training in Italy.[1] Immediately on his return to St. Petersburg in 1786 he composed the five-act ballet opera *Novgorodskïy bogatïr' Boeslavich* (Boeslavich, the Novgorod Bogatyr), with a libretto by Catherine II. The subject of this was taken 'from a fairy-tale, Russian songs, and other compositions'. Although the music has survived only in the form of orchestral parts,[2] it is apparent from these that the composer was able to write freely in the Russian folk idiom. A curious feature is that one ballet represents fisticuffs ('kulachnïy boi').[3]

The following year saw Fomin's best-known opera *Yamshchiki na podstave* (The Post-drivers at the Post-station)[4]—a one-act comic opera with libretto by N. A. Lvov, who collaborated with Prach in his folk-song collection. The story is very slender and describes how the villain, Filka Prolaza (lit. 'Filka the sly one'), endeavours to have the hero, Timofey, called up as a recruit instead of himself. The plot misfires, however, and with the help of a passing officer Filka is himself conscripted. The dialogue in this is quite well developed. The folk-songs employed are diverse in character ranging from the slow protracted ('protyazhnaya') song to the lively *chastushka* type. Again Fomin writes music in the folk idiom and this is employed not only in the solo numbers but in the choral ones also. Of the total of eleven numbers, two (the overture and a march) are instrumental. The overture is an excellent example of its kind and to some commentators has suggested a troika whirling across the Russian plain. It employs two folk-songs, the first subject being the folk melody 'Kapitanskaya doch'.[5]

Ex. 134

[1] Fomin was elected a member of the Bologna Accademia filarmonica in 1785 and on all three of his surviving orchestral scores he signed himself 'Academico filarmonico'. For accounts of his work, see Rabinovich, op. cit., pp. 85–105; Finagin, 'Evst. Fomin, Zhizn' i tvorchestvo' in *Muzïka i muzïkal'nïy bït staroy Rossii*, p. 70 (though this has a number of inaccuracies); B. Dobrokhotov, *E. I. Fomin* (Moscow–Leningrad, 1949); G. F. Fesechko, 'Novïe materialy o kompozïtorakh P. A. Skokove i E. I. Fomine', in *Muzïkal'noe nasledstvo*, ii, part 1 (Moscow, 1966), p. 9.
[2] Parts in Leningrad, Gos.-Tsen. bibl. Ms. I 1 ф 762.
[3] Excerpts from this and other ballet-numbers in Keldïsh, op. cit., pp. 329 ff.
[4] Score in Leningrad, Gos.-Tsen. bibl. Ms. I 1 ф 762.
[5] Printed in Rabinovich, op. cit., p. 92.

The second chorus of the opera, 'Vïsoko sokol letaet', is striking on account of the fact that it attempts to reproduce the characteristic features of folk *podgolosnaya* ('underpart') polyphony. Though this bears only a slight resemblance to genuine folk choral polyphony, nevertheless it is of historical importance as a precursor of a practice that was later frequently employed in Russian opera. The third number is a solo song 'Retivo serdtse molodetskoe' sung by Timofey, in which he laments his forthcoming enforced separation from his wife. The strings are marked *con sordino*. This takes the form of a protracted song essentially in the urban-folk tradition. The melody is almost identical with the tune as it appears later in Prač. Of the other numbers, the trio with chorus (No. 8) uses variations on the folk-song 'Vo pole berëza stoyala', the orchestral accompaniment imitating the sound of balalaikas.[1] No. 9 is a short instrumental march-intermezzo which leads directly into the final chorus. This consists of a Russian dance theme, 'Vy razdaytes, rasstupites, dobrïe lyudi', accompanied by an unchanging eight-bar figure in the bass.[2] The full orchestra (comprising flutes, oboes, clarinets, bassoons, trumpets, horns, timpani, and strings) is heard for the first time.

Of Fomin's other major operas *Amerikantsy* (The Americans)[3] and *Zolotoe yabloko* (The Golden Apple), which were performed in 1788 and 1803 respectively, neither makes use of the folk element. What is generally held to be Fomin's best work, however, is the two-act melodrama *Orfey i Evredika* (Orpheus and Euridice) which was written in 1791–2 and based on a libretto by Knyazhnin.[4] Fomin's *Orfey i Evredika* was by no means the first time this subject had been treated in Russia, for Torelli had already made a setting of the same Knyazhnin libretto a decade previously, while Gluck's *Orfeo* had had its St. Petersburg première on 13 December 1782. Fomin's melodrama was successful from the start and was performed frequently in Petersburg and Moscow from 1792 to 1802. Apart from the adventurousness of the harmonic and melodic language, *Orfey* abounds in musical innovations, not the least being the employment of two piccolos and the introduction of a Russian horn band to strengthen a chorus of bass voices (symbolizing the Gods) heard off-stage and to accompany the final dance of the Furies: an anticipation of the men's chorus heard in the giant's head in Glinka's

---

[1] The overture and the three numbers just mentioned are printed in Ginzburg, op. cit., pp. 304–31; Timofey's song also in Livanova, op. cit., ii, pp. 193–6, and Dieter Lehmann, *Russlands Oper und Singspiel in der zweiten Hälfte des 18. Jahrhunderts* (Leipzig, 1958), pp. 117–19.
[2] Quoted in Keldïsh, op. cit., p. 340.
[3] Overture and four numbers in Ginzburg, op. cit., pp. 332–82.
[4] Score in Leningrad, Gos.–Tsen. bibl. Ms. I 1 ф 762.

Ruslan. The overture is well written, and one of its themes occurs again in the first number of the melodrama.[1]

No survey of early Russian opera would be complete without mention of the part played by Dmitry Bortnyansky (1751–1825), whose three operas *Creonte*, *Alcide*, and *Quinto Fabio* were written during his residence in Italy. On his return he received an Imperial commission to write a further two operas—*Le Faucon* (1786) and *Le Fils rival* (1787), the libretti of which were written by F. H. Lafermière.[2] They are models of their kind, faultlessly written and in impeccable taste, but void of any national colouring.

The evolution of Russian opera was notably quick: in the space of a mere thirty years it rose from literally nothing to a standard of competent professionalism. Although Russian composers of the period were incapable of undertaking anything of a complex nature, nevertheless, within the framework of the melodrama, the *Singspiel*, and the *opéra comique*, they were able to achieve some significant successes, and through their willingness to draw on the native musical tradition they produced a number of works which are as unique as the cultural environment which engendered them.

(c) SPANISH OPERA

By Gerald Abraham

ITALIAN OPERA IN SPAIN

The accession in 1759 of Charles III, who had already been King of Naples since 1735, brought considerable changes at the Spanish court. Unlike his brother and sister-in-law, Charles was no passionate lover of music; Farinelli was pensioned off and during the period 1767–76 only twelve Italian operas were performed at court. The most notable of these was Piccinni's *La buona figliuola* (1769), but it is significant that this had not only been given in Barcelona (1761) and Seville (1764), but in a Spanish adaptation, *La buena hija*, with additional music by Pablo Esteve (d. 1794), in Madrid itself (1765) before it reached the court theatre at Aranjuez. (In such adaptations, *recitativo secco* was replaced by spoken dialogue.) Perhaps even more significant is the fact that, when the Infanta Maria Luisa was married to Leopold of Tuscany in 1764,

---

[1] Excerpts from *Orfey* (including the overture) in Ginzburg, op. cit., pp. 383–405.
[2] On Bortnyansky, see B. Dobrokhotov, *D. S. Bortnyansky* (Moscow, 1950). Manuscript copies of both these opera scores in London, Brit. Mus., Egerton 2506 and 2507.

the festivities included a performance of Gassmann's *Gli uccellatori*, not with Goldoni's libretto but in a Spanish translation, *Los cazadores*, by Ramón de la Cruz,[1] who took the place Cañizares had filled in the previous generation as the leading Spanish librettist.[2] Thus, while Italian opera no longer enjoyed special royal favour, it flourished in the public theatres of Madrid, Barcelona, Seville, Valencia, and other centres, both in its original form and language and also in adaptations in the form of *zarzuelas*. It was even composed by natives; in 1760 a setting of Metastasio's *Antigono* by José Durán, a Catalan apparently trained in Naples, was produced in Barcelona, and a generation later the Valencian Vicente Martín y Soler (1754–1806) won European fame with *Una cosa rara* in 1786 and went on to contribute even to Russian opera,[3] while the numerous Italian operas[4] of the Portuguese, Joãs Carvalho (1745–98) enjoyed great success in his own country.

At the same time the *zarzuela* was given fresh life by the libretti of Ramón de la Cruz; other native forms of musical play developed, and one must ask to what extent these were influenced by the vogue of Italian opera. Apart from the frank cannibalization of operas into *zarzuelas*, not very much. As José Subirá has put it:[5] 'Our composers, in their cultivation of national genres, especially the *tonadilla escénica*, certainly introduced in these works superficial traits of Italian vocal music, turning them into clichés belonging to the common stock. But operas, actual operas, were a different matter.'

THE LATER *ZARZUELA*

Ramón de la Cruz began his career as a librettist in 1757 with *Quien complace a la deidad acierta a sacrificar* (He who pleases the god makes the right sacrifice), composed by the oboist, Manuel Pla, a typical eighteenth-century affair of a king with a brother who pretends to his throne. Cruz continued for ten years to produce both original works and adaptations of Italian operas by Bertoni, Giuseppe Scarlatti, Galuppi, and others, but it was not until 1768 that he met the musical collaborator he needed: Antonio Rodriguez de Hita (1704–87), up to then known only as a church-musician and author of a short treatise on the study of counterpoint, *Diapasón instructivo* (Madrid, 1757).[6] The first fruit of their partnership was a *zarzuela heróica*, *La Briseida*, produced

---

[1] See Emilio Cotarelo y Mori, *Don Ramón de la Cruz* (Madrid, 1899).
[2] See Vol. V, chap. 2.
[3] See supra, p. 277.
[4] Manuscript scores in Lisbon, Bibl. da Ajuda.
[5] *Historia de la música teatral en España* (Barcelona, 1945), p. 122.
[6] Hita's views are summarised by Rafaël Mitjana in Albert Lavignac and Lionel de La Laurencie, *Encyclopédie de la musique*, 1re partie, iv (Paris, 1920), p. 2118.

at the Teatro del Principe, Madrid, on 11 July 1768, all the parts except that of Calcas (bass) being sung by women. Between the two acts was performed a *sainete* (intermezzo) on a Don Quixote subject. *Briseida* was an enormous success, even financially, but it was still an Italianate opera, with a Homeric subject treated in the manner of Metastasio. But Cruz was not happy with true opera; in the 'prologue' to the ten-volume collection of his dramatic works (Madrid, 1786–96) he remarks on 'the incredibility of music in many situations'. 'How can one endure or accept that a father finding his son dead, a gallant discovering his lady in the arms of another, a lady repulsing a gallant soliciting favours abhorrent to her, should expound the most grievous passions in an aria? And when an actor is in a great hurry, how opportune is this for a cantata lasting, with ritornellos and repeats, a quarter of an hour?' The objections are familiar enough but they come strangely from an extremely successful librettist.

Less than two months after the production of *Briseida*, Cruz struck out on the right track. On 3 September at the same theatre he brought out *Las segadoras de Vallecas* (The reapers of Vallecas), a *zarzuela burlesca*, again with music by Hita. *Las segadoras* is essentially the Old Testament story of Ruth transposed into terms of more or less contemporary Galicia, with scenes and characters from popular life and imitations of folk-instruments, such as the bagpipes (*gaita gallega*), in the music—a formula which gave the eighteenth-century *zarzuela* twenty years of new life. On Christmas Day of the same year another composer, Pablo Esteve—the adaptor of *La buona figluola*—produced *Los jardineros de Aranjuez* in the same vein and to his own libretto; Esteve was highly literate and in the 'prologue' to the libretto (Madrid, 1768)[1] he emphasises both that his work is 'puramente Castellana' and that the audience should be familiar with the *words* of the 'airs, cavatinas and cantilenas'. However he composed a Cruz libretto, *Los zagales de Genil* (The young shepherds of Genil), the following year. But it was Cruz's collaboration with Hita which produced the outstanding masterpiece of the genre: *Las labradoras de Murcia* (Teatro del Principe, 16 September 1769). Like *Las segadoras*, it is a pastoral but concerned with Murcian silk-workers instead of Galician reapers. The popular superstition that the sound of thunder is fatal to silkworms, and must be drowned at all costs, was made the pretext for a spectacular finale to Act I when the stage fills with workers singing and dancing the *jota murciana* and playing guitars and mandolines, tambourines and castanets; similarly the Second Act ends with choral *seguidillas*. But the score is by no means merely an affair of national colour and comic

[1] See Mitjana. op. cit., p. 2167.

characterisation; Hita could also strike a serious note, as in the calmer middle section of the agitated song sung in Act II by the heroine Teresa as she waits for her lover.[1]

Ex. 135

O cielo que miras mi mal rigoroso, mi mal rigoroso,

(O heaven that looks on me so harshly . . .)

Las labradores was Hita's last *zarzuela burlesca*, though he wrote a *Scipión en Cartagena* (1770). Cruz's later libretti were set by other composers, e.g. *Las Foncarraleras* (The girls of Fuencarral) by Ventura Galván (1772)[2] and *El licenciado Farfulla* (The lawyer Farfulla) (1776), based largely on popular airs with some original music by Antonio Rosales, which enjoyed enormous popularity and, with various modifications, went on being performed for more than thirty years. In the three-act *comedia de música, La espigadera* (The gleaner) (1778), another variation on the theme of Ruth, and its sequel *La espigadera y la vendimia* (The gleaner and the grape-harvest) Cruz collaborated once more with Esteve, who composed a descriptive overture depicting night, the dawn chorus of birds, and sunrise. These really marked the end of the eighteenth-century *zarzuela*, for as Subirá says[3] it lasted only as long as Ramón de la Cruz provided libretti.

THE *TONADILLA ESCÉNICA*

The—usually—two-act *zarzuela* was always rivalled and ultimately supplanted as a popular antidote to Italian opera by miniature forms

[1] Quoted from Mitjana, op. cit., p. 2165. The score is in Madrid, Bibl. Municipal.
[2] Score in Madrid, Bibl. Municipal.
[3] Op. cit., p. 131.

such as the *zarzuelita* (one-act *zarzuela*), the already mentioned *sainete* or intermezzo, and the *tonadilla escénica*, of which the last is by far the most significant.[1] Like the *sainete*, it originated as a quasi-parasitic form: first as a solo song (*tonadilla*) in another theatrical piece, then a dialogue, and finally a short independent piece for as few as two or three characters (*tonadilla a dúo* or *a tres*) or for the whole company (*tonadilla general*). It is, in Subirá's definition, 'a short comic opera lasting no more than twenty minutes, to serve as interlude in a theatrical performance'. They were ephemeras, produced in vast numbers and seldom performed for more than a few days—although individual songs from them might live on. The composers included most of those mentioned in connection with the *zarzuela*—Esteve, Galván, Rosales—as well as many others.

The outstanding composer of theatrical *tonadillas* at the beginning of their heyday was the Catalan flautist Luis Misón (d. 1766), a member of the royal orchestra who became its director in 1756. Misón wrote only three *zarzuelas* but a great number of *tonadillas*.[2] One of these, *Los ciegos* (The blind men) (1758) has been published in full score[3] and is typical of this slight but distinctive genre. The form is common to many of them:

1. Introduction: presentation of the characters and situation.
2. Main part: often a series of strophic verses.
3. Finale: *seguidillas*, with free expansion in the middle part, or sometimes in the form of *tirana* or even *polacca*.

Los ciegos has three characters, Relación, Gaceta and Diario; the orchestra consists of oboes (in the plural but always playing in unison, and almost always doubling the first violins), two horns, first and second violins, *violón* and *contrabajo*. (The viola appears so rarely in Spanish theatre music of this period that its occasional use, as in Rodríguez de Hita's *Labradoras*, calls for comment.) Each blind man is introduced in turn by three or four Adagio bars based on a single figure, coming to rest on a long-held chord, above which each announces in monotone the contents of what he is selling: Relación, 'New narrative and curious ballad which gives an account and clear outline of the great affair that happened between a coachman, an innkeeper, a valet, a mason . . .' (on G); Gaceta, 'Great news. The Gazette. Booklets and prints for learning the art of cooking, reckoning, adding, subtracting,

---

[1] The standard works on the subject are by Subirá: *La tonadilla escénica* (three vols., of which the third consists of libretti and transcriptions of the music, Madrid, 1928–30); *Tonadillas teatrales inéditas; libretos y partituras* (Madrid, 1932); *Los maestros de la tonadilla escénica* (Barcelona, 1933).
[2] List in *Die Musik in Geschichte und Gegenwart*, ix, col. 368.
[3] Subirá, *Tonadillas teatrales inéditas*, following p. 283.

multiplying . . .' (on C); Diario, 'Economic diary. Sales, losses or findings; curious things that anyone may see who gives me two *cuartos* . . .' (on A). Each instrumental ritornello is a little louder and in a different key: *con sordina* cadencing in C; *sin sordina* cadencing in F; *ff* cadencing in D; the rest of the piece is entirely in D major. The central part of *Los ciegos* consists of an orchestral *jota*, to which Relación at first sings his ballad, but he breaks off and all three speak against the music: 'Business is bad', 'Let's go somewhere else'. Presently they decide to sing and the piece ends with their *seguidillas*, the first two bars of which are borrowed from the *jota*:

Ex. 136

(My unhappy love, you lasted briefly.)

It is surprising that such an ingenuous form of art should have existed so long, but its decline came—around 1790—through the very loss of its ingenuousness and raciness. It expanded in form, sometimes even introducing choruses, lost its element of satire, and became 'bourgeois and moralistic'. Worst of all, it began to borrow elements from Italian opera; in the *seguidillas epilogales*[1] of *Los signos del año* (The signs of the zodiac) (1785) Esteve makes the solo voice compete in coloratura echo-effects with two trumpets. Finally, like the *zarzuela* before it, the *tonadilla escénica* succumbed altogether to the rivalry of *opera buffa*.

[1] Printed in full score by Subirá, ibid., musical supplement, p. 18.

IV

CHURCH MUSIC AND ORATORIO

By Edward Olleson

STYLISTIC PROBLEMS IN SACRED MUSIC

The second half of the eighteenth century, unlike the first, was not typically a period of great choral music. At its best it produced some supreme masterpieces of church music and oratorio, but the Age of Enlightenment clearly had its centre of gravity not here but in the fields of instrumental music and opera. Choral music underwent little of the organic growth that was shaping and transforming the symphony, string quartet, and concerto; rather than developing inwardly, it tended more to mirror the stylistic and formal developments that were taking place in other genres. The Italian *missa solemnis* was written by the same composers, for the same singers, and to a considerable extent on the same musical principles as was the *opera seria*. A solo aria in a Mass by Mozart may well be in the same idiom and form as a movement from one of his concertos. The six great Masses that Haydn wrote after his final return from London have been called the composer's 'symphonic legacy'.

This process of cross-fertilization between musical genres was a fruitful one, but it also had its dangers. The oratorio, as a dramatic form, could properly employ operatic means. In church music, however, the problem was more acute. There is today little sympathy with the view that an essential difference must exist between sacred and secular idioms, and that the operatic and instrumental style of the eighteenth century was inherently unsuitable for sacred music. At the same time, there is no denying that the wholesale adoption of the methods of the opera house by composers for the church, without regard for the differences in musical function, could give rise to works that were little more than sacred contrafacta, and frankly out of place. Burney was one of many writers who criticized the sacred music of their time for its 'secularity':

I do not call every modern oratorio, mass, or motet, *church music:* as the same compositions to different words would do equally well, indeed often better, for the stage. But by *Musica di Chiesa*, properly so called, I mean grave and scientific compositions for voices only, of which the excellence consists more in good harmony, learned modulation, and fugues upon ingenious and sober subjects, than in light airs and turbulent accompaniments.[1]

Many composers of Burney's generation, without perhaps wishing to

[1] *The Present State of Music in Germany* (London, 1773), i, pp. 329–30.

commit themselves to his funereal prescription, would have agreed with him in principle.

The problem of style in sacred music was one of which the eighteenth century was well aware. It is no defence of 'operatic' church music–if indeed any defence is needed—to say that it was the product of an innocent age which made no stylistic distinction between sacred and secular. On the contrary, the rift between the two was already long established. There was a very real, if not always clearly defined, concept of a 'true church style'. Some composers, Haydn and Mozart among them, chose to use the current language of their time for their sacred music. But there were many who preferred a deliberately archaic idiom. The same men who produced operas in the modern Neapolitan manner with one hand wrote church music in the *stile antico* with the other.

The *stile antico* of the eighteenth century was by no means a mere imitation of Palestrina.[1] Within the traditional contrapuntal texture, composers made more or less free use of the resources of tonal harmony. In the hands of a man like Antonio Lotti (1667–1740), the *stile antico* could still be an extremely expressive medium. But if it was not a dead language, it was not a truly living one either. It survived only in the church, and owed its survival to the virtue of being archaic.

The composer who wished to write his church music in a modern idiom faced a twofold problem. Not only had he to reconcile to the requirements of the liturgy a style that was evolving—and was frankly more at home—outside church walls. He also had to make his peace with the past. Between the two extremes of ancient and modern no reconciliation was possible, and none attempted: the *missa a cappella* and other works in the *stile antico* made few concessions to the present, while the motet for solo voice and orchestra was often completely and unashamedly operatic. But in works that combined soloists, chorus, and orchestra, particularly in settings of the Ordinary of the Mass, some sort of compromise had to be reached.

CHURCH MUSIC OF THE NEAPOLITAN SCHOOL

The Neapolitan School was as decisive for the history of church music as it was for opera. Yet operatic methods were not ideally suited to liturgical music. The trouble was not incompatibility so much as inadequacy. In the opera, with its focus ever more on the solo singer, the chorus was of minimal importance. In church music it was vital. True, there was no purely musical reason why a short text, as of a Gradual or

---

[1] Cf. Karl Gustav Fellerer, 'Die vokale Kirchenmusik des 17./18. Jahrhunderts und die altklassische Polyphonie', *Zeitschrift für Musikwissenschaft*, xi (1928–9), p. 354.

Offertory, should not be composed in the manner of an operatic aria. But the sheer quantity of words to be set ruled out any possibility of applying this sort of treatment to the whole of the Mass. Here the chorus had to serve as the backbone of the work, and the homophonic choral writing that was sufficient to round off an Act had not the strength to carry the structure of the *missa solemnis*. The operatic style, if transferred bodily to the church, had its weakest element brought into prominence.

One can never talk of a 'solo Mass', as one can of the 'solo opera' of the Neapolitan School. The subdivision of the long texts of the *Gloria* and *Credo* into several smaller sections, each potentially an independent musical movement, admitted closed aria forms to the Mass, but the choral sections always remained predominant in quantity, if not in quality. One advantage of a declamatory choral style was that it disposed rapidly of large portions of the text, allowing a more extended treatment of others as arias and ensembles. In this respect it can be compared with operatic *recitativo secco*, and on occasions it served much the same function. But there were other ways of handling the chorus as well. The older concertante style, with the chorus alternating in ritornello fashion with one or more soloists, continued to be used. Where more imposing choral music was demanded, and traditionally for the final sections of the *Gloria* and *Credo*, composers turned to the now archaic contrapuntal manner. These extended fugues, however, all too often betrayed the modern preference for homophony by a quality of academic worthiness in place of spontaneous vitality.

The *missa solemnis* of the Neapolitan School was not a homogeneous work. It set the text as a series of independent arias, ensembles, and choral movements, a procedure which has earned it the label of 'cantata Mass'. There was always the danger of fragmentation, a lack of cohesion between the different subsections. In addition, there was the inevitable disunity between homophony and counterpoint: homophony in the operatic style of the solo numbers, and counterpoint, quite foreign to modern opera, in the most important choral movements. This uneasy cohabitation was recognized, and often deplored, by contemporary writers as the 'stilus mixtus'.[1] Contrapuntal writing made little impression on the basic homophony of the period, but survived in isolation within its own preserves as 'the strict style'.

These were pitfalls of the Neapolitan Mass, not necessarily shortcomings. The music for soloists could at its best have exquisite sensitivity and grace. The choral writing, in which one feels that some composers made a simple choice between the perfunctory and the dull, could be

---

[1] Cf. Johann Joseph Fux, *Gradus ad Parnassum* (Vienna, 1725), p. 273.

both vigorous and strong. Bach's B minor Mass, though written neither as a Catholic Mass nor in the Neapolitan manner, is a 'cantata Mass' in structure. Mozart's C minor Mass, unfinished though it is, triumphantly vindicates the formal and stylistic principles of the Neapolitan school.

The characteristic features of a mid-eighteenth-century *missa solemnis* in the Neapolitan manner had already been present in the work of Alessandro Scarlatti (d. 1725). Though most of his church music was written in the *stile antico*, his works with orchestral accompaniment—most especially the 'Messa di Sancta Cecilia' of 1720[1]—were progressive. His successors, such as Francesco Durante (1684–1755), Leonardo Vinci (1690–1730), and Leonardo Leo (1694–1744), followed the same principles but moved with the style of the times. In general, opera gained more and more the ascendancy, and the severity that can still be felt in Scarlatti had its corners rounded off.

HASSE'S CHURCH MUSIC

By the middle of the century the leadership of what must still be called the Neapolitan school had moved north. Many of the composers resident in Catholic Germany were Italian by birth. Of those who were not, most were none the less Italian by musical nationality. The chief of these was Johann Adolf Hasse (1699–1783)—'Giovanni Adolfo Hasse, detto il Sassone'—for thirty years Kapellmeister to the Saxon Court in Dresden. Hasse represents a peak in Neapolitan church music,[2] as he does in Metastasian opera, demonstrating the best characteristic of the school while often avoiding its greatest weaknesses. Two excerpts (i) from the Gloria of a Mass in D,[3] (ii) from a 'Salve Regina' in G,[4] will show firstly how his great gifts as a melodist were combined with a sure sensitivity for harmonic effect, and secondly how his writing for the solo voice, unmistakably operatic in idiom, can employ coloratura for expressive purposes (Ex. 137).

Hasse's writing for the chorus is typical of its time. Outside the solidly worked fugues that recur at the appropriate places, much of it consists of homophony of the most basic kind, sometimes to the extent of being devoid of melodic or even motivic interest. The musical substance is carried by the concertino of soloists, and also by the orchestra. A fundamental principle in the structure of choral movements is the systematic

---

[1] Modern edition by John Steele, London, 1968; see also E. J. Dent, *Alessandro Scarlatt* (London, 1905), pp. 181–7.
[2] Cf. W. Müller, *Johann Adolf Hasse als Kirchenkomponist* (Leipzig, 1911).
[3] Vienna, Nat. Bibl., SA 67D 70.
[4] Vienna, Nat. Bibl., SA 67D 79.

Ex. 137

use of some orchestral figure, on occasions so persistent as to come close to a real ostinato. Given strong orchestral material, this could produce music of splendid vigour and impetus. But the chorus, providing a harmonic filling between violin figuration and a running bass, tended to be relegated to the function of a continuo instrument.[1] And if the composer was satisfied, as many seem to have been, with note-spinning instead of genuine thematic work from the orchestra, there was little enough real music to go round.

This sort of texture still has both feet in the Baroque camp. Church music of the mid-eighteenth century is rarely notable for its orchestration. In general, the orchestra supports the soloists without adding much of its own, doubles or perhaps decorates the fugues, and seeks to provide a backbone to the other choruses. The change to a more modern orchestral technique was a slow one, and, allowing for a time-lag, more or less in step with the growing supremacy of German symphonic music.

At its best, the music of Hasse's generation can bear comparison with Mozart in its sheer mellifluous beauty of sound. Yet the undeniable grace and smoothness are often accompanied by a feeling of superficiality. The church music of Italian and Italianate composers seems to inherit the spirit as well as the techniques of the opera, which can be disturbing. Settings of the most solemn part of the Mass, the 'Et incarnatus est', are rarely concerned with the mystery of the Incarnation. Instead, as Hermann Abert tellingly observes,[2] they commonly portray a Nativity scene, such as may be found in the painting of the time, with charm as the main ingredient.

VIENNA AND SALZBURG

Not everywhere was the Neapolitan manner adopted with equal readiness. Within Italy Padre Martini (1706–84) advocated a more restrained

[1] Some of these points are illustrated in the 'Lacrymosa' of the Requiem in C minor, Arnold Schering, *Geschichte der Musik in Beispielen* (Leipzig, 1931), p. 469.
[2] *W. A. Mozart* (Leipzig, 1919–21), i, p. 305.

idiom for church music. In Vienna the famous contrapuntal treatise of Johann Joseph Fux, *Gradus ad Parnassum* (1725), had a lasting effect. Both here and in Salzburg there was a strong local tradition, which was influenced, but never quite overcome, by Neapolitan opera.

The fourth decade of the eighteenth century had brought to a close a brilliant era of Viennese music. Charles VI, the last of four successive Emperors notable for their practice and patronage of music,[1] died in 1740, and Fux, his Kapellmeister, the following year. In a sense a new era, even more brilliant than the last, had already begun: 1740 was also the year of that D major symphony by Monn,[2] which in its four-movement structure happens to correspond to the mature works of Haydn and Mozart. But it was to be many years before the music of Vienna regained its former eminence. Under Charles VI's successor, Maria Theresa, the musical complement at Court sank in numbers and distinction. Johann Georg Reutter the younger (1708–72), her Kapellmeister for over twenty years, did little to halt the decline. Yet Vienna never quite threw off the influence of the 'admirable old music composed by Fux', which Burney still heard performed in St. Stephen's in 1770. The middle of the century produced a curious mixture of old and new, the pomp and solemnity of the late Baroque alongside the melody and homophony of the Rococo. The change in Viennese style can be seen in the work of Reutter, under whom Haydn sang as a chorister. The music he wrote for the conservative taste of Charles VI's court shows him to have been a reputable composer, and still has something of Caldara about it.[3] But it seems to have gone over increasingly to the Neapolitan manner. His most individual characteristic is the accompaniment of bald, non-thematic choral homophony by scurrying, equally non-thematic string passage-work—the proverbial 'violins à la Reutter' that left their mark on Haydn's first two Masses. The low ebb to which he allowed the Hofkapelle to drop was no doubt partly the fault of financial restrictions. The apparent haste of much of his composition may be due to the fact that from 1756 he held in plurality the posts of first and second Kapellmeister both at court and at St. Stephen's.[4] Whatever the reasons, Reutter often contrived to adopt the facile tone of Neapolitan church music at its worst, without even inheriting its grace and charm.

[1] Cf. Guido Adler, 'Die Kaiser Ferdinand III, Leopold I., Joseph I. und Karl VI. als Tonsetzer und Förderer der Musik', *Vierteljahrsschrift für Musikwissenschaft*, viii (1892), p. 252.

[2] See *infra*, pp. 395–7.

[3] Selected church music by Reutter in *Denkmäler der Tonkunst in Österreich*, lxxxviii (1952), ed. Norbert Hofer.

[4] L. Stollbrock, 'Leben und Wirken des K. K. Hofkapellmeisters und Hofkompositors Johann Georg Reuter jun.', *Vierteljahrsschrift für Musikwissenschaft*, viii (1892), pp. 161–203 and 289–306.

PLATE V

INTERIOR OF THE ABBEY CHURCH AT OTTOBEUREN (*see p. xviii*)
By Johann Michael Fischer (1748–66)

Few composers went as far as Reutter. The works of Matthias Georg Monn (1717–50) and Georg Christoph Wagenseil (1715–77) have something of both worlds. Solo numbers in a contrapuntal style are still found, as in this duet from the 'Christe' of Wagenseil's Mass in G:[1]

Ex. 138

Wagenseil in particular uses counterpoint freely, alongside a declamatory chordal texture, in his writing for chorus—not only in formal fugues in the 'strict style' but as a natural part of his musical language.

The development of church music in Vienna to the more homogeneous style of Haydn's late Masses can be seen in the work of three composers who successfully held the position of Imperial Kapellmeister after Reutter: Florian Leopold Gassmann (1729–74),[2] Giuseppe Bonno (1710–88),[3] and Antonio Salieri (1750–1825).[4] If the Masses of the first two lean heavily on the Neapolitan tradition, the shaping of the *Gloria*

[1] Vienna, Nat. Bibl., Cod. 17039.
[2] Selected church music in *Denkmäler der Tonkunst in Österreich*, xlv (1938), ed. Franz Kosch. Cf. Kosch, 'Fl. L. Gassmann als Kirchenkomponist', *Studien zur Musikwissenschaft*, xiv (1927), p. 213.
[3] Alfred Schiernerl, 'Giuseppe Bonnos Kirchenkompositionen', ibid., xv (1928), p. 62; also Egon Wellesz, 'Giuseppe Bonno (1710–88). Sein Leben und seine dramatischen Werke', *Sammelbände der internationalen Musikgesellschaft*, xi (1909–10), p. 395.
[4] Rudolf Nützlader, 'Salieri als Kirchenmusiker', *Studien zur Musikwissenschaft*, xiv (1927), pp. 160–78.

and *Credo* into a complex of few interlocking sections, rather than several independent movements, is a Viennese characteristic throughout the century. Bonno, especially, shows how little careful part-writing is needed to lift the homophonic chorus from the level of mere utility music. In technique, the much younger Salieri was a late representative of the Neapolitan School, but his music belongs unmistakably to the age of Haydn and Mozart. To give him his due, the man who could on one occasion accuse Haydn of 'gross sins against the church style' was himself generally scrupulous in his avoidance of superficiality and of incongruity between words and music. Looking ahead to a work of Salieri's maturity, his Mass in D minor,[1] one can see that church music was leaving behind the old stylistic foundations of concerto and *opera seria*.

Ex. 139

Here one can no longer talk of an opening ritornello. The chief influence on church music was by now the modern symphony.

The other main centre of Austrian church music was Salzburg. Music for the liturgy naturally had an important part to play at the seat of an archiepiscopal court. Like everywhere else, Salzburg came under the influence of the Neapolitan style. But, with its choir school, it maintained a tradition of choral singing which favoured counterpoint. The two motets of Johann Ernst Eberlin (1702–62) printed in the Austrian *Denkmäler*[2] show both sides of the picture: the one written contrapuntally for chorus, the other consisting of an accompanied recitative, a solo duet in *da capo* form and a homophonic choral finale. In the same volume, the two motets by Eberlin's pupil, Anton Cajetan Adlgasser (1728–77), are completely modern in approach, but they are representative of only part of his output. Salzburg retained a conservative streak. Even a piece like the 'Litaniae Venerabili'[3] of Leopold Mozart (1719–87), for all its theatrical effects, has its share of counterpoint too. The young Mozart's regard for his two most distinguished colleagues at Salzburg, Adlgasser

[1] Vienna, Nat. Bibl. HK 485.
[2] Ed. Karl A. Rosenthal and Constantin Schneider, *Denkmäler der Tonkunst in Österreich*, xliii (1) (1936).
[3] Max Seiffert (ed.), *Denkmäler der Tonkunst in Bayern*, ix (2) (1909).

and Michael Haydn, was significantly as 'excellent masters of counterpoint'.

Salzburg church music reached a peak in the work of Michael Haydn (1737–1806),[1] who entered the Archbishop's service in 1763 and stayed for the rest of his life. Though never rising higher than the position of Vice-Kapellmeister, he became probably the most respected church composer in Austria, not excepting his more famous brother. Michael Haydn, like Joseph, began by writing in much the same manner as the Viennese composers whose music he would have known and sung in St. Stephen's as a chorister. The early 'Missa in honorem Ssmae Trinitatis' (1754) has similarities with Joseph's first two Masses, written at about the same age, in the declamatory choral style with scurrying violins (*à la*

Ex. 140

[1] Anton M. Klafsky, 'Michael Haydn als Kirchenkomponist', *Studien zur Musikwissenschaft*, iii (1915), p. 5.

Reutter) and the more florid solo parts. But a greater integration between voices and orchestra becomes increasingly a feature of his music. Not only is the orchestra handled in a more modern fashion. The chorus parts also gain in significance. Within a basically homophonic texture, the chorus has real thematic interest of its own, as in the *Credo* (Ex. 140) of his 'Missa Sti Amadi' (1776),[1] instead of being secondary to orchestral figuration.

Michael Haydn was almost alone among the notable composers of his generation in working first and foremost for the church. He was not a startling innovator. Rather, he applied the methods of his own time to the established practices of church music. Much of his 'Missa in Dominica Palmarum'[2] consists of unmeasured settings of plainsong, in which the old chant melody is subjected to tonal harmonization in four parts. The same procedure is found in the 'Missa Tempore Quadragesimae'. But whether it is in simple choral Masses like these, or in festive settings such as those written for the Viennese Court, Haydn seems to keep the question of liturgical propriety in view. The essentially functional nature of his church music is demonstrated by the cycle of Gradual settings for the whole year,[3] ordered by Archbishop Hieronymus Colloredo to replace the instrumental substitutes (such as Mozart's so-called 'Epistle Sonatas') that had been used previously. The extended movements of the Masses often owe their musical coherence to a formal organization that is symphonic in origin. In Michael Haydn more than in most of his contemporaries, however, the words count. Here again, the form is put to liturgical use, rather than the text crammed into an uncongenial framework.

SYMPHONIC INFLUENCES

The age of Metastasian opera had found its characteristic solution to the formal problems of church music in the 'cantata Mass', but its piecemeal methods left the question of internal unity unanswered. The age of the symphony, with its greater breadth and continuity, could put the pieces together again. The late Masses of the two Haydns show not so much a rationalization of the 'cantata Mass' as a more expansive treatment of the *missa brevis*, where each liturgical unit remained intact. At Salzburg, indeed, there was no choice but to write compact settings, even for the most solemn occasions, since, as Mozart complained to

[1] Vienna, Nat. Bibl., Cod. 16542.
[2] Klafsky (ed.), *Denkmäler der Tonkunst in Österreich*, xxii (1915).
[3] A selection, ed. Klafsky, ibid., xxxii (1) (1925). The Gradual 'Prope est' is recorded in *The History of Music in Sound*, vii.

Padre Martini in 1776, 'a Mass ... must not last longer than three quarters of an hour'.[1]

To some extent the Ordinary of the Mass suggests its own musical forms. The ternary structure of the *Kyrie* and the responsory pattern of the *Agnus Dei* are obvious. The jubilant tone of the *Gloria* is interrupted by the greater solemnity of the 'Qui tollis'. The affirmations of the *Credo* surround the central 'Et incarnatus' and 'Crucifixus'. Symphonic methods, in particular thematic development, gave composers the means of setting these lengthy texts accordingly, without having to resort to further subdivision. The old ritornello form long continued in use. But the sonata increasingly took its place beside the concerto as a basic formal principle. The function of the soloists as a Baroque concertino moved more and more towards that of a lyrical subsidiary group.

The application of instrumental formal procedures to church music was a useful tool. But it was no more than that. It did not provide a ready-made solution to all the composer's formal problems. There is little to choose between splitting the liturgical text into a series of more or less disconnected sections as a 'cantata Mass', and fitting the words willy-nilly into 'sonata form'. The considerations of purely musical balance could still, and often did, take precedence over those of faithfulness to the text, as is shown by the frequent settings of the ternary *Kyrie* in extended binary form. Despite the plea for peace which closes the *Agnus Dei*, few composers could resist the temptation of ending a Mass as they would a symphony, with a rollicking finale.

Important as the symphony was for its effect on form, its most far-reaching influence was on the texture of church music. The Baroque treatment of the orchestra, with its emphasis on treble and bass and its use of wind as either obbligato or ripieno instruments, survived in church long after it had been succeeded by a more modern orchestral technique in secular surroundings. Within such a texture the position of the chorus as a sandwich-filling—except that in this case the bread was tastier than the middle—was natural. The alternative was counterpoint, meaning for most composers the ossified 'strict style'. The evolution of a more homogeneous texture, in which the continuo, if present, played a less essential role, gave greater freedom of movement, not only to the inner parts and wind instruments of the orchestra but also to the chorus.

The biggest single gain in Catholic church music in the later eighteenth century was that of a melodic chorus. The tunefulness of Joseph and Michael Haydn may have something to do with *Volkstümlichkeit*, a popular native tradition. But it is most of all the consequence of a

[1] *The Letters of Mozart*, tr. and ed. Emily Anderson (London, 1938), i, p. 386.

relaxed musical texture, in which there is less distinction than previously between harmony and counterpoint. The incongruity of the Neapolitan Mass, in which the solo voices dominated insignificant orchestral accompaniment, the orchestra in turn dominated casual homophonic choral writing, while the chorus took the lead for the formal fugues, gave way to a greater evenness of style.

JOSEPH HAYDN

Joseph Haydn's church music spans almost the whole of his creative life. His Masses were not written at regular intervals, and so do not demonstrate the composer's steady development in the same way as do his symphonies or string quartets. But they do represent Haydn from his earliest compositions to the mastery of his last major work, the 'Harmoniemesse' of 1802.

Haydn's first two Masses, composed about 1750, show little promise of the great contributions he was later to make to the form. The 'Missa Rorate coeli desuper',[1] formerly supposed lost but rediscovered in Göttweig Abbey in 1957, and the 'Missa Brevis' in F are typical, if undistinguished, examples of their time. In their setting of different phrases of the text simultaneously in two or more voices, a procedure deplored by the Church but none the less widely practised, they belong to the most drastic type of *missa brevis*—the entire *Gloria* of the 'Rorate' Mass is telescoped into a mere nine bars. Both are for four-part choir, from which two sopranos step forward as soloists in the F major Mass, and an orchestra of two violins, bass, and organ continuo. The whole style of the music, particularly the instrumental writing with the violins scurrying about in unison, points clearly to the influence of Reutter,[2] while the composer's youthful inexperience is revealed by an occasional awkwardness in the part-writing and a few grammatical errors by way of consecutive fifths and octaves. Yet these little works have a quality of freshness—'a certain youthful fire', as Haydn himself said when he rediscovered the F major Mass in 1805. The latter is carefully tied together by the use of identical settings of the final 'Amen' in both *Gloria* and *Credo*, and by repeating the music of the opening *Kyrie* at the end, to the words of the 'Dona nobis pacem', a common enough practice throughout the period. There are also features that remain characteristic

[1] H. C. Robbins Landon (ed.) (London, 1957). Haydn's other Masses are published in *Joseph Haydn. The Complete Works* (ed. Carl M. Brand) (Boston, 1950–1), series 23, i; and *J. Haydn, Werke* (Munich and Duisburg), ser. 23, ii–v.

[2] The 'Rorate' Mass has in fact been claimed as one of Reutter's compositions; cf. Erich Schenk, 'Ist die Göttweiger Rorate–Messe ein Werk Joseph Haydns?', *Studien zur Musikwissenschaft*, xxiv (1960), p. 87.

in his most mature Masses, such as the poignant harmony of the 'Incarnatus' and the affectionate handling of the 'Benedictus'.

After these two unpretentious works, the 'Missa in honorem Beatissimae Virginis Mariae', probably written some sixteen years later in 1766, is altogether more ambitious. Perhaps it was intended as something of a showpiece: Franz Gregor Werner, under whom Haydn had served up to this time as Vice-Kapellmeister in Eisenstadt, died on 5 March 1766, and there may have been an element here of his young successor's wish to show his true mettle.[1] At all events, the 'Great Organ Mass', as it is usually called, is a work on a large scale, approaching the 'cantata Mass' in treatment. Its name derives from the prominent obbligato organ part, a common feature in the late eighteenth century which is found in three other Masses by Haydn. The writing for organ is scarcely idiomatic, being in a florid, perhaps even mannered harpsichord style, similar to that of the C major organ concerto of 1756. The organ is most important in the *Kyrie* and 'Benedictus', which is in a fully developed concerto form, with chorus, organ, and orchestra set against the concertino of the solo quartet. But the greatest gain in this Mass is that of breathing-space. The larger time-scale allows more lyricism and expansiveness, and there is a notable amount of contrapuntal writing. It is no accident that the two most memorable sections have fugal texture: the *Sanctus*, with its solemn swing of syncopated movement in slow triple time, and the 'Crucifixus' (Ex. 141), where the diminished third of the subject and the chromatic descent of the counter-subject combine to produce a superbly expressive effect.

The expansiveness of the 'Great Organ Mass' is found in even greater measure in the 'Missa Sanctae Caeciliae',[2] the longest of all Haydn's

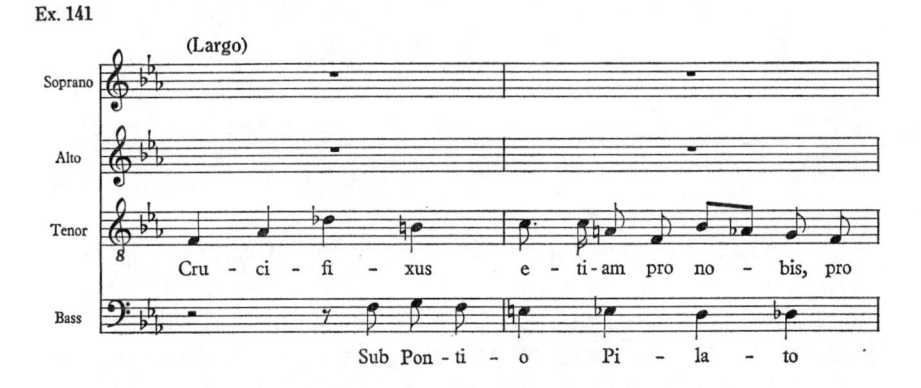

Ex. 141

[1] Brand, *Die Messen von Joseph Haydn* (Würzburg, 1941), p. 36.
[2] *Complete Works*, ser. 23, i. In the only other published full score, the first edition issued by Breitkopf and Härtel in 1807, the Mass is severely cut.

Masses, which must have been composed in the early 1770s. It seems likely that it was intended for a service to celebrate the patronal festival on 22 November of a musicians' guild.[1] If so, and it was written for a congregation (or audience) of professional musicians, then this may explain why it is really too long for normal liturgical use, even on the most festal occasions. It is noticeable that the first half of the Mass re-

---

[1] Brand, op. cit., pp. 51 ff.

ceives far more extended treatment than the second; the *Sanctus* of only ten bars (or twenty-one in all, including the 'Pleni sunt coeli' and 'Osanna', may indeed be felt to be too short. But up to the *Credo* the work belongs wholeheartedly to the genre of the 'cantata Mass'. The *Gloria* is set as seven quite independent movements, of which two are arias for soprano solo, the 'Quoniam' being in a particularly brilliant concerto style, with coloratura, ritornelli, and with trumpets and drums in the orchestra. In the *Credo*, the repeated affirmations of the initial word are nothing unusual, much less prophetic of Beethoven's 'Missa Solemnis', as some have claimed. They serve the musical function of providing formal articulation, and, despite the official disapproval of the Church, they also make liturgical sense in a text where there is a danger of losing sight of the all-important verb. As might be expected in a work of this size, contrapuntal writing plays an important part. It is a symptom of the Neapolitan leanings of the 'Cecilia' Mass, however, that it tends to keep its harmony and counterpoint apart. Counterpoint comes into its own chiefly in the massive formal fugues, which sometimes seem to miss Haydn's characteristic spontaneity and freshness. Even the 'Et vitam venturi', with its magnificent impetus, is of a pattern with which Haydn's audience would be well familiar—a fugue on a subject of neutral character, cast in the standard mould of church counterpoint. Far more original, and indeed one of the high points of the Mass, is the 'Gratias', which uses fugal texture but is not a fugue as such. Here Haydn, like Mozart in the finale of his G major quartet, K. 387, uses fugue and homophony as deliberate contrasts in a movement that is basically in sonata form.

Haydn's mastery of fugue is unquestioned, as is shown by the 'Cecilia' Mass and the more or less contemporary Op. 20 string quartets. But he has his own view of the form. Haydn's fugues are continually coloured by his symphonic thinking. Their middle sections often take on the character of a development section, in which the subject is worked out, not as a whole but in its component parts. Many subjects contain some harmonic twist, which becomes the starting-point for dramatic modulations and sequences. The end of the exposition may mark the last complete entry of the subject. The final section, rather than growing out of the continuous contrapuntal texture, will probably begin afresh, almost in the manner of a recapitulation. After the exposition, the part-writing tends to become less real, and fugal movements frequently end with a homophonic coda. The result is often less truly fugal, but certainly more idiomatic of its time and its composer than many of the carefully worked-out fugues of Haydn's contemporaries.

The 'Cecilia' Mass was a work in the grand manner. By contrast, the other two Masses of the 1770s are modest pieces: the 'Missa Sancti Nicolai' of 1772, presumably composed for Prince Nicholas Esterházy's name-day on 6 December, and the 'Missa brevis Sancti Joannis de Deo', or 'Little Organ Mass' (*c.* 1775), whose original title suggests that it was written for the Barmherzige Brüder in Eisenstadt, the religious order founded by St. John of God, later its patron saint. To the same decade belongs what was perhaps Haydn's best-known piece of church music during his lifetime, the *Stabat Mater* of about 1771, which went through several editions in Germany, France, and England before 1800. (None of the Masses was printed in the eighteenth century.) The 'St. Nicholas' and the 'Little Organ Mass' belong to the genre of the *missa brevis*. The first of them, despite its brevity, is relaxed in mood, and some have felt a seasonal Christmas spirit in the music. The second, in which the orchestra is cut down to two violins and bass, is more compressed. Yet both show the same economy of material that was noted in the early F major Mass: the 'St. Nicholas' Mass had its *Credo* in ABA form, with an Adagio tenor solo as the central 'Incarnatus', and again repeats the music of the *Kyrie* to the words of the 'Dona nobis pacem'; the 'Little Organ Mass' has matching final sections to *Gloria* and *Credo*. Both,

Ex. 142

particularly the later work, use the device of setting different clauses of the text simultaneously (Ex. 142). Another feature they have in common is the extended setting of the *Benedictus*, which is a focal point of each. That of the 'Little Organ Mass', a leisurely cantabile aria for soprano, is the only movement to employ the obbligato organ that gives the work its name. But the most striking part of this Mass is its ending. Instead of being in the more customary Adagio/Allegro pattern, the *Agnus Dei* and 'Dona nobis pacem' are composed in the same slow tempo throughout, and the close is a magical *perdendosi* in place of the usual *strepitosissimo*.

The finest of Haydn's earlier Masses is the 'Missa Cellensis', or 'Mariazell' Mass, of 1782, commissioned by a certain Anton Liebner as a votive offering at the pilgrimage church of Mariazell on his ennoblement as Edler von Kreutzner. As a whole it is not quite even in quality. The rather everyday declamatory opening of the *Credo* does not reach the same level as that of the *Gloria*, which is written in much the same manner but with real rhythmic and melodic interest. At its best, however, the 'Mariazell' Mass surpasses all its predecessors. It is noteworthy that here the concerto form noted previously, with its important structural ritornelli, has largely given way to sonata construction; *Kyrie*, 'Gratias', and 'Benedictus' are all in straightforward sonata form, with two subject-groups and complete recapitulations. This last movement is deservedly the most famous part of the work. It is in fact an adaptation of an alto aria from Haydn's opera *Il mondo della luna* (1777), though no one would guess it, reworked for solo quartet and chorus, the soloists being entrusted with the lyrical material of the extended second subject group. This was not the first time Haydn had contrasted the solo quartet against the full choir, but it was becoming an increasingly prominent feature of his church music. The recapitulation brings one of the most beautiful moments: while Mozart's movements in minor keys often produce their most telling effect by the return of the subsidiary material, first heard in the relative major, now in the unrelieved tonic minor, here Haydn uses the technique, more typical of Schubert, of bringing back his second subject with a melting change to the tonic major.

THE JOSEPHINE RESTRICTIONS ON CHURCH MUSIC

It was to be fourteen years before Haydn composed another Mass, a gap that has often been accounted for by the restrictions imposed on church music by the Emperor Joseph II in 1783. Joseph's reign was a turbulent one for the Catholic Church in Austria. Among the reforms that he implemented in the name of 'Enlightened' liberalism, many seemed to strike directly at the roots of the Church's authority. It would now appear that Joseph's opposition was not, as his critics claimed at the time, to the Church itself, but to the political power of the clergy. The effects, however, were none the less drastic: monasteries were dissolved, their revenues transferred to the state exchequer; the number of religious holidays was severely cut. The 1780s were years of a more relaxed censorship, of religious tolerance—and of tolerance towards freethinkers and Freemasons. Austria came close to following England's example of two hundred years earlier, though for different reasons, in severing connections with Rome and establishing a national church with the monarch as titular head.

The measures that concerned music[1] were of small enough importance in the total context of these religious reforms. They did have their effect, however. As late as 1799 Haydn's biographer Georg August Griesinger could write—though with gross exaggeration—shortly after his arrival in Vienna: 'There has been no church music here since Emperor Joseph.'[2] The use of music with elaborate instrumental accompaniment was restricted, thus giving composers less incentive to write for the church. But there was never any question of an absolute ban. Had the occasion arisen, a new Mass by Haydn need not have lacked an opportunity for performance. Neither the long pause in Haydn's output nor Mozart's puzzling failure to complete the C minor Mass can be ascribed solely to the Josephine restrictions.

MOZART

When Haydn composed the 'Mariazell' Mass, in 1782, Mozart's last complete work in the genre was already in existence. By the time he wrote the next, Mozart had been dead for almost five years. Church music takes a rather different place in Mozart's work than it does in Haydn's. The older composer's Masses are crowned by the six great examples of his old age. (It is worth bearing in mind that all but three of Haydn's extant Masses were written at an age that Mozart never lived to see.) Mozart too reached his peak in the latter part of his life, but the majority of his church music is early. From his last Viennese years, so fruitful in other fields of composition, there are only three liturgical works, of which one, the *Ave verum corpus*, is a tiny gem, while the two large-scale masterpieces, the C minor Mass and the Requiem, remain unfinished.

Mozart was acquainted with the church music not only of his native

---

[1] Cf. Reinhard G. Pauly, 'The Reforms of Church Music under Joseph II', *Musical Quarterly*, xliii (1957), p. 372.
[2] Edward Olleson, *Haydn Yearbook*, iii (1965), p. 8.

Salzburg but of Catholic Europe at large. At home he had a fine tradition on which to build, and he was no stranger to the church music of Vienna. He would have known the Italian operatic style in the first place as an Austrian import, and his boyhood travels gave him first-hand experience of this approach. His studies with Padre Martini brought him into contact with more conservative ideas. At the other extreme, he knew (and deplored) the predominantly instrumental church music of Mannheim[1]: 'you must write principally for the instruments as you cannot imagine anything worse than the voices here'. Mozart's cosmopolitan upbringing, together with the fact that so many of the sacred works were written in his youth, may to some extent explain why his church music as a whole is less consistent in style and in quality than Haydn's.

Mozart's first sacred work of any size was the Mass for the consecration of the orphanage church (Waisenhauskirche) on the Rennweg in Vienna, on 7 December 1768. The Mass in question was the one in C minor, K. 139 (47a),[2] once thought to belong to a later date. The identification of K.139 with the 'Waisenhauskirche' Mass was proposed long ago, despite widespread incredulity that Mozart, then still a month short of his thirteenth birthday, could have composed so mature a work at such an early age. Now that more recent research has provided confirmation, however, the matter may be regarded as settled.[3]

This C minor Mass is certainly an astonishing achievement for a boy of twelve. It is a *missa solemnis* in the grand manner, scored for oboes, four trumpets, trombones, drums, and a string section that includes divided violas—a sure sign, incidentally, that the work was not intended for Salzburg, as some have assumed. Stylistically the work owes most to Hasse, who was resident in Vienna at this time, and it faithfully follows the conventions of the Italianate 'cantata Mass' in its sectional treatment of the text and its use of solo voices and concerto forms. The *Credo* is bound together by the violin ostinato figure that is common to all the fast sections, including the customary final fugue, while the *bel canto* duet of the 'Et incarnatus' is in the typical 'Nativity scene' manner of the Neapolitan School. In Mozart no less than in Hasse, this sort of writing can come dangerously close to the superficial, and the more serious sections, with the opportunities they offer for pathos and chromatic harmony, are generally the most successful parts of the Mass. But

---

[1] See the selection, *Kirchenmusik der Mannheimer Schule*, in *Denkmäler der Tonkunst in Bayern* (*Neue Folge*), xi, ed. Eduard Schmitt.

[2] Figures in brackets refer to the sixth edition of Köchel's catalogue (Wiesbaden, 1964).

[3] *W. A. Mozart. Neue Ausgabe sämtliche Werke* (ed. Ernst F. Schmid *et al.*) (Salzburg, Kassel and Basel, 1955–), ser. I, Werkgruppe 1, Abt. 1, i, p. 37. Cf. Wilhelm Kurthen, 'Studien zu W. A. Mozarts kirchenmusikalischen Jugendwerken', *Zeitschrift für Musikwissenschaft*, iii (1920–1), pp. 209 ff; and Karl Pfannhauser, 'Zu Mozarts Kirchenwerken von 1768', *Mozart–Jahrbuch 1954* (Salzburg, 1955), p. 150.

the language is basically that of the opera house—even in the 'Crucifixus', where trombones and muted trumpets produce a splendid theatrical solemnity.

Of a similar type, though without the same degree of pomp, is the 'Dominicus' Mass in C major, K. 66,[1] written in October of the following year for the first Mass of Cajetan, now Father Dominicus, Hagenauer, son of the Mozarts' landlord in Salzburg and a friend of the family. The orchestration is less lavish than in K. 139,[2] but the formal and stylistic principles are identical. The *Credo* again makes use of a unifying ostinato figure, and, as in the earlier work, contrapuntal writing is by and large restricted to the formally fugal movements. In these, not only here but throughout his life, Mozart was normally more conservative than Haydn. His fugues tend to be more 'real', following the old-established fugal procedures, and less inclined to revert to a homophonic texture.

Apart from these two festal Masses, the years 1768–9 saw the composition of two works of the *missa brevis* type, one of them, K. 49 (47d) in G major, written in Vienna towards the end of 1768, the other, K. 65 (61a) in D minor, shortly after Mozart's return to Salzburg early in the new year. The small scale of these pieces leaves no room for extended treatment: between them they contain only one movement that could be called an aria, the bass solo of 'Et in Spiritum sanctum' in K. 49; the fugues that end the *Gloria* and *Credo* of each consist of no more than a four-part exposition plus coda. The *Gloria* of the earlier work, set in one continuous piece, overcomes the problem of cohesion by its effective use of thematic cross-reference:

Ex.143

[1] *Gesamtausgabe der Werke Mozarts* (ed. Johannes Brahms *et al.*) (Leipzig, 1876–1905), ser. 1, iii; *Neue Ausgabe*, ser. I, Werkgruppe 1, Abt. 1, i, p. 185.
[2] At a later date further wind parts were added; cf. Köchel, 6th edn., p. 91.

Hints of the same thing can also be found in the D minor Mass. Particularly remarkable is the *Gloria* of K. 65, presumably written so as to make up a complete setting of the Ordinary, since it cannot have been performed at the service for which the Mass was originally intended (the inauguration of a forty-hour period of intercession): the expected relative F major is only touched upon in passing, and the whole movement hovers between the minor keys of D and G.

The G major and D minor Masses show a decided contrast to the two big works already discussed, not only in size but also in texture. With their loosely contrapuntal choral writing, they are closer to the Salzburg tradition of such composers as Eberlin and Adlgasser than to the modern Neapolitan manner. This contrast between counterpoint and opera becomes still more marked in the works of the next few years up to 1773, the period of Mozart's three Italian journeys, during which he wrote no complete Masses, but several other pieces of church music. If it was principally opera that took him to Italy, his travels also gave him a closer familiarity with the *stile antico*. His studies with Padre Martini in 1770 had the greatest effect, giving rise to a number of works in an austerely contrapuntal style. Not all of them are unquestionably by Mozart: some may be his own copies of music by other composers. But the point remains: together with the contrapuntal exercises of the same period (e.g. K. 73x) they show an interest in polyphonic technique that is in some ways comparable to the preoccupation with Bach and Handel during 1782 and 1783.

Perhaps the most finished of these contrapuntal pieces is the little *Kyrie*, K. 90,[1] composed in Salzburg between Mozart's first and second journeys to Italy, in the summer of 1771. Yet the almost contemporary setting of the *Regina coeli*, K. 108 (74d), like that of the following year, K. 127, is completely operatic in style. The most substantial work of this period, the 'Litaniae de venerabili altaris sacramento', K. 125, is also in a similar vein, though it still has close ties with earlier Salzburg settings of the same Litany.[2] At the farthest extreme from Padre Martini stands the motet 'Exsultate jubilate', K. 165 (158a), composed in January 1773, significantly for Venanzio Rauzzini, Mozart's leading castrato in *Lucio Silla*, which is in all but name a three-movement concerto for soprano and orchestra. These differences of style cannot be equated directly with differences in quality. Nevertheless, it may be felt that Mozart is at his most characteristic when he is stylistically least hide-bound, somewhere between the two poles of *stile antico* and *opera seria*, as in the

[1] Published by Alfred Einstein, 'Mozart's Kyrie, K. 90', *Musical Quarterly*, xxxvii (1951), p. 1.
[2] Karl A. Rosenthal, 'Mozart's Sacramental Litanies and their Forerunners', ibid., xxvii (1941), p. 433.

unpretentious but charming Offertory 'Inter natos', K. 72 (74f).

The return from the third Italian journey brought with it a return to Mass composition. (From the intervening period there is only the fragment of a *missa brevis* in F, K. 116 (90a), dating from 1771.) The first of the two Masses composed in 1773 was never finished, the *missa brevis* in C for four voices and organ continuo, K. 115 (166d), which breaks off after nine bars of the *Sanctus*. Written in the contrapuntal style of his home town, it would have been unique among Mozart's Masses, had it been completed, in being the only one to do without orchestral accompaniment. The 'Missa in honorem Ssmae Trinitatis', K. 167, on the other hand, dispenses with soloists, presumably for the sake of brevity. This work seems tailor-made to fit the requirements of Hieronymus Colloredo, who had succeeded to the Archbishopric in 1772. As Mozart said in the letter already quoted:

... a mass with the whole Kyrie, the Gloria, the Credo, the Epistle sonata, the Offertory or Motet, the Sanctus and the Agnus Dei must not last longer than three quarters of an hour. This applies even to the most solemn mass said by the Archbishop himself ... At the same time, the mass must have all the instruments—trumpets, drums, and so forth.[1]

The 'Trinity' Mass is a *missa brevis* in length, but not in manner: despite its conciseness, it has 'all the instruments'. The absence of soloists naturally precludes the more extravagantly operatic features of Neapolitan church music. The work as a whole has a greater homogeneity of style, and in its structure owes more to instrumental forms than to opera. This is particularly true of the rondo-like plan of the *Credo*, in which the final fugue is rounded off by the reappearance of the orchestral motifs that have dominated the movement.

The lengths to which instrumental organization could go may be seen in the 'Litaniae Lauretanae', K. 195 (186d), of 1774.[2] The *Kyrie*, for example, is a beautifully balanced movement in sonata-form, prefaced by a slow introduction. But the text seems to have had no part in determining the shape of the movement or the character of the thematic material. The two Masses of the same year, K. 192 (186f) in F, and K. 194 (186h) in D, however, achieve a nice balance between homophony and counterpoint, voices and orchestra. Both are of the *missa brevis* type and use the same small orchestra of two violins and bass. If the F major Mass is the superior, this is due to the quality of its choral writing and particularly to the fine *Credo*. The constant recurrence of the first

[1] Op. cit., i, pp. 386–7.
[2] The *Agnus Dei* is recorded in *The History of Music in Sound*, vii. On Mozart's two 'Litanies of Loreto' see Renate Federhofer-Königs, 'Mozarts "Lauretanische Litaneien"', *Mozart-Jahrbuch 1967*, p. 111.

word to the same motif (which is incidentally the same as the well-known opening figure from the finale of the so-called 'Jupiter' Symphony) produces a remarkably coherent single movement, whose structure depends not on the orchestra, as so often, but on the voices. This device can be related to a host of earlier examples,[1] including Haydn's 'Cecilia' Mass, and was used again by Mozart in K. 257.

Mozart's visit to Munich for *La finta giardiniera* produced another of those contrasts that so often crop up in his church music. On the one hand, he wrote early in 1775 the Offertory 'Misericordias Domini,' K. 222 (205a), at the express request of the Elector 'to hear some of [his] contrapuntal compositions'; on the other, he composed what is probably the most perfunctory of his Masses, K. 220 (196b) in C, whose chirpings in the *Sanctus* have earned it the irreverent but not inapt title of 'Sparrow' Mass. Padre Martini's comments on the Offertory show how far Mozart's counterpoint now stood from the *stile antico* he had learned in Bologna: that it had 'everything that modern music requires'. The Mass, though written in Munich, appears to have the requirements of Salzburg in mind; it is short, but still employs trumpets and drums. (Only one of the subsequent Masses, K. 275 (272b), does without.) But for the date and place of composition, K. 220 would seem to epitomize the attitude expressed in Mozart's letter to Padre Martini in 1776, when he wrote that, for want of adequate opera in Salzburg, he was 'amusing himself by writing chamber music and music for the church'.

The two and a half years in Salzburg after the return from Munich represent the longest period Mozart had spent at home since infancy. The first year produced no church music, but the works of the next eighteen months, from March 1776 to September 1777, include five Masses and a substantial Litany. To some extent, Mozart made up for the irksome lack of opera by using the church as his stage. The 'Litaniae de venerabili altaris sacramento', K. 243, for example, uses in its solo numbers all the apparatus of opera. At the same time it displays the inherent contradictions of the *stilus mixtus*, as in the two consecutive movements for solo soprano, 'Dulcissimum convivium' and 'Viaticum', the first an operatic aria, the second using the old 'Pange lingua' melody as a *canto fermo*.

The so-called 'Missa longa', K. 262 (246a), however, has little recourse to operatic methods. It is not a multi-sectional 'Cantata Mass', and there are no solo arias as such. Its length, which suggests that it was intended for some church other than the cathedral in Salzburg, derives from the extended treatment of relatively few movements. There is more

[1] Georg Reichert, 'Mozarts "Credo–Messen" und ihre Vorläufer', *Mozart-Jahrbuch 1955*, p. 117.

fugal writing than in the average *missa brevis*. In its use of instrumental forms the work may be compared to Haydn's 'Mariazell' Mass, written six years later. Both set the *Kyrie* in regular sonata form. But Mozart, unlike Haydn, identifies the words 'Christe eleison' with his lyrical second subject:

	Exposition	'Development'	Recapitulation
Haydn:	*Kyrie*	*Christe*	*Kyrie*
Mozart:	I: *Kyrie*		I: *Kyrie*
	II: *Christe*-codetta	*Kyrie*	II: *Christe*-codetta
	Kyrie		*Kyrie*

Mozart's musical logic in associating words with their own thematic material overrides the simple ABA pattern of the text. Another instance of the precedence of formal considerations over the words is the 'Benedictus', where the 'Osanna' not only appears in its orthodox place at the end but is interpolated almost as a choral refrain within what is basically a sonata-form movement for soloists.

The three C major Masses written in November and December 1776 show a retreat from this instrumental style. They are in a sense less highly organized than the 'Missa longa', and their structure hangs more closely on the words. Extended fugues are lacking, but, as is often the case in Mozart's shorter Masses, there is an altogether freer use of contrapuntal texture. The 'Credo' Mass, K. 257, owes its name to the device already noted in the F major *missa brevis*, K. 192 (186 f), that of reiterating the first word of the Creed throughout the course of the movement, though here the repetitions are less of a structural backbone than they were in the earlier work. Another point of contact is the fact that the 'Credo' motif of K. 192 reappears in the *Sanctus* of this C major Mass. The 'Spaur' Mass, K. 258, so called because it was supposedly written for the consecration of Count von Spaur, represents a further step away from instrumental organization, in favour of a more vocal style. Its 'Benedictus' is built round a choral motto-theme of four notes, from which the soloists take their departure. The 'Dona nobis pacem' does not serve its usual function of a quick finale, but continues at the flowing speed of the *Agnus Dei*. The long plagal coda, in which the tonality never truly returns from the subdominant to the tonic, forms a remarkable ending to the work, described by Einstein as a 'reverent "Lydian" close'. Mozart's 'Organ Solo Mass', K. 259, goes to the utmost brevity. In this respect, as well as in its use of obbligato organ, it parallels Haydn's 'Little Organ Mass'. Mozart is not so ruthlessly concise as Haydn, who managed to deal with the whole *Gloria* in the space of thirty-one bars. Nevertheless, his main concern is clearly the rapid disposal of the text, and the Mass contains a good deal of pure utility music. This does not of course apply to the 'Benedictus', which receives the most extended treatment of the work and, as in Haydn, is the only movement to have a solo organ part, written in a similar, rather rococo manner.

Stylistically the *missa brevis* in B♭, K. 275 (272b), of 1777 belongs together with the Masses of the previous year. It is short, but not so condensed as to leave no time for a certain amount of free counterpoint. The most arresting feature of the work is the opening of the *Gloria*, where the feeling of hushed awe is in contrast to the usual jubilant tone.

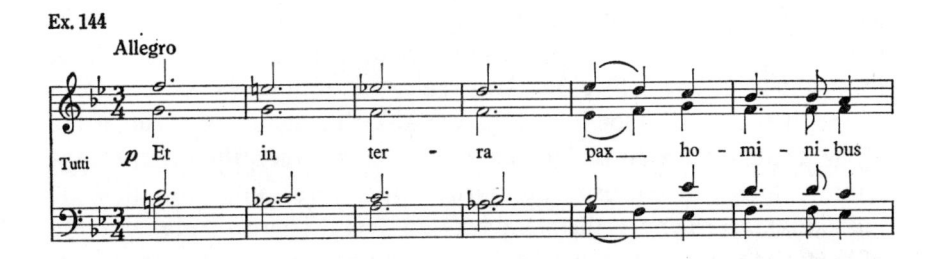

Ex. 144

But the tuneful character of the Mass as a whole is exemplified in the attractive rondo finale of the 'Dona nobis pacem'.

In August 1777 Mozart resigned his position in Salzburg, and the following month set out 'to seek his fortune elsewhere'. Some sixteen months later, after an abortive tour which had brought little but disappointment, he returned cap in hand to the post of Court Organist. Mozart's travels to Paris and back, like the other foreign journeys, produced little by way of church music, though a major work seems to have been begun in Mannheim in 1778.[1] Once again it was his return home that prompted a new series of sacred compositions, including the two Vespers settings and the Masses in C major, K. 317 and 337, all written during 1779 and 1780. The 'Vesperae de Dominica', K. 321, and the 'Vesperae solennes de confessore', K. 339 (both, incidentally, on identical texts, despite their different titles), follow the same general principle of conciseness as do most of the Salzburg Masses, and closely resemble one

---

[1] Cf. K. 296a–c in Köchel (sixth edition), and *The Letters of Mozart*, ii, p. 711.

another in layout. In each of them the 'Laudate pueri' is set contrapuntally, followed by a soprano aria for the 'Laudate Dominum'—an especially telling contrast in the 'Vesperae solennes', with the juxtaposition of the old fugue subject based on a falling diminished seventh and the almost sensuous smoothness of the solo melody. The quality of serene beauty in the vocal melody that is so conspicuous in this 'Laudate Dominum' is also present in the two Masses, and its operatic nature is brought home by the similarities that their settings of the *Agnus Dei* bear to the two great arias of the Countess in *Figaro*—in the 'Coronation' Mass, K. 317, to 'Dove sono', and in K. 337 a less marked resemblance to 'Porgi amor'. The Masses rely a good deal on instrumental forms for their structure; the 'recapitulation' in the *Gloria* of the 'Coronation' Mass, for instance, is unusually exact. This is another of those works that finish as they began: the 'Dona nobis pacem' takes up again the music of the *Kyrie*, though with an undeniable loss of effect when the original Andante changes to Allegro con spirito. But more important than the individual ingredients is the blend between them. There is a greater sense of balance than ever before, particularly between voices and instruments. The obbligato writing for oboe, bassoon, and organ in the *Agnus Dei* of K. 337 is the most spectacular piece of orchestration in the two Masses, but felicitous touches in scoring occur throughout both works. Quite exceptional, however, not only in the Masses of 1779 and 1780 but in Mozart's church music as a whole, is the 'Benedictus' of K. 337, in which the customary idyllic mood is replaced by uncompromising counterpoint in an unrelenting minor key.

These works represent the peak of Mozart's Salzburg church music. Yet, even at his best, and whether or not he was writing specifically for the Cathedral, and therefore within the limitations imposed by the Archbishop, Mozart seems in some degree frustrated in his home town. What he might have done in less restricting surroundings is shown by the magnificent *Kyrie* in D minor, K. 341 (368a), written in Munich at the time of *Idomeneo*, which is the most fully scored of his sacred works, and surpasses all the previous choral music. Ironically, the artistic freedom that produced Mozart's greatest masterpieces also removed the incentive to compose for the church. In Vienna, after the break from the Archbishop's service in 1781, there was little occasion to write Masses.

Mozart's C minor Mass, K. 427 (417a), poses a puzzle second only to that of the Requiem. It was written in fulfillment of a promise, the exact terms of which are not clear, connected with the composer's marriage to Constanze Weber. But, despite the patent sincerity of his intention to complete it, the Mass was never finished. It was performed notwithstanding, apparently as a votive offering, when Mozart took his wife home to Salzburg for the first time in the summer of 1783,[1] and on this occasion Constanze sang one of the solo parts. Presumably the missing movements were made good with music from earlier Masses.[2] Any present-day attempt at completion on these lines,[3] however, can only result in mere cobbling, for in the rest of Mozart's church music there is nothing of the scale and quality equal to supplying the sections that are missing—the second half of the *Credo* and the whole *Agnus Dei*. Unfinished as it is, the C minor Mass ranks among the very finest of all Mozart's works.

The years 1782–3, during which the Mass was written, were a revelation to Mozart. It was at this time that he came to know and admire the works of J. S. Bach and Handel, chiefly through the agency of Baron Gottfried van Swieten, who was later responsible for commissioning his arrangements of *Acis and Galatea*, *Messiah*, the *Ode on St. Cecilia's Day*, and *Alexander's Feast*.[4] Mozart's preoccupation with counterpoint at this time can be seen in such works as the Fantasia and Fugue in C, K. 394 (383a), and the Suite 'in the style of Handel', K. 399 (385i). It reaches its complete fruition in the C minor Mass. Yet the work is by no means wholly contrapuntal. Alongside movements which are as close as Mozart ever came to Bach there is music which is wholeheartedly operatic in style. The C minor Mass is the ultimate degree of the *stilus mixtus*, but the stylistic contrast gives rise to no sense of disunity or incongruity. Here, one feels, the contrapuntal writing is no mere traditional gesture. One can no longer, as was perhaps reasonable in some of the earlier works, identify homophony and counterpoint respectively with the quick and the dead. Both are complementary parts of Mozart's current musical language.

The wide range of style in the C minor Mass is already evident within the single movement that sets the complex of *Kyrie–Christe–Kyrie*, in which the mellifluous soprano solo of the 'Christe' is framed by the contrapuntal choral writing of the outer sections. In treating the *Gloria* as a series of independent movements. Mozart uses the structural methods of the 'cantata Mass'. Three of the numbers are for soloists only, the 'Laudamus te', for instance, being a florid soprano aria in concerto form which calls for considerable virtuosity from the singer. The slightly archaic

[1] Otto E. Deutsch, *Mozart. Die Dokumente seines Lebens* (Kassel, etc., 1961), p. 194.

[2] Cf. H. C. Robbins Landon's introduction to the Eulenburg miniature score (Zürich, etc., 1956).

[3] See, for instance, Ernst Lewicki, 'Die Vervollständigung von Mozarts grosser C-Moll Messe durch Alois Schmitt', *Die Musik*, Jg. V (2) (1905–06), pp. 1 ff. and 168 ff., and 'Über Mozarts grosse C-Moll Messe und die Endgestalt ihrer Ergänzung', *Mozart-Jahrbuch* I (ed. Abert), (Munich, 1923), p. 71.

[4] Cf. *The Letters of Mozart*, iii, p. 1192 and *passim*; Edward Olleson, 'Gottfried van Swieten, Patron of Haydn and Mozart', *Proceedings of the Royal Musical Association*, lxxxix (1962/3), p. 63.

flavour that is sometimes to be felt in this aria is more prominent in the 'Domine Deus' duet and the 'Quoniam' trio, with their Handelian echoes and astonishing variety and ease of counterpoint. The focal point of the work as it stands is the massive 'Qui tollis' for double choir, whose persistent jagged rhythms, relentless dissonance, and reliance on the old chaconne bass of a chromatically descending fourth seem to recall both Handel and Bach. Contrapuntal brilliance is most conspicuous in the 'Cum sancto spiritu' fugue and in the 'Osanna', which, though left by Mozart in four vocal parts, was clearly—like the same movement in Bach's B minor Mass—conceived in eight. The only movement to have aroused misgivings is the 'Et incarnatus', in which some of the accompanying parts remain unfinished. It undeniably belongs to the 'nativity scene' tradition of the Neapolitan Mass, and, with its florid cadenza for solo voice and obbligato instruments, has sometimes been frowned upon for its secularity. When in 1785 Mozart recast the C minor Mass as the cantata *Davidde penitente*, K. 469, the 'Et incarnatus' was one of the movements to be omitted, and critics have seen this, together with its incomplete state, as proof of Mozart's dissatisfaction with it. True, the aria has nothing of a 'church style' about it. Yet its sheer loveliness seems to transcend all boundaries between the sacred and the secular.

The C minor Mass is unsurpassed, and in Mozart's church music is equalled only by the Requiem. From the years between them there is no major work for the church, only the beautifully simple 'Ave verum corpus', K. 618, less than fifty bars long, which was composed in 1791 for Anton Stoll, the choirmaster of the little town of Baden, near Vienna, doubtless out of personal gratitude for his kindness to Constanze on her visits there to take the waters. In Vienna Mozart was concerned principally with opera, concerto, and chamber music. But the lacking incentive for him to compose for the liturgy was supplied by the commission in 1791 to write a Requiem Mass.

Mozart's Requiem has enjoyed greater popularity than any other piece of eighteenth-century Catholic church music. The mystery which surrounds it has undoubtedly added to its appeal. Mozart's supposed fatalistic conviction that he was writing the Requiem for his own impending death has lent a certain macabre *frisson*. The doubts concerning its authenticity have only heightened the interest. No work has aroused so much controversy,[1] and many questions still remain unanswered and unanswerable.

---

[1] Cf. Otto Jahn, 'Die Kontroverse über das Requiem', in Abert, *Mozart*, ii, p. 1019; Friedrich Blume, 'Requiem but no Peace', *Musical Quarterly*, xlviii (1961), p. 147; Ernst Hess, 'Zur Ergänzung des Requiems von Mozart durch F. X. Süssmayr', *Mozart–Jahrbuch 1959*, p. 99; K. Marguerre, 'Mozart und Süssmayr', *Mozart–Jahrbuch 1962/63*, p. 172.

The commission for the Requiem came anonymously from Count Franz von Walsegg, whose reason for concealing his identity was that he wished to pass the work off as his own. But it was never finished: progress was held up by the intense pressure of the summer and autumn of 1791, during which *La Clemenza di Tito* and *Die Zauberflöte* were written, and Mozart was still working on it at his death in December. The Requiem as we know it[1] was completed by Mozart's pupil Franz Xaver Süssmayr, and here the difficulties begin. What Süssmayr wrote down can be determined from the handwriting, but this is not necessarily the same as what he actually composed. For all his statement admitting, apparently with ingenuous modesty, that 'the greatest part' of the work was his own,[2] it cannot be overlooked that Süssmayr had every reason for making the most of his contribution to the Requiem, since he never before or thereafter produced anything of comparable stature.

The Introit and *Kyrie* present no problems of authenticity, as every note is by Mozart. Here there is the same rigorous polyphony that was noted in the C minor Mass. Mozart's visit to Leipzig in 1789, when he was so impressed by Bach's motet 'Singet dem Herrn',[3] seems to have left its mark, especially on the almost chorale-prelude treatment of the old *tonus peregrinus* melody at 'Te decet hymnus' and the *Kyrie* fugue on the well-worn subject spanning a diminished seventh. The sombre mood of the D minor tonality is underlined by the dark colour of the orchestral sound, with basset horns as the highest woodwind instruments and trombones doubling the three lowest voices.

Süssmayr's work begins with the Sequence, most of which Mozart left in draft only. Mozart's score contained the complete voice-parts and bass, together with the most important orchestral material, up to the middle of the 'Lacrimosa', but much of the instrumentation remained to be filled out. The change to Süssmayr can sometimes be felt, for instance in the 'Tuba mirum', where the solo trombone surely exceeds his brief to wake the dead. Occasional cases of heavy-handedness in the scoring, however, do little damage to the substance of Mozart's music. The six movements balance terror and consolation, the pomp of the 'Rex tremendae' being succeeded by the magical 'Recordare', which may be compared to the 'Domine Deus' of the C minor Mass for the ease and subtlety of its contrapuntal writing. This is in turn succeeded by the deeply disturbing 'Confutatis', whose enharmonic modulations in the final section come close to a distintegration of the tonality.

[1] The portions in Mozart's autograph (Vienna, Nat. Bibl. 17561) have been published in facsimile by Alfred Schnerich (Vienna, 1914).
[2] Jahn, op. cit.
[3] Ibid., ii, p. 628.

The last movement of the Sequence, the 'Lacrimosa', brings the question of authenticity to a head, since after eight bars Mozart's manuscript breaks off altogether, and the rest is apparently all Süssmayr's work.[1] The 'Domine Jesu Christe' and 'Hostias' that make up the Offertory were left in the same state as the greater part of the Sequence, complete in substance but with the scoring unfinished, while of the *Sanctus*, 'Benedictus', and *Agnus Dei* nothing in Mozart's hand remains. These last sections Süssmayr, according to his own account, composed entirely anew, except that from the words 'Lux aeterna' he took up the music of Mozart's opening movement at 'Te decet hymnus'. The work thus ends, as Mozart is said to have directed it should,[2] with the *Kyrie* fugue repeated to the words 'Cum sanctis tuis'.

The problem of Mozart's Requiem is simply one of credulity. If we can accept Süssmayr's testimony—and some can—then no difficulties arise. On the other hand, many have felt, on the evidence of their ears, that at least parts of the music ostensibly by Süssmayr bear the unmistakable stamp of Mozart himself. Such aural evidence, unlike calligraphic, cannot be proved, but it is no less admissible for that; to dismiss it out of hand, and rely solely on the handwriting of the score, is altogether too glib. The test is the 'Lacrimosa': could Süssmayr have written the magnificent passage, so at one with Mozart's first eight bars, from the point where the original stops up to the F major cadence? If so, then it is easy to see him as the true composer of the three movements he claimed as his own.

It must remain an open question as to whether, and to what extent, Süssmayr received guidance from Mozart, either in the shape of sketches or verbal instructions. Opportunity certainly existed, for the two worked much together during 1791. Süssmayr is said to have taken away from Mozart's death-bed a number of slips of manuscript paper, which could have been sketches for the Requiem.[3] Among the many attempts to explain away the anomaly of what appears to be Mozart's music in what is unquestionably Süssmayr's hand, one should be mentioned here. A proposal by Friedrich Blume[4] resurrects two reports which have generally been discredited up to now: that most of the Requiem existed in fair copy in August 1791; and that the whole work was performed the following month. Blume suggests that Mozart, recognizing that his

---

[1] For an alternative completion, see Wilhelm Fischer, 'Das "Lacrimosa dies illa" in Mozart's Requiem', *Mozart–Jahrbuch 1951*, p. 7.

[2] *Wolfgang Amadeus Mozart. Briefe und Aufzeichnungen*, ed. Wilhelm A. Bauer and O. E. Deutsch, iv (1963), p. 234.

[3] Cf. Abert, op. cit., ii, p. 852; and Wolfgang Plath, 'Über Skizzen zu Mozarts "Requiem"', *Kongress-Bericht, Kassel 1962*, (Kassel, 1963), p. 184; Gerhard Groll, 'Briefe zum Requiem', *Mozart–Jahrbuch 1967*, p. 12.

[4] Op. cit., pp. 164–8.

other commitments would prevent him from fulfilling the commission for the Requiem on time, may have had it completed by Süssmayr, under his own more or less close supervision, during the summer. After his return from Prague and the completion of *Die Zauberflöte*, he will then have taken it up again to finish it himself. Blume's theory, which he admits is 'no more than a hypothesis', is the only fresh idea to have emerged in recent years. It can easily be challenged, and is by no means the last word on the subject. It merely adds a new and stimulating question-mark to the puzzle of Mozart's Requiem.

HAYDN'S LATE MASSES

The death of Prince Nicholas Esterházy in 1790 had freed Haydn, and enabled him to undertake his two visits to London. While remaining titular *Kapellmeister* to Prince Anton, he was no longer burdened with the responsibilities of his post. The succession in 1794 of Nicholas II, however, meant for Haydn a resumption of his practical duties, though on a smaller scale than before. Music in the Esterházy household never regained the magnificence of its heyday, but under the new prince the musical establishment, which had lapsed during Anton's rule, was reconstituted. By far the most important consequence of this revival was the group of six Masses that Haydn composed between 1796 and 1802, all apparently intended for the name-day of Princess Maria Hermengilde, wife of Prince Nicholas. Beethoven followed in Haydn's footsteps in 1807, when he wrote his C major Mass for the same occasion.

In the fourteen years since the 'Mariazell' Mass Haydn had become an international celebrity. The late Masses share many characteristics with the symphonies that had captured his London audiences. Though written in the first place for home consumption, they have a popular appeal that reaches far beyond the festivities for the name-day of the princess in Eisenstadt. Like many of the London symphonies—the 'Surprise', 'Military', 'Drum Roll' and so forth—the Masses typically contain some feature that makes each of them immediately memorable, and often gives rise to a descriptive nickname. They have the same quality of easy intelligibility combined with the utmost freedom and subtlety of form, making them a constant delight to the listener but sometimes a headache to the doctrinaire analyst. They continue Haydn's tendency towards ever more colourful orchestration, particularly in the use of the wind instruments.

Not everything, of course, is new. Haydn rarely discards anything altogether, and the late Masses freely employ earlier techniques. The first of them, the 'Missa in Tempore Belli' or 'Paukenmesse' of 1796, contains passages in the trio texture of decades before:

Ex. 145

The *Gloria*, which has the usual fast–slow–fast layout, is unified by the common material of its outer sections. But here the old principle of the orchestral ostinato is handled with a new flexibility, and the three movements as a whole, with the central 'Qui tollis' in the key of the submediant major, show a wider range of tonality than is found in any of the previous Masses. The most strikingly novel part of the work, however, is the *Agnus Dei*, whose menacing drum-rolls and fanfares clearly symbolize the 'time of war' referred to in Haydn's original title.

There are several points of contact between the 'Paukenmesse' and its predecessor, the 'Mariazell' Mass, not least in the radiant turn to the tonic major towards the end of the 'Benedictus' in each. A specific parallel occurs between the 'Mariazell' Mass and the 'Missa Sancti Bernardi de Offida', begun in 1796 but probably not finished until the following year, both of which, allowing for transposition, share identical openings to the *Gloria*. The tendency, noted earlier, for the soloists to work together and in conjunction with the chorus, rather than alone, becomes more pronounced in the late Masses, where there is little by way of solo arias as such. One notable ensemble passage is the canonic 'Et incarnatus est' of the 'Missa Sancti Bernardi'. The title 'Heiligmesse', by which this Mass is generally known, derives from the appropriate quotation in the *Sanctus* of the hymn tune 'Heilig, heilig, heilig'. Again one is reminded of an older practice: the presentation of the melody in an inner part, doubled by wind instruments (here two bassoons), seems to hark back to Haydn's use of *canti fermi* in such symphonies as the 'Lamentatione', written some thirty years earlier.

A conspicuous feature of Haydn's late choral style is its freedom of texture. Just as no structural division is made between aria and chorus, so there is no dogmatic distinction between homophony and counterpoint. This is not to say that formal counterpoint goes by the board, however; an example of canon was mentioned above, and the six Masses contain magnificent fugues. Two of Haydn's finest contrapuntal movements are found consecutively in the 'Missa in Angustiis', or 'Nelson' Mass, of 1798. The fugue at the end of the *Gloria* combines tunefulness and enormous rhythmic energy, while the opening section of the *Credo* is an extended canon at the fifth for two pairs of voices, sopranos singing in octaves with tenors, and altos with basses. The whole Mass sustains a consistent level of mastery which is exceptional even among these works of Haydn's old age. How Nelson comes into the picture is far from clear. Picturesque though the story is that associates the fanfares in the 'Benedictus' with the Battle of the Nile, the news of Nelson's victory cannot have reached Haydn until after the Mass was finished. In any case, these strident trumpet calls are equally appropriate to the 'in angustiis' of Haydn's original title.

The 'Nelson' Mass has an entirely individual sound, due to its scoring for three trumpets, drums, obbligato organ, and strings, without woodwind. On its publication in 1803, however, wind instruments replaced the organ—apparently with Haydn's connivance, though the arrangement was certainly not his own[1]—and some of the trumpet parts were altered as well. It was in this form that the work was generally known until recently, when the original version was published for the first time.

The scarcity of wind players at Eisenstadt, said to have been the cause of this unusual though extremely telling scoring,[2] also affected the so-called 'Theresienmesse', composed in 1799, which employs only clarinets, two trumpets, and drums in addition to the string orchestra. The organ resumes its normal function of continuo instrument. Curiously enough, the clarinets, adopted by Haydn in his second set of London symphonies and used affectionately in *The Creation*, have little that is idiomatic. When playing independent parts, rather than doubling, they tend to live up to their etymology as 'little trumpets'.

The 'Theresa' is the least spectacular of the late Masses, having neither the brilliance of the 'Nelson' nor the same variety of colour as the others, but this is no criticism of the music. The longest movements, it is true, scarcely equal those of the 'Nelson' Mass, and the first section of the *Credo*, with its *moto perpetuo* writing for the violins, has a hint of the old workaday declamatory style, though here the voices have far more melodic and contrapuntal interest. The 'Et incarnatus est' that follows, however, is a profoundly expressive Adagio in the minor, whose closing words 'et sepultus est' are underlined by the quiet persistence of a repeated tonic pedal from trumpets and drum. The same sensitivity can be felt in the middle section of the *Gloria* and in the long 'Benedictus'.

The Empress Maria Theresa, consort of Francis II, has as doubtful a connection with 'her' Mass as Nelson with his. She certainly did not commission it, as she did the fine C major *Te Deum* which Haydn wrote in 1799 or 1800. In fact she has a closer link with the next Mass, dating from 1801, of which she received a copy.[3] The 'Schöpfungsmesse', or 'Creation' Mass takes its name from the fact that it contains a conspicuous quotation from the oratorio. A phrase from the duet of Adam and Eve appears, rather surprisingly, to the words 'Qui tollis peccata mundi' in the *Gloria*, preceding the change to a slower speed and unashamedly cheerful. It is no doubt partly this, together with the rococo style of the concertante organ in the 'Et incarnatus est', that has earned the 'Creation' Mass the reputation from some critics for superficial brilliance and little else. But it is a splendid work, if perhaps uneven. The sudden fortissimo change from F major to D♭ at 'judicare' in the *Credo* uses the same tonal contrast, and has the same impact, as the dramatic entry of 'Endless

[1] Cf. Olleson, 'Georg August Griesinger's Correspondence with Breitkopf and Härtel', *Haydn Yearbook*, iii (1965), p. 40.
[2] Olleson, loc. cit.
[3] Brand, *Die Messen*, pp. 409 ff.

God' in *The Seasons*. The exhilarating first section of the *Gloria*, with its powerful recurrent fanfare for wind, is second to none.

In 1800 Prince Esterházy had augmented his musical staff by eight members, so that the wind section was now at full strength.[1] This had a marked effect on Haydn's last two Masses. The 'Creation' Mass, unlike its two predecessors, calls for a large orchestra of oboes, clarinets, bassoons, horns, trumpets, and drums as well as strings and organ. The prominence of the wind instruments has given the name of 'Harmoniemesse' ('Wind-band Mass') to Haydn's last major work, composed in 1802, which uses the same forces, but without the obbligato organ and with the addition of a flute. (Perhaps significantly, the organ part of the 'Creation' Mass is headed 'Flautino'.)

In June 1802 Haydn, in a letter to Prince Esterházy, referred to himself as 'labouring WEARILY on the new Mass'.[2] The weariness does not show in the 'Harmoniemesse', as it occasionally does in *The Seasons*, which had caused him so much trouble before its completion the previous year. A certain mellowness may perhaps be felt in the grand sonata-form *Kyrie*, which, unusually, remains Poco adagio throughout and finishes pianissimo. But the opening of the *Gloria* has the old man's characteristic youthful freshness. He did not spare himself: the Mass is on the largest scale, with fugues at the end of the *Gloria* and *Credo* that are huge both in dimensions and strength. None of his works apart from *The Creation* and *The Seasons* is so fully and imaginatively scored. All the instruments are obbligato. The clarinet, sometimes the Cinderella of Haydn's orchestra, eloquently opens the 'Et incarnatus est'. The beginning of the *Agnus Dei*, in F major, has the beautiful sonority of solo oboes and bassoon with pizzicato strings. Returning to the tonic key of the work, B♭ major fanfares—such a typical feature of the late Masses —herald the 'Dona nobis pacem', which brings to a fitting conclusion not only the 'Harmoniemesse', but Haydn's long career.

CHURCH MUSIC AND ORATORIO IN ENGLAND AND FRANCE

No other country in Europe could challenge Austria in the quality and importance of her church music, though practical necessity ensured that composers everywhere continued to write for the liturgy. In France, men like Gossec and Grétry supplied their tithe of church music, but it formed no substantial part of their total output. Jean-François Lesueur produced a quantity of liturgical works of real stature, particularly during his time at Notre Dame in Paris (1786–8), but even in his case one

[1] Olleson, op. cit., p. 16.
[2] *The Collected Correspondence ... of Joseph Haydn*, ed. Landon (London, 1959), p. 205.

cannot quarrel with the judgement that remembers him chiefly for his contributions to opera. One would scarcely expect the country of Voltaire to have found its natural artistic medium in sacred music, and the Revolution brought all such composition to a halt. A great revival was to take place at the hands of Luigi Cherubini, who settled in Paris in 1787, but the period of his finest sacred works began only in 1809.

Nor was oratorio cultivated in France. After Charpentier, the genre was as good as totally ignored by French composers until the last thirty years of the eighteenth century. At the Concert Spirituel, where one might have expected to find oratorios alongside the motets and other sacred works that were given, they were admitted to the programme only when the directorship passed in 1773 to Gossec, who the following year performed his own *La Nativité*. Even after this oratorio performances were infrequent, and the awakening interest in the works of Handel, which was making steady progress in German-speaking countries, seems to have passed France by. French oratorio, like French church music, had to wait till the nineteenth century for its revival.

English sacred music during the later eighteenth century fared little better, if for different reasons. The traditions of the Anglican church could not, except on special ceremonial occasions like coronations and royal weddings, offer the opportunities for ambitious music that the Roman Catholic liturgy did. And English church music had no composer of the first rank. As in the first half of the century, the leading figures in English music were for the most part foreigners domiciled in London, such as J. C. Bach and Karl Friederich Abel. The native Englishmen who served the Anglican church tended to be more conservative by inclination, and none of them was completely successful in applying the modern instrumental style to his church music.

In a sense, the greatest achievement of the period was not the creation of a new repertoire of sacred music but the preservation of the treasures of the past. A collection of English church music of the sixteenth and seventeenth centuries was begun by Handel's younger contemporary, Maurice Greene, but remained unfinished at his death in 1755. Taken over by William Boyce, Greene's successor as Master of the King's Music, this was now published in three volumes between 1760 and 1773 under the title *Cathedral Music*, forming a corpus of music beside which the original anthems and services of Boyce and his contemporaries, though very considerable in quantity, seem small enough. A further four volumes with the same title appeared in 1790, edited by Samuel Arnold. It is surely no accident that the finest new sacred pieces of the second half of the century are often those that owe most to the idioms of a previous era. An anthem like Jonathan Battishill's 'O Lord, look down from heaven' has little of the conventional charm that is characteristic of so much of the church music of the time. In its strength and rigorous part-writing it belongs firmly to the traditions that made Boyce's *Cathedral Music* such a notable collection.

Oratorio, carried along on the momentum generated by Handel, continued to flourish in England after his death. The oratorio performances which Handel himself had directed at Covent Garden continued under J. C. Smith, the composer's former amanuensis, and John Stanley. Rival concerts at Drury Lane were directed by Thomas Arne and, later, Samuel Arnold. All these men produced oratorios of their own, among the most popular being Arne's *Judith* (1761) and Arnold's *The Prodigal Son* (1773). Smith's *Paradise Lost* (1758), on a libretto derived from Milton, is one of a small minority of works not strictly on Old Testament historical themes, and in its subject-matter (though nothing else) is a precursor of Haydn's *Creation* of some forty years later. But none of the English composers was big enough to free himself in his own music from the dominating influence of Handel, and it was Handel's oratorios that formed the staple diet at the concerts they conducted. While on the Continent Handel had to wait for a revival of interest in the music of the past before he won universal recognition, in England no such revival was needed: his oratorios never went out of circulation. The cultivation of Handel's oratorios reached a peak in the centenary celebrations that were held one year prematurely in 1784. This was the first of a series of Handel Commemorations, at which vast numbers of singers and instrumentalists took part.

The tradition of oratorio was stronger in England than in any other country, but it was to bear its chief fruits elsewhere. At the last of the Handel Commemorations, in 1791, Joseph Haydn was present, and the music he heard in London provided him with the stimulus to attempt a different type of oratorio from the Neapolitan model that was predominant in Vienna. The direct result was what is unquestionably the greatest oratorio of the later eighteenth century: *The Creation*.

THE ORATORIO IN CATHOLIC EUROPE

To criticize the oratorio of Catholic Europe, as many have done from Burney onwards, for its inadequacy both as church music and as choral music is to do it an injustice, for it made no attempt to be either. Oratorio was predominantly Italian, and its history for most of the eighteenth century is the history of Italian *opera seria*. Like the opera, it had undergone reform at the hands of Zeno and Metastasio, and now the two genres shared the same formal and stylistic principles.

The oratorio, of course, was not normally staged,[1] and had two acts to the opera's three, but otherwise its only fundamental distinguishing feature was its sacred subject.

Nor was oratorio any more sober, less histrionic, than opera, rather the reverse. Full use was made of every available means to compensate for the lack of action in what was none the less a dramatic form. The proportion of recitative accompanied by the orchestra, always higher than in opera, increased as time went on, until in such a representative late Italian oratorio as Giovanni Paisiello's *Passione* (1782) it has predominance over *recitativo secco*. The oratorio moved steadily towards a greater sense of dramatic continuity, and was less inclined than *opera seria* to degenerate into a steeplechase of more or less disconnected arias.

In terms of musical quality the oratorio could more than hold its own. It is almost as if the music, as the sole centre of interest, received as a bonus the share of attention which the stage would claim in opera. The care that composers took over their oratorios is particularly evident in the painstaking treatment of the orchestra, in recitative and aria alike. True to Metastasian conventions, however, the focus was on the solo singer. The chorus had little more to do than finish off each act. To be sure, the choral writing was often more weighty than it was in opera, perhaps taking the form of a fugal finale, and thus giving rise to the same mixture of old and new styles that has been noted in church music. But no composer of Italian oratorio followed Handel's example in creating choral oratorio within a dramatic framework.

German oratorio, which was eventually to eclipse Italian, had at first little place in the south. The tradition of school drama in Salzburg fostered a number of notable works in German and Latin as well as Italian, with Johann Ernst Eberlin (1702–1762) as their most prolific and distinguished composer.[2] In these circumstances Mozart at the age of ten or eleven collaborated with Adlgasser and Michael Haydn in composing *Die Schuldigkeit des ersten Gebotes*, K. 35. But his first and only true oratorio was an Italian one on a libretto by Metastasio. *La Betulia liberata*, K. 118 (74c), apparently written for Padua in 1771, is clearly modelled on Hasse, and for all its fingerprints of Mozart's youthful originality belongs to the mainstream of Neapolitan oratorio.

During the almost thirty-year reign of Charles VI, Vienna maintained a splendid independence, in oratorio as in church music. But after 1740 the sponsorship of the Court quickly declined, and the strength of Fux, Caldara, and Francesco Conti gave place to the easier, more mellifluous,

[1] But see Schering, *Geschichte des Oratoriums* (Leipzig, 1911), p. 241.
[2] Cf. Robert Haas, 'Eberlins Schuldramen und Oratorien', *Studien zur Musikwissenschaft*, viii (1921), p. 9; *Der blutschwitzende Jesus*, ed. Haas, *Denkmäler der Tonkunst in Österreich*, xxviii/1 (1921).

more modern, yet undeniably less virile Neapolitan style. The conservatism that characterizes much Viennese church music is little in evidence in oratorio after the middle of the century. Works such as Wagenseil's *Redenzione* (1755)—significantly subtitled 'Componimento drammatico'—and Bonno's *Isaaco* (1759) are virtually indistinguishable in style from those of Italianate composers elsewhere. The foundation of the Tonkünstler-Societät in 1771, whose twice-yearly performances gave Vienna its first truly public concerts, might have been expected to encourage oratorio in the vernacular. Some German works indeed appeared on the programmes, but more often than not the language of the words was that of the music, the language of Italian opera. It was for the Tonkünstler that Haydn in 1775 composed *Il Ritorno di Tobia*, and Mozart ten years later arranged his C minor Mass as *Davidde penitente*.

Il Ritorno di Tobia[1] was perhaps the most ambitious work that Haydn had written to date, and is a magnificent example of Neapolitan oratorio at its best. Its greatest weakness is its length, as Haydn apparently recognized, for he seems to have made cuts for its revival in 1784, and certainly sanctioned its performance in an abridged version in 1808—the last occasion that the Tonkünstler-Societät presented an Italian oratorio. In consisting largely of alternate recitatives (for the most part accompanied) and florid arias with long ritornelli, it follows the normal pattern of its time. But from the overture, which leads without a break into the first duet and chorus, it immediately impresses by its musical quality and particularly its rich orchestration. Sara's exquisite aria 'Non parmi esser fra gl' uomini' from Part II, for instance, has obbligato flutes, oboes, cors anglais, bassoons, and horns. It is in the choral writing, however, that Haydn most clearly demonstrates his supremacy. Even the three choruses in the first version of 1775 show the hand of the composer of the 'Cecilia' Mass. And in 1784[2] two more were added, including the oratorio's finest number, 'Svanisce in un momento', which has been rescued from the oblivion into which the rest of the work has fallen by its use as a motet to the words 'Insanae et vanae curae'.

One has to admit that *Il Ritorno di Tobia* is scarcely ideal as a whole. Its huge arias, for all their quality, are more satisfactory individually than strung together. The fault lies less with Haydn than with the contemporary conception of the genre. Neapolitan oratorio was outgrowing its conventional structure, but it had no Gluck or Calzabigi to question its basic principles, while to follow the trend towards *opera buffa* was clearly impossible. It lived on in Vienna for some time after the effective

[1] J. Haydn: *Werke*, ser. 28, i.
[2] On the ornamented version of the tenor aria, 'Quando mi dona', which Haydn made in 1784, see Schmid, 'Joseph Haydn und die vocale Zierpraxis seiner Zeit', *Bericht über die internationale Konferenz zum Andenken Joseph Haydns* (Budapest, 1961), p. 117.

death of its twin form of *opera seria*. Haydn himself, with *The Creation*, dealt it the *coup de grâce*.

CHORAL MUSIC IN PROTESTANT GERMANY

If in the south oratorio was neither church music nor choral music, in the north it was to some extent both. The Protestant oratorio of the eighteenth century had its roots in Lutheran church music, and, though it outgrew its liturgical function and became a concert-piece in its own right, it never completely cast off its connections with the church. The chorus continued to be of importance, and the chorale held its place long after the congregation had become an audience.

To these origins the oratorio of northern Germany owed much of its strength. Even outside the church it still spoke to the same cross-section of the community that would have heard it there—and, unlike the oratorio in Dresden or Vienna, it spoke to them in their own language. The wide audience it reached may be judged from the large number of oratorios that were published in vocal score. Its essentially popular appeal had little of the refinement of the more exclusive Italian oratorio. Compared to Hasse's *Conversione di Sant' Agostino* (1750),[1] Telemann's *Tag des Gerichts* (1761)[2] is full-blooded almost to the point of vulgarity in its melodramatic scene-painting. Operatic influence was strong in north and south alike, but in drawing on the dramatic techniques of opera Protestant composers did not inevitably at the same time take over its structural conventions.

The dramatic oratorio with a continuous, usually Old Testament story, established by Mattheson in Hamburg and continued there by Telemann, found its chief exponent during the later eighteenth century in Johann Heinrich Rolle (1718–85) of Magdeburg. The popular tone of Rolle's melodies, which at their best have an attractive simplicity, can result in the obvious or even banal, but his dramatic instinct is undeniable, and his approach to oratorio is typified by the stage directions that sometimes occur in his scores. Rolle's most famous work, *Der Tod Abels* (1771), has a sense of forward-moving action such as is rare in Italian oratorio of the time, and in Abraham's 'Herr, wende nicht dein Angesicht' contains a magnificently sustained *scena* of changing moods. The freedom with which Rolle moves from effective accompanied recitative to aria and back again, in order to achieve continuity, is still more noticeable in the later *Lazarus* (1779).

These oratorios of Rolle may truly be described as sacred dramas.

Schering ed.), *Denkmäler deutscher Tonkunst*, xx (1905); excerpt in Archibald T. Davison and Willi Apel, *Historical Anthology of Music* (London, 1950), ii, p. 212.

[2] Max Schneider (ed.), ibid., xxviii (1907); excerpt in Davison and Apel, op. cit., p. 191.

Most composers from the middle of the century onwards, however, inclined towards a type of oratorio which, while retaining the trappings of a dramatic form, was in reality more devotional by nature. The difference can be clearly seen in Karl Heinrich Graun's *Tod Jesu* (1755), perhaps the most popular German oratorio before Haydn's *Creation*. The libretto by Karl Wilhelm Ramler tells the Passion story, not in the biblical narration of an Evangelist but as seen through the eyes of supposed onlookers.

Nun klingen Waffen, Lanzen blinken bey dem Schein der Fakkeln, Mörder dringen ein: Ich sehe Mörder: ach es ist um Ihn geschehen! Er aber unerschrocken nahet sich den Feinden selbst; grossmüthig spricht er: Sucht ihr mich? so lasset meine Freunde gehen.

(Now weapons clash, lances flash in the torches' gleam, murderers close in. I see murderers. Ah, He is done for! But He, unflinching, Himself approaches His enemies. Magnanimously He speaks: Seek ye me? Then let my friends go.)

This can scarcely be called dramatic. The action takes place as it were off-stage, and the continuous use of the first person in the present tense rather gives the impression of a running commentary. The obvious danger is sentimentality. All too often one feels that oratorio libretti were compounded from the dignified narrative of the Bible by the simple recipe of adding sugar and water to taste.

This subjective view of religion produced countless libretti of a semi-dramatic, semi-reflective character, among them some of real literary merit, notably Herder's *Kindheit Jesu* and *Auferweckung Lazarus*, both of which were composed in 1773 by Johann Christoph Friedrich Bach.[1] Whether or not the prevailing sweetness of the time is to our liking, Graun's *Tod Jesu* is one of the finest works of its kind, and little deserves its reputation in some quarters as typifying the depths to which sacred music had sunk. Graun's vocal lines, it is true, have on occasions a song-like quality that comes close to being merely facile. But his handling of recitative, particularly when it crosses the borderline into arioso, is masterly, and if the chorales of the work cannot compare with J. S. Bach for pathos, its best contrapuntal writing can:

Ex. 146

---
[1] Georg Schünemann (ed.), *Denkmäler deutscher Tonkunst*, lvi (1917), and article 'Johann Christoph Friedrich Bach', *Bach–Jahrbuch 1914* (Leipzig, 1915), particularly pp. 64–86.

Sei - ne See -le__ ist voll Jam - - - - - (mer)

(His soul is filled with grief)

Graun, however, for all his considerable stature, is a minor figure beside his colleague at the Prussian court, Carl Philipp Emanuel Bach, who is as pre-eminent in North German choral music as he is in instrumental. C. P. E. Bach composed his best-remembered work, the *Magnificat*, in 1749, during the long period he spent in the service of Frederick the Great. The fact that it was written while Johann Sebastian was still alive, in surroundings where the vogue was for modern Italian music, might be said to sum up the *Magnificat*, with the stylistic contrasts it contains. The old is represented, for example, by the massive fugal texture of 'Sicut erat in principio', the new by the more graceful charm of the solo 'Suscepit Israel'. But little sacred music was written by Bach in Berlin. Most dates from the years in Hamburg, from 1768 onwards.

When C. P. E. Bach succeeded Telemann as musical director in Hamburg, he stepped into a position which demanded, as his father's in Leipzig had, a formidable quantity of music for church use, and it is not surprising that much of his work is in the nature of occasional compositions. That church music nevertheless had a following in its own right, not merely as a pendant to the Sunday services, is shown by the repeat performances that were given, for purely musical reasons, of pieces written specifically for some church festival, such as the great eight-part 'Heilig' for Michaelmas 1776.[1] But most rewarding were the full-scale concerts that Bach mounted, in which he performed not only his own but also other composers' works, including *Messiah* in 1785 and the *Credo* of the B minor Mass a year later.

With respect to its subject, Bach's *Die Israeliten in der Wüste* (1769) apparently belongs to the old Hamburg tradition of dramatic oratorio. In fact its second half is entirely without action, and Moses in the desert looks forward to the New Testament:

[1] Cf. Heinrich Miesner, *Philipp Emanuel Bach in Hamburg* (Heide, 1929), pp. 93–4.

Er wird, wenn nun der Zeiten Lauf erfüllt,
In sterbliche Gestalt verhüllt,
Die menschliche Gestalt erhöhen.

(Now when the course of time is fulfilled, He, veiled
in mortal form, shall elevate the nature of
mankind.)

The most memorable parts of the work, however, are the dramatic ones like the wild descriptive 'Symphony, in the manner of an overture' that precedes the words 'What a tumult sounds in my ear'. And Moses's prayer, 'Gott, meiner Väter Gott', continually interrupted by the angry shouts of the crowd, is one of the most vivid pictures in eighteenth-century oratorio.

Bach's *Auferstehung und Himmelfahrt Jesu* (1777/8), on the other hand is a setting of Ramler's devotional oratorio on the Resurrection and Ascension, a companion-piece to *Der Tod Jesu*. That it never achieved the widespread popularity of Graun's Passion oratorio in the same vein is surely due to the very features that make it far superior, the daring and imaginative strokes which can seem at odds with the armchair religiosity of the words. Here, in a strictly non-dramatic work, it is again Bach's sense of drama that makes the biggest impact. There is little comfortably conventional in the jagged dissonance of the first recitative, 'Judaea zittert'. The most brilliantly striking moment of the oratorio is reserved until the final chorus, when, after a cadence in C minor, the voices break in, unaccompanied and in unison, with the words 'The Lord is King' in D flat.

Ex. 147

No discussion of C. P. E. Bach could do better than end with the magnificent 'Heilig' for double chorus, which, though not his last work, he intended to stand as his 'swan-song in this sort of composition'. It was to be 'an attempt to arouse, by quite natural harmonic progressions, far more attention and stronger emotions than is possible by any amount of uneasy chromaticism'.[1] The opening *Ariette* for solo alto is little more than commonplace, but the remainder, entirely choral, is music of

[1] Hermann von Hase, 'Carl Philipp Emanuel Bach und Joh. Gottl. Im. Breitkopf', *Bach-Jahrbuch 1911*, p. 95.

extraordinary vision and power. The two choirs, each accompanied by its own orchestra of oboes, trumpets, drums, strings, and organ, are superbly contrasted: the first, the chorus of angels, begins on a quiet E major chord, after the G major close of the introduction, and is almost mystical in the breadth of its modulation, while the second, representing the people on earth, is loud, forceful and diatonic.

Ex. 148

This antiphonal treatment is succeeded by a mighty fugue, during the course of which appears as a *canto fermo* the first part of the Lutheran *Te Deum* melody intoned in unison. The 'Heilig' lasts no more than a few minutes, yet it is one of the most remarkable masterpieces of German choral music.

HAYDN'S *CREATION* AND *SEASONS*

By 1800 both the German and Italian oratorio could look back on what had been, with a bare handful of outstanding exceptions, fifty years of indifferent achievement. The spread of Italian style in the north, and the increasing use of the German language in the south, had brought about a certain rapprochement from both ends, with sentimentality as the all too common factor. Beethoven's *Christus am Oelberge* (1803) is something of a hybrid, a devotional oratorio of the German type, yet retaining features of the Neapolitan school. But neither had a great future, nor can Haydn's *Creation* and *Seasons* be said to result from any union between them. The two works that crown the period are more truly descended from the great oratorios of the earlier part of the century, those of Handel.

Handel's oratorios were not unknown to Vienna. Apart from isolated performances earlier, some of them had been given regularly since the 1780s in the private concerts of the so-called Gesellschaft der Associierten under the leadership of Baron van Swieten.[1] Mozart had played the biggest part in these, with his arrangements of *Messiah* and other works, but Haydn may have been involved too. In any event, he seems to have been little impressed by the performances of the Associierten, though he was evidently commissioned in about 1793 to compose an oratorio, *Die Vergötterung Hercules*, 'in the spirit and manner of Handel'. But when the Handel oratorios he heard in London fired him with enthusiasm to write a large choral work of his own, he had a ready-made platform in Vienna. The circumstances in which the vocal version of *Die Sieben Worte* (The Seven Last Words) (1796) arose[2] set the pattern for the two oratorios proper which were to follow: van Swieten made himself responsible for the text, in this case drawn in large measure from Ramler's *Tod Jesu*, and the first performance took place privately under the auspices of his society of aristocratic sponsors.

Die Schöpfung—The Creation—owed Handel more than inspiration and, indirectly, financial backing. Its libretto was modelled on an English text which is said to have been written in the first place for Handel himself, and although this anonymous original is now lost it clearly underlies the greatest part of *The Creation* as we know it. The oratorio has a plan quite untypical of its time, particularly in Parts I and II, which are built on a strong framework of biblical narrative at the beginning of each day of creation and chorus at the end. In between there was room for more lyrical and descriptive matter, while Part III, which introduces Adam and Eve blissfully contemplating each other and the newly created world, is predominantly idyllic in mood.

This simple scheme gave Haydn opportunity for the widest variety of musical treatment. The choruses that proclaim each successive stage of creation, some of them, like 'Mit Staunen sieht' (The glorious work

---

[1] For a more detailed discussion of this and the following, cf. Olleson, 'The Origin and Libretto of Haydn's "Creation"', *Haydn Yearbook*, iv (1968), p. 148.

[2] *J. Haydn: Werke*, series 28, ii. See Adolf Sandberger, 'Zur Entstehungsgeschichte' von Haydns "Sieben Worte des Erlösers am Kreuze"', *Ausgewählte Aufsätze zur Musikgeschichte* (Munich, 1921), p. 266.

behold amazed) and 'Die Himmel erzählen' (The Heavens are telling), incorporating one or more solo voices as well, have a magnificently jubilant tone. At the other extreme is the opening 'Representation of Chaos',[1] a remarkable depiction by means of ambiguous tonalities of an earth without form and void, whose darkness is only dispelled by the triumphant blaze of C major at the creation of light. Haydn's sense of orchestral colour, always prominent, seems to have been particularly sensitive to light in general: among the most memorable passages in *The Creation* are the sunrise at the beginning of the third day, together with the 'softer beams' of the moon, and the ethereal sonority of three flutes and pizzicato strings for the dawn of Part III. Yet 'endless night' is represented too, Hell's spirits falling headlong through a C minor fugato within a movement in A major.

The most directly pictorial music occurs when Gabriel, Uriel, and Raphael in the persons of the three soloists elaborate on the biblical account of creation, often paraphrasing Milton's *Paradise Lost*. Haydn's portrayal of the various natural phenomena, geographical features, and much of the vegetable and animal kingdom besides, is both vivid and sympathetic, with frequent touches of humour like the double bassoon of the heavy beasts or the lion's rude trombone blast.

This naïvely picturesque side to Haydn's music, which we now take for granted as an essential part of the charm of *The Creation*, came in for considerable criticism in his own time. If any scapegoat is needed, the blame can be laid on van Swieten. One is tempted to feel that the cost to Haydn of van Swieten's sponsorship was van Swieten the librettist, whose views he did not always share but whom he could not afford to offend. Certainly van Swieten's influence extended beyond the words into the music. The margins of his libretti to both the oratorios contain suggestions as to musical treatment,[2] which may be in fact less presumptuous than they seem, since it is likely that they were requested by Haydn himself. Whether called for or not, they were for the most part closely followed. But one need only recall Haydn's indignant protest that he had been forced to imitate the croaking of a frog in *The Seasons*, to see that van Swieten's penchant for the picturesque sometimes prevailed on Haydn to go against his better judgement.

Haydn's complaints about *Die Jahreszeiten* (The Seasons) (1801) were legion, and his dissatisfaction may account for the difficulty he had in finishing the work. In a sense he was right. James Thomson's poem,

[1] On Haydn's original conception, see Geiringer, 'Haydn's Sketches for "The Creation"', *Musical Quarterly*, xviii (1932), pp. 306–7.
[2] Printed in Carl F. Pohl and Hugo Botstiber, *Joseph Haydn*, iii (Leipzig, 1927), pp. 358–9; and Max Friedländer, 'Van Swieten und das Textbuch zu Haydns "Jahreszeiten"', *Jahrbuch der Musikbibliothek Peters*, 1909, pp. 47–56.

however drastically butchered, could never provide material with the simple dignity of Genesis, and the bucolic Simon, Hanne, and Lucas hardly measure up to the Archangels Gabriel, Uriel, and Raphael. Yet, taken on its own terms, *The Seasons* need not suffer by comparison with *The Creation*. It is essentially a series of tableaux of country life, and what it lacks in continuity it amply makes up for in diversity and colour.

The Seasons has much in common with *The Creation*. 'Summer', for example, opens with another dawn, this time including a cock-crow from the solo oboe. The orchestral introduction which 'paints the thick fogs at the beginning of Winter' is a feat of evocative writing comparable to the 'Representation of Chaos'. Haydn's notorious frog is only one of the creatures that appear in much the same way as they do in the earlier oratorio. But *The Seasons*, making little pretence of being a sacred work, can accommodate a wider range of subject-matter and style. 'Spring' has the ploughman whistling Haydn's own 'Surprise' Symphony. The hunting scenes of 'Autumn' culminate in a superbly vigorous chorus, which in the excitement of the chase rises from D major to E flat, and the season closes, not with a psalm of praise but with a drinking chorus, merriment to the bagpipes, and an intoxicated fugue. Different again is the atmosphere of domestic conviviality conjured up by the spinning song and the tale with which Hanne (Jane) entertains the company in 'Winter'.

The oratorio ends on a more solemn note. The seasons become an allegory of life, winter is man's old age. Optimism prevails, however, in a majestic final movement for soloists and double chorus. The words of the closing fugue, 'Uns leite deine Hand, o Gott! verleih uns Stärk' und Mut' (Let Thy hand lead us, Lord; grant us strength and courage), might have served Haydn as a motto in his intention to write another choral work. But nothing came of it.

V
SOLO SONG
By Rosemary Hughes

It is remarkable that solo song, so essential a part of the musical life of the Middle Ages, Renaissance, and early seventeenth century, should by the beginning of the eighteenth century have shrunk to a mere shadow. Still more remarkable is the lop-sided pattern of its gradual renewal. At the middle of the century the Mediterranean countries, France, and Austria still have little to show, whereas in the countries of northern Germany published song collections are on the increase, and in England they are appearing in quantity. By the last decade of the century the picture has changed once more. In England, songs are no less abundant, but they have hardly altered in character or in quality. France is the scene of a modest revival, of which the main feature is its almost antiquarian devotion to the past. Italy, and those countries in which the Italian musical language was still almost exclusively spoken even by native composers, still show little or nothing. But in Germany the resurgence has brought vast changes in character, quality, and range, while the Austrian revival, though barely two decades old, has already thrust forward towards the inner core of lyrical song.

To offer an explanation of this curiously uneven development would lead us outside the workings of purely musical cause and effect into a network of interacting forces, social, political, and religious as well as cultural. But if it be accepted that the eclipse of lyrical solo song at the outset of the century is in large measure due to the predominance of opera and the operatic style throughout Europe, it is also significant that opera flourished most powerfully in the areas of the Catholic Counter-Reformation, whereas lyrical poetry and song flourished, or revived, most strongly in the Protestant regions, particularly Northern Germany and England. The resurgent vitality and expansiveness of Catholicism—linked, in Austria, with that of the Habsburg dynasty and, in France, with the reign of the *Roi Soleil*—found its natural expression in dramatic spectacle, sacred and secular, spoken and musical. And underlying all this is the capacity of Catholicism, with its strongly corporate character, and its dogmatic grasp of objective truth, to maintain, even at this epoch, a religious culture within which the arts could find expression. But where, on the other hand, religious culture as such was slowly losing its hold on the realms of the intellect and the arts, men's minds had begun to seek a substitute in personal and subjective experience and its utterance; and this, supremely, lyrical poetry provides. It was in the Protestant areas of Europe that this emphasis on personal feelings and intuitions led most directly and swiftly to that flowering of lyrical poetry, and its corollary, lyrical song, that is but one aspect of the vast transformation of outlook and perspective known as the Romantic movement.

This trend, intersected or offset by many others, is not put forward as a complete explanation. It is, moreover, complicated by local factors which will be taken into account as they arise.

ENGLAND

In England solo song flourished throughout the century, in the teeth of the operatic invasion, and fostered by the London pleasure gardens, which offered public musical entertainment to a far wider social circle than was able to enjoy it in most European countries.[1]

So many songs were composed year by year for the Gardens and for the individual singers who appeared there that, as Frank Kidson wrote, 'if we eliminate from the published music of the time all that had its first hearing at the public gardens, there would be very little to show what English music was like in the eighteenth century'.[2] Such music, however, was sheer diversion, not an occupation demanding mental effort or the artistic spiritual energies no longer exercised in the service of a unified religious culture; for those energies, Englishmen in the eighteenth century found their outlet, on the one hand, in public life—politics, administration, large-scale agriculture and commerce, philanthropy—and, on the other, in direct religious revival movements. Even in the arts, the finest achievements of the century were on the practical side, in architecture, domestic elegance, and garden design, while the thinkers of the period were largely occupied with legal, political, and economic theory, and not, as in the states of northern Germany, with such matters as the theory of poetry or the relationship of text to music in song.

It is thus not surprising that eighteenth-century English song should be touched with the easy charm of pure entertainment music, and, at that, of music composed in the first instance for public performance. It

---

[1] Vauxhall and Marylebone Gardens were already in existence in the seventeenth century: Vauxhall was the 'New Spring Garden' visited by Evelyn and Pepys. Ranelagh, with its famous Rotunda, was opened in 1742. See Mollie Sands, *Invitation to Ranelagh* (London, 1947) and *The Gardens of Hampton Court* (London, 1950).

[2] 'The Nurseries of English Song', *Musical Times*, lxiii (1922), pp. 394 and 620.

lacks the intimacy inherent in music designed for private music-making, although it transplants readily enough to the home: witness the abundance of elegantly produced collections for domestic use.[1] What it lacks in depth and inwardness it makes up in its inexhaustible flow of easy, attractive melody. The good verbal accentuation, too, that has in every century characterized English song at its best, now takes the form of a rhythmic and syllabic crispness, especially in humorous, topical, or patriotic song, allowing the words to make their point in public performance. This is seen in songs as divergent in character and date as the sturdy 'Orpheus and Euridice' by William Boyce (1710–79)[2] and James Hook's (1746–1827) arch 'He'll stay a great while'.[3]

Ex. 149 (i)

When Orpheus went down to the Regions below, Which men are forbidden to see, He tun'd up his Lyre, as old histories show, To set his Euridice free, to set his Euridice free. All hell was astonish'd a person so wise Shou'd rashly endanger his life. And venture so far, but how vast their surprise When they heard that he came for his wife, how vast their surprise When they heard that he came for his wife.

[1] The character of these collections is indicated by such titles as *Universal Harmony, or the Gentleman and Ladies* [sic] *Social Companion* (1745), *The Universal Musician or the Songster's Delight* (1738), and *Orpheus Britannicus, or the Gentleman and Lady's Musical Musaeum: consisting of One Hundred favourite SONGS, compiled from the most approved Vocal Performances at the Theatres, Vaux-hall, Mary-bone Gardens, Sadlers-Wells, or any other polite places of public Entertainment* ... (1760). See Frank Kidson, 'Some Illustrated Music-Books of the Seventeenth and Eighteenth Centuries', *Musical Antiquary*, iii (1912), p. 195.

[2] *Universal Harmony, or the Gentleman and Ladies Social Companion* ... (London, 1745).

[3] *A Collection of Songs sung by Mr. Cubitt, Mrs. Wrighton, Mrs. Weichsell and Mrs. Kennedy at Vauxhall Gardens* ... (London, 1782).

(ii) *Allegretto*

Blith Co-lin, a pretty young swain, to court me came many a mile, I bid him return back again tho' I wish'd him to stay a great while.

Phrasing in general is square-cut, and the constant use of anapaestic metres in the current topical, comic or pseudo-rustic verse brings a stultifying monotony to much of the musical rhythm. Boyce, however, while he treats this hackneyed pattern conventionally in the example just quoted, proves, in his famous 'Heart of Oak', that it is possible to handle it with freshness and energy; Thomas Augustine Arne (1710–78) also achieves originality and freedom with his frequent irregular phrase-lengths. Modulation is almost entirely confined to the dominant, or to the relative major from the minor; the only romantic or expressive turn of harmony is (and rarely) that to the tonic minor, as in the second verse of Arne's 'The Happy Bride'.[1]

Minuet songs abound, and are in many cases arranged from popular instrumental minuets, including large numbers of Handel's; but there are also original compositions among them. Songs in the pastoral and rustic convention were likewise the fashionable stock-in-trade, and many of them, like Arne's immensely popular duet, 'Colin and Phoebe', are very conventional indeed. But his spacious and poised 'Address to Caelia'[2] shows the distinction with which he could, on occasion, handle a well-worn style. A variant on the pastoral theme is that in which some English name is substituted, with deliberate effect, for the Arcadian Phyllis and Chloe. This type, leaning towards folk-song and bluffness, gave us Arne's 'Polly Willis' and 'Peggy Wynne' and Hook's immortal 'Lass of Richmond Hill'.

A period of expansion and mainly successful war produced a heavy crop of topical and patriotic song, in which the hardiest strain is that glorifying the British sailor. Nourished by the topical stage[3] and by ballad operas such as Arne's *Thomas and Sally*, it came to fruition in those one-man entertainments with which Charles Dibdin (1745–1814)

---

[1] Arne, *Lyric Harmony consisting of ... new ballads, with Colin and Phoebe ...* (London, 1745).

[2] Arne, *Vocal Melody. An entire new collection of English songs ... sung ... at Vaux-Hall, Ranelagh, and Marybon-Gardens*, 4 books (1746–52), Book II.

[3] 'Heart of Oak', inspired by the victories of Lagos and Quiberon Bay, is among Boyce's music for Garrick's pantomime of 1759, *The Harlequin's Invasion*.

captured London's imagination from 1789 onwards. Self-taught, Dibdin was too versatile, and too little conscious of his technical limitations,[1] to fulfil the promise of his superb melodic gift. But his humanity and his sense of the stage enabled him to depict the British sailor in the round, and alongside 'Tom Bowling' (his elegy on his own brother), 'Ben Backstay', and the famous 'Poor Jack', we find rollicking songs like 'The Flowing Can', in the true comic tradition.

Another salient feature of British song throughout the eighteenth century is the vogue for Scottish song and the Scottish idiom. Although this was no new thing, the immediate impetus was given by the publication, in 1725, of William Thomson's *Orpheus Caledonius*, a volume of fifty songs, all drawn from Allan Ramsay's widely read *Tea Table Miscellany* of Scottish song-texts. These songs, genuine, if somewhat edited, both in words and music, achieved an immense popularity, which composers were quick to exploit, turning out 'Scotch' songs in quantity and adopting the pentatonic idiom, the wide leaps and the 'Scotch snap', as found in their models, sometimes with absurdly exaggerated effect, but often with real skill. Arne's 'The Broom of Cowdenknowes' is both attractive and convincing until set beside the bare simplicity of the original; and of Hook's 'Scotch' songs, 'Within a mile of Edinboro' Town' and the endearing 'Doun the burn, Davy' have both been taken for genuine specimens of traditional Scottish song. Thus Haydn, in the arrangements of Scottish songs which he made during and after his visits to England, was simply following up a well-established and extremely popular tradition.

If the public gardens set their mark on the character and temper of English song at this period, they also exerted an influence, and a retarding one, on the purely musical plane, for the fact that the accompaniments were conceived and written in the first place for orchestra held back the development of keyboard accompaniment. While the songs in the elegant anthologies are on two staves only, melody and bass (figured or unfigured), Arne's first publication, *Lyric Harmony*, like the countless succeeding sets of songs 'as performed at' the public gardens, is 'in score', that is, laid out for strings, with or without wind, and continuo. It is not until the last two decades of the century that we begin to find music published for voice and keyboard on three staves, with corresponding independence of accompaniment, or even such stock figuration as the Alberti bass. By then, isolated instances occur in which composers seem to be reaching out not only towards a truer integration of the song with its accompaniment but also towards a deeper vein of expression: such are Shield's 'When ev'ry charm of life is fled', or

[1] See also pp. 261–3.

Stephen Storace's setting of the opening verses of Gray's 'Elegy written in a Country Churchyard':[1]

Ex. 150

[Largo. *p* The Cur-few tolls the Knell of part-ing Day, The low-ing Herd winds slow-ly o'er the lea,]

But these are isolated instances, and for the most part British composers remained untouched by the inner vision that irradiated the finest work done by English poets and landscape painters as the century drew to its close.

FRANCE

In France, owing to the central position held by Paris and by the Court in the social and artistic life of the country, opera continued to dominate the musical scene, even while, at the same time, evolving a national genre of its own, the *opéra comique*. As a result, France's direct contribution in the field of song was of less consequence, and indeed, for over half a century, the songs in general circulation were very largely dance songs, or *ariettes* drawn from the current *opéra comique* repertory. Genuine, independent songs appeared in published collections, but such collections tended to be few in number and—a unique feature—were deliberately antiquarian, making a point of the fact that their contents

[1] William Shield, *A Collection of Canzonetts and an Elegy, with an Accompaniment for the Piano Forte or Harp* (London, 1796); Stephen Storace, *Eight Canzonetts, with an Accompaniment for a Piano Forte or Harp* (London, 1782).

dated almost entirely from past centuries.[1] Yet through these anthologies, which became widely current in the francophile Prussia of Frederick the Great, the French past affected the European future, for they exerted a formative influence on the new minds at work in Berlin and elsewhere. Moreover, the idealization of the past which they embodied, although not creative, at least kept alive an almost submerged conception of true song.[2]

In the second half of the century the latent musical patriotism aroused by the 'Querelle des bouffons' and the Gluck–Piccinni controversy, reinforcing the earlier nostalgia for the simplicity of bygone ages, gave rise to what was in effect a new genre, the *romance*. This was a deliberately simple and artless strophic narrative song, harking back to medieval prototypes. Rousseau, in his *Dictionnaire de musique* of 1767, defines the *romance* as an

air to which is sung a little poem of the same name, divided into verses . . . as the *romance* should be simple, touching and somewhat archaic in style, the tune should match the character of the words: no ornaments, nothing mannered, the melody gentle, natural, rustic . . . a well-written *romance*, having no salient features, makes no impression at first; but each verse adds something to the effect made by the ones before . . . and sometimes one finds oneself moved to tears, yet unable to say wherein lies the charm that has brought this about. It is common experience that all instrumental accompaniment weakens this impression.

This definition is full of significance in the light of the formative influence exerted by Rousseau, not only through his political theory but also, through his heightened response to nature and his idealization of the natural man, on the incipient Romantic movement in Germany.

Coming when it did, the *romance* caught up and embodied one aspect of the ideals and aspirations that were afoot in Europe, and anticipated by some years the revival of the ballad in German-speaking countries. It also gave practical expression to the contemporary urge towards greater simplicity in song-writing, though neither Rousseau nor his German fellow-musicians who advocated the discarding of accom-

[1] See the preface to the three volumes of *Brunettes ou Petits airs tendres*, published by Christophe Ballard between 1703 and 1711, quoted in Paul-Marie Masson, 'Les "Brunettes"', *Sammelbände der internationalen Musikgesellschaft*, xii (1910–11), p. 347. Cf. also the title of Jean Monnet's *Anthologie française ou Chansons choisies depuis le 13e siècle jusqu'à présent* (Paris, 1765). The term 'brunette', denoting a pastoral love-song, is derived from the refrain of 'Le beau berger Tircis', 'Ah, petite Brunette, Ah, tu me fais mourir'.

[2] Masson, op. cit., quotes the following extract from Le Cerf's *Comparaison de la musique italienne et de la musique française*, which appeared shortly after Ballard's second collection: 'tous ces jolis airs champêtres qu'on appelle des *Brunettes*, combien ils sont naturels! . . . Ces Brunettes sont doublement à estimer dans notre Musique, parce que cela n'est ni de la connaissance, ni du génie des Italiens, et que les tons aimables et gracieux, si finement proportionnés aux paroles, en sont d'un extrême prix.'

paniment went so far in practice. Rousseau did, however, put his principles into effect in a number of *romances*, many of them contained in the posthumously published *Consolations des misères de ma vie* (1781).[1] In a *romance* from a slightly earlier source[2] France and Germany meet and diverge: the theme, that of the dead lover returning by night to carry off his bride to their nuptials at the open grave, is the same as that of Bürger's famous poem 'Lenore' (see p. 349), but whereas the German settings of that ballad are expansive and descriptive, the French composer (his name is not stated) sets the narrative to a single strophic melody, relying entirely, in accordance with Rousseau's theory, on cumulative effect.

Ex. 151

C'ét-oit l'hi-ver, mi-nuit ét-oit pass-é, Ber-gers, trou-peaux, tout dor-moit au vil-la-ge, Li-se rê-voit à son jeu-ne fian-cé, de-puis deux mois ab-sent pour un voy-a-ge.

Similarly all the texts in another collection of *romances*,[3] although dealing, as the title suggests, with a variety of subject-matter, have straightforward strophic settings. Again the effects are obtained through Rousseau's gentle, natural, rustic melody.

[1] 'Echo' from this collection is reprinted by Fritz Noske, *Das ausserdeutsche Sololied* (*Das Musikwerk*), (Cologne, 1958), p. 54.
[2] *Romances par M. Berquin*, published in 1776. Arnaud Berquin was the poet; the composers' names are given as Blois and de Gramaignac.
[3] *Recueil de Romances historiques tendres et burlesques* . . . M[athis] D[e] L[usse]. 2 vols. (Paris, 1767 (1774)).

Simple strophic and unaccompanied settings of texts are not limited to the *romance* however, but appear also in the lighter songs published in contemporary collected editions.[1] In one such anthology[2] all the settings are strophic and no accompaniments are provided. Here there is also evidence of that curious mixture of classical didacticism and sardonic humour which is so characteristic of the French song even at its lightest level. The *vaudeville* is described in the preface as 'la pierre de touche de tous les bons Chansonniers. Il divertit, il raconte, il instruit même . . .', and the texts in this and also in another similar collection of *bagatelles*[3] are drawn from a wide range of mythological and anacreontic sources.

The *Mille et une bagatelles* is particularly rich in the variety of its forms. In addition to the strophic *vaudevilles*, *brunettes* and *rondes de table* it contains songs formally based on suite movements (and entitled *minuet*, *musette*, etc.), *fanfares*, *caprices*, brief *da capo* arias, *ariettes* in the form of dialogues and even stylized recitatives. But perhaps the most noticeable quality of all, and indeed the essence of these songs, is the freshness and expressiveness of the melody. In the *airs tendres*, *sérieux* and *gracieux*, in particular, with their pure lyricism and perfectly balanced tonal and rhythmic contrasts, and the total lack of accompaniment, we have the successors to the seventeenth-century *air de cour*.

The most numerous of all these contemporary collections are those of songs from operas. One anthology[4] consists entirely of *ariettes* taken from the French operas of the preceding thirty years, and several publishers issued opera periodicals[5] which ran with great success for some considerable time. Many of these *ariettes* in the periodical collections, with their instrumental accompaniments, must be regarded as nearer the art song than the *romance* or *air tendre*. But influences are frequently reciprocal, and the telling simplicity of the unaccompanied forms cannot have been lost on the composers of *opéras comiques*. It was assuredly not lost on Gluck.

GERMANY

It is in northern Germany that at last we find a favourable climate for

[1] The same appears to be true of the little-known song literature of Freemasonry. In a *Recueil de Chansons des Franc-Macons* . . . [Paris, 1750], all the settings are strophic and unaccompanied.

[2] *Recueil de Chansons nouvelles et vaudevilles. Tirées des pièces de théatre, comédie italienne, opéra comique, chansons de la foire*, &c. (Paris, 1737).

[3] *Les mille et une bagatelles*. [Paris, n.d].

[4] *Dictionnaire lyrique portatif, ou Choix des plus jolies Ariettes de tous les genres . . . mis en ordre par M. Dubreuil*. 2 vols. (Paris, 1764).

[5] For instance, De La Chevardière's *Journal Hebdomadaire ou recueil d'airs choisis dans les opéra-comiques* (1764–83), which was continued by Le Duc as the *Journal Hebdomadaire composé d'airs d'opéra et opéra comiques* . . . (1784–1808).

the revival of lyrical song. Here is a region where, as dogmatic religion gradually lost its hold, the mental and spiritual energies thus left uncanalized either issued in the more subjective and emotional manifestations summed up in the term 'pietism', or found a substitute for direct religious experience in poetry; significant here is the volume and quality of the religious poetry produced throughout the seventeenth and eighteenth centuries, as also the persistence of the *geistliches Lied* even through the leanest years of song. As time passed, even the specifically religious emotions that found expression in pietism were deflected from the worship of the Creator to that of created nature and of human feelings and relationships—again, fruitful material for lyrical utterance. All these tendencies, moreover, were at work within that large intellectual middle class—civil servants, lawyers, university teachers, and students—to whom the host of despotic principalities into which the region was split up offered a livelihood but no satisfactory outlet in public life: restless minds open and exposed to the new winds of thought from all directions—France, England, Germany itself—that were soon to blow with gale force in the *Sturm und Drang* movement of the 1770s.

In the first half of the century these stirrings had begun to make themselves felt, indirectly, in passionate and partisan conflicts such as that between the advocates of the classic rhyme-patterns and the pioneers of the newer rhymelessness, or disputes over the perennial problem of the relationship between words and music. This problem was the more acute in that, during this period of sterility, it had become common practice to produce songs by the expedient of writing texts to pre-existing keyboard pieces. The well-known Leipzig collection of 1736, the *Singende Muse an der Pleisse*, proclaims in its subtitle that its purpose is to provide 'agreeable keyboard practice and pleasant recreation', and in fact it contains a high proportion of pure keyboard music, mainly dance tunes already familiar, such as minuets and polonaises, to which words have been fitted in defiance of verbal accentuation and, often, of vocal compass.

Already there were stirrings of a new conception. Men as widely contrasted as the amateur Friedrich Gräfe (1711–87) and the highly professional Georg Philipp Telemann (1681–1767) brought out collections of songs designed expressly as a counterblast to the *Singende Muse* and claiming, in their elaborate titles and prefaces, that their song melodies were easy to sing and composed expressly to fit the words.[1] But it was with the emergence of the Berlin group of song composers in the following decade that the urge towards simplification was carried on to the intellectual plane. Its leading figures were not only musicians but

[1] See Vol. VI.

also theorists and men of letters: Karl Wilhelm Ramler (1725–98) and Christoph Gottfried Krause (1719–70) with their two volumes of *Oden mit Melodien* in 1753 and 1755,[1] and Friedrich Wilhelm Marpurg (1718–95), who, as editor and composer, brought out from 1756 onwards a succession of song collections, including the three volumes of *Berlinische Oden und Lieder*. The preface to the Ramler–Krause *Oden mit Melodien* elaborates, at some length, a reasoned theory of song composition. The simplicity of the older French *chanson* is held up as model, as against the artificialities of the operatic convention, and we meet for the first time a constantly recurring theme: that melody alone is the essence of a song, and that composers should conceive their melodies away from the keyboard and without thinking of a bass. This conception spells open and articulate revolt against the continuo. Driven to its logical conclusion it would have killed any attempt at independent accompaniment; but practice was apt to mitigate the full rigours of theory, and we find, among the arid tracts of these collections, such imaginative dance songs as the anonymous 'Einladung zum Tanz', described as being 'in der Bewegung einer Passepied', with its coda in which snatches of the opening verse are sung against the dance movement played on the accompanying instrument.[2] Greater stress is laid at this stage of development on the simplicity of the melody itself than on its relationship to the words and some of the melodies are still so instrumentally conceived as to ruin the verbal accent. Karl Heinrich Graun (1704–59) however, besides carrying on the unbroken tradition of the *geistliches Lied* with his fervent 'Die Auferstehung',[3] charms us in pastoral vein with the excellent declamation of his 'Belinde' and 'Die Rose';[4] and in Marpurg's 'Die Bekehrung'[5] good verbal accentuation, neatly matching all verses and not merely the first, brings out the somewhat prim humour of the text:

Ex. 152

[musical notation: Etwas munter — Mein Vor-mund straf-te mich, und sprach: Sohn, schä-me dich, du]

[1] Ramler was a poet, and wrote a number of oratorio libretti (see *supra*, pp. 329 and 331); Krause, a lawyer by profession, was an essayist as well as a composer. In 1767 they brought out a revised and enlarged version of the *Oden mit Melodien*, under the title *Lieder der Deutschen*.
[2] *Lieder der Deutschen*, Book II, no. 4 (Berlin, 1767).
[3] *Geistliche Oden, in Melodien gesetzt von einigen Tonkünstlern in Berlin* (Berlin, 1758).
[4] *Berlinische Oden und Lieder*, Book II, nos. 1 and 3 (Berlin, 1759). Graun's amusing 'Das Töchterchen–Das Söhnchen' is reprinted in Hans Joachim Moser, *Das deutsche Sololied* (*Das Musikwerk*), (Cologne, 1957), p. 43.
[5] Ibid., Book, I, no. 6 (Berlin, 1756).

(My guardian punished me and said, 'My lad, be ashamed of yourself, you're too young for love! Curb your instincts! Feelings change. It's all too easy to get tired of your girl before you've had her'.)

It is characteristic of the serious and high-minded C. P. E. Bach (1714–88) that his chief fame as a song composer, among his contemporaries, rested on his settings of Gellert's religious poetry.[1] Of these, some are in the direct tradition of the Schemelli song-book, with their grave flow of melody: such are the meditative E minor 'Bitten', and the two songs on the Passion, 'Herr, stärke mich, Dein Leiden zu bedenken', in A flat major, and 'Erforsche mich, erfahr' mein Herz', restless and syncopated in G minor. Others are affected by the dotted rhythms of the *galant* style, which, while lending an excessively jaunty air to the 'Danklied', impart a fine rhythmic vigour to 'Die Ehre Gottes aus der Natur' and the Easter hymn 'Jesus lebt'. His finest religious songs, however, are found among his settings of poems by Christoph Christian Sturm, published over twenty years later:[2] 'Jesus in Gethsemane', 'Über die Fin-

---

[1] *Geistliche Oden und Lieder mit Melodien von Carl Philipp Emanuel Bach*. The work first appeared in 1758 (Berlin) and went into four editions. For a detailed study, see Hertha Wien-Claudi, *Zum Liedschaffen Philipp Emanuel Bachs* (Reichenberg, 1928) and Gudrun Busch, *C. P. E. Bach und seine Lieder*, 2 vols. (Ratisbon, 1957). Modern selections of Bach's songs have been edited by Johannes Dittberner (Leipzig, 1918), Herman Roth (Leipzig, 1922) and Vrieslander (Munich, 1922); one Gellert setting in Arnold Schering, *Geschichte der Musik in Beispielen* (Leipzig, 1931), p. 455, another in Moser, op. cit., p. 51.

[2] *Geistliche Gesänge mit Melodien zu singen bey dem Klaviere* (Hamburg, two parts, 1780 and 1781).

sterniss kurz vor dem Tode Jesu', and 'Der Tag des Weltgerichts', in which the pulsating bass builds up a cumulative tension.

Ex. 153 **Ernsthaft**

Wann der Er - de Grün - de be - ben, und in Tod - ten - grüf - ten Le - ben und im Stau - be Ju - gend-stär-ke wallt: wann des Auf - er-weckers Stimme schallt: Gott! Gott! er - barm dich un - ser!

(When earth's foundations shake, life lies in the tomb and our youthful strength in the dust, when the voice of the Awakener resounds: God! God! have mercy on us!)

Here voice part and accompaniment are fused in a true imaginative unity.

The gathering movement away from Italianate operatic elaboration towards unstudied simplicity, and the groping search for a more essentially German form of expression, received a fresh access of strength through the rise of the *Singspiel*, and the warm-hearted and tuneful airs in

Johann Adam Hiller's *Die verwandelten Weiber* (1766)[1] and its successors in the field of vernacular opera brought far more to the development of German song than the more mannered *Lieder* of his formal song collections. This trend was also powerfully strengthened by the new forces making themselves felt in literature, and in the revival of the ballad are united the urge towards simplification, the idealization of country life and country virtues, and the attraction of past history and legend, often fused with an element of the supernatural—all elements in the incipient Romantic movement. Gottfried Bürger's poem 'Lenore' is an inspired example of a modern ballad of genuine power and directness of appeal, using the Seven Years War to give immediacy to the tale of the missing soldier, his mysterious return to his despairing bride, and their night ride together to the grave that is to be their marriage bed. Johann André (1741–99), founder of the publishing-house at Offenbach, and Johann Friedrich Reichardt (1752–1814) both set it to music: André's version, published in 1775, is the first ballad setting that may claim to be *durchkomponiert*. In this he was followed, with greater power and imagination, by Johann Rudolf Zumsteeg (1760–1802) at the turn of the century.[2]

It is no mere coincidence that the previous year, 1774, saw the appearance of the young Goethe's first novel. *Werther* swept contemporary readers off their feet by its moving advocacy of what Keats was to call 'the holiness of the heart's affections', while the quotations from Ossian further quickened the growing response to immemorial and heroic legend. In the same spirit Klopstock, his earlier classicism abandoned, brought out his bardic odes, his ardent love poems and elegies, and his patriotic songs to fire the imagination. Christian Gottlob Neefe (1748–98), Beethoven's teacher, set Klopstock's impassioned love poems with immense fervour and conviction,[3] and although neither he nor Emanuel Bach nor Gluck can make the 'Vaterlandslied' ('Ich bin ein deutsches Mädchen') sound other than faintly ridiculous, the elegiac poems 'Sommernacht' and 'Die frühen Gräber'[4] touched Gluck's finest vein of imaginative poetry; 'Sommernacht' (Ex. 154) reaches forward towards the nineteenth century in its romantic evocation of atmosphere. Gluck's seven Klopstock settings[5] are his sole incursion into the field of

[1] See *supra*, p. 79.
[2] See Vol. VIII.
[3] One of Neefe's Klopstock settings, 'Hermann und Thusnelda', is reprinted in Moser, op. cit., p. 44.
[4] Ibid., p. 46.
[5] Gluck's Klopstock odes first appeared in the *Göttinger Musenalmanach* in 1774 and 1775. They were published in Vienna by Artaria in 1785 under the title *Klopstocks Oden und Lieder beym Clavier zu singen, in Musik gesetzt von Herrn Ritter Gluck*, and reprinted in 1917, *Veröffentlichungen der Gluckgesellschaft*, iii.

Ex. 154 Moderato e ligato

Wenn der Schim- - -mer von dem Mon- - -de nun her-ab___ in die Wäl- - -der sich er-giesst, und Ge-rü- - -che mit den Düf- - -ten von der Lin- - -de in der Küh- - -lun-gen weh'n.

(When the shimmering light of the moon streams down into the woods, and scents are borne with the fragrance of the linden blossom on the cool breezes. . . .)

solo song as such; but by his expressed belief that music should subserve the dramatic situation, as well as by the power of his operas themselves, he exerted a strong influence on both the theory and practice of songwriting.

Goethe's full and direct impact on composers was felt only with the appearance of the first complete edition of his works in 1789; then, in 1795, came *Wilhelm Meister*, its first edition containing settings by Johann Friedrich Reichardt (1752–1814) of eight of the songs. Reichardt, too many-sided, and too cerebral, to achieve the single-mindedness of genius, only fulfilled himself as a composer in the deeply felt Goethe settings which he brought out in the first ten years of the nineteenth century[1]; but among his songs of the 1780s are some, notably his setting of Goethe's declamatory 'An die Einzige', which show that the operatic convention has something positive to give to lyrical song. In these years his importance was, however, primarily as a thinker and controversialist. With him, and with his contemporaries André and Schulz, the quest for simplicity took a new turn, both in theory and practice, and folk-song now becomes the embodiment of the qualities to which all true song should aspire; Reichardt's extreme views on the essentially melodic and unharmonizable character of folk-song even anticipate later findings in certain areas of that vast field of study. André, meanwhile, wrote copiously in patriotic and popular vein. Although a lesser talent, his immense fluency was matched by a real care for verbal accentuation, and one of his songs, the drinking song 'Bekränzt mit Laub den freudenvollen Becher', has achieved folk-song status.[2]

But it was left to Johann Abraham Peter Schulz (sometimes spelt Schultz) (1747–1800), who worked in Berlin for part of his mature life, to lift the theory and practice of the Berlin school on to a new and higher plane, and to give classic expression to the 'folk-song' theory of song composition. His views on the relationship of music to text in a song are expressed in the famous preface to Part I of his *Lieder im Volkston* (1782), and are a direct echo of Gluck's principles in regard to opera:

> For only if the musical and the poetic expression of the song are closely matched, only if the melody is such that it neither outsoars the text nor sinks below its level, only if it moulds itself to the metre and accentuation of the words as a garment to the body, only if it moves in singable intervals ... and in the easiest of modulations ... only then will the song strike that note of uncontrived artlessness, of familarity, of which I speak: in a word, the note of true folk music ...

> And that should be the aim of the composer who wishes to remain true to the only aim worth pursuing in this field—to make good song texts universally known. His melodies should not themselves attract attention: their task is to focus it on the good poet's verses. We must therefore discard all useless ornament, alike in melody and accompaniment, all the paraphernalia of ritornelli and interludes, which deflect attention from the main issue to unessentials, from the words to the musician ...

Once more, and still more fortunately, Schulz's lyrical impulse was stronger than his obedience to the full rigour of his own reasoning. Of the hundred and thirty-two songs in the three volumes of his *Lieder*

---
[1] See Vol. VIII.
[2] It appeared in his *Musikalischer Blumenstrauss für das Jahr 1776, den Freunden deutschen Gesangs gewidmet*, a title reflecting the patriotic impulse which contributed to the resurgence of song at this period.

im Volkston[1] many are, indeed, so simple as to be, musically, nonentities. But he often achieves a remarkable rhythmic freedom within a small compass, as in the six-bar stanzas of 'Arete zu ihren Gespielinnen' and the irresistible verve of 'Im Grünen'. Nor is Schulz so austere in practice as in theory where his accompaniments are concerned, and it is when he allows his imagination free flight that he achieves some of his best results: the gay little 'Ständchen', with its ritornelli imitating the serenading lute, the solemn tread of the 'Elegie auf ein Landmädchen', and 'Die Spinnerin', a foreshadowing in miniature of 'Gretchen am Spinnrade':

Ex. 155

Etwas langsam

Ich ar - - mes Mäd-chen! Mein Spin - - ne-räd-chen will gar nicht gehn, Seit - dem der Frem - de in weiss - em Hem - de uns half beim Wai - zen-mähn!

(Poor girl that I am! My spinning-wheel doesn't want to turn since the stranger in the white shirt came to help us harvest the wheat.)

In Southern Germany the same impulse is at work in Christoph Rheineck (1748–97) and in the stormy and versatile Christian Friedrich Daniel Schubart (1739–91), whose verses, often set to his own music, are charged with real humanity.[2]

AUSTRIA

The intellectual and artistic movements at work in Northern Germany were slow to make their impact in Austria, insulated as she was by her

[1] Selections ed. Bernhard Engelke (Leipzig, 1909) and Fritz Jöde (Wolfenbüttel, 1925); one example in Moser, op. cit., p. 54.
[2] A Claudius setting by Schubart is reprinted in Moser, op. cit., p. 52. The four poems by Schubart including 'Die Forelle', set to music by Schubert, are well known.

strongly Catholic outlook and by her own vigorous and individual culture. But this insulation was, of course, only relative, and when the Emperor Joseph II succeeded in 1780 to the Austrian and Hungarian domains of his mother Maria Theresa (with whom he had previously been co-regent) his liberalizing—and to a certain extent anti-clerical—outlook opened Austria to outside influences which hitherto had touched her but little; it is an odd and ironic sign of the times that Klopstock's bardic element in poetry was represented in Austria by a former Jesuit priest, Michael Denis, using his name in reverse to produce the bardic pseudonym 'Sined'.[1] And it is not for nothing that the first upsurge of Austrian song should have virtually coincided with Joseph II's short reign. It began, indeed, in 1778, with the publication of the *Sammlung deutscher Lieder für das Klavier*, by Josef Anton Steffan (1726–97); a second volume followed in the ensuing year. A third *Sammlung deutscher Lieder* appeared in 1780, this time by Leopold Hoffmann and Carl Friberth; the last-named had been leading tenor at Esterház under Haydn. Haydn himself brought out his first set of songs at the end of 1781, followed by a second set in 1784. Steffan had meanwhile published a fourth volume of his own, and from then on hardly a year passed without the appearance of at least one new collection.

The result of the long dormant period is at once apparent. Simply by hibernation, song in Austria has escaped both the cramping influence of the continuo style itself and the inhibitions set up by the theoretical controversy which, in northern Germany, formed a part of the reaction against it. The vocal line is unashamedly Italianate, borrowing freely from aria and canzonetta, even in those songs which, in their square-cut tunefulness, reflect the influence of the German *Singspiel*.[2] Moreover, the fact that this reawakening came at the very period in which the harpsichord was being edged out by the newer and more flexible fortepiano meant that the accompaniments were conceived from the outset in the idiom of the piano and in the harmonic language of the current keyboard music.[3] Although in most cases the songs are set out on two staves only, with the vocal melody incorporated into the right-hand part, they are astonishingly rich and pianistic by comparison with their

---

[1] Mozart began a setting of his ode on the defence of Gibraltar (K. 386d) but did not finish it.

[2] In 1778, the years of Steffan's first volume of songs, the Emperor Joseph II's new National Theatre opened with Umlauff's *Singspiel, Die Bergknappen*.

[3] The term 'Clavier' was applied to both harpsichord and fortepiano alike; but the letter which Mozart wrote to his father from Augsburg about the pianoforte-maker Stein and his instruments on 17–18 October 1777 makes it clear that from then on he thinks, writes, and composes in terms of the piano. It is also evident that Hiller is contrasting the two instruments in the preface to his *Lieder für Kinder* of 1784, where, expressing his desire for a legato style of playing the accompaniments, he writes: 'to this end I would almost ask that they should never be played on a harpsichord (*Flügel*) or spinet, but on a good clavier'.

north German counterparts, expanding freely in interludes and opening and closing ritornelli.

This freedom and richness of vocal and instrumental technique held limitless promise. If its fulfilment was delayed, it was, in the last resort, because there had not yet been time to build up that accumulation of routine practice and collective experience which is the normal seed-bed for all great art, even taking into account the power of genius to transcend it. And if full achievement in this field eluded even Haydn and Mozart, their contemporaries were men of talent, working within the vocal and harmonic conventions of their musical language and of the stock types of text then current in Austria: pastoral, humorous (whether bluff or artlessly naïve), sententious, amorous, elegiac. The wonder is that the music so often transcends these banalities, whether by such melodic and rhythmic vitality as we find in Friberth's 'Warnung an die Mädchen' or Johann Holzer's 'Die gute Stunde' and 'Der verschwiegene Schäfer', or by the imaginative use of keyboard technique for descriptive or evocative purposes, as in Wilhelm Pohl's *Ländler*-like 'Amor im Tanz' and his 'Das Mädchen am Ufer', or Steffan's setting of the same poem.[1] Modulation, and the harmonic palette, are on the whole restricted, but the alternation of tonic minor and tonic major, besides being treated as an element of design in an A–B–A pattern, as in Kozeluch's 'Der Langmut Lohn' and Steffan's charming 'Gold'ne Freiheit', is also freely used by Steffan to lend expressive depth of shadow. And there are also, here and there, more dramatic uses of harmonic colour, ranging from the tiny chromatic postlude to Grünwald's 'Die tote Nachtigall' to the powerful and unconventional modulation to the dominant minor in Holzer's 'Liebeslied' and the sombre touches of harmony that lend real depth of feeling to Friberth's 'Abschied an Adelinen' and Steffan's 'Seid mir gegrüsst, ihr Täler der Gebeine':

Ex. 156

[1] All the examples here quoted are to be found in *Denkmäler der Tonkunst in Oesterreich* liv (Jg. 27 (2)) (Vienna, 1920), ed. Irene Pollak–Schlaffenberg and Margarete Ansion. See also Pollak–Schlaffenberg, 'Die Wiener Liedmusik von 1778 bis 1789', *Studien zur Musikwissenschaft*, v (1918), p. 97.

(... receive me, that I may weep unseen where my Doris rests.)

There are, moreover, instances where the composer's inspiration either transfigures a mediocre text, as in the songs just quoted, and in others such as Holzer's fiery 'Zwei Augen', or is quickened by response to true poetry. Steffan may have failed to match Goethe's 'Das Veilchen' with a comparable inspiration, but his tragic ballad 'Edward' conveys something of the drama and horror of the story, and in his setting of Klopstock's 'Dein süsses Bild' he draws operatic idiom and new keyboard technique together in a finely imaginative fusion.

HAYDN'S GERMAN SONGS

Among Haydn's songs there are a number which suffer from the prevailing stock response to stock types of text. But a more subtle danger sprang from his own qualities—his strongly symphonic and structural cast of mind and the vigorous and personal keyboard style which he had evolved in his piano sonatas, both tending to make him develop his musical thought independently of the words. The 'Gebet zu Gott' is among the rare instances in Austria of the *geistliches Lied*, but its character is far more that of a rich and impassioned instrumental slow movement, and in 'Gegenliebe', although text and music are closely interwoven musically, there seems to be no inner connection between the warmth of Bürger's verses and Haydn's graceful, subtly organized but emotionally non-committal melody.[1] Where, however, Haydn succeeds in drawing text, melody, and accompaniment into a true unity of

---

[1] This melody has, in fact, an independent existence as the principal theme of the slow movement of Symphony No. 73 (*La Chasse*). Both song and symphony were composed in 1781, and H. C. Robbins Landon, *The Symphonies of Joseph Haydn* (London, 1955), pp. 385-6, considers that 'it is not possible to decide if *La Chasse* borrowed the song, or if the song was taken from the symphony, though the former seems more likely'.

expression as well as of technique, the result can be very satisfying indeed. In 'Die zu späte Ankunft der Mutter', as in 'Gegenliebe', voice and accompaniment are interlocked in a manner foreshadowing Schumann, but here the lyrical charm of the music perfectly matches the gay and innocently *risqué* little pastoral. The wayward hesitancy of 'Lachet nicht, Mädchen' is brought out by its piquant rhythm and its three-bar phrasing, and in the delectable 'Lob der Faulheit'[1] Haydn uses chromaticism and remote harmonies as a perfect reflection of the whimsicality of Lessing's poem. Nor are these achievements among the lighter songs only. The dramatic 'Die Verlassene' may, like the 'Gebet zu Gott', bear the stamp of an instrumental slow movement, but it is more vocal and is fired with a genuine passion, and the grave tenderness and long-sustained lines of 'Der erste Kuss' lift it on to a level well above the average aria-type song. Most individual of all, perhaps, is the F minor 'Trost unglücklicher Liebe', strangely Schubertian in its tranquil sadness and in its sudden shift to the relative major.

Ex. 157

[1] Moser, op. cit., p. 68.

(Hours of unsatisfied longing, how great your number! Bring more pain, more wounds, then, and kill me once and for all!)

HAYDN'S ENGLISH SONGS

Haydn published no songs between the appearance of his second set of *Lieder* (1784) and his journey to London. But his career as a song composer was by no means over, and a first set of *VI Original Canzonettas* appeared in 1794, to words by Mrs. Anne Hunter, wife of the famous surgeon, who had entertained him on his first visit to London; a second set was published in 1795. To this venture Haydn brought a refined and perfected technique, as well as the heightened creative vitality which England had awakened in him, and the songs are in many ways an advance on the Viennese sets. They are laid out on three staves, and the accompaniments, though often incorporating the vocal melody, constantly break into free pianistic figuration or independent counter-melody. As sheer sound, moreover, they are ravishing, recalling again and again, in their crystalline translucency, Haydn's magical last piano trios of the same decade.

It is always a *tour de force* to set a foreign language to music, and although Haydn achieves a superficial correctness of declamation, to frame his music to the inner life of the words is beyond his power. This inevitable lack of response to the language has the effect of bringing out, even more strongly than before, the instrumental character of Haydn's approach. The design is paramount, the words merely a framework to support it. The fiery F minor 'Fidelity' could well stand on its own as an admirable 'song without words', but the verbal repetitions which carry the music produce an effect of emotional anticlimax. 'Despair', again, is closely akin, both in its keyboard writing and in its warmth and tenderness, to Haydn's finest late slow movements for piano, but its mood is so far removed from despair that one is tempted to wonder if Haydn understood the spirit of the words at all.

Yet in the end it was in his settings of two English texts that Haydn achieved fulfilment as a song composer. 'O Tuneful Voice' was the valedictory poem addressed to him by Mrs. Hunter on his final departure from London; Haydn set it to music with a gloriously Schubertian fervour and modulatory freedom, as if (as Marion Scott suggests) it were a song in praise of music itself.[1] 'The Spirit's Song' is also a setting of a poem by Mrs. Hunter,[2] though Haydn seems to have thought it was by Shakespeare. Here, at last, Haydn makes his musical design carry the text, so that the expressive power of the song springs directly from its architectural strength. This is evident where the piano interlude which follows the first stanza is incorporated into the accompaniment towards the close, thus at the same time unifying the design and building up the rising tension towards its climax; then, a final stroke of genius, it returns, this time beneath a falling line, in the short and brooding coda.

Ex. 158

---

[1] 'Some English Affinities and Associations in Haydn's Songs', *Music and Letters*, xxv (1944), p. 1.
[2] Otto E. Albrecht, 'English Pre-Romantic Poetry in Settings by German Composers', in H. C. Robbins Landon (ed.), *Studies in Eighteenth-Century Music* (London, 1970), pp. 31–2.

Of the few songs which Haydn subsequently wrote, none touches this height (the incomparable 'Emperor's Hymn' is left out of account, because it was designed for massed singing). But in this moment of vision he points forward in the direction in which the land of promise lay.

MOZART'S LIEDER

Mozart's relationship to the Viennese School is more complex than Haydn's, for he had been a composer of songs, albeit casually and at intervals, from boyhood onwards, and thus, before the Viennese School had come into being at all. These earlier songs are youthful essays in the current styles: minuet songs like 'Daphne, deine Rosenwangen' (1768) and 'An die Freundschaft' (1772), studies in the north German manner such as 'Geheime Liebe' and 'Die grossmütige Gelassenheit' (1772), and the two French *ariettes*, 'Oiseaux, si tous les ans' and 'Dans un bois solitaire', written on his way to Paris in 1777-8. A further batch of three songs, composed in 1780 to texts from a sentimental novel of the day, shows the north German influence, and in particular that of Emanuel Bach, touched by the emotional subjectivity of the 1770s.

Mozart left Salzburg for Vienna in 1781, and for the next four years wrote no songs at all; for him, song composition was a mere overflow from the main channel of his creative effort, and he had more important matters in hand.[1] When he once more turned to song writing, in 1785, he had become completely Viennese in the richness and variety of his accompaniments (from now on he invariably uses three staves), completely personal in his rhythmic freedom and in the range of his modulations, and inveterately operatic in his approach. The result of this combination of qualities is that the best of his mature songs are, in an odd way, songs in spite of themselves. They have a compressed, explosive quality, and seem to demand a larger space in which to unfold. If this applies even to the lighter songs, 'Der Zauberer', 'Die betrogene Welt' and the canzonetta-like 'An Chloe',[2] it is still more strongly felt in the two tragic love-songs of 1787, 'Das Lied der Trennung' and 'Als Luise die Briefe ihres ungetreuen Liebhabers verbrannte', which are so dramatic that they appear to be striving to convey a whole operatic *scena* within the compass of a song; 'Das Lied der Trennung', indeed, opens as a strophic song, but breaks away, in the last three verses, into what is in effect the middle section and free repetition of a *da capo* aria. Paradoxically, it is the smaller and less powerful songs that are most truly song-like: such songs as the graceful 'Die Verschweigung' and

---

[1] Mozart published only four of his songs; these appeared in 1789 in two books, the first containing 'Abendempfindung' and 'An Chloe', the second 'Das Veilchen' and 'Das Lied der Trennung'.

[2] Moser, op. cit., p. 69.

the two 'naïve' songs, 'Das Kinderspiel' and 'Sehnsucht nach dem Frühling', written on the same January day in 1791.

There are, however, two exceptions: 'Abendempfindung' and 'Das Veilchen'. 'Abendempfindung', in lesser hands, might have become a mere replica of a dozen other Viennese songs of the elegiac type. Mozart, however, transcending the sentimentality of the text, creates at the outset an atmosphere of serene tranquility, intensified by the recurring echoes in the accompaniment, throughout the song, of a vocal cadence in the opening verse.

Ex. 159

([It is evening, the sun has vanished] and the moon gleams with silver; so life's fairest hours fleet by, as in a dance.)

In 'Das Veilchen', by contrast, Mozart is at grips with a true poem, and, with unerring perception, subordinates everything, verse-structure, declamation, descriptive and dramatic expression, to the unity of the narrative, to which he moulds his music with sensitive economy. The result is, in its delicate and reticent way, a model of what the *durchkomponiertes Lied* can achieve.

MOZART'S CONCERT ARIAS

In southern Germany the habits of a hundred years of Neapolitan activity died hard. However artificial the traditional *fioriture* of *bel canto* there was still a demand in the middle of the eighteenth century for a formal display piece in which a brilliant singer could display technical skill. Hence the solo cantata—in principle still ideal but in practice already an anachronism—was succeeded by the concert aria, a compromise which satisfied both traditional and progressive taste and which reached a high point in the hands of Mozart.

In all Mozart contributed some fifty-six items to the repertoire of the genre, including *licenze* (epilogues or personal tributes) and insertions into existing operas as well as the true concert arias. Formally they are modelled on the operatic recitative-and-aria pair, of which they are basically only a more elaborate version. Initially Mozart follows the model closely, as for instance in the repetitive 'Voi avete un cor fedele', K.217, with its A–B–A'–B'–A"–C structure, but frequently the arias are extended into two contrasting sections, and increasingly Mozart displays that cavalier attitude to classical form which is so characteristic of his mature style. There is no recurrent formal pattern as such in these concert arias; they are not however formless, but rather derive their musical logic from the exigencies of text and situation. The fact that the first aria in 'Ah, lo previdi', K.272, is in sonata form, and the second in a type of rondo form, is only coincidental to the overriding fact that these were the sequences of musical ideas which Mozart felt to be the most appropriate interpretation of his text. In 'Sperai vicino il lido', K.368, for instance, a passage of recitative breaks in before the return of the opening aria theme, thus dramatically replacing any stilted repetition of the instrumental ritornello.

Mozart's treatment of recitative is an important aspect of these works. He adds to it an increasingly participatory accompaniment, which not only gives it more thematic coherence (as in 'Ah, non son io che parlo', K.369) but also inspires the voice to arioso (as in 'Non temer, amato bene', K.505, an interesting comparison with an earlier and less lyrical setting of the same words in K.490).

The style of the concert arias, written throughout his career, developed with Mozart's increased dramatic experience, although he had always to consider the characteristics of the singer for whom he was writing, and was hence not necessarily able always to write precisely as he might have wished. In 'Popoli di Tessaglia', K.316 (300b), for instance, the splendidly dramatic effect of the recitative is later dimmed by the *passaggi* included for Aloysia Weber.

There are nevertheless examples of all Mozart's moods, from the remote modulations underlying the text of '... trasportar mi sento fra le tempeste' in K.368, to the wonderful simplicity of one of the last arias, 'Vado, ma dove?', K.583, or the Don Basilio Mozart of 'Alma grande e nobil core', K.578. The most remarkable concert arias, however, are perhaps 'Ch'io mi scordi di te', K.505 and 'Bella mia fiamma', K.528. The former is scored for solo soprano with the accompaniment of an orchestra and obbligato pianoforte, so that here we almost see, in all the

(I go ... alas! farewell for ever! This effort, this step is terrible for me.)

subtlety of Mozart's concerto style, a double concerto for voice and pianoforte. In K.528 (written five days after the première of *Don Giovanni* in Prague), with its contrapuntal opening reflecting the esoteric late pianoforte sonatas, its poignant beauty in the descending bass line to the words 'Vado ... ahi lasso' (Ex. 160) and the succeeding tortuous chromaticism, we have not only a great concert aria but also one of Mozart's greatest works.

THE SOLO CANTATA

Of all the Neapolitan Baroque forms inherited by Europe in the eighteenth century, the secular solo cantata was one of the most artificial and convention-ridden. It was therefore inevitable that when new ideals of simplicity and naturalism spread, the cantata was one of the first of the forms to topple. But the extent of its downfall varied in each country according to the degree to which the new philosophies were accepted: in north Germany, for instance, a revolutionary spirit ultimately quite altered the old Neapolitan form, but further south it was modified rather than overthrown. The country in which the least change took place was Italy herself, where such composers as Paër, Zingarelli, Fioravanti and Crescentini were content to retain the traditional four-part framework of two *da capo* arias introduced by recitatives. Works like Ferdinando Paër's (1771–1839) unpublished cantata *Saffo* and Girolamo Crescenti's (1762–1846) *Sei Cantate e dieciotto Ariette a voce sola con accomp. di Fortepiano*[1] continued to present a marked distinction between brief and relatively insignificant recitatives and expansive, wholly lyrical arias. A blurring of the clear-cut differences, however, between these component parts is seen in Paër's *L'amor timido*,[2] with a rich instrumental accompaniment to the recitative and a

[1] Milan, Ricordi, n.d.
[2] Op. 5. Leipzig, n.d.

loosening of the rigid *da capo* scheme. Similarly in Nìcolò Antonio Zingarelli's (1752–1837) *Armida*[1] the text is freely treated as a dramatic *scena*, but such freedom is relatively isolated and the genre lived on into the nineteenth century in the plural form of the choral cantata.

In England the high point of cantata composition was reached in the time of Handel. The most prolific of the few subsequent English cantata composers was the blind organist John Stanley (1713–86), but on the whole his music is confined within the strait-jacket of *secco* recitative and *da capo* and only occasionally emerges in the freshness of the national idiom. The English cantata is perhaps at its sorry best as used by James Oswald (1711–68) in *The Dust Cart*,[2] where the stylized structure adds mock dignity to Tinkering Tom's declaration of love to the Dustgirl.

The lifespan of the solo cantata in France was by contrast short, but although in its traditional form (or rather in its traditional French form, of three paired recitatives and arias), it reached a peak with Rameau, it was simultaneously undermined by the delicate and briefly-flowering *cantatille*.[3] The height of *cantatille* composition was reached in the work of Louis Antoine Le Febvre (also known as André Le Febvre, *c.* 1700(?)–1763), published between 1745 and 1763. His *Le Bouquet de l'Amour* shows this simple form at its charming best, particularly in the first aria, where the flight of birds is depicted in flowing triplets moving contrapuntally through all the concerted instruments. A later work, *Andromède*,[4] illustrates the link between the *cantatille* and solo cantata and the French dramatic tradition, with its expressive chromatic harmony in Andromeda's opening air, and its vivid portrayal of the *tempête* in the strings.

In Germany the development of the Italian cantata and of an indigenous form proceeded together for a time, but in the north the dramatic poetry of Johann Elias Schlegel, Ramler and Gerstenberg kindled a flame already flickering in the naturalism of Friedrich Gräfe's *Oden* of 1744.[5] In Johann Adolph Scheibe's (1708–76) settings of texts by these poets[6] the divisions between recitative and aria were now dictated by the text, not by musical convention, and in Johann Friedrich Reichardt's (1752–1814) *Ariadne*[7] the whole merges in a continuous flow of recitative

---

[1] In *Stanze del canto vigesimo della Gerusalemme Liberata di Torquato Tasso*. (*c.* 1790).
[2] *The Dust Cart, a favourite cantata . . . sung in The Old Woman's Oratory . . . in manner of the Moderns* (London, *c.* 1753).
[3] See Vol. VI.
[4] *Andromède* (Paris, n.d.).
[5] See p. 345.
[6] *Tragische Kantaten für eine oder zwo Singestimmen und das Clavier* (Copenhagen and Leipzig, 1765).
[7] *Ariadne auf Naxos. Eine Cantate von Herrn von Gerstenberg . . .* (Leipzig, 1780).

and *arioso* styles. The final step was taken by Reichardt in his settings of Goethe's *Lyrische Gedichte* in 1794[1]; although these are entitled *Deklamationen* they are, in fact, a combination of *Lied* and solo cantata which brings the latter to the threshold of Schubert's *durchkomponiertes Kunstlied*. Haydn's contribution to the genre was small, amounting to less than half a dozen works, but includes one masterpiece, *Arianna a Naxos*, written in 1789 for mezzo-soprano with keyboard accompaniment. As in Reichardt's *Ariadne*, the conventional divisions into recitative and aria are discarded in favour of an almost continuous recitative broken by only two short arias, a form which allows the composer fully to exploit the numerous dramatic possibilities of the text.

[1] For a modern edition, by Walter Salmen, of Reichardt's settings of Goethe based on the later edition of 1809–11, see *Das Erbe Deutscher Musik*, lviii (Munich, 1964).

VI

THE EARLY SYMPHONY

By Egon Wellesz and F. W. Sternfeld[1]

To open a discussion of the early symphony with generalizations would be a great mistake, for the characteristics of the period are diversity and ramification. Any attempt at neat categories would misrepresent the character of a development that moves in all directions. For one thing, the number of compositions is much larger than has been generally suspected. In his *Eighteenth Century Symphonies* (London, 1951) Adam Carse tabulates 1,643 published symphonies or overtures but makes no attempt to estimate works in manuscript, which, for most composers, far exceed their works in print. Paisiello's published symphonies, for example, are very few indeed, yet there is scarcely a music archive in Europe which does not contain at least one manuscript of an overture-symphony by him, dozens of which became popular in concert use. To arrive at a more accurate assessment of the total output we must multiply the number of printed symphonies by a large factor. Research suggests that well over 7,000 symphonies (or overtures used in concerts) dating from the period 1740–1810 are still extant and there is evidence of many more that have disappeared.

As might be expected in such a large repertory, the types of the eighteenth-century symphony are bafflingly diverse. The modern concepts of symphony, concerto, and chamber music were at that time habitually blurred in the practice of composers, not to mention their copyists. When a *partita* in one archive is called a *sinfonia* in the next, and these titles alternate inconsistently with overture, divertimento, serenade, cassation, trio, quartet, quintet, concerto, concertino, sonata, and even the archaic intrada and preludio, the flexibility of nomenclature indicates stylistic uncertainty as well. Even after the symphony became clearly established, it could not remain entirely aloof from other genres. Repeated stylistic invasions from opera, chamber music, and concerto produced the *da capo* symphony, the quartet-symphony, and the *symphonie concertante*.

In attempting to trace the threads of development, many problems of attribution and chronology arise. A surprisingly large number of symphonies bear conflicting attributions in different sources, and a similar

---

[1] This chapter has been prepared on the basis of material provided by Jan LaRue. The editors are responsible for its presentation.

uncertainty exists in chronology, since most of the manuscript sources are undated. But by recourse to indirect evidence, such as newspaper announcements and dated publishers' catalogues,[1] much of the chronology can be clarified, although a number of crucial questions remain to be answered.

Since the evolution of the symphony can be apprehended more intelligibly by geography than by chronology, the following discussion is arranged according to areas.

ITALY: GALUPPI AND JOMMELLI

The symphony shares with all other extended musical forms the problem of finding a satisfactory adjustment between unity and contrast. The early ascendancy of Italian composers in this field rests upon a century of experience with opera, where a vocabulary of contrast and a syntax for achieving unity had gradually evolved. The constant reciprocal relationship between operatic and symphonic styles must be emphasized to avoid any lingering misconceptions resulting from the conventional division between vocal and instrumental music. To opera the symphony owes not only its name and fast–slow–fast arrangement of movements but also its basic instrumentation (two oboes, two horns, and strings) and the formal principle of recapitulation after contrast. In addition to these broad legacies, composers inherited a wealth of detailed solutions to problems in articulation, texture, and thematic differentiation.

Although resting on this operatic background, the Italian symphony in the eighteenth century falls into two distinct branches, the opera overture and the concert symphony. Theoretically any overture could be used in a concert, and hundreds were printed and copied for these nontheatrical performances, often without any identification of the opera from which they were culled. Alongside the overture a second tradition grew up: namely of symphonies written specifically for performances outside the theatre, though initially the overture outweighed the concert symphony in numbers, though not in artistic achievement. (As is well known, many Italians made their careers in foreign regions and those of particular significance will be discussed in connection with their adopted countries.)

The first revealing steps in the transition from Baroque to Classical in the Italian overture took place gradually and unsystematically from about 1715 to 1730.[2] Although the style of Alessandro Scarlatti (1660–1725) tended to recall the heritage of the high Baroque, he nevertheless greatly influenced those composers who wrote in the newer style in his

[1] Carl Johansson, *French Music Publishers' Catalogues of the Second Half of the Eighteenth Century* (Stockholm, 1955).
[2] See Vol. VI.

use of a fast–slow–fast pattern, but he did not always follow this pattern, nor was it universally adopted by later composers. Porpora, for instance, abandoned it in his work published by Venier in 1755.[1] But the fast–slow–fast pattern, once adopted, began to expand rapidly, especially as regards length of phrase and the overall pattern of the movement. The most advanced composers of the first phase of the eighteenth century were Vinci and Leo. In the works of these composers and others, one can see the beginnings of a differentiation of thematic material; but the concept of ritornello still predominated. Leonardo Vinci (1690–1730), for instance, tended to write in a more modern idiom while often still using Baroque forms. The opera overtures of Leonardo Leo (1694–1744) also show the same trend in development of thematic usage, as well as other characteristics common to early symphonies of this period.

The second stage of the Italian overture consolidated the gains of Leo and Vinci by eliminating some of the Baroque techniques while retaining others. Clearly, many Baroque procedures furnish indispensable technical background for the Classical processes, notably the use of sequences in modulation sections. The outstanding composers of the second generation were Rinaldo di Capua (c. 1715–c. 1775), Galuppi, and Jommelli. Even on the basis of the relatively few surviving works it is evident that Rinaldo made a considerable advance over Vinci and Leo in achieving thematic differentiation and rudimentary development without disruption of the recapitulation.

A fresh emphasis in the second generation derived from Baldassare Galuppi (1706–85), a composer more deeply involved with *opera buffa* and keyboard composition than with *opera seria* or church music. In search of piquant melodies and rhythms Galuppi popularized several formulae that soon became hackneyed, particularly various types of turn with preceding grace-notes. Another Italian cliché that crystallized in this generation was a combination of triadic and sequential themes, in which a pattern applied to the root then moves up to the third and fifth, an elaboration of the triadic types seen in earlier symphonies. Galuppi's turns and sequences are well illustrated in the opening bars of *Il filosofo di campagna* (1754), an overture which also displays an effective development as well as a full recapitulation (London, Brit. Mus. Roy. 22.c.20). In other instances, his interest in melodic freshness prevents a mature consideration of formal concerns. In *Antigono* (1746) a long exposition of five ideas leaves no energy for development, and a debilitated recapitulation brings back only three themes. Galuppi's slow movements are usually in the A–B–A form of the operatic aria, but the

[1] *Sinfonie da vari autori* (Paris).

themes employ the fussy rhythms reminiscent of his keyboard style rather than broad cantabile. The finales add new forms to the minuet already noted: a 3/8 Presto, a fast 2/4, and a gigue-type. These four species may be seen in the publisher Venier's *Sinfonie da vari autori* (Paris, 1755) III/6, *Antigono*, a Symphony in D major in Genoa (Civico Liceo Musicale, T.C.7.2. (Scatola 100)) and *Siroe* (1754).

The contributions of Niccolò Jommelli (1714-74) lie chiefly in the clarification of first-movement form. Less spontaneous than Galuppi, he avoids Galuppi's impulsive tendency to expand one section of the form beyond its appropriate size. As a result, Jommelli produced overtures of excellent effect, such as *Il Ciro riconosciuto* (1744),[1] in which four thematic areas clearly emerge. The secondary theme, though not strongly contrasted in material, makes a particular mark by its minor mode and the sharp articulation achieved by rests and changes in texture and dynamics:

Ex. 161

Brit. Mus. Roy. 22.5.3.

Note the recurrence of elements (*x*) and (*y*) as well as the thematic relation between the primary and closing material. These unifying touches, and the occasional attention to parts other than the top (see the secondary theme) reflect a creative ability well above the average of Jommelli's contemporaries.

In later works Jommelli tried a number of experiments in avoiding conventional forms. Apart from the unique two-movement symphony with chaconne, most of these experiments involved a truncation of the first movement and connection of all three movements to give the impression of a single inclusive scheme. In a manuscript symphony in D (Genoa Conservatory) the first movement modulates to the dominant, only to introduce an Andante in the tonic minor. This slow movement is cut short by a surprise return of the Allegro, which again comes to a swift end after the modulation, this time continuing directly with a conventional Presto 3/8 finale. Experiments of this sort led to a conciseness that ultimately established the one-movement overture as predominant.

Among Italian composers Jommelli stands out for his dynamics, not only in forte-piano dialogue themes (*Caio Mario*, 1746) but more significantly in the use of the orchestral crescendo. Already in *Merope* (1741) the score teems with dynamic indications, including crescendos effected by successive gradations from *pp* to *ff* or *forte assai*: Jommelli moved in the same direction as Johann Stamitz in exploiting orchestral crescendos. In many cases they mark the opening of the modulating section, with characteristic tremolos in the violins and a transfer of thematic fragments to the bass. This use of crescendo as a device of formal differentiation rather than mere dynamic sensation again reflects Jommelli's broad concern with form. It was perhaps this formal clarity that appealed to eighteenth-century listeners, for Jommelli was even more popular than Galuppi.

In the last third of the century experiments with overture form increase, thus gradually widening the split between the three-movement tradition and the newer one-movement trend, with many hybrids in between. One recurrent type, the *da capo* symphony or overture, consists of an allegro exposition that is immediately followed by a slow movement, ending with the direction 'da capo al 𝄋'. The 𝄋 sign is usually placed at the point of modulation, directing us to an alternate section that resumes the tonic like a normal recapitulation. This effective scheme occurs in the work of many composers, such as Piccinni and Guglielmi, and continues into the nineteenth century.

By 1770 one would expect to find some influence of the concert symphony on the overture, but the growing strength of the concert symphony seems rather to have turned the overture in upon itself. The Italian opera composers continued to stress rhythmic drive and to favour the main melodic line, so that one need listen to only a few bars of an overture to notice the absence of the full texture, sophisticated phrasing and imaginative orchestration which were characteristic of the concert symphony. These inferiorities of the overture did not reduce its popularity, for about 1780 the one-movement overture holds its place statistically in both printed collections and in manuscript sources.

LATER ITALIAN OPERA OVERTURES

Among the large number of successful Italian composers in the latter half of the century, the most prominent are Anfossi, Cimarosa, Guglielmi, Paisiello, Piccinni, Sacchini, and Sarti. The overtures of Pasquale Anfossi (1727–97) display an occasional firm line in a secondary theme, but the trite construction can barely sustain interest throughout the movement. The great melodic gifts of Domenico Cimarosa (1749–1801) tempted him to string together tuneful episodes without much formal organization. He favoured the one-movement form, as in *L'impresario* (1786)[1] or his ever popular *Il matrimonio segreto* (1792). Though he rarely developed themes, he often used the development section to introduce fresh harmonic colours. Pietro Guglielmi (1728–1804) offers little more interest in texture or phrasing than Anfossi, but as a relief from the conventional turns and staccato articulation customary with his countrymen he occasionally introduces a cantabile element in the primary themes, as in *Il carnovale di Venezia*[2] and *Le pazzie d'Orlando*.[3] Judging by the number of surviving sources, Giovanni Paisiello (1740–1816) appears to have been the most popular of overture composers.

[1] Modern edition by Carse (London, 1946). Carse's are 'practical' editions, textually unreliable.
[2] 1772 (London, c. 1775).
[3] 1771 (London, 1771).

This general esteem undobutedly grew out of the unparalleled success of his *Barbiere di Siviglia* (1782),[1] next to Mozart's *Figaro* the most enduring work in the late *buffa* repertory. Paisiello began his career with three-movement overtures, later adopting mainly the one-movement style; but his wide range includes many experiments such as *da capo* overtures and a single two-movement work (D major, Manchester, Henry Watson Library), Allegro—Rondo Andante, a sequence similar to the *Symphonie concertante*. Like Cimarosa, Paisiello commanded a rich flow of melodic invention, but he organized movements with more logic and balance, so that established themes do not suddenly disappear in irruptions of new material.

Of all the Italians, Niccolò Piccinni (1728–1800) concentrated the most on sheer rhythmic motion. Even his secondary themes employ the crisp rests, syncopations, and driving figures that propel his movements. The following pattern from his *L'amante ridicolo deluso* (1757),[2] shows the accelerating effect of his energy:

Ex. 162

In spite of the breakneck speed of composition required by operatic deadlines (about a hundred and twenty operas in forty years), he still had time for constructional niceties, such as the relationship between primary and secondary material in his most famous overture *La buona figliuola* (1760).[3]

Ex. 163

When Piccinni was called to Paris to oppose Gluck his style underwent several noticeable changes. He tried at first to imitate French pomp, an uncongenial task for a *buffa* composer. His art profited, on the other

[1] Overture ed. Antonio de Almeida (Paris, 1961).
[2] Brit. Mus. Roy. 22.m.20.
[3] Ed. Giacomo Benvenuti, *I classici musicali italiani*, vii (Milan, 1942).

hand, from the rich possibilities of the French orchestra, and from the first (*Roland*, 1778) his Paris operas exploit many effects absent from his Italian works, such as frequent passages for solo wind instruments, particularly clarinets. Most revealing of French influence is Piccinni's *Diane et Endimion* (1784), a two-movement, slow–fast overture, leading directly into Act I at the point where we would normally expect a recapitulation. In making this close connection of the overture with the dramatic action Piccinni surprisingly becomes a link between Gluck and early Romantics such as Méhul.

Unlike Piccinni, Antonio Sacchini (1730–86) did not change styles when he changed residences by moving to England and France. In his early operas we find many three-movement works, but also convincing one-movement overtures. These two types continue with little change in the years up to his masterpiece, *Oedipe à Colone*. The main advance consists of an enlargement of the development section: in *Semiramide* (1763) it functions as an eight-bar transition to the recapitulation; in *Oedipe* (1786)[1] he carries an expressive theme through twenty-two bars, reaching the recapitulation in B♭ through the darker areas of F minor, A♭ major, and the tonic minor.

Sacchini was undoubtedly one of the finest overture composers of the group under discussion. Where others composed in a constant bustle of raw energy, he harnessed the energy to propel phrases at varying speeds suitable to the different phases and areas of the form. To the Italian sense of line he added much-needed feeling for contrast, not only melodically but also in harmony and orchestration. The quality of Sacchini's movement with its rhythmic variety grips the listener right at the opening of *Oedipe*:

Ex.164 Allegro spiritoso

[1] Overture ed. Almeida (Paris, 1961).

Giuseppe Sarti (1729–1802) stands next to Sacchini in musical imagination, more varied in his formal experiments if less subtle in melody and inner construction. In addition to three-movement and one-movement overtures he tried unusual combinations such as the scheme of *Le gelosie villane* (1776), an allegro exposition and curtailed andante directly connected to the finale. Sarti's slow movements include rondo forms, in addition to the common two-part and A–B–A patterns. In his orchestration he shows a quite un-Italian interest in variety and colour: *Le gelosie villane*, for example, exploits the pizzicato of the first violins near the beginning of the allegro, later presenting the secondary theme on the first violins against horn chords and pizzicato accompaniment in the second violins. Preceding Rossini, Sarti was one of the first to employ effectively the orchestral crescendo as a curtain-raiser at the end of one-movement overtures.

In the half-century just reviewed, the overture begins on a par with the concert symphony but soon declines in both relative size and artistic weight. Where in earlier years borrowings from opera helped to fill out the scanty orchestral repertory, after 1760 the large production of independent symphonies fully satisfied all requirements. Thus at the end of the century the overture maintained a somewhat ephemeral position based less on its own merits than on the popularity of the opera from which it came.

SAMMARTINI AND THE SYMPHONY

Coincident with the height of the late Baroque style, a new direction in instrumental music was established by Giovanni Battista Sammartini (1700/01–75), a Milanese steeped in the north Italian sonata-concerto. Attempts to establish Sammartini's priority as a symphonist have foundered on difficulties of chronology: we cannot date any works with certainty before 1742, when his Op. 2 appeared in a Paris sale catalogue as *XII Sonate a due e tre violini col basso* by his elder brother Giuseppe.[1] Numerous symphonies, variously titled sinfonia, ouvertura, trio, concertino and sonata appear in the Fonds Blancheton of the Paris Conservatoire, a collection dated 1740–4 by Lionel de La Laurencie.[2]

When one compares the symphonies of Sammartini generally with the works of his notable predecessors, such as Vinci and Leo, the Fonds

[1] See Georges de Saint-Foix, 'La Chronologie de l'oeuvre instrumentale de Jean Baptiste Sammartini', *Sammelbände der internationalen Musikgesellschaft*, xv (1913–14), p. 308; Saint-Foix gives the incipits of Op. 2. Op. 2, no. 11, is printed complete in Karl Nef, *Geschichte der Sinfonie und Suite* (Leipzig, 1921), p. 318.

[2] *Inventaire critique du Fonds Blancheton*, 2 vols. (Paris, 1930 and 1931). On problems of chronology and attribution, see Bathia Churgin and Newell Jenkins, 'Sammartini', *Die Musik in Geschichte und Gegenwart*, xi, cols. 1337–8, and Churgin, *The Symphonies of G. B. Sammartini* (Radcliffe, 1961).

Blancheton symphonies are larger in size and exhibit more variety in the character of the movements (especially finales), more development of ideas, and far greater textural interest. In Sammartini's symphonies we observe the same conflicts of the Baroque–Classical transition already observed in the overture. Three distinct styles coexist in his music, noticeable even in the incipits of the early symphonies:

    1. The post-Vivaldi style, emphasizing rhythm with strongly marked beats and ritornello elements as in Fonds Blancheton, nos. 6, 69, 87, 145;

    2. The early Classical overture style, with neatly symmetrical repetitions as in Fonds Blancheton, no. 17;

    3. The *style galant*, basically a chamber rather than orchestral style, with playful rather than forceful themes, frequent ornamentation, and elaborate lines often cast in facile ♫ rhythm.[1]

Ex. 165

A number of these early works differentiate clearly primary, modulatory, secondary, and closing themes, yet without losing sight of the large form by over-preoccupation with melodic details. In the Symphony in G major, Fonds Blancheton, no. 150,[2] Sammartini achieves rhythmic continuity by reducing transitional matter and arranging phrases asymmetrically, two procedures that foreshadow Haydn's close-knit forms.

Still more important is Sammartini's infusion of interest into the recapitulation in a variety of ways. Let us briefly consider certain movements of four of his symphonies. None of the first movements is rounded off by a ritornello-coda in the manner of Emanuel Bach, nor by a developmental coda in the manner of the later Viennese composers. In the already mentioned Fonds Blancheton, no. 150, the end of the exposition (bars 9–17) returns unchanged to complete the first movement (bars 43–51). The sole spice of variety is the inevitable transposition from dominant to tonic. The third movement is of interest in regard to Haydn. This Allegro assai consists of 107 bars in 3/8 time. At bar 25 the opening theme reappears in the dominant and, as one would expect

[1] Paris, Bibl. Nat. Cons., Fonds Blancheton, nos. 46 and 113.
[2] Miniature score, ed. Jenkins (London, 1956).

in such a monothematic pattern, the theme is played only once in the recapitulation; the movement concludes, however, with the same cadential figure that provided the ending of the exposition at the double bar.

In the C major symphony edited by Fausto Torrefranca,[1] the re-arrangement of the material from the exposition is more varied. For one thing, the commonplace theme, so famous from the finale of Mozart's last great symphony, is melodically altered in that the exposition emphasizes the opening ascending whole-tone step (G–A–C–B), and the recapitulation the ascending semitone (E–F–F–E), although the harmony remains the same. By and large the recapitulation is exact, but a short snatch from the modulating group (bars 8–9) is omitted at bar 45 and tagged on to the closing group instead (bars 59–61). Obviously, such reshuffling of the component passages, however brief, provided a certain amount of interest towards the end of the movement.

A G major symphony[2] is more radical, introducing a slight amount of new material in the first movement (bars 62–4) though the distinctive feature that lends interest to the recapitulation is its omissions. These are sizeable, and the passages that do not reappear (bars 7–13, 16–28) have not been worked over in the development. Strategic, if not dramatic, considerations seem to have dictated the ordering of the material.

Perhaps the C major symphony edited by Bonelli[3] approaches most closely the expanded recapitulation which Haydn preferred in his movements without coda. In the first movement some passages are omitted (bars 12–15), others are abbreviated (bars 24–37 are reduced to 105–13), others are re-ordered (bars 37–40). The main interest resides in the expansion of the subsidiary group. By a variety of devices, including the recall of material from the development section, a passage of six bars (19–24) is expanded three-fold (87–105).

In slow movements Sammartini surpasses those of his operatic contemporaries in size, and sophistication of harmony and texture; at the same time he yields to no one in warmth of cantabile:[4]

Ex. 166 Andante

[1] Milan, 1936.
[2] Ed. Torrefranca (Milan, 1931).
[3] Padua, 1956.
[4] Ex. 166 is from Fonds Blancheton, no. 45.

The tendency towards expressive chromaticism and the use of such intervals as the two successive augmented fourths in the second bar are characteristic. So, also, are the occasional employment of false relations and the juxtaposition of ordinary and lowered leading notes in cadences. In his orchestration Sammartini achieves less distinction than in other aspects of his style, though by comparison with the opera composers he finds more interest for the wind instruments and produces better part-writing generally. In one respect, however, he is unique: he may be called the patron saint of the second violin. He organized string texture by interlacing the parts so that, in repetitions of thematic elements, the violins exchange material; moreover, the usually repressed second violins in numerous cases supply a vital rhythmic core of broken arpeggios or tremolo semiquavers against the themes of the first violin. This independence becomes even more marked in slow movements:[1]

Ex. 167 Largo

By 1760 few composers had so successfully resurrected counterpoint and made it part of the Classical style. Most early symphonists carefully avoided Baroque counterpoint, sensing its disruptive effect on the balanced unfolding of Classical form in a homophonic texture. To be sure, such change of focus is not inappropriate for developmental excursions, where identity of themes and the tonalities towards which they move are often intentionally obscure; but this function of counterpoint was little realized by early Classicists. Sammartini stands virtually alone in solving the conflict of styles by evolving a non-imitative, harmonically controlled counterpoint.

A last major contribution of Sammartini concerns the minuet. While most opera composers write a fast 3/8 minuet with the bar felt as one pulse, Sammartini increasingly favoured a 3/4 minuet of dignified tempo directly related to the minuet of the later four-movement symphony. Fonds Blancheton no. 150 actually consists of four movements though the minuet comes last, curiously following a fast finale-type of

[1] Ex. 167 is from ibid., no. 148.

movement. Since this minuet occurs in the key of E flat as the finale of one of Sammartini's trios (Fonds Blancheton, no. 121, also published by John Simpson of London as Op. 1, no. 2) it was probably transposed and added to an existing symphony by the compilers of the Fonds Blancheton collection. With this ambiguous origin, the symphony does not represent as firm a precedent for the four-movement symphony with minuet as the 1740 autograph of G. M. Monn discussed below, though the Sammartini work surpasses Monn in maturity of form and style. Both of these works precede the Stamitz four-movement symphonies that can be dated, yet it is Stamitz alone who follows the precedent with consistency.[1]

Among Sammartini's contemporaries, one might have expected a significant contribution from Giuseppe Tartini (1692–1770); but, like Vivaldi, the great virtuoso saved his best effort for his concertos, and his relatively few symphonies are surprisingly backward-looking. More important in the field of the symphony is Antonio Brioschi, a composer not frequently met with in modern works of reference though his works occur in many European libraries. His popularity at mid-century can be gauged by his representation in the Fonds Blancheton and in the first Breitkopf catalogues (1762), a record nearly as strong as that of Sammartini. In certain prints and manuscripts Brioschi's symphonies are confused with those of Sammartini,[2] which they resemble in miniature, even to a similar cultivation of the second violin. The most distinctive parts are the development sections, which sometimes exceed the expositions in length, with effective episodes in related minor tonalities. Brioschi's wide skips and rhythmic emphasis (using repeated notes even in lyric movements) reflect a genuinely orchestral thematic style which was now gradually replacing the operatic, vocal influence formerly predominant in the symphony.

LATER ITALIAN SYMPHONISTS

In addition to Sammartini, two other Milanese composers, Melchior Chiesa (*fl.* 1760) and Count Giorgio Giulini (1714–80), further contributed to the position of Milan as a symphonic centre. The Chiesa symphonies seem more primitive than Sammartini in all respects except the clear punctuation before the secondary theme. Sammartini's pupil

[1] The four-movement symphonies with minuets of Tomaso Albinoni (1671–1750) dated 1735 by Remo Giazotto (*Tomaso Albinoni*, Milan, 1945, pp. 259–92) were destroyed in the Darmstadt bombing of the Second World War. From Giazatto's copious quotations these works appear to belong more to the Classical than to the Baroque style. By his dating, based on a mention of six Albinoni symphonies in a Darmstadt repertory list of 1735, these symphonies precede those of Monn and Sammartini.

[2] Notably in Le Clerc's publication, *Sonate a due e tre violini*, Op. 2 (see p. 530), of which nos. 2, 6 and 12 are really by Brioschi.

Giulini apparently attained popularity in Paris, since the publisher Venier included him in four of his *Vari autori* collections (*c.* 1755–1764). Although his themes lack personality, the consistently adequate developments and recapitulations surpass the construction of most overtures of the time.

The dearth of immediate successors of Sammartini's calibre ends abruptly with the rocket-like rise to fame of Luigi Boccherini(1743–1805). Prolific and imaginative, possessing an instinct for formal balance and fluent lyric gifts, Boccherini barely missed the highest artistic rank. Unfortunately, his emotional range is restricted as a result of his innate placidity; he also overworked the device of symmetrical repetition. No one who has heard his Symphony in C major of 1771[1] can fail to be impressed by the opening phrase: the falling octave in the second bar embodies the century-old practice of expressing the sigh 'ahimè' melodically. (To identify this sigh with the Mannheim School, as Riemann did, does not seem tenable in view of its universal occurrence.) This phrase is a fair and felicitous example of Boccherini's poignant melancholy, a significant precedent for Mozart's lyrical allegro. At other times, Boccherini commands a sharp wit and satirizes the clichés of the *buffa* overture (Op. 35, no. 1). Still, it is in his cantabile passages that he is most memorable, as in the beginning of the slow movement of Op. 37, no. 4.[2] The rise and fall in the bass of over two octaves creates unusual intensity, and above it the oboe projects an expressive arc. Also notable are the full texture and co-ordinated polyphony of this passage with its proto-romantic doubling of oboe and viola:

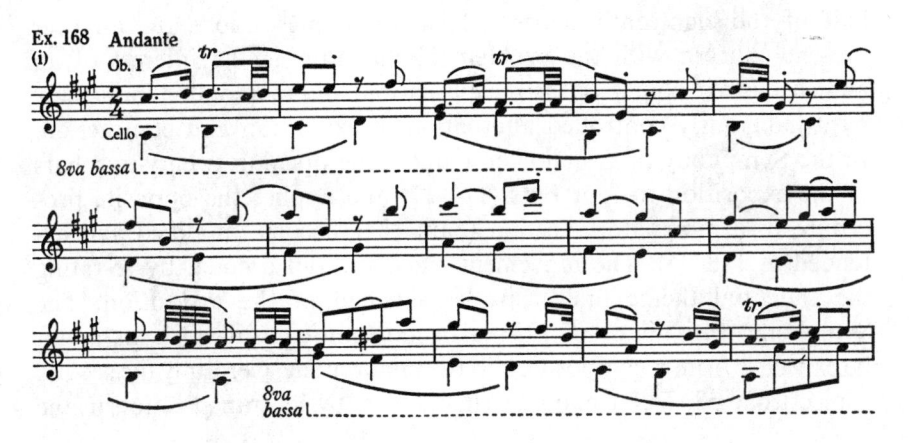

Ex. 168 Andante

[1] No. 505 in Yves Gérard, *Thematic, Bibliographical, and Critical Catalogue of the Works of Luigi Boccherini* (London, 1969).
[2] ibid, no. 518; Karl Geiringer (ed.) (Vienna, 1937).

The same passage showing the orchestration.

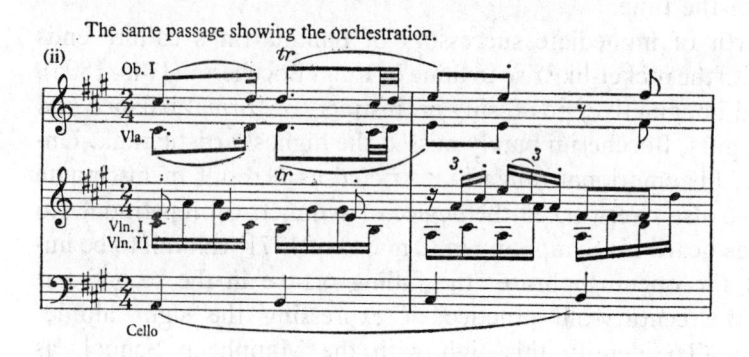

The subtleties of Boccherini's orchestration deserve further study. His originalities of timbre extend beyond details to entire movements: in the *Sinfonia funebre* (1782), between the conventional instrumentation of the first movement and the finale, Boccherini scored the second movement for wind instruments, the third movement for strings alone.

As regards Boccherini's treatment of form, one may note the omission of the main theme in the recapitulation of his cello concerto in B flat major.[1] A similar procedure is to be observed in the C major symphony which is actually a rearrangement, made in 1799, for concertino and orchestra, of an earlier quintet.[2] Obviously the usefulness and popularity of the A B : : C B pattern penetrated far into the second half of the eighteenth century. His symphonies also show an ever present concern with the problem of maintaining the interest of an audience in the course of the recapitulation, and of avoiding monotony by a judiciously controlled alternation of expansion and contraction. In the Symphony in C major he reduces the opening twenty-two bars of the exposition to four bars (114–17) and applies the opposite procedure to a modulatory section (bars 22–7 become modified and extended in 118–34). The movement ends, without a coda, by restating the cadential theme first heard at the end of the exposition. The Symphony in C minor of 1788[3] is a more thoughtful work, as might be expected from a composition in the minor mode. Certainly the second subject (bar 58, E flat major, strings only), by its transposition in the

[1] See p. 445.
[2] Nos. 523 and 268 respectively in Gérard, op. cit.
[3] No. 519 in Gérard, op. cit.; ed. P. Carmirelli (Milan, 1956).

recapitulation to the tonic minor (bar 164) contributes both to musical variety and at the same time to the overall emotional unity of the movement in a manner that goes beyond the fashionable, posed melancholy of the day. And the new passage (bars 181–91) which does not appear in the exposition is balanced by the radical reduction of the opening material (bars 1–55 against 147–55). Following these and other changes, the return of the closing theme from the exposition, with its concerto dynamics, provides a welcome structural point of stability at the conclusion of the movement.

Resembling Boccherini in lyric emphasis, another North Italian, Gaetano Pugnani[1] (1731–98) nearly equalled his popularity, especially in England. Despite occasional activity as an opera composer, Pugnani favoured the concert tradition of four movements in both overtures and symphonies. Within this form he experimented widely with unconventional arrangements such as opening slow movements (not mere introductions).[2] In his best-known overture, in E flat (Welcker, Op. 8, no. 2; Venier, Op. 9, no. 2), he adopted the extremely unusual sequence Andante–Allegro–Minuet and Trio, a grouping more usual in his quintets.

In Pugnani's first movements we find advanced thematic articulation, but without a proper balance between the main sections. In the symphonies of Op. 4 the themes move in related sentences, not in isolated words and phrases, e.g. no. 1 of this set:

Ex. 169 Allegro assai

In the same set of symphonies Pugnani developed another progressive feature, a decisive pause to signal the beginning of the modulating section, in contrast to a mere change in dynamics and orchestration. (The operatic cliché was the violin tremolo, forte.) On the other hand, Pugnani, in this same symphony, omits the development section. In

[1] E. von Zschinsky-Troxler, *Gaetano Pugnani* (Berlin, 1939) contains a detailed thematic index.
[2] See Welcker's publication of Pugnani's Op. 4 and 8 (London, *c.* 1770), especially Zschinsky-Troxler, nos. 28, 29, 32, 34.

another symphony, with an excellent development section (Op. 4. no. 3), the primary theme does not return in the recapitulation.

The passion somewhat lacking in Boccherini and Pugnani overflows in the vigorous music of Gaetano Brunetti (*c.* 1740–1808), who, like Boccherini, worked mainly in Spain. In a period when most symphonists preferred the major mode, Brunetti wrote a number of poignant and even stormy works in the minor. His obscurity may be traced largely to his patron, the Duke of Alba, who permitted him to print only a few pieces of chamber music; even manuscript copies of his works are extremely rare. Working in an isolation even more severe than that of Haydn at Esterház, Brunetti developed a similarly strong and individual musical personality. Curiously enough he resembles Haydn also in his attention to rhythmic continuity.

Brunetti's fresh melodic style ranges from jagged or sweeping energy to a Mozartian lyricism, as in the third movement of his Symphony in C minor:[1]

Ex. 170

In his handling of the third movement he abandoned the minuet tradition and experimented with various types of scherzo, inventing a scheme in which a woodwind 'quintetto' plays the first section, the tutti entering only for the contrasting episode. This quintetto–tutti–quintetto pattern is the opposite of the textural scheme of the minuet–trio–minuet arrangement.

The Italian symphony created few significant innovations and only a handful of masterpieces. Yet its emphasis on easy, natural movement

[1] Ed. Jenkins, *Classici italiani della musica*, iii (Rome, 1960).

was important in the evolution of the symphony. French concern for elegant detail and German preoccupation with contrapuntal texture might have run the whole idea of the development aground; but the earthy rhythmic vigour and clear melodic objectives of the Italians served as channel markers to keep the others on a straight course.

THE GRAUN BROTHERS AND HASSE

Nowhere does the Italian opera more clearly demonstrate its strength than at the Court of Frederick the Great. Surrounded by imported French culture, the Italian style nevertheless dominates the development of the north German symphony. Although one can find a few French overtures in the work of each composer, the dignified dotted rhythms and fugal allegros remain a conscious stereotype that was not carried over into the symphonic style in general. The composers important in the north German group were the brothers Carl Heinrich and Johann Gottlieb Graun, Johann Adolf Hasse, Johann Wilhelm Hertel, and Carl Philipp Emanuel Bach.

Carl Heinrich Graun (1704–59), an opera composer now best known for his fine passion-cantata, *Der Tod Jesu*, wrote overtures in a three-movement form similar to those of Jommelli and Galuppi. Few of these works appeared in print separately,[1] but the Breitkopf Catalogue (1762) offers no less than twenty-two overtures for sale in manuscript. Mennicke[2] severely criticizes Graun's stereotyped themes and ubiquitous 'drum' basses, such as those of *Rodelinda* (1741). These characteristics stemmed in a general way from the Italian overture, but Graun clung to the old-fashioned Baroque manner with his persistent quaver-rhythm in both melody and accompaniment.

As if to compensate for his thematic shortcomings, Graun's handling of development sections extends far beyond the normal Italian practice. In *Montezuma*[3] (1755) the development carries motives from the exposition through an extensive episode in the relative minor, leading back to the recapitulation with further modulatory excursions. Another progressive feature is Graun's texture, which he tightens and unifies by distributing thematic fragments to parts other than the treble.

The older brother, Johann Gottlieb Graun (1703–71), is less famous; yet in the field of the symphony he is the more deserving. He also favoured a conservative version of the Italian three-movement overture.

---

[1] One of the few is *Il giudizio di Paride* (Leipzig, 1757). Etienne Mangean's strangely confused publication, *Six Simphonies . . . del Signor Sans Martini et Brioschi* (Paris, c. 1750), contains Graun's *Adriano* and *Cajo Fabricio* as nos. 5 and 6, quite without identification. No. 4 in this set is a symphony by J. G. Graun (Mennicke, no. 40), similarly unidentified.

[2] Carl Mennicke, *Hasse und die Brüder Graun als Sinfoniker* (Leipzig, 1906), pp. 199 ff.

[3] *Denkmäler deutscher Tonkunst*, xv (Leipzig, 1904), pp. 1–10.

Although his themes often use the Baroque rhythms noted in Carl Heinrich's work he occasionally broadens the motivic sequences into true phrases, several bars in length. At his most progressive, Graun enlarges his thematic structure to permit balanced phrase-segments, the first stage in the evolution of the question–answer theme typical of late Classicism.

Like his brother, Johann Gottlieb excelled in development sections, which often surpass the expositions in length. Short stretches of developmental imitation give welcome relief from the mid-century glut of homophonic texture, as in the Symphony in G[1] published by Breitkopf in 1762.

Ex. 171 [Allegro]

Here, as so often in the early symphony, however, a strong and extended development stunts the following recapitulation. The achievement of the Grauns is incomplete, for it is rare to find a symphony of theirs with all movements of equal worth.

Johann Wilhelm Hertel (1727–89), a prolific symphonist, was Court composer at Schwerin. Though he was younger than the others of the North German group, Hertel's works share many of their characteristics. Generally, however, he employs a larger wind instrumentation: two each of flutes, oboes, and horns, with—on the evidence of occasional solo passages in slow movements—bassoons. His relatively colourful orchestration contrasts sharply with the attitude that permitted 'oboi e corni ad libitum'.

Most famous of the North German group was the Dresden Kapellmeister, Johann Adolf Hasse (1699–1783). To appreciate his value one must look beyond the beginnings of his symphonies, for the opening themes fall into stereotyped forms even more rigid than those of the younger Graun. Frequently repeated notes in the melodic line charac-

---

[1] Quoted from Mennicke, op. cit., pp. 210–13.

teristic of the Baroque style combined with the slower harmonic rhythms of the Classical style give an impression of sterility, as in the opera-symphonies *La clemenza di Tito* (1738), *Atalanta* (1737), *Artaserse* (1730), and *Il Ciro rinconosciuto* (1751):[1]

Ex. 172

In other respects, however, Hasse gives evidence of a lively imagination. Already in *Arminio* (1730) he sets off secondary material with a short rest, highlighting a quasi-lyrical theme quite unlike the arpeggio beginning, a differentiation fully as successful as the gestures of Vinci and Leo in this direction.[2]

Ex. 173

Hasse tried many experiments in his slow movements, ranging from a brief eleven-bar connecting movement (*Leucippo*, 1747) to long, differentiated binary forms (*Cleofide*, 1731). Significant is his treatment of the minuet finale as a miniature rondo with two episodes (*Asteria*, 1737). By breaking away from the heavy punctuations of the minuet–trio–minuet sequence Hasse obtained a continuous flow and created a precedent for later rondo finales. In orchestration Hasse's originality and evident open-mindedness lead him to search for unusual colours such as the two solo cors anglais in the slow movement of *Il trionfo di Clelia* (1762) two years before Haydn's use of this combination in his Symphony no. 22.

C. P. E. BACH

In Carl Philipp Emanuel Bach (1714–88) the North German group possessed a composer of the boldest imagination. Endowed with a

[1] Ibid., pp. 500 ff.
[2] Rudolf Gerber (ed.), *Das Erbe deutscher Musik* xxvii (Mainz, 1957).

fertile and versatile mind, he established a position of almost oracular authority, in spite of the fact that few of his works can be described as balanced masterpieces. In a number of transitional composers we have seen the conflict between Baroque and Classical styles, to which Bach joined a third, even more disparate element: a genuine Romanticism half a century before its general acceptance. The chief components of Baroque, Classical, and Romantic so uneasily coexisting in Bach's works may be characterized as:

1. A deeply rooted interest in Baroque polyphony which deepens musical as well as intellectual interest while it conflicts with the larger-scale Classical designs. True polyphony articulates each line independently, obscuring the co-ordinated punctuations required by Classic form. Furthermore, polyphonic textures reduce the listener's awareness of broader contrasts and developments.

2. A rhythmic structure emphasizing small units, as in the opening bars of the C major symphony, no. 3 of the set of six composed at Hamburg.[1] Dating from 1773, these two bars might have been written half a century earlier, say, by Pergolesi:

Ex. 174
Allegro assai
bars 1–4

3. A profound interest in and command of development: in this essentially Classical process Bach has no equal before Haydn and Beethoven. He explores line extension and permutation, rhythmic fragmentation, harmonic variation, contrapuntal combination, re-orchestration of themes—every conceivable device enriching the original material receives subtle and probing attention.

4. Expressive ornamentation: Bach uses ornaments partly as an elegant refinement, as in the *style galant*, but more as a delicately adjustable means of expression. In his hands the harmonic, dynamic, and rhythmic aspects of ornamentation reach a high degree of sophistication. It is this integration of ornament with the core of the musical thought that distinguishes *Empfindsamkeit* from *style galant*, for in the latter ornamentation comes as a secondary process, an overlay, refined but superficial. In performance the nature of the ornamentation calls for soloists suggesting a chamber ensemble; hence, for orchestral works this element tends to produce more confusion than enhancement.

[1] On the Berlin symphonies of 1741–62, see p. 389.

5. Strong Romantic leanings. Bach's striking individualism, worthy of any full-blown Romantic, affects almost every movement he wrote. No clearer sample can be found than the unexpected continuation of the theme just cited:

Ex. 175 bars 5–8

We are startled not only by the dramatic rests (did Mozart hear this work or the opening of the *Orchester Sinfonie* in F before he wrote the C minor piano concerto?) but also by the juxtaposition of the A flat and F sharp against the bland beginning and simple continuation. In typically Romantic fashion Bach values the vivid impulse of the moment above the long-range design and one senses in his music a conscious exploitation of paradox. His works abound in what appear to be deliberate contortions of form, explicit in the *Sonaten mit veränderten Reprisen* (1760). Viewed by the Romanticist these exhibit the genius of the free imagination; to the Classicist they often appear as excessively subjective.

In addition to proliferations from these five major aspects of Bach's style, a great number of conflicting details can be found in his works. To mention only orchestration, it is possible to find a romantically colouristic use of solo woodwind nearly side-by-side with block alternations of tutti–concertino forces typical of the Baroque. In these circumstances Bach could furnish leadership only to men of a calibre sufficient to appreciate content when forms are equivocal. The average composer is able to imitate a clear form or procedure with adequate and often attractive results—hence the astounding spate of Baroque trio sonatas and Classical symphonies. But there are few neat formulae in C. P. E. Bach, and the *Kleinmeister* were incapable of extracting his nuggets of genius from their unconventional surroundings. Though universally respected and widely admired, Bach influenced the course of the symphony only through the transmutations of Haydn, Mozart, and Beethoven.

From the treasury of Bach's ideas any selection seems hopelessly inadequate. His forms contain lessons of ingenuity and freedom, particularly in the flexible connection of movements and in variety of types in slow movements. The sweep of his tonalities is wide indeed, as may be seen in the first of the four *Orchester-Sinfonien mit 12 obligaten Stimmen* of 1776, a D major work with slow movement in E flat. Artistic deception in rhythmic matters, surprises in metre and phraseology, concerned

Bach nearly as much as Haydn. He is equally a master of pregnant silence. The following example, from the C major symphony already quoted, combines certain of these traits, particularly the imaginative development of the opening motive, the dramatic excursion to the remote tonality of B flat minor, and the sparse accompaniment spaced with significant rests:

Ex. 176

FORM IN C. P. E. BACH'S SYMPHONIES

Emanuel Bach's handling of form is of such interest, both in its own right and as a transition to the practice of Haydn and Mozart, that it deserves separate consideration. His Symphony in E minor (1756) contains features which remind us of Vivaldi, whose works he would have known, both directly and through their influence on the compositions of his father, as well as on Handel and Telemann. Of the eight symphonies composed before Emanuel moved to Hamburg in 1768 this E minor, highly praised by Hasse and others, best repays study.[1] The opening movement is certainly as long and as serious as one would expect from a German symphony in the minor mode: 140-odd bars, in 4/4 time, containing a development that occupies more than a third of the total length. It is an open question, however, whether this imposing middle section is properly termed 'development'. Bars 39–51 sound more like a restatement of the opening ritornello in the key of the relative major, and bars 62–70 like a further restatement in the dominant. This is not to deny that occasional minute bits of thematic development occur, but their brevity and relative unimportance in the whole scheme hardly go beyond Corelli and Vivaldi. The aspects in which it does differ from the baroque concerto of Italy are its magisterial seriousness, its length, and the expressive modulations. On the other hand, the tutti passages, in true concertato fashion, are punctuated by concertino episodes scored for a trio of two violins and viola (bars 52–4, 59–61). Whether this procedure derives from Corelli or Lully or both the movement is clearly organized by dynamics and texture, rather than by themes or thematic work. Even more interesting in this respect is the final section which, in Haydn and Mozart, would be called the recapitulation. True, it does deserve this term in that both the first and the second subjects reappear in the tonic (bars 90 and 125). But several aspects are more reminiscent of Baroque practices. For instance, the reappearance of the first subject is reduced in size and modified, which removes the sense of an unmistakable restatement so essential for the clarity of design of the later sonata forms. The impression conveyed to an audience, without score, is one of an intermediate ritornello which in no way usurps the traditional finality of the ritornello at the end of the movement. In fact, this recapitulation tends to sound as 'incomplete' as the

[1] Karl Geiringer (ed.), *Music of the Bach Family* (Cambridge, Mass., 1955), pp. 141–55. The symphony was originally published at Nuremberg in 1759 by Balthasar Schmid, whose beautiful workmanship also served the compositions of Telemann, Emanuel's Prussian Sonatas, and his father's *Goldberg Variations*. The version published by Schmid is for strings only, though manuscript parts for flutes, oboes and horns exist.

A B::C D forms of Sebastian Bach and Domenico Scarlatti, because the A which precedes the final B is tentative and inexact.

Another Baroque element is the manner in which the trio-episode from the middle section just mentioned keeps turning up in this pseudo-recapitulation (bars 95 and 122). As in a Vivaldi concerto, the only exact and striking correspondence exists between the opening and closing ritornellos (bars 1 and 132). This closing ritornello, incidentally, is complete and literal except that in its second half it modulates towards the key of the slow movement, for Emanuel is ever fond of obscuring the division between his opening movements. Now what should one call this final reappearance of the main theme: a coda or a ritornello? Clearly, it is both and neither. Indeed, the entire work is a hybrid. It partakes of the Baroque in a vital and effortless manner, while the disposition of tonalities, the spaciousness, the individualism of harmony and expression, look forward to Haydn, Mozart, and Beethoven. In discovering the earlier eighteenth century after achieving a familiarity with later composers we must beware of censuring Emanuel Bach's work when it differs from the formal patterns established one and even two generations later. True, from the point of view of 1800 his recapitulations are abbreviated and incomplete. But is this a fault in either dramatic cogency or musical originality? Emanuel was able to write movements of a high degree of balance and symmetry, movements as regular as the textbooks of the nineteenth century require. This suggests that he retained Baroque elements because it suited his purpose, in the same way that Mozart used the chorale of the armoured men in *Die Zauberflöte*. Both Emanuel Bach and Mozart, among others, became harbingers of Romanticism when they employed the expressive and formal devices of an earlier age. In short, it was natural for the proto-Romanticists of the eighteenth century to fall back upon stylistic elements of the Baroque. Only by going out of their own epoch and searching for apt phrases in the vocabulary of their parents and grandparents could they vary and relieve the monotony and predictability of the fashionable symphonies of their day, which were characterized by homophony, simplicity, and lucidity. By tempering the austere textures of the Enlightenment with Baroque obbligato writing, by inserting a fugato into a straightforward sonata-form section, in effect, by casting a backward look, the greatest masters looked forward to the fashions to come.

The six symphonies composed in 1773 were dedicated to Gottfried van Swieten, in whose library they were available to the Viennese composers. Without doubt, the main characteristic of these symphonies was their uncompromising seriousness. Reichardt, who visited the composer at Hamburg in the 1770s, recounts that in these six great symphonies 'he gave his imagination full rein in accord with van Swieten's wishes (*in welchen er sich, nach Swietens Wunsch, ganz gehen liess*) and did not consider the difficulties (*ohne auf die Schwierigkeiten Rücksicht zu nehmen*) which would be encountered in performance'.[1] Indeed, one need only consider the main theme (or ritornello) of the Symphony no. 4 in A major, with its surprising introduction of G natural and F natural within the tonality of A major and within the short space of four bars. Or the remarkable development of that figure in the middle section (bars 53–61), where the initial motive appears six times, its characteristic downward leap being successively reduced from an octave to a minor seventh and, finally, to a diminished seventh. This last variant receives additional emphasis at the end of the movement (bars 100–8).

Ex. 177

It is an open question which passage should be called the subsidiary theme: the concertino passage, again scored for a trio of two violins and viola, (bars 22–7, A minor, E minor–E major) or the return of the primary theme (bars 33–6, E major). If one chooses the latter, the design looks much like Haydn's monothematic construction. What is

[1] *Allgemeine musikalische Zeitung*, xvi (12 January 1814), cols. 28 ff.

incontestable is that the duality of keys so essential to sonata form is present, but that the vigorous returns of the primary material (bars 4, 33, 53, 100) have an impetus and a manner of dominating the entire movement which hark back to the older Bach's ritornello, and at the same time point forward to Beethoven's main themes. The dramatic alternation of tutti and concertino cannot fail to bring to mind such a work as the *Eroica*. But Emanuel Bach's work lacks sizeable modulating sections in contrast to Haydn and Beethoven. The distance between the tonic and dominant tonalities (bars 15–22) would be too short for the harmonic rhythm of late Haydn, and one is tempted to censure these sudden harmonic twists as regressive or old-fashioned. Yet the ease with which the last bar of Emanuel's first movement, which seems to anticipate A major, turns instead to the F major of the second movement looks forward to Beethoven, Schubert, and Brahms, rather than back to Vivaldi. We must accept then, that the many ritornello-like returns, unchanged in instrumentation and character, are motivated by a delight in block-like construction, which in no way impedes the composer's exploration of new thematic and harmonic paths.

Of the six symphonies which Emanuel Bach dedicated to van Swieten five are available in modern reprints.[1] In these may be observed the characteristics already discussed in the other works. In Symphony no. 2, notable features include the long and serious development section in the first movement, occupying more than a third of the entire movement; the ritornello returns of the main theme after the exposition, to open the middle section, and after the recapitulation to round off the movement; the trio concertino episodes which perform an articulating function; and the expressive harmony at bars 18–28, which takes us from F major to F minor, to B flat minor and, by way of an interrupted cadence, to a G flat major chord.

In Symphony no. 3[2] the opening theme or ritornello of the first movement dominates to an even greater degree: in unison at bars 1, 51, and and 124; in the bass at bars 28, 61, 97; in the treble at bar 69; and in a trio-concertino passage in the viola at bar 57. On the other hand, the recapitulation is much longer than any in Sebastian Bach or Vivaldi. Starting in the subdominant, it is full of significant harmonic changes, after which the ritornello conclusion acts as a much-needed anchor of stability, particularly as it precedes a wild leap into an adagio which begins on a diminished seventh chord on B flat. This proves to be the

---

[1] No. 1 in G (ed. Hugo Riemann) (Langensalza, 1897); No. 2 in B flat (ed. Ernst F. Schmid) (Celle, 1933); No. 3 in C (ed. Schmid) (Celle, 1931); No. 4 in A (ed. Ernst Suchalla) (Wiesbaden, 1965); No. 5 in B minor (ed. Schmid) (Celle, 1937).
[2] See the previous discussion of this work, p. 386–8.

opening note of the famous musical motto B–A–C–H, played by the bass in a tutti passage whose dynamics are marked *ff–p–pp–ff–p–pp*.

Symphony no. 5 has an opening movement in the minor mode, a circumstance which, in the case of both Emanuel Bach and Haydn, seems to function as an inducement to experiment. Concertato dynamics endow both the primary and the secondary material with a nervous intensity far removed from *galanterie*. The main theme in B minor begins with two bars of a trio concertino which are answered by two bars of tutti; the secondary material, in the relative major, changes every half-bar between forte (lower strings plus continuo) and piano (violins without continuo), six such changes taking place within three bars. The development starts in true ritornello fashion (bar 18) as does the recapitulation (bar 35). But this latter section is of a highly experimental nature: beginning in the subdominant its harmonic scheme allows digressions of all kinds, and thus facilitates some surprising appearances of the main theme in addition to those that might be expected in places corresponding to the exposition. Such miniature developments, inserted before the end of the recapitulation, are not uncommon in Emanuel's works, though they are more frequently met with in Haydn, but both the harmonic scheme, progressing from A minor to the dominant of the tonic, and the dynamics, rising in crescendo from *pp* to *p* to *mf* and to *ff*, make for an unusual intensity (bars 48–54). With so many reappearances of the main theme in the development and recapitulation (bars 18, 33, 35, 48, 55) a final ritornello would be anticlimactic. Consequently, the recapitulation ends exactly as did the exposition (bars 58–62 correspond to 14–17). This procedure, another instance of which occurs in the fourth of the *Orchester-Sinfonien* (first movement), foreshadows a characteristic practice of Haydn.

In 1775–6 Emanuel Bach, then over sixty years of age, composed his four famous *Orchester-Sinfonien* (printed in 1780),[1] scored for horns and woodwind in addition to the usual strings and continuo. No. 1 in D major is the only one of Emanuel's symphonies included by Tovey in his analytical essays.[2] Among its most interesting features are a development which boasts fortissimo variations (bars 119, 132) of material taken from the exposition and a coda which is not a ritornello return of the main theme but a development of another theme (bars 56, 191, 207). In Symphony no. 2 in E flat interest centres on the harmonic and thematic scheme. In the exposition, when the opening theme reappears in the subdominant it seems to fulfil the function of a second

---

[1] Reprinted in Rudolf Steglich (ed.), *Das Erbe deutscher Musik*, xviii (Leipzig, 1942). No. 3 in F is recorded in *The History of Music in Sound*, vii. On these four works, see Fritz Tutenberg, *Die Sinfonik Johann Christian Bachs* (Wolfenbüttel, 1928), pp. 97–113.

[2] Vol. VI (London, 1939), pp. 10 ff.

theme in a monothematic movement; it continues rather unexpectedly in D flat major and F minor. Some of this material is omitted in the recapitulation and other material takes its place; also, the harmonic course now turns to A flat and E flat major, instead of D flat major and F minor. The entire movement is another instance of the composer's harmonic and architectural adventurousness.

These symphonies were dedicated to Crown Prince Frederick William of Prussia (1744–97), who succeeded Frederick the Great to the throne in 1786 and to whom Haydn and Mozart dedicated string quartets and Beethoven two cello sonatas. Frederick William was a notable champion of German music (his patronage also extended to Gluck, Stamitz, and Dittersdorf), and it was for his orchestra that this set of symphonies was composed. Bach seems to have enjoyed the opportunity to employ a richer orchestral palette: the work was published in 12 orchestral parts (2 horns, 2 flutes, 2 oboes, bassoon, 2 violins, viola, violoncello, continuo), and it is likely that when the resources were available two players each performed the flute and oboe parts, and six players each the violin parts, resulting in a total orchestra of about 40. The German poet Klopstock writes about the first performance in 1776: 'How often we wish you were with us, my dear Schönborn, for example, yesterday, when we heard four new symphonies by Bach, performed by 40 instruments...'[1] As one would expect from the composer, the role of the strings is a prominent one; sometimes the violins dominate the tutti in tempestuous unison passages (in the finale of no. 2 the rapid figuration demands virtuoso playing), at other times the two violin parts are interlaced in a thin concertino texture (often without continuo). The group of wind instruments is too small to be used as a contrasting body to the string band, hence it is frequently employed to double the strings or to sustain chords. But short fragments for solo wind instruments are numerous, and several passages are more extended, such as the concertino passage in the first movement of no. 1 (bars 35, 170), set for two oboes and bassoon; in the second movement of the same symphony two solo flutes are the main protagonists.

Enough has been said to show that to dismiss Emanuel Bach as a mere pioneer and to criticize his Baroque strength as reactionary or old-fashioned would give an incomplete assessment of his achievements. To ignore the excitement that his compositions generate as the products of first-rate musicianship, intelligence, and originality, would be to overlook both their historical importance and their artistic stature.

In most contemporary collections of eighteenth-century symphonies —the publications of Venier, La Chevardière, and such—the works of

[1] Steglich, op. cit., p. vii.

North Germans occupy relatively little space (Breitkopf is an exception, but he was a German publisher). The implied verdict rests on the unlucky transitional position of the chief northern composers, who were old-fashioned before they reached their prime. It is a typical tragedy of such composers that they tend to dissipate their creative energies with attempts at renovation and adjustment. Yet Baroque styles lack charm when refurbished to fit a Classical mode. By an accident of chronology the north German composers were never fully at home in the Classical style. Hence, despite their intellectual talent for development of ideas and their marked originality in many details, they wrote few symphonic works of lasting significance.

VIENNA

The Viennese School drew strength from the long coexistence in the Austrian capital of operatic overture and concert symphony. The two styles exercised a vigorous influence upon each other through a competition more direct than that in Italy, where the concert symphony developed as a small island in an operatic sea. A number of Viennese composers wrote both overtures and symphonies: Caldara, Wagenseil, Gassmann.[1] Yet the genres never developed a hybrid: the overture retained the Italian flair for activity without introspection, the symphony soon developed impressive size and subtle differentiations of musical ideas, although the symphonies of J. J. Fux and Georg Reutter the younger, many of them operatic in origin, contribute practically nothing to the advance of Classical style. On the other hand, the partitas of Matthaeus Schloeger (1722?–66),[2] which one might assume to be unimportant dance suites, include new stylistic elements of great promise. Thus, although the Viennese symphony adopts the framework of the three-movement opera overture, the building stones within the frame owe more to chamber music.

MONN AND WAGENSEIL

The independent development of the Viennese symphony between 1730 and 1750 may be seen principally in the work of Monn and Wagenseil. The significance of Georg Matthias Monn (1717–50) has been exaggerated by some musicologists in a pointless controversy. In 1740 Monn wrote a symphony[3] with the following movements: Allegro–

---

[1] On the earliest Viennese symphonies see Vol. VI.
[2] One partita in *Denkmäler der Tonkunst in Österreich*, xv, (2) (Vienna, 1908).
[3] Dated autograph, Vienna, Nat. Bibl., 18334; published in *Denkmäler der Tonkunst in Österreich*, xv (2) (Vienna, 1908); minuet in Kurt Stephenson, *Die musikalische Klassik* (*Das Musikwerk*) (Cologne, 1962), p. 33; finale in Archibald T. Davison and Willi Apel, *Historical Anthology of Music*, ii (London, 1950), p. 246.

Aria: Andante un poco–Menuet–Allegro. While this may be the first four-movement symphony with minuet, it evidently exercised no decisive influence, for neither Monn nor other Austrian composers adopted the four-movement cycle at this time.[1] In other respects this symphony harks back to the Baroque: all movements employ the same key; in omitting the violas the orchestration is reminiscent of the trio-sonata texture; the wind instruments play a concertato role, alternating squarely with the tutti.

Monn's other symphonies are in three movements and usually call for strings only; the use of church-sonata designs in three instances (opening slow movements followed by quasi-fugal allegros) emphasizes the close connection of the early Austrian symphony with its chamber-music background. The short breath of Monn's themes and harmonic turns becomes more accentuated by the brevity of the complete symphonies. The first movement of the symphony of 1740 occupies only forty-one bars, and other (presumably later) works have a full exposition, development, and recapitulation in less than sixty bars. Monn's themes reveal an acquaintance with both the North Italian hammer-stroke concerto and the Neapolitan–Venetian overture.[2]

Ex. 178

His symphony of 1740, with all movements in the same key, tends to mislead for his general policy favours contrasted tonalities in slow movements, including tonic and relative minors as well as subdominant and dominant. His tonal curiosity shows also in a B major symphony, a key so unusual that only one other eighteenth-century symphony (Haydn, no. 46) has thus far been found in it. Many individual movements contain welcome touches of harmonic colour, such as major–minor passages and expressive cross-relations. Monn's vigorous motion depends in part on unexpected repetitions within the phrase, later a favourite technique of Haydn. This design from the third

---

[1] The other four-movement symphony with minuet attributed to Monn in *Denkmäler der Tonkunst in Österreich*, xv (2), was probably written by Franz Xavier Pokorný (1729–94); see LaRue, 'Major and Minor Mysteries of Identification in the 18th-Century Symphony', *Journal of the American Musicological Society*, xiii (1960), particularly p. 191.

[2] Vienna, Ges. der Musikfreunde, XIII 1317, 8552, 6371; Stift Melk V 398. Thematic catalogue in *Denkmäler der Tonkunst in Österreich* xix (2), ed. Wilhelm Fischer (Vienna, 1912).

movement of the 1740 symphony (A B B C) develops much more energy than conventional groupings such as AB AB, yet avoids the fragmentary effect of excessive variety:

Ex. 179 Menuetto

In contrast to Monn, who had little importance outside Austria, Georg Christoph Wagenseil (1715–77) achieved a wide European reputation, with many publications both in France and England. Wagenseil succeeded early as a composer of Italian opera, and many of his symphonies originated as overtures. Even in early works, however, he sought a path independent of the Italian style. The overture to *I lamenti d'Orfeo* (1740) is in an unusual two-movement form of fugal allegro with effective strettos followed by a brief presto 3/8. In *Ariodante*, written for Venice in 1745, Wagenseil has six main thematic units.[1]

Ex. 180

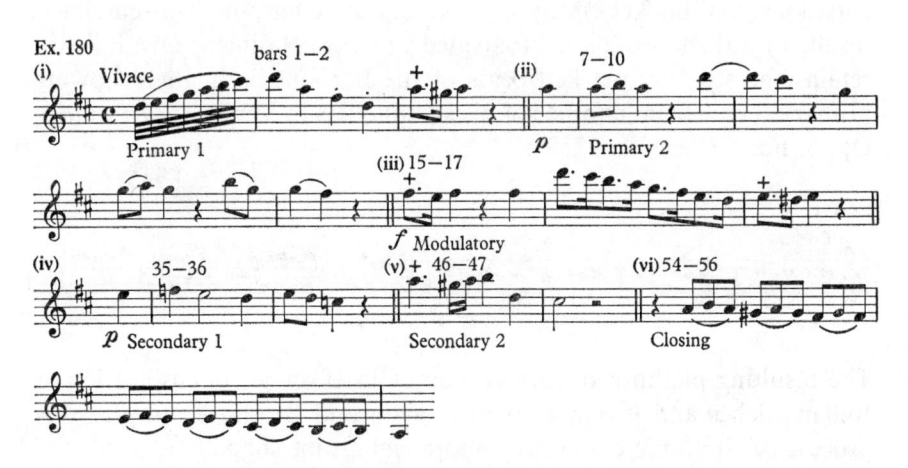

Here, though following the Italian formula of an immediate bridge to the recapitulation rather than true development, Wagenseil manages to insert a long developmental episode into the recapitulation. Another example of his experimentation may be seen in the number and order of movements. The presumably early Symphony in D major[2] has four movements with a minuet as second movement while a symphony of 1746,

[1] From *Six Symphonies*... (Paris, *c.* 1765).
[2] *Denkmäler der Tonkunst in Österreich*, xv (2), p. 28.

also in D major,[1] follows the three-movement plan (Allegro–Andante–Tempo di menuetto) also found in his Op. 8, no. 6, published by Huberty twenty years later. Wagenseil excelled in formal clarity, exploiting a variety of means to set his themes apart, such as the minor tonality of the secondary theme in *La clemenza di Tito* (an alternative title for the symphony in D major of 1746, just referred to). It is likely that he inherited this technique from Monn. Differentiations by modal colour continue through the 1750s, as in the Venier publications, *Sinfonie da vari autori*, Opp. 6, no. 5; 7, no. 3; and 8, no. 3. It is tempting (though as yet not proven) to think of this technique as predominantly Viennese, perhaps an early phase of the major–minor shift endemic in Schubert.

Wagenseil early developed procedures for relating and unifying the various sections of the exposition, commonly by a recurring motive. This procedure may be seen in the recurrence of the trill motive in *Ariodante* (Ex. 180 above), developed more than a decade later in Venier's *Vari autori*, Op. 5, no. 1, where all themes are related to a triadic arpeggio. This work was in the repertory of the Esterházy orchestra and may have influenced Haydn's monothematic expositions.

Like Haydn, Wagenseil tended to stress rhythm and to concentrate upon motives rather than phrases. The sweeping upbeats, frequent syncopations, and hocket effects increase rhythmic tension. This emphasis results in a theme which is broadened to classical dimensions, but still retains the strongly marked beats of the Baroque as in the following primary theme from another of his symphonies in Venier's *Vari Autori*, Op. 5, no. 5 (Paris, *c.* 1759):

Ex. 181

The resulting plethora of turns becomes, in effect, an intensification of Italian clichés and it remained for Haydn and Beethoven to give this process of rhythmic emphasis a more significant shape.

Although Wagenseil employed orchestral contrast to highlight thematic differentiation, he rarely attempted unusual or subtle orchestration, writing works suited to the requirements of small orchestras in which the wind parts are dispensable. Wagenseil occasionally employed a complex texture but his basic fabric displays a trio texture, even in late symphonies. He took care to achieve subtle effects where appropriate, as in the distinction of mezzo–piano (a dynamic marking rare in

---

[1] Ibid., p. 16.

print before 1760) in Op. 7, no. 3, and Op. 8, no. 3, of Venier's anthology, *Vari autori*.

GASSMANN'S OVERTURES AND SYMPHONIES

Florian Leopold Gassmann (1729-74) absorbed Italian elements more fully than either Monn or Wagenseil. Not less active but less intense, Gassmann leaves room for breath, pausing for a crotchet here or a minim there. He composed operas continuously for both Vienna and Italy (mainly Venice), yet he remained active in concert life as well, as we can see from the independent symphonies in the Breitkopf Catalogue supplements from 1766 to 1775. He did not make a consistent distinction between concert and theatre styles until about 1770, when his symphonies turned increasingly to the four-movement cycle including minuet. Before this time, his works in both styles were in three movements. Also in five late concert works, though in only a single overture, *Amore e Psiche* (1767),[1] we find slow introductions or opening slow movements. In this respect Gassmann developed earlier than Haydn. By contrast with Wagenseil, Gassmann experimented unceasingly. In his first extant opera, *Issipile* (1758),[2] he uses a variant of the Baroque modulating ritornello form: after the primary group (tonic) and the secondary group (dominant) have been introduced, both groups reappear in the customary order of binary form (dominant, followed by tonic), after which a final reappearance of the primary material in the tonic takes place. Again in a Symphony in B minor[3] an expanded design has no restatement of the primary material in the tonic at the beginning of what might be called the recapitulation, but instead at the end of the movement. Preceding this final statement there have been ritornello-like appearances in mediant and submediant. Obviously, Gassmann did not feel the need to restate the primary material in the manner of a recapitulation. Thus his designs become a combination of binary and ritornello forms rather than fully fledged sonata form. Transitional types are to be found in his overtures (*La Contessina*, 1770) and his symphonies (e.g. the C major: Vienna, Nationalbibl. Sm 3667).

Gassmann frequently unified his expositions by thematic interrelationship between primary and secondary material. Sometimes the continuation of the opening theme reappears in the subsidiary group, sometimes the secondary theme is old, but the accompaniment is new (Ex. 182(i)),[4] sometimes rhythmically related motives provide the connection,

---

[1] All Gassmann's operas are preserved in Vienna, Nationalbibliothek.
[2] Overture ed. H. C. Robbins Landon (Vienna, 1965).
[3] Ed. Geiringer (Vienna, 1933).
[4] *Il viaggiatore ridicolo* (1766): Paris, Bibl. Nat. Cons. D4353.

at other times, as in *La contessina*,[1] a prominent opening interval functions in that capacity (Ex. 182(ii)).

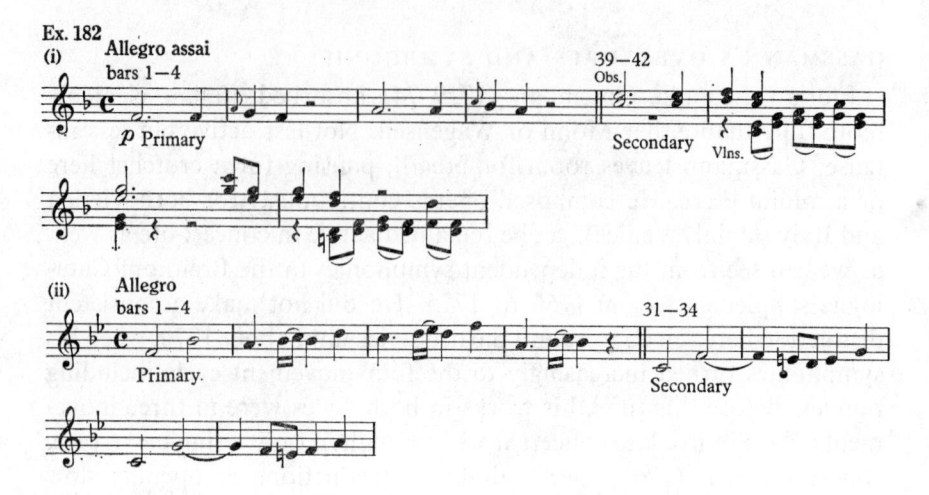

Ex. 182

(i) Allegro assai bars 1—4 ... 39—42

p Primary   Secondary   Vlns.

(ii) Allegro bars 1—4 ... 31—34

Primary.   Secondary

Among other of Gassmann's contributions to the Viennese symphonic tradition we may single out:

1. First-movement coda (Vienna Nationalbibl., Sm 3667).
2. First-movement fugue (ibid., Sm 3685).
3. Rondo form in slow movement (*I rovinati*, 1772).
4. Connection of slow movement to finale (*Il filosofo innamorato*, 1771).
5. Rondo finale, in which a folk-song-like theme with a characteristic Viennese flavour suitable for rondo treatment is used (Vienna, Nationalbibl., Sm 3667).

In the overtures Gassmann largely followed the Italian 3/8 minuet tradition for finales, but in the symphonies he helped to build an independent tradition of duple metres and more significant forms.

About a decade and a half separate the formative years of Wagenseil and Gassmann; and the younger composer profited from the tendency towards expressive manipulation of the orchestra which began to be fashionable in Europe in the 1750s. Among Gassmann's progressive features are the occasionally thematic rather than harmonic function of oboes and horns, and the increased role played by the violas, sometimes as bass, sometimes as solo. His textures, too, are more interesting than those of Wagenseil, showing, perhaps, the influence of his two years of contrapuntal study under Padre Martini. Certainly his basses are more melodic, and imitation is more frequently encountered.

[1] Ed. Robert Haas, *Denkmäler der Tonkunst in Österreich*, xxi (1).

ORDOÑEZ AND LEOPOLD HOFFMANN

The extensive musical activity in Vienna stimulated local composers and attracted others from all parts of Europe. Carlos d'Ordoñez (1734–86), a violinist of Spanish extraction, composed more than sixty symphonies, some known now only by entries in eighteenth-century catalogues. At least two of his works have had the honour of being attributed to Haydn.[1] Ordoñez, like Wagenseil, preferred the three-movement symphony. Among his early works is an unusual symphony, in C major, with a slow first movement connected to a following Allegro, which is dated 1756 in a copy preserved in the Göttweig Monastery. This slow–fast sequence might have established a valuable direction, but it proves to be as exceptional for Ordoñez as the 1740 symphony was for Monn: both works are accidents rather than precedents. Of his later symphonies there are a few four-movement works with minuet; the earliest is a B flat major symphony at Göttweig dated 1765.

Ordoñez's themes have a distinct rhythmic profile and, as in the case of Wagenseil, his beats are strongly marked. This attention to rhythmic detail operates within extensive thematic sentences, carefully developed in regard to phrase structure and motivic work. The string writing shows the daring of the professional with experience in orchestras as well as chamber music ensembles.

Modern works of reference have rather summarily dismissed the Viennese cathedral Kapellmeister Leopold Hoffmann (1738–93), possibly as a result of Haydn's letter to Artaria of 20 July 1781: '... the braggart thinks that he alone has ascended the heights of Mount Parnassus'.[2] Hoffmann's contemporaries, on the other hand, Burney and Hiller among them, approved of his popularity which is implicit in the number of Hoffmann's publications and surviving manuscripts. He leaps into prominence in the development of the symphony because he was one of the earliest composers who consistently wrote four-movement symphonies with both slow introductions and minuets. The Göttweig Catalogue records works of this type as early as 1761, and at least a dozen symphonies before 1770 confirm the trend. The distribution of Hoffmann's symphonies in all parts of Europe suggests that his example was an early influence in the establishment of the mature Classical pattern. There is, for instance, a contemporary score of a Hoffmann four-movement symphony in Genoa (Civ. Liceo Mus. M 4.27.9), copied

[1] Landon, *The Symphonies of Joseph Haydn* (London, 1955), Appendix II, nos. 13 and 119. See also Landon's article 'Ordoñez', *Die Musik in Geschichte und Gegenwart*, x (1962), cols. 194–6.
[2] Landon, *Collected Correspondence and London Notebooks of Joseph Haydn* (London, 1959), p. 31.

in an Italian hand. Full scores, except for autographs, were rarely made in the eighteenth century, and the Italian handwriting is in fact more important than the location of the score.[1] This same symphony occurs in the Göttweig Catalogue dated 1762, the Breitkopf Catalogue of 1766, the Lambach Catalogue (1768), the monastery of Melk, the library of the Berlin Hochschule für Musik, and falsely under the name of Haydn in Prague.[2] In addition to his formal achievements Hoffmann is remarkable both for the lyrical quality of his allegro themes which sometimes anticipates the second Mannheim generation, and for the professional competence of his orchestral practice.

DITTERSDORF AND VAŇHAL

During the second half of the eighteenth century Austria and Bohemia, and particularly Vienna, exported instrumentalists and Kapellmeisters much as Italy exported singers and opera composers. Among the travelling symphonists who nevertheless maintained allegiance to Viennese traditions the most important were Ditters (later von Dittersdorf) and Vaňhal.

Carl Ditters von Dittersdorf (1739–99) belongs to that select group which includes Joseph Haydn, Johann Molter, and F. X. Pokorný,[3] who wrote more than a hundred symphonies.[4] Two characteristics set him apart. First, his interest in descriptive titles, though they did not always follow the proposed subject matter in the precise manner of the later programme-symphony. About 1785 he composed a dozen symphonies[5] *'exprimant les Métamorphoses d'Ovide'*. Most of this series are entirely regular (if slightly dull) four-movement symphonies. They include some elementary tone-painting, however, such as the hunting 6/8 of *Acteon's Transformation into a Stag* (generically related to Haydn's 6/8 stag in *The Creation*) and the treble and bass croaking of the farmers changed into frogs. A decade earlier Dittersdorf had attempted to contrast the humours of mankind in a six-movement symphony (*Il superbo, Il umile, Il matto, Il contento, Il melancolico, Il vivace*), again without conspicuous descriptive fidelity. Earliest of all, yet most attractive of his quasi-programmatic works, is the *Sinfonia nel gusto di cinque nazioni* (1767)

---

[1] Many manuscripts in Modena and Florence are in the handwriting of Viennese copyists, imported there because of the dynastic connections with the Habsburgs.

[2] Anthony Van Hoboken, *Joseph Haydn: Thematisch-bibliographisches Werkverzeichnis* (Mainz, 1957), Gruppe I: D 27.   [3] On Molter and Pokorný, see p. 433.

[4] In 1900 Carl Krebs compiled a thematic catalogue (*Dittersdorfiana*, Berlin) which contains some internal duplications. Nevertheless, many additional symphonies, discovered since, may bring Dittersdorf's total to about one hundred and fifty, second only to Molter.

[5] Six of them, with two other symphonies, reprinted in Joseph Liebeskind (ed.), *C. Ditters von Dittersdorf; Ausgewählte Orchesterwerke* (Leipzig, 1899). On the Ovid symphonies, see Frederick Niecks, *Programme Music* (London, 1906), pp. 88 ff., and Otto Klauwell, *Geschichte der Programm-musik* (Leipzig, 1910), pp. 88 ff.

containing a German Allegro, an Italian Andante, an English Allegretto, a French minuet with Turkish trio, and a polyglot finale.

The second point of individuality in Dittersdorf is the strong folk element in his melodic style, in which he nearly equals Haydn in variety and originality. Where earlier composers, such as Wagenseil and Gassmann, occasionally inserted folk-like material into minuets, trios and rondo finales, Dittersdorf uses rustic themes even to open a symphony. Formally, Dittersdorf did not follow Hoffmann's precocious example. His symphonies in the 1760s took the three-movement pattern of Wagenseil, with many minuet finales, as in Op. 1, no. 3 (Krebs 6). About 1770 Dittersdorf began to write consistently in four movements with minuet, but he never adopted the slow introduction as standard. In the single movements he constructed well-balanced sonata forms, placing the usual Viennese emphasis on recapitulation of the primary theme. The exuberant charm of his themes, whether flowing or energetic, rescues his symphonies from triteness. Another attractive, Haydnesque feature is the frequent humour, particularly the rhythmic sallies and displacements.

Born in the same year as Dittersdorf, the Czech Jan Vaňhal (Johann Wanhal) (1739–1813) settled in Vienna and first attracted attention there as a symphonist about 1767 with his *Trois symphonies,* Op. 10. In England Robert Bremner brought Dittersdorf and Vaňhal to public attention in the *Periodical Overture,* nos. 38 (1773) and 42 (1774), the latter being Vaňhal's most popular work for many years. Of the two composers Vaňhal caught the English fancy, and in the next five years Bremner issued five more Vaňhal symphonies, completely neglecting Dittersdorf. The catalogues of Breitkopf and Hummel give Vaňhal equal (or greater) space with Dittersdorf, and in northern Europe he exceeded Haydn in popularity until the last years of the century.

This great popularity rests on the range of Vaňhal's melodic expression. In such cantabiles as the following[1] he rivals Gassmann, Hoffmann, and Dittersdorf.

Ex. 183

[1] (i) *Six Overtures* ... no. 2, pub. Welcker (London, 1773); (ii) Op. 7, no. 2, pub. Hummel (Amsterdam, 1770).

On other occasions he does not lack vigour, nor is the humorous element entirely neglected, though it played a smaller part than in Haydn and Dittersdorf. Distinctive in Vaňhal, however, is the broad scale of pathos found in no less than a dozen of his symphonies in the minor mode, an unusually high proportion. A more typical distribution may be seen in Dittersdorf, who among all his many symphonies wrote only half as many as Vaňhal in minor keys. (Haydn nearly equals Vaňhal, with ten symphonies in the minor, not counting slow introductions.) In the following examples in A minor and D minor,[1] the pathetic vein ranges from gentle melancholy to urgent tragedy:

Ex. 184

Another trait, the folk aspect so common in central European symphonists, has received attention from several scholars.[2]

Vaňhal made few experiments with the conventional order and type of movements and rarely employed slow introductions. Even in the 1780s he wrote a good many three-movement symphonies (without minuet), possibly in response to the preferences of French and English publishers, who sometimes published works originally in four movements without the original minuet. But within this formal framework Vaňhal's control of phrasing and motion makes him approach Haydn more nearly than the master's other contemporaries. We can feel the control of movement clearly by comparing a Vaňhal theme (Ex. 183(i)) with a similar though earlier work by the Mannheim composer Anton Filtz. In the former, the absence of such dead spots as Filtz's final crotchet is notable:

Ex. 185

[1] (i) Op. 7, no. 4, pub. Hummel (Amsterdam, c. 1770); (ii) *Simphonie périodique*, no. 3, pub. Jolivet (Paris, c. 1774).
[2] Antonín Sychra, 'W.-A. Mozart et la musique populaire tchèque' in *Influences étrangères dans l'œuvre de W.-A. Mozart*, ed. André Verchaly (Paris, 1958), pp. 190–1; see also the articles by Václav Dobiáš and Dénes Bartha in the same volume.

Like Haydn, Vaňhal discovered a precious source of motion in the uncommitted phrase, a hint of irresolution that chains our attention to following ideas. The surprise pauses found so frequently in Haydn, the phrase extensions on a suspended dominant, the overlaps caused by phrase compression—all these are shared by Vaňhal.

In one characteristic Vaňhal reminds us of Mozart: he frequently reserves a special measure of imagination for the moments immediately before the recapitulation. A Symphony in B flat of no apparent distinction (Breitkopf Catalogue, supplement, 1770)[1] suddenly arrests our attention in the retransition:

Ex. 186 Allegro moderato

At the same point in its finale, a similarity of moods and harmonic pathways suggests an intentional parallel, a design anticipating Beethoven. It has been assumed that Vaňhal imitated Haydn, yet in many cases the same technique apparently occurred to both composers at approximately the same time.

MICHAEL HAYDN

In completing the Viennese survey we turn finally to Michael Haydn (1737–1806; at Salzburg from 1763 until his death). The thematic catalogue of his works[2] lists fifty-two symphonies, the last in 1789. The

[1] *Quatre Ouvertures composées par . . . Vanhal* (and others), pub. Bailleux (Paris, n.d.).
[2] Thematic catalogue of instrumental works only in *Denkmäler der Tonkunst in Österreich* xiv (2), ed. Lothar Perger (Vienna and Leipzig, 1907). Two symphonies are included in this volume, in C and E flat major, pp. 1 and 34. Hans Jancik in *Die Musik in Geschichte und Gegenwart*, v, col. 1940, mentions only 46 symphonies.

majority of these works, including the early ones, consist of the conventional four movements, with the minuet as second or third. After 1780 the sonata form of the first movement is fully developed, with a contrasting subsidiary subject. Also, in this later period, the number of movements is more likely to be three, with a slow movement in the middle, as in the Symphony in G of 1783 long attributed to Mozart (K. 444) because he wrote a slow introduction for it; there is even an instance of one work in two movements.[1] A very few works recall the organization of the old *sonata da chiesa*; the four movements of a Symphony in F of 1789 are: Adagio; Presto; an unmarked movement in 6/8 time which is, in effect, a scherzo; and a final Vivace assai. Two C major symphonies (1784 and 1788) have fugal finales anticipating that of Mozart's *Jupiter*. Haydn also composed symphonies which have programmatic titles (an undated Symphony in F, for instance, is called *Wahrheit der Natur*), but these works are not descriptive in the manner of, say, Kuhnau's *Biblical Sonatas*.

In Michael Haydn's work there is a quality curiously inhibited in most of his contemporaries: harmonic imagination. In Joseph Haydn harmonic ingenuity consists more in astonishing key juxtapositions than in subtleties of chord structure or details of dissonance. Michael's chromaticism takes sinuous forms, probably one of the elements of style that influenced Mozart, but he also injects sudden accents or pivot points of harmonic colour, as can be seen in this example from the second movement of a Symphony in B flat.[2]

[1] Symphony in D major (1786). The movements are Vivace assai—Rondeau.
[2] No. 1 of *Tre Sinfonie a Grand Orchestra* (Vienna, 1785).

Even so selective a review of the Viennese background may help to explain the extraordinary flowering concentrated in the music of Joseph Haydn and Mozart. Nowhere else were so many diverse sounds in the air, such varied procedures, such challenging experiments.

MANNHEIM: THE FIRST GENERATION

For music-lovers the name Mannheim will always suggest, first of all, the magnificent musical establishment created in the eighteenth century by the Palatine Electors. Within this establishment a remarkable collection of orchestral musicians—many of them composers as well—achieved new standards of co-ordination and discipline.

If the Viennese School may be regarded as a pyramid with Mozart and Haydn as its apex, the Mannheim School represents the opposite picture: the entire school depended on the forceful imagination of a single man, Johann Stamitz (1717-57), whose effective symphonic concepts were adopted by many composers as their standard. Yet Stamitz's widespread influence probably led to a loss of individuality that was more evident in Mannheim and its creative dependencies than elsewhere.

In execution of dynamics there can be little doubt that the Mannheim orchestra surpassed all others, but specific effects such as the alternation of forte and piano, or crescendo, were not in themselves new. In this respect Hugo Riemann exaggerated the accomplishments of the school.[1] De Brosses,[2] for example, commented on the 'clair-obscur' of Roman

---

[1] Preface to *Denkmäler der Tonkunst in Bayern*, iii (1) (Leipzig, 1902).
[2] *Lettres familières écrites d'Italie*, no. 50 (Paris, 1858), ii, p. 382.

orchestras in 1740, and Jommelli specifically required crescendo in *Eumene* (1742). It is similarly untenable that the melodic appoggiatura or 'Seufzer' may be specifically credited to Mannheim.[1] The sigh motive as well as certain other melodic flourishes were already fairly commonplace; they became so popular in Mannheim that they were reduced to expressionless clichés, as can be seen in the following examples:[2]

Ex. 188

The first generation of Mannheim composers included Johann Stamitz, Richter, Holzbauer, and Filtz, personalities that contrast more clearly than those of the second generation, since (except for Filtz) their styles had already crystallized before they joined forces. Stamitz dominated the group not only by his inspiration but by his firmer grasp of the Classical models. He early perceived that the long-range tensions necessary for a large design required a thematic apparatus that would exploit many categories of contrast. Many composers felt this need, but in struggling between two styles they satisfied only a part of the Classical requirements. Stamitz, however, combined articulation, harmonic stabilization, enlargement of melodic design, differentiation of melodic types, and widening of colour contrast. Only by the conjunction of all these techniques could the broad balances of Classicism succeed.

Stamitz's control of harmonic stability represents his most radical break with the past, for isolated cases of all the other procedures occurred far back in the Baroque period. He achieved stability in two ways: by the use of markedly slower harmonic rhythm, the basis for broader phrase dimensions; and by emphasis on harmonic rather than melodic bass lines, thus concentrating attention on the main thematic line. In this way the focus was not on the momentary Baroque polarity between treble and bass but on long-term thematic oppositions and reconciliations. In making these innovations Stamitz did not reject counterpoint altogether but, like Sammartini, he manipulated elements so that their articulations coincided with the broader plan of the movement.

[1] Lucian Kamieński, 'Mannheim und Italien', *Sammelbände der internationalen Musikgesellschaft*, x (1908–9), p. 307.
[2] (i) Richter, Symphony in G (London, 1760); (ii) J. Stamitz, Symphony in A (Paris, c. 1755); (iii) Toeschi, Symphony in G; Regensburg, Turn u. Taxische Hofbibl.

Similarly, he did not completely abandon the melodic bass but valued its contrast in unstable areas such as modulation and development sections.

The slower harmonic rhythm most notably affected Stamitz's openings. In the following example from the Symphony in D, *La melodia Germanica*, Op. XI, no. 1 (Paris, *c.* 1756),[1] the listener senses the large form to come from the length of the opening phrase, whose eight bars are sharply distinguished from the succeeding scale passage by harmonic stability and terraced dynamics.

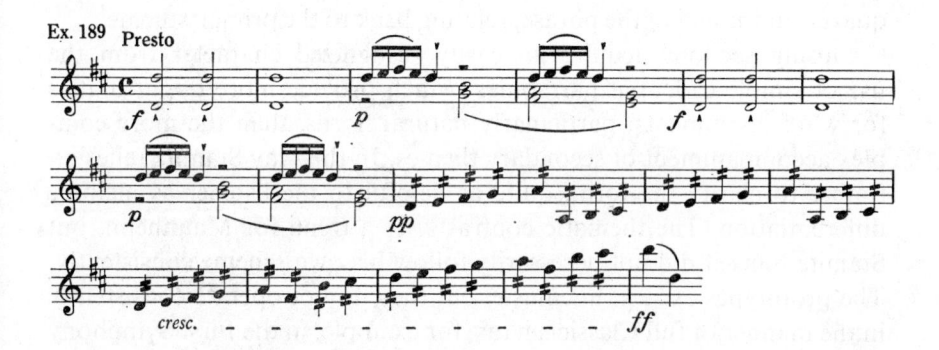

Ex. 189 Presto

The rhythmic contrasts of this example are somewhat reminiscent of the question-and-answer theme of mature Classicism. But in his desire to connect and relate themes, and to increase their span, Stamitz employed many modes of rhythmic variety. In the following example from the finale of the same symphony, the activity of the second violin part in the eighth bar helps to extend the length and interest of the phrase.

Ex. 190 Prestissimo

Starting from dignified, annunciatory openings, Stamitz proceeded to differentiate modulatory, cantabile, and closing-type themes. His modulations were not the mere bustling of broken chords but were characterized by distinctive motives, long crescendos, and melodic sequences in the bass. Once arrived in the dominant, the different type of

[1] *Denkmäler der Tonkunst in Bayern*, iii (1), p. 14.

melody and the relaxation in orchestral force achieved a remarkably advanced degree of contrast, as is apparent in the secondary theme of the movement already quoted in Ex. 189:

Ex. 191 Presto

Even here, however, Stamitz's irrepressible vigour explodes in semiquavers at the end of the phrase, relating back to the primary theme.

Closing sections acquire an easily recognized character from the use of simple cadential harmonies, which provide more opportunities for wind instruments, particularly natural horns, than the more complex accompaniment of secondary themes. In this way Stamitz relies on timbre to clarify the form, quite as helpful to the listener as melodic differentiation. The thematic contrasts set a trend for Mannheim, but Stamitz himself did not necessarily follow his own scheme consistently. The prototypes exist in his music, but they do not operate consistently in the manner of full Classicism (as, for example, in the First Symphony of Beethoven).

Stamitz's first-movement form must be viewed in terms of his own day. More frequently than not he was wont, as were his disciples, to begin the recapitulation with the secondary rather than the primary theme. Since these movements were fundamentally in binary form, with an emphatic middle statement of primary material in the dominant, it would be anachronistic to speak of them as abbreviated recapitulations. The return of the secondary material in the tonic completed the normal pattern of polythematic binary forms. Occasionally the primary theme also reappeared, though at the very end, as in the first movement of another symphony (in E flat) from *La melodia Germanica*, Op. XI, no. 3.[1] To listeners of the 1750s this would suggest not a reversed recapitulation but rather a survival of the ritornello device. It is more likely, however, that the occasional return of the primary material, after the recapitulation of the secondary group in the tonic, was an attempt on Stamitz's part to create more weight at the end of the movement in order to balance the development.

In addition to his sharply contrasted and carefully graduated dynamics, Stamitz was of importance in several other respects. The earliest recorded use of clarinets in a symphony seems to have occurred at a Concert spirituel (Paris) of 26 March 1755, with a symphony by Stamitz

[1] Ibid., vii (2), p. 1. The first two movements are recorded in *The History of Music in Sound*, vii.

'avec clarinets (!) et cors de chasse.'[1] Stamitz and his followers also devoted considerable attention to the melodic value of the viola line. Most important, however, were his forward-looking techniques of mixing string and wind colours (oboes and horns over a violin pedal point, for example) and the selective punctuation of one colour by adding other instruments at the phrase end.

Stamitz's place in history rests securely on his establishment of the four-movement symphony with minuet. The priority of Monn's 1740 symphony means little historically, since it had no appreciable influence on the course of the Austrian symphony, even in Monn's own work. Stamitz, however, adopted four movements as a norm for many symphonies printed in Paris and elsewhere. The wide distribution of these works altered the course of the symphony fundamentally, splitting it irrevocably from the overture and redefining the function of the minuet as a movement of relief and contrast rather than as an innocuous finale.

Franz Xaver Richter (1709–89), born eight years earlier than Stamitz, is a typical example of a composer caught between two styles. For the most part he inclined backwards, using small forms, conservative orchestration, motival themes of short dimensions, imitation as a frequent textural device, and the 'walking' bass reminiscent of the Baroque. Yet, occasionally, he begins a symphony in a progressive manner, as in the Symphony in A, Op. 4, no. 5,[2] with its lyric Allegro. More characteristic, however, is the beginning of the finale of this same symphony:

Ex. 192 Presto

Textures of this sort with their interplay of motives obscure the broader thematic dimensions and relationships.

Richter resembles C. P. E. Bach in combining old-fashioned traits with progressive flashes. He experiments with links between movements, uses wind instruments in slow movements more freely than Stamitz, and

---

[1] *Mercure de France*, mai 1755, p. 181. See Georges Cucuel, *Études sur un orchestre au XVIIIe siècle* (Paris, 1913), pp. 16–23. In opera clarinets were used at least as early as Rameau's *Zoroastre* (1749).
[2] *Denkmäler*, iii (1), p. 118.

freshens the harmonic palette with incisive chromaticism derived from the secondary dominants. His works are full of unexpected pauses on dominants and sudden reductions in dynamics and texture. Not all of these experiments succeed, but Richter's evident artistic curiosity increased the range of musical experience upon which the younger Mannheimers drew.

Ignaz Holzbauer (1711–83), born in Vienna, was self-taught, studied Fux's *Gradus ad Parnassum*, and wrote church music as well as symphonies. He aspired to become a pupil of Fux, but the old composer found Holzbauer's technique so good that he told his young colleague that, as he was born a genius, he had nothing to learn from him. The significant part of Holzbauer's career began in 1745 as Director of Music at the Vienna Court theatre. In 1750 he was appointed Court composer in Stuttgart and in 1753 in Mannheim, where he worked under Johann Stamitz. Of Holzbauer the young Mozart wrote in 1777: 'I heard a Mass by Holzbauer ... which is very fine. He is a good composer, he has a good church style, he knows how to write for voices and instruments, and he composes good fugues.'[1] In view of such a tribute it may seem unfortunate that Riemann reprinted only one symphony.[2] But it must be said that Holzbauer's symphonies do not match his church works. His early trio symphonies in three movements, much like early Wagenseil, were followed by works employing a larger orchestra and by a number of four-movement symphonies, particularly in his Op. 3. The size of the orchestra does not entirely conceal primitive aspects of the texture, however, such as frequent doubling of the two violin parts.

One of the regressive features of Holzbauer's style is lack of differentiation: primary and secondary themes are not well contrasted, sometimes all three movements are in the same key, and in regard to time signatures, too, there is an instance of an outmoded 3/8 finale succeeding a minuet. On the other hand, there is a surprising sophistication in the construction of the themes themselves, incorporating contrasting motives, and in the continuation and development of phrases.

Anton Filtz (*c*. 1730–60), as the youngest member of this first generation of Mannheim composers, was troubled by fewer of the stylistic conflicts that mar Richter's and Holzbauer's symphonies. Though much of Filtz now seems lacking in musical substance, he did attract players and listeners of his time by a seemingly naïve lack of complication and by a natural gracefulness exemplified by the Andante of his Symphony in E flat (*Symphonie périodique*, no. 4, published by La Chevardière):

---

[1] *Letters of Mozart and his family*, ed. Emily Anderson, 2nd edn. (London, 1966), p. 356.
[2] Op. 4, no. 3, in E flat, with a finale entitled 'La Tempesta del Mare', *Denkmäler der Tonkunst in Bayern*, vii (2), p. 117.

Ex. 193 Andante

Indeed, informality and a certain folk element, though different from Haydn's and Dittersdorf's, are frequently met in Filtz. A country dance atmosphere is not restricted to minuets (see Ex. 185 above), and melodic reminiscences of folk-song are numerous; some scholars have attributed these to an indebtedness to Czech folk music. Certainly, the raised fourth in the manner of a Lydian folk-mode (Slovak?) is used with charm in the finale[1] of the *Symphonie périodique* no. 10.

Some of Filtz's critics did object to his unusually long pedal points where astonishingly little material is spread over long stretches, as in an A major symphony, *Symphonie périodique*, no. 2, where a tonic pedal of 31 bars occurs in a finale of 113 bars.[2] Yet behind this facile exterior one soon notices skilful planning, as in the opening movement of the same work:

Ex. 194 Allegro

[1] *Denkmäler*, vii (2), p. 115.
[2] Ibid. iii (1), pp. 153–4.

Here the multiplicity of ways in which phrases (bars 1–6, 7–12, 12–16) interlock and in which harmonic interest (D sharp at bar 16) intervenes where rhythmic variety wanes, is notable. Comparison of such a passage with an average Italian overture of the time points to Filtz's exceptional control over movement and tension.

THE YOUNGER MANNHEIM COMPOSERS

The leadership of Stamitz affected, as one would expect, a whole younger generation of Mannheim composers, of which the most important were Toeschi (of Italian origin), Cannabich, Eichner, Beck, and Carl Stamitz. By 1760 symphonic production had grown so plentiful that it becomes more difficult to evaluate composers and to trace influences and contributions. It is safe to say that none of the younger group wielded an influence comparable to Johann Stamitz, and from 1770 onwards the Mannheim style increasingly absorbed influences from other centres. We must now expect less in the nature of discoveries, and must look more for refinements within established conventions.

Concerning the biography and works of Carl Joseph Toeschi (1732–88) recent research has shed new light.[1] It would be a mistake to consider the Symphony in B flat major[2] a typical work. It is in four movements, whereas Toeschi favours the more old-fashioned three-movement form; also, the dominating motive of the opening movement rambles imitatively between the parts, whereas the composer tends generally to avoid contrapuntal complications. A Symphony in D major[3] is more representative. The form of the opening movement is that hybrid between binary and sonata forms, discussed in connection with Johann Stamitz. The flourish at the beginning of the movement does not recur at the beginning of the recapitulation; on the other hand, the motive is worked out in the development section, and there is real contrast between the primary and secondary groups.

Toeschi's texture and articulation remind one of Filtz, but he lacks the latter's originality and rhythmic drive. His cantabile melodies were praised by contemporaries, such as Daniel Schubart, as 'sweet', and his effective and progressive violin figuration betrays the virtuoso background. On the other hand, he easily descends to the trite, or at least the hackneyed. Stamitz's striking openings, in the hands of Toeschi and others of his generation, develop into a convention of stately dotted

---

[1] In his dissertation on Toeschi's symphonies (Munich, 1956) Robert Münster corrects the composer's birthdate and provides thematic indices and chronological tables.
[2] *Denkmäler*, vii (2), p. 143.
[3] Paris, Bur. d'ab. mus. 'a più str.', no. 1.

rhythms that influenced Mozart's concerto openings. A typical example is the *Symphonie périodique* no. 26 (La Chevardière, Paris, n.d.):[1]

Ex. 195 Allegro

Like Toeschi, Christian Cannabich (1731–98) depended heavily on thematic clichés, particularly on semiquaver turns, which he often used adroitly to get a movement under way, as in the *Symphonie périodique* no. 5 (La Chevardière, Paris, n.d.):[1]

Ex. 196 Allegro

Cannabich used four movements much more than Toeschi. He also employed a slow introduction as early as 1763, only slightly later than Leopold Hoffmann, though admittedly his cultivation of that formal device was less consistent than on the part of such Viennese composers as Hoffmann and Haydn.

In a series of late works, not published during his lifetime, Cannabich developed a mature Classical style of surprising depth and expressiveness, of which his Symphony in B flat major[2] is a distinguished example. Particularly impressive in the opening movement are the use of the minor mode and the interrelationships between the various themes. The manner in which the figure of the turn (bar 1) pervades primary, secondary, and closing themes, appearing in treble and bass, in strings and in clarinets, is reminiscent of Haydn's more advanced techniques. Throughout the work, the orchestration is thoroughly idiomatic: the liquid

[1] Paris, Bibl. Nat. Cons. H 159
[2] *Denkmäler*, iii (2), p. 3.

quality of the clarinets, the lyrical register of the bassoon, repeated notes on the French horn producing a tolling effect, are all exploited. The precise date of this symphony is uncertain, but if it stems from the 1790s it would appear that Mozart repaid his early debts to Mannheim, for the scoring recalls his.

Ernst Eichner (1740–77) in his short life composed only about a third as many symphonies as the long-lived Cannabich. Like Toeschi he wrote mostly three-movement works. His sonata forms seem unusually well articulated, and the different thematic groups clearly endowed with their appropriate characteristics. In some instances Eichner builds tension steadily by an increase of rhythmic focus. In the following example[1] the compression of units of one bar, marked (a), to progressively shorter dimensions, marked (b) and (c), is steadily maintained until the figure marked (cx). The derivation of the succeeding phrase from motive (c) is characteristic of the composer's ability to create a smooth flow and unified structure of paragraphs.

Ex. 197 Allegro maestoso

Franz Beck (1723–1809) was one of the few composers of the group who was actually a native of Mannheim. A Romantic, born a generation too early, he anticipated the nineteenth century with experiments in which the emotional impact of the moment tended to submerge the long-range structural goals, a spontaneity that was out of tune with the prevailing currents of Classicism.

An unusual feature of Beck's symphonies was his choice of the minor tonality in four out of more than two dozen symphonies (Opp. 1, no. 1;

[1] *Denkmäler*, viii (2), p. 162.

THE YOUNGER MANNHEIM COMPOSERS

2, no. 2; 3, no. 3; 3, no. 5). In his Opp. 1 and 2 he used three movements, shifting thereafter mainly to four movements, unlike Toeschi. The formal designs of Beck do not show much originality, but the details within the movement are characterized by dramatic individualism. For instance, he sometimes assigns to the basses passages of melodic and thematic importance, at other times the basses are silent in favour of the violas, even at the outset of a symphony. His dynamics, too, are highly idiosyncratic, employing often a proto-Romantic exaggeration. Where Johann Stamitz used forte and piano, Beck resorted to rapid shifts from fortissimo to pianissimo. In fact, his dynamics do not enhance the musical substance; as in the case of the Romantics, they are part of that substance. The following example from the Symphony in G minor, Op. 3, no. 3,[1] exemplifies several of these aspects: the whispered echo of a fortissimo climax; the expressive contrasts of full harmony and unison, of diatonicism and chromaticism; and the exploitation of the melodic and harmonic possibilities of the minor mode:

Ex. 198 Allegro con spirito

Cello solo

[1] Pub. Venier (Paris, 1762).

[musical example]

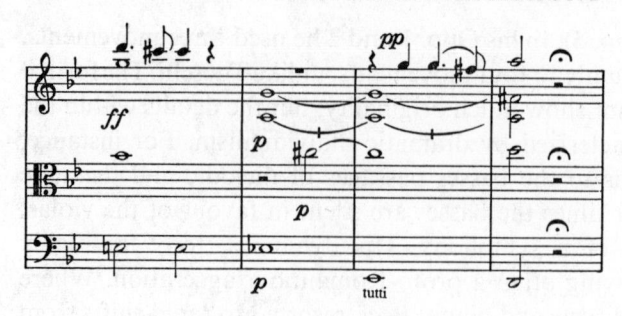

Beck's symphonies also display, at times, remarkable powers of thematic development, for instance, in the reversal of constituent motives and in rhythmic compression. If such features remind us of Haydn and even Beethoven, it must be admitted that clarity and balance sometimes suffered. Beck often failed to differentiate the secondary group as lucidly from the primary group as other Mannheim composers had done, and he was not consistently in control of his larger dimensions. This may explain his relative obscurity in an age that considered formal clarity as the highest ideal.[1]

At the conclusion of a discussion of the Mannheim School, one must turn to the founder's elder son, Carl Stamitz (1745–1801). Comparison shows the inevitable evolution of a style from innovation to convention. The son refined many of the gestures conceived with raw strength and incomplete self-comprehension by his father. No other Mannheimer had better control of thematic differentiation. The two symphonies reprinted by Riemann[2] offer a characteristic sample of Carl Stamitz's style. His melodic talent shows in well-chosen groupings of attractive themes. From various short passages one surmises that Stamitz might have been a better composer than he was, and a slow movement like that of Op. 16, no. 4,[3] reveals his potential scope:

Ex. 199 Andantino
[musical example]

Too often, however, Stamitz surrenders to his own polished conventions, and the predictability of his style reduces his stature.

As virtuoso on both violin and viola, Stamitz took particular interest

[1] The symphonies by Beck edited and published by Robert Sondheimer (Berlin, Basle, London, 1927–53) are compilations of movements from different works.
[2] *Denkmäler*, viii (2) (Leipzig, 1907).
[3] Ibid., p. 98.

in the new French form of the *symphonie concertante*, usually a two-movement scheme consisting of a concerto-form first movement, followed by a comparatively insignificant rondeau. Stamitz brought this form closer to the symphony by the occasional addition of a middle slow movement. But these pieces properly belong to the concerto rather than the symphony tradition.

The mature symphony owes its orchestral garb and thematic differentiation more to Mannheim than to any other school. In matters of form, however, the Mannheim group did not travel the main road of symphonic evolution. Even late in the century these composers occasionally used the limited binary scheme that Johann Stamitz never entirely outgrew; yet they failed to follow his lead in establishing the four-movement symphony.

THE SYMPHONY IN FRANCE

The limited contribution of French composers to the early development of the symphony, in relation to other countries, brings to light an astonishing paradox. One would expect that a nation renowned for its rationality and systematic thought would excel in the application of these approaches to an abstract art-form. There was no lack of interest on the part of audiences, and programmes of new symphonies at the Concert Spirituel in Paris drew nearly as careful attention from critics as did the premières of operas. The records of concert life outside Paris (the Académie Royale in Lyons, for example) show that symphonies were important in the provinces as well. Finally one may cite the French music publishers, whose catalogues demonstrate a lively demand for symphonies. Yet, despite its evident importance in French musical life, the majority of French composers did not find the symphony a natural channel of expression. One explanation may be that French rationalism dealt more successfully with concrete facts than with abstractions such as instrumental forms, resulting in the mid-century preference of French composers for opera over symphony.

Notwithstanding this penchant towards drama, the French symphonic output later in the century grew to a surprising total of approximately one thousand works by more than one hundred composers. In an important study, *La Symphonie française dans la seconde moitié du XVIIIe siècle*[1] Barry S. Brook divides the development into five periods:

1750–56   Birth of the style: Rousseau, Martin, L'Abbé, Gossec, Blainville.
1757–67   Establishment of the style; the foreign contribution: Ruge, Leemanns, Roeser.

[1] Three vols. (Paris, 1962). The account below frequently draws on Brook's study, with occasional differences of emphasis. The *symphonie concertante* is discussed in the next chapter.

1768-77 Maturity of the French symphony; birth of the *symphonie concertante*: Le Duc, Davaux.
1778-89 Apogee of the symphony; rise of the *symphonie concertante*: Rigel, Saint-Georges.
1790-1800 Decline of the symphony; survival of the *symphonie concertante*: Bréval, Cambini.

In reviewing earlier French symphonies[1] it becomes clear that from about 1740 onwards they followed the Classical trend. Hence, the French development lagged slightly behind Italy but was parallel to that of Vienna and Mannheim.

The most significant early symphonist was Louis-Gabriel Guillemain (1705-70), whose 6 *Symphonies dans le goût italien en trio*, op. 4 (Paris, 1740) suggest that France looked to Italy for models at this time. Except in thematic style, however, it is hard to find any close precedent for Guillemain. He grafted textural features and a melodic style related to the older trio sonata upon the fast-slow-fast plan of the *sinfonia*. His themes often remind one of the Corelli-Vivaldi background, and his strongly marked beats, syncopations, cut-off phrases, and symmetrical echo-repetitions all stem from an obsolescent style. Guillemain used these materials in a fully recapitulated sonata form which is to be found in all the fast movements of his Op. 6. The thematic functions of primary, secondary, and closing themes are easily distinguishable, though not specialized or strongly contrasted, as in Op. 6, no. 2:

Ex. 200 Allegro
(i) bars 1-4
Primary
(ii) 20-23
Secondary
(iii)
Closing

The full return of the primary theme in the dominant after the double-bar robs the recapitulation of freshness, and (reinforced by the old-fashioned style) reminds one of the central ritornello in a movement by Vivaldi. Nevertheless, these middle sections genuinely develop the material of the exposition, extracting elements for sequential elaboration. The following example shows the opening of the development section of the same symphony:

[1] Listed in La Laurencie and Saint-Foix, 'Contribution à l'histoire de la symphonie française vers 1750', *L'Année musicale*, i (1911), p. 122.

Ex. 201
bars 46—56

Guillemain's interesting mixture of precocity and backwardness becomes clearer when we examine the symphonies just a decade later of François Martin (1727–57). Martin profits from Guillemain's balanced sectional design but turns away from the Baroque thematic style. His melodies may sound somewhat naïve, but it is a Classical, rather than a Baroque, naïveté, and they focus our attention on the phrase as a structural unit rather than on the individual beat. In dynamic indications Martin shows special care ('fortissi', 'mezzo piano' 'più forte') and his explicit direction, 'en diminuant le Son', in his *Symphonies et ouvertures,* Op. 4, no. 1 (Paris, 1751), is one of the earliest printed examples of diminuendo.

The role of the French overture as a precedent for the slow introduction of the symphony is controversial. Certainly no composer writing a slow introduction could be unaware of the long overture tradition. Yet, to demonstrate historical relationships, one requires a continuity between two phenomena. The title of the Martin publication just mentioned indicates a common area, but, curiously, it demonstrates a separation rather than a transfer of styles. Here we find overtures with slow beginnings but symphonies without. Furthermore, the overtures retain the traditional fugato as a second movement, a feature absent from the symphonies.

Apart from Martin, the continuity between the French overture and the slow introduction is hard to find. For example, only two of Gossec's first thirty symphonies (Opp. 3–6, 1756–62) have slow introductions (Opp. 5, no. 3; and 6, no. 1), neither of which seems to derive from the Grave of the earlier overture. At the same time, Austrian composers such as Hoffmann, less directly associated with the overture tradition, show more interest in the slow introduction than the French. This suggests that the relationship between French overture and symphonic slow introduction is, at most, incomplete and indirect.

François-Joseph Gossec (1734–1829) not only helped to lay the foundations of the French symphony but, by virtue of an astoundingly long professional career (from about 1752 to 1809), his works form a reference point for the entire development. In his first six symphonies, Op. 3 (1756), Gossec adopts many mannerisms from the Italian overture, such as patterned triadic themes or Scotch-snap rhythms, spaced with rests.

Gossec's design displays decisive modulations, but the area in the dominant tonality produces few well-differentiated themes. There is no double bar, and the development area carries less weight than in Martin. On the other hand, his textures show great care, maintaining the integrity of the inner lines; and detailed dynamics—recalling Martin—include long crescendos similar to those of Jommelli and Stamitz. In Op. 3, no. 6, there is a *pp* in the bass against a *p* in the violins, and at another point a written-out *ritard*.[1]

The maturity of Gossec's symphonies Op. 4 (before 1759) is conspicuous. Slow movements and finales are frequently in sonata form, and all six symphonies include minuets with trios. By comparison with Op. 3 clarity of articulation and contrast between thematic groups has been improved, and the melodic dimension markedly broadened. With Op. 5 Gossec established a secure pattern of four movements with controlled logical processes within movements. In later symphonies he made a surprisingly large number of experiments in form as well as scoring. Despite these irregularities, the movements of Gossec's late works have a distinctive profile, though evidently clarity and specialized function of thematic groups meant less to the aged composer.

In any overall assessment of Gossec's symphonies the excellence of his musical materials as such must be stressed. His rhythmic variety and asymmetrical phrase structure remind one of Haydn. His interesting parts for the second violin recall Sammartini, and the many (though short) passages of imitation show careful attention to part-writing and texture. Most rewarding are his slow movements, as in a symphony in D, where long melodic threads build emotional tension.

Ex. 202 Andante un poco allegretto

Brook, op. cit., iii, pp. 25, 31.

PARISIAN COSMOPOLITANISM

The development of the French symphony after 1750 presents a curiously cosmopolitan picture in which it is virtually impossible to identify specifically French characteristics. This cosmopolitanism was the result of two causes, both of them peculiar to Paris. First, as an international centre it attracted musicians from all parts of Europe. The early Italian influence continued in the work of such residents as Filippo Ruge and Giuseppe Cambini, as well as many opera composers, notably Piccinni. In addition to Gossec, a number of composers from the Low Countries worked in Paris, including Antoine Mahaut and H. Leemans. In 1754-5 Johann Stamitz came there for a year on the invition of La Pouplinière; and many Mannheimers, including Toeschi, visited Paris regularly on tour. One imitator of Stamitz, Valentin Roeser, settled for an extended period, and Stamitz's pupil, Franz Beck, worked in Bordeaux.

A second source of cosmopolitanism may be traced to the Paris music publishers. French publishers issued more foreign than native music, including such distant and obscure symphonists as the Swede Johann Agrell, the Viennese Spaniard Carlos d' Ordoñez, and the Czech Joseph Mysliveček. In this whirlpool the French contribution cannot properly be described as a school.

The early death of Simon Le Duc 'l'Aîné' (c. 1745-77) robbed France of a composer of great originality. The few symphonies that he completed are among the best of the eighteenth century. In a period marked by widespread conventionality he managed to evade clichés without resorting to eccentricity. In the symphonies he first arrests our attention by bold chords and pauses, then unleashes an Allegro of vigorous rhythmic continuity. Two procedures contribute to this vigour and power. First, he extends and contracts phrases with great flexibility, so that the flow never ceases. Second, he augments textures to support the rhythmic cumulation of the phrase (sometimes also accelerating the harmonic rhythm). The resultant polyphony may incidentally produce secondary lines of melodic interest, but the chief purpose is rhythmic. The Symphony in E flat major of 1777[1] offers many examples of Le Duc's virtues. The first movement illustrates flexibility of phrasing and postponement of cadences (bars 189-96) and growth in rhythm and texture (bars 20-4). But most remarkable is the slow movement[2] which surpasses Gossec in emotional depth and does not stand far below Mozart:

---
[1] Brook, op. cit., iii, p. 55.
[2] Ibid., p. 70.

Ex. 203

[musical notation: Adagio sostenuto]

Henri-Joseph Rigel (1741–99) was born in Germany and studied, according to Laborde,[1] in Mannheim under Richter; he settled in Paris about 1767. The quantity of Rigel's work, eighteen symphonies, is not large, but the quality demands notice. Like so many composers of Paris and Mannheim, he favoured the three-movement form without minuet. The Mannheim influence may also be responsible for the occasional occurrence of incomplete recapitulations, as in the Symphonies in G major (*c.* 1767) and D major (*c.* 1780).[2]

Rigel's rhythmic control of movement and phrase extensions remind us sometimes of Le Duc, but it is his gift for melody that is most impressive. His expression ranges from phrases of turbulent passion to lilting dance measures, and some themes have an insinuating and haunting quality that approaches Mozart and Schubert. In the following example from the slow movement of Op. 12, no. 2, a tragic mood is evoked by remarkable harmonic colour from a series of appoggiaturas over a pedal point:

Ex. 204 Adagio

[musical notation: vla. *8ve higher*]

[1] *Essai sur la musique ancienne et moderne* (Paris, 1780).
[2] See also Brook's article on Rigel, *Die Musik in Geschichte und Gegenwart*, xi (1963), col. 508.

SYMPHONIE CONCERTANTE AND SYMPHONIE PÉRIODIQUE

From about 1770 on the rise of the *symphonie concertante* drew more and more composers away from the symphony. Examples are Jean Baptiste Davaux (*c.* 1737–1822) and Joseph de Saint-Georges (1739–99), and an extreme case is Giovanni Cambini (1746–1825), whose devotion to the new form was almost exclusive. On the other hand, Ignaz Joseph Pleyel (1757–1831), a pupil of Vaňhal and Haydn, transmitted the conventions of the Viennese School to Paris, among them the four-movement symphony. The results are to be seen in Pleyel's own work as well as that of younger composers such as Méhul; indeed, even the aged Gossec returned in his last symphony (1809) to the four-movement form of his earlier years. The Austrian Pleyel moved to Strasbourg in his twenties as assistant to Richter (who had come there from Mannheim earlier). A steady stream of his *Symphonies périodiques* came off the press of the Parisian music publisher Imbault both before and after the Revolution. His experiments and innovations are interesting and were influential. Sometimes he inserts a fast section into a slow movement (no. 1, *c.* 1778), sometimes a transition section between trio and return of minuet (no. 2, 1778), a valuable idea exploited later by Haydn in his London Symphony, no. 104. Pleyel's symphonies are more spacious than the average of his period, particularly his first movements (e.g. no. 4, *c.* 1783). This enlargement is due to his treatment of the development section where, not content with a single episode, Pleyel constructs several adventures, so to speak. In his D major symphony (no. 7, *c.* 1785)[2] a negligible fragment of the primary section is worked into five episodes:

Ex. 205   bars 26–29

[2] Manchester, Henry Watson Library.

One of the characteristics of Pleyel's music is tidiness. Melodically, this leads at times to an excess of regular phrasing, but in orchestration his care for colour is a virtue. He adds wind instruments to strings with discrimination and avoids the crude block entrances so common with his contemporaries. When scoring for strings only he often makes the violas function as basses in soft passages; at other times he makes a thoughtful distinction between contrabass and cello.

The real contribution of France to the history of the symphony was to provide, through its centralized publishing industry, a forum for the exchange of ideas. Paris alternately drew material from remote areas, and in turn produced new approaches. This function was more important than the creation of a national school, and the French symphony, as such, was one of the by-products of this function.

GERMAN SYMPHONISTS IN ENGLAND

In the eighteenth century foreign influences dominated British music no less in the symphonic field than in opera. Concerts and music publishing paralleled the Parisian pattern, though on a smaller scale and at a slightly later date. In the last third of the century the expansion of publishing made a wide repertory available. For instance, the *Periodical Overtures*, published by Robert Bremner, included in their first fifty numbers works by twelve Austrian, twelve Italian, eight Mannheim, seven French, six English, and five resident Anglo-German composers. (The most popular single composer was Vaňhal.) This representation was quite as broad as that in the serial offerings of most Parisian publishers.

The foreign influence may be termed a Saxon invasion, for the dominating figures were Abel and J. C. Bach, and both these men continued the trend of emigration to England established by Handel. But, unlike Handel, they did not adopt any specifically English features of musical style, and they are included here on geographical and historical grounds.

Carl Friedrich Abel (1723–87) came first to England in 1759 and became a partner in the Bach–Abel concerts in 1764. His six sets of published symphonies[1] were extraordinarily popular, to judge from their representation in European libraries. Abel's style joins Italian with Germanic features. The former are reflected in the three-movement form with frequent minuet finales, and in well-differentiated themes in the expositions. He shows no flair for original orchestral effects, and this conservatism may also be Italianate. On the other hand, the vigour and squareness of Abel's rhythm, and the attention lavished on the development section, point to the north. The bass lines proceed with a sense of

[1] See Gwilym Beechey, 'Carl Friedrich Abel's Six Symphonies, Op. 14', *Music and Letters*, li (1970), p. 279.

direction, and the part-writing is forceful. One senses competence and conviction, but originality and profundity are rare. The symphonies of Op. 1 (*c*. 1759) already exhibit his characteristically mature sonata form, so much appreciated by the young Mozart. His legato themes, with chromatic appoggiaturas which were to become a Mozart cliché, are appealing, and his melodic lines are sometimes of impressive length. Abel did not progress much beyond this, and the pattern was bound to become outmoded two decades later. There was an advance, though, in the manner of contruction of his themes, which is well illustrated by the main theme of the Symphony in E flat major, Op. 10, no. 3 (pub. Bremner, 1773). It shows a compound formation of question and answer, perhaps influenced by J. C. Bach. The balance between four bars of tonic and four bars of dominant is notable and emphasizes incidentally, the unsymmetrical formation of Beethoven's 'Eroica' theme, in the same key and time signature.

Ex. 206

Abel's friend and partner, John Christian Bach (1735–82) was the greatest of the composers of symphonies in England.[1] At his best he approached Haydn and Mozart. He has been accused of superficiality, but that charge cannot be maintained against his work as a whole. In his best instrumental works, the symphonies and quintets, he established the essential characteristics of the component sections of sonata form more firmly than anyone before Mozart. Where others were content to contrast successive sections, Bach distinguished the thematic types appropriate to each formal division. For his general framework, he took the Italian three-movement overture. In early works such as *Orione* (1763) the first movement may be without development, but usually it is expanded to full sonata form. The slow movements, too, differ from their Italian models by their more spacious design (e.g. Op. 9, no. 1). In the finales the 3/8 tradition is often followed, but stalwart 2/4 finales of Teutonic flavour (e.g. Op. 9, nos. 1, 3) are also found.

Bach's contribution to the contrast between primary and secondary themes is well known. His groups are marked in the Italian manner by

[1] Regarding his symphonies in general, see F. Tutenberg, *Die Sinfonik Johann Christian Bachs* (Kiel, 1926).

rests and changes of scoring, but beyond that the opposition gains depth by the nature of the phrasing and the rhythmic articulation. In addition to the thematic contrast, Bach developed the structure of the themes themselves. The breadth of advanced Classical form owes a good deal to his expansion of thematic building-blocks. Particularly in opening themes he perfected a compound that consisted of fanfare balanced by contrasting response. Whatever the dimensions, this procedure lent a broader aspect to the form than was possible with a theme of simpler construction, as in an F major symphony published as Op. 8, no. 4 by Marchandt (Amsterdam, *c.* 1773) and one in B flat, Op. 9 (in some editions, Op. 21), no. 1, published by Longman, Lukey & Co. (London, 1775):

Ex. 207

Equally distinguished was the subtlety with which brief motives were used to knit together all sections of the exposition, as in Op. 18, no. 4 (*c.* 1781):[1]

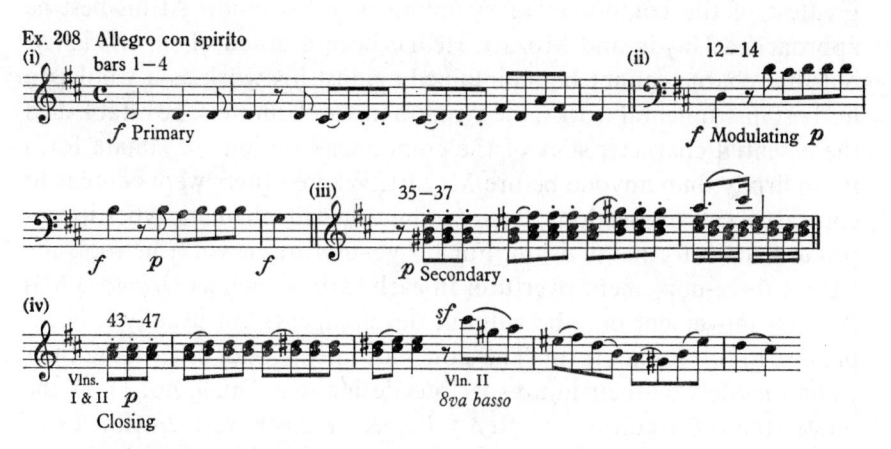

Ex. 208

In his orchestration Bach avoided experimental sonorities, yet often arrived at fresh combinations. Solo cellos in thirds and sixths answer the flutes in *Orione*, and there is a trio of 'clarinetti d'amore' in

[1] Miniature score, ed. Einstein (London, 1934).

Temistocle[1] (1772). Most interesting are his three symphonies for double orchestra (Op. 18, nos. 1, 3, 5), an idea gleaned not so much from the unequal groups of the concerto grosso as from earlier overtures for double grouping such as Jommelli's *Merope* (1741).

Among other foreign composers who influenced the English musical scene were Friedrich Schwindl (1737–86) and Anton (or Antonín) Kammel (*c.* 1740–*c.* 1788). Both belonged by background and training to the German-speaking world, though one was born in Holland, the other in Bohemia. Schwindl's compact works are, in fact, Mannheim symphonies in miniature, with orchestral crescendos, abbreviated recapitulations, and even thematic resemblances to Johann Stamitz. Schwindl's symphonies were issued by several London publishers with great success. Even more popular was Kammel who wrote, principally, chamber music for strings. His *Six Overtures*, Op. 10, however, also called for oboes, flutes, and French horns on the title page, and were published by Welcker in London about 1775. They maintain a sense of motion well, but the repetitions are rather inflexible and one welcomes the appearance of new material in the development sections.

NATIVE ENGLISH SYMPHONISTS

In spite of foreign domination, the English symphony managed to put down some native roots.[2] William Boyce (1711–79) published in 1760 *Eight Symphonys in Eight Parts*,[3] most of them compiled from dramatic overtures extending back as far as *Solomon* (1743). Although Baroque in style, the quality of these works and their distinctly English melodic flavour set an encouraging precedent.[4] Thomas Arne (1710–78) proved more adaptable to the changing stylistic currents. Beginning in a post-Handelian style with dotted-rhythm largos and fast fugatos, by 1764 Arne had caught the spirit of the Italian comic opera in his *Guardian Outwitted*, one of the few English pieces to appear in the Breitkopf Catalogue (Supplement of 1771). His later works show a consequent broadening of phrase dimensions.

Possibly as the result of close connections with the theatre, many English symphonies tended to be small in size and informal in mood.

---

[1] The overture to *Temistocle* and the Symphony, Op. 18, no. 5, ed. Fritz Stein, *Das Erbe deutscher Musik*, xxx (Wiesbaden, 1956); Symphonies, Op. 18, nos. 1 and 3, ed. Stein (Leipzig, 1930–1).

[2] Charles Cudworth, 'English Symphonists of the Eighteenth Century', *Proceedings of the Royal Musical Association*, lxxviii (1953), p. 31, and *Thematic Index of English Eighteenth Century Overtures and Symphonies* (London, 1953).

[3] Ed. Constant Lambert (London, revised edition 1967), and M. Gobermann (Vienna, 1964). No. 8 is recorded in *The History of Music in Sound*, vii.

[4] See also Boyce's collected Ode overtures, ed. Gerald Finzi, *Musica Britannica*, xiii (London, 1957).

Three-movement form predominated with a good many minuet finales, as well as gavottes, rondeaux, jigs, marches, chaconnes, and the exceptional Andante amoroso finale of Arne's *Guardian Outwitted*.

Thomas Erskine, Earl of Kelly (1732–81), studied the violin and composition with Johann Stamitz. On his return to England he received recognition as performer and composer from numerous critics, including Burney. His works are somewhat entangled in attribution with those of Stamitz,[1] but the undisputed works demonstrate exceptional command of articulation and thematic differentiation. The propulsive rhythms and sharply contrasting dynamics follow the style of Stamitz, as may be seen in No. 5 of *Six Simphonies in 4 parts* published by Bremner, *c.* 1764:

Ex. 209

John Collett (fl. 1765), cruder than Kelly as a composer, nevertheless shares his rhythmic vigour, clear grasp of form, and even some aspects of Mannheim dynamics, though applied on a smaller scale. Collett's Op. 2, no. 5 is the only English symphony of this time in four movements, but the composer hedges his radicalism with the direction before the minuet: 'Either or both of the following movements to be played.'

John Abraham Fisher (1744–1806) fashioned his six symphonies (*c.* 1770) with more skill than Collett. Particularly sensitive to orchestral effects, Fisher exploits pizzicato (Symphony no. 2), wind instruments (notably bassoon solos in slow movements of nos. 2 and 4), distinction of cello from contrabass, and careful dynamic gradation, including what may be the earliest printed *ppp*, at the end of the slow movement of Symphony no. 2.

William Smethergell (*fl.* 1780) published two sets of overtures that show influences of the thematic style of the second Mannheim generation. Even at this comparatively late date Smethergell continues to rely on minuet or 3/8 finales, an atavism equally observable in Fisher and Collett.

At the end of the century John Marsh (*c.* 1752–1828) made a partial break with this earlier tradition. In several cases his symphonies take four-movement form, and the individual parts, especially slow movements, develop to a more normal size than the Lilliputian dimensions of his immediate predecessors. Significantly, his only published sym-

[1] See Cudworth, 'English Symphonists', p. 37.

phony with minuet finale is subtitled, 'In the Ancient Style' (c. 1797). Of particular interest is Marsh's *Conversation Symphony*, printed under the anagram of his name, Sharm. This work for double orchestra does not follow the Jommelli–J. C. Bach plan of similar groups but mainly plays off treble instruments in one orchestra (violins, oboes, first cello, and bassoon) against alto and lower instruments in the other (first and second violas, horns, second cello and contrabass). The following example with a melody for solo viola is appealing:

Ex. 210 Andante

Overpowered by the giant shadow of Handel, the English symphonists lacked the vigour and momentum necessary for a positive and individual achievement. In this period the conspicuous excellence of England was that of critical appreciation. As an audience she called forth the best from Bach, Abel, and many other distinguished performers and composers. In response to English appreciation Haydn composed the crowning achievements of his symphonic career.

THE PERIPHERIES

Apart from the main centres, many of the minor Courts of the period supported a number of competent and productive composers. A brief selection may suggest the wide ramifications of symphonic activity.

The great monasteries obviously played a part in fostering the Classical style. In Austrian Benedictine monasteries, such as Göttweig, Kremsmünster, and St. Florian, monks often performed and composed as part of their duties, notably Georg Pasterwitz (1730–1803), Amandus Ivanschiz (*fl.* 1758), and Marian Carl Paradeiser (1747–75), and in Poland a similar role was played by monasteries, churches, and the houses of the nobility.[1]

Among the natives and residents of Sweden, Johan Roman,[2] Johan

---

[1] See Jan Węcowski, 'La musique symphonique polonaise du XVIIIe siècle', *Musica Antiqua Europae Orientalis* (ed. Zofia Lissa) (Warsaw, 1966), p. 334, and Gerald Abraham, 'Some Eighteenth-Century Polish Symphonies', in H. C. Robbins Landon (ed.), *Studies in Eighteenth-Century Music* (London, 1970), p. 13.

[2] Ingmar Bengtsson, *J. H. Roman* (Uppsala, 1955) includes an English summary and thematic index.

Agrell, and Joseph Kraus deserve mention. Johan Roman (1694–1758) started his career by writing in the Baroque manner, but made a considerable reorientation later towards the new style. Agrell (1701–65), born in Sweden, moved to Nuremberg in 1746. His attractive themes move farther from the Baroque than those of many of his German contemporaries. The German Kraus (1756–92) went to Sweden in 1778. His symphonies are few, but distinguished for thematic development, dramatic use of harmony, and subtly graduated orchestral effects.

Placidus von Camerloher (1718–82) was Kapellmeister to the Prince Bishop of Freising, Johann Theodor, who also functioned as Bishop of Liège. His peripatetic patron was wont to travel from Bavaria not only to Belgium but also to Paris. This may account for the wide distribution of Camerloher's symphonies, of which over fifty are known in various European libraries. Camerloher's musical style, praised by Gerber, is distinguished by harmonic variety, unusually detailed indications of dynamics, and differentiation between primary and secondary material.[1]

J. M. Molter (d. 1765) was Court composer to the Margrave of Baden. His amazing total of 169 symphonies has already been mentioned.[2] These works tend to be conservative, though they are remarkable for their mastery of the idiom of individual instruments, particularly the woodwinds. On the other hand, it is the thoroughly Classical phrase structure and the smooth linking of ideas that are notable in the work of the Belgian Pierre Van Maldere (1729–68).[3] He wrote about fifty symphonies, several of them misattributed to Haydn.

Two Bohemian-born composers who were active at Bavarian courts also deserve mention: F. X. Pokorný (1729–94) and F. A. Rösler (or Rossetti) (c. 1750–1792).[4] Pokorný, in the service of the Thurn and Taxis Court at Regensburg, wrote symphonies which rarely rose above a level of general competence, except in his advanced writing for brass instruments. Rösler, in the service of the Ottingen–Wallerstein Court at Wallerstein, wrote symphonies of a mature Classicism. Here we find a cantabile and an effortless counterpoint which approach Mozart, while the tightly knit forms are reminiscent of Haydn. The career of this provincial Court composer emphasizes the unique decentralization of

---

[1] See B. Ziegler, *P. von Camerloher* (Munich, 1920), and Karl Gustav Fellerer's article in *Die Musik in Geschichte und Gegenwart*, ii (1952), col. 722; Andante of a C major Symphony (c. 1760) in Arnold Schering, *Geschichte der Musik in Beispielen* (Leipzig, 1931), p. 461.

[2] See p. 402. See also H. Becker's remarks on Molter in *Das Erbe deutscher Musik*, xli (Wiesbaden, 1957), p. vii; and Friedrich Hermann's article in *Die Musik in Geschichte und Gegenwart*, ix (1961), col. 446.

[3] Suzanne Clercx, *P. Van Maldere* (Brussels, 1948).

[4] On Pokorný see p. 402; concerning French horn passages in both composers, J. M. Barbour. *Trumpets, Horns, and Music* (East Lansing, Mich., 1964); for five of Rossetti's symphonies, *Denkmäler der Tonkunst in Bayern*, xii, part i (Leipzig, 1912).

Classicism. Of the Czechs who did not emigrate, one of the most notable was František Adam Míča (1746–1811), composer of a symphony in D major formerly attributed to František Václav Míča (1694–1744).

VII

THE CONCERTO

By Egon Wellesz and F. W. Sternfeld[1]

EVOLUTION OF THE CONCERTO

Of the various developments in the Classical period, one of the hardest to explain is the evolution of the concerto. If we speak of 'Classical concerto form', we over-simplify, for the concerto in the second half of the eighteenth century was neither a stable form nor was it wholly Classical. We owe this situation to the high development of the Baroque concerto about 1740 in the hands of such composers as Vivaldi, Handel, and Albinoni. Their successful procedures tended to overshadow the infusions of Classical elements; and while the primitive symphony sought a structure of its own by testing every aspect of the new Classical language, the concerto persisted in applying the formulae of the Baroque. These circumstances explain in part the popularity after mid-century of conservative concertos such as those of Arne, Avison, and Stanley in a period otherwise devoted to experiment.

Fundamental aspects of the Baroque concerto survive even in concertos usually regarded as typically Classical, such as those of Mozart. The entrance of the tutti at the end of the solo exposition, for example, adheres to the ritornello plan matured by Torelli and Vivaldi two generations earlier. This point in concerto form bears little resemblance to the double-bar of sonata form, by comparison a point of rest. The central tutti also reflects Baroque influence in its habit of recapitulating earlier material in the dominant key, a procedure that may weaken the impact of the recapitulation.

Notwithstanding the domination of the ritornello plan, characteristic details of Classical style such as broadly balanced melodic phrases and thematic contrast can be found in progressive concertos just as early as in the symphony or sonata. Any attempt, therefore, to explain Classical concerto form as a later development from sonata form risks confusion and historical inaccuracy. The forms developed simultaneously as exploitations of dominant tension on a large scale; but the concerto, owing to its prior commitments, reached markedly different conclusions. We should view the development of the concerto not as in two distinct periods, Baroque and Classical, but rather as an evolutionary process.

[1] This chapter has been prepared on the basis of material provided by Jan LaRue. The editors are responsible for its presentation.

The ritornello principle supplied a basic plan that could be filled with varying materials.

One might suppose that the treatment of the analogous medium of the solo voice in the operatic aria would contain significant precedents for the Classical concerto. Where the *da capo* aria is concerned this idea seems far-fetched, for the first section of the aria ends in the tonic key, a design basically different from the modulating ritornello plan of the concerto. Later in the Baroque period, however, there are parallels between the enlargement of the aria and that of the concerto. For example, Handel designs 'Ev'ry Valley' (*Messiah*) as a miniature of Classical concerto form, complete with contrasting themes, development, and recapitulation. In terms of precedents, however, it appears that here the aria has adopted the concerto plan, rather than the reverse.

In view of the Baroque influence on the Classical form, a review of the earlier development of the concerto will place the Classical concerto in perspective. The Baroque background included three phases:

1. *The concerto grosso* (Corelli): a random alternation of slow and fast movements with simple exchange of brief passages between tutti and concertino.

2. *The early solo concerto* (Torelli): enlargement of the tutti section by differentiation of thematic material; characterization of solo sections by brilliant figuration; establishment of a fast–slow–fast sequence of three movements.

3. *The mature solo concerto* (Vivaldi): further enlargement by more extensive thematic differentiation within both tutti and solo sections; development as well as contrast in the solo sections; enlargement of movements by additional episodes and returns.

At this point the Baroque concerto had reached a plateau, owing mainly to the limitations of motivic themes and quick harmonic rhythm which tended to produce forms of small dimensions. The great achievements of the late Baroque concerto, exemplified particularly by J. S. Bach, present refinements of detail rather than new lines of development. This long and successful tradition inhibited the development of a Classical concerto style. Even such original composers as Sammartini and C. P. E. Bach could not rid their minds of Baroque preconceptions. The problem of adjustment between two frequently incompatible styles explains in part the confusions of the succeeding decades.

The Classical development may be understood as an increasing control of various stylistic processes, three of which demand special attention. First, tonality: in the Baroque concerto, modulation touched upon a series of related keys, all of approximately equal attraction. Classicism intensified key relationships, dramatizing tonic-dominant tension in large forms. For effective opposition of tonic and dominant, both must be clearly defined, and in Classical design this stabilization replaces the more active but less clearly organized modulation of the Baroque.

Second, form: the Baroque style tended to mix the functions of exposition and development indiscriminately throughout a piece. In the Classical period, the exposition is restricted to the beginning, the development furnishes contrast and continuation, and the time span is gradually increased. Within each section the character of themes matches the functions of beginning, transition, contrast, and close. Baroque harmony tends to move consistently from start to finish; in Classical pieces we can often identify a thematic section merely by its harmonic rhythm. In Mozart and Beethoven, for example, primary and closing sections contain accelerations, transitions maintain almost perfect regularity, and secondary sections employ slower or more varied harmonic rhythm.[1]

Third, co-ordination of musical elements: the Baroque excluded full co-ordination by the independence of the bass line and the overlapping of contrapuntal textures. Characteristic examples of Classicism, however, stressed simultaneous control of all components according to an overall plan, whereby the major divisions of a piece emerge with equal clarity whether we consider harmony, melody, rhythm, or orchestration. The interaction of these distinctive Classical processes with the Baroque ritornello scheme produced fundamental modifications. Although the concerto never entirely escaped from its Baroque background, the Classical evolution attained three objectives:

1. *Thematic differentiation in the tutti.* By studying Vivaldi's larger tuttis we can see that mere contrast of thematic material, despite its interest, may produce a sense of oscillation rather than direction. Classical composers designed themes to indicate the function of a particular passage in the total plan. Thus, rhythmic, harmonic and orchestral factors were employed to create themes with formal associations which, in turn, gave a sense of motion and direction.

2. *Heightened contrast between solo and tutti.* Various devices for distinguishing solo and tutti existed in a primitive state even in the middle Baroque, for example, thematic contrasts, alteration to minor mode, and change in orchestral texture or colour. Classicism carried this contrast further by associating the soloist's new themes with the heightened tension of the dominant tonality. In the most mature ex-

[1] Jan LaRue, 'Harmonic Rhythm in the Beethoven Symphonies', *Music Review*, xviii (1957), p. 8.

amples of the concerto (Mozart), the opening tutti does not modulate to the dominant: the freshness of the new tonality is reserved for the soloist. This device makes a point of special interest in the concerto, and since in other Classical forms we expect the modulation, the concerto achieves a keen advantage for the soloist by holding back the dominant key. Classical concertos also increased the range of relationship between solo and tutti, on the one hand sharpening the opposition by all possible contrasts (chiefly in the exposition), on the other hand forming alliances between tutti and solo through exchange of material (chiefly in developments and recapitulations). As a final touch, the increased importance of the cadenza in the Classical concerto further distinguishes the personality of the soloist.

3. *Large-scale unification of the form.* Since large musical forms can be sustained only by tension of various sorts, Classical symphony composers gradually discovered that co-ordination of harmonic tension with thematic expectation, rhythmic drive, and varied orchestral colour could extend and unify a form more successfully than the less co-ordinated procedures of the Baroque. In the concerto, however, the Baroque heritage apparently blinded composers for a time to the powers of unification. Only slowly did they realize the strength of a development section that uses the expositional material, as opposed to an unrelated contrasting episode. Also retarded was the full mastery of the recapitulation, the fulfilment of returning to the tonic with the opening material of the concerto. Not until high Classicism do we find concertos that fully exploit the subtle tensions of thematic expectation, such as the significant and sensitive interchange of orchestral and solo ideas which can emerge only from a unified concept of concerto form.

These three achievements give us a base for judging the gradual stylistic evolution of the Classical concerto.

PATTERNS AND CLICHÉS

The concerto shows less tendency to develop characteristic local or national patterns than the symphony. This tendency towards homogeneity doubtless owed much to the travelling virtuosi, who accelerated the exchange of stylistic innovations throughout Europe, and whose compositions often represent a cross-fertilization of styles. They form a unique genre of superbly idiomatic music; yet too frequently they conform to the most desiccated of conventions, a justification for critics who view Classical form as a mould into which ideas were poured. These tendencies are easily understood as most of the virtuosi were performers first and composers second, writing mainly to show off their own talents. They tended to copy any successful model, applying their ingenuity to the solo elaborations rather than to the basic thematic material. About 1770 two thematic clichés began to appear with tiresome frequency in concertos from many parts of Europe. A pompous opening rhythm in some such combination as $\frac{4}{4}\ \downarrow\ \ \downarrow.\ \ \downarrow|\downarrow\ \_\ \ |$ reminds us of the development of a similarly predominant rhythm in the Renaissance canzona. Even more frequent was a syncopated stress on the second beat of common time, occurring most characteristically in the second bar of two- and four-bar phrases. Triple and other metres are much rarer than in symphonies. Among thousands of variants the following give some idea of the nature and distribution of these clichés:

Ex. 211
(i)
FEYER
    Allegro con spirito

FRAENZL
    Allegro spiritoso

(ii)
PLEYEL
    Allegro

KRUMPHOLTZ
    Allegro moderato

(iii)
ROSSETTI
    Allegro maestoso

ANTON STAMITZ
    Allegro

Despite its conventionality of themes, the concerto showed surprising diversity in forms. It lent itself to aberrations such as slow movements based on popular operatic melodies; finales 'à la russe'; interjections of foreign tempi that disturb the flow of a movement; and connection of two or three movements into one continuous piece. We find an astonishing variety of settings, from cembalo alone to massive concertante structures with five soloists and full orchestra. Thus, during the last quarter of the eighteenth century the concerto employed conventional material in diverse forms, in contrast to the symphony with its more varied thematic material yet comparatively settled forms.

PREFERENCE FOR THE SOLO CONCERTO

Several overlapping changes of direction can be observed in the development of the concerto in the later eighteenth century. The concerto grosso persists with surprising vigour, notably in England, but finally gives way to a Classical preference for the solo concerto. The choice of solo instrument also changes. While violin concertos predominate in late Baroque and early Classical repertories, preferences begin to shift about 1750 to keyboard concertos, as reflected some years later in various publishers' catalogues, notably those of Breitkopf between 1762 and 1770. Flute concertos held their own and clarinet concertos did not become popular until after 1780 as one would expect.[1]

It might be thought that the increasing predominance of solo concertos over the concerto grosso relates to the domination of a single upper line in the homophonic Classical style, as opposed to the polyphonic texture of the concerto grosso. Actually, the attractions of a concertino containing several instruments soon found expression in the new form of the *symphonie concertante*. This abbreviated concerto (normally two movements, Allegro and Rondo Allegretto) took Paris by storm, temporarily overshadowing the conventional concerto and even challenging the popularity of the symphony. Elsewhere the trend was weaker, and in the early nineteenth century the solo concerto emerged across Europe as the dominating form. The problem of misattribution for concertos is as confusing as for symphonies.[2] Concertos seem on the whole to be less numerous than symphonies but it has been possible to catalogue well over five thousand incipits so far.

PERFORMANCE

The performance of concertos poses a special problem. Although contemporary convention encouraged flexible attitudes, modern soloists must remember the implied boundaries of good taste. Today it is not much help to give rules, as good taste is essentially creative and tends to escape definition. Yet to avoid gross anachronisms we must assemble evidence from contemporary manuscripts and establish norms of per-

[1] The Breitkopf catalogue should be supplemented by the Hummel catalogue (Amsterdam, 1768) and the Ringmacher catalogue (Berlin, 1773). A catalogue for flute and oboe concertos has been made by Raymond Meylan; see 'Documents douteux dans le domaine des concertos pour instruments à vent au XVIIIe siècle', *Revue de musicologie*, xlix (1963), p. 47.

[2] LaRue, 'Major and Minor Mysteries of Identification in the 18th-century Symphony', *Journal of the American Musicological Society*, xiii (1960), p. 181.

formance as foundations of eighteenth-century taste. One problem in keyboard concertos concerns improvised addition to the solo part. Recently considerable attention has been given to ambiguous passages in Mozart piano concertos.[1] Other contemporary sources provide us with further hints. In a number of solo keyboard parts surviving in manuscript sources,[2] right-hand harmonies in small notes have been sketched in tutti sections, showing that the soloist played a normal thoroughbass background when not involved in solo passages. The existing contemporary examples use surprisingly simple textures, mainly three-part, changing to two or four parts as required. Since few keyboard concertos before 1800 use heavy textures even in solo passages, these simple realizations may represent what was actually played, and not a shorthand version to be amplified in performance.

Another important question concerns cadenzas. The rule of simplicity suggested for thoroughbass realization applies with even greater force to cadenzas. We tend to credit the eighteenth-century performers with uncanny powers of improvisation, and discussions of the concerto often assume that soloists frequently improvised at any occurrence of a fermata. Many of these fermate require only a simple lead-in, perhaps only a short connecting scale. We should not assume, merely because editions and manuscripts often lack cadenzas, that these were always improvised. That we lack cadenzas for many works is no surprise; the soloist was certainly expected to provide, but not necessarily to improvise, the cadenza, and naturally he tended to take his prepared cadenza along with him more often than he left it behind, loose among the other parts.

A final point concerns the nature of the cadenza itself. In dozens of eighteenth-century cadenzas found in all parts of Europe, the majority make no reference to the thematic material of the concerto. Extensive thematic development must be considered as unnecessary and inappropriate for the typical Classical concerto. Cadenzas consisted mainly of brilliant but simple figurations exploiting the possibilities of the instrument and sometimes of the individual soloist.

THE TRANSITIONAL CONCERTO IN ITALY

As the cradle of the concerto, Italy might have extended her century-long leadership into the later eighteenth century. Yet the very successes of Corelli and Vivaldi limited the imaginations of their followers. About

---

[1] Paul and Eva Badura-Skoda, *Interpreting Mozart on the Keyboard* (New York, 1962), p. 177.

[2] Particularly interesting is a performing copy of Haydn's D major cembalo concerto, Anthony Van Hoboken, *Joseph Haydn: Thematisch-bibliographisches Werkverzeichnis* (Mainz, 1957), Gruppe XVIII: 11; formerly in the Breslau (Wrocław) University Library, now in the Warsaw University Library; this copy includes realizations and cadenzas.

1730 the concerto was predominantly a medium for violin and strings, despite Vivaldi's many wind concertos. Walther's *Musicalisches Lexicon* (1732), in the entry for 'concerto', speaks of 'Violin-sachen ... wo unter vielen Violinen, eine mit sonderlicher Hurtigkeit hervorraget'. Deeply rooted in this tradition, the Italians continued to concentrate on violin concertos. Among these composers we can distinguish three groups, not always separable chronologically: (1) composers steeped in the Baroque tradition who break away towards Classicism in various essential characteristics; (2) writers of more clearly Classical spirit who cannot entirely escape the past; (3) thoroughgoing Classicists who accept the new models but contribute no particular vitality of their own.

The first group includes Leo, Brescianello, Locatelli, Padre Martini, and G. B. Sammartini.[1] The cello concertos of Leonardo Leo (1694–1744) are significant early examples of the genre, but contribute little towards development in form, except possibly in the finales, and tend towards the Baroque in their small dimensions and diatonic sequences. The very little known Stuttgart Kapellmeister Giuseppe Antonio Brescianello (d. 1751) wrote both old-fashioned concerti grossi and also concertos which foreshadow the later *symphonie concertante*.[2] Pietro Locatelli (1695–1764) was one of the first in the tradition of composers who wrote violin concertos of a very high virtuoso standard. His layout was entirely in the Baroque tradition, especially in his choice of tempi for the various movements. One can, however, see certain places where a short cadenza was inserted, and his use of the soloist in general is forward looking. The style of Padre Giovanni Battista Martini (1706–84) shows both Baroque and Classical elements. The solo instruments vary a great deal, from concerto grosso combinations to real *symphonie concertante* ones. The concertos of G. B. Sammartini (1700–75) were few and unimportant compared to his symphonies, and, written mostly before 1740, are for various instruments. Sammartini follows Vivaldi in his movement patterns, as in other things, but looks forward in many ways to the classical concerto.

The composers of the second group, moving towards Classicism yet unable to cast off Baroque influence, include Platti, Tartini, and Nardini. Giovanni Benedetto Platti (*c.* 1690–1763), a versatile instrumentalist active mainly in Würzburg, gives us a date for early Classical tendencies with his *VI Concerti* for cembalo, Op. 2 (Nuremberg, 1742).[3]

---

[1] See Vol. VI.
[2] Barry, S. Brook, 'The Symphonie Concertante: An Interim Report', *Musical Quarterly*, xlvii (1961), pp. 493–516.
[3] Fausto Torrefranca, *G. B. Platti e la sonata moderna* (Milan, 1963). Torrefranca claims the somewhat unlikely period of 1720–5 for the actual composition of these works, citing merely style as evidence; see his editorial introduction to Concerto no. 1 (Milan, 1949).

Not only do these concertos antedate some of the works mentioned above, but they include true recapitulations and are more balanced. The thematic material, however, is in small motives that remind us of the early date, and the keyboard style is undemanding. In addition to later cembalo concertos, Platti's competence on several instruments resulted in a violin concerto and numerous concertos for cello.

Giuseppe Tartini (1692–1770), famous as violin virtuoso, teacher, and theorist, illustrates the stylistic conflicts of a transitional composer. His prodigious output includes approximately a hundred and twenty-five violin concertos and several for cello and gamba.[1] In early works Tartini follows the manner of Vivaldi fairly closely. In those of his middle years (1735–50) Dounias calls attention to Tartini's preoccupation with the affective possibilities of music, reflected in his complex ornamentation.[2] There is also a significant broadening of dimension in a theme such as the following, from an E major violin concerto,[3] where the motive proliferates to form an answering phrase, as indicated by the brackets:

Ex. 212

Although his later concertos (1750–70) are more concerned with large-scale structural problems, Tartini never outgrew the main Baroque procedures. Most of the concertos adhere to the pattern of alternating ritornellos and solo episodes. The emphasis on the central ritornello overbalances the frequently inconspicuous recapitulation in the tonic key. The full coupling of the principal material with the tonic often occurs only in the final tutti and shows that Tartini still viewed musical form more as a perpetual unfolding than as a balance of harmonic tensions and thematic oppositions.

The restless imagination that led Tartini to become a master of fencing as well as the discoverer of combination tones[4] also produced some

[1] Minos Dounias, *Die Violinkonzerte Giuseppe Tartinis* (Wolfenbüttel and Berlin, 1935) includes an excellent thematic catalogue; Antonio Capri, *Giuseppe Tartini* (Milan, 1945) gives thematic lists of solo and trio sonatas as well as concertos, unfortunately without locations.
[2] Op. cit., pp. 117 f.
[3] Ibid., p. 266.
[4] First described in his *Trattato di musica secondo la vera scienza dell'armonia* (Padua, 1754), but discovered in 1714, according to Tartini's account in his *De' prinzipi dell'armonia* (Padua, 1767), p. 36.

unique forms, such as the Violin Concerto in A minor,[1] which alternates short sections of Andante cantabile 3/4 with Allegro assai.[2] Tartini also uses capriccios,[3] mainly in finales in early concertos, and unlike Locatelli he relates these episodes, enriched with occasional contrapuntal passages, to the main material. Despite his virtuosity, his concertos offer less spectacular technical difficulties than those of Locatelli, though the intricacy of his ornaments severely challenges the technique of the performer as in the second movement of the G major, Op. 2, published by Witvogel (Amsterdam, *c.* 1745):

Ex. 213

Tartini's most famous pupil, Pietro Nardini (1722–93),[4] played in the Court orchestras of Stuttgart and then of Florence. His six violin concertos, op. 1 (Amsterdam, *c.* 1765) and four violin concertos in manuscript[5] are less advanced than those of his teacher. Formal balance is sometimes upset by the emphasis on solo episodes, while a deficiency of thematic contrast is shown in the Baroque repetition of rhythmic motives. J. B. Cartier's edition of Nardini's violin sonatas 'avec les Adagios brodés'[6] suggests that performance of concertos may also have been more elaborate than the written version.

THE CLASSICAL CONCERTO IN ITALY

In the decade 1760–70 the problem of integrating the concerto ritornello within the sonata form was solved by a number of leading composers in various parts of Europe. Most of them abandoned Baroque practices almost entirely in favour of the more dramatic new form. The fluent, well-trained Italians absorbed the Classical clichés with especial ease, and many Italian virtuosi all over Europe composed in the new

[1] Dounias (op. cit.) catalogues this concerto as no. 115. The manuscript is in Padua, Bibl. Antoniana, autogr. 76.
[2] Dounias quotes part of this work, op. cit., p. 230.
[3] See Dounias 39 (Paris Bibl. Nat. Cons. 11227/11), which has a capriccio 54 bars long; Dounias 43 and 47 also include lengthy capriccios.
[4] Clara Pfäfflin, *Pietro Nardini: seine Werke und sein Leben* (Stuttgart, 1935) contains a thematic index.
[5] Vienna, Ges. der Musikfreunde, Q 16732, Q 16733, Q 16734, and Q 16735.
[6] In *L'Art du violon* (Paris, 1798).

style. As a result, the third Italian group–the mature Classicists—includes numerous competent if not always inspired composers, among whom Sirmen, Giordani, Lolli, Pugnani, and Rolla are representative, to whom one might add the Italianized foreigners Giornovichi (Jarnovič, Jarnowick) and Mysliveček.

Among the Italian virtuoso composers is the woman violinist, Maddalena Lombardini–Sirmen (c. 1735–after 1785), the pupil of Tartini, to whom he addressed his well-known letter (Venice, 1770), later published as *L'arte dell'arco*. Her six violin concertos, Op. 3 (London, 1772) are competent though conventional works, the first movements of which often contain opening ritornellos modulating to the dominant, which, as Tovey has pointed out,[1] spoils the later effect of the solo modulation.

By comparison with Tartini, the two other pre-eminent virtuosos of the time, Pugnani and Lolli, contribute little to the history of the concerto. Of Gaetano Pugnani (1731–98) only the Concerto in E flat major survives in Brussels. It is unusual in that it lacks any fast movement, its plan being Andantino tempo giusto–Adagio–Andantino grazioso.[2] Pugnani's phrase details often approach a Classical balance, but in larger dimensions he uses the ritornello plan more than the new sonata form. The rondo finale, though somewhat irregular, heralds a style that soon became the convention for concerto finales. Antonio Lolli (c. 1730–1802) published eight concertos between about 1765 and 1790, leaving three further works in manuscript. These concertos require exceptional command of the upper register, but otherwise lack originality and pursue conservative forms much like Tartini's. One of Lolli's best pupils, Giovanni Mane Giornovichi (c. 1740–1804), a violinist of Croatian origin,[3] far surpassed his teacher as a composer. From 1774 onwards he published more than fifteen large-scale violin concertos, which generally follow the conventional pattern of late eighteenth-century form, but also show some experiment in the form of four-movement works and recitative movements. Two rondos 'à la russe' (third movements of Concertos nos. 7 and 14) illustrate a trend towards local colour more noticeable in the concerto than in the symphony.

Josef Mysliveček (1737–81), a composer of opera rather than a virtuoso, received little contemporary notice for his concertos. Surviving examples include a half-dozen each for keyboard and violin, as well

---

[1] *Essays in Musical Analysis*, iii (London, 1936), p. 20.

[2] Two further concertos are known merely by their incipits in the Breitkopf Catalogue (Supplements 1770 and 1776/77). Elsa M. von Zschinsky-Troxler, *Gaetano Pugnani* (Berlin, 1939), pp. 80–1, 169–70; see also Albert Müry, *Die Instrumentalwerke Gaetano Pugnanis* (Basle, 1941).

[3] Stana Djurič-Klajn, 'Un contemporain de Mozart, Ivan Mane Jarnovič', *Bericht über den internationalen musikwissenschaftlichen Kongress, Wien 1956*, ed. Erich Schenk (Graz, 1958), p. 134.

as single works for cello and flute.[1] As the product of a professional composer for whom Mozart recorded his admiration in several letters,[2] they command a degree of technical finesse rarely found among the virtuosos, and the richness of texture and complexity of thematic structure lend them enduring interest.

Public and scholarly appreciation of Luigi Boccherini (1743–1805) has grown in the past two decades. His full stature, however, cannot be properly measured without further research, both to recover lost or unknown works and to correct impressions derived from unauthentic works or from the use of bad editions. His concertos have suffered from editors who have 'corrected' the originals with inevitable misrepresentation. The well-known B flat cello concerto (Op. 34), for example, is usually performed in a version with a recomposed first movement, a substitute slow movement, and augmented and revised orchestration.[3] Four other cello concertos published by the Bureau d'Abonnement Musical in 1770–1 can be more securely associated with Boccherini; but a sixth cello concerto, a flute concerto (generally referred to as Op. 27), a violin concerto, and a cembalo concerto, all are doubtful or falsely attributed works.[4] In addition there are several *symphonies concertantes* of varying instrumentation.

Boccherini's concertos do not achieve a perfect adjustment between the ritornello principle and sonata form. Although he usually reserves the dominant modulation for the solo exposition, he may not highlight the new key with solo themes; and the recapitulation does not always enter strongly with both tonic key and initial material (a confusing aspect of Op. 34, for example). In the development section Boccherini gives us more genuine mutation of ideas than most composers. His attitude towards the finale is serious; whereas most concertos have rondo finales a number of his develop a more complex concerto–sonata form. These experiments counteracted a late eighteenth-century tendency towards lightweight finales using variations and rondos based on popular songs or other inconsequential themes.

In Boccherini's harmonic scheme, one notices a richness in chromaticism frequently resulting from secondary dominants (often in the

[1] Incipits of two Mysliveček violin concertos appear in the Breitkopf Catalogue Supplements 1769–1770. One violin concerto has been edited by Karel Moor and Ladislav Láska with piano accompaniment (Prague, 1948).

[2] Notably the letter of 13 November 1777, *Mozart. Briefe und Aufzeichnungen*, ed. Wilhelm A. Bauer and Otto E. Deutsch (Kassel, 1962), ii, p. 12.

[3] F. Grützmacher (ed.) (Leipzig: Breitkopf and Härtel, 1896, repr. 1923, 1951). A much better edition, in miniature score, also with considerable revision, has been ed. Richard Sturzenegger (London, 1949).

[4] The flute concerto has been shown to be a work of F. X. Pokorný. Questions of authenticity are discussed in Yves Gérard, *Catalogue of the Works of Luigi Boccherini* (London, 1969).

diminished-seventh form, without root, like Mozart) as in the B flat concerto:[1]

Ex. 214
Allegro moderato

His reputed femininity in melody is equalled by his vigour and intensity. In the following phrase for solo cello, from the second movement of the G major,[2] the unusual and rhythmically intensified upward drive is placed in relief by the descending octave:

Ex. 215
Adagio

Although Boccherini's instrumentation is old-fashioned—strings only, or with one or two pairs of winds—he discovers fresh sonorities. The slow movement of the G major cello concerto is accompanied throughout by the first and second violins, a rare texture. Boccherini comes close to Mozart in his sensitive integration of solo and orchestra. He realizes the beauties of alliance as well as the drama of opposition.

The Classical concerto style may be seen in fully evolved form in the twenty-nine violin concertos of Giovanni Battista Viotti (1755–1824), Pugnani's most renowned pupil and the founder of the new French violin school. Of these concertos several were arranged for flute and no less than eleven were adapted for piano. Viotti also composed two *symphonies concertantes* for two violins and orchestra in connection with his appearances at the Concert Spirituel in 1787. Although he worked mainly in France and England, his style owes more to Italy and Vienna. Even today his idiomatic concertos form an indispensable stage of every violinist's training, with no. 22 in A minor,[3] as a particular favourite. Possibly influenced by the brilliant Paris orchestras, he soon turned from the modest instrumentation of Tartini and Boccherini, and in his late works included not only pairs of all woodwind and horns

[1] Sturzenegger's edition. No. 482 in Gérard, op. cit.
[2] Paris, 1770. No. 480 in Gérard, op. cit.
[3] Miniature score, ed. Alfred Einstein (Zürich, 1929).

but trumpets and kettledrums as well. The orchestration includes touches such as the doubling of solo themes by flute and bassoon in the first movement of Concerto no. 22 and solo woodwind echoes in the finale. Viotti's technical demands are high and never unrewarding: in the solo violin he obtains great sonority and contrast, giving unusually full play to the lower strings.

The thematic style, while often obvious and occasionally insipid, at its best has impressively balanced phrases with features that later break up naturally for development, as in the A major, no. 13:[1]

Ex. 216
Allegro brillante

The dramatic finale of Concerto no. 22 (1803/4) sets a quite different mood from the bucolic rondos so common a few years earlier:

Ex. 217
Agitato assai

[1] Sieber (Paris, c. 1785).

Despite some outstanding works, Italy played a far less important role in the development of the concerto than in that of the symphony. The great virtuoso violin tradition entailed some detrimental side-effects, for Italian concertos were mainly produced by men who were virtuosi first and composers second, Also, as we have seen, the noble echoes of Corelli and Vivaldi rang in the ears of Italian composers, inhibiting their originality even after mid-century. By then it was too late: the leadership in the concerto had migrated to northern Europe.

NORTH GERMANY

North German composers made a greater contribution to the history of the concerto than to that of the symphony. As we have seen, a number of these composers belonged to a generation slightly too early to feel a complete and instinctive sympathy with Classicism. Since the Classical concerto perpetuates various Baroque procedures, such as the ritornello principle and the textural opposition between tutti and solo, these Baroque continuations may have provided a propitious climate of transition for the Northern imagination. The North German School is outstanding for the cultivation of the keyboard concerto. Although we can find Italian concertos for many different instruments, south of the Alps the violin was mainly favoured. It is tempting to relate this preference to the perennial vocal emphasis in Italy: of concerto instruments the violin is nearest to the human voice in sostenuto and expressive flexibility. Moreover, the age-old identification of the North with polyphony may have exercised some influence on the predominant choice of the keyboard as solo instrument, and the strength of the German organ tradition undoubtedly furnished a direct background and stimulus for the emphasis on keyboard concertos in the North.

The major composers include three sets of brothers: Carl Heinrich and Johann Gottlieb Graun; Franz and Georg Benda; and Wilhelm Friedemann and Carl Philipp Emanuel Bach. Three important North Germans, Frederick the Great, Quantz, and Hasse, have no place in a discussion of the Classical concerto, since both their forms and themes are typically Baroque. Hasse and Quantz in their numerous flute concertos (mostly for the use of Frederick) make few departures from the modulating ritornello form characteristic of the late Baroque. Even slow movements use the ritornello structure, a practice already long obsolescent in Italy and South Germany.

The Graun brothers wrote better concertos than symphonies, perhaps because the concerto medium would appeal to an opera composer (Carl Heinrich, 1704–59) or to a violin virtuoso (Johann Gottlieb, 1703–71). Although the numerous concertos are difficult to assign between the brothers, the keyboard concertos (about thirty-five) are mostly by Carl Heinrich, the violin concertos (at least sixty) by Johann Gottlieb. Though less famous than his brother, Johann Gottlieb excels him in concerto composition even more than in symphonies. In the following example,[1] the articulated four-bar phrase and the stability resulting from repeating the first bar reveal a type of theme quite different from the Baroque:

Ex. 218

As a pupil of Tartini, he included some traits reminiscent of an earlier phase of the Italian violin school, such as the short motivic imitations found in Torelli. But his sense of line co-ordinates rhythm and melodic climax: in the following phrase from an F major violin concerto[2] he maintains continuity in three expanding arches (rising third, fifth, and seventh) with the quickest notes at the climax and slower rhythms at the beginning and end:

Ex. 219

The Benda family produced at least five talented performer-composers mainly in the north, of whom the brothers Franz (1709-86) and Georg (1722-95) are best known. Franz Benda, the pupil and successor of J. G. Graun as leader in Berlin, though widely admired as a virtuoso, composed rather dull concertos, which show the violin to advantage but in musical content fall far behind those of his brother.

Georg Benda's instrumental works demonstrate the inhibiting atmosphere of the conservative North German style. Though a leader of the

---

[1] Cembalo Concerto in F major from *Six Concertos for the Harpsichord or Organ* of J. G. Graun and J. J. Agrell, Op. 2 (Walsh, London, 1762; modern edition by H. Ruf, Heidelberg, 1959).
[2] Stockholm, Kungl. Mus. Akad., Violinkonserter. Rar. (VO-R).

avant-garde in melodrama, in his concertos Benda continues old-fashioned Baroque elements quite incompatible with the rest of his style. A G major cembalo concerto surviving in autograph shows the conflicts in Benda's musical personality:[1]

Ex. 220
Non tanto allegro

The opening bar recalls a mid-century or earlier style, the following triplets are Rococo, and the legato and articulation of bars 3 and 4 fully Classical. The sinuous chromatic detail in bar 6 is characteristic of Benda's *Empfindsamkeit* (highly expressive but not as clearly pre-Romantic as similar passages in C. P. E. Bach, e.g. Ex. 228), and in great contrast to the reversion to Baroque rhythms in bar 7. This emphasis on emotional expression derives from his dramatic vocal music, and his interest in the minor mode is seen in several of his cembalo concertos[2]:

Ex. 221
(i) Allegro
(ii) Allegro

In the work of Georg's son Friedrich Ludwig (1746–92) we finally escape the iron hand of Potsdam. In his three concertos for flute, Op. 4 (Berlin), and a similar set for violin (published by Schwickert of Leipzig), the progressive influence of Mannheim on the north is evident in the enlarged dimension of the theme, as in a C major violin concerto:[3]

---

[1] Leipzig, Musik–Bibliothek, PM 5199.
[2] The concertos in F minor and B minor, with a third concerto in D major, ed. Vratislav Bělský, *Musica Antiqua Bohemica*, xlv (Prague, 1960).
[3] Lund, Univ. Bibl., Wenster Litt. X. Nr 1.

Ex. 222

The Schwerin Kapellmeister, Johann Wilhelm Hertel (1727–89), though even younger than Georg Benda, reminds one more of the Grauns in his use of Baroque rhythmic figures. In an opening tutti such as that of his G minor violin concerto,[1] he has not moved far from Vivaldi:

Ex. 223

but the noble cantilena of the solo entry above supersedes any sense of outworn influences. The Adagio of the same concerto contains expressive harmonies and dramatic rhythms:

Ex. 224

Hertel wrote for other instruments, including flute, cello, cembalo, and —somewhat unusual at this time—high trumpet.[2]

[1] Stockholm, Kungl. Mus. Akad., Violinkonserter. Rar. (VO–R).
[2] The Library of the Royal Conservatory in Brussels contains numerous autograph scores of Hertel's concertos, apparently part of the Westphal Collection purchased from Hamburg.

The conservative Berlin style apparently inhibited composers in other northern cities as well, although in Dresden J. B. G. Neruda (1706–80), a Court violinist of Bohemian origin, struggled in his concertos to progress beyond the shorter motivic phrases of the Baroque.

The conservatism of northern concertos may even be a matter of geography and climate: it seems to increase as we look farther north. The Swedish-born Johan Agrell (1701–65), Kapellmeister at Nuremberg wrote concertos for cembalo, flute, oboe, and violin with Baroque rhythms and ritornello forms as clear (and often as uninspiring) as a book-keeper's balance sheet. Agrell's concertos may have been written earlier than his symphonies: the latter have more charm and originality.[1]

FRIEDEMANN AND EMANUEL BACH

Wilhelm Friedemann Bach (1710–84) illustrates in almost every bar the central problem of northern composers: the need either to evolve or to escape from the Baroque tradition. Friedemann's music contains many appealing details of melody, harmony, and rhythm, but he too rarely gives a sense of larger goals. He foreshadows Romanticism not merely in effective details but more in his expressive ideas. Thus even in an opening theme he may repeat a figure insistently, carrying the emphasis far beyond a merely momentary expressive colouring[2]:

Ex. 225

Despite Friedemann's attractive material, his phrases and paragraphs often lack contrast and balance; in his rhythms particularly he loses emphasis by overloading with details. Among northern composers he is outstanding for his effective use of imitation; yet his polyphonic textures defeat any emerging Classical spirit by focusing our attention on small dimensions. He expanded forms merely by adding segments to the modulating ritornello form; and even after five or six returns of a tutti he repeated the whole ritornello at the end, an unselective and old-fashioned approach.

[1] See Hugo Daffner, *Die Entwicklung des Klavierkonzerts bis Mozart* (Leipzig, 1906), pp. 70–3, and Hans Uldall, *Das Klavierkonzert der Berliner Schule* (Leipzig, 1928), p. 93.
[2] Concerto for 2 cembali in E flat major, 3rd mvt., ed. Hugo Riemann (Leipzig, 1895).

Friedemann's concertos all involve the keyboard, usually with a string orchestra. He continued his father's rather uncommon medium of multiple keyboards in the concerto just quoted from for two claviers and a larger orchestra (with horns and kettle drums), one of his finest works.

Carl Philipp Emanuel Bach (1714–88), the greatest composer of the north, in some ways stood curiously aside from the Berlin Court where he worked so long. (C. H. Graun, not Bach, was Frederick's Kapellmeister.) Bach devoted himself almost exclusively to harpsichord concertos with string accompaniment, a few of them also arranged as concertos for flute, cello, or oboe.[1] They follow the Baroque plan (typically with four or five tuttis) even in works written after Bach retired from Potsdam to Hamburg (1767). Because of this conservative framework, Bach's concertos seem rather more consistent in style than his symphonies, yet on closer examination his concertos also prove to be daring and original. Only by contrast with conventional composers can one fully appreciate the freshness of Bach's approach, for example, in his concertos with slow introductions (see nos. 41 and 43/5 in Alfred Wotquenne's *Thematisches Verzeichnis der Werke von Carl Philipp Emanuel Bach*, Leipzig, 1905). With a restless imagination (more dramatic than that of Haydn but less well controlled), Bach foreshadows the flexibility of Romantic form in his connection of movements without pause, his skilful thematic interrelationships, and his insertion of episodes in different tempi, sometimes relating to an earlier movement with a brief quotation. By contrast, Bach's ritornello forms reflect surprisingly little influence of the newer symphonic distinctions: his solo episodes are usually modulatory and rarely introduce significant new material. In several early concertos he even ignores tonic-dominant tension by placing the second tutti in the subdominant (Wotquenne 23 and 26). As we have seen in the symphonies,[2] Bach's motivic rhythms stem from the driving style of Vivaldi, transmitted to him by his father[3]:

Ex. 226
Allegro assai

In some works,[4] the repetition of small dimension figures even when

[1] See Leon Crickmore, 'C. P. E. Bach's Harpsichord Concertos', *Music and Letters* xxxix (1958), p. 227.
[2] See pp. 386–94.
[3] Cembalo Concerto in A minor, Wq. 26, ed. Wilhelm Altmann (London, 1954).
[4] For example, the Cembalo Concerto in F major Wq 33/II, ed. Fritz Oberdörffer (Kassel, 1952).

combined with affective appoggiaturas and balanced melody, prevents any feeling of Classical breadth. But the tremendous range of his imagination occasionally touches a genuinely Classical style, a broader, more balanced melodic arch. The theme of Wotquenne 171[1] is remarkably advanced for its time (1751):

Ex. 227

The slow movement of the same concerto demonstrates Bach's superb control of melodic line in which the peaks of the phrases form a strong progression:

Ex. 228

Bach is at his best in fiery, sweeping allegro themes, as in his D minor cembalo concerto, Wq. 23 (Potsdam, 1748):[2]

Ex. 229

After such a masterly opening, however, he often fails to sustain the rhythmic drive or the bold stride of the melody. As in the symphonies, this conflicting wealth of ideas tends to detract from any unified impression. His original harmonic treatment suffers similarly: the marvellously free dissonances supply momentary, vivid colour more than structural emphasis. This tendency to view harmony as a chain of incidents rather than as a span of tension reveals the Baroque undercurrents

[1] Cello Concerto in B flat, ed. Paul Klengel (Leipzig, 1931).
[2] Arnold Schering, *Denkmäler deutscher Tonkunst*, xxix/xxx, p. 62; and G. Wertheim (Wiesbaden, 1956).

in his thinking. Bach's richly varied range and texture in keyboard writing affected later composers such as Haydn and Beethoven. True to *Empfindsamkeit*, he preferred extremes, very high and very low ranges, sudden contrasts of thin and full textures or close and distant spacing. This expressiveness at the keyboard strangely did not influence his orchestration, where he showed no particular aptness in either choice or treatment of instruments. At times, however, drawing upon his contrapuntal mastery, he interlaced thematic fragments between soloist and accompaniment with admirable effect.

It is even possible that Emanuel's conservatism resulted in large part from the old-fashioned atmosphere of the Prussian Court, for in 1772, five years after going to Hamburg, he published a set of six concertos (Wq. 43) specifically for the new pianoforte and in a far more modern style, with flutes and horns added to the orchestra and an enlarged dimension:[1]

Ex. 230

Despite stylistic changes, he had lost none of his originality of approach: the entry of the solo in the first movement (Allegro di molto) is andante, a startling idea repeated in the recapitulation; the slow movement is in the tonality of the supertonic; and all three movements are connected. The ageing master thus showed a surprising adaptability to new trends without compromising his individuality.

MINOR NORTH GERMANS

Next to those of C. P. E. Bach the most original keyboard concertos are the few surviving works of Johann Gottfried Müthel (1728–88),[2] a pupil of J. S. Bach. As well as following Philipp Emanuel in expressive features of rhythm, dynamics, and harmony, Müthel also experimented with form freely and episodically, with 'recitative adagio' sections in the Allegro of one concerto. He made effective use of the various keyboard registers, employing techniques such as the crossing of hands, by no means common at that time.

The inability of North German composers to adjust their Baroque background to the Classical ideas affects even such men of the second generation as the famous critic Johann Friedrich Reichardt (1752–1814). He wrote more than a dozen cembalo concertos, a violin concerto, and

[1] Ex. 230 is from the Concerto in D, Wq. 43, no. 2 (Hamburg, 1772).
[2] See Daffner, op. cit., pp. 51–7, and Uldall, op. cit., pp. 95–6.

a double concerto for cembalo and violin. But although thoroughly conversant with the new style, he still used Baroque elements, and in his Op. 1 the poverty of ideas revealed in the extremely similar themes hardly carries out the courtly compliment implied by the title page: 'Six concerts pour le clavecin à l'usage du beau sexe.'

Composers of this younger generation who were born and trained elsewhere could apparently escape the inhibiting northern pattern. Johann Balthasar Tricklir (c. 1745–1813), a famous cellist at Dresden, wrote a number of cello concertos that sound much like the Mannheim school. In the older group it is striking evidence of northern isolation that relatively outstanding men such as Christoph Schaffrath (1709–63), Christian Friedrich Schale (1713–1800), Christoph Nichelmann (1717–62),[1] and Christlieb Siegmund Binder (1723–89) composed long after mid-century in a largely outmoded style.

Owing to the large number of piano concertos in the output of the North German school, historians often credit the establishment of the piano concerto to these composers. Their priority and diligence is indisputable. But the antiquated language and confusion of styles that characterized their works limited their influence: it is significant that the successors of the Grauns, Bendas, and Bachs turned more to Mannheim and Vienna for their models. This choice shows that the earlier North German concerto had pursued an isolated, obsolescent road, far removed from the central evolution of the Classical concerto.

MANNHEIM

One might expect that the nature of Mannheim's prestige, a specifically orchestral fame identified mainly with the symphony, would lessen its contribution to the development of the concerto. Yet this great orchestra was made up of outstanding virtuosos, some of them more important as composers for their instruments than as symphonists. Through their works, many published in Paris or London and others widely circulated in manuscript copies, the Mannheim concerto exerted quite as important an influence as the Mannheim symphony. The gift for inventing characteristic themes that we associate with Johann Stamitz and his followers fitted the requirement of the concerto for contrast between tutti and soloist. Furthermore, the concerto form minimized a typical Mannheim defect, the frequent lack of a complete recapitulation mentioned during the discussion of Mannheim symphonies.[2] Since the concerto form until relatively late in the century continued to depend on Baroque ritornello designs, the uncertainty of Mannheim

[1] See Daffner, op. cit., pp. 47–50, and Uldall, op. cit., p. 76. A cembalo concerto in A, has been ed. C. Bittner (Kassel, n.d.).
[2] See p. 410.

composers in handling recapitulations was less damaging to their concertos than to their symphonies.

The fanfare rhythms and standard syncopations of the Classical concerto have already been mentioned,[1] two mannerisms that Riemann might have traced to Mannheim with more justice than the ubiquitous *Seufzer*, the sigh heard all around Europe. It would be difficult to prove that the concerto clichés first emerged from the Mannheim school, but we should notice the frequent incidence of such ideas in Mannheim concerto themes.

At first the older generation of Mannheim composers adopted the treatment of motives and ritornellos of the flourishing Baroque tradition, as observed in the North German school. Richter, who wrote only a few concertos, never outgrew the older style. But earlier than in the north, most Palatine composers began to broaden the internal dimensions and to differentiate the thematic materials of the concerto.

Johann Stamitz (1717–57) began his career as a violin virtuoso, and although he soon wrote mainly symphonies, he composed concertos for violin, oboe, and flute. The attribution of other Stamitz concertos for harpsichord and clarinet is at present dubious. His Flute Concerto in D major, published by Welcker (London, 1765)[2] eight years after Stamitz's death, in several respects illustrates the first stage of the Mannheim concerto. The tutti opening in octaves and unisons with undifferentiated rhythms belongs to the Vivaldi tradition:

Ex. 231

When the solo enters, Stamitz adds a prefix of two minims before the tutti material, giving the solo an individuality from the start. Later he consistently differentiates the solo personality with idiomatic passage-work such as the rising leaps so effective on a flute. The Oboe Concerto[3] has a more advanced tutti theme and the sweeping lines of the solo entry make an equally strong impression:

---

[1] See p. 438.
[2] Miniature score, ed. Walter Lebermann (London, 1961).
[3] Ed. H. Töttcher (Hamburg, 1957). The Breitkopf Catalogue for 1762 lists its incipit as a violin concerto, the Supplement for 1768, as a flute concerto.

Ex. 232

It is not always easy at first glance to recognize the progressive elements in Stamitz's music, but he stabilizes the repetitive Rococo syncopations by slower harmonic change, foreshadowing Classical emphasis on the tonic at the beginning of large forms.

In slow movements Stamitz moves away from Baroque ritornello forms, and uses designs vaguely related to two-part form: after a central modulation to the dominant he does not necessarily recommence with a transposition of the initial material to the dominant, but may insert a more loosely related episode or development of previous material. This is balanced at the end by bringing back the closing section in the tonic. Stamitz also increased the variety of concerto finales, writing not merely the light 3/8 Italian type, but also 2/4 and 4/4 allegros and tempi di minuetto in 3/4.

Neither Richter nor Holzbauer devoted as much attention to concertos as to symphonies. Franz Xaver Richter (1709–89) wrote a set of six concertos for cembalo and strings printed in London. There are works in manuscript for flute, oboe, and trumpet, with evidence in catalogues of works for horn and cello. Apart from occasional striking harmonic details and imitations, these works reflect mainly Baroque procedures without Stamitz's progressive touch. Ignaz Holzbauer (1711–83) left fewer but more interesting works, including violin and cello concertos, and an unusual double concerto for viola and cello.

In two 'concertanti'[1] Holzbauer experimented with a modification of the concerto scheme: in addition to a 'violino principale' he adds concertato passages for solo viola and cello. It is noteworthy in comparing Mannheim and North Germany that, though born a decade earlier than Georg Benda, Holzbauer retains far fewer traces from the Baroque.

It is no surprise that Anton Filtz, born a decade later than Benda (1730–60), should leave all Baroque procedures behind—perhaps too far behind: Filtz's instinct for formal clarity occasionally leads him into superficiality of texture and phrasing. As a cellist, he left concertos for his own instrument and for flute and oboe (those for violin and cembalo are of doubtful attribution) in which his melodic gift, already noted

[1] Possibly written for Frederick the Great (Berlin, Deutsche Bibl., K.H. 2383 and 2384).

in his symphonies,[1] plays an even more important part in the differentiation of themes between tutti and solo. As we shall see with Mozart, a correlation exists between melodic fluency and success in the concerto form. Filtz occasionally seems somewhat light-minded, but at his best he writes well-balanced, clearly articulated themes, as in this Cello Concerto in B flat:[2]

Ex. 233

Despite his early death, Filtz made an extraordinary contribution to Classicism, particularly in his clear formulation of thematic paragraphs, and the unification of relationships between primary and secondary material without loss of contrast. In the following example from a cello Concerto in F, the secondary theme recalls the triad of the primary theme but continues with more lyrical lines:

Ex. 234

The finale is a rondo and in that respect anticipates the final form of the concerto. Its main theme is so remarkably similar to the first movement that one is tempted to credit Filtz with deliberate unification:

Ex. 235

---

[1] See p. 412–3.
[2] Hans Weber, *Das Violoncellkonzert des 18. und beginnenden 19. Jahrhunderts* (Diss., Tübingen, 1922), p. 63.

It is dangerous to assume that such relationships are intentional, since the common vocabulary produced so many unintentional coincidences,[1] but this one certainly seems significant.

THE LATER MANNHEIMERS

The achievements of Filtz laid a foundation for the second generation of Mannheim composers who evolved a tradition for the concerto that persisted until the end of the century. Christian Cannabich (1731-98) never fully exploited Filtz's advances, but in concertos for violin and flute seems closer to Johann Stamitz, with rhythms in small syncopations and rococo figuration, including the ever-present Cannabich turns mentioned as part of his symphonic style. Perhaps this talent for small dimensions explains his skilled development of motives in concerto episodes. In later works he progressed towards the broader thematic style of the later Mannheim composers, marked by articulations such as the crotchet rest in bar 2 of this Flute Concerto in D:[2]

Ex. 236

In an exceptional triple concerto (flute, oboe, bassoon) with large orchestral accompaniment and fully written-out cadenzas, Cannabich approached the style of the *symphonie concertante*.

C. J. Toeschi (1732-88), long the leader of the Mannheim orchestra, brings an Italian suppleness to his themes that minimizes the squareness of the old-fashioned syncopations, as in this Flute Concerto in F:[3]

Ex. 237

---

[1] See LaRue, 'Significant and Coincidental Resemblances between Classical Themes', *Journal of the American Musicological Society*', xiv (1961), p. 224.

[2] Munich, Bay. Staatsbibl. Mus. 1828.

[3] Ed. Lebermann, *Das Erbe deutscher Musik*, li (1964). See also the expanded role of syncopations in a later Flute Concerto in G major (Paris, Bibl. Nat. D. 10311). This has been edited by Robert Münster (Munich, 1962); in the preface he discusses the difficulties of attribution of other Toeschi concertos.

These small concertos have novel experiments in their finales—insertions of adagio sections as contrasts in 3/4 minuets.

A Mannheim composer, and one of the most significant of the whole period before Beethoven, was Carl Stamitz. Born late enough (1745–1801) to grow up with Classical instead of Baroque sounds in his ears, he was a virtuoso and an original and competent composer. He acquired experience of many styles during a long career of performance throughout Europe. He applied his melodic talent to themes suited to Classical forms, i.e. of large dimension and contrasting character, and developed the dialogue theme, contrasting a forceful opening with an answering cantabile of Italianate grace, as in this F major bassoon concerto:[1]

Ex. 238

He favours the second-beat syncopation and the slurred-quaver appoggiatura figures so much that they become regrettably stereotyped in his style. The great success of Carl's concertos in publication and the influence of his tours may be to blame for the plague of this cliché in all concertos at this time. Although he usually finds some new melodic twist for each work, his melodic style—particularly in opening themes—is remarkably consistent. The regrettable sameness of many of the Mannheim concertos was due as much to an exaggerated enthusiasm for the new, articulated style as to lack of invention. The enormous production of these composers and the pressure of their daily requirements rarely permitted the experimentation that Beethoven and later composers brought to the process of composition.

Carl Stamitz was certainly one of the most competent and industrious of these hundreds of composers and his impact on the composition of concertos resulted both from the enormous number he wrote and the variety of solo instruments. He wrote solo concertos for cembalo, violin, viola, viola d'amore, cello, flute, oboe, clarinet, bassoon, and horn; double concertos for clarinet and bassoon, oboe and bassoon, violin and viola, and two violins; in the new form of the *symphonie concertante* he wrote works chiefly with two violins and also a triple concerto for violin, viola, and cello. Stamitz's writing for solo instruments goes beyond mere display; he shares in at least a minor degree Mozart's gift for using material that shows an instrument to best advantage. We see in Stamitz's works the same clarity in forms as in his primary themes: principal sections are clearly marked by orchestral or textural changes. The

[1] Ed. J. Wojciechowski (Hamburg, 1956).

solo exposition, which generally has new material, is more often followed by a new episode than by a genuine development—a feature distinguishing the concerto from the symphony of the time. His closing themes are highly characteristic and the return to the tonic is often treated in typical Mannheim fashion by not coinciding with a return of the initial material, which may return at the end or not at all.

In slow movements, usually in the subdominant, Stamitz simply expands the earlier two-part form by organizing the second part more tightly, usually restating and developing primary material in the dominant and other keys, returning to the tonic with the secondary and closing material. Stamitz's cantabile produces many beautiful moments in slow movements, as in that of a B flat clarinet concerto:[1]

Ex. 239

His preference in rondo finales for clear articulations sometimes unduly emphasizes the squareness of the form, but this is relieved by the rhythmic verve inherited from his father.

Anton, the younger Stamitz brother (1754–1809), produced a few good concertos for violin and viola in a style less thematically stereotyped than Carl's. Though his phrasing is equally articulated, on occasion he sustains an astonishingly broad melodic span.[2]

Ex. 240

The relatively few concertos (bassoon, flute, oboe, clarinet, cembalo) of Ernst Eichner (1740–77), who was a bassoonist, are by reason of their mastery of form and characteristic woodwind writing among the best that Mannheim produced. The cembalo concertos do not make brilliant use of the keyboard, but the themes are (as in the C major, Op. 6)[3] precocious in balance and articulation:

[1] Ed. J. Michaels (Hamburg, 1958).
[2] Second movement of Flute Concerto in D, ed. Lebermann, op. cit.
[3] Dresden, Sächs. Landesbibl. Mus. 3428/0/3.

Ex. 241

The second Mannheim generation includes a number of composers who, as virtuosos in the orchestra, wrote negligible symphonies but worthy and often strikingly idiomatic concertos. Johann B. Wendling (c. 1720–97), an outstanding flautist mentioned favourably by Mozart, composed attractive flute concertos; Ludwig A. Lebrun (1752–90), an oboe virtuoso, wrote for both flute and oboe. More important was Ignaz Fränzl (1726–1811), at least seven of whose violin concertos were published by Götz at Mannheim and Bailleux in Paris. The Mannheim procedures fitted concerto better than symphonic style, which had run its course; and the proportion of concertos rises in comparison with symphonies in the later productions of the school.

The chamber music of the cellist Franz Danzi (1763–1826) has received considerable attention to the neglect of his excellent concertos (flute, clarinet, bassoon, cello, cembalo). His large-scale *Symphonie concertante no. 1* maintains a three-movement concerto form, showing comparatively little influence of the lighter French two-movement genre. Peter Ritter (1763–1846), also a cellist, wrote concertos particularly for cello, but also for piano and woodwind, as well as double concertos for horn and cello and two violins. His style is attractive thematically and clear in form.

The history of the Mannheim concerto includes a famous figure who does not merit special attention as a symphonist, Abbé Georg Joseph Vogler (1749–1814). We owe the original idea of a Mannheim School not to Hugo Riemann but to Vogler, who wrote a monograph on *Die Churpfälzische Tonschule* (Mannheim, 1778), following it with three volumes of *Betrachtungen der Mannheimer Tonschule* (Mannheim, 1778–81). Despite his vivid imagination and the penetration of his critical writings, Vogler taught others more successfully than himself; his three sets of six keyboard concertos[1] make extensive use of bass octaves and expressive dynamics. The harmony, more than the dull thematic material, reflects Vogler's inquiring mind in its remote modulations and expressive chords.

A large group of Mannheim pupils and imitators worked in other

---

[1] 6 *Clavier Concerte con stromenti*, 6 *Concerti facili di Cembalo*, 6 *leichte Clavier-Concerte*.

parts of Europe. Joseph Reicha (1746–95), cellist at the Oettingen–Wallerstein Court, wrote cello concertos and *symphonies concertantes* for two violins. The concertos of the brilliant Paris pianist Johann Schobert (1720–67) reflect Mannheim melodic style. Father Joseph Schmitt (1734–91)[1] in a piano concerto and one for two flutes reminds us of the elder Stamitz. Friedrich Schwindl (1737–86) wrote flute concertos that could easily be taken for Mannheim works. Most important was Franz Anton Rösler (*c*. 1750–92) already discussed as independent in his symphonic style.[2] In concertos he reminds us of Carl Stamitz. Apart from a great variety of solo concertos, his double concertos for two horns bring a fresh sound into the concerto literature, expert technically and attractive musically. Perhaps because he wrote fewer concertos than Stamitz, Rösler does not fall into such obvious stereotypes of theme and form, though he was far from immune to the slurred-quaver appoggiaturas and the second-beat syncopation. His themes are often bolder than the typical Mannheim product, but he can also charm us, as in this D major flute concerto,[3] with a cantabile that resembles Mozart:

Ex. 242

This opening of an E flat horn concerto,[4] with its skilfully extended phrase at bar 9, shows the mature techniques of Classicism:

Ex. 243

[1] Albert Dunning, *Joseph Schmitt* (Amsterdam, 1962), includes a thematic index.
[2] See p. 432.
[3] Hummel (Amsterdam, n.d.).
[4] Ed. Oskar Kaul, *Denkmäler der Tonkunst in Bayern*, xxv (1925).

Rösler adoption of the Mannheim style for his concertos is evidence of its attractive power, for in the symphony he followed the lead of Vienna, a minor corroboration of Vienna's pre-eminent position in the symphonic evolution.

Apart from the achievements of Mozart, the Mannheim School made the most significant contribution to the evolution of the concerto, and we owe particularly to Carl Stamitz the crystallization of a thematic language and form that solved the long conflict in the concerto between the Baroque and the Classical styles.

THE CONCERTO IN AUSTRIA

To understand the development of the Viennese concerto we must remember the situation in the Viennese symphony, which very early emphasized full recapitulation as a balance to the dominant tension generated by the modulation in the exposition. Since the themes recurred in the symphonic recapitulation, it soon became evident that something else should be done with them in the development section, which therefore became highly organized in Viennese compositions. This admirable preoccupation with large dimensions caused Vienna to lag behind Mannheim in creating significant themes and clear melodic sentences. This affected the symphony less than the concerto, which may succeed without highly organized development or full recapitulation but not without contrast of memorable themes between tutti and solo.

A second influence on the background of the Viennese concerto was the emphasis on church composition in an antiquated imitative style. The clarity of articulation and balanced demarcation of formal elements essential to Classical style were obscured by imitative complications in the musical fabric, and the Viennese concerto was only slowly converted from the Baroque to the Classical point of view.

Although the chronology of the Viennese concerto still requires much clarification, Georg Monn (1717–50) was probably the first to write concertos with Classical elements. In his small but well-constructed concertos (for cembalo, violin, cello) the Classical balance in miniature can be seen despite the old-fashioned patterns. The repetition of tiny motives sometimes produces completely frustrated themes (i), whereas in better works, a clear direction in line is present (ii):[1]

Ex. 244

[1] Themes of cembalo concertos, quoted from the index by Wilhelm Fischer in *Denkmäler der Tonkunst in Österreich*, xix (2) (1912).

Allegro

(ii) [musical notation]

The ritornello influence in Monn's form is strong; clear recapitulations are rare. Quite unusual is his Concerto for Cembalo in four movements, a form recalling his oft-cited early four-movement symphony.[1] Monn's harmonic inventiveness is seen in a Cembalo Concerto in E flat major which at one point passes through the minor keys of C sharp, F sharp, and B.[2] His Cello Concerto in G minor[3] makes advanced use of the solo instrument, particularly in the low range, considering its early date—1746. In the opening tutti we find an astonishing sample of Monn's expressive chromatic harmony.

Ex. 245

Allegro

[musical notation]

Many of Monn's concertos have only a three-part orchestral tutti, two violins and bass, omitting the viola (if available, violas would simply have played the bass). This combination, which is not exclusively characteristic of Vienna, may be a survival of the Baroque trio-sonata texture found in many concerti grossi and, since many full-scale concertos employed it, does not indicate an informal divertimento character. But as in the late Baroque there is often an independent viola line, the trio accompaniment may most likely be explained by the fact that concertos were often played as chamber music.

The three-part tutti is characteristic also of Georg Wagenseil (1715-77), one of the most prolific of Viennese concerto composers (about sixty for cembalo, others for two cembalos, violin, bassoon, trombone). These are mostly exceedingly dull works[4] and although the themes show slightly more breadth than those of Monn, Wagenseil subjects many a rhythmic motive to insensitive repetition, and he often falls into a superficial, *galant* style, with aimless triplets as its hall-mark. Accompaniments often consist of reiterated left-hand chords, frequently repeated thirds without any rhythmic differentiation. Wagenseil's emphasis,

---

[1] See pp. 395-7.
[2] See the example in Hans Engel, *Das Instrumentalkonzert* (Leipzig, 1932), p. 161.
[3] Ed. Fischer, op. cit.; first movement recorded in *The History of Music in Sound*, vii.
[4] But see Daffner, op. cit., pp. 87-90, and Uldall, op. cit., pp. 86-7, on the cembalo concertos.

however, on a genuine keyboard style is important as a foundation for later, more talented men. His use of broken-chord figures, scales, dashing arpeggios, and broken octaves is added to many trills and turns, and comfortable pianistically idiomatic figures occur in primary thematic material. In works with violinistic themes, when the solo piano enters the essential elements of the original line are translated into effective keyboard figures. More important is that instinct for balanced form noticed in his symphonies.[1] He understood the importance in the concerto of a clear recapitulation, and a development section related to the exposition. The balance between the movements is not so successful and his small minuet finales hardly bear comparison with the stronger Mannheim concerto finales of this period.

Wagenseil may claim priority in one respect: at Kroměříž there is a manuscript of a small trombone concerto in two movements attributed somewhat confusingly to 'Wagenseil und Reiter'. This may be a unique pasticcio, for collaboration in concerto sources is exceedingly rare.[2] The solo lies mainly in the octave above middle C.

Johann Georg Albrechtsberger (1736–1809), Kapellmeister at St. Stephen's cathedral and briefly a teacher of Beethoven, falls into the second generation chronologically but possibly owing to his interest in theory and church music his thematic treatment often recalls Baroque procedures. In an Organ Concerto in B flat[3] as late as 1762 the repetition of the opening theme is typically Baroque though offset by recommencing on the half bar. Such attention to small detail and his detailed dynamics emphasize the expressiveness of individual bars and distract us from the larger aspects of form. But in compensation, Albrechtsberger's forms are particularly clear and his cadenzas in this concerto refer to previous thematic material, a rather rare occurrence in the eighteenth century. The broad melody and balanced phrases of the slow movement are quite the opposite of the first movement:

Ex. 246

---

[1] See pp. 398–9.
[2] So far neither Wagenseil nor Reiter has been established as the true composer. 'Reiter' may be incorrect spelling for 'Reutter', the Imperial *Opernkapellmeister* in Vienna.
[3] Ed. László Somfai (Budapest, 1963).

Among his several works for brass, a trombone concerto of 1769[1] still has small syncopations and dotted motives, but the lively finale approaches mature Classicism in its phrases:

Ex. 247

Albrechtsberger also left a concertino for chromatic solo trumpet, violin, viola, bass, and cembalo[2] which, though backward-looking in thematic style and texture, antedates Haydn's trumpet concerto by almost a quarter-century: the source is dated 1771.

In Vienna, as in Mannheim, the second generation contributed most to the development of the concerto. Leopold Hoffmann (1738–93) wrote more than thirty cembalo concertos, works for two cembalos, violin, cello, and flute, and experimented with intermediate forms such as concertanti for two cembalos, and a variety of other concertinos. (Most of these are preserved in the archiepiscopal archives at Kroměříž, possibly the finest collection of eighteenth-century keyboard works.) Some have four movements, not unlike the Monn concerto mentioned above, but because of their smaller size are related more to the divertimento tradition. Though Hoffmann's melodies are often more lyrical than Wagenseil's, the stiff style of the earlier Viennese generation is found particularly in opening movements. Stereotyped rhythms and syncopations are relieved by alternation with legato material (i), or placing of small motives in a broad melodic line (ii):[3]

Ex. 248

[1] Ed. Gábor Darvas (Budapest, 1966).

[2] Originally in the Esterházy collection, this concerto is now in the National Library in Budapest. See Mary Rasmussen, 'A Concerto for Chromatic Trumpet by Johann Georg Albrechtsberger', *Brass Quarterly*, v (1962), p. 104.

[3] Cembalo concertos in A and F major (Dresden, Sächs. Landesbibl., Mus. 3301/0/4 and Mus. 3301/0/5).

THE CONCERTO IN AUSTRIA

Like Wagenseil, Hoffmann developed themes with pianistic elements such as broken octaves and five-finger swirls. Though less original than Monn in harmonic treatment, he experiments with unusual key schemes between movements: one of the C major cembalo concertos has a slow movement in A flat major.

Carl Ditters von Dittersdorf (1739–99) wrote in a more advanced style, possibly owing to his broader contact through travel with varied aspects of the Classical evolution. Though he composed fewer concertos than symphonies, he wrote for a wide variety of instruments—violin, viola, double bass, flute, oboe, oboe d'amore, and cembalo. In an early flute concerto (dated 1760 in Regensburg) the Italian Baroque style still persists, but although some other works show the small-dimension thinking we associate with Monn and Wagenseil, Dittersdorf avoids these Baroque effects by a sharper sense of direction in his line:[1]

Ex. 249

Many passages suffer from the rigid extension of ideas by unrelieved sequences, spoiling an idea that initially had some charm. In others, however, there is a well-balanced melodic and rhythmic curve, as in the second movement of a Violin Concerto in C:[2]

Ex. 250

In later works, such as a *symphonie concertante* with large solo group (two horns, two oboes, bassoon) dated 1795, Dittersdorf develops a broader thematic phrase, though still depending too often on sequences. In mature works the solo has new themes, including transition, secondary, and closing material, which make excellent differentiation between solo and tutti. Recapitulation, therefore, may involve as many as six themes and Dittersdorf, in the Viennese tradition of complete recapitulation, met this challenge better than Mannheim composers. In such

---

[1] (i) Viola Concerto, F major, ed. Lebermann (Mainz, 1966); (ii) Oboe Concerto, G major, ed. G. Rhau (Wiesbaden, 1948).
[2] Ed. Lebermann (Mainz, 1961).

works as a cembalo concerto published by Hummel (Amsterdam, 1772) in which all thematic elements are clear to the end, there is a confluence of the thematic differentiation of Mannheim with the Viennese instinct for recapitulation, a juncture of forces that Mozart carried to perfection.

Even more than Dittersdorf, Johann Vaňhal (1739–1813) assimilates the Mannheim melodic style: first the small syncopations and other unimaginative rhythms and later the full Mannheim influence with the familiar slurring and second-beat syncopations. Apart from a few concertos for flute and bassoon, Vaňhal wrote mostly keyboard concertos, often designated 'pianoforte o organo', though never specifically idiomatic for organ. He obtains some characteristic Bohemian colour by occasional use of folk-like melodies, especially in finales. Vaňhal's themes are unusually clear, as in a late piano concerto published in *Storace's Collection of Original Harpsichord Music*, Vol. I (Birchall and Andrews, London, 1788), in which the primary theme reminds one of Mannheim:

Ex. 251

The secondary and closing sections contrast clearly both with the primary section and with each other:

Ex. 252

Later the solo adds a new secondary theme, differentiated by its dotted rhythm and imitation. The slow movement illustrates Vaňhal's melodic simplicity:

Ex. 253

Despite their apparent naïvety, such melodies often reveal balanced curves and careful rhythmic control.

Next to Mozart, the most advanced Viennese concerto composer was a man almost forgotten today, Josef Anton Steffan (Štěfán) (1726–97), a pupil of Wagenseil. Steffan was not neglected by his contemporaries, for his concertos are listed in the Breitkopf Catalogue supplements from as early as 1763 until 1774. He wrote about forty concertos[1] for keyboard and at least one for two cembalos. In some manuscripts Steffan specifies 'per il Fortepiano' or 'per il clavicembalo d'espressione', and he treats the piano with sensitivity to its sonorities and dynamic capabilities. The rhythms and finger swirls of his early concertos sound like Wagenseil (with whom there are confusions of attribution) and Hoffmann, over whose concertos these early works make a few advances. There are attractive moments in slow movements but Wagenseil's superficial 3/8 finales and the thin three-part accompaniment noted particularly in the Viennese tradition are continued.

In eight large-scale and presumably late works, however, Steffan breaks with the Wagenseil–Hoffmann tradition, suddenly discovering a strikingly personal style. These concertos all have slow introductions made up of expressive dialogues between the solo piano and orchestra, in which the syncopations, pauses, impulsive rhythms, and sudden dynamic changes foreshadow Romantic devices. In these introductions, Steffan's power is similar to that of C. P. E. Bach, and he anticipates the early Romantic concerto in his concentration on consistent growth of tension. The D minor of the introduction is an unusual key relationship to the B flat major of the following Allegro. This high level of invention is not maintained, for Steffan's flashes of inspiration do not make a pattern of consistent strength. Discursive episodes impede his forms and his first movements are usually better than the others. He is at his best in

[1] Largely surviving in Kroměříž, Archiepiscopal Library (e.g. one in D, *Musica Antiqua Bohemica*, xxxix), with a few works each in Budapest, Vienna, Prague, and Brussels. See the preface to Steffan's piano works, ed. Dana Šetková, *Musica Antiqua Bohemica*, lxiv (Prague, 1963).

cadenzas, and here, where his imaginativeness might have free play, he surprisingly establishes clear links with the main thematic material.

Among the numerous concertos of Michael Haydn (1737–1806)—for violin, viola, viola and cembalo, flute, trumpet, one and two horns, cembalo, and organ—there are outstanding movements and many satisfactory works. The decrescendo of interest found in many Viennese concertos when, after the imaginative first movement, the concerto degenerates through a desultory slow movement to a pale finale is not found in his works. Michael's concerto slow movements occasionally surpass those of his symphonies in quality. In the Violin Concerto in B flat of 1760[1] a noble Adagio co-ordinates line and rhythmic tension in typically Classical manner:

Ex. 254

Where Michael uses 3/8 finales he often expands the form into an extended rondo by means of additional episodes. One flute concerto has a forceful finale in common time;[2] and the Violin Concerto in B flat ends with a long, sturdy Allegro molto that bears no resemblance to the minuet tradition.

HAYDN AND THE CONCERTO

The many-sided genius of Joseph Haydn (1732–1809) did not reach fullest expression in his considerable variety of concertos.[3] These excel most concertos of his contemporaries, but with the exception of the Trumpet Concerto they fall below the quality of his own symphonies and quartets. Several explanations may be advanced to account for this curious and disappointing situation. In the first place, most of the concertos are early works; secondly, as they are fewer than symphonies and quartets Haydn had less opportunity to mature his concerto technique; thirdly, he did not excel as a player on any instrument. Probably the

[1] Ed. P. Angerer (Vienna, 1960).
[2] Ed. H. C. Robbins Landon (Salzburg, 1959).
[3] For violin, cello, double bass, oboe, flute, keyed trumpet, horn, cembalo, organ—and a large *symphonie concertante*—some unfortunately known only through entries in catalogues.

main reason lies in the fundamental incompatibility between Haydn's approach to music and the requirements of the concerto, in which duality rather than unity is the point of departure. The contrast of complete and characteristic themes between tutti and solo runs counter to Haydn's concept of form as an evolving unity in which themes unfold from a possibly undistinguished musical germ as in the monothematic expositions in his symphonies.

Haydn's early concertos are generally in the three-movement style initiated by Wagenseil. Though he uses the pallid triplets and dotted rhythms so common about 1760, he already shows marked originality in phrase structure, and rarely permits undistinguished material to lead to undistinguished phrasing. All too often Wagenseil would double the dullness of a musical platitude by repeating it. The indispensable Classical principle of repetition, essential in stabilizing tonality and making themes memorable, could become a two-edged sword. Haydn's inimitable flexibility in phrasing rescues much otherwise neutral and even dull material, as in an Organ Concerto in C major[1] which opens with a five-bar phrase.

Haydn's music is best understood not as a construction of themes but rather as a creation of momentum by finely adjusted relationships in motive, phrase, section, and even between main parts, exposition versus development and recapitulation. One instinctively feels a rhythmic unity in some pieces even taken as a whole. The proportions emerge naturally from the various parts; a shorter section may easily balance longer sections because of its intensity in line, dynamics, modulations, textural complication, or orchestral virtuosity. Thematic style and development in Haydn depend on the rhythmic substructure, and even in early works the irregular phrasing results from the evolutionary aspect of his music. In a Concertino in C for cembalo (1760)[2] Haydn expands the first subphrase (1½ bars) to two bars by repeating motive m, a procedure that most other composers would use only after establishing a thematic entity:

Ex. 255

The concertino opens with a full sonata-form movement. The concertinos of Steffan and Hoffmann, by contrast, often use a simple two-part form with double bars and repeats like any dance form.

[1] Ed. Max Schneider (Wiesbaden, 1953).
[2] Hoboken, op. cit. XIV: 11; ed. Landon (Vienna, 1959).

One of the best of the early concertos is the Cello Concerto in C major.[1] It shows another procedure typical of Haydn—the insertion of a small secondary idea, *x*, between repetitions of a larger element, to prevent squareness in the repetition:

Ex. 256

The slow movement opens with a three-bar phrase, ending with a turn on a cadence. Haydn immediately develops the turn figure to form a four-bar phrase:

Ex. 257

The finale of this concerto is important historically, since it departs from the innocuous 3/8 tradition and has an Allegro molto in full concerto first-movement form.

Among Haydn's small, early horn concertos, the first in D major[2] opens with a long, ascending triad and the theme continues with a typically irregular phrase pattern. Strangely, Haydn makes fewer demands on the horn in these concertos than in the concertato parts of some of the symphonies (no. 31, for example). The naïve charm of the D major cembalo concerto[3] furnishes a musical oasis among the 'average' piano concertos of the last quarter of the century. Despite the folk-like material, the motion is enhanced by small flexibilities. At the beginning the first phrase is extended to six bars and a motive from this theme is transferred to the bass in the development—a type of unification rare in concertos. The theme of the rondo finale is enlivened by repeating bars 3–4 as an echo in the bass.

[1] Hoboken VII b: 1; ed. Oldřich Pulkert (Prague, 1962).
[2] Ed. H. H. Steves (London, 1949).
[3] Miniature score, ed. Kurt Soldan (London, 1949).

During the 1930s the authenticity of Haydn's Cello Concerto in D major fell under a cloud though Tovey found nothing in his analysis committing him 'to uphold this charming concerto as a great work'.[1] Certainly, one can hardly maintain that this concerto belongs with the greatest of Haydn's music. The charm of the opening theme with its gentle slurs and graceful chromatics make it sound more like Mozart or Carl Stamitz:

Ex. 258

This theme is interesting because of the similarity of motive *x* to the opening of the slow movement.

Ex. 259

It is dangerous to assume intentional relationships merely on the basis of melodic resemblance, because of the numerous stock phrases of the time. But here, when motive *x* occurs twice in the closing bars of the first movement and then opens the second movement, the connection cannot be dismissed as a coincidence.

The autograph of the *Symphonie concertante* in B flat major (oboe, bassoon, violin, cello) shows unusually frantic haste, even considering that Haydn's notation is typically hasty and abbreviated. No existing editions have fully solved the inconsistencies of this autograph, which have led editors to various unsatisfactory solutions of its problems,[2] but it is evident that this relatively late work (1792) is not up to the normal standard of the symphonies of the same period. The unity essential to Haydn's concepts was more fragmented in a concerto for

[1] Donald Tovey, *Essays in Musical Analysis*, iii (London, 1936), p. ix. For a summary of the bibliographical history, see Leopold Nowak, 'Das Autograph von Joseph Haydns Cello-Konzert in D-dur, op. 101', *Österreichisches Musikzeitschrift*, ix (1954), p. 274, and the review by Frederick Sternfeld, *Music and Letters*, xliv (1963), p. 85, of the score based on the autograph, ed. Nowak, *Veröffentlichungen der Österreichischen Nationalbibliothek* Neue Folge, Dritte Reihe (Vienna, 1962).

[2] The only good text is that of the miniature score, ed. Christa Landon (London, 1969).

four soloists than in a solo concerto. In an attempt at unity between solo and tutti, Haydn brings the soloists into the closing section of the orchestral tutti. But the result is ambiguous, particularly as the soloists play instruments already in the orchestra. (Mozart omits clarinets from the orchestration of his clarinet concerto.)

Haydn's last concerto, that of 1796 for keyed trumpet,[1] may be his best. This attractive small work does not depend on its rare solo instrument for its success: it combines piquant themes with tidy forms to create a well-balanced whole. The repeated notes so common in Haydn's style fit the trumpet well, but the vein of lyricism brings out unsuspected cantabile. The chromatic compass of Anton Weidinger's extraordinary keyed trumpet led not only to expressive chromaticism but to unusual modulations contrasting colour and mood (particularly the effect of C flat major in the A flat slow movement, bars 22–26). The conflicts between Haydn's unifying instincts and the duality of the concerto medium disappear because of the strong personality of the solo instrument, and already in the first entry (bar 37) Haydn embeds the solo in a fabric of orchestral echoes, without losing its identity.

In the generation slightly younger than Haydn, the Austrians combined the best of Mannheim and Vienna in a mature style. (Mozart, of course, furnishes the high point of this development.)[2] Among the more prominent composers associated with Vienna are: Anton Kraft (1752–1820), cellist in the Esterházy orchestra, whose cello concertos are good enough to create serious confusion with those of Haydn; Anton Zimmermann (1741–81), Kapellmeister at Bratislava (Pressburg), who composed concertos for flute and cembalo; Wenzel (Václav) Pichl (1741–1804), active in Milan, who wrote violin concertos; the publisher Franz Anton Hoffmeister (1754–1812), who began in Vienna and moved to Leipzig, writing numberless flute concertos and excellent works for other woodwind; Joseph Fiala (1748–1816), cellist in many princely orchestras, and who wrote for his own instrument; Leopold Koželuh (1738–1814),[3] like Hoffmeister a composer-publisher, who wrote his best concertos for the piano.[4]

In the evolution of the concerto, unlike that of the symphony, the function of the Viennese school was contributory rather than dominant —the early Viennese composers understood the necessary compromises between the Baroque inheritances of the concerto and the Classical formal requirements, but failed to discover a thematic style that matched this formal control until relatively late in the century. The final style,

[1] Miniature score, ed. Hans Redlich (London, c. 1955).
[2] See p. 487.
[3] Milan Poštolka, *Leopold Koželuh* (Prague, 1964) contains a thematic index.
[4] On the work of the later Viennese concerto-composers, see Vol. VIII.

therefore, owed much to Mannheim, especially in thematic formation and differentiation. By a curious stroke of history, the Mannheim style lost its impetus when the Electoral Court moved to Munich in 1778. Thus it remained for Vienna to take the contributions of Mannheim and capitalize them in the final form of the Classical concerto.

PARIS AND THE CONCERTO

For the concerto just as for the symphony, Paris acted as a point of special magnetism. All travelling virtuosos hoped for an invitation from the Concert Spirituel, and composers felt a sense of arrival when their works appeared in Paris editions. The noble amateurs of central Europe augmented their music libraries and copied new concertos and symphonies during yearly trips to Paris. Despite the great production of Paris publishers, copyists existed here and in Hamburg, Leipzig, Vienna, and Venice until after 1800. There are fewer concertos than symphonies in publishers' catalogues and fewer still surviving, but this may be explained by the more constant use and wearing out of concerto parts by travelling virtuosos.

The popularity of concertos from Mannheim at mid-century may explain in part the seeming lack of native compositions. Gossec and other Parisians were apparently too occupied with symphonies and other projects to write concertos. As a result the French concerto springs rather suddenly and late into its Classical phase. French composers of Haydn's generation began without the encumbrance of a strong tradition and their early works are comparatively free from Baroque influences. Pierre Gaviniès (1727–1800) continued the tradition of Leclair in his brilliant exploitation of the violin, but his concertos show Classical phrasing and clear articulation of form up to the recapitulation, where, like many Mannheim composers, he does not always make a pointed return to events of the exposition. His trilled scales and sonorous double-stops are more notable than his thematic material. To extend his rather thin invention, Gaviniès introduces much figuration and repetition which, particularly in slow movements, furnishes opportunities for improvised embellishment, and he himself intersperses many grace notes in his melodic lines.

THE *SYMPHONIE CONCERTANTE*

The next decade brought two important developments peculiar, at least in their degree, to France: the rise of the *symphonie concertante*[1] and

[1] According to Barry Brook, *La Symphonie française dans la seconde moitié du XVIIIe siècle* (Paris, 1962), i p. 69, the first actual *symphonies concertantes* were probably Louis-Gabriel Guillemain's *Simphonies d'un goût nouveau, en forme de Concerto ... Op. XVI* (1752), the music of which has been lost. See also Brook, 'Symphonie concertante', *Die Musik in Geschichte und Gegenwart*, xii, col. 1902.

the growing significance of the amateur composer. The popularity of concerted symphonies, which were usually concertos for multiple soloists rather than symphonies with solo interjections, probably rests on the long tradition of the concerto grosso, stimulated by the new Classical proportions and the Parisian partiality for grand effects. The introduction of two or more soloists in the Classical concerto form posed more serious problems than the solo concerto: characteristic thematic variants must be provided for each soloist and the longer piece resulting from this complexity tested the composer's capacity to sustain interest and strained the listener's attention. Furthermore, enlargement endangered the balance with the finale which, taking simpler forms, did not enlarge correspondingly. The new *symphonie concertante* solved these problems by frequently having only two movements: an allegro first movement in concerto–sonata form with orchestral introduction, followed by a rondeau, usually allegretto, of lighter character and smaller size. Some of the lyricism of the missing slow movement could be transferred to contrasting themes in the first movement or cantabile episodes in the rondo. The problem of balance became nearly irrelevant, for in the two-movement sequence there is no implication of symmetry between balancing parts. The rondeau of the *symphonie concertante* has more the function of an *envoi*. The simplifications and instrumental brilliance of the *symphonie concertante* won immediate success, persisting into the nineteenth century. Some French composers turned to it almost exclusively (Cambini, for example) and throughout Europe there is scarcely a concerto composer of significance who did not try his hand at the form. The Mannheim school also contributed to it and the French repertory penetrated deep into the continent: we find editions and manuscripts of *symphonies concertantes* by Davaux and Bréval in Budapest, Bratislava, Prague, and Warsaw.

The second important development concerned the musical amateur, whose significance in the eighteenth century has long been recognized, but perhaps more as a performer than as a producer. Among the most significant of these was the violin virtuoso Chevalier de Saint-Georges (1739–99). He adopted the Mannheim style but deserves credit for his well-balanced phrases and compelling musical flow, exemplified in his D major concerto, Op. 3, no. 1 (Paris, 1774).

Ex. 260
Allegro maestoso

The clear articulation of themes extends to sections as well, but in place of a true development Saint-Georges often has new material. His demands on the violin are more modest than Leclair's, but he uses the total compass skilfully with effective contrast of pitch. In addition to concertos, he also wrote a number of *symphonies concertantes*. Concertos of Marie-Alexandre Guénin (1744–1835) dating from about the same period strongly resemble those of Saint-Georges in form, thematic style, and violin technique. One of the most original amateurs was Jean-Baptiste Davaux (1742–1822). His solo parts require less technique than some of his contemporaries, but he excels in clearly defined thematic style, strongly influenced by the Mannheim school. Davaux gives more care to his accompaniments than most amateurs, and printed sources of his works contain detailed phrasing and dynamics. He is more advanced than Saint-Georges, particularly in developments where expositional material is used rather than mere figurations or episodes.

Simon Le Duc 'l'Aîné' (*c.* 1745–77) left three violin concertos and at least one *Symphonie concertante* (Paris, 1775) for two violins, the favourite combination of the French school. For a time leader of the Concert Spirituel, Le Duc reflects his orchestral experience in fuller, more idiomatic accompaniments. Remembering the power of his E flat symphony,[1] one is disappointed in the rather pedestrian ideas in his violin concertos though the solo writing is masterly. The *Symphonie concertante* is unusual with its three-movement form, and the main theme, though simple, offers relief from the concerto clichés and provides characteristic rhythms for later reference:

Ex. 261

Not all the French composers were violinists, of course. Jean-Baptiste Bréval (1753–1823), an outstanding cellist, wrote concertos for his own instrument (in deference to prevailing taste and practice, the title-pages employ the phrase 'pour violon ou violoncelle'). They belong to the best of the French school. Unlike most of his contemporaries, he differentiates the solo by adding new themes both in primary and secondary sections. His modulations are more interesting, as in the C major Cello Concerto (no. 6, Op. 26), where he touches both E flat major and D minor in the development. In two concertos he uses the popular operatic *romance* as the basis for slow movements, maintaining the

[1] See pp. 423–4.

characteristic phrasing like a slow gavotte that Haydn used in the slow movement of Symphony no. 85. Bréval's lines reveal a more-than-average gift of melody, as in this Cello Concerto no. 3 in F major, Op. 20:

Ex. 262
Romance
[musical notation]

Wind concertos occur rarely in the French repertory, but some excellent flute concertos and *symphonies concertantes* were written by François Devienne (1759–1803). His personality shows in spite of his use of the Mannheim thematic vocabulary. Phrases have now expanded to a spacious four-bar dimension, the ascending rhythmic drive of the opening balancing the descending legato response:

Ex. 263
Allegro
[musical notation]

These eight bars from his Flute Concerto no. 3 contain a wealth of motives for later development and rigidity of phrasing is avoided by the two phrases ending on different beats.

One of the most prolific of Parisian composers was Giovanni Giuseppe Cambini (1746–1825), who wrote *symphonies concertantes* for two violins as well as for other combinations of wind and string. He also wrote a few solo concertos for violin and flute, the latter being replaceable by oboe or bassoon after the fashion of the period. The graceful chromatic touches of his line we now call 'Mozartean', though Mozart did not invent them. The lack of variety in Cambini's rhythm, as in his *Symphonie concertante* in F (Paris, 1782), contrasts with the subtlety of Devienne's phrasing:

Ex. 264
Allegro
[musical notation]

Several composers in the Low Countries wrote concertos. Unlike the central Parisian tradition, these included a higher proportion of keyboard concertos by composers such as Josse Boutmy (1697–1779), and Pieter Van den Bosch (1763–1803). H. J. de Croes (1705–86) wrote excellent concertos for flute and violin which, like the works of Boutmy, are more Baroque than Classical.

In the last decades of the eighteenth century the French concerto became almost completely international. The two-movement *symphonie concertante* became less popular and there was renewed interest in solo concertos and three-movement *concertante* symphonies. The elements which distinguished the French violin school from the cantabile style were now relegated to exercise books and tutors. Typical of those who now absorbed techniques from all of Europe is Ignaz Pleyel (1757–1831) whose concertos combine Mannheim style with Viennese solidity in development and recapitulation derived from his early studies with Haydn. Pleyel also goes beyond the French tradition in the variety of his concertos and his emphasis on solo works, though he also wrote a number of *symphonies concertantes* for various combinations of strings and wind. Among the secondary masters of the late eighteenth century Pleyel is one of the best.[1] Like Devienne he avoids rigidity at phrase ends, and is skilful in the handling of a flowing line. Pleyel's brilliant success, both musical and commercial, in the most sophisticated capital of Europe did not entirely obliterate his memories of simpler things. A charming *Bauerntanz* in a late concerto published by André demonstrates how broad the assimilations of the French concerto had become.

THE CONCERTO IN ENGLAND

The cosmopolitanism of English life and its hospitality to foreign artists were nowhere more evident than in the eighteenth-century concerto. Foreigners dominated the composition of concertos even more than of symphonies. The lack of native activity in large musical forms is mainly explained by the boundless devotion to the works of Handel, which diminished the search for new styles. English concertos simply continued in Handelian types and remained essentially Baroque when continental composers were evolving the language of Classicism.[2] The English symphony was beneficially influenced by the native dramatic overtures, but the concerto had no influence independent of the Handelian tradition. However, the demand for new works as well must explain the success and emigration to England of so many continental musicians. Haydn's

[1] His work is examined more extensively in Vol. VIII.
[2] See Vol. VI.

invitations to London were part of an established pattern. The concertos of these foreign musicians rarely show any English characteristics.

The virtuosity of Carl Friedrich Abel (1723–87) on the gamba must have inspired his concertos, for they are far more spontaneous than his symphonies. After his early flute concertos which follow the conservative North German pattern, in a set of six piano concertos, Op. 11 (London, 1774), he turned to the Mannheim style, adding significant touches of individuality. Incipit (i) (Op. 11, no. 1, in F) shows the usual syncopations and slurred quavers, relieved by a smooth phrase ending; the first two bars of incipit (ii) (Op. 11, no. 5, in G) could easily have been written by Cannabich, but the chromaticism in the following bars carries Abel's stamp:

Ex. 265

The *symphonie concertante* influenced these small, two-movement concertos, several of which have a *tempo di minuetto* as the second movement. Abel's cello concertos are larger, three-movement works of sharper individuality as we see in the following virile theme from one in C major[1] which uses ordinary but less stereotyped material:

Ex. 266

The unusual refinement of line noticed in Abel's symphonies, particularly in slow movements, is evident in concertos also. In another work for cello, in B flat,[2] Abel achieves melodic continuity in the Adagio by returning with varied rhythm to an upper E flat with the same leap of a fourth with which he began:

Ex. 267

[1] Berlin, Deutsche Bibl. K.H. 20.
[2] Ed. W. Knape (Cuxhaven, c. 1960).

His best work is a *symphonie concertante* (violin, cello, oboe) in three movements—surprising, in view of Abel's two-movement forms in the piano concertos. Here he adapts sonata form to the needs of the multiple concerto, and his intimate knowledge of instrumental possibilities results in unusually effective passages for the three soloists. Johann André published the work long after Abel's death, a significant tribute to its enduring quality.

JOHANN CHRISTIAN BACH

The concertos of Johann Christian Bach (1735–82) stand with the best that the eighteenth century produced. His facile but not superficial melodic invention, a special advantage to a concerto composer, underlies his success in varied ways. A wealth of thematic ideas facilitates not only differentiation of solo and tutti, but, in a multiple concerto, variants that individualize the soloists' parts. He also differentiates the sections of the exposition by themes of special character. Primary themes are usually triadic, with the familiar syncopations improved by careful rhythmic phrasing instead of dull repetition; transitions are sequential, stressing rhythm more than melody; secondary themes are cantabile for contrast; closing themes elaborate cadence patterns and end with active rhythms. Although these characteristics could be found here and there in works of Bach's more perceptive contemporaries, few understood the importance of consistent identification of formal functions with appropriate themes. His thematic style is less advanced in the five early works[1] where small-dimension ideas show the influence of his Berlin background, though he wrote more interesting rhythms than most of the North Germans, for example in no. 2 in F minor:[2]

Ex. 268

[1] On these, see particularly Heinrich Peter Schökel, *Johann Christian Bach und die Instrumentalmusik seiner Zeit* (Wolfenbüttel, 1926), pp. 27–37.
[2] Ed. E. Martini (Kassel, 1953).

The two concertos published at Riga in 1770 and 1772 were probably written as early as 1754–55; the influence of Carl Philipp Emanuel still affects them strongly in the impulsive leaps and relatively undifferentiated rhythmic style.[1] Bach reached a personal style only with his Op. 1, six concertos published by Welcker (London, 1767). He reduced the orchestral accompaniment from four strings to the two violins and bass found so commonly at this time, retaining this combination for the next six concertos (Op. 7, 1770), and returning to a 'normal' eighteenth-century orchestra only in the last group of six concertos (Op. 13, 1777). A number of the works in Opp. 1 and 7 have only two movements, Allegro and minuet, possibly influenced by the *symphonie concertante*, like Abel's Op. 11.

Though Bach emphasized keyboard concertos, he wrote also for flute, oboe, and violin. Among his maturest works are a half-dozen *symphonies concertantes* for various combinations of strings and wind. The most impressive is for flute, oboe, violin, and cello.[2] Bach contrasts annunciatory triadic material in the tutti with more lyric themes for the solo instrument, which present them with variants appropriate to their characteristics:

Ex. 269

In many concertos Bach has an admirably flexible relationship between tutti and solo, conceiving their participation as interchange as much as contrast, undoubtedly influencing Mozart in this respect. A good example is the use of flutes and horns accompanying the soloists in the *symphonie concertante* in E flat for two violins.[3]

[1] No. 1 in E flat, ed. Ernst Praetorius (London, *c.* 1937); no. 2 in A, ed. Li Stadelmann (Mainz, 1935), first movement recorded in *The History of Music in Sound*, vii.
[2] Miniature score, ed. R. Maunder (London, 1961).
[3] Miniature score, ed. Fritz Stein (London, *c.* 1936).

Bach's textures appear simple, but his gift for melody enables him to insert figurations and momentary imitations, much like Mozart's lively enrichments of inner parts. Perhaps Bach's most significant accomplishment is his co-ordination of musical elements as a means of expression, a skill in which he influenced Mozart. In the slow movement of the Cembalo Concerto, Op. 7, no. 5,[1] the line moves from an upper G to E flat a tenth below. Its apparent simplicity conceals a subtle construction: note the peaks in bars 6, 8, 9, which carry the phrase forward. The co-ordination of increasing rhythmic activity with this long-drawn phrasing creates momentum, which culminates in the semiquavers of bar 9 and the final triplets:

Ex. 270

With co-ordination of this sort Bach ushers in the culminating phase of the Classical concerto in the works of Mozart.

OTHER FOREIGNERS IN LONDON

Two other Germans resident in England wrote significant concertos. Johann Christian Fischer (1733–1800), the outstanding oboist, published nine lively oboe concertos. His treatment of concerto form is interesting; though he adds new transitional, secondary, and closing themes in the solo exposition, usually only the closing themes return in the recapitulation, which concentrates on tutti material. In his eighth concerto, like J. C. Bach in the finale of his Op. 13, no. 4, he introduces a British tune—in this case 'Lango Lee'. The rondo finale of the first concerto provided the theme of Mozart's piano variations, K. 179.

Johann Samuel Schroeter (1750–88) wrote a number of carefully constructed concertos, mostly about 1775, drawing on Mannheim precedents, particularly in skilful balancing of subphrases whose incisive motives are used in development passages, as in the Piano Concerto, Op. 3, no. 4, in D (London, 1774):

[1] Published by Welcker (London, *c.* 1775); ed. Christian Döbereiner (Leipzig, 1927).

Ex. 271

Allegro

Mozart thought highly enough of these concertos to write four cadenzas for Op. 3 (K. 626a); 'Schrötter' concertos are mentioned in letters of 3 and 20 July 1778.[1]

London musical establishments included not only Germans but also many Italian virtuosos and composers. Luigi Borghi (c. 1745–after 1792), a pupil of Pugnani, attained a considerable reputation in England from about 1772 to 1792. Six of his nine violin concertos (Op. 2, Paris, c. 1775; Op. 3, Berlin, c. 1775) were listed in the supplement to the Breitkopf Catalogue for 1776, and a cello concerto dated 1788 makes brilliant use of the solo instrument in a more expansive form than the smaller, less technically demanding violin concertos.

Tommaso Giordani (c. 1730–1806), an opera composer active in London and Dublin between about 1770 and 1785, published a dozen concertos for flute and at least fifteen for 'pianoforte or harpsichord'. (Placing the piano first is not necessarily significant, but it is worth notice that German and English publishers place it first at an earlier date than the French.) Like many works composed in England, Giordani's concertos are smaller in scale than most continental ones, but have mature forms with balanced phrases and thematic contrast. Occasionally Giordani produces melodies of outstanding quality, scarcely surprising in a successful opera composer.

NATIVE BRITISH COMPOSERS

English production of concertos appears to have been slender indeed. 'The favourite Concerto' for piano by George Rush (*fl.* 1770) found a place in Hummel's catalogue for 1768, a rare distinction for an English work, except for those of the *émigrés*—Hummel published many works of Abel, J. C. Bach, and Schroeter. Like Giordani, Rush was principally concerned with dramatic music to the benefit of his slow movements.

The concertos of James Hook (1746–1827) are disappointing. The best English concertos came from the Oxford professor Philip Hayes (1738–92), who published in 1769 six competent keyboard concertos not entirely free from the Baroque flavour found in so many English concertos.

One notable feature of the English concerto, already mentioned, was

---

[1] *Mozart. Briefe und Aufzeichnungen*, ed. Wilhelm A. Bauer and Otto E. Deutsch, ii (Kassel, 1962), pp. 390, 410. See also *Die Musik in Geschichte und Gegenwart*, xii, col. 88–90.

the use of popular tunes as thematic material. Not only Fischer but also François Barthélemon (1741–1808) used 'Lango Lee' in finales. The Irishman Philip Cogan's Op. 5 (Edinburgh, 1793) makes use of the 'Favourite Air of Malbrouk'; Charles Wesley brought 'Rule, Britannia' into a finale; John Peter Salomon, Haydn's friend and London impresario, based a rondo on 'Hillisberg's favourite Pas Seul'.

MOZART

The incomparable achievement of Mozart was the culmination of the development of the Classical concerto. Except geographically, he cannot be grouped with any one school, even the Viennese, since he absorbed influences from many directions, in each case carrying a received procedure far beyond its earlier state, realizing new potentialities on a higher plane. In his concertos he derived precedents from three main sources: formal unity from Vienna, thematic sophistication from Mannheim, and rhythmic continuity from Italy; the direct model of J. C. Bach, however, probably affected Mozart more significantly in melody and form than any generalized influence. Both as a co-ordinator of the essential trends of Classicism and as an originator of its culminating refinements. Mozart stands alone. Except for opera, there is no form in which Mozart stands forth so supremely as in the concerto. Haydn, though he was Mozart's revered equal in the symphony, quartet, and sonata, failed to reach the same level in the concerto. The dual supremacy of Mozart in opera and concerto is no mere coincidence, for the two media can be related in various respects. The presentation of an instrument against the orchestra has analogies with that of a singer against a similar background. A subtle balance of contrast and co-operation is as necessary in the aria as in the more complex concerto. Many of the large separate arias, which stretch over a decade (1778–88, K. 294 to K. 538) parallel to his greatest concerto activity, show a concerto-like complexity of thematic style and effective leaps to demonstrate an impressive range, a device equally frequent in concertos. The influence of aria on concerto most affects slow movements, which often use a cantilena that approximates to a wordless aria (the slow movement of K. 467 is a good example). The dramatic presentation of the soloist's episodes is obviously due to the composer's operatic experience, and the sense of timing with which Mozart matches music to stage action surely accounts for the inevitability in the unfolding of his concertos. Analogies such as that between concertos with several soloists and ensemble finales in operas illuminate his control of contrast and co-ordination. A conception of the relationship of tutti and solo as going beyond the mere opposition of two instrumental forces is the key to Mozart's accomplishment. His mastery of this concept may be viewed in several different aspects:

1. *Form.* The orchestral tutti is larger with clear primary, transitional, secondary, and closing sections. Modulation, except in passing, is reserved for the solo exposition. The break between orchestral introduction and solo entry is bridged by various means. The solo exposition elaborates orchestral themes and adds new ones at any point, but mainly in the secondary section, often in the minor mode. In contrast to Baroque practice, primary material rarely returns either in the central tutti or in the development section. The development usually modulates to remote tonalities, using comparatively unimportant and sometimes unrelated material. Mozart's open structure in place of 'true' development is a natural and necessary contrast to the intensely organized exposition and the recapitulation. In the latter, Mozart brings back all essential elements of the exposition, changing the order and assigning orchestral themes to the solo and vice versa. His closing sections show a special finesse: when an opening tutti includes two or more closing themes, one will disappear at the end of the solo exposition, returning at the recapitulation. Mozart's cadenzas, unlike most of those by his contemporaries, are almost always related thematically to the movement but stress modulation and passagework rather than thematic exploration as in Beethoven's cadenzas. His slow movements include two-part and A–B–A forms, sonata form, rondo, and variation. In finales, he expands and tightens the conventional rondo form by various combinations with sonata form, which supplies greater tonal direction and thematic unity.

2. *Thematic style.* March rhythms and syncopations appear constantly in Mozart's concertos but are overshadowed by more interesting adjacent material. In fast movements the thematic dimension has increased to basic four-bar units, but interspersed with much irregular phrasing. Ambivalent bars that serve both as the end of one phrase and the beginning of the next often lend an apparent regularity to both phrases (see Ex. 272). Although Mozart's concerto themes conform less to a norm than do his symphony and sonata themes, probably because contrast of solo and orchestra outweighs the principle of contrasting sections, the following observations hold good for most concertos: primary themes are triadic with a responding phrase; secondary themes stress legato phrases, often with chromaticism and appoggiaturas; closing themes have first a loud cadence, then a pause, followed by a lighter orchestration of a second cadential pattern before the final chords.

3. *Orchestration.* Beginning with the piano concertos of the Viennese period, Mozart expands the orchestral devices of interchange with the solo in a manner closer to chamber music than to symphony. The tradi-

tional solo and tutti oppositions and accompaniments are revitalized particularly by the use of woodwind. Mozart fully exploited the technical capacities of solo instruments, but with few passages intended for sheer effect. He made comparatively few genuine additions to technique; the piano concertos contain far fewer experiments than those of C. P. E. Bach.

4. *Technical mastery.* Mozart's effortless technical command enhances all the procedures mentioned above. His textures are constantly interesting owing to imaginative part-writing with many brief but exquisitely dovetailed imitations. Harmonic tension is built up by using a richer vocabulary of chords and tonalities. Most significant is his coordination of musical elements by harmonic or rhythmic emphasis of the distinctive features of a melodic line.

Most eighteenth-century composers specialized in works for their own instrument with perhaps a few lesser works for other instruments, e.g. Tartini and Viotti, but comparatively few rivalled Mozart in his great variety. Complete concertos survive for flute, oboe, bassoon, horn, violin, and piano, with multiple concertos for violin and viola, a *sinfonia concertante* for four wind instruments, and double and triple concertos for piano. Though Mozart specialized in piano concertos, his works for other instruments influenced the whole later literature of the concerto, so that it is painful to hear of the lost and incomplete works. In a letter of Leopold Mozart dated 12 November 1768 we learn that 'Wolfgangl' had written a trumpet concerto for the consecration ceremonies of the Rennweg Orphanage in Vienna. There is also a lost bassoon concerto (K. 196d, not fully authenticated). The incomplete works for horn, such as the Rondo, K. 371, and probably unrelated concerto movements, K. 412/514, are fortunately balanced by three fine concertos that have survived complete. The only Mozart cello concerto (F major, K. 206a, possibly only a fragment) was once part of Charles Malherbe's famous collection of autographs, but disappeared before the manuscripts reached the Paris Conservatoire after his death in 1911. Surviving fragments are more tantalizing than complete losses: there are 120 bars of a concerto for violin and piano (K. 315f) intended for an 'académie des amateurs' in Mannheim. The fragment equals in quality the best works of this period, which include another splendid torso, 134 bars (not all completely scored) of a triple concerto for violin, viola, and cello, K. 320e. These lost and fragmentary works show us that Mozart's accomplishments and intentions were even more richly varied than we might suspect from the complete sources.

The condition of these more-or-less complete sources, however, is at times peculiar and inconsistent. None of the violin or wind concertos was published during Mozart's lifetime, and their survival is due to the purchase of the autographs from his widow Constanze by the publisher André, who later issued the first publications. Some of these autographs, however, have subsequently disappeared, leaving us entirely dependent on André. Before the Second World War the autographs of all twenty-three concertos for piano, except the first (K. 175), had survived, and seven of these concertos were published during Mozart's lifetime. Owing to the irregularity of his professional life, he composed almost entirely for commissions. Fragments such as the concerto for violin and piano were abandoned when circumstances no longer required the piece. Since most concertos were connected with specific occasions, their authenticity may be supported by our rich documentation of Mozart's external circumstances. The existence of the *Sinfonia concertante*, K. 297b, for flute, oboe, horn, and bassoon, composed in Paris for four Mannheim virtuosos is mentioned frequently in Mozart's letters (notably 5 April 1778). Since the autograph has not survived, the non-correspondence of these circumstances with a manuscript of a *sinfonia concertante* discovered in the late nineteenth century by Otto Jahn raises doubts as to authenticity. In this obviously garbled work the upper winds are oboe and clarinet instead of flute and oboe. Since this alteration is mentioned nowhere in Mozart's correspondence and there are also stylistic doubts, the authenticity of the wind *concertante* remains in dispute.[1]

MOZART'S CONCERTOS WITH VIOLIN

The following brief discussion of individual concertos makes no attempt at completeness;[2] rather, the aim is to illustrate the principles of Mozart's concertos as a whole. The violin concertos are not only early works, giving us an insight into the beginnings of Mozart's concerto style, but no less than five were written within nine months (April to December 1775) for the Salzburg leader Brunetti, showing Mozart's rapid mastery of the form. The first three concertos (B flat, K. 207; D, K. 211; G, K. 216) are on a small scale thematically, compared to the remaining two, but in the manipulation of the solo, orchestration, and balanced recapitulation they are advanced for 1775. In the D major concerto, K. 218, the themes have broader phrases and contrasting elements, while the sinuous cantabile of the adult composer has arrived with the love of surprise found mainly at this period, here seen in the

[1] Friedrich Blume has made a survey of concerto sources in *The Mozart Companion*, ed. Landon and Donald Mitchell (London, 1956), pp. 200–33.
[2] Cuthbert M. Girdlestone, *Mozart and his Piano Concertos* (London, 1948; first published in French, Paris, 1939), is the most extensive study in English. Girdlestone discusses relevant parallels in other works of Mozart.

sudden forte of bar 180. The A major concerto, K. 219, is marked by a strikingly fresh way of introducing the solo. After the orchestral exposition, the solo enters with an apparently unrelated adagio melody; after only six bars, however, it resumes the original tempo with a new phrase, also elaborating the triad in addition to the orchestral theme, a return of the idea that opened the concerto. This highly original treatment of concerto relationships finds no precedent in earlier composers. The finales of the early violin concertos are less mature than such a first movement. They recall the small scale of the divertimento and the minuet finales of Wagenseil and J. C. Bach.[1]

The *Sinfonia concertante* in E flat major for violin and viola, K. 364, is in three movements rather than the two of the French style, and is more serious in character. The march rhythm of the first subject shows Mozart's absorption and ennoblement of convention in contrast to Haydn's avoidance of clichés. (In the orchestral exposition a 'Mannheim crescendo' is used as a final climax more impressively than as a Stamitz-style opening.) The answering quavers and rests, learned from Italy via J. C. Bach and Abel, pass immediately into the bass, a sample of Mozart's distribution of thematic responsibility throughout his textures. The entry of the soloists is a stroke of genius: their sustained high note over the final cadence of the orchestral exposition descends to their gentle initial phrases, avoiding the heavy articulation so usual at this point. The personalities of the solo instruments, despite their use of similar material, are individualized often by the simplest means. At the opening of the slow movement, the viola repeats the melody but in modulating from minor to relative major makes a fresh impression. The remarkable sense of continuity in all three movements emerges in part from ambiguities in phrase connection. At points of articulation, Mozart frequently arranges two consecutive strong bars to increase momentum. Near the beginning, after symmetrical two-bar phrases, the grouping (3 + 2 + 3) produces this effect:

Ex. 272

[1] Two later violin concertos (K. 268 and K. 271i) pose problems of authenticity though most scholars feel the latter has the stronger claim. The authenticity of K. Anh. 294a is in even greater dispute.

The descent of the violas through an entire octave in the last bars of this example enhances the continuity.

MOZART'S WIND CONCERTOS

The wind concertos belong to Mozart's earliest period of concerto writing. The Bassoon Concerto in B flat, K. 191 (1774), a small work in three movements with minuet finale, lacks true Mozartean individuality of thematic style. It commands attention for its transparent accompaniments that permit the bassoon to penetrate the orchestral background. The unfortunate textures that must often have resulted from the concertos of other composers 'for flute, oboe, or bassoon' are unthinkable in Mozart. The Oboe Concerto in C major, K. 271k, survives only in a set of parts. It apparently formed the basis for the later Flute Concerto, K. 314, in which Mozart fundamentally reworked the solo part with resultant changes for the accompaniment. The commission to write three simple flute concertos and some flute quartets for the Dutch amateur De Jean was troublesome, and Mozart completed only one new concerto, K. 313 in G major. In this work he returned to the proportions and much of the style of the early violin concertos. The Concerto for Flute and Harp, K. 299, commissioned by the Duc de Guines, was more stimulating, possibly because both the duke and his daughter were superlative players. Though Mozart apparently disliked the mild character of both flute and harp, the concerto is superbly idiomatic, with one or two passages that challenge even a modern harpist, and unusual low notes for the flute. If the material seems a trifle bland, the profusion of themes (which characterizes many of Mozart's early concertos) prevents our tiring of any single idea.

The three horn concertos, all in E flat (K. 417, 447, 495), belong to Mozart's great period in Vienna, and were written for Ignaz Leutgeb, a Salzburg horn player who came to Vienna. Despite their lighthearted tone and almost miniature dimensions, the thematic style and formal construction are mature and they give an impression of control and economy quite different from early works of similar size. Mozart's full maturity affected only one wind concerto, the beautiful Clarinet Concerto, K. 622, composed shortly before his death.[1] The unforgettable impression made by this concerto rests on the pathos in all three movements, partly in melodies, partly in use of related minor keys, and also in chromatic alterations, with emphasis on the diminished seventh. The part-writing equals the late piano concertos in the skilful intertwining of orchestra with solo. Harmonic refinements are matched by textural subtleties as in the first movement, where the clarinet is accompanied by first violins only (bar 86), but shortly serves as bass to violins doubled an octave higher by flutes. The expressive atmosphere of the concerto can be illustrated by a passage near the end of the slow movement. The upper line remains the same as in its first appearance (i), but for the return (ii) Mozart recasts the texture, greatly enriching the harmonies. The descent of the bass to B flat, producing a minor subdominant chord, concentrates in one progression the mood of autumnal resignation characteristic of this great work:

Ex. 273
bars 30–33
Adagio
(i)

bars 80–83
(ii)

[1] Originally for a special instrument owned by Anton Stadler, with compass extended by a lower third: see George Dazeley, 'The Original Text of Mozart's Clarinet Concerto', *Music Review*, ix (1948), p. 166; Jiří Kratochvíl, 'Betrachtungen über die Urfassung des Konzerts für Klarinette und des Quintetts für Klarinette und Streicher von W. A. Mozart', *Bericht: Internationale Konferenz über das Leben und Werk W. A. Mozarts* (Prague, 1956), p. 262; Ernst Hess, 'Die ursprüngliche Gestalt des Klarinettenkonzertes KV622', *Mozart-Jahrbuch 1967* (Salzburg, 1968), p. 18.

MOZART'S PIANO CONCERTOS

In numerous ways the piano concertos stand apart from the rest of Mozart's output of concertos. Writing most often for himself, and for an instrument that not only contrasts better with the orchestra but also most nearly maintains a balance in volume (if we use a properly modest eighteenth-century instrumentation), Mozart exploited these advantages to reach many pinnacles of composition. Although his very first and next-to-last concertos are for piano, the concentration of works in his Viennese period (all after K. 413, i.e. seventeen of the twenty-three) makes these concertos important as a group. For proper appreciation the pre-Vienna concertos need to be considered against the prevailing standard of piano concertos (J. C. Bach, for example) rather than against Mozart's own later works.[1] In this milder light, the first original concerto, D major, K. 175 (1773) appears as a work of considerable distinction, relatively large in size, clear in form, brilliant for the solo, and rich in thematic ideas. It is notable for large orchestration (trumpets and drums in addition to the usual oboes and horns) and for the use in the finale of an opening fugato (which relaxes into freer writing) rather than the minuet finale so common at the time. The next three concertos (B flat, K. 238; F major for three pianos, K. 242; C major, K. 246), two years later, found Mozart in his *galant* period, attempting to graft a facile salon style over his sound early training.[2] None of these works equals the earlier D major in flow of ideas or originality of form, for there is more repetition of phrasing, emphasized articulation, ornamentation, and written-out elaborations.

In the following year Mozart passed out of his *galant* phase, and the E flat concerto, K. 271 (1777), written for the outstanding French pianist Mlle Jeunehomme, shows astonishing originality and power. The work opens with a witty thrust and parry of motives between orchestra and piano; equally original is the next entry of the solo, a right-hand trill over the closing theme of the orchestra. This overlapping of solo and tutti represents Mozarts's attempt to soften the break at the end of the orchestral exposition, going beyond the idea of an adagio insertion (A

---

[1] See Edwin J. Simon, 'Sonata into Concerto. A study of Mozart's first seven concertos', *Acta Musicologica*, xxxi (1959), p. 170. Mozart's early arrangements of sonatas by other composers as piano concertos (K. 107, 37, 39, 40, 41) show that even as a child he viewed the concerto as a broadly balanced form (the Classical view) rather than merely as a series of solo episodes between modulating ritornelli (the Baroque view). The three of K. 107 have been ed. Heinrich Wollheim (Mainz, 1931); the other four are in the *Gesamtausgabe der Werke Mozarts*, ed. Brahms *et al.* (Leipzig, 1876–1905), series 16, nos. 1–4. These four concertos have also been edited and arranged for two pianos by Artur Balsam (London, 1966) with an introduction by A. Hyatt King.

[2] A copy of K. 246 at St. Peter's, Salzburg, has Mozart's autograph realization of the Keyboard continuo part in the tuttis of the first two movements.

major violin concerto) and forming a close precedent for the passage in the *Sinfonia concertante* mentioned above. Mozart emphasizes long-range relationships as in the recapitulation where the repartee of the opening is reversed: humorously, the piano now leads off. More significantly, a device mentioned above (p. 488) and used in a number of late concertos, is employed in the closing section. The orchestral introduction had two closing themes, in the solo exposition we hear only the first, but in the recapitulation both themes return—emphasizing a long-range symmetry. The C minor slow movement reaches great expressive depths. A close canon between the violins is answered with a phrase astounding for its details of harmony:

Ex. 274

Here the F sharps and A flats (bar 9) clash not only against the sustained Gs but also against the F natural of the trill. Its finale, a mixture of rondo and sonata form, has a short minuet as part of the development. This represents a later stage of the experiments Mozart had made in finales of earlier concertos, although the presto tempo and sonata-rondo design anticipate his mature style, in which he rarely risked loss of continuity by extraneous episodes.

Although there is less formal experimentation in the Concerto for Two Pianos, K. 365 (1779) than in K. 271, Mozart shows great resourcefulness in the kaleidoscopic exchanges between the two solo pianos. The three concertos that mark the beginning of Mozart's years in Vienna (F major, K. 413; A major K. 414; C major, K. 415), autumn and winter 1782–3, actually regress somewhat in size and originality as compared with K. 271 and K. 365. Though lacking in thematic distinction, they have smooth control in form, elegant use of the solo, and skilful orchestration. Mozart may have used these works to test the Viennese reaction to his concertos, hesitating to go too far beyond accepted patterns, yet meanwhile perfecting various technical aspects. This conflict can be seen in the finale of K. 413, old-fashioned in its use of *tempo di minuetto*, yet one of the most individual pieces of part-writing that Mozart had produced up to this time.

Mozart's personal thematic catalogue (*Verzeichnis aller meiner Werke*)[1] begins with the Piano Concerto in E flat, K. 449 (1784), written for Barbara von Ployer. It initiates a period of astounding productivity during which piano concertos formed the core of Mozart's development, and in the production of twelve significant works in less than three years, the quality of his work being already high, he extended his horizons in a fascinating range of compositions. K. 449 stands slightly outside the group by reason of slighter technical demands and smaller size and instrumentation. The first movement is unusually active harmonically and has a modulation to the dominant for the secondary section of the orchestral exposition where Mozart almost always maintains the tonic. The finale begins like a fugal exercise, but soon becomes a non-stop rondo. The next two concertos (B flat major, K. 450; D major, K. 451) Mozart wrote for his own concert appearances, adding bassoons and a single flute (finale only) to oboes and horns in K. 450, and trumpets and drums in K. 451. Mozart himself comments on the brilliance of the solo parts as 'to make the player sweat' (letter of 26 May 1784). The solo exposition only begins after the soloist has freely elaborated the tonic chord for twelve bars, ending with a trill and fermata: another new device to bridge any harsh gap at this point. A striking feature of this concerto is the use of wind instruments, not only in orchestral sections but in characteristic Mozartean interchange with the piano, especially in the last movement. The D major concerto, K. 451, illustrates Mozart's exploitation and improvement of a convention. The opening theme contains the march-rhythm cliché, the usual answering quavers, and then a typical rising Mannheim crescendo. After the climax (bar 10) a lesser

---

[1] Facsimile edition, ed. Deutsch (Vienna, 1938); ordinary edition, ed. Erich Müller von Asow (Vienna, 1943).

composer might have continued with a more active semiquaver figure; Mozart has a new rhythmic figure ♩ 𝄾♫ 𝄾♩ imitated in the lower parts. The long and complex exposition has well-contrasted sections. As a foil to this emphasis on thematic ideas, the development stresses modulation through long stretches of uninterrupted passage-work, a typically Mozartean approach for which Hermann Abert invented the useful term 'fantasia development'.

Just three weeks later Mozart completed the G major concerto, K. 453, also for Barbara von Ployer. The sunny mood of this work is outstanding. The musical explanation of its atmosphere of peace and relaxation is in the slow-moving harmony of the themes and transitions, with frequent pedal points and other long values in the bass. In the finale Mozart forms a theme from a starling's song he had noted down. He adds three other phrases and treats it in four variations and a long presto coda.

Later in the same year (1784) Mozart wrote K. 456 in B flat and K. 459 in F major. The B flat concerto, although smaller and less significant than the works surrounding it, includes several unusual features. The slow movement is a fine set of variations in the relative minor, a rare form for the piano concertos, and the finale has a highly original episode in B minor. The F major concerto, K. 459, written for himself, is more characteristic and combines the pomp of the D major, K. 451, with the expansiveness of the G major. It is striking for the unity of the first movement in which the conventional march rhythm ♩ ♫♩ ♩ pervades the exposition and development with unusual persistence. The sonata–rondo finale utilizes the basic contrast between chordal and contrapuntal textures to clarify the form, with first a harmonic theme, then a fugato, then other more vertical textures.

With the D minor concerto, K. 466 (1785), Mozart reaches an entirely new realm of expression. Secondary composers rarely sustain their momentary inspirations in the minor mode, but in the D minor concerto Mozart introduces and maintains intensity and mystery, recalling the D minor quartet, K. 421, and anticipating the finale of *Don Giovanni*. The opening hints at the rhythmic and dynamic power of the full tutti (including trumpets) at bar 16. The secret of this powerful passage is the exact opposite of a Mannheim crescendo, and typifies Mozart's search throughout the work for expanded means of expression. Despite the rising parts and quickening rhythmic figures, Mozart permits no crescendo, thus building suspense to give the sudden tutti additional impact. The slow movement in B flat has a passionate episode in G minor, and then, like the major mode conclusion of the D minor finale, the return of the peaceful B flat theme heightens in retrospect our perception of the dark passages that have gone before.

The C major concerto, K. 467 (1785), somewhat resembles in its majestic mood the D major, K. 451. Few of the mature concertos are as rich in thematic material. After the orchestral exposition the solo adds new elements and parts of the primary theme are brought back in transitional and closing sections. The depth of expression heard in the D minor concerto does not entirely disappear, for the piano enters with a secondary subject in G minor, including a thrice-repeated quaver motive (the same that opens the G minor symphony). For the entry of the solo Mozart has found a better way to avoid the break after the orchestral introduction. Where in the B flat concerto, K. 450, he preluded on the tonic, emphasizing a chord which creates an effect of inappropriate stability, in K. 467 the soloist has flourishes on the dominant, maintaining harmonic tension so that the tonic resolution carries the motion forward.

In the winter season 1785-6 Mozart wrote two concertos that again change the pattern of evolution. The E flat concerto, K. 482, is smooth and expert, but less personal and more conventional thematically than other works of this period. The first movement lacks the tight planning of the preceding concertos, with looser development, though interesting modulations. The strongest movement is the C minor Andante, a leisurely rondo, unusual for slow movements. The orchestra includes clarinets for the first time in the piano concertos. The A major concerto, K. 488, is smaller in size and instrumentation. The smooth lyricism of the primary theme of the first movement results not from conjunct motion alone but from a typically Mozartean co-ordination of elements: the stable harmony, the slow harmonic rhythm over a pedal point which counteracts the melodic leaps, and the rhythmic curve of the phrase:

Ex. 275

The slow movement, in the rare key of F sharp minor, illustrates Mozart's mastery of chromatic effects. As in the Clarinet Concerto, he reharmonizes phrases with secondary diminished sevenths that change a conventional harmonic bass to a highly expressive motion in semitones. The finale moves with the incomparable *élan* that one comes to expect of Mozart's third movements, and as in all concertos of the Viennese period, maintains a balance of quality with the preceding movements, a problem rarely solved by lesser composers.

In all three movements of the concerto in C minor, K. 491 (1786), but most obviously in the finale, the woodwind share significant aspects of the thematic material and vie constantly with the solo in textures that approach the intricacy of Mozart's chamber music. The first movement deserves special attention in that almost all the material relates to the opening twelve-bar theme:

Ex. 276

Significant aspects of this theme are submitted to fragmentation and recombination. Mozart isolates the descending motive of bar 5, the semitone motive of bars 3–4 and the rhythmic pattern of bars 5–6 for special attention:

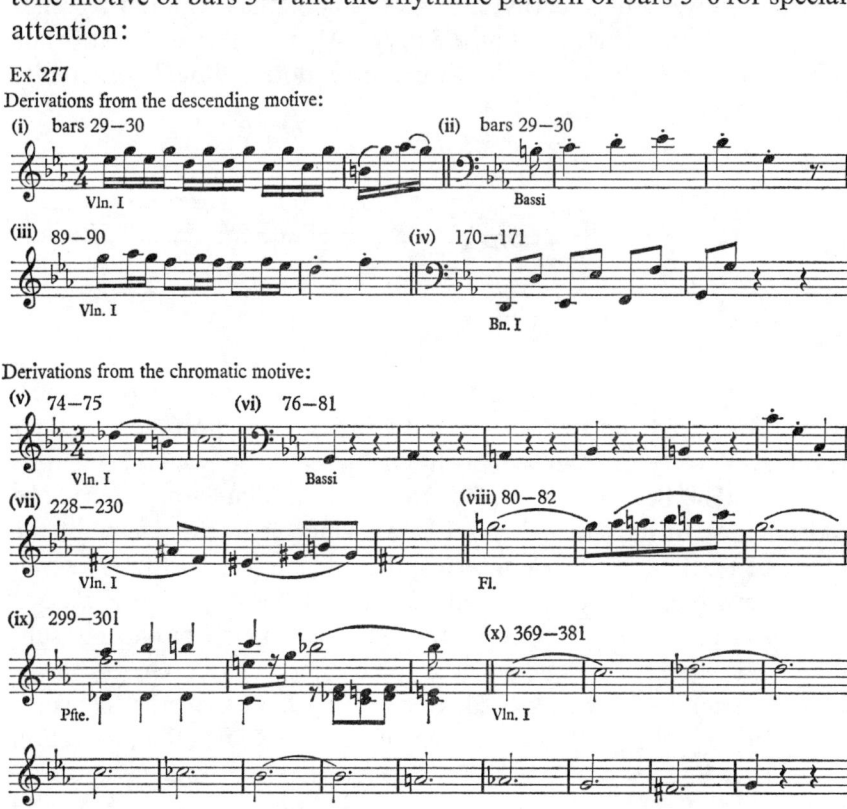

Ex. 277
Derivations from the descending motive:
(i) bars 29–30
(ii) bars 29–30
(iii) 89–90
(iv) 170–171

Derivations from the chromatic motive:
(v) 74–75
(vi) 76–81
(vii) 228–230
(viii) 80–82
(ix) 299–301
(x) 369–381

Derivations from the rhythmic motive:

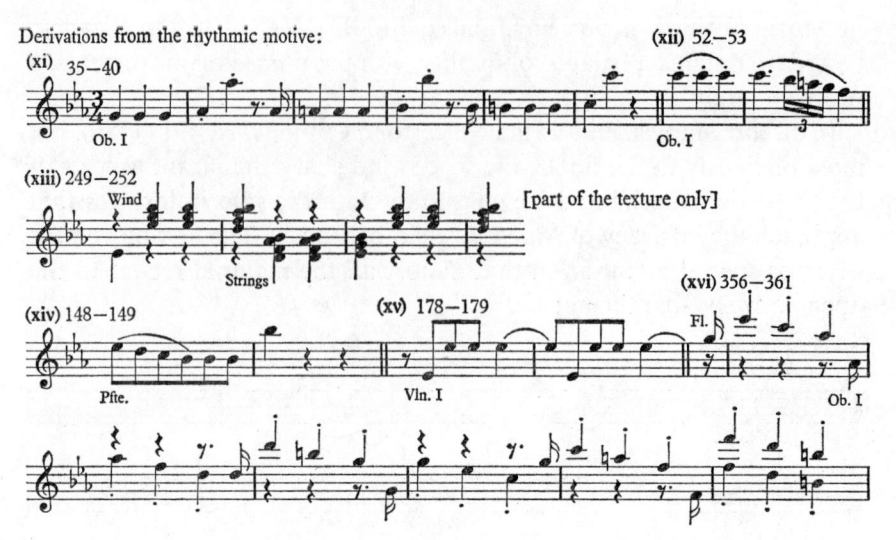

[musical examples (xi) 35–40, (xii) 52–53, (xiii) 249–252, (xiv) 148–149, (xv) 178–179, (xvi) 356–361]

Cross-relationships also intensify the formal structure. The entrance of the solo at bar 100 combines the descending line of bars 3–8, in a modified version, with the chief motive; the most important closing theme not only derives from the rhythmic motive combined with the descending line in dotted rhythms, but the progression C, E flat, A flat in the first notes of each bar is the same three notes, though differently arranged, that begin in bars 1–3:

Ex. 278
bars 91–96

[musical example]

The last of the dozen concertos of 1784–6, the great C major K.503, forms a splendid end to a group so diversified that chronology is their main tie. Yet Mozart's lines of evolution are apparent even through this diversity. The beauties of K. 503 are not immediately apparent. The individuality of its rather formal themes emerges in the course of the piece. More than in other concertos, the influence of Haydn is seen in continuous thematic development throughout the movement.[1] K. 503 advances in treatment of tonality, touching particularly on the flat, subdominant side of C major and the tonic minor. The orchestration is more imaginative particularly in wind writing than any other concerto except for K. 491. In the transition of the solo exposition, a section

[1] See Hans Keller, 'K. 503. The Unity of contrasting Themes and Movements', *The Music Review*, xvii (1956), pp. 48–58, 120–9.

PLATE VI

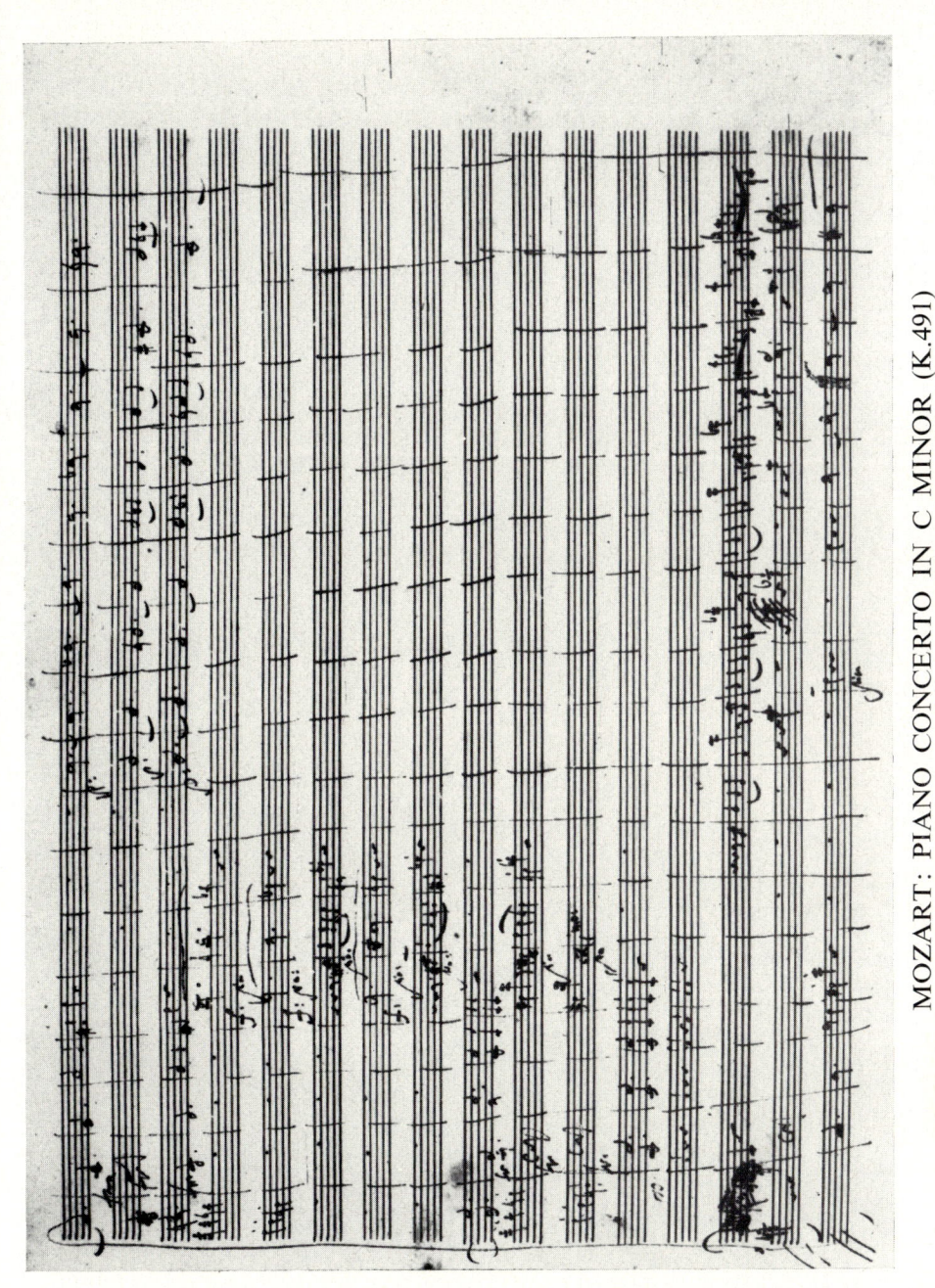

MOZART: PIANO CONCERTO IN C MINOR (K.491)

First movement, beginning of the recapitulation (bars 361–77). The autograph shows that Mozart thought of the piano as not only solo but also continuo instrument, playing with the orchestra ('c B') through bars 362–5.

normally involving sequential passagework, the following inverted imitation is combined with a swiftly changing harmonic scheme:

Ex. 279
Allegro maestoso
bars 130—134

This material originated in the primary group, bar 19, and its rhythmic motive ♪♪♪♪ recurs in the secondary and closing sections. The unification here surpasses the interesting derivations of K. 491 not so much in imagination as in systematic arrangement.

The D major concerto, K. 537 (1788), nicknamed 'The Coronation' from its performance at the coronation of Leopold II in Frankfurt in 1790, requires a more casual, eighteenth-century attitude after the intellectual depth of K. 503. It is a conscious stereotype and, viewed as such, it is an entirely successful work. It summarizes the state of concertos about 1790, standardized not so much by the works of Mozart as by those of countless minor composers, and its relative simplicity emphasizes the originality of Mozart's other concertos. On grounds of authenticity, however, one should avoid a final judgement of K. 537. The version most commonly played stems from the first printed edition, André's (Offenbach, 1794), in which the solo part, incomplete in the autograph, was probably completed by André himself.

Mozart's final concerto, K. 595 in B flat (1791), is more characteristic and original again. Mozart's flexible phrase structure is obvious right at the beginning where string phrases are punctuated by interjections from the wind that produce irregular phrases quite unlike the symmetry of K. 537. These exchanges provide material for later dialogues between solo and strings. The development is original in its use of remote tonalities such as B minor and a rather rare section of true development where the primary theme is treated imitatively:

Ex. 280

Allegro
bars 225—228

The restrained atmosphere of the first movement continues in the Larghetto, but the rondo finale is one of Mozart's most rollicking ideas. The contrast of such carefree gaiety with the tragic circumstances of Mozart's last year reminds us of an interesting analogy: the boisterous finale of Beethoven's Second Symphony, written in the same year in which he recorded his desperation in the tragic Testament of Heiligenstadt (1802).

Viewed against the efforts of his contemporaries, Mozart's concertos rose early to a much higher level. The gap between Mozart and Vaňhal, for example, seems greater in the concerto than in the symphony. In each of his works there is a wide distribution of qualities: captivating themes, piquant orchestration, ingenious modulations, subtle counterpoint, brilliantly idiomatic solo passages. Where lesser composers may be original in one of these aspects, in each masterpiece Mozart uses his superlative talents in all directions. Supreme among these, for the purposes of the concerto, was his gift of melody. The duality of tutti and solo require an unusual wealth of characteristic material to clarify and animate the complex form. Only a melodist of Mozart's imaginative fluency and depth could fully meet this requirement. With the confidence of true genius he apparently rejoiced in the challenge of the concerto, for under its special stimulation he produced many of his greatest works.

VIII

THE DIVERTIMENTO AND COGNATE FORMS

by GÜNTER HAUSSWALD

The divertimento and related forms[1] played a decisive role in late eighteenth-century instrumental music. In the second half of the period especially, the genre developed to a point where it appreciably influenced the musical outlook of the time. In its most mature forms it clearly reflected the tastes of the aristocratic and wealthy middle-class patrons who commissioned them. Frequently we do not know these patrons by name, but occasionally they are revealed by dedications or by our knowledge of the occasion of a particular performance. This social conditioning of the divertimento style must be borne in mind in any attempt to define the term, a task made the more difficult by the circumstance that different genres are often concealed by loose and inconsistent terminology.

The divertimento never had a formal structure peculiar to itself. It is characterized by its musical content, rather than by the number of movements, which may vary from a single movement to a twelve-movement cycle. For its formal structure at the peak of its popularity, it drew upon the sonata principle as well as the suite-like succession of dance movements. A resemblance to classical sonata form is often obvious, although the duality of the basic thematic structure is not always realized; soon, too, rondo forms of various kinds appear, or a set of variations may alternate with movements of an aria type. The old minuet, which was elsewhere losing its importance, continued to play an essential role in the divertimento, as did other old-fashioned movements from the partitas. The very fact that the divertimento did not respond to current formal trends, and did not exhibit a stable formal structure, made possible an interchange of forms, so that material very different from most contemporary instrumental music may be incorporated within a piece designated divertimento. Forms such as sonata, trio, and quartet, which were already acquiring clear contours in the second half of the eighteenth century, are often styled divertimenti, and examples of divertimento style may be found in works of the sonata type.

[1] See Vol. VI.

The instrumentation of divertimenti is also extremely diverse, ranging from a single instrument, such as a harpsichord, to ensembles of as many as thirteen instruments. There are divertimenti for wind alone, for strings alone, and for mixed string and wind combinations. In the last case the music is almost always orchestral in nature, and demands doubling of the string parts, while pure string or wind ensembles, especially the latter, were almost always groups of soloists.

SERENADE, CASSATION, AND NOTTURNO

Besides the divertimento actually so-called, there were a number of closely related forms—serenade, cassation, notturno—which sprang from the same social demands, yet were musically based on other principles. Here again, the boundaries are indeterminate, though recent research[1] has given us criteria which help to define them: Hans Engel, for instance, has shown that the serenade is essentially orchestral, the divertimento chamber music. As outdoor evening music, the serenade had a special function. Mozart's serenades always originated in specific occasions, as, for example, the so-called Haffner Serenade K. 250 (248b), composed in 1776 for the wedding-eve celebrations of a Salzburg citizen, Anton Spaeth, and Elizabeth Haffner, the daughter of a wealthy former mayor of the town. Recent research[2] has shown other serenades of Mozart to have been composed for the musical entertainments which Salzburg students presented before their professors at the end of term in the Mirabell Garden or in front of the university. The serenade K. 100 (62a), dating from 1769, is an example. Mozart's serenades always consist of several movements approaching the style of the sonata, preceded by typical processional music in the form of a march; with a degree of probability bordering on certainty, marches which have been preserved separately can now be reunited with their serenades;[3] these works are indisputably orchestral music. Doubled string parts with single wind parts are called for, and the parts merely described as *basso* are probably to be imagined as being performed by bassoon and double bass, rather than by the violoncello (which required the player to be seated). How much trouble was taken in adapting serenades to be used more than once is shown by the fact that by the elimination of complete movements and the addition of timpani a four-movement form could

[1] Hans Engel, 'Divertimento, Cassation, Serenade', *Die Musik in Geschichte und Gegenwart*, lii, col. 597; Günter Hausswald, *Mozarts Serenaden* (Leipzig, 1951) and 'Der Divertimento-Begriff bei Georg Christoph Wagenseil', *Archiv für Musikwissenschaft*, ix (1952), p. 45; Reimund Hess, *Serenade, Cassation, Notturno und Divertimento bei Michael Haydn* (Mainz, 1963).

[2] See Günter Hausswald, Foreword to the *Neue Mozart Ausgabe*, series IV/12/2 (Kassel, 1961), pp. vii–ix.

[3] See Hausswald, *Mozarts Serenaden*, pp. 19–20.

be created. This form was called *sinfonia* and was transferred to the concert room, whereas serenades were performed in the open air. The Neue Mozart-Ausgabe (Series IV, Band 7) includes three symphonies derived in this way from the Serenades K. 204 (213a), 250 (248b) and 320. To take the first case, K. 204, subtraction of three inner movements has left a normal four-movement symphony (copy in the Preussische Staatsbibliothek):

	Serenade		*Symphony*
1.	Allegro assai	1.	Allegro assai
2.	Andante moderato		
3.	Allegro		
4.	Minuetto/Trio		
5.	(Andante)	2.	Andante
6.	Minuetto/Trio	3.	Minuetto/Trio
7.	Andantino grazioso—	4.	Andantino grazioso—
	Allegro		Allegro

The other two cases are similar. How fluid the terms were is shown by the orchestral Divertimento K. 113, which was described as a *Concerto ò sia Divertimento*. All Mozart's serenades remain closely allied to the divertimento, with the exception of the *serenata teatrale*, which developed out of festive theatrical offers of homage such as Gluck's *Le Cinesi* or Mozart's own *Ascanio in Alba*, K. 111.[1]

The cassation and the notturno were also related to the divertimento. A convincing linguistic interpretation of the term cassation has so far eluded scholars. The Latin *cassatio* or Italian *cassazione*, meaning 'annulment' makes no sense in connection with a musical form. The derivation from *gassatim gehen* (literally, go about the alleys) with the meaning of 'give a serenade' is an ingenious invention but hardly carries conviction. It seems equally impossible to establish a connection with the word *cassa*, the original meaning of which is 'box' or 'chest'. Nor does the special Italian use of *cassa* for 'drum' offer any help. All we can say is that during the eighteenth century the word 'cassation' came into use as one of the terms for a set of short instrumental pieces.

Mozart composed such works, of which K. 99 (63a) is an example, as ensemble music in the divertimento style, as did Joseph Haydn. The *notturno* was treated by Mozart as typical evening music in the three-movement *Serenata notturna*, K. 239, for two orchestras and in the *Notturno* for four orchestras, K. 286 (269a), in both of which features of the divertimento style are prominent. The *Kleine Nachtmusik*, K. 525, for two violins, viola, and bass was probably conceived as chamber

[1] See p. 117.

music; the divertimento character is emphasized by the second movement, a *Romanze*, the serenade style by the fact that, according to Mozart's own thematic catalogue, there was originally another minuet between the first movement and the *Romanze*.

The divertimento, specifically so called, in the second half of the eighteenth century thus exhibits a complex and varied picture. On the one hand, its character as entertainment causes it to overlap with related forms; on the other hand it becomes more clearly defined and consequently, to an increasing extent, stands out from the serenade, the cassation, and the notturno.

FRENCH AND ITALIAN DIVERTIMENTI

The following cursory survey will serve to show how many and how various were the composers who wrote divertimenti for keyboard, strings, wind or mixed ensemble. The divertimento idea was indeed widespread. And formally—with its relatives the serenade, notturno, and cassation—it was embodied in many different ways. So far as musical fashion was concerned, it occupied a central position in music between 1750 and 1800, side by side with the only just developing symphony. Its principal exponents were a circle of French and Italian masters, the so-called Viennese school, and the Viennese classics. Among the French composers should be noted the relatively late works of Michel Corrette (1709–95) for musette, vielle, flute, and violin, such as *Les récréations du berger fortuné*, as well as a *Divertissement pour le clavecin ou le forte-piano, contenant les échos de Boston et la victoire d'un combat naval remportée par une frégatte contre plusieurs corsaires réunis* (1780), a programmatic piece of battle music for harpsichord, arranged in the manner of a divertimento. In Italy the Neapolitan Francesco Durante (1684–1755) composed *Sei sonate divise in Studi e Divertimenti*[1] (1732) for harpsichord and a set of *Divertimenti ossia Sonate per Cembalo*; whilst the Paduan composer Giuseppe Antonio Paganelli (1710–60) is represented by a *Divertissement de le beau Sexe*[2] (1755) which consists of keyboard sonatas. By Niccolò Jommelli (1714–74) we have *Due Divertimenti per stromenti* for string quartet, and the Lucca-born Luigi Boccherini (1743–1805) wrote divertimenti which he published as Op. 11 for string quartet. Mention should also be made of the keyboard divertimenti of Giovanni Sammartini of Milan (1698–1775) including *Sei sonate notturne*,[3] as well as similar works by the Venetian Giovanni Ferrandini (1710–1791). The range of the Italian divertimento

[1] *Sei studi e sei divertimenti per cembalo*, ed. Bernhard Paumgartner (Kassel, n.d.).
[2] Ed. Giovanni Tagliapetra (Milan, 1936).
[3] Ed. Carlo Perinello, *I classici della musica italiana*, xxviii (Milan, 1919).

is rounded off by a work of Stefan Pauselli (1748–1805) who came from the South Tyrol, the *Sei Divertimenti*[1] of which one for wind instruments begins with a march. The list should perhaps be completed by mention of the *Sei Divertimenti à Quadro* by Alessandro Lodovica, *Sei Divertimenti* for two cellos by Giacomo Cervetto (1682–1783) who was active in London, and four-movement sonatas by the Bolognese composer Bartolommeo Campagnoli (1751–1827), described as *Divertissement ou L'exercise des sept principales positions*, Op. 18.

VIENNA AND MANNHEIM

The focal point of the classical divertimento on a wide scale was formed by the Austrian (including Bohemian) musicians, particularly those of the so-called Viennese and Mannheim schools. In the works of these minor composers the craftsman element always asserts itself more strongly and the formal element is clarified and refined, so that it comes closer to the sonata, and for the most part remains chamber-like in its instrumentation. Gradually the genre freed itself from the suite, of which basically only the minuet was preserved. In this process of transition a long line of composers was involved. If for example one analyses one of the ten *Divertimenti a 3*, for two violins and bass, by the Viennese composer Johann Christoph Monn or Mann (1726–82), which have from three to seven movements, one finds influences of the suite and even of the popular *Singspiel*, but complete freedom from all formality. A Divertimento in D by him[2] opens with a cantabile Andante using concertante elements.

Ex. 281

[1] Divertimento in F, ed. Walter Senn, *Denkmäler der Tonkunst in Österreich*, lxxxvi (Vienna, 1949).
[2] Ed. Wilhelm Fischer, *Denkmäler der Tonkunst in Österreich*, xix (2) (Bd. 39) (Vienna, 1912).

Its festoon-like stringing together of motives shows that playful relaxation so characteristic of the divertimento style. The second movement, an Allegro which one might have expected to find put first, suggests by its sprightly upbeat phrasing and by its inversion of the motive-complex a completely new loose *musikantisch* attitude:

Ex. 282

The minuet, on the other hand, with its triad-built melody reminds one of old Austrian popular song with its sharp dynamic contrasts:

Ex. 283

A sparkling finale ends the work, which represents the very archetype of the pre-classical Viennese divertimento style. Monn's better known brother, George Matthias (1717–1750), has left a similar divertimento in G major.

In contrast to these, however, is the Divertimento in C[1] of another Viennese, Josef Starzer (1726–87). The opening theme of the first movement is as follows:

Ex. 284

Here there is no short-breathed, smooth, playfully relaxed melody-building. This is the controlled spinning-out of a melodic idea and thus basically symphonic. Closer to the true divertimento are the works of

---

[1] Two divertimenti, ed. K. Horwitz and K. Riedel, *Denkmäler der Tonkunst in Österreich*, Jg. xv (2) (Bd. 31) (Vienna, 1908).

Franz Aspelmayer (1728–86), Wenzel Pichl (1741–1804), and Karl Ditters von Dittersdorf (1739–99), composer of entertainment music of various kinds—divertimenti, serenades, cassations, and notturni, including a *Divertimento dell'umane Passioni*. The thirty divertimenti of Georg Christoph Wagenseil (1715–77) are of particular importance.[1] Composed for harpsichord in three movements (fast–slow–minuet), they represent genuine keyboard entertainment music of the *galant* period. Peter Winter (1754–1825) of Munich, whose twelve divertimenti contain a march, a minuet, and movements approaching the sonata pattern, provides the bridge to the Mannheimers, for he was born and trained there, as was Franz Beck (1723–1809), the composer of two divertimenti. The Alsatian Johann Friedrich Edelmann (1749–94) wrote divertimenti for harpsichord, two violins, and viola, and Franz Xaver Richter (1709–89), who was active in Mannheim and Strasbourg, wrote works for harpsichord, flute, and violoncello. In the Stamitz family Johann (1717–57), in addition to conventional divertimenti, composed *Deux divertissements en Duo pour un violon seul sans basse,* while his son Karl (1745–1801) assembled a number of operatic melodies for flute, violin, and bass under the title *Six Divertissements ou Airs choisis des Opéras français*. Herein are found the origins of the potpourri character of the later divertimento. Among others who must be mentioned are Anton Stamitz (1754–1809), Carlo Giuseppe Toeschi (1732–88), Placidus von Camerloher (1718–82), and Joseph Anton Liber (1732–1809), whose divertimenti display a preference for the clarinet after the model of Joseph Riepel (1709–82). These last-named composers give some indication of the circle who cultivated the divertimento outside Mannheim. It is astonishing how extensive was the preoccupation of composers in the second half of the eighteenth century with this genre, the development of which was crowned by Haydn and Mozart.

THE HAYDN BROTHERS

Michael Haydn (1737–1806), born at Rohrau like his brother Joseph, produced numerous divertimenti for strings and wind instruments, in which lively experiments with form and content can be seen both in the number of movements and in the texture. In from four to eight movements, and in four to eight parts, they already show the structure of the classical divertimento. A Divertimento in G major,[2] dated Salzburg 17 June 1785, enjoys that transparency of sound so typical of the chamber divertimento in its combination of flute, horn, violin, viola, and bassoon:

[1] *Vier Divertimenti da Cembalo*, ed. Friedrich Blume, *Nagels Musik-Archiv 36* (Hanover).
[2] Ed. L. H. Perger, *Denkmäler der Tonkunst in Österreich*, Jg. xiv (2) (Bd. 29) (Vienna, 1907).

Ex. 285

Likewise characteristic of the pure divertimento style is its sequence of movements—Marcia, Allegro spiritoso, Minuet and Trio, Andante, second Minuet and Trio, Polonese, Allegretto—the opening of which is shown in Ex. 285—and a Presto finale.

As for Joseph Haydn (1732–1809) the greater part of his chamber music might be described as close to the divertimento in style. In addition to the string quartets, string trios, and duos for various instruments, it includes works specifically entitled Divertimenti for four or more instruments, *notturni* for two *lire organizzate* (hurdy-gurdies furnished with one or two sets of organ pipes), *scherzandi* (which, however, were not so called by Haydn), and *Feldparthien* (partitas for open-air performance) scored expressly for wind instruments. There also exist numerous divertimenti for various string or mixed three-part combinations, including some with *clarinette d'amour* or lute. To be added to these are the divertimenti for string or wind instruments with piano, and a few for keyboard alone, pieces in cassation style, the trios and duos with baryton, and finally keyboard sonatas and pieces, including some *per un Cembalo solo a quattro mani*. Even these are often styled 'divertimento' in the sources. The divertimento character perhaps shows itself most clearly in Haydn in one of his *Divertimenti a tre per il Baryton, Viola e Basso*.[1] Note the relaxed but ingenious theme of the minuet:

[1] *Werke*, series 14, ii, no. 25.

Ex. 286

[musical example]

or the fine workmanship of the finale:

Ex. 287

[musical example]

The rhythmic reinterpretation at *b'* is particularly characteristic of the special divertimento style.

THE MOZARTS AND THE DIVERTIMENTO

Leopold Mozart (1719–87) similarly cultivated this art of an aristocratic and middle-class society, mainly in divertimenti for two violins and violoncello. But he also composed for orchestra a delightful *Divertimento militare sive Sinfonia mit zwei Sweggl-Pfeifen*[1] (military flutes) consisting of a march:

Ex. 288

[musical example]

[1] Ed. Max Seiffert, *Denkmäler der Tonkunst in Bayern*, ix (2) (Leipzig, 1908).

followed by a Presto, Andante, Minuet and Trio, and Presto finale.

It was, however, in the works of Wolfgang Amadeus Mozart (1756–91) that the genre reached its culmination. Mozart's divertimenti grew entirely out of the specific Salzburg tradition; they were in the best sense music written to order for patrons, and reflect in their style a light-hearted chamber-music tradition that is almost unique. The scoring is varied, yet characteristic, whether it be for wind or strings or—one of Mozart's favourite combinations—strings with horns. Here the art of the divertimento reaches its fulfilment. All traces of accidental and improvisatory elements have disappeared, and all references to other genres. Mozart cultivated the divertimento especially in his early and middle creative periods; other problems absorbed him later on. The three divertimenti K. 136 (125a), 137 (125b), 138 (125c) are pure three-movement string quartets. Among the wind divertimenti the two works K. 186 (159b) and K. 166 (159d) for two oboes, two clarinets, two cors anglais, two horns, and two bassoons are outstanding. These five-movement compositions display not only the characteristics of idiomatic wind writing, but also serenade-like qualities in their thematic ideas. Of the eight-part works the two Munich divertimenti K. Anh. 226 (196e) and

K. Anh. 227 (196f) are worthy of note. Five Viennese divertimenti, K. Anh. 229 (439b) are scored for two basset horns (or clarinets) and bassoon, or alternatively for three basset horns. More unusual scoring occurs in the divertimento for flutes, trumpets, and drums, K. 188 (240b), a Salzburg work, probably dating from 1776. Then follows the superbly scored group of wind divertimenti for two oboes, two horns, and two bassoons, K. 213, 240, 252 (240a), 253, 270, 289 (271g), all from the Salzburg period, and finally the divertimenti for strings and wind, K. 131, 205 (173a), 247, 251, 287 (271b), and 334 (320b).

To demonstrate the form at its consummate stage it is only necessary to cite the first movement of the Divertimento in E flat major, K. 289 (271g), for two oboes, two bassoons, and two horns, composed in Salzburg in the early summer of 1777. A short Adagio:

Ex. 289

prefaces this four-movement work in which the minuet appears second. The main part of the first movement proper, a sonata-form Allegro, presents first and second subjects in the usual manner, but with no dramatic opposition:

Ex. 290
(i) Allegro

(ii)
dolce

The music flows with infinite playful elegance and charm. In the concise development and recapitulation, the thematic ideas succeed each other immediately. A psychical conflict is neither sought nor offered. It is in the apparent ease and obviousness with which the rich filigree web of parts is spread before the listener that the uniqueness and greatness of Mozart's divertimenti lie.

These works represent a fulfilment of the spirit of the eighteenth century. It is easy to understand why the classically balanced form of the divertimento soon declined in the nineteenth century. The sociological assumptions, the relationship between patron and composer, changed fundamentally. Romanticism with its literary orientation was a hindrance rather than a help to a free, playful unfolding of pure music, and the once highly regarded divertimento quickly declined into the motley potpourri.

IX

THE RISE OF CHAMBER MUSIC

By KARL GEIRINGER

INTRODUCTION

IN the period from 1745 to 1790 chamber music displayed a bewildering variety of content, combination of instruments, and form.[1] The pompous grandeur and powerful emotions which characterized Baroque art gradually disappeared. Domestic elegance came to have a stronger appeal than sumptuous splendour and the intimate art of chamber music flourished. The luxurious concerted style with its dramatic competition between different instruments and its rich polyphony gave way to plain homophony and the preponderance of a single melody. The young school of composers born during the first quarter of the eighteenth century in Italy, Austria, and Bohemia abhorred the heavy formality of their predecessors. Lightness, carefree gaiety, and the expression of natural feeling were their artistic aims resulting in simple, almost primitive compositions.

In Northern Germany the reaction against the Baroque style assumed somewhat different aspects. Here an idiom of a more subjective character emerged. While sentimental and languorous at the outset, it assumed subsequently a passionate intensity conforming with the ideals of the contemporary *Sturm und Drang* movement in literature.

During the last quarter of the century the leading composers of the time increasingly felt the need to take stock of the vast potentialities disclosed by their predecessors. After exploring the different new trends and even returning to the idiom of the Baroque, they achieved at last a perfect blend and fusion of the various elements. The classical art which thus came to the fore was based on the integration of all the ideas presented by the creative writers of the century.

Even more significant than the change of content was the new diversity displayed in the choice of instruments. The chamber music compositions of the Baroque period used as a rule one to four melody

---

[1] Cf. Wilhelm Fischer, 'Zur Entwicklungsgeschichte des Wiener klassischen Stiles', *Studien zur Musikwissenschaft*, iii, 1915, p. 24, Karl Geiringer, *The Bach Family* (London, 1954), and *Joseph Haydn* (Mainz, 1959), Hans Engel, 'Die Quellen des klassischen Stiles', in *Report of the Eighth Congress of the International Musicological Society* (Kassel, 1961), p. 285, Reinhard G. Pauly, *Music in the Classic Period* (Englewood Cliffs, 1965), Charles Rosen, *The Classical Style* (London, 1972).

instruments accompanied by a *basso continuo*. The elaboration of this continuo part, which was intended to fill the gap between the bass and the melodic lines, was usually entrusted to a keyboard instrument, particularly the harpsichord, whose bass line was occasionally reinforced by a violoncello, a viola da gamba, or a bassoon. The situation changed after the middle of the century, when the harpsichord with its inflexible tone was gradually superseded by the more expressive fortepiano. The earlier instrument was endowed with a tone quality which made it equally suitable for blending with the sounds of strings or wind instruments. It was the ideal continuo instrument, easily fitting into any ensemble which it enriched without ever becoming too prominent. The fortepiano, on the other hand, produced a hitherto unknown tone which did not mix well with that of other instruments. Thus the cembalo's modest task of providing support and filling the tonal texture could not be entrusted to the new instrument, an attitude that found reinforcement in the growing tendency of composers to write out the middle parts and not leave the clavier player to elaborate them from the figured bass.

To adjust to these altered conditions composers of chamber music began about the middle of the century to employ two diametrically opposed methods. Either they removed the keyboard instrument from the ensemble, adding where necessary a string or wind instrument in the middle range, or they went to the other extreme by allotting a leading position to the fortepiano while the string or wind instruments were mostly treated as reinforcement or accompaniment. In rare cases only did composers provide the piano with equal partners, thus establishing true balance between the members of the chamber music group.

Yet the old ensembles maintained a certain life even in the third quarter of the century, and in many cases it was left to the discretion of the performers whether or not to employ a continuo instrument. Thus the chamber music between 1745 and 1790 offers a wide variety of combinations.

Remarkable changes also occurred in the formal structure of chamber music. The Baroque era showed great variety in the use of cyclical forms. The sequence of movements slow–fast(fugue)–slow–fast was often employed, and related to it was the French overture. This started with a homophonic Grave introduction which was followed by a somewhat more animated fugal section, the conclusion being often formed by a second Grave. In contrast to it the Italian *sinfonia* and concerto forms consisted of a fast, a slow, and a concluding fast movement. Sequences of dance pieces known as suites or *sonate da camera* were frequently employed; sometimes these were headed by a French overture or a *sinfonia*.

In the second quarter of the century new forms like the divertimento and the *cassazione* gradually replaced the Baroque suite. Most of the movements shed their connection with the dance; only the minuet and, to a lesser extent, the march were preserved. Rondos and sets of variations in which the individual instruments alternately were allotted solo parts played an important role in the divertimento. At the same time the Italian *sinfonia* enjoyed great favour, occasionally with a minuet as an additional middle movement. More and more it became the habit to use this form for ensembles of four or more instruments, while smaller groups—particularly in Italy—contented themselves with three or even two movements chosen at random from the larger form.

Within individual movements an important structural evolution took place. Of greatest significance was the change that occurred in the binary form commonly used in the first movement of the *sinfonia* and in dance movements of the Baroque period. Originally this consisted of two almost equally long sections. But the second section was gradually enlarged and subdivided in a manner which eventually led to the development of the so-called 'sonata-form'.[1] This plan assumed an ever-increasing significance in eighteenth-century chamber music. Some form of it became the rule in fast first movements, was often used in finales, and even occurred at times in the slow movements. Other forms such as the plain ternary structure and the rondo often adopted features of sonata-form.

Turning now to the discussion of individual compositions, we start with works which—although their authors were born after the turn of the century—are composed for ensembles known already in the Baroque period.

THE 'SOLO' SONATA

The so-called 'solo' sonata may be considered as a preliminary step towards the chamber music of the second half of the eighteenth century. Only rarely does it occur as a real unaccompanied solo for a melody instrument *senza basso* and then it frequently assumes the character of a technical study such as we find in the famous *24 Matinées* by Pierre Gaviniès (1728–1800) which are among the most valuable studies in violin literature.[2]

Less conspicuous is the technical and educational purpose in the unaccompanied solo sonatas by Johann Friedrich Reichardt (1752–1814) published in 1778, or in the two brilliant sonatas of 1795 by

[1] For a more detailed account of this process, see chapter VI.
[2] Cf. Lionel de La Laurencie, *L'École française de violon* (Paris, 1922–24) ii, pp. 328–32.

Friedrich Wilhelm Rust (1739-96),[1] though they still require first-class virtuosos for their performance.

It is interesting to note that unaccompanied solos were published even for so unlikely an instrument as the flute. In C. P. E. Bach's *Sonata per il Flauto traverso solo, senza Basso* of 1747 (Wq. 132)[2] the composer creates the illusion of an accompanying bass instrument by interrupting the cantilena with low-pitched notes, a device his father had already employed in similar cases.

Much more common is the accompanied 'solo' sonata, which is in fact a duet for a melody instrument and continuo. As one of the main forms in the seventeenth century it maintained its vitality through the pre-classical era and even occurs in the last quarter of the century (cf. C. P. E. Bach's *Solo a flauto traverso col basso*, Wq. 133, Hamburg, 1786).[3]

Various instruments were used in the 'solo' sonata, the violin taking first place and the flute enjoying hardly less favour. Oboe, viola da gamba, cello, and others made occasional contributions. In accordance with the general trend of the time various alternatives were suggested to the performer. Typical is the title of a composition by the famous viola da gamba virtuoso, C. F. Abel, published after 1759 by J. J. Hummel: *Six Easy Sonattas* [sic] *for the Harpsichord or for a Viola da Gamba/ Violin or German flute with a Thorough-Bass Accompaniment*.[4] Thus there are four different possibilities of performance. The pieces may be played on a harpsichord alone, the melody being executed with the right hand and the bass with the left, with the addition of filling-in notes according to the figures in the bass. A better method of performance is to give the melody to a viola da gamba while the keyboard instrument merely has to realize the thorough bass. In the absence of a viola da gamba the melody may be transposed one octave upwards and played by a violin or flute. But such routine transfer from one instrument to another is not always carried out mechanically. In the Sonata for Flute or Violin, Op. 9, no. 7 (Paris, 1738) by J. M. Leclair the elder (1697-1764) the third movement, an aria, is provided with a separate violin part which in each of the four repeats employs double stops:

---

[1] It is significant that the great violinist Ferdinand David, who edited Rust's D minor Sonata in 1867 for Peters, felt it necessary considerably to simplify the violin part, as he was afraid the work's brilliance might discourage his contemporaries. Cf. Andreas Moser, *Geschichte des Violinspiels* (Berlin, 1923), p. 332.

[2] Cf. Ernst F. Schmid, *C. P. E. Bach und seine Kammermusik* (Kassel, 1931), p. 92. The abbreviation 'Wq' is used for Alfred Wotquenne, *Thematisches Verzeichnis der Werke Ph. E. Bachs* (Leipzig, 1905).

[3] Schmid, op. cit. p. 102.

[4] J. Bacher (ed.), (Kassel, 1937).

Ex. 291

(musical notation: Aria, Original version, Repeat)

The solo sonata was cultivated throughout the musical centres of Europe. In Italy virtuoso pieces were offered by Pietro Nardini (1722–93) who continued the tradition established by his teacher, Giuseppe Tartini. His sonatas Op. 2, nos. 5 and 6 in D major and B♭ major (published Amsterdam, c. 1770?), with their fine cantilenas and the skilful handling of the form, belong to the best, and at the same time to the most difficult, violin solos published in this era. On the other hand, the sonatas by Gaetano Pugnani (1731–98), avidly printed by publishers in Amsterdam, Paris and London, interest merely for their technical brilliance while their artistic substance is rather disappointing.[1] A completely different approach is found in the solos for violin or flute or oboe by the Bolognese composer Santo Lapis.[2] Meant for amateurs, they consist of three playfully light miniature movements and offer no technical difficulties.

Among the solos for cello the works by Giuseppe dall'Abaco (1710–1805), a son of the renowned Baroque composer Felice dall'Abaco, deserve mention. He wrote over thirty works, mostly preserved in manuscript in the British Museum, among which the attractive G major sonata in three movements was long erroneously ascribed to G. B. Sammartini.[3] His C major sonata has as finale a gay Allegro headed 'La Sampogna': with humour and skilful realism the sounds of a bagpipe are imitated here by means of a virtuoso idiom. In other pieces the composer succeeds in imitating a viola da gamba, an organ and a large bass viol.[4]

In 1760 there appeared (Hummel, Amsterdam) six Sonatas for Cello and Bass, Op. 3, by Carlo Graziani (d. 1787).[5] These are again extremely

---

[1] Op. 3, no. 1 in C major, ed. Claude Arrieu (Paris, 1957); Op. 7, no. 4 in E major, ed. Gustav Jensen (Mainz, 1911).
[2] *3 leichte Sonaten*, ed. Hugo Ruf (Mainz, n.d.).
[3] Cf. Grove's *Dictionary of Music and Musicians*, 5th edn. (London, 1954), vii, p. 396.
[4] Cf. Edmond Van der Straeten, *History of the Violoncello* (London, 1915), pp. 164–5.
[5] Giacomo Benvenuti (ed.), *I classici musicali italiani*, xv (Milan, 1943).

brilliant showpieces which provide wide scope for the solo instrument's virtuosity, particularly in the variation movements frequently employed as finales.

Not only destined for, but also composed by, an amateur are some hundred and twenty sonatas for flute and bass which Frederick the Great wrote for his own use.[1] These are skilfully written pieces, displaying neither great theoretical knowledge nor deep emotions. The Sonata no. 84 in C minor, however, shows interesting links with the works of two members of the Bach family. It starts in the manner of C. P. E. Bach with a dramatic recitative by the flute, changes into an arioso and then once more intones the recitative. There follows an Andante e cantabile, and in conclusion one of the few fugues written by the king. It employs a subject reminiscent of the one Frederick gave to Johann Sebastian for elaboration, at their meeting in 1747:

Ex. 292

More progressive in character are the eleven flute solos by the king's harpsichordist, C. P. E. Bach. They display a brilliant idiom and one of them, the already mentioned Wq. 133,[2] impresses with its numerous wide leaps and its uncommon range, reaching up to high G.

In France the solo achieved its climax during the first half of the eighteenth century in the works of the great Jean-Marie Leclair.[3] Among his successors the versatile Jean Joseph de Mondonville (1711–72) ought to be mentioned; his output included sonatas both for violin with continuo accompaniment and for clavier with violin accompaniment.

England was so interested in importing Italian and German music that her native artists were not given sufficient encouragement. Yet there is no lack of attractive solos by English composers. One might mention the solidly constructed sonatas for flute or violin with bass by John Stanley (1713–86), a blind organist and master of the king's band. His Op. 1 consisting of eight compositions appeared in 1742; six other sona-

---

[1] Cf. *Musikalische Werke*, ed. Philipp Spitta (Leipzig, 1889). The Adagio from no. 22 is reprinted in Arnold Schering, *Geschichte der Musik in Beispielen* (Leipzig, 1931), p. 462.
[2] Cf. Schmid, op. cit., *Notenanhang*, nos. 38–48.
[3] See Vol. VI.

tas, Op. 4, followed in 1745. His G minor sonata in four movements[1] is lively and melodious, while strongly dependent on the great Italian traditions of the past. About John Collett, who was active by the middle of the century, we have no biographical information. His Op. 1, *Six Solos for the Violin with a Thorough-Bass for the Harpsicord* [sic] were published in 1755 in London. The A major sonata[2] with an expressive Largo reveals an artist familiar with the potentialities of violin technique. Likewise James Lates (c. 1710–77), trained in Italy and active at Oxford, seems to have been an excellent violinist. The six sonatas of his Op. 3, published 1768, make clever use of the solo instrument's capabilities and in their structure reveal a progressive spirit, although the melodic invention is somewhat dry and study-like.[3]

Altogether the solo sonata belongs to the less significant ensembles of eighteenth-century chamber music. The great movements towards the development of a new style by-passed this form, which was firmly anchored in the past and displayed more retrospective than progressive tendencies.

THE TRIO SONATA

A different situation prevailed with the trio sonata which had played a dominating role in the Baroque era. This genre, scored for two melody instruments and a keyboard instrument with cello *ad libitum*, was still widely cultivated by the younger generation. They nevertheless strove for a different style and tended to replace the competition between two equally endowed melody instruments by the preponderance of one instrument.

The gradual change from the Baroque to a lighter and gentler idiom is illustrated by the fourteen sonatas formerly ascribed to the Neapolitan Giovanni Battista Pergolesi (1710–36),[4] and a further step forward in the evolution of chamber music forms may be observed in the works of the two brothers Sammartini. Giuseppe, the elder of the two, who was active in London, lived from about 1693 to 1770. His Trio in A minor Op. 3, no. 9,[5] of 1743 consists of four movements, fast–slow–fast–minuet.[6] The first starts on an expressive unison of all parts with wide melodic leaps stressing the Baroque aspect. But after this introduction the texture is loosened and surprisingly enough there is a clear tendency

---

[1] Alfred Moffat (ed.), (London, 1907).
[2] Moffat (ed.), (London, 1907).
[3] Cf. his Sonata in G major, ed. Moffat, (London, 1907).
[4] See Vol. VI.
[5] Hugo Riemann (ed.), *Collegium Musicum*, xxvii (Leipzig, n.d.).
[6] In the bass part of the set printed by Walsh (London, 1743) we find the remark 'a violoncello e cembalo se piace'.

towards a contrasting second subject. The development section presents cadenza-like passages in the first violin pointing to a stylistic relationship with the concerto. Similarly, in the third movement, solo passages for the first violin playing in double-stops are contrasted with the tutti. The final 'Minuet grazioso' has two trios, one major and one minor, and gives a truly suite-like conclusion to the composition.

Giuseppe's younger brother, Giovanni Battista (1701–85), wrote a considerable amount of chamber music among which his trio sonatas again deserve attention. Particularly attractive are the six *Sonate notturne*, Op. 7.[1] Each consists of two movements only, a minuet usually forming the conclusion. In these amiable, warm-hearted pieces an approach to the style of 'sensibility' is noticeable with such headings as 'affettuoso', 'larghetto cantabile', and 'allegro dolce assai'. These *notturni*, though probably composed after the middle of the century, still embody the aesthetics of a by-gone age by not clearly distinguishing between the styles of orchestral and chamber music. A certain *al fresco* technique may be noticed in the third *notturno*. Similarly in the minuet of no. 6 the two violins are constantly presented in unison, thus departing from the true chamber music spirit. Mostly, however, the two upper voices co-operate, the first violin maintaining preponderance, according to the general trend:

Ex. 293 Larghetto affettuoso

Among the last masters of the trio sonata Pugnani and Antonio Sacchini (1734–86) should be mentioned.[2] Pugnani wrote various trios, some of which, e.g. Op. 9 of 1771, offer the virtuoso an opportunity to display technical brilliance. On the other hand his Op. 1 of 1754 is primarily meant for amateurs as it makes only limited demands on the performer's skill. No. 5 includes a fugue, but also a finale, 'La Caccia', with programmatic elements pointing to Rousseau's motto of return to nature. Throughout, a fresh and youthful spirit seems to be struggling against a more formalistic attitude. Sacchini's Op. 1 of 1772, with its tendency towards singing melodies, discloses an affinity with the music of J. C. Bach and Mozart. The primacy of the first violin is undisputed,

---

[1] Paris, *c*. 1759–62; Carlo Perinello and Enrico Polo (ed.), *I classici della musica italiana*, xxviii (Milan, 1919); one movement of no. 4 in Kurt Stephenson, *The Classics* (*Anthology of Music*) (Cologne, 1962), p. 21.

[2] Cf. Erich Schenk, *The Italian Trio Sonata* (*Anthology of Music*) (Cologne, 1955), introduction, p. 13, and first movement of Pugnani, Op. 1, no. 4, p. 63.

the texture solid, and filling-in chords of the keyboard instrument are hardly needed. Obviously the trio sonata was making ready to surrender its rights to the new string trio.

North of the Alps the trio sonata occupied an even more prominent place in musical life. Of several centres of music culture where Austrian and Bohemian composers played an important part, the town of Mannheim was of particular significance. The oldest among the resident composers was the renowned Czech violinist and singer Franz Xaver Richter (1709–89). His twelve trio sonatas Opp. 3 and 4[1] reveal stylistic elements which bring to mind the chamber music ascribed to Pergolesi. Richter employed Baroque sequences and fugues, permeating them, however, with homophonic elements. Of greater significance were the trio sonatas by the eminent Bohemian violin virtuoso Johann Stamitz[2] (1717–57), one of the first composers to conjure with vivid emotional contrasts within a short space. His dynamic scale does not restrict itself to *p* and *f*; he also prescribes *pp*, *ff*, and even *cresc.* Thus in the first movement of Op. 1, no. 5 over the repeated bass note B flat an upward melodic sweep of the violins is combined with a crescendo:

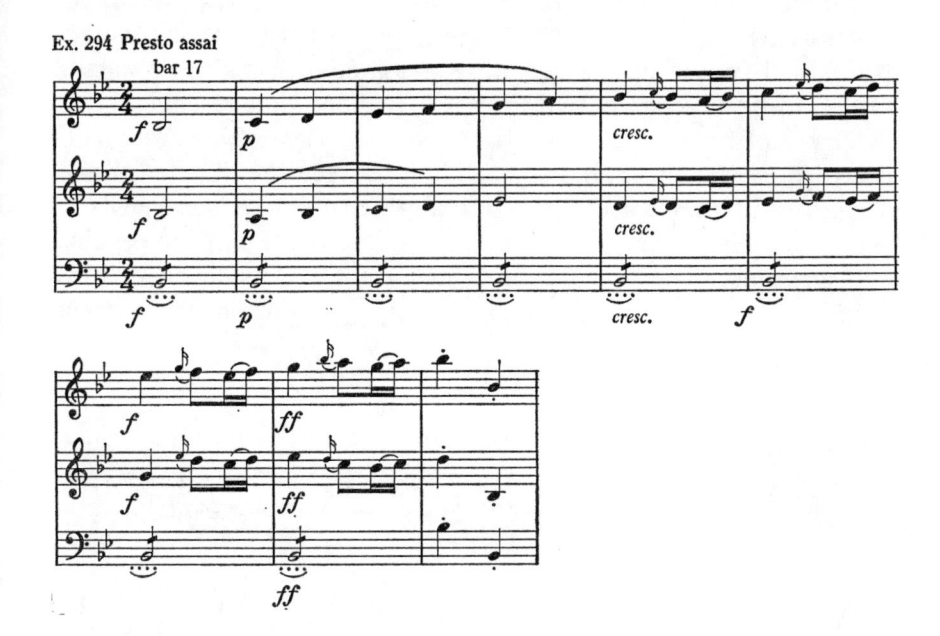

Ex. 294 **Presto assai**
bar 17

Significant also is the almost excessive contrast between first and second subject in the finale of Op. 1, no. 1. This Op. 1 is probably not his first

[1] Riemann (ed.), *Denkmäler der Tonkunst in Bayern*, xv/xvi (Leipzig, 1914–15).
[2] Riemann (ed.), ibid. iii (1) and *Collegium Musicum*, i–vii and xlviii–xlix (Leipzig, n.d.). Op. 1, nos. 1 and 15 also ed. Christian Döbereiner (Mainz, 1936–7).

work; it is a mature master's product exhibiting the structural sequence fast–slow–minuet–fast which was to achieve so important a rôle in the future. On the other hand, this set does not appear to be pure chamber music. A contemporary Paris edition speaks of trio sonatas... *pour exécuter ou à trois, ou avec toute l'orchestre*... and some of these 'orchestra trios' reveal indeed a symphonic character.

Of the numerous other representatives of the Mannheim School two composers might be singled out, Stamitz's pupil, the cellist Anton Filtz (*c.* 1730–60), probably likewise a native of Bohemia, and Stamitz's eldest son, Carl (1746–1801). In Filtz's Op. 3 the transition to the string trio may be noticed. The greater mobility of the continuo part and the comparatively compact instrumental texture seem to point towards performance by strings only. The second trio of this group[1] closes with a curious 'fuga con stylo mixto' whose piquant rhythms and syncopations may have been inspired by Czech folk music. Carl Stamitz's Six Trios, Op. 14, for flute, violin, and bass[2] clearly reveal elements of the concerto. Attractive, warmly singing solo passages are entrusted not only to the two effectively contrasting upper parts, but also to the cello, which the composer sometimes places above the violin part. Occasionally rests are prescribed for the filling-in keyboard instrument; for other passages, however, its participation is essential. Thus Carl Stamitz moves in the direction of the string trio, without quite reaching it.

Ignaz Holzbauer (1711–83), who was born in Vienna but subsequently settled in Mannheim, represents a link between the Mannheim and Viennese schools. He wrote trios in both three and four movements in which a leaning towards a gay popular idiom is matched by genuine craftsmanship. The *Sinfonia* in G major for two violins and *basso continuo*[3] presents as finale a 'fuga villanesca' introducing an Austrian peasant dance as subject:

Ex. 295 Allegro molto

In his *Sinfonia a tre* in F major[4] we are captivated by the warmth of the middle movement, Larghetto ed amoroso, in which the spirit of

---

[1] *Denkmäler der Tonkunst in Bayern*, xvi, p. 50.
[2] No. 1, ed. W. Upmeyer (Hanover, 1928).
[3] *Ignaz Holzbauer: Instrumentale Kammermusik*, ed. Ursula Lehmann, *Das Erbe deutscher Musik*, xxiv (Kassel, 1953), p. 99.
[4] H. Zirnbauer (ed.) (Mainz, 1940).

'sensibility' makes itself felt. The thematic relationship between first and last movements which is not uncommon in compositions of the time,[1] is particularly noticeable in this work, the finale moreover exhibiting piquant rhythms with a slight Slavic touch:

Ex. 296

The music of the Viennese masters displays some of the mannerisms to be found in the works of the Mannheim composers. Georg Matthias Monn (1717–50), one of Vienna's most distinguished musicians, still seems to be somewhat rooted in the idiom of the past, It is significant that his A major sonata[2] opens like a Baroque overture with a slow introduction and a subsequent fast fugue. This is followed, however, by the more progressive sequence of Andante, Menuetto, and Allegro assai. In a lighter vein are the works of the clavier composer, Georg Christoph Wagenseil (1715–77), whose trios reveal a striving for the new formal ideals.[3] His Symphony in D major[4] displays in its very concise first movement all the elements of a fully developed sonata form and the finale presents a contrasting second subject in a minor key (a feature frequently to be found in this transitional period). It is interesting to compare such works with the trios by Wagenseil's Bavarian contemporary Placidus von Camerloher (1718–76). These are likewise imbued with grace and gaiety, but their overall structure frequently maintains the Baroque sequence slow–fast–slow–fast, and in the C major sonata[5] a strict canon on the two violins serves as middle movement.

The compositions of the younger Austrians lead to the idiom of the Viennese classical masters. The exuberant gaiety of the Allegro in Johann Christoph Mann's (1726–82) *Divertimento a tre*[6] and the sensitive colouristic effects achieved in the trio of its minuet, where first violin

---

[1] Cf. Hans Engel, 'Haydn, Mozart und die Klassik', *Mozart-Jahrbuch 1959* (Salzburg, 1960), p. 46.

[2] Karl Horwitz and Karl Riedel (ed.), *Denkmäler der Tonkunst in Österreich*, xv (2) (Vienna, 1908), p. 60.

[3] Cf. his *Sonata a tre* in F, ed. Geiringer (Vienna, 1934), and the Sonata in B flat, Op. 1, no. 3, ed. Schenk (Vienna, 1953).

[4] Horwitz and Riedel (ed.), *Denkmäler der Tonkunst in Österreich*, xv (2), p. 28.

[5] No. 2 of *Vier Sonaten*, ed. A. Hoffmann (Mainz, 1939).

[6] W. Fischer (ed.) *Denkmäler der Tonkunst in Österreich*, xix (2) (Vienna, 1912), p. 107.

and cello play pizzicato while the second violin intones *pp* and arco a portamento middle part, remind one of similar features in Haydn's chamber music. Franz Aspelmayr (1728–86) was a violinist, and in 1782 he took part in a public performance of Haydn's quartets. His fifteen sonatas for two violins and bass, of which six *Trios modernes*[1] were published in 1765 as Op. 1 by Huberty, Paris, contain lively, skilfully written pieces for which the dynamic interpretation is prescribed with special care. The C major *Divertimento a tre*[2] by Florian Gassmann (1729–74) reveals both sensitive melodic invention and solid contrapuntal knowledge. Leopold Hoffmann (1738–93) was ridiculed by Haydn[3] but his little C major Trio[4] is attractive enough to make Haydn's jealousy appear not wholly unfounded.

A comparison of such works with the trios by Joseph Haydn does not always work to the disadvantage of the lesser masters. To Haydn music for two violins and bass was merely a stepping-stone on his path towards the mastery of the string quartet and only a few of these pieces show a more serious concern.[5] In his own catalogues Haydn listed no less than twenty-one trios which probably originated between *c.* 1750 and *c.* 1765.[6] They adhere to the traditional *sinfonia* form, fast–slow–fast, or emphasize a suite character with the sequence Adagio–Allegro–Minuet. Although the harpsichord is not specifically prescribed, the thin musical texture makes its co-operation seem imperative. Moreover, in the first movement of one in F major[7] there occurs a passage where the first violin moves below the bass line, thus causing an undesirable 6/4 chord only to be avoided if the cembalist plays octaves with the left hand. In the early pieces little demand is made on technical proficiency, and the melodies assume the superficial, dashing character of Neapolitan overtures. In the later trios, however, the part of the first violin is brilliant, bolder modulations are introduced and the emotional content is more serious and significant. Thus the trios reveal an evolution from Haydn's earliest style to an idiom preparing for his middle creative period.

Mozart too wrote trios[8] which shed light on his creative development. They were meant as instrumental interludes in the Mass and were prob-

---

[1] No. 4 ed. Schenk (Vienna, 1954); Op. 5, no. 1, ed. Riemann, *Collegium Musicum*, xxxix (Leipzig, n.d.).

[2] Schenk (ed.), (Vienna, 1953).

[3] Letter to Artaria, 20 July 1781.

[4] Schenk (ed.), (Vienna, 1953).

[5] Cf. Geiringer, *Haydn, A Creative Life in Music*, 3rd ed. (Berkeley and Los Angeles, 1968) pp. 230 and 246.

[6] For a list of modern reprints, see *Die Musik in Geschichte und Gegenwart*, v, col. 1919.

[7] Anthony van Hoboken, *Joseph Haydn: Thematisch-bibliographisches Werkverzeichnis*, (Mainz, 1957), Gruppe V: 2.

[8] *Gesamtausgabe der Werke Mozarts* (1876–1905), series 23; *Neue Mozart-Ausgabe*, (1955 ff.), series VI/16.

ably played between the reading of the epistle and the gospel. Despite their liturgical destination these pieces are throughout lively and gay; they are brief single movements in a miniature sonata form. In view of their use in the church the organ is chosen as the continuo instrument, its rôle gradually undergoing a noteworthy change. In the majority of the sonatas, which Mozart began to write as early as 1767, a figured bass is prescribed in addition to the two violins, and consequently the organ part is to be improvised by the performer. In no. 9 of 1776 (K. 224), however, the organ part is for the first time written out and the keyboard instrument treated as a soloist competing with the two violins. Particularly interesting is no. 15 of 1780 (K. 336), a kind of concerto with fully elaborated organ part in the solo sections and a figured bass for the tutti passages. Mozart thus seems to revive the aspects of a Baroque keyboard concerto in which the clavier is entrusted with the two-fold task of soloist and continuo instrument.

Among the composers of the North German School Wilhelm Friedemann Bach (1710–84), Johann Sebastian's eldest son, continued the tradition adopted by his teacher, Johann Gottlieb Graun.[1] Both composers show a predilection for the use of contrapuntal devices and for a sequence of movements which gradually increase in speed. Friedemann's Trio[2] in A minor for two violins and bass even employs a fugue as introductory movement and in the three other trios of this series (one for two violins and bass, and two for two flutes and bass) we find an abundance of the playful imitations favoured by this composer.

Friedemann's brother, Carl Philipp Emanuel Bach (1714–88), wrote some twenty trios,[3] partly for flute, violin, and bass, partly for two violins and bass.[4] According to the custom of the time the same work was often presented in both versions and even in a third one for a melody instrument and cembalo obbligato, the part of the second violin being entrusted to the right hand of the keyboard part. Only three of the trios were printed in the composer's lifetime. The most interesting among them is the one in C minor (Wq. 161/1)[5] (Nuremberg, 1751) which, according

[1] Geiringer, *The Bach Family* (London, 1954), p. 328.
[2] Cf. *4 Trios*, ed. Max Seiffert (Leipzig, 1934).
[3] Sonata in G major for 2 violins and continuo (Wq. 157), ed. B. Hinze-Rheinhold (Leipzig, 1924); Sonata in B flat major for 2 violins and continuo (Wq. 158), ed. Georg Schumann (Leipzig, 1910); 2 sonatas in F major and D minor for 2 violins and continuo (Wq. 154 and 160), ed. Paul Klengel (Leipzig, 1933); Sonata in B flat major for flute, violin, and continuo (Wq. 161/2), ed. Ludwig Landshoff (Leipzig, 1936); Sonata in B minor for flute, violin, and continuo (Wq. 143), ed. Rolf Ermeler (Leipzig, 1932); Sonata in E major for 2 flutes and continuo (Wq. 162), ed. Kurt Walther (Leipzig, 1935).
[4] Cf. Geiringer, op. cit., p. 361.
[5] Cf. Hans Mersmann, 'Ein Programmtrio Karl Philipp Emanuel Bachs', *Bach–Jahrbuch*, 1917, p. 137; Charles Burney, *A General History of Music*, iv (London, 1789), p. 643.

to the author's preface, represents 'a conversation between a Sanguine and a Melancholic who endeavour to convince each other'. At the end the Sanguine is triumphant and this is symbolized by the second violin taking over the subject of the first. Of greater musical value than this somewhat pedantically didactic composition is Emanuel's G major trio of 1754 (Wq. 157). Its beautifully singing melodies and the logical derivation of each movement's thematic material from a single germ-cell testify to the artistic eminence of this composer so greatly admired by the Viennese classical masters.

By the middle of the century Paris and London provided centres for the publication of chamber music. Here the compositions of leading Italian, Czech, and German masters were printed and there was an almost unceasing demand for the importation of foreign music. That continental composers were stimulated to provide chamber music for the English market may be seen in the six trio sonatas for two violins and bass by Gluck[1] (1714–87) printed in 1746 by Simpson, London,[2] while the composer was visiting Britain; it seems likely that these works were also composed there. They are in three movements with a minuet-like conclusion. Stylistically these trios bear a resemblance to the works of Gluck's teacher, G. B. Sammartini. Occasional passionate expression is not to be taken too seriously and quickly gives way to gaiety. Some imitation occurs, but by and large the idiom is homophonic and even the canon concluding the C major Trio displays in its lilting melody a typical Rococo character:

Ex. 297

In the movements in sonata form a contrasting second subject is not infrequent and in the development sections there are indications of the

[1] C. W. von Gluck, *Sämtliche Werke*, v (1), ed. Friedrich-Heinrich Neumann (Kassel, 1961).
[2] Three other trios by Gluck remained in manuscript during the composer's lifetime; one of them, ed. Riemann, *Collegium Musicum*, no. 38.

'thematic elaboration' of a later era, while the recapitulations are generally incomplete. Gluck's trios are by no means pioneer works; yet this is genuine chamber music belonging to the most attractive specimens of the form produced about the middle of the century.

The number of native artists active in the Western capitals as composers of trios was small indeed when compared to those from the south and east. William Boyce[1] (c. 1710–79) contributed twelve sonatas[2] (printed by Walsh in 1747) about which Burney[3] wrote that they were 'longer and more generally purchased, performed, and admired than any productions of the kind in this kingdom, except those of Corelli'. The reference to Corelli is by no means accidental; his influence is obvious in the dignified slow movements and the sprightly dances with their occasional imitations. Canon, fugue, and double fugue are employed in this set (nos. 9, 3, and 11 respectively) but in a rather careless manner, as one would expect in this later age.[4] The publication of Thomas Arne's seven trios,[5] Op. 3, by Walsh may have taken place at about the same time.[6] Like Boyce, Arne (1710–78) showed interest in the traditional tempo sequence slow–fast–slow–fast, but occasionally he added a dance as a fifth movement. The first trio offers as finale a minuet which after the *minore* section presents a variation instead of the *da capo*, a feature also to be found in works of Handel. Arne's trios are melodious and amiable, displaying a definite leaning towards the *style galant*. Compared to the works of Boyce they appear more progressive, but also somewhat superficial in character.

In France, during the first half of the century, the general predilection for Italian art in the field of opera was also noticeable in chamber music. The successful violinist Louis-Gabriel Guillemain (1705–70) wrote a number of trios 'dans le goût italien'.[7] The designation *amusement à la mode* given to his Op. 8, published in 1740, well characterizes his light and playful Rococo style. But the trios, Op. 1, of 1753 by François-

---

[1] Cf. Stanley Sadie, 'The Chamber Music of Boyce and Arne', *Musical Quarterly*, xlvi, (1960), p. 425.

[2] No. 2 in F major, ed. Murrill (London, 1951); No. 3 in A major, ed. Jensen (London, 1894); No. 6 in B flat major, ed. Sadie (London, 1967); No. 7 in D minor, ed. Moffat (London, 1908); No. 8 in E flat major, ed. Sadie (London, 1961); No. 9 in C major, ed. Sadie (London, 1961); No. 11 in C minor, ed. Moffat (Berlin, 1902); No. 12 in G major, ed. Sadie (London, 1961).

[3] op. cit., iii, p. 620.

[4] The old edition leaves the player the choice of performing the bass 'on the violoncello or harpsichord'. Cf. also the Walsh edition of Arne's trios containing a similar remark.

[5] No. 1, ed. Seiffert, *Collegium Musicum* no. 57 (Leipzig, 1928); nos. 2–3, ed. Herbert Murrill (London, 1939 and 1951); no. 7, ed. Moffat (London, 1907).

[6] William S. Newman in *The Sonata in the Baroque Era* (Chapel Hill, 1959), p. 327, dates them at approximately 1740, the *British Union Catalogue of Early Music* (London, 1957), at 1757. Sadie, op. cit., p. 434, accepts the later date.

[7] La Laurencie, op. cit., ii, p. 15.

Joseph Gossec[1] (1734–1829), a native of Belgium, residing in France, reveal familiarity with the idiom the young generation had adopted in Vienna and Mannheim. Although these trios are skilfully devised and offer effective passages for the first violin, they yet confirm Mozart's verdict[2] that Gossec was 'a dull person'.

From the *a tre* combination there is only a step towards the *a quattro* with *basso continuo*. In 1742 there appeared under the imprint of the Parisian publishing house LeClerc *XII Sonate a 2 e 3 Violini col Basso del Signor Giuseppe San Martini*, Op. 2.[3] Half of these are real trios for two violins and figured bass. In the other half we find in the second violin part, and printed underneath it, music for a third violin. The latter has mostly an accompanying and filling-in function, and is placed in so low a register that it may easily be played by a viola. We may presume that it was occasionally omitted since the figured bass makes it dispensable. In any case, it is noteworthy that the publisher considered it unnecessary to produce a separate partbook for the third violin.

This cautious advance led to a new combination, which actually belongs to orchestral rather than chamber music. Compositions for two violins, viola, and *basso continuo* are not only frequently described as *sinfonia* or *ouverture*; their style also points to the use of more than one instrument for each part. Nevertheless the *a quattro* also has significance for chamber music as may be seen in the *Echo*,[4] Op. 8, in D major for 'flauto traverso, oboe, ovvero violino, viola da braccio e cembalo con violone' (Berlin, 1760) by the Silesian composer J. Gottlieb Janitsch (1708–63) or the *Conversation galante et amusante*,[5] Op. 12, no. 1, for flute, violin, bass viol, and continuo (Paris, 1743) by Louis-Gabriel Guillemain. The unusual combination of soloistically treated instruments and their intricate rhythms show clearly that these gay and playful works were designed for individual players.

The ensembles employing clavier obbligato were to a large extent intended for amateurs, whose enthusiasm was only too often matched by lack of skill. Their music had therefore to be free of technical difficulties. It was also an advantage if the work could be performed by different combinations of instruments—indeed, post-Baroque amateurs felt this even more keenly than those of the Baroque period. Countless works were presented for performance on either flute or violin—the choice between fortepiano and harpsichord being, up to the nineteenth century, left to the discretion of the performer—and an equally large

---

[1] No. 2 in Georges Cucuel, *Études sur un orchestre au XVIIIe siècle* (Paris, 1913), p. 3.
[2] Letter of 5 April 1778.
[3] Really by his brother, Giovanni Battista, and Antonio Brioschi: see p. 374.
[4] Hellmuth Christian Wolff (ed.), *Collegium Musicum*, no. 68 (Leipzig, 1938).
[5] P. Klengel (ed.), *Collegium Musicum*, no. 58 (Leipzig, 1930).

number of clavier compositions provided an optional accompaniment for string instruments. A typical example is J. B. Vaňhal's (1739–1813) sonatas for the pianoforte or harpsichord with accompaniments for a violin and violoncello, published by Longman & Co. (London, *c.* 1790). The cello part hardly differs from that of the clavier's left hand; moreover, the violin solos are inserted into the clavier part with the designation 'violino', and supported by a figured bass. If the violinist is available, the keyboard-player ignores the violin passages but realizes the figured bass. In the absence of the violinist he plays both the violin notes and the bass. An original line was taken by Mondonville in his *Pièces de Clavecin avec voix ou violon* (Op. 5) published in 1748. He explains in his preface that the pieces may be performed with the co-operation of a singer or a violin or both or without either. The ingenious Abbé Vogler[1] went even further and devised six different performing possibilities for his six *Pièces de musique dans un genre nouveau*, Op. 4, published by Schott (Mainz, n.d.). They could be played by (1) clavier alone, (2) clavier and violin, (3) clavier and flute, (4) clavier, violin, viola, cello, (5) clavier, flute, violin, viola, cello, (6) flute, violin, viola, cello.

THE EVOLUTION TO THE ENSEMBLE WITHOUT CONTINUO

The demand for chamber music, which was sizeable in the first half of the century, seems to have increased even more when the clavier part was written out. After 1750 there was such an abundance of printed editions, especially in Amsterdam, Paris, and London, that it is possible only to single out a few significant contributions by composers of different nationalities. As the use of string instruments was only too often optional, there is no clear dividing line between the various ensembles, which therefore will be discussed together.

The evolution from the ensemble depending on a continuo to one without it is excellently illustrated by the *Sei Sonate per Cembalo con Violino o Flauto Traverso*, Op. 3,[2] by Felice de Giardini (1716–96), published around 1751 in London. These are real 'trios' intended, however, for a melody instrument and a keyboard part of two melodic lines. The violin is frequently accompanied by the figured bass only; but when the keyboard-player's right hand starts on a melody of its own, no figures are to be found in the bass. The harpsichord is used alternately as an accompanying continuo instrument and as a combination of melody instrument and supporting bass. Typical keyboard features also occur, such as the Scarlatti device of crossing the hands, or the playing of

[1] Riemann (ed.), *Denkmäler der Tonkunst in Bayern*, xv (1915), p. xxiv.
[2] Polo (ed.), *I classici musicali italiani*, iii (Milan, 1942).

chords. The melodic idiom of these two-movement sonatas reveals a preference for brief phrases reminiscent of the *opera buffa*, and lacks strong thematic contrasts.

An entirely different picture is offered by the famous six *Sonates pour clavecin et violon*, Op. 5[1] (published as Op. 6), of Luigi Boccherini (1743–1805). They were composed in 1768, issued in the following year and frequently reprinted throughout the eighteenth century. In Boccherini's work the clavier accompaniments are fully elaborated and there are no passages with figured bass. The technique is adapted to the new pianoforte; in lieu of the repeated notes in the bass, characteristic of the harpsichord, preference is now given to the broken 'Alberti bass'. Most of the sonatas are in three movements in the order fast–slow–fast, but deviations from this conventional pattern may also be noticed, as for instance in no. 6 (E flat) which consists of an heroic march and a light rondo finale. In the melodic language there is no longer any predilection for short phrases. Tender, soft, and singing melodies are employed, while subsidiary subjects display a decisive contrast to the main idea and still use at times the device of canonic imitation:

Ex. 298 Allegro con moto

These works are among the most remarkable violin sonatas of the time. Looking at the 'Cantabile ma con un poco di moto' of no. 5 in G minor one cannot help wondering whether Mozart and possibly also Beethoven knew this music.

Less interesting are Boccherini's twelve piano quintets, Opp. 56 and 57.[2] These pieces in three or four movements, while revealing Boccherini's amiable charm, are equipped with an extremely simple, almost primitive piano part which achieves a certain stature only through the cooperation of the strings. The technique is curiously lacking in assurance and there is a striking gap between these works and his string quintets.[3]

The six quintets[4] for organ or harpsichord and string quartet by the Spanish composer Antonio Soler (1729–83), organist and later conductor at the Escorial, are true chamber-music pieces which allow the

[1] Ibid. iv (Milan, 1941). Nos. 25–30 in Yves Gérard, *Catalogue of the Works of Luigi Boccherini* (London, 1969). Ex. 298 is from no. 1.
[2] Nos. 407–18 in Gérard, op. cit.
[3] See pp. 567–9.
[4] Ed. Roberto Gerhard, with an introduction by Higini Anglès (Barcelona, 1933) and a complete list of works.

keyboard instrument and strings to co-operate or alternate in an attractive manner. In the middle sections of the frequently occurring minuets the four string instruments play alone, and these sections are quite logically designated *quartetto* instead of *trio* as usual. These works display no more specifically organ technique than do Mozart's organ trios dating from the same time, and the optional use of a harpsichord seems justified all the more as the technique of Soler's teacher, Domenico Scarlatti, is reflected in the keyboard part. The works display the character of divertimentos—there is little conciseness but much carefree spirit. No. 6 in G minor starts, for example, with an extensive rondo-like structure, three Andante sections being interrupted by two Allegros; there follows a minuet in E flat and the work ends with another rondo. These dainty and playful Rococo pieces make it hard for us to realize that their composer was a Spanish monk active in the austere abode housing the mausoleum of Spain's royal family.

In Germany the Mannheim composer Franz Xaver Richter stands, like the Italian Felice de Giardini, at the borderline between the old and the new era. His *VI Sonate da Camera a Cembalo obbligato, Flauto traverso o Violino concertato, e Violoncello*,[1] published by Ulrich Haffner (Nuremberg, 1764), still tend to have a figured bass when the violin has the leading melody. The cello doubles and strengthens the keyboard bass, and may be omitted without noticeable detriment to the overall effect. On the other hand, the violin part is significant, though it is not always independent of the clavier. Powerful, skilfully devised bass lines give these works vigour and energy. The loose fugal forms mainly to be found in the finales are reminiscent of Baroque music; but Richter's intimate chamber-music style, his careful harmonic language, free of shallowness, and his warmly singing, flexible melodic idiom, point towards the works of the Viennese classics.

The small output of chamber-music works by Ignaz Holzbauer includes two interesting quintets in G and B flat major *a Cembalo obbligato, Flauto obbligato, Violino obbligato, Viola e Basso*.[2] These still reveal features of the old trio: one melody instrument (flute) competes with the right-hand part of the clavier, while the strings mainly serve to solidify the texture. Both quintets end with a minuet whose trio takes the form of a theme with five variations. Here Holzbauer presents a different combination of instruments in each variation, entrusting the leadership each time to another member of the group. These two quintets are examples of the pleasant, skilfully written utility music so greatly in demand in this era.

[1] Upmeyer (ed.) (Kassel, 1951).
[2] *Das Erbe deutscher Musik*, xxiv, pp. 1 and 14 respectively.

Among the artists who helped to replace the Baroque preponderance of string instruments by writing chamber music with clavier obbligato, the Silesian composer Johann Schobert (c. 1740–67), who was active in Paris, deserves mention. We owe to him a number of valuable *Sonates pour le clavecin avec accompagnement de violon et basse* as well as *Sonates en quatuor pour le clavecin avec l'accompagnement de deux violons et basse*.[1] As the titles show, the string parts are mostly treated as accompaniment. Some experimentation does occur, however, for in certain minuets (cf. the trios of Op. 16, nos. 1 and 4) violin and cello take the lead, while the Allegro moderato of Op. 14, no. 3, is written for clavier alone. Schobert's music is imbued with deep feeling while at the same time displaying a virtuoso character. He likes broadly contoured cantilenas and employs both hands of the keyboard-player in brilliant passages which occasionally assume an almost orchestral nature:

Ex. 299

The composer explores the darker and more passionate ranges of expression; stormy tremolos may be effectively succeeded by delicate sighs. It is not surprising that this music exercised great influence on the receptive mind of the young Mozart and indeed is reflected in the works of Beethoven.

The attitude of the younger members of the Bach family towards this type of chamber music is significant. For Friedemann, born in 1710 and firmly rooted in the music of the past, it was of no interest and he contented himself with writing trio sonatas with continuo. But his brother Emanuel, born only four years later, reacted quite differently.

Although he wrote a number of works for ensembles with continuo, chamber music with a clavier part elaborated by the composer him-

[1] Riemann (ed.), *Denkmäler deutscher Tonkunst*, xxxix (Leipzig, 1909).

THE EVOLUTION TO ENSEMBLE WITHOUT CONTINUO   535

self[1] played a more important role in his output. In the early works for harpsichord and violin or flute, beginning about 1731, we still find the Baroque sequence of slow–fast–slow–fast (e.g. Wq. 71), canonic episodes, and the harmonic language of the past. The compositions of the fifties and sixties, however, employ neither a polyphonic nor a *concertato* style; the melody instrument contents itself largely with supporting the right hand of the keyboard-player. In the seventies and eighties C. P. E. Bach's chamber music gains in diversity, two melody instruments, such as violin and cello or flute and viola, joining the clavier. More care is given to dynamic indications, and the chamber music assumes the strongly subjective character to be found in the clavier solo works. The *Claviersonaten mit einer Violine und einem Violoncello zur Begleitung* of 1775–7 (Wq. 89–91) in particular[2] contain music of a strong emotional impact. The rondo, which allows the composer to reveal new facets of a musical idea, also appears frequently in the late chamber music. It is mostly to be found in the finales and, at times, also in the first movements.[3] A noble formal structure is now matched by profound emotional content, and the idiom approaches that of Haydn's mature works.

An intimate chamber-music character is particularly obvious in C. P. E. Bach's short works such as the twelve pieces for flute (or violin) and clavier (Wq. 82) published in 1770 at Hamburg.[4] These are exquisite miniatures, graceful or fiery, in which the melody instrument either co-operates with the clavier or appears without it. Related to them are the transparent six *Piccole Sonate* for two flutes, two clarinets, two horns and bassoon of 1775 (Wq. 184), four of which also exist in versions for clavier, clarinet, and bassoon (Wq. 92). It is significant for the composer, so greatly concerned with the clavier, that for those few of his chamber works which do not employ a keyboard instrument he offered an alternative version which does.

Emanuel's cousin, Johann Ernst Bach (1722–77) wrote six fine sonatas[5] for clavier and violin which appeared in two sets in 1770 and 1772. Here

[1] Two sonatas in B minor and C minor for cembalo obbligato and violin (Wq. 76, 78), ed. Hans Sitt (Leipzig, 1864); Sonata in G minor for cembalo obbligato and viola da gamba (Wq. 88), ed. Friedrich Grützmacher (Leipzig, 1881); Sonata in C major for cembalo obbligato and flute (Wq. 87), ed. Arij van Leeuwen (Leipzig, 1932); Sonata for cembalo obbligato and violin in D major (Wq. 71), ed. Schmid (Karlsbad, 1932); Sonata in B flat major for cembalo obbligato and violin (Wq. 77), ed. Landshoff (Leipzig, n.d.).

[2] Trios for clavier, violin, and cello in C major, B flat major, and G major (Wq. 89), ed. Schmid (Kassel, 1932).

[3] See the expressive Andantino of the Quartet for clavier, flute, viola (violoncello *ad lib.*) (Wq. 93), written in 1788, ed. Schmid (Kassel 1952); also the Quartets in D and G major (Wq. 94 and 95), ed. *idem*.

[4] Richard Hohenemser (ed.) (Berlin, 1928).

[5] Sonata in D major for clavier and violin, ed. Albert Küster (Hanover, 1927); Largo and Allegro from Sonata in F major for clavier and violin, ed. Geiringer, *Music of the Bach Family* (Cambridge, Mass., 1955), p. 159.

the violin complements the clavier as a partner with equal rights. Both instruments are skilfully handled, with understanding for their peculiar capacities, and there is frequently an attractive interchange of ideas. Though the composer evidently had the harpsichord in mind, there is no lack of passages which seem to be inspired by the pianoforte's more flexible tone. The sonatas are constructed in three concise movements, the second often leading with a half-close to the finale. They are merry and witty, but free of the shallow gaiety of conventional *galant* music.

A much larger output of chamber music with clavier has been preserved from the pen of J. C. Friedrich Bach (1732–95), a son of J. S. Bach by his second marriage. Among the various duets, Friedrich's fine Sonata in A[1] for violoncello and clavier of 1789 deserves mention. This work, which allows the cello a sizeable degree of independence, tends towards the old solo form, with mellow cantilenas effectively supported by the pianoforte. It is an attractive contribution to the rather sparse cello literature of the time. His trios[2] too show the composer not completely free from the Baroque style. In addition to an engaging sonata for harpsichord, flute (or violin), and cello, there is a work for flute, violin, and cembalo (piano) and another for violin, viola, and cembalo (or piano) in which the combinations of instruments seem to be influenced by the *sonata a tre*. A climax is reached in his Sextet[3] for pianoforte, two horns, oboe, violin, and cello, probably written about 1780. As the horns mainly provide filling-in parts, the effect is of a trio of melody instruments contrasted with the clavier. Gaiety and energy pervade this music, which approaches the art of the Viennese classics in its fresh, easily flowing and melodious idiom:

Ex. 300

The unusual combination of instruments suggests that the composer was not writing for average amateur groups; the sextet is evidently meant for professionals eager to display their proficiency.

It is interesting to compare the achievements of Friedrich Bach with those of his contemporary Haydn. Haydn did not consider the clavier

[1] Transposed edition, ed. John Smith (Leipzig, n.d.).
[2] C major for flute, cello, clavier, and G major for violin, viola, clavier, ed. Schünemann (Leipzig, 1920).
[3] Schünemann (ed.) (Leipzig, 1920).

his main instrument; consequently his chamber music with clavier does not reveal that independent pioneering spirit so evident in his other compositions, especially those for strings alone. The sonata for violin and clavier or flute and clavier apparently did not interest him at all, and the various editions of such works printed in his lifetime have all proved to be arrangements probably made by other musicians. His divertimenti for harpsichord with accompaniment of two violins and cello[1] do not concern us here, as the dominating rôle allotted to the keyboard instrument marks them as concertos. The only sizeable group of ensemble works is supplied by the thirty-odd trios[2] for clavier, violin (or flute), and cello which reach from an early period to the composer's maturity. The trios of the fifties and sixties occasionally approach the suite in character, and are by and large clavier sonatas with violin accompaniment and a reinforced clavier bass. After an extensive pause Haydn resumed the composition of trios in the eighties and gradually the picture changed. Though his former method was by no means discarded, he now began to write pieces like the first movement of Hob. XV/9 of 1785, in which violin and cello are one closely knit unit contrasted with the clavier:

Ex. 301

[1] Hoboken, op. cit., Gruppe XIV, p. 669.
[2] Ibid., Gruppe XV, p. 681.

Haydn's interest in this ensemble continued to grow in the nineties, and in these years he wrote more than half his clavier trios. The form increased in size, the content deepened, the modulatory idiom expanded. The great E minor middle movement of Hob. XV/28, probably inspired by the Baroque passacaglia, would at an earlier date hardly have been conceived by Haydn as a clavier trio. The turbulent Presto finale of Hob. XV/30 (1795) seems to forecast a Beethovenian scherzo. Particularly stirring is the Adagio cantabile of Hob. XV/26[1]; it represents a concise version of the slow movement in Symphony no. 102, a piece which evidently held a special meaning for the composer.

In the works of J. S. Bach's youngest son the tastes of the musical amateurs are again taken into consideration. The chamber music with clavier by Johann Christian Bach (1735–82) was not primarily addressed to professionals, and thanks to the lack of technical difficulties and their easily accessible content these works were immediately successful. In 1763 Christian started with the publication of six sonatas, Op. 2, for harpsichord with accompaniment of violin (or flute) and cello.[2] In these short two-movement compositions the cello part as usual has no life of its own. Apparently the public did not attach any importance to the instrument—in any case, it is no longer employed in the numerous works for keyboard and accompanying violin subsequently published. These duos are all in the major key, with not more than three flats or sharps. Usually they consist of two movements only, the first in rudimentary sonata form (with contrasting subjects, a short development, and incomplete recapitulation), the last an Allegretto or Tempo di menuetto in *da capo* or rondo form. In his first violin sonata[3] (Op. 10, no. 1, of 1773), J. C. Bach offered a tribute to his father, whom he had lost at the age of fifteen. The main subject of the first movement is taken from the

---
[1] Recorded in *The History of Music in Sound*, vii.
[2] No. 3 in D major, ed. Riemann (Leipzig, 1903).
[3] Sonatas, Op. 10, nos. 1–5, ed. Landshoff (London, 1938).

beginning of Partita no. 1 in Sebastian's *Clavierübung*, the Baroque melody having been skilfully transformed into a classical four-measure phrase:

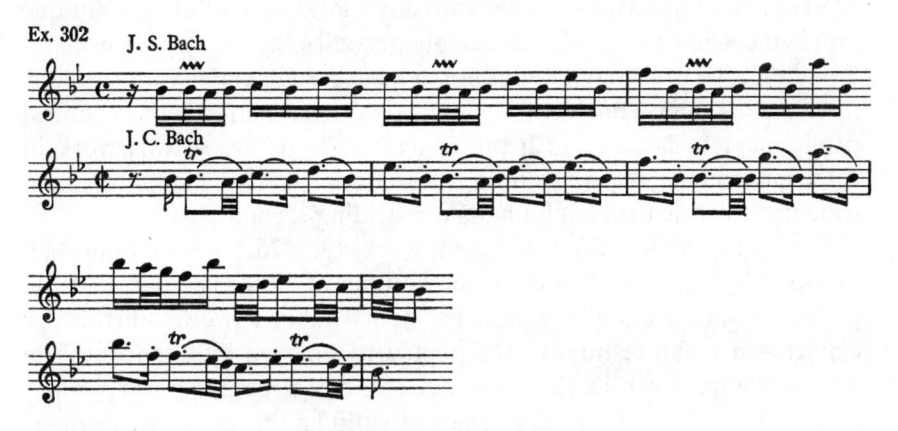

Ex. 302 J. S. Bach

J. C. Bach

MOZART'S VIOLIN SONATAS

The pliability, grace, and elegance of J. C. Bach's idiom, his singing allegros, and the warmth and tenderness of his subsidiary subjects, made a deep impression on the young Mozart, a fact clearly to be noticed in the younger artist's chamber music with clavier. It was Mozart who brought the form to a high point, and his output far exceeds that of other composers in quality. The core of this group is formed by over thirty works[1] for clavier and violin which stretch from Mozart's childhood to the period of his highest mastery. Mozart's first sonatas, written between the ages of six and ten, do not deviate fundamentally from the traditional clavier sonata with accompanying violin *ad libitum*. After a pause of twelve years he started to cultivate the form again and now the works reveal a decisive stylistic change. Real dialogues occur between the two instruments, whose utterances alternate or supplement each other in a nineteenth-century manner. Occasionally, it is true, there are still works which allow the piano a dominating rôle, but such compositions are at this stage very rare indeed.

The Sonatas K. 296 and 301–6 were written in 1778, partly at Mannheim, partly at Paris. The fact that K. 301–6 appeared in print as Op. 1 has a certain symbolic significance. Mozart's very first violin sonatas (K. 6, 7) had many years earlier been published as Op. 1 also, and the works of 1778 may be considered a new start in this form. In K. 296 he pays homage to his model; his Andante sostenuto recalls J. C. Bach's aria 'Dolci aurette',[2] though against a more sophisticated harmonic

[1] *Gesamtausgabe*, series 18; *Neue Ausgabe*, series VIII/23.
[2] J. C. Bach, *Konzert-und Opernarien* (ed. Landshoff) (Leipzig, 1930), p. 90.

background. Most of the sonatas consist of but two movements, and are light, witty, optimistic, and amusing. Strikingly different is K. 304 in E minor; the first movement (written perhaps under the impact of his mother's fatal illness) is imbued with a tragic passion of almost antique grandeur, while a delicate melancholy pervades the finale. The brilliant Sonata K. 306 in D major seems not to have been intended for amateurs, as it makes quite considerable demands on the performers' technical proficiency. In keeping with the concerto-like nature of this work in three movements, the concluding Allegretto includes an elaborate piano cadenza, to which the violin adds a sparkling second part.

Sonata K. 296 and five subsequent works (K. 376–80) were published as Op. 2 by Artaria, Vienna, in the autumn of 1781. The fact that the young composer could within a few years publish twelve sonatas for clavier and violin testifies to the popularity enjoyed by this form. The works of Op. 2 are in three movements, and a contemporary critic[1] rightly claims that 'they require just as skilful a player on the violin as on the clavier'. Here again are works of enchanting diversity offering a wealth of contrasts. K. 376 is gay and exuberant. K. 377, on the other hand, is turbulent in its first movement; a serious, plaintive D minor tune is the theme for the middle movement's variations, and only in the gentle and serene Tempo di menuetto is the conflict resolved. K. 379 is somewhat irregularly constructed. It starts with a broadly flowing, pathetic Adagio in G major which leads to a vigorous Allegro in G minor. A graceful Andantino cantabile with variations forms the conclusion. K. 380 places a brooding chromatic Andante con moto between two powerful Allegro movements in E flat. The rondo finale presents as episode a free C minor variation of the main theme, an agitated section which, with its runs of chromatic semiquavers, seems to forecast the mood of *Don Giovanni*.

Curiously, after these brilliant compositions of 1781, Mozart began to experiment in the form. The acquaintance with Baroque music, which he made at that time through Baron van Swieten, evidently stimulated him to practise polyphonic writing. Thus K. 402 consists of a pompous prelude followed by a fugue in which the violin is entrusted with one part, and the piano with three. As this sounded unsatisfactory the composer broke off in the middle of his work. In K. 403 Mozart, apparently influenced by C. P. E. Bach's trios, tried to write in three parts, only occasionally supplying some filling-in notes. This style was no longer in use, and consequently this work too remained a torso.[2]

Such failures were more than counterbalanced by the three 'great'

---

[1] In K. F. Cramer's *Magazin der Musik*, i, p. 485 (Hamburg, 4 April 1783).
[2] Both compositions were subsequently completed by Maximilian Stadler.

sonatas which constitute the peak of Mozart's activity in this form. K. 454 was composed in April 1784 for the Vienna recital of the young violinist Regina Strinasacchi, in which Mozart played the piano part. Here the traditional relationship of the two instruments has almost been reversed, as again and again the violin is given preference (though the composer's own part has by no means been neglected). A forceful Largo introduction prepares for the gay and energetic Allegro. In the ensuing Andante deep emotion merges with supreme artistry, and a style is achieved that is completely free of the last remnants of conventional expression. 'The middle section, with its deep glow of passion and its romantic harmonies, leads straight to Schubert.'[1] Likewise, the concluding Allegretto is more serious and substantial than the customary finales.

K. 481, composed in December 1785, is hardly inferior. In the development section of the first movement Mozart surprises us by presenting, instead of the subjects introduced in the exposition, a new idea for elaboration, one to occur again at the outset of the 'Jupiter' Symphony finale. The Adagio with its fantastic modulations, and the concluding, beautifully climaxed Allegretto with variations, are among those masterly achievements which explain why the young Beethoven was eager to study with Mozart.

In K. 526 the most important movement again occurs in the middle of the work, a sensitive Andante, devoid of sentimentality, which precedes a breathless Presto finale. Mozart's last contribution to the form, K. 547 (1788), is a rather problematic work, tending alternately towards light music for beginners and virtuoso brilliance, and fluctuating between suite and sonata.

MOZART'S PIANO TRIOS

Mozart's output in the form of the piano trio[2] is related to that in the violin sonata, though it includes fewer works. He starts in the traditional way, allowing limited independence to the violin and hardly any to the cello. The decisive step forward was taken only with the G major Trio (K. 496) of 1786. The first movement of this trio presents in the development a dramatic dialogue between cello and piano bass which may have seemed revolutionary to contemporary listeners:

[1] Hermann Abert in *Cobbett's Cyclopedic Survey of Chamber Music*, 2nd edn. (London, 1963) ii, p. 176.
[2] *Gesamtausgabe*, series 17; *Neue Ausgabe*, series VIII/22, Abt. 2.

Ex. 303

Likewise in the ensuing Andante, with its striking modulations, the two string instruments carry on a conversation joined at times by the piano, which, however, always leaves the initiative to them. In conclusion there is an Allegretto with variations. This starts at first in a somewhat pedestrian manner. However, in the fourth variation in G minor, and subsequently in the coda, it conjures up a subdued and oppressed mood of almost tragic impact, a sudden emotional reversal revealing Mozart's inclination for mixing dark colours into otherwise bright pictures.[1] The second of the 'great' trios (K. 502) was also written in 1786. Here the realization of the new 'quartet-style', allotting two parts to the string instruments and two to the piano, made further progress. Transparency of texture, unobtrusive contrapuntal virtuosity and a melodic idiom imbued with lightness and grace distinguish this work. Its stylistic relationship to Mozart's contemporary piano concertos has justly been noted. The trio displays the same *concertato* features of brilliance and elegance,

[1] Also among the trios there are incomplete pieces. They were completed by Stadler and published as a single D minor trio, K. 442. This curious amalgamation is rather uneven in both style and quality.

though it is more intimate in character. Between K. 496 and 502 there is another piano trio, K. 498, for which Mozart chose an uncommon combination of instruments; here clarinet and viola join the keyboard. In this magnificent work Mozart's perfect sense of instrumental colouring reveals itself. The rich and sensuous-sounding clarinet is juxtaposed with the dark, brooding, and somewhat dry tone of the string instrument, while the piano serves as partner or accompanist. Even Mozart did not often succeed in writing a work like the Clarinet Trio, which so wholly satisfies performers as well as audience.

In 1788 the composer reverted to the piano, violin, and cello and composed three trios. Two of them (K. 548, 564) were written during, and soon after, the time when Mozart was engaged on his last great symphonies, and reveal a certain lack of interest in the smaller form. Quite different is K. 542, which was completed earlier. This E major trio almost surpasses the three masterworks of 1786. Mozart himself thought highly of it. He wanted it to be heard by Michael Haydn, whose verdict he respected, and played it himself at the Dresden Court. The first movement is especially interesting for the way it subjects insignificant motives to brilliant contrapuntal and modulatory treatment in the development:

Ex. 304

The Andante grazioso of the second movement achieves a classical sublimation of Rococo poetry, and the finale is a virtuoso piece in which brilliance and verve are matched by the intricacy of the thematic elaboration.

MOZART'S PIANO QUARTETS AND QUINTET

In 1785 Mozart wrote his first quartet[1] for pianoforte, violin, viola, and cello (K. 478). The traditional combination of string instruments—two violins (or flute, violin) and cello—common in earlier compositions, is here replaced by that of string instruments in high, middle, and low range. This combination is better suited to balance the keyboard instrument and to achieve the character of true chamber music. Mozart's work was printed by Hoffmeister, but according to Nissen it had little success, and the publisher, who had intended to present three Mozart quartets, withdrew from the contract. It is not difficult to understand the public's reaction, for this work was bound to appear problematical to the lover of music in the eighteenth century. The first movement, in G minor, has a demonic fury and passion. The coda, with its rise to a thundering *ff* and the Baroque unison conclusion, displays a vehemence of expression quite foreign to the taste of the time. The following movements are, it is true, less unconventional: a simple and serene Andante in B flat major, followed by a gay rondo in G major. The latter introduces a cantabile melody (later employed in the Rondo for piano, K. 485) which appears like a bow to Johann Christian Bach[2]:

Ex. 305

[1] *Gesamtausgabe*, series 17, no. 2; *Neue Ausgabe*, series VIII/22/Abt. 1.
[2] A quartet for violin, viola, cello, and piano, attributed to Bach (cf. Charles Sanford Terry, *J. C. Bach*, London, 1929, p. 310) ends likewise with a rondo in G major.

Despite the public's lukewarm reception Mozart wrote a second quartet[1] in the following year. By contrast with its predecessor, this work, in E flat major (K. 493), has gaiety and warmth. Composed shortly after the completion of *Figaro*, it is pervaded by some of the opera's mediterranean serenity.

The composer's only piano quintet[2] (K. 452) is again in the key of E flat major. Composed in 1784, it is one of the earliest of Mozart's 'great' chamber-music works with piano obbligato. The composer here set himself a novel problem, as four wind instruments—oboe, clarinet, horn, and bassoon—are combined with the piano. The former are, however, anything but homogeneous, and the composer never tired of exploring their differences in sonority. Features of the *stile concertato* noticeable in the first two movements become even more conspicuous in the rondo finale. Here one finds an elaborate cadenza, though the character of chamber music is never relinquished and Mozart avoids preferential treatment for any of his five instruments. The mastery evident in this work was admired by the young Beethoven, who in 1797 wrote his quintet for the same group of instruments. This, however despite its distinction, does not match the glory of its model.

DUETS FOR STRINGS OR WIND

More important than the chamber music with *basso continuo*, and even with clavier obbligato, are the works for strings alone or for string and wind instruments, as they represent some of the great innovations of eighteenth-century chamber music. As mentioned before, these ensembles were formed either by omitting the clavier part or by partially replacing it with a melody instrument in the middle range. In view of the vast output of works in this field, they will be grouped according to the combination of instruments employed.

Among the amateurs and music students of the period the duet for two string or wind instruments enjoyed particular favour as it was meant both for instruction[3] and for the fashionable drawing-room. Ignaz Pleyel (1757–1831) wrote eight books of duets[4] for strings and Anton Stamitz (1754–c. 1809) in the first forty years of his life composed about a dozen sets[5] each comprising six numbers. Naturally works of such

---

[1] *Gesamtausgabe*, series 17/3; *Neue Ausgabe*, series VIII/22/Abt. 1.
[2] *Gesamtausgabe*, series 17/1; *Neue Ausgabe*, series VIII/22/Abt. 1.
[3] Characteristic is the title of a work by the Dresden conductor J. Gottlieb Naumann, *Six duos faciles pour deux violons à l'usage des commençants*; modern edition by Paul Bormann (Kassel, c. 1951).
[4] e.g. *6 petits duos pour 2 violons*, Op. 8, ed. Ferdinand David (Leipzig, n.d.) and 3 duos, Op. 61, ed. Friedrich Hermann (Leipzig, n.d.).
[5] Cf. *Denkmäler der Tonkunst in Bayern*, xvi (Leipzig, 1915), p. xxi.

limited technical means offered only modest possibilities of expression; yet there was so great a demand for duets that they even invaded the concert hall.[1]

In the duets for two violins the string instruments may also play double stops and even full chords. In the duets for two flutes, where only two parts are possible, the harmonic progressions are more hinted at than clearly expressed, resulting in a floating quality.

Though the form achieved its full growth in the second half of the century, examples of it appeared before this time.[2] Even an artist aloof from fashionable ideas like W. Friedemann Bach (1710–84) could not rid himself of the general trend and wrote four duets for two flutes[3] while serving at Dresden, i.e. before 1746. These avoid, however, the studied simplicity so often noticeable in this form. Vigorous use is made of the Baroque crossing of parts and the style is truly polyphonic, the G major sonata even containing a carefully worked out two-part fugue. The harmonic language reveals at times a surprising boldness as the 'Lamentabile' in the F major sonata shows:

Ex. 306

In the last years of his life the composer wrote two other flute duets besides three duets for violas.[4] In these late works he is even less prepared to make concessions. Canon and fugue are now more frequently used and the composer maintains two parts without resorting to the customary expedient of employing double stops to enrich the texture. Unconventional pieces such as these seem to explain why Friedemann died a lonely embittered man, forgotten by the world around him.

[1] Cf. Carl Stamitz's *The favorite Duet for Violin and Tenor as performed by Messrs. Cramer and Crosdill* and the brilliant show-pieces by Paganini's master, Alessandro Rolla (1757–1841).
[2] See Vol. VI.
[3] ed. K. Walther (Leipzig, n.d.).
[4] Cf. Martin Falck, *Wilhelm Friedemann Bach* (Leipzig, 1913), pp. 119–21, and thematic catalogue, nos. 54–62.

An unbridgeable gulf lies between Friedemann Bach's works and the compositions of Emanuele Barbella (c. 1710–73). The G major duet[1] of 1760 by this Italian violinist is completely homophonic and devised so skilfully that even an amateur of modest technical proficiency may produce the illusion of some brilliance. Double stops of the easiest type are frequent; the second violin is almost always accompanying and moving at a lower range than the first. In the final rondo the occasional use of the minor mode produces a temporary clouding-over of the sunny atmosphere, thus achieving a piquant contrast.

Somewhat related in character are the graceful *Sei duetti per violini*, Op. 3 (Paris, 1769, as Op. 5), composed by Boccherini[2] and the set similarly entitled by Gossec published 1765 in Paris as Op. 7.[3] Gossec's short B flat major duet Op. 7, no. 5, in two movements does not move beyond the first three positions and is evidently meant for beginners. Yet a suggestion of Gallic splendour and pomp endows the work with unexpected attractiveness.

The six duets for violin and viola which Haydn wrote at the beginning of the seventies are particularly interesting. The composer, who was studying Baroque music at that time, presented 'violin solos with the accompaniment of a viola', as he noted in his *Entwurfkatalog*.[4] Melodic interest and thematic development are concentrated in the upper part, while the lower instrument mostly provides harmonic support. It is significant that the first printed version issued in 1775 by Bailleux described the work as *Six Sonates à Violon seul avec la Basse*, thus possibly implying the co-operation of a keyboard instrument, while the first edition of the original version for violin and viola was not published until 1799.[5] The sonatas are distinguished by well-rounded form, exhibiting the wealth of invention and the large-scale planning characteristic of Haydn's compositions of that period. This is idiomatic music, offering the violin an opportunity to display a solid technique which, however, never degenerates into empty brilliance.

Though Haydn's work did not meet with popular success it seems to have been appreciated by connoisseurs. The composer's own brother, Michael (1737–1806), wrote in 1783, by order of the Archbishop of Salzburg, four duets[6] for the same instrumental combination which clearly follow Joseph's example. These pieces are likewise in three movements with a rondo or a set of variations as finale. The viola is assigned almost

---

[1] In Bormann, *Das Violinduett im 18. Jahrhundert* (Hamburg, 1954), i, p. 4.
[2] Nos. 2, 5, and 6 in ibid. Nos. 56–61 in Gérard, op. cit.
[3] Nos. 5 and 6 in ibid.
[4] Jens Peter Larsen, *Drei Haydn Kataloge in Faksimile* (Copenhagen, 1941), p. 15.
[5] By André (Offenbach), cf. Hoboken, op. cit. i, p. 512.
[6] J. Siderits (ed.) (Vienna, 1950).

as little independence as in Joseph Haydn's 'solos', and the leading character of the violin part is still emphasized by fermatas, which appear twice near the end of a slow movement and invite the violinist to insert a cadenza. This is amiable entertainment music to suit the taste prevailing at the Salzburg Court. From a historical viewpoint the duets are important, as they caused Mozart to compose two masterly works.

A frequently repeated anecdote relates that Michael Haydn fell ill after completing four duets. As his patron had demanded six works, Mozart came to the rescue and supplied the two missing compositions,[1] authorizing his friend to hand these pieces over as his own works. Whatever the truth of this story, Mozart's works (K. 423, 424)[2] certainly originated in the second half of the year 1783 and in their formal construction and some details resemble the works by the two Haydns. There is a significant difference, however. Mozart, an excellent viola player himself, did not neglect the lower part, and endowed it with almost as much brilliance as the violin. Frequently the traditional relationship is reversed; the parts cross, and the violin accompanies in the low register while the melody is in the viola. These duets are reminiscent of a related work which Mozart had composed in Salzburg four years earlier: the *Symphonie concertante* for violin and viola (K. 364). The wealth of sonorities in these duos and the wide range of expression prove that Mozart gave his best even within such narrow confines.[3]

With these two Mozart works, the duet for two melody instruments reached its climax. Equality became more and more the rule, and in duets combining instruments of different range there was even an occasional tendency to favour the lower part. The employment of two flutes, two violins, or violin and viola, still predominated, but works in more varied tonal colours began to appear, as in Gottlieb Naumann's (1741–1801) Duet for oboe and bassoon.[4] The form, moreover, continued to be cultivated until far into the nineteenth century.

STRING OR WIND TRIOS

The trios, without continuo or clavier obbligato, are direct descendants of the Baroque *sonata a tre*, and it is by no means easy to draw the line between old and new. The titles of the contemporary editions hardly offer a clue, and the customary heading *due violini e basso* is intentionally ambiguous. '*Basso*' may designate a violoncello alone or the bass part of a keyboard instrument with or without cello. Nor can the presence of

[1] Georges de Saint-Foix, *W. A. Mozart*, iii, (Paris, 1936), p. 384.
[2] *Gesamtausgabe*, series 15/1, no. 2.
[3] Mozart did not from the outset achieve this independence for the second part. About 1775 he wrote a duet for bassoon and cello (K. 292) which is more like a 'solo' for bassoon.
[4] Bormann (ed.), (Hamburg, 1953).

figures in the bass provide clarification, since the publishers liked, for practical reasons, to offer music with figured bass even when a keyboard instrument was not really required. On the other hand, many manuscripts of works which were probably intended for an ensemble with clavier lacked bass figures, since the cembalist could easily improvise. In the chamber music of the transitional period the only criterion is the style of the composition itself. When the bass participates in the thematic work, when repeated notes in the bass are not in the typical harpsichord manner, when the gaps between the upper and the lower parts are not unduly pronounced, then the use of a keyboard instrument does not seem to be called for, and a cello is sufficient. The transition occurred slowly; before 1760 there are but few compositions dispensing with the keyboard instrument; after 1770 the opposite is the case. From a technical point of view three-part writing presents some problems, and the trio was unable to hold its own against the quartet with its superior artistic potentialities. Furthermore, the combination of three players was not as easily obtainable as that of two, and the trio therefore never enjoyed the popularity won by the duet. Nevertheless, the leading composers took an interest in this challenging form that had been mainly favoured by connoisseurs.

An interesting example of music from the transition period is offered by Johann Christian Bach's six *sonate notturne*[1] published in 1765 in Paris with the designation *pour deux violons et alto viola ou basse obligée*. The part of the viola lies close to that of the two violins, resulting in a compact texture which makes the collaboration of a harpsichord superfluous. On the other hand, the title-page suggests that the viola could be replaced by a *basse obligée*. Actually an old manuscript has been preserved in which this substitution is made.[2] The notes of the lowest instrument are here transposed an octave down and written in the bass clef. The resulting gap between upper and lower parts and the absence of lively thematic action in the bass pose the question whether for this version a string instrument alone or one joined by the harpsichord was to be used. Each sonata consists of two movements: an extensive slow piece and a minuet with trio. This is unpretentious music, its delicacy fitting the instrumentation for viola and violins which was no doubt the composer's first choice.

The trio without cello or harpsichord is particularly well suited for the co-operation of the flute, since its tone enhances the pastel character of the medium. This is evident in the C major Trio for flute, violin (or

[1] Sydney Beck (ed.), (New York, 1937).
[2] Washington, Lib. of Congress, M 350/M 28/Case. For a similar handling of the problem in duos, cf. p. 547.

second flute) and viola, Op. 3, no. 3, by the Bückeburg conductor Franz Christoph Neubaur (1760–95).[1] The work consists of an Allegro, a slow variation movement, and a rondo (*tempo di minuetto*) and entrusts the viola with as interesting a part as the two upper voices. It is written with great skill and attracts by its colouring and its graceful idiom. Somewhat related in character is the G major Trio[2] for two flutes and viola by Wilhelm Friedrich Ernst Bach (1759–1845), a grandson of J. S. Bach. In his capacity as music teacher of the children of Queen Louise of Prussia he may have found good use for this playful work. As a curious contrast to these compositions, two trios by Giuseppe dall'Abaco expertly written for three cellos[3] ought to be mentioned. One is in three movements, the other in four, with the sequence Moderato–Adagio–Capriccio–Allegro. This is entertaining, technically not too easy music, well suited for instructional purposes.

Boccherini's sixty-odd trios[4] are among the most significant contributions to this form. At seventeen years of age he wrote as his Op. 2, later renumbered 1, *Sei tercetti per due violini e violoncello obbligato*. Several works of this kind followed until in 1772 Boccherini employed in his Op. 14 a new instrumental combination which had a strong impact on the evolution of the form: the trio for violin, viola, and cello. In replacing the second violin with the deeper viola he removed the last reason for the employment of filling-in middle parts. Moreover, Boccherini liked to give the cello part such difficult passages that it assumed an almost concerto-like character. Particularly attractive in this set are the Trio no. 4 in D major with a middle movement of almost impressionistic delicacy, and no. 6, in F major, which starts with a most expressive Larghetto and concludes with a dance-like rondo. This imposing *opera grande*, as the composer designated it himself, was followed in 1793 by the *opera piccola*, Op. 47 (pub. as 38), for the same instruments. The trios are in two movements, usually ending with a minuet. Grace and a somewhat languid elegance pervade these attractive miniatures. Though successfully handling the new instrumental combination, Boccherini by no means discarded the traditional ensemble. Between his Opp. 14 and 47 he wrote in 1781 the Six Trios for two violins and cello, Op. 34 (pub. as 35), which show him at the summit of his art. These are broadly conceived works, brilliant and full of charm. Particularly interesting is no. 4 which begins with an Allegro moderato assai. The following Grave is condensed to a four-measure introduction leading to a second Allegro. At its end the brief Grave reappears, this time

[1] Bormann (ed.), (Hamburg, 1954).
[2] Ermeler (ed.), (Kassel, 1943).
[3] Washington, Lib. of Congress, M 350/M 28/Case.
[4] Nos. 77–142 in Gérard, op. cit.

leading to the concluding *tempo di minuetto*. Such attempts to provide firmer cohesion to his work are characteristic of Boccherini's idiom. On the other hand, other trios of this set show a leaning towards the classical structure, fast–slow–minuet–rondo, as do works in Op. 54 (1796).

Boccherini wrote three times as many works for the customary trio of two violins and cello as for the new combination of violin, viola, and cello, and many other composers continued to employ the older ensemble. As typical examples there are two works by Mannheim composers, available in reprints, which may be singled out. Wilhelm Cramer's (1745–99) Trio in B flat major, Op. 3, no. 2,[1] is an effective and brilliant piece introducing dramatic contrasts between the major and minor modes, and offering careful dynamic markings. Anton Stamitz's Trio in E flat major, Op. 4, no. 1,[2] on the other hand is brief and unpretentious, its dignified old-fashioned minuet creating an attractive contrast to the prevailing *galant* idiom.

Among the leading composers of the eighteenth century no one made as large a contribution to the trio literature as Joseph Haydn. The early works for two violins and bass have already been discussed as trio sonatas.[3] Between 1762 and 1775 Haydn composed no fewer than a hundred and twenty-six other trios for a rather unusual instrumental combination. The main part is entrusted to the baryton, of which Haydn's patron, Prince Nicholas Esterházy, was an enthusiastic player. This instrument is related to the bass viol, and besides the six or seven strings over its fingerboard has another set of strings attached underneath. These serve a double function: they sound in sympathetic vibration with the upper strings and may also be played pizzicato by the performer's left thumb, the neck of the baryton being open at the back. A viola, replaced by a violin in three works, and a cello supply the remaining voices. These trios[4] in three movements are carefully elaborated and prove that Haydn knew how to produce works of art, even when forced to something like mass production. Quotations and arrangements from the composer's own symphonies and operas, and even from Gluck, may have amused his august patron.[5] Modern listeners, for their part, admire the characteristic features in these remarkable works: the occasional derivation of subsidiary subjects from the main ideas, intricate contrapuntal devices, interesting harmonic progressions,

---

[1] *Denkmäler der Tonkunst in Bayern*, xvi, p. 102.

[2] Ibid., p. 136.

[3] See p. 526.

[4] *J. Haydn: Werke* (Munich and Duisburg, 1958 ff.), series 14 (ed. Hubert Unverricht, Michael Härting, and Horst Walter).

[5] See Unverricht's prefaces, ibid., and H. C. Robbins Landon, *The Symphonies of Joseph Haydn* (London, 1955), p. 260, n. 22.

and delightful sound effects achieved with the baryton's peculiar pizzicato (prescribed by numbers in the score):

Ex. 307

The frequent attempts to arrange baryton trios for conventional string trio have unfortunately proved a failure, as the pieces need the baryton's distinctive sound.

In 1767 Haydn wrote an attractive trio in two movements for horn, violin, and cello[1] which offers the horn-player excellent opportunities to exhibit his technical skill. Much later, during his visit to London in 1794, he contributed several trios for the fashionable combination of two flutes and cello.[2] Perhaps he wished to give amateurs a special treat and so chose the flute, which enjoyed great favour in England.

Mozart wrote a single string trio, the Divertimento K. 563[3] of 1788 for violin, viola, and cello. His arrangements of Bach's fugues for violin, viola, and cello, which he scored in 1782 (K. 404a),[4] may be considered a kind of preliminary study. With no more than three instruments at his disposal, Mozart achieved a polyphonic loosening of the texture, a sonority and diversity usually to be found in string quartets only. He enlarged the traditional structure of four movements by inserting two extra movements in the middle, and thereupon entitled the work a divertimento. In this music 'for entertainment', however, dark hues intermingle with brilliance. Particularly moving is the set of variations on a simple folk-song-like theme in the Andante, for instance the passage when the viola intones the theme like a *canto fermo*.

THE STRING QUARTET

Among the new eighteenth-century chamber-music ensembles, the string quartet for two violins, viola, and cello assumed the leading role.[5]

---

[1] H. C. Robbins Landon (ed.) (Vienna, 1957).
[2] Hob. IV/1–4. L. Balet (ed.) (Hanover, 1931).
[3] *Gesamtausgabe*, series 15, no. 4.
[4] Concerning these works, see Warren Kirkendale, 'More slow introductions by Mozart to fugues of J. S. Bach?' *Journal of the American Musicological Society*, xvii (1964), p. 43; idem, *Fuge und Fugato in der Kammermusik des Rokoko und der Klassik* (Tutzing, 1966); Andreas Holschneider, 'Zu Mozarts Bearbeitungen Bachscher Fugen', *Die Musikforschung*, xvii (1964), pp. 51–6, 463–4; Gerhard Croll, 'Eine neuentdeckte Bach–Fuge für Streichquartett von Mozart', *Österreichische Musikzeitschrift*, xxi (1966), p. 508.
[5] Cf. p. 617.

It is hardly possible to ascertain at what precise time the string quartet was first developed. Four-part compositions for strings were no rarity in the first half of the eighteenth century. They were, however, closer to orchestral than to chamber music, and depended as a rule on the co-operation of a continuo instrument. On the other hand, the idea that the string bass part should be played alone, at times, without a keyboard instrument either to double or to add chords, was well known to the Baroque era, and occasionally whole pieces were written without a clavier. To this category belong the works of a composer not usually associated with instrumental music. Alessandro Scarlatti (1660–1725), the great master of Neapolitan opera, wrote in the last decade of his life *Sonate a quattro: Due Violini, Violetta e Violoncello—senza Cemb[al]o*.[1] The remark *senza cembalo* deliberately distinguishes this work from the contemporary *a quattro* literature with basso continuo.[2] We do not know whether it was really meant for four players only. Occasional indications such as *solo* and *tutti* seem to point to a concerto-like arrangement, but, in view of the liberty taken in performing practice during the Baroque era, other possibilities need not be excluded. It is certain, at any rate, that the compact, frequently polyphonic, texture of these works makes unnecessary the addition of a continuo instrument. Scarlatti's quartets employ the sequence fast–slow–fast, with an occasional minuet as finale. Other composers, too, wrote works of this kind which, in most cases, are closer to the symphony and concerto than to the string quartet proper.

HAYDN'S EARLIER QUARTETS

The contribution of Haydn to the form of the string quartet was vital. His first twelve quartets (Op. 1, nos. 1–4, 6; Op. 2, nos. 1–6, and the E flat major quartet known as 'no. 0')[3] clearly reveal a divertimento-like character. Usually, fast movements occur at the beginning and end, a slow movement framed by two minuets appearing in the middle. The music is popular and simple in character. In the F minor Adagio of Op. 2, no. 4 the naïve Austrian idiom is replaced by the North German 'sensibility' of C. P. E. Bach, whose music Haydn greatly admired. Dialogues between the two violins occur frequently; the viola is almost wholly subordinate to the cello, which it often doubles at the octave. The resultant predominance of three voices suggests the evolution of

[1] Edward J. Dent, 'The Earliest String Quartets', *Monthly Musical Record*, xxxiii (1903), p. 202. *Sonate a quattro* in D minor and G minor, ed. Hans David (New York, 1940).

[2] Ignoring the indication on the manuscript, the publisher Benjamin Cooke issued movements from this with figured bass (London, *c.* 1740). Similarly, Haydn's early quartets were frequently published with figured bass.

[3] No. 0 is available in two editions; ed. Marion Scott (London, 1932), and ed. Geiringer (Hanover, 1932).

this form from the trio sonata rather than the Baroque *a quattro*, and this derivation from a basically different genre may account both for the youthful freshness of the style and for the groping uncertainty in solving its problems. Haydn's biographer, August Griesinger, claims—evidently on information from the aged composer—that the first string quartet originated in 1750.[1] The other quartets written in similar style were no doubt composed in the fifties as well. But we cannot know whether these works were conceived as real chamber music or were meant for a small orchestra. The facts that Op. 2, nos. 3 and 5 were originally scored with two horns and that Op. 1, no. 5 exists also in a symphonic version with two oboes and two horns[2] provides food for thought.

The six quartets known as Op. 3 belong to a somewhat later period. Their authenticity has been challenged by László Somfai,[3] and it seems possible that they are compositions by one of Haydn's pupils, Romanus Hofstetter.[4] In the six quartets, Op. 9, composed before 1769, the structure in four movements has become the rule. This set clearly reveals the elaboration of detail so significant for the true chamber-music style. It is interesting to note that Haydn now allots greater significance to the development; in the first movements he so extends the middle section as to make it almost equal in length to the exposition. Moreover, the somewhat stereotyped modulation- and sequence-technique used in the development sections of the earlier quartets gives way to careful selection, those musical ideas in the exposition which offer the best scope for thematic elaboration being given preference. There is also much evidence of an approach to the idiom of C. P. E. Bach. In the slow movement of no. 2 an introduction full of dramatic tension dissolves into a nostalgic song. The D minor quartet, no. 4, has not only a passionate first movement, but also a minuet in a similar mood, while the finale reverts to the opposite pole of emotion. Besides such sharp contrasts in mood, a certain leaning towards a rhapsodic idiom—evident, for instance, in the brilliant passages in the first violin—points to Bach, whose influence was stressed by Haydn himself.

The six quartets, Op. 17, of 1771 go one step farther. The first violin's virtuosity is as evident as in Op. 9, but there is no lack of passages in which the second violin takes the lead while the first merely accompanies. In the adagios of this remarkable set one notices harsh and bold harmonic progressions; on the other hand, a typical Austrian note is un-

[1] *Biographische Notizen über Joseph Haydn* (Leipzig, 1810). Engl. translation by Vernon Gotwals in *Joseph Haydn, Eighteenth Century Gentleman and Genius* (Madison, 1963), p. 13.
[2] Landon, op. cit., Appendix.
[3] 'A klasszikus kvartetthangzás megszületése Haydn vonósnágyeseiben' (with abstract in German), *Haydn Emlékére* (Budapest, 1965), p. 295.
[4] See Landon and Alan Tyson, 'Who Composed Haydn's Op. 3?' *Musical Times*, cv (1964), p. 506.

mistakable in the effervescent minuets. Development now assumes an even greater importance; for instance, in the first movement of no. 5 the middle section is longer than the preceding exposition.[1] With the six 'Sun' quartets,[2] Op. 20 (1772)—*divertimenti a quattro*, as the autograph calls them—Haydn's work in this medium reached its first climax. Most conspicuous in these quartets is the conscious reversion to the Baroque style. The Adagio of no. 2 starts with a four-bar introduction, the unison of which reminds us of the tutti-ritornello in an old concerto. Moreover, no less than three times in this set a fugue serves as the finale. With a somewhat naïve pride Haydn pointed out his artistry, explaining in the heading that he was presenting a fugue *a due* or *a tre* or, even, *a quattro soggetti*. Stretto sections are marked *in canone* and inversions in somewhat careless Italian as *al roverscio*. All this shows Haydn to be quite aware of the unusual character of these quartets and anxious to account for his methods. Again, the influence of C. P. E. Bach is clearly noticeable. Deep emotion often pervades this music, and it is significant that the designation *affettuoso*, often employed by Bach for his slow movements, occurs twice in the 'Sun' quartets. The minor mode is given a prominent place. Two quartets are in the minor key, and the other works modulate again and again to the minor. At the same time, the aim towards strong characterization leads to the inclusion of folk elements (cf. the Menuetto alla zingarese of no. 4 and the ensuing, typically Hungarian, Presto scherzando). These six quartets reveal a striving for deeper and stronger expression,[3] and it is not surprising that Beethoven was led to make a copy of the first number of the set.

OTHER STRING QUARTETS OF THE PERIOD

Between the completion of the 'Sun' quartets and that of the next group there occurred a pause of nine years. Before proceeding to the second half of Haydn's output of string quartets, it seems advisable to survey the production of other composers of the time. Although several were born before Haydn, their work probably did not precede Haydn's first quartets.

Franz Xaver Richter's six quartets, Op. 5,[4] were published between 1767 and 1771 in London. These are attractive works in true quartet style with independent parts for viola and cello. Crossing of voices is no

---

[1] Cf. the extensive analysis of this set in Friedrich Blume, 'Joseph Haydns künstlerische Persönlichkeit in seinen Streichquartetten', *Jahrbuch Peters* (Leipzig, 1931).

[2] The designation is due to the sun on the title-page of the Hummel edition (Amsterdam and Berlin, 1779); it has also been given a symbolic interpretation, as Haydn's genius shines forth with full brilliance in these quartets.

[3] For an extensive analysis of the F minor quartet, no. 5 of the set, see pp. 618–20. The fugal finale of the A major, no. 6, is recorded in *The History of Music in Sound*, vii.

[4] *Denkmäler der Tonkunst in Bayern*, xv.

rarity, and in the slow movement of the first quartet we find the two violin parts below those of the viola and cello. The works exhibit solid craftsmanship, and fugue-like pieces appear in two of them as finales. Richter's quartets are mostly in three movements, frequently with a minuet as the concluding piece. They reveal a sensitive artist who avoided cheap effects and the type of shallow music that was fashionable in the drawing-rooms of the Rococo period.

Somewhat similar in nature are the divertimenti[1] composed by the Austrian Josef Starzer (*c.* 1726–87) at the beginning of the sixties. Here, again, skill is evident in the handling of the four parts, the imitative treatment of the subjects in the development sections testifying to solid craftsmanship:

Ex. 308

The slow movements present singing melodies, the fast ones are resolute and witty in character. While the sonata form is not yet fully developed and lacks a complete recapitulation, the works as a whole are organized into four movements with minuet and slow movement in the middle.

Ignaz Holzbauer left few, though rather remarkable, contributions to the form. His E flat major quartet, and especially his F minor *Sonata da camera*[2] reflect the literary 'Storm and Stress' of the time. Suspensions and appoggiaturas, diminished and augmented chords, frequent dynamic changes and the use of sforzandos characterize this music, which is always imbued with forceful expression:

[1] Horwitz and Riedel (ed.), *Denkmäler der Tonkunst in Österreich*, xv (2) (Vienna, 1909), pp. 94 and 105.
[2] *Das Erbe deutscher Musik*, xxiv, pp. 80 and 89.

Ex. 309 Andantino con moto

Like Haydn's works of the early seventies Holzbauer's quartets employ remote tonalities. Thus, the *Sonata da camera* in F minor has a slow middle movement in the unusual key of B flat minor. Holzbauer's expressive quartets must be classed as rather conservative in some respects. Viola and cello frequently move in octaves, and the two violins also play in unison at times. Moreover, extensive rests are allotted, first to the cello and subsequently to the viola. It is obvious that the composer entertained certain reservations concerning the new idea of four-part writing without continuo.

The six quartets, Op. 23, by Felice Giardini, printed about 1780, are light and extremely brilliant compositions, skilfully offering effective passages to each of the four partners, and displaying a certain leaning towards a gay idiom. His fondness for diversity extends to the combination of instruments: two of the works are designated for violin, oboe, viola, and cello, two for violin, two violas and cello, and two for the customary string quartet.[1] One can well understand why the London public acclaimed these contributions by the celebrated violin virtuoso.

[1] Op. 23, nos. 3 and 4, ed. Alberto Poltronieri, *I classici musicali italiani,* vi (Milan, 1941).

Boccherini probably wrote more string quartets than any other composer of his time. The hundred-odd works produced by him extend throughout his career. Op. 2 (published as Op. 1), composed at the age of eighteen, was a set of quartets, as was his very last work, the Op. 64, left incomplete forty-one years later.[1]

The C minor quartet of 1761, Op. 2, no. 1, which, in part, still displays orchestral features,[2] leans to some extent on the styles of Pergolesi and Sammartini. It is a somewhat plaintive composition in three movements with a certain predilection for the cello which Boccherini was henceforth to maintain. Particularly attractive is the finale, an Allegro risoluto, stressing the contrast between an energetic subject played forte, mostly in unison, and a melodious piano theme harmonized, an effect dear to preclassical composers:

Ex. 310

The promising start made with this work is matched by the five other quartets of Op. 2. The three movement-structure is also to be found in the six quartets, Op. 8, of 1769. Besides the sequence fast–slow–fast they also employ that of slow–minuet–fast, which has an effective twofold increase in tempo and is not unusual in compositions produced north of the Alps. While Boccherini's Op. 2 had been dedicated to *dilettanti e conoscitori di musica*, his third set, Op. 9 of 1770, was, significantly enough, inscribed only *alli signori dilettani*, and in pursuance of this tendency the Op. 15 of 1772 was an *opera piccola* of the type already encountered among Boccherini's trios, containing pieces on a smaller

---

[1] Nos. 159–258 in Gérard, op. cit.
[2] The Paris original edition by Venier has the title *Sei sinfonie ò sia quartetti*.

scale. More and more the composer paid heed to his growing popularity, although virtuoso features did not disappear from his chamber music. Thus in the *Quartetti concertanti* Op. 24, of 1777,[1] the cello part was treated with such brilliance as to prove detrimental to the circulation of the work. Boccherini did not repeat this mistake. Thereafter he returned to the small and easy forms in his quartets, even producing sets of *quartettini* (Op. 44 of 1792, Op. 48 of 1794), playful pieces in two movements which show that the evolution of the classical style through Haydn and Mozart had made but a slight impact on Boccherini. Similarly, Op. 58 (1799), the last set of quartets published in Boccherini's lifetime, consisted of unpretentious works, this time in four movements, indicating that the ageing composer had lost contact with contemporary trends.

For Mozart, the composition of string quartets was probably not the result of the same spontaneous, creative urge that generated his works for piano and his operas. Lacking a specific motive, he was apt to neglect the form. But when the occasion arose, he could create quartets of consummate beauty and form. Between the ages of fourteen and seventeen he wrote ten quartets,[2] K. 80, 155–60, and the Divertimenti K. 136–38. The first experiments show his attempts to familiarize himself with the form. They are orchestral in conception, while both the melodic idiom and the emphasis on three-part writing may be said to derive from the Italian trio sonata. But as Mozart gradually became aware of the potentialities inherent in this form, an intimate chamber-music style and a more personal idiom made their appearance. The quartets K. 155–60, written in Italy at the end of 1772 or the beginning of 1773, have singing Allegro subjects and show a predilection for romantic middle movements in the minor key. How carefully these quartets were elaborated is shown in the manuscript of K. 156, where the completed E minor Adagio is crossed out, to be replaced by a new movement.

These first works were quickly followed by the quartets K. 168–73, composed in August and September 1773 in Vienna. It may have been a commission which induced Mozart to turn again to quartet writing, though the principal cause was provided by his acquaintance with Haydn's Op. 17 and, especially, his Op. 20, the 'Sun' quartets. Mozart starts K. 170 with a set of variations, as Haydn did in Op. 17, no. 3; in K. 168 and 173 fugues serve as finales, thus clearly following the model of the 'Sun' quartets. Fugue-like elements are to be found also in the first movement of K. 171, and in addition the Baroque force of the

[1] Published as Op. 27; minuet from no. 3 in Archibald T. Davison and Willi Apel, *Historical Anthology of Music*, ii (London, 1950), p. 270.
[2] *Gesamtausgabe*, series 14.

introductory Adagio which precedes the Allegro assai conjures up the beginning of the Adagio in Haydn's Op. 20, no. 2. The older master's music seems at first to have had an almost paralysing impact on Mozart, and only from the fourth quartet on did the young composer find himself. The last piece of the set especially, K. 173 in D minor, with its dark and tragic Allegro, its vigorous and energetic minuet, and the remarkable chromatically descending fugal subject of the finale, shows that Mozart succeeded in fighting his way through mere imitation to a more individual expressive style.[1] As soon as this goal was attained, however, the composer's interest waned once more. He neglected the form for a decade, until a new set by Haydn provided a compelling inducement to compose string quartets again.

Fugues in quartets were no rarity at that time. Leopold Gassmann[2] (1729–74), probably also under the influence of the 'Sun' quartets, composed six works of this kind, each containing an introductory slow movement, a fugue, a minuet with trio, and a second fugue serving as finale. The four movements are in the same key, and the fugues exhibit the character of contrapuntal fantasias in a strongly conservative style, which cannot stand comparison with Mozart's works. In this connection one may also mention the six *Quatuors en Fugues*, Op. 2, by Johann Georg Albrechtsberger (1736–1809), published about 1780 by J. J. Hummel, Berlin,[3] as well as a later work of the same nature, the A flat major sonata[4] of 1792, which consists of a prelude and double fugue for string quartet. The sixty-odd quartets by Albrechtsberger are mostly gay and unassuming, but some of them are in the strict, fugal style which explains why the composer was respected as a theory teacher by so exacting a pupil as Beethoven.

STRING QUARTETS OF THE 1780S

Haydn himself seems to have felt doubt concerning the wisdom of continuing the use of fugues in string quartets. In the last quarter of the century this method of ensuring equal rights for all four players was bound to appear rather antiquated and mechanical. He therefore avoided the form altogether for some time and returned to it only after having found a different solution of its problems, a solution which was fully in keeping with the spirit of the time. In 1781, nine years after the 'Sun' quartets, he completed the 'Russian' quartets, Op. 33,

[1] For further discussion of K. 168 and 173, see pp. 624–5.
[2] Cf. Geiringer, op. cit., p. 279.
[3] Cf. *British Union Catalogue*, i, p. 18.
[4] *Denkmäler der Tonkunst in Österreich*, xvi (2), p. 54: cf. also the bibliographical list in Somfai, 'Albrechtsberger-Eigenschriften in der Nationalbibliothek Széchényi, Budapest,' *Studia Musicologica*, i (1961), p. 175.

dedicated to Grand Duke Paul Petrovich, wherein the principle of 'thematic elaboration' is systematically employed. In the course of a movement the composer did not use complete subjects; rather, in his developments he worked with short motives derived from the subjects which had been heard complete earlier in the movement. This method manifested itself in various transitional passages and, in particular, in the development sections in which contrapuntal work abounded. The four instruments were allowed to take their turns, alternating between a leading and a subordinate role. Thematic elaboration was by no means a new invention: Haydn, Mozart, Starzer, and many others had previously resorted to it. Yet, so far, no other composer had used it so consistently. Thus, in the Allegro moderato of Op. 33, no. 2, the end of the four-bar principal subject (i) is worked out in the transitional passage (ii):

Ex. 311

Similarly, the cuckoo-call, G–E (in the main subject of the finale of Op. 33, no. 3) gives rise to a wealth of unforeseen results. A decisive advance was also achieved through the fusion of the *galant* light Rococo style with the idiom of 'sensibility' and with Baroque polyphony. Thus a wide range of human emotions finds expression in Haydn's string quartets. It is significant that in the 'Russian' quartets the minuets are mostly designated as scherzo or scherzando. This is more than a mere change of nomenclature; a piece like the 'scherzo' of no. 5 seems somewhat to anticipate the fiery piquancy of Beethoven's movements bearing the same name.

Haydn's short, rather unpretentious quartet, Op. 42, of 1785, was followed by the six quartets, Op. 50, published in 1787, which were dedicated to the King of Prussia, an enthusiastic performer on the cello. Noteworthy, again, is the method of thematic elaboration and the preference for a monothematic structure, which Haydn shared with C. P. E. Bach. In so many of his sonata forms, Haydn liked to achieve cohesion by effacing rather than stressing the contrast between first and second subjects. Tendencies of this kind may have prompted him to employ a set of variations in his slow movements instead of the tripartite form with a contrasting middle section. No. 4 is in the unusual key of F sharp minor, the opening Allegro spiritoso affording scope for a great deal of chromaticism and a wide dynamic range. Yet even here Haydn was eager to maintain contact with the past, and the finale is again built as a fugue.

In 1789 and 1790 the quartets, Op. 54, nos. 1–3, and Op. 55, nos. 1–3, were published, and in 1790 Haydn composed six other quartets which appeared before long as Op. 64. All twelve seem to have been dedicated to the violinist Johann Tost. These works, displaying Haydn's art at the peak of classical perfection, do not exhibit any fundamentally new features, but the former devices have now been intensified and developed to full maturity. We more frequently find movements in sonata form constructed from a single subject. To create greater diversity Haydn occasionally inserts fugato passages into his development sections; he also likes to surprise the listener with false recapitulations, which create the illusion that the development is ending prematurely. His modulations grow richer and more romantic. He employs a device, subsequently used by Beethoven, whereby he concludes a passage with a cadence in a certain key and after a general pause starts in another key, usually a semitone higher. The Tost quartets often present the first violin with difficulties suggesting a concerto; yet brilliance is never an end in itself. For instance, at one point (Op. 64, no. 6, trio) the first violin is carried up to E flat, in the fourth octave above middle C, but the purpose is to set off a subsidiary voice, in colour, against the second violin which carries the melody proper. In Op. 64, no. 5, justly nicknamed 'The Lark', the three deeper instruments suggest solid earthiness while the first violin soars upwards. Humour has an important role in the Tost quartets; indeed, some finales (such as those in Op. 64, nos. 1 and 2) belong to the most amusing instances ever produced in chamber music.

Before dealing with Haydn's last fifteen string quartets, we should consider works by other composers who followed the lead of the pioneer in this form and were influenced by his compositions in the eighties.

Carl Ditters von Dittersdorf (1739–99) published in 1788 six string quartets printed by Artaria. They are works revealing a strong sense of humour in presenting unexpected effects and striking harmonic contrasts. Dittersdorf's dynamic scale is unusually varied, and he works with small motives which he elaborates, thus achieving a rich texture. Occasionally, as in his C major quartet, he links two movements by employing the same thematic material. His E flat major quartet, which consists, like all his works of the kind, of three movements, has unusual dramatic power.

Ignaz Pleyel, Haydn's pupil and publisher, wrote a considerable number of quartets, of which the earlier ones merit particular attention. His flute quartets, Op. 20,[1] published in 1786 by J. Schmitt) Amsterdam), show the influence of both Mozart and Haydn. This is graceful and amiable utility music written with technical competence and not lacking in artistic value, the sort of music for which there was always a demand about the turn of the century.

Friedrich Wilhelm Rust provides an instance of the uncommon instruments that were occasionally used in chamber music, as in the Quartet for nail violin, two violins and cello (1787).[2] The composer, who had earlier written a brilliant trio for viola d'amore and two flutes, here skilfully uses that rare bowed instrument in which the strings are replaced by tuned nails,[3] producing delicate and ethereal sounds. The A major Adagio, where muted strings join the flute-like tone of the nail violin, is especially remarkable for the interplay of instrumental colour.

MOZART'S MATURE QUARTETS

After the appearance of Haydn's 'Russian' quartets Mozart openly acknowledged him as his model. Indeed, it may have been the acquaintance with Haydn's newest contributions that induced him to take up quartet composition again.[4] He now wrote six further quartets (K. 387, 421, 428, 458, 464, 465) which appeared as Op. X and were dedicated to Haydn. Mozart was engaged on this new set for more than three years (1782–5), discarding, changing, and improving; and his

[1] Hans Albrecht (ed.) (Lippstadt, 1949).
[2] R. Czach (ed.), *Das Erbe deutscher Musik*, 2nd series, Mitteldeutschland, i (Wolfenbüttel, 1939).
[3] On the nail violin see Karl Geiringer, *Musical Instruments* (London, 1943), p. 229.
[4] See p. 625.

dedication justly speaks of 'long and arduous work'. The fame of these compositions rests on a unique combination: an unmistakable indebtedness to Haydn, paired with the equally conspicuous imprint of Mozart's own genius. An innate dramatic quality may be noticed in these compositions, which induced one writer to establish a direct connection between each of the six quartets and one of Mozart's master operas.[1] K. 421 concludes, like Haydn's Op. 33, no. 5, with a set of variations, and there is even a certain affinity between the subjects of these two movements. Yet, while Haydn's G major finale exudes unencumbered gaiety, the younger composer presents a tragic, pessimistic piece in D minor. In K. 387 Mozart wrote a fugal finale, as Haydn and he himself had done in the seventies. On closer scrutiny one becomes aware, however, that Mozart was mainly concerned here with fitting his fugue into the sonata form, a task he set himself again later in the so-called Jupiter Symphony. The chromatically changing harmonies in the Andante con moto of K. 428 produce a romantic and mysterious effect which made Hermann Abert think of Wagner's *Tristan [und Isolde]*.[2] In the last movement of the Quartet in B flat (K. 458) we seem to watch a comedy scene, doubly poignant by contrast with the lofty Adagio. It is significant that Mozart discarded a first sketch for this finale, since its beginning was too complex for such a nimbly moving piece. In the finale of K. 464 Mozart adopted a device sometimes used by Haydn: he postponed the entrance of the second subject until it assumed the character of a concluding idea. To compensate, he introduced a new theme in the development section, a Mozartean feature foreign to Haydn. Beethoven was so impressed by the superb contrapuntal treatment in this finale that he copied it with his own hand. The Adagio introduction to the first movement of K. 465 is responsible for its nickname of 'Dissonance Quartet'. It took some time before musicians learned to see in these harsh progressions not errors but a deliberate artistic intention. Even in the following Allegro the nightmarish atmosphere of the introduction is not completely discarded, and a feeling of profound unrest prevails throughout this deeply felt composition.

In 1786 Mozart wrote a single string quartet in D major (K. 499). It starts with a deceptively simple tune intoned in unison by the four instruments. Before long so many possible aspects of this theme are explored that the introduction of a significant second subject seems superfluous.

In the years 1789–90 Mozart wrote his last three quartets (K. 575,

---

[1] See Walther Siegmund-Schultze, 'Mozart's Haydn-Quartette', *Bericht über die internationale Konferenz zum Andenken Josef Haydns* (Budapest), 1961, p. 137.
[2] op. cit., ii, p. 158.

589, 590), destined for the cello-playing King of Prussia to whom Haydn had earlier dedicated his Op. 50. In each of Mozart's works the cello has a part that is particularly expressive, at times even brilliant. Significant roles are allotted to the other instruments also, and thus the quartet form is imbued with elements of the concerto. In the finale of K. 589 the main subject shows a striking resemblance to that of the last movement of Haydn's Op. 33, no. 2. In K. 590 also, with its first movement built on a single subject and the Hungarian gipsy tune suddenly appearing in the finale, we seem to feel Haydn looking over Mozart's shoulder. It was the young composer's last greeting to the old friend who had been his mentor.

Finally, the Mozart quartets[1] employing a woodwind instrument instead of the first violin must be mentioned. The three quartets with flute (K. 285, 285a, 298) were composed in 1777 and 1778,[2] the one with oboe (K. 370) early in 1781. These are gay compositions in two or three movements, where the woodwind instrument is at times treated as soloist. Despite the prevailing light character, passages of an elegiac mood (e.g. the D minor Adagio of the oboe quartet) also occur. Soon, however, Mozart turned to string quartet composition in the grand style, and lost interest in the fashionable quartet ensembles with a woodwind instrument, in which a true balance was impossible.

HAYDN'S LAST QUARTETS

Haydn himself wrote fifteen further quartets in the decade between 1793 and 1803, which appeared as Op. 71, nos. 1–3; Op. 74, nos. 1–3; Op. 76, nos. 1–6; Op. 77, nos. 1–2, and Op. 103. It is interesting to observe how in these products of his old age, which at times even surpass the earlier works, the pattern of development begins to come full circle. Haydn's earliest quartets had emerged from orchestral music, and now again he produces quartets influenced by orchestral and symphonic conceptions. More and more he employed introductions of the sort used for his symphonic first movements. In the quartets they often consist merely of chords intoned by all instruments (cf. Op. 71, nos. 1 and 3; Op. 74, no. 3); however, in Op. 71, no. 2, there is a real Adagio introduction. In general the first movement of this D major Quartet with its wide leaps and passages in rushing semiquavers reveals a powerful technique, reminiscent of *al fresco* painting, that goes far beyond the customary chamber-music style. In his zeal for experimentation Haydn now tried in various ways to solve the problems of

[1] *Gesamtausgabe*, series 14; *Neue Ausgabe*, series VIII/20/Abt. 2.
[2] K. 298 possibly as late as 1787. Concerning K. Anh. 171, cf. Ralph Leavis, 'Mozart's Flute Quartet in C, K. App. 171', *Music and Letters*, xliii (1962), p. 48.

sonata form. In Op. 74, no. 3, so great a stress is laid on the introduction as to make the main subject comparatively insignificant: here only the subsidiary idea achieves greater importance. In these works there are many vistas into the territory of romanticism. The aim for intensification is reflected in the increase of tempo within the individual movements (cf. finale of Op. 76, no. 4). Likewise Haydn now often prescribes presto for a minuet (cf. Op. 74, no. 1) thus approaching Beethoven's scherzos. In his melodies there is also a typically Austrian quality that foreshadows Schubert's language (cf. trio of the minuet in Op. 74, no. 1). The sequence of keys shows even greater boldness than appeared in the 1770s. An F major minuet (Op. 74, no. 2) is followed by a trio in D flat major; the G minor quartet (Op. 74, no. 3) has a Largo in E major, the D major quartet (Op. 76, no. 5) a Largo in F sharp major. Within individual movements, the modulatory and enharmonic progressions are equally daring. A Fantasia (Op. 76, no. 6) moves from B major through a variety of unexpected keys, including B flat and A flat major. Following the model of C. P. E. Bach, Haydn temporarily omits the key signature, thus giving his work a curiously twentieth-century appearance.

With these quartets, which represent the climax of eighteenth-century chamber music, a high plateau was reached on which Beethoven was to erect his mighty edifices.

THE STRING QUINTET

The production of quintets in the eighteenth century was far less extensive than that of quartets. For one thing, composing in five parts involved problems of scoring, and quite a number of different instrumental combinations were experimented with. Moreover, surprisingly many quintets are to be found also in arrangements for ensembles other than strings.

The combination of two violins, two violas, and a bass, treating the parts in the traditional manner of seventeenth-century orchestral music, enjoyed favour in eighteenth-century chamber music as well. We find it, for instance, in the six quintets[1] of the Czech composer Josef Mysliveček (1737–81), who was mainly active in Italy. In these works the bass part hardly participates in the thematic elaboration and the large number of repeated notes seems to indicate that the composer expected the addition of a harpsichord. These quintets are in three movements, without a minuet, and are closer to the *sinfonia* than to the divertimento. The frequent use of tremolo and the occasional unisons of the two violins or the two violas point to the possibility of performance by an

[1] ed. Jan Racek and Vratislav Bělský, *Musica antiqua bohemica*, xxxi (Prague, 1957).

orchestra. In the fast movements Czech folk music is in evidence and the earthy, vigorous character of this music may have appealed to listeners unaccustomed to such fare.

More in the nature of a divertimento is a youthful work[1] by Haydn (Hob. II/2) known in different versions, of which that for two violins, two violas and bass appears to be the original. This quintet, which probably dates from the beginning of the 1750s, exhibits the symmetrical structure noticeable also in Haydn's earliest string quartets. It has an introductory fast movement, the result being a sequence of Presto–Allegro moderato–Minuet–Adagio–Minuet–Presto. Though graceful, it is of interest mainly as a preparatory study for the composer's subsequent great contributions for strings.

The three divertimenti[2] by Holzbauer which have been preserved in the composer's autograph must be considered as arrangements. He wrote them originally for a sextet of wind and string instruments, and adapted them subsequently for two violins, two violas, and bass. These consist of a slow and a fast movement, to which, in the E flat Divertimento, a 'Menuetto grazioso' is added as finale. Frequent consecutive thirds and octaves, as well as other factors, produce works that are light both in texture and character. In a similar vein we have the little F major quintet, Op. 3, no. 6,[3] by Giuseppe Toeschi (1732–88), an unpretentious serenade in miniature, scored for flute, violin, viola, cello, and bass, which results in a well-balanced ensemble. Significantly enough, this Mannheim composer also shows a certain reserve towards the quintet medium.

Quite different was the attitude of Boccherini, who preferred the quintet to any other form, reaching in it the peak of his achievements in the field of chamber music. Through a period of some thirty years (1771–1801) he wrote nearly two hundred quintets for various combinations,[4] particularly favouring the string quintet for two violins, viola, and two cellos, a combination for which he composed more than a hundred works.[5] As Boccherini himself was an eminent cellist, he liked to entrust the two cellos with virtuoso tasks.

In 1771 Boccherini composed two sets of six quintets Opp. 10 and 11 in his own numbering, the next year a further six, Op. 13. The derivation

[1] Walter Höckner (ed.), (Copenhagen, 1953).
[2] *Das Erbe deutscher Musik*, xxiv, pp. 34–68.
[3] *Denkmäler der Tonkunst in Bayern*, xv.
[4] Nos. 265–453 in Gérard, op. cit.
[5] The collection of parts published in Paris by Janet and Cotelle in 1829 comprises 93 such quintets transcribing, with an alternative sixth part, the music of the first cello for an 'alto-violoncelle'. This instrument was probably a 'violoncello piccolo', a smaller type of cello, which besides the regular four strings had a fifth, tuned to E'. However, the part, which is notated in both alto and treble clefs, can also be played by a second viola.

of these from the quartet and from symphonic music is clearly noticeable, as the two cellos often alternate or play in unison. The quintets are in either three or four movements. Op. 11, no. 5, contains the graceful A major minuet, one of the most famous examples of Rococo musical art. There is a clear resemblance to the divertimento in most of the quintets. Thus Op. 10, no. 6, consists of a pastorale (in part of which the instruments are muted), an Allegro maestoso, and a minuet with four variations. Similarly, Op. 11, no. 6, *l'Uccelliera*, written ten years before Haydn's 'Bird' Quartet, presents, after a slow introduction, an Allegro giusto filled with the twittering of birds. Another Allegro inscribed *I Pastori e i Cacciatori* includes the sound of bagpipes alongside that of hunting horns. After the minuet the finale reverts to the first movement, whose last section is quoted exactly, a 'romantic' fusion of first and last movements for which Boccherini showed a definite predilection. One senses the dawn of a new era in other features of these products of the 1770s. The Largo of the first quintet is highly expressive and the first movements of Op. 10, no. 2 and Op. 11, no. 5, have the characteristic heading 'amoroso'. Quintets in a minor key are no rarity and the F minor minuet of Op. 13, no. 3, is inscribed 'appassionato'. In the same work, the first movement bears the very unusual tempo-indication 'prestissimo'. We find also in Boccherini's works of the time a return to Baroque means of expression: the finale of Op. 13, no. 5, composed in the same year as Haydn's 'Sun' quartets, ends with a fugue.

The desire for intense emotional expression is still noticeable in the six quintets, Op. 18, of 1774. One work of this set is in the unusual key of E major, two others are in a minor key. In the C minor finale of no. 1 a high pitch of passionate expression is reached. Picquot[1] tells us that Louis Persuis (1769–1819) successfully employed this movement in his ballet *Nina* (1813) for the scene where the heroine learns of her lover's death.

In the later sets the amiable charm of Boccherini's artistic personality, which had been temporarily obscured by the fashionable emphasis on strong expression, came once more to the fore. Thus, in the A major quintet from Op. 28 (composed in 1779) only the Larghetto of the third movement, with its Schubertian modulations, points to the sentiments (and sentimentality) of the era, while the brisk first movement taken up in the finale, and the minuet with its piquant trio are far removed from romantic subjectivity. To the year 1779 also belongs Op. 29, no. 6, concluding with a *ballo tedesco*, a rousing dance tune.

[1] Picquot, *Notice sur la vie et les ouvrages de Luigi Boccherini* (Paris, 1851; ed. Saint-Foix, Paris, 1930).

In addition to the full-sized quintets, Boccherini wrote in the seventies a number of smaller works for five instruments, some in two, some in three movements. Occasionally he scored for string quartet plus a flute, the favourite instrument of the time; yet in such cases he treated the single cello part so generously that it made up for the elimination of the second bass instrument. Six such works for two violins, flute, viola, and cello, Op. 17, were composed in 1773; six others, Op. 19, originated in 1774, while in Op. 55 an oboe is added to the quartet of strings. In 1801 and 1802 there followed as *opere grandi* six quintets Opp. 60 and 62 for two violins, two violas, and cello, dedicated to 'cittadino Luciano Bonaparte', a brother of Napoleon serving at that time as French ambassador in Madrid. Although traces of thematic development and elaboration may be observed in some of Boccherini's later compositions, by and large Fétis's[1] famous statement concerning Boccherini that 'one would be tempted to believe that he knew no other music but his own' is borne out by the quintets. Even works written during the last decade of the composer's career show no specific innovations.

MOZART'S QUINTETS

The most significant quintets of the eighteenth century were composed by Mozart.[2] Michael Haydn seems to have been responsible for the young composer's interest in the form.[3] When the seventeen-year-old Mozart came to know Michael Haydn's Quintet in C major,[4] completed 17 February 1773, he was inspired to write a work of this kind in B flat major (K. 174), and worked on it from March to July 1773. Mozart's work shared with its model the sequence of movements, the use of echo effects, the codas at the end of the movements, and the preference for the first violin and first viola. The work did not fully satisfy its author, and when Michael Haydn completed a Quintet in G major, on 1 December 1773, this had so great an impact on the young genius that in the same month he radically altered his own composition. He rejected the trio of the minuet, replacing it with a much more extensive piece constructed on the echo principle; the finale was given greater solidity through added counterpoint and the insertion of a large development section. The seriousness with which Mozart applied himself to this quintet proves that he was greatly attracted by the form. Yet fourteen years were to elapse before he felt ready to cope with it and attempt to solve its problems.

During this time six quintets were composed by another musician

[1] *Biographie universelle des musiciens.* 2nd edn. (Paris, 1860–5), i, p. 454.
[2] *Gesamtausgabe*, series 13.
[3] Cf. Wyzewa and Saint-Foix, op. cit., ii, (Paris, 1911) p. 28.
[4] Albrecht (ed.), (Lippstadt, 1952).

whose work greatly influenced Mozart. By the middle of the seventies J. C. Bach had written his Op. 11, six quintets for flute, oboe, violin, viola, and bass.[1] Although the bass part is figured, the texture of these pieces is so transparent that the inclusion of a harpsichord would surely produce too massive and clumsy an effect. In these works the five instruments are frequently grouped as trios, since Christian liked to set the two string instruments with bass against the two wind instruments with bass. The quintets are in two or three movements; their sonority and rich melodic invention earned Mozart's admiration.

We cannot be certain just what rekindled Mozart's interest in the genre of the quintet. Michael Haydn had written another work of the kind in 1784, after a considerable pause, and Boccherini's compositions enjoyed a wide circulation. In any event, in the spring of 1787 Mozart once more began to work on quintets. The C minor Quintet, K. 406, should be considered as a kind of preliminary study, since it is an arrangement of the Serenade for eight wind instruments, K. 388, of 1782. Mozart may have felt that the sombre tonality of the octet and its intricate polyphony were not apt for the serenade-like orchestration. In the second version, however, one misses the rich colours of the original. By contrast, the C major Quintet, K. 515, written in April 1787, reveals a perfect balance of form, content, and technique. Its unhurried, leisurely breadth forecasts Schubert, and it seems like an anticipation of nineteenth-century *Lied* technique when in the initial movement the subsidiary subject appears first as an independent melody and immediately afterwards as accompaniment to a new idea. The slow movement, built on a duet between first violin and first viola, recalls the middle movement of Mozart's *Sinfonia concertante*, K. 364. The finale is humorous and relaxed, yet the use of chromaticism and unexpected harmonic progressions gives even this movement a slightly nostalgic character.

Among Mozart's great G minor works the String Quintet, K. 516, composed in May 1787, occupies a place of honour. A tragic mood pervades the first movement. It is significant that the composer does not follow the usual practice of introducing the second subject in the relative major, but maintains the pessimistic key of G minor. The development, too, after a short burst of despair, breathes weary resignation and a similar sequence of moods is evoked in the coda which reverts to the development (a device later also adopted by Beethoven). Rarely has a composition borne the heading 'minuetto' with as little justification as the ensuing G minor movement. Nor does the E flat major Adagio ma non troppo bring relief. Of this movement Tchaikovsky wrote to Nadezhda von Meck: 'No one has ever with such beauty expressed in

[1] Steglich (ed.), *Das Erbe deutscher Musik*, iii (Hanover, 1935).

music the feeling of resigned, helpless grief.'[1] The finale, anticipating a device later employed in Brahms's First Symphony, starts with an Adagio in which the dark spirit of the preceding movement is echoed, while in true Mozartean fashion the concluding rondo, an Allegro in G major, is in a joyous and affirmative mood. Such dramatic changes seemed as natural to the eighteenth century as the happy ending (*lieto fine*) following a tragic scene in an opera.

The three last string quartets were followed again by two mighty quintets: K. 593 in D major composed in December 1790 and K. 614 in E flat major composed in April 1791. Mozart's idiom is now even bolder and more subjective, though he observes the formal rules. The D major quintet starts with a slow introduction which reappears in the coda to round off the movement. Mozart's aim towards unification is also apparent in the Allegro, where a canonic version of the rhythmical main subject becomes the second subject.

The E flat major quintet, sunny and graceful, was Mozart's last chamber-music work. Interestingly enough, not only the beginning of the finale but also that of the minuet show a certain relationship to the opening of the first movement, a feature which was to assume even greater significance in the nineteenth century:

Ex. 312 Allegro di molto

Menuetto, allegretto

Allegro

Besides the string quintets Mozart also wrote two quintets each of which included one wind instrument.[2] K. 407 in E flat major (1782) is scored for horn, violin, two violas, and cello. This piece is more in the nature of a double concerto for horn and violin, accompanied by three low-pitched string instruments. In accordance with its concerto-like character it consists of three movements only and lacks a minuet. The work was written for the horn-player Ignaz Leutgeb.[3] K. 581, the Clarinet Quintet in A major (1789), was written for the clarinettist Anton

[1] Letter of 16/28 March 1878.
[2] *Gesamtausgabe*, series 13; *Neue Ausgabe*, series VIII/19/Abt. 2.
[3] See p. 492.

Stadler. It is a piece for five virtuosos, the usual string quartet plus the solo clarinet, though special attention is paid to the potentialities of the wind instrument. In accordance with the work's divertimento-like character Mozart provided an extensive minuet with two trios, the second of which is an Austrian peasant dance. The finale is a series of variations which likewise recall South German folk music. As a concluding movement Mozart had originally planned another piece which he rejected after writing some ninety bars. Thus the playful, unencumbered character of the Allegro con variazioni is the result of careful deliberation, an attitude characteristic of the whole work, which matches freshness of invention with technical mastery.

LARGER ENSEMBLES

The study of ensembles employing more than five instruments discloses a surprising tendency towards variety of instrumental combinations. Even among sextets the choice of instruments is varied, and as the parts become more numerous new possibilities of scoring are exploited. Boccherini wrote seventeen sextets,[1] among which one finds no fewer than four types of instrumentation, varied mainly by the introduction of one or more wind instruments. Haydn and Mozart produced fewer sextets and displayed a preference for the pure wind sextet of two oboes, two horns, and two bassoons, as well as the string quartet with two horns or with flute and oboe. In works for seven, eight or more instruments even less uniformity may be noticed. Although for practical reasons sets of three or six works might be scored identically, as a rule composers avoided repeating the same instrumental combination. Occasionally unusual instruments such as the tiny post-horn,[2] the unwieldy serpent[3] (a bass horn equipped with finger holes) or the *lira organizzata*[4] (a hurdy-gurdy supplied with organ pipes) made their appearance in the larger ensembles.

Extreme diversity prevailed also in the length of the compositions. Pieces in two, three, or four movements were still frequent, but as more and more variation sets, contredanses, polonaises, minuets, and marches were employed, the number of movements increased. Works with six, seven, and eight movements, taking as much as three-quarters of an hour to perform, were not infrequent.

[1] Nos. 454–73 in Gérard, op. cit. Modern editions include the sextets Op. 42, nos. 1, 2, ed. Bormann (Hamburg, 1954 and 1956) and the Sextet in B flat major (flute, oboe, bassoon, strings), ed. Kurt Janetzki (Leipzig, 1955).
[2] Cf. Mozart, Serenade, K. 320 (*Gesamtausgabe*, series 9, no. 11).
[3] Cf. *Feldparthien*, attributed to Haydn, Hob.II/44–46; no. 46, ed. Geiringer (Leipzig, 1932).
[4] Cf. Haydn, 8 *Notturni*, Hob. II/25–32; no. 25, ed. Schmid (Karlsbad, 1932); no. 27, ed. Adolf Sandberger (Munich, 1936); nos. 28–9, ed. Geiringer (Vienna, 1931); no. 30, ed. Edvard Fendler (New York, 1946); nos. 31–2, ed. Schmid (Leipzig, 1936).

PLATE VII

THE WIND PLAYERS OF THE WALLERSTEIN COURT ORCHESTRA
A gold silhouette of c. 1785.

The function of these compositions was different from that of the trios, quartets, and quintets discussed earlier. They were not primarily intended for amateurs or pupils but were meant as a tribute to persons of distinction for birthday or wedding celebrations. Such entertainment music was in great demand by the well-to-do of the eighteenth century, compositions for outdoor use frequently alternating with those for indoors.[1]

Works for larger ensembles increasingly lack the true spirit of chamber music. The idea of co-operation between equal partners becomes more and more neglected in favour of a more orchestral or concerto-like character. Thus Mozart's *Serenata notturna*, K. 239, joins a concerto grosso of string orchestra and timpani to a concertino of four stringed instruments. In K. 63 and K. 250, solo violins are prescribed, while in K. 286, four orchestras compete with each other. Haydn's *notturni*, written for the King of Naples, were adapted and performed as orchestral pieces by the composer himself and Mozart's second Haffner Serenade had only to be shortened and strengthened in its scoring to become a real symphony (K. 385).

[1] See chap. VIII.

X

KEYBOARD MUSIC

By Philip Radcliffe

THE development of keyboard music was in many ways less significant in the second than in the first half of the eighteenth century. So long as the continuo system lasted, music for a solo keyboard instrument was almost the only kind of which, in performance, every note was the composer's own, and, in the hands of such men as François Couperin in France, Domenico Scarlatti in Italy and Spain, and J. S. Bach in Germany, it rose to heights as great as those of any other branch of music. But the gradual disappearance of the continuo brought with it a change of emphasis; the distinction between orchestral and chamber music became more clearly defined, and with this came a new standard of sensitiveness to instrumental colour. The output of keyboard music continued, more copiously in some countries than in others, but the quality was less consistent than in the earlier part of the century, and only in Germany and Austria was much really important work produced.

ITALY

By 1750 the counterpoint that to J. S. Bach was the lifeblood of anything that he wrote, from the most elaborate fugue to the gayest gigue, had become a luxury rather than a necessity; it was still liable to appear, sometimes with admirable effect, but more and more with a feeling of archaism, as of classical scholars conversing elegantly in Greek or Latin. This was particularly the case in Italy, where, since the beginning of the century, increasing stress had been laid on accompanied solo melody, preferably against a stage background. It is interesting to reflect that Domenico Scarlatti and Clementi both spent the greater part of their lives outside Italy; between them, chronologically, came a fair number of Italian composers who wrote keyboard music, often of considerable merit, but usually as a sideline. Inevitably there is a similarity of idiom in most of their works, but it is interesting to see the idiom itself gradually changing as the century proceeds, and the music of some of the composers shows the precise characteristics that might be expected from their careers. For instance, the sonatas of Giovanni Battista Martini (1706–84), well known as a musical historian, theorist, and teacher, are far more solid in texture than those of the other Italians. They often include fugal and dance movements reminiscent of the older suite, while some have preludes of the grandiose, improvisatory kind. The well-known Gavotte, in F, from the twelfth of his first set of sonatas, published in 1742,[1] is a good example of his easy and spontaneous canonic writing, and a Siciliano from the ninth sonata of the same set, in F minor, combines a flowing Italian lyricism with a contrapuntal texture in a very attractive way:

Ex. 313 Adagio

In his treatment of variation form he is generally less mechanical than his contemporaries; in a set from the fourth sonata, in C major,[2] the variations are alternately in the major and minor modes; in another, from the seventh sonata, in E minor, they are alternately in duple and triple time. Interesting in another way is an Adagio from the eleventh sonata, in C minor, in which the rhythm of the first two bars is repeated with a strange persistence, covering an unusually wide range of modulation. The number of movements in these works varies considerably, and the form of those that are neither dances nor fugues is often surprisingly free.

Baldassare Galuppi (1706–85), born in the same year as Martini, wrote more than fifty keyboard sonatas,[3] but, as might be expected from a composer whose main interest was in the stage, their texture is far less contrapuntal, and there is far less kinship with the suite. They rarely consist of more than four movements, usually less, and, at any rate in the two sets published by Walsh as Opp. 1 and 2,[4] the music is often slight. Galuppi had an attractive lyrical gift, which is pleasantly apparent in some of the slow movements, especially in the Adagio with which Op. 1, no. 4 begins. This sonata is one of the best; it contains a

[1] Modern editions, ed. Louise Farrenc, *Le Trésor des pianistes*, iii, (Paris, 1862), and ed. M. Vitali, Milan, n.d. A second set, containing six sonatas, was published in 1747; modern edition, ed. Lothar Hoffmann–Erbrecht, (Leipzig, 1954). A selection from the two sets is to be found, ed. D. Cipollini, *I classici della musica italiana*, xviii (Milan, 1920).

[2] Also in Kurt von Fischer, *Die Variation* (*Das Musikwerk*) (Cologne, 1956), p. 29.

[3] See Fausto Torrefranca, 'Per un catalogo tematico delle sonate di B. Galuppi', *Rivista musicale italiana*, xvi (1909), p. 872, xviii (1911), pp. 276 and 497, xix (1912), p. 108, and Charles Van der Borren, ibid. xxx (1923); additions and corrections in F. Raabe, *Galuppi als Instrumentalkomponist* (Frankfurt a. O., 1929), pp. 54 ff.

[4] In 1756 and 1759 respectively, *British Union Catalogue of Early Music* (London, 1957).

striking third movement, marked 'Spiritoso e staccato', that resembles a transcription from an operatic overture. Occasionally Galuppi writes passages of an almost Mozartean sensitiveness, as in the following, from Op. 1, no. 1.

Ex. 314

He is least interesting when most obviously preoccupied with brilliant keyboard effects. Many of his sonatas remained unpublished in his lifetime, including a late set of six sonatas with the title *Passatempo al Cembalo*, written in 1781.[1] These show a greater variety of texture than the Walsh sets; the opening Larghetto of the second sonata begins with dotted rhythms characteristic of the French overture, but there is also more employment of the Alberti bass, as in the first movement of the first sonata, where it is used almost continuously. Formally most of the movements follow the binary plan of Domenico Scarlatti, with the ends of the two sections corresponding thematically; in these sonatas, however, this second group of themes is far more clearly defined than in Scarlatti. Occasionally a complete sonata-form movement appears, as for example in the last movement of the fifth sonata.

While the sonatas of Galuppi are on the whole slighter in texture and content than those of Martini, they must certainly have seemed more up-to-date to contemporary listeners, and there is much in them that still sounds fresh. More varied and resourceful in keyboard technique than either of them are the twelve sonatas of Domenico Paradies or Paradisi (1707?–91), published in 1754 by John Johnson in London.[2] They are all in two movements only, of which the first is always the longer; the second varies considerably in character, being sometimes a gigue, sometimes a rapid *moto perpetuo*, as in the well-known Sonata in

[1] Modern edition, ed. F. Piva, *Collana di musiche veneziane*, vi (Venice, 1964). Twelve others, ed. Giacomo Benvenuti (Bologna, 1920), contain some of his best works.
[2] Ten in Farrenc, op. cit., xii (Paris, 1870), also in a complete but 'enriched' edition by Benvenuti and Cipollini, *I classici della musica italiana*, xxii (Milan, 1919).

A (no. 6), and sometimes quiet and lyrical. Except in some of these last there is little sustained melodic invention, nor is the texture at all polyphonic, but there is abundant skill in constructing long paragraphs built on phrases of varying lengths that sometimes seem to look at the same time back to Domenico Scarlatti and forward to Haydn. The influence of Scarlatti can also be seen in some of the unexpected harmonic digressions, and in the keyboard writing of such passages as the following from the eleventh sonata, in F major:

Ex. 315

Although Paradies was a composer of opera, there is hardly any trace of operatic influence in his sonatas; in the keyboard music of many younger Italian composers, however, it is very prominent, and shows itself not only in the tunes themselves but in the increasingly stylized nature of the accompaniments, including the familiar 'Alberti bass'. Domenico Alberti himself (c. 1710–c. 1740) was a singer, and his eight harpsichord sonatas published by Walsh as Op. 1 in 1748 are melodious in a mild and undistinguished way.[1] It can be seen at once that whenever he began to use his favourite accompaniment formula he found it remarkably hard to abandon it, but it is only fair to add that there are movements in which it does not appear, and he can no more be said to have invented it than can Puccini be considered the inventor of 'Puccini octaves'.

In the latter part of the eighteenth century, Domenico Cimarosa (1749–1801) wrote a number of one-movement sonatas[2] which, though not notably individual, are attractive enough. They may originally have been played in groups, like those of Scarlatti. But, with the exception of

[1] Modern edition of no. 2, ed. Franz Giegling, *Die Solosonate* (*Das Musikwerk*) (Cologne, 1960), p. 78, and no. 8, ed. William S. Newman, *Thirteen Keyboard Sonatas of the 18th and 19th Centuries* (Chapel Hill, 1947).
[2] Thirty-two sonatas, ed. Felice Boghen, 3 vols. (Paris, 1925–6).

Clementi, whose work is dealt with in volume VIII, Italian keyboard music in the last decades of the century is disappointing; the following, from a sonata by Giambattista Grazioli (1746–1820)[1] is typical of many works of the period, pleasant, but saying little that was not more vitally expressed in other genres.

Ex. 316

FRANCE

The same can be said of much of the keyboard music in France at this period. That produced by native French composers can be virtually disregarded. Of far greater interest are the works of a group of composers of German or Alsatian origin, active in Paris shortly after the middle of the century, among whom must be especially mentioned Johann Schobert (c. 1740–67), Johann Gottfried Eckard (1735–1809), Leontzi Honauer (c. 1735–c. 1790), and Hermann Friedrich Raupach (1728–78). The young Mozart evidently found their sonatas sufficiently attractive to arrange movements from them as piano concertos, K. 37, K. 39, and K. 41.[2] The works of Schobert merit particular attention,[3] for although only two of his sonatas are specifically for keyboard alone, the instrumental parts of the others are almost always optional in character and often designated as such. His keyboard style is marked by a propensity for imitating orchestral idioms, such as *tremolandi* and repeated bass notes, and his music owes much of its effect to his strong bass lines which produce firm harmonic progressions, occasionally of an arresting nature, as in the development of the first movement of the C minor sonata.[4] In exploitation of the keyboard's resources Schobert was probably surpassed by Eckard, himself a brilliant performer, whose sonatas[5] begin to show characteristics of a definite piano style, a fact not surprising when it is remembered that he was closely associated with the piano-maker Johann Andreas Stein.

[1] Published in a set of twelve sonatas in Venice, c. 1800; modern edition, ed. R. Gerlin, *I classici musicali italiani*, xii (Milan, 1943).
[2] Cf. Edwin J. Simon, 'Sonata in Concerto', *Acta Musicologica*, xxxi (1959), p. 170.
[3] Selected works, ed. Hugo Riemann, *Denkmäler deutscher Tonkunst*, xxxix (Leipzig, 1909).
[4] Ibid., p. 25.
[5] Complete edition of the eight sonatas, Opp. 1 and 2, and the *Menuet d'Exaudet*, ed. Eduard Reeser (Amsterdam and Basle/Kassel, 1956).

SPAIN

In Spain the predominant figure is that of Antonio Soler (1729-83),[1] who was a pupil of Domenico Scarlatti. It is natural that a composer of Scarlatti's peculiarly marked individuality should have exercised a strong influence on his pupil, and it can be seen at once in the design, texture, and to some extent the spirit of many of Soler's sonatas; the following passage, with its slightly modal colouring, is characteristic:

Ex. 317
Allegretto

But the strange guitar-like harmonies that often give such a marked Spanish flavour to Scarlatti's sonatas appear far less often than might be expected in those of Soler; perhaps to him, a native of Spain, they sounded less exciting than to Scarlatti, a visitor. He is less successful than the Italian in his inconsequent modulations, but he quite often shows a vein of lyrical tenderness that only occasionally finds expression in Scarlatti's music, as, for example, in the Sonata in E flat (no. 16 in the Rubio edition).

ENGLAND

The output of keyboard music in England at this time was quite large in quantity, but of uneven value and curiously varied in style. For instance, the *Suites of Lessons* of Thomas Chilcot (d. 1766), who was organist at Bath, are well-planned works in a solidly Handelian style, while those of William Felton (1715-69) are unpretentiously tuneful. The suite was gradually merging into the sonata, with such works as the harpsichord lessons of James Nares (1715-87) forming a kind of link between the two, as they sometimes contain allemandes and other dance movements of the older kind, and sometimes not. But at this stage the

---

[1] Twenty-seven sonatas published by Birchall (London, c. 1796). Complete modern edition in progress, ed. S. Rubio (Madrid, 1957). Thirty-four sonatas, ed. F. Marvin, 3 vols. (London, 1957-61).

difference between the suite and sonata types of movement is often slight; many of the binary allegros are to all intents and purposes allemandes, and the finales are gigues or minuets, even if they are not so described. The sonatas of Joseph Kelway (*c.* 1702–82), published in 1764, have only three movements, but they are mostly of a type that could well be found in a suite. The texture of these works is sometimes bare, sometimes grandiose, but the general impression is oddly laboured. Of the eight harpsichord sonatas of Thomas Arne (1710–78), published by Walsh in 1756,[1] the fourth, in D minor, is an interesting and successful blend of styles. The homophony of the first movement is certainly modern:

Ex. 318

the third is a fugue, and the fourth a gigue that is polyphonic without being definitely fugal. The short second movement provides a very attractive example of Arne's lyricism. This sonata is his most ambitious keyboard work; of the others the eighth, a superficial set of variations, may be disregarded, but the remaining six are all rewarding to play.[2]

Nares' style is in many ways similar to that of Arne; his melodic gift is perhaps less individual, but his keyboard texture is often richer and more varied, and his harmonic range wider. The slow movement of a Lesson in A major, no. 5 of his first set published by Johnson in 1747, contains a chain of modulations of an almost Schubertian kind:

Ex. 319

[1] Facsimile edition, ed. Thurston Dart and Gwilym Beechey (London, 1969).
[2] Modern edition, ed. Ernst Pauer (London, n.d.).

and there are other things, such as the end of the fugue in the Lesson in G from Op. 2, published by Johnson c. 1759,[1] that are unusual for their date. There are some delightful specimens of his more lyrical movements in all the collections of lessons, one of the best being the *pastorale* that ends the fifth of the lessons included in his treatise *Il Principio*[2] He and Arne are certainly the most distinguished writers of keyboard music in England of that time, and anyone who turns from their work to that of their successors will at once feel the superiority of their style to the amiable emptiness of such composers as Samuel Arnold (1740–1802) or Thomas Dupuis (1733–96), or the unconvincing freakishness of John Worgan (1724–90), whose attempts at harmonic boldness sound for the most part merely ungrammatical. The lessons of John Jones (1728–96), however, are notable for the frankly orchestral texture of their keyboard writing. Towards the end of the eighteenth century there was a great vogue for programme music of a highly flimsy and unsatisfying kind, usually written by foreign composers who had settled in England; Franz Kotzwara's *The Battle of Prague* (*c.* 1788) was the most famous, but there are other equally quaint specimens. It was many years before any keyboard music of distinction was produced by an English composer, and the strong influence of Johann Christian Bach (1735–82), who lived in London from 1762 until his death, as well as the continuing Handel adulation, was not conducive to much independence or originality of thought.

GERMANY

Turning from England to Germany, mention must first of all be made of the works of the Italian *émigré* Giovanni Benedetto Platti (*c.* 1698–1763), who was resident in Würzburg, and whose two sets of keyboard sonatas, Opp. 1 and 4, were published by Haffner in Nuremberg in 1742 and *c.* 1745. They are of interest particularly for their expressive use of appoggiaturas and harmonic colouring, even though they are neither as progressive nor as important as Torrefranca maintains.[3] The keyboard works of Wilhelm Friedemann Bach (1710–84), on the other hand, give a peculiarly fascinating picture of the changing musical trend in the eighteenth century. The eldest of Johann Sebastian's sons, he was the one of whom his father had the highest hopes and he inherited at least some of his contrapuntal instincts, even if counterpoint was a less

[1] Modern edition of no. 3, ed. Henry G. Ley (London, 1926).
[2] Published by Weckler, London; date variously given as 1759 (*Grove*), *c.* 1765 (*Die Musik in Geschichte und Gegenwart*), and 1777 (British Museum Catalogue).
[3] Cf. Fausto Torrefranca, 'Giovanni Benedetto Platti e la sonata moderna', *Istituzioni e monumenti dell'arte musicale Italiana*, nuova serie, ii (Milan, 1963); this includes an edition of all eighteen keyboard sonatas; cf. also the review by W. S. Newman, *Musical Quarterly*, l (1964), p. 526.

constant feature of his style. So far as the nine authentic sonatas[1] are concerned, it is most in evidence in the *Sei Sonate* written in Dresden between *c.* 1733 and 1744. For instance in the fine Sonata in D,[2] published in 1745, the opening of the Adagio:

Ex. 320

Adagio

might almost have been written by Johann Sebastian and, apart from the passages that lead to the final cadence of each section, this texture is maintained consistently throughout the movement. The rest of the sonata is of similar quality, and is unified, intentionally or not, by a cadential figure that recurs in slightly differing forms at the end of each movement. The Sonata in E flat from the same set,[3] published in 1748, also has a contrapuntal slow movement, while the first movement of another, in G major,[4] has the unusual feature of a slow introduction that returns twice. The later sonatas are smoother and more homophonic, as in the Sonata in D of 1778,[5] but on the whole they are of less interest. Although these sonatas of his last years inclined more towards the *galant* style, his feeling for counterpoint found expression in other channels. In 1778 he published a set of keyboard fugues[6] in a style highly unfashionable at the time. Now and then there are passages such as Exx. 321 and 322 that betray their date, but the general texture is

Ex. 321

---

[1] Modern edition, ed. Friedrich Blume, 3 vols. (Hanover, 1930–40).
[2] Ibid., no. 4.
[3] Ibid., no. 6.
[4] Ibid., no. 1.
[5] Ibid., no. 5.
[6] Modern editions, ed. Walter Niemann (Leipzig, n.d.), Carl de Nys (Paris, 1961), and others.

Ex. 322

strongly reminiscent of Johann Sebastian, and at the same time the music is sufficiently alive to avoid any suggestion of the sham antique. The twelve polonaises,[1] written before 1768, are less consistently polyphonic, but their richness of texture is retrospective, and they are among Friedemann's finest works. Particularly striking are no. 6, in E flat minor, and no. 10, in F minor, which have something of the intimacy and depth of feeling to be found in his father's sarabandes. The fantasias[2] also have interesting features; here the keyboard writing is more brilliant but never empty, with *bravura* passages sometimes alternating with more fugal or lyrical sections, and in these works Friedemann shows that he had inherited some of his father's power of rhapsodizing in the grand manner without becoming incoherent. The 'concerto' in F for two harpsichords[3] dates from around 1733, and was at one time attributed to J. S. Bach;[4] it makes for a fascinating comparison with Sebastian's Italian Concerto also written about this time.

Friedemann Bach was undoubtedly a composer of great gifts, but his life, though long, was singularly unsettled, especially in later years, and his eccentric and unreliable character may well have prevented him from developing as fully as might have been expected. His work is certainly most vital when following in the tradition of his father's style, and weakest when conforming most to the fashions of his time.

C. P. E. BACH

Friedemann's equally long-lived brother, Carl Philipp Emanuel (1714–88), was only four years younger, but his music was far less deeply rooted in the past. His early sonatas sometimes contain contrapuntal writing of a high order, but this tends to become rare in the later works. This did not, however, as in the music of his brother Friedemann, result in a decrease of musical interest, and it is significant that in the

[1] Modern editions, ed. Julius Epstein (Vienna, n.d.), Niemann (Leipzig, n.d.), and others.
[2] Six in modern edition, ed. C. Banck (Lippstadt, n.d.); Fantasia in C major, ed. Hoffmann–Erbrecht (Lippstadt, 1963).
[3] A number of modern editions, beginning with that by Brahms (Winterthur, 1864).
[4] On its authenticity, see Martin Falck, *Wilhelm Friedemann Bach* (Leipzig, 1913), pp. 62 ff.

small handful of fugues that he wrote for keyboard,[1] the most striking features are usually the least contrapuntal. His first set of sonatas (Wq. 48), dedicated to the King of Prussia, was published in 1742,[2] and it shows an interesting mixture of tendencies, though the style is already mature and convincing. In the first sonata, in F, the opening movement shows a 'sonata form' construction, with most of the formal characteristics that are later to be found in the Haydn–Mozart period, albeit on a small scale (eighty-one bars of 3/4 time). The abbreviation of the first subject in the recapitulation is an almost invariable feature of Emanuel's sonata-form movements. In the early works particularly, the longer the development section the shorter the recapitulation tends to be, so that the second part of a movement (from the double bar) remains in a balanced proportion to the first. In other allegro movements he often dispenses with a recapitulation of the first subject, so reverting more to the older binary form of J. S. Bach and Domenico Scarlatti. This form is particularly common in the final movements, as for example in those of nos. 1 and 2 of the 'Prussian' set. On the whole the allegro movements contain little in the way of vivid contrasts between first and second subjects, and variations in the dynamics generally have an expressive rather than a formal role in these works. The Adagio of the first sonata has the unusual character of an operatic arioso, interrupted twice by recitatives that involve surprising enharmonic modulations. The third sonata, in E, has an entirely lyrical first movement, and the Adagio is far more polyphonic, with occasional reminiscences of Johann Sebastian, as here:

Ex. 323

[1] Three of these, Wq. 119, nos. 2, 4, and 6, are printed as an appendix to Philip Barford, *The Keyboard Music of C. P. E. Bach* (London, 1965).
[2] Modern edition, ed. Rudolf Steglich (Hanover, 1927).

The next set of six sonatas, Wq. 49,[1] dedicated to the Duke of Württemberg, subsequently the patron of Jommelli and Noverre, are of similar quality, but on a larger scale and more massive in texture. This is especially true of the first movements, where the frequent dynamic markings show an increasing reliance on variety of colour; the general style is more rhetorical than in the earlier sonatas, with unexpected pauses and harmonic digressions.

Ex. 324

With the exception of that of the fourth sonata, in B flat, these first movements are all in the moderately paced common time that is so often found in Haydn's keyboard works, and that gives so much scope for varied phrase-lengths. The fourth and fifth sonatas have contrapuntal slow movements, that of the latter, in the key of E flat minor, being of particular beauty; the others are rich in harmonic colour and melodic decoration, and in all six of them there is a pause for a cadenza in the final bars, a feature also to be found in all but one of the slow movements of the 'Prussian' set. The finales of the 'Württemberg' sonatas share in the general lengthening of the movements, four have recapitulations with both subjects, and the mood often foreshadows Haydn in its vivacity, especially perhaps the finale of no. 5, in E flat.

In 1753 C. P. E. Bach published his celebrated treatise on keyboard playing, and the six *Probestücke*, Wq. 63,[2] with which he accompanied it, mark an important stage in his development as a composer. They all contain the usual succession of three movements, but with no unity of key; the first three are comparatively small and slight in texture, but the others are the richest and most elaborate works that he had yet written. Even in these, however, the first movements are less elaborate than those of the 'Württemberg' sonatas. The slow movement of the fifth looks back, in its first theme, to that of the first of the 'Prussian' set, but is far more ornate in texture, while that of the sixth has an almost Beethovenian breadth and richness. The finales of all three works are striking; that of the fifth is an amiably lyrical movement, with varied repeats that look

[1] Idem (Hanover, 1928).
[2] Modern edition, ed. Erich Doflein (Mainz, 1935).

ahead to the next set of sonatas. The fourth ends with a delightful siciliano and the sixth with a remarkable fantasia,[1] rhapsodical in character and strangely prophetic in some of its modulations. The grandiose, improvisatory character of this movement does not recur until some of the much later fantasias. The set is also of interest for the unusually detailed tempo instructions, for example, 'Allegretto arioso ed amoroso' or 'Adagio affettuoso e sostenuto', as well as for the numerous dynamic marks often indicating extreme contrasts, such as *ff–pp*. From these pieces, and from the treatise itself, we can gain an exceptional insight into Emanuel's own manner of performance.

The next set of sonatas, Wq. 50,[2] published by Winter of Berlin in 1760 are entirely different in their aim. They are described as *Sonaten mit veränderten Reprisen* and in the movements in sonata or binary form both sections are followed by varied repeats. This procedure was not on the whole conducive to the more adventurous aspects of C. P. E. Bach's style; the most vigorous of these movements, the opening Presto of the third sonata, in A minor, is comparatively empty, and the others are concerned mainly with gracefully flowing lyricism, with none of the striking contrasts of colour or dramatic gestures that are to be found in the first movements of the 'Württemberg' sonatas. On the other hand the slow movements, though usually short, are of decidedly emotional character. In the first sonata, which is to be played without a break, the Largo serves as a kind of dramatic interlude, while that of the fourth is a fine instance of subtly balanced design combined with a broad, half rhapsodical manner. But the most remarkable slow movement is the Larghetto of the fifth sonata, which has a curiously haunting and poignant main theme:[3]

Ex. 325 Larghetto

[1] Recorded in *The History of Music in Sound*, vii.
[2] No complete modern edition. No. 1 in Hans Fischer, *Musikalische Formen in historischen Reihen*, xviii (Berlin, 1937); no. 5, ed. K. Herrmann in *C.Ph. E. Bach: Sonaten and Stücke* (Leipzig, 1938). On the copies of the original edition in the British Museum, London, and Bibliothèque Nationale, Paris, with Bach's autograph alterations of 1788, see Barford, op. cit., pp. 101–2, and 'Some Afterthoughts by C. P. E. Bach', *Monthly Musical Record*, xc (1960), p. 94, and also pl. VIII of the present volume.
[3] For the version of 1788, see Barford, 'Some Afterthoughts', p. 98.

PLATE VIII

A PAGE FROM NO. 3 OF C.P.E. BACH'S *SONATEN MIT VERÄNDERTEN REPRISEN*, 1760 (*see p. 586*)

The composer's own copy showing emendations and variants made by him probably not long before his death.

and a harmonic restlessness that gives it a distinctive character. The finale of the same work is notable for the emphatic cadential phrase in octaves that occurs from time to time, and which towards the end of the movement shows a tendency to end on a wrong note. The sixth sonata of this set consists of a single extended movement in which the principle of varied repetition is applied, not to the usual sonata form but to a pair of alternating themes, one in the minor and the other in the major. This idea, partially anticipated by Martini, was probably the model for the many movements of this kind written by Haydn, but its material has not enough character or contrast for it to be of great musical interest.

If Emanuel Bach had died in 1760 there would have been no doubt about his gifts, but in some ways his work might have seemed curiously diverse in its aims; the vigour and rhetoric of the 'Württemberg' sonatas and the delicate ornamentation of the *Sonaten mit veränderten Reprisen* must have appeared to point in different directions. In the works after 1760 he was able to gather up the various threads and blend the rhetorical and lyrical sides of his personality. This can be seen in his next two sets of sonatas, Wq. 51 and 52,[1] which appeared in 1761 and 1763 respectively. In the earlier set the first movement of the fifth sonata has varied repeats; those of the others are more in the manner of the 'Württemberg' sonatas, but with greater continuity and concentration. The second sonata, in B flat, has a few bars of slow introduction, which are recalled, though not repeated, at the beginning of the fine and solemn slow movement. The finale of the third, in C minor, is very striking, and its mysterious and dramatic closing bars are worth quoting:

[1] No complete modern edition. Wq. 51, no. 2, and 52, no. 2, ed. Elizabeth Caland in *Neues C. Ph. E. Bach Album* (Münster, 1929); Wq. 51, no. 3, and 52, no. 3, ed. Herrmann, op. cit. Copies of first edition of Wq. 51 in British Museum, London; King's College, Cambridge; Reid and Public Libraries, Edinburgh: copies of first edition of Wq. 52 in the same libraries and also in the Bodleian Library, Oxford.

The set of 1763 is similar in general calibre, though more sombre as a whole. Of the two works in major keys the fifth, in E, though pleasant enough, is the slightest of the set, and the most remarkable feature of the first, in E flat, is its gloomy and powerful Adagio. The third has an unusual scheme, an Andante in G minor being followed by two contrasted movements in G major, the second of which is in a simple ternary form, A–B–A', with the B section in the minor mode. But the outstanding feature of this set is the first movement of the sixth sonata, in E minor, which has a remarkably imaginative development section, covering a wide range of modulation. The next two sets, the *Sechs leichte Klaviersonaten* (Wq. 53) of 1766 and the *Six Sonates de Clavecin à l'usage des dames* (Wq. 54)[1] of 1770, are smaller in scale, though they contain some very agreeable music; the latter, as might be expected, chirp demurely, with occasional unexpected touches, such as the oddly impish first movement of the sixth sonata. Of the 1766 set the most interesting is the sixth, in F, which has features which foreshadow the orchestral symphonies of some ten years later;[2] not only are the three movements joined, which is often the case in the sonatas, but the first movement lacks the usual double bar, and makes no clear division between the exposition and development, the whole work being conceived in a very idiomatic keyboard style.

The sonatas that have been discussed give a good idea of the development of C. P. E. Bach's style up to 1770, but they are far from being the only keyboard works that he wrote during that period. All through his life there was a steady output of smaller pieces, fantasias, solfeggi, and dance movements, in addition to many other sonatas, a number of which are still unpublished, making a total of around 350 keyboard works. From 1779 onwards appeared the six sets of sonatas, rondos, and fantasias, *für Kenner und Liebhaber* (Wq. 55–59 and 61),[3] though many of these were written some years before they were published. The Sonata in F (Wq. 55, no. 2) was written as early as 1758; it is notable for the unexpectedly dramatic development of the opening Andante, and

---

[1] Modern edition, Halle, n.d.
[2] See pp. 393–4.
[3] Modern edition, ed. Carl Krebs (Leipzig, 1895), revised by L. Hoffman–Erbrecht (Leipzig, 1953).

the impressive link between this and the Larghetto that follows. It is also the only piece in the *Kenner und Liebhaber* sets to indicate the use of *Bebung*—the vibrato effect obtainable on the clavichord. No instrument is specified by Bach for the first set, but the other five sets are all designated as for 'forte-piano'. The Andante of the G major sonata (Wq. 55, no. 6) is a fine instance of C. P. E. Bach's improvisatory manner, which increasingly comes to dominate the slow movements in his later years. The F minor sonata (Wq. 57, no. 6), whose kinship to Beethoven's sonata in the same key, Op. 2, no. 1, has often been noted, is perhaps the most powerful of the sonatas dating from the early 1760s (the others being Wq. 55, nos. 4 and 6, and Wq. 58, no. 4). Besides the bold harmonic progressions in the development of the first movement, we also find definite preparation for the recapitulation by the creation of an anticipatory mood, a feature to be found also in the A major sonata (Wq. 55, no. 4). The Sonata in D minor, (Wq. 57, no. 4) contains a magnificent slow movement not unlike that in the *Reprise* Sonata in B flat quoted in Ex. 325, but more chromatic and more polyphonic in texture. The tonal restlessness that shows itself from time to time in the earlier works is even more in evidence in those written after 1770, and sometimes appears at singularly unexpected places. In the first *Kenner und Liebhaber* set, for instance, the Sonatas in B minor and F (nos. 3 and 5) deliberately avoid the tonic in the opening bars, in a manner highly uncharacteristic of the eighteenth century:

Ex. 327 Allegretto

Ex. 328 Allegro

In the B minor sonata this restlessness is intensified by the fact that the short slow movement opens in the remote key of G minor and modulates gradually and very effectively to the dominant of B minor. More curious still is the key-scheme of the Sonata in G (Wq. 58, no. 2), in which the first movement is in G major, the second in G minor, and the third in E major. Most of these late sonatas are very compressed and epigrammatic, and their unexpected harmonic turns must have seemed bewilderingly breathless to contemporary audiences. A characteristic instance is the finale of the Sonata in E minor (Wq. 59, no. 1), written in 1784, which opens in a bland and innocent manner but soon plunges into remote and unexpected modulations, and in its last bars appears to fall asleep in the middle of a sentence. There are a few movements with varied repeats, but they are on a smaller scale than those in the earlier works. There is an attractive specimen in the two-movement Sonata in F (Wq. 56, no. 4), the finale of which might almost be poking fun at the first movement of the earlier work in the same key quoted in Ex. 328. Of these late sonatas the largest is the work in B flat (Wq. 59, no. 3), composed in 1784. The first movement combines the usual sonata form with a rhapsodical and improvisatory manner. Ten years before, Bach had attempted this with less success in the first movement of the A minor sonata (Wq. 57, no. 2), where the rhetoric is rather flowery and empty; here the music has more force and a surer sense of direction. Here too we have virtuoso music which seems to demand the forte-piano rather than the intimate clavichord. Finer still is the slow movement; the main theme is a formula used by countless composers of the period, but soon mysterious chromatic shadows appear, and when it is introduced in the dominant it quickly passes into a remote key with a wonderful sense of poetry:

The flowing lyricism of the finale looks back to the *Reprisen* sonatas, and the work as a whole gives a clear and convincing picture of the various aspects of its composer's personality.

The first *Kenner und Liebhaber* set contains six sonatas, the second and third contain three sonatas and three rondos, and in the others there are two sonatas, two fantasias, and two or three rondos. This suggests that in his last years Bach was finding the sonata a less congenial form of expression, and in his last two specimens, written in 1785, the extreme compression amounts in places almost to sketchiness. On the other hand, he clearly felt that when writing rondos and fantasias he was free to make his explorations with the utmost leisure. He had used the rondo form with gentle precision in the finale of the B minor sonata (Wq. 55, no. 3); in the separate rondos the themes are equally unpretentious but they are treated with an extravagant spaciousness, with extraordinary harmonic digressions, so that the pieces often have the inconsequent charm of stories or plays in which the most homely characters are made to undergo the most fantastic adventures. They were widely admired in Bach's life, and even those who were bewildered by the remote modulations would have had no difficulty in appreciating the simple geniality of the themes. With the exception of the comparatively terse Rondo in C minor (Wq. 59, no. 4), these works do not have the wealth of episodic material that is to be found in the rondos of Mozart; the all-important feature is the main theme, which often undergoes ingenious variations and transformations on its subsequent appearances. The contrast between the melodic naïvety and the harmonic adventurousness is often fascinating, but in some of the more diffuse rondos there is a feeling of strain upon the simple material that makes them, in the long run, less satisfying works of art than the finest of the sonatas.

The fantasias are similar in character to the beautiful finale with which the last of the *Probestücke* ends; bar-lines are frequently dispensed with, and the general style is improvisatory. Sometimes, as in the Fantasias in F (Wq. 58, no. 7) and G (Wq. 59, no. 5), this style leaves a chaotic impression, but in several of the others the planning is considerably less haphazard than it seems at first. Usually there is a highly varied assortment of material, to which the capricious and unexpected treatment is more suited than to the single themes of the rondos. One of the most interesting is the last, in C major (Wq. 61, no. 6), in which not only the main theme itself, but also its treatment in introducing it in unexpected keys, is suggestive of Haydn. The transitions are often wildly abrupt, but the whole composition is admirably proportioned; the interrupted cadences near the end look back to a passage in one of the *Reprisen* sonatas mentioned before (Wq. 50, no. 5). It should be remembered, however, that Emanuel was doing little more in this form than continue, in the tradition of the organ and clavier, rhapsodic fantasias of the late baroque, including many of his father's works. The fantasia was the home of harmonic experiment, as may be seen in Johann Sebastian's Chromatic Fantasia or the G minor Fantasia for organ.

Among Bach's short pieces there are a number that have French titles, such as *La Xénophon et la Sybille*, *La Complaisante*, and *Les Langueurs tendres*;[1] these often show a delicate intimacy worthy of Couperin, though simpler and more direct in style. In 1781, when presenting his Silbermann clavichord to an amateur composer, Dietrich Ewald von Grothius, he accompanied it with an elegiac piece, *Abschied von meinem Silbermannischen Claviere in einem Rondeaux*,[2] with an expressive use of *Bebung*. In 1786 he wrote six sonatinas (Wq. 63) for a new edition of his treatise, each consisting of a single movement only. Though on a very small scale, they have considerable individuality, such as the characteristic waywardness of the unexpected harmonic turn at the end of the beautiful Largo in E.

C. P. E. Bach was composing at a time when his father's work was generally regarded as dry and remote, and he himself may well have felt that the particular kind of *Empfindsamkeit* at which he was aiming was something that had no place in the world of the previous generation. But we can see now that the gulf between the two personalities was less wide than it seemed at the time. They both had the same deep sensitiveness to harmonic colour; with the one it softened the outlines of a contrapuntal texture, and with the other it enriched a precise and limited harmonic scheme. Sometimes the two styles come oddly near to each other: the Prelude in F minor from the second book of the 'Forty-eight' might almost be by C. P. E. Bach; and similarly the following, from one of the *Kenner und Liebhaber* sonatas, Wq. 55, no. 6, could easily appear in a keyboard prelude by Johann Sebastian.

Ex. 330
Allegro di molto

[1] In Arnold Schering, *Geschichte der Musik in Beispielen* (Leipzig, 1931), p. 458.
[2] Modern edition, ed. Alfred Kreutz (Mainz, 1950).

As for the younger generation, Haydn generously, but with ample justice, admitted his great debt to C. P. E. Bach; in both composers there was a streak of impishness, and a love for building long paragraphs containing phrases of unequal lengths. At times Emanuel Bach's music looks still farther ahead, though the most obviously prophetic passages are not necessarily the finest; the daring may sometimes seem unsuited to the material. He was far more versatile than any of his brothers and, while constantly moving with the times, he inherited sufficient harmonic imagination to avoid the rather insipid amiability into which the music of the latter half of the eighteenth century was liable to fall in its weaker moments. Comparison of the Sarabande from J. S. Bach's English Suite in D minor, the Adagio maestoso from C. P. E. Bach's Sonata in F, Wq. 55, no. 5, and the Largo e sostenuto from Haydn's Sonata in D, no. 37, shows how the second of these seems at the same time to look back to the first and onward to the third. Though far from being exclusively a keyboard-composer, C. P. E. Bach always wrote for it with sensitiveness and imagination.

OTHER GERMAN AND AUSTRIAN COMPOSERS

Of the many lesser composers writing keyboard music in Germany and Austria at this time, the most solidly conservative was Johann Ludwig Krebs (1713–80), a pupil of J. S. Bach, whose suites and fugues imitate the style of his teacher with remarkable skill. Primarily an organist, with an outstanding pedal technique, Krebs also wrote clavier sonatas less imitative of Bach than his organ works, although their concession to progress is restricted to a thinning of the contrapuntal texture rather than a total adoption of the *style galant*. Another J. S. Bach pupil, the theorist and violinist Johann Philipp Kirnberger (1721–83), likewise composed keyboard works mainly in contrapuntal style. His uncompromisingly strict fugal writing, however, enjoyed little more popularity than his unorthodox theories on harmonic construction and his bizarre *Methode Sonaten aus'm Ermel zu schüddeln*,[1] describing how to produce 'new' works simply by modifying old ones. Georg Christoph Wagenseil (1715–77), a Viennese composer of opera, wrote keyboard sonatas in an Italianate manner, though with but little distinction. Himself an accomplished performer on the clavier, and Maria Theresa's *Hofklaviermeister* from 1749, Wagenseil composed with an eye to the capabilities of his Viennese public, and his writing, especially for the left hand, is frequently dull and repetitive, yet it was his very simplicity, tunefulness, and avoidance of contrapuntal complexity which attracted

[1] Berlin, 1783. Translated in full as 'Method for Tossing Off Sonatas', in William S. Newman, *The Sonata in the Classic Era* (Chapel Hill, 1963), p. 442.

the young Mozart to his music; like J. C. Bach, with whom he has strong affinities, Wagenseil played a major part in the formation of Mozart's keyboard style. Nevertheless, none of his clavier works possesses the character and individuality of a sonata in E flat[1] by J. H. Rolle (1718–85) which is spaciously designed, and has a slow movement of considerable beauty opening with a particularly striking phrase:

Ex. 331 Adagio

This prolific composer was a violinist and viola player at the court of Frederick the Great from 1741 to 1746, and therefore had every opportunity to study the music of C. P. E. Bach, which is reflected in his own keyboard works, displaying imaginative harmonies and modulations as well as occasional passages of an improvisatory nature. The keyboard works of the Czech composer Georg Benda (1722–95) not surprisingly also owe much to C. P. E. Bach, since Benda spent several years in Berlin from 1742 onwards, and often show an interesting balance between homophonic and more contrapuntal writing. The slow movement of a sonata in C minor,[2] with its modulations from E flat through E flat minor to F sharp major, returning by way of G sharp minor, B flat minor, and F minor, illustrates both the debt to Emanuel Bach and Benda's own individuality, for only a composer of independent mind could work such a scheme convincingly.

The two youngest surviving sons of J. S. Bach, Johann Christoph Friedrich (1732–95) and Johann Christian (1735–82), both wrote pleasantly for the keyboard, though without the vitality and enterprise of Emanuel, their senior by over ten years, or Haydn, their contemporary. Johann Christian, whose devotion to the keyboard found expression in his concertos rather than in solo works, published only two sets of solo sonatas each containing six pieces,[3] whilst a further three sonatas were brought out posthumously by Bonin of Paris as

---

[1] Printed in Ernst Pauer, *Alte Meister, Sammlung wertvoller Klavierstücke des 17. und 18. Jahrhunderts* (Leipzig, 1868–85).

[2] No. 12 in *Musica Antiqua Bohemica*, xxiv, ed. Jan Racek and Václav Jan Sykora (Prague, 1956).

[3] Op. 5, without *ad libitum* violin parts (Amsterdam, 1768) and Op. 17 (London, *c.* 1779). Modern edition of ten sonatas, ed. Ludwig Landshoff (Leipzig, 1927).

Op. 21, of which only the first movement incipits survive. In many ways, Christian's approach to the medium contrasts strongly with Emanuel's: the former soon began to prefer the forte-piano to the harpsichord, whilst his brother remained faithful to the older instrument; moreover, Christian's writing seldom incorporates elements of *Empfindsamkeit* but depends instead on melodiousness and an intimate knowledge of the capabilities of the keyboard. Significantly only two of his fifteen sonatas are in the minor, of which the first, Op. 5, no. 6 in C minor, looks back rather than forward, consisting of a prelude-like slow movement, a fugue more reminiscent of Handel than of J. S. Bach, and a gavotte, all in an idiom that must have sounded somewhat archaic at the time they were published.[1] The other C minor work, Op. 17, no. 2, is the nearest J. C. Bach has ever approached to the idiom of the *Sturm und Drang* school, especially in the restless urgency of the prestissimo finale, but the remaining sonatas are firmly in the *galant* idiom, full of the turns of phrase which are generally associated with Mozart, but which had already been made common property by the symphonists of the Mannheim school. The lyrical element predominates, not only in the slow movements but in many of the others, such as the Rondo from the Sonata in E flat, Op. 5, no. 4. Some of the first movements too are mainly lyrical, as in the Sonata in G, Op. 17, no. 4:

Ex. 332

which has a strong likeness to the opening of Mozart's Sonata in B flat, K. 333, and in others there is the familiar contrast between a ceremonious opening theme and a singing second subject, for instance in Op. 5, no. 5 in E. This work employs a more markedly virtuoso idiom in its outer movements than any other of Bach's sonatas, yet in his boyhood Mozart selected nos. 2, 3, and 4 of the same set for conversion into the piano concertos of K. 107. The years that Johann Christian spent in Italy in his youth influenced his style considerably. The language of Italian opera—and he continued to write in that genre in England—had a noticeable effect on his instrumental style, and that in

[1] Heinrich Peter Schökel, *Johann Christian Bach und die Instrumentalmusik seiner Zeit* (Wolfenbüttel, 1926), pp. 156-7, shows that it was probably written considerably earlier, c. 1756-7.

itself would have made Mozart particularly sympathetic to his music. There are no formal innovations in Bach's sonatas: he shows a slight preference for the two-movement over the three-movement form, with seven of the twelve extant sonatas in the former category. Most of the fast movements adopt a form which is basically binary, with the first subject returning immediately in the dominant (or relative major) after the double bar, and the second subject making its final appearance in the tonic. However the second section is never an exact copy of the first; Bach always expands his material in the latter half, either by extending his first subject by a few bars as in the opening movement of Op. 5, no. 1, or by replacing it with new, though related, material as in the first movement of Op. 17, no. 3. Very rarely in these works can one identify a distinct 'development' section, for Bach was not interested in creating the tensions and sharp contrasts, motivic repetitions and wandering tonality that such a term implies, though the first movement of Op. 5, no. 2 in D does contain such a section, with an opening motive derived, interestingly, from bar two of the second subject, and with modulations into E minor, B minor, G major, and A major before the return to a clearly defined 'recapitulation' in the tonic. Texturally the sonatas are thin; Bach seldom employs full-blooded chords, preferring a light, two-part texture, with the striking exception of the early Op. 5, no. 6, where thickly scored harmonies, combined with the sombre tonality, produce a sonority unique in his keyboard music. Johann Christian also wrote half a dozen sonatas for four hands, which together with those of Mozart (whom they may have influenced) can be said to have established the genre.

HAYDN

The keyboard works of Haydn cover a period of over thirty years, beginning in the 1760s or earlier. It was not until the last years of that decade that they began to show much individuality, though the very early sonatas now and then show interesting features, such as the surprisingly emotional slow movement of no. 2,[1] the trio of the minuet in no. 12, which is unusually chromatic for its date, and the lively finale of no. 13. These works are all on a small scale; rather longer are the Sonatas in E flat, no. 45, written in 1766, and in D, no. 19, written in 1767. Here the influence of C. P. E. Bach can be seen,

[1] The numbering follows that of Anthony van Hoboken, *Joseph Haydn: Thematisch-bibliographisches Werkzeichnis*, i, Gruppe XVI (Mainz, 1957). This corresponds to the numbering in *Joseph Haydns Werke: Erste kritisch durchgesehene Gesamtausgabe* (Leipzig, 1908–33), series XIV. *J. Haydn: Werke* (Munich and Duisburg, 1958–), series 18 (ed. Georg Feder) adopts a different order, as does Christa Landon in her edition (Vienna, 1963–6).

especially in the leisurely pace and varying phrase-lengths of their first movements. The Sonata in D has an equally leisurely slow movement, which, to judge from the cantabile passages in the lower keyboard register, might almost be a transcription from a violoncello concerto, and a finale in rondo form, less common in these works than might be expected. In the piano sonatas, as in the symphonies and quartets, there is a notable increase in maturity in the works written after about 1770. The actual range of the keyboard writing is wider, the high F above the treble stave being used for the first time, the texture is more varied and the emotional content richer. The Sonata in A flat, no. 46, which was published in 1786 but is thought to have been composed about 1768, has a slow movement which is by far the subtlest thing that Haydn had yet written for the piano; it is full of beautifully clear and delicate contrapuntal writing, and ends with an unusually eventful coda. Finer still is the twentieth sonata, in C minor, which is a masterpiece comparable to the contemporary string quartets, Op. 20. The first and last movements are on a broad scale, and, especially in the latter, there is a remarkable urgency and passion; the slow movement, less immediately attractive, has a strange undercurrent of agitation that brings it into line emotionally with the other two.

This work, written when Haydn was in his fortieth year, holds a position among his sonatas very similar to that of the work in A minor (K. 310) among the sonatas of Mozart. Both are comparatively early works of peculiar intensity in which the composer is giving rein to a more vehement and uninhibited emotion than in most of the works that come before or immediately after. In the sonatas that follow the C minor, there is much that is delightful and individual, but it is generally more subdued. The set of six written in 1773 contains the pleasant work in E, no. 22, whose finale provides the first instance in the sonatas of Haydn's favourite form of variations on two alternating themes, one in the major and the other in the minor. The first three sonatas of this set, nos. 21–3, are notable for the irregular features of the recapitulations in their first movements; the last three, nos. 24–6, have optional violin parts, which, as is usual in Haydn, contribute singularly little to the general effect. With the exception of one or two very early works none of the sonatas has more than three movements: Haydn however had a special affection for the minuet and frequently substituted it for either the slow movement or the finale. He was equally fond of variation form and one or other of these appear in all of the next set of six sonatas, published in 1778. The Sonata in F, no. 29, is perhaps the richest in its pianistic texture; in no. 30 the movements are played without a break, as in some of C. P. E. Bach's sonatas, the join between the first and second movements coming with particular dramatic effect. The Adagio itself has no formal structure, and its twenty-one bars quickly lead back from the F sharp minor of the opening to A major (the key of the first movement), ending on the dominant chord of that key in preparation for the final minuet with variations. No. 31 is remarkable for its second movement,[1] an Allegretto in E minor written as a short binary movement in lucid three-part counterpoint throughout. But the strongest of the set is undoubtedly the last, in B minor, which in its first movement and finale shows a fierce and defiant energy that has a marked foretaste of Beethoven; between them comes a minuet with some typical examples of irregular phrase construction.

Something of the same energy reappears in the first movement of the Sonata in E minor, no. 34, which also provides a fine instance of Haydn's resourcefulness in thematic development. Not gifted with Mozart's inexhaustible flow of melody, he was more concerned with making the most of the material at hand and so often, at moments where Mozart would introduce a new idea, Haydn instead produces a new version of an already existing theme. In the first movement of the E minor sonata almost everything grows from one or the other of the two figures announced in the opening bars; at the end of the recapitulation the extension of closing group followed by a coda is far longer than is usual in piano sonatas of this period, and the sudden conclusion is most imaginative. In 1780, nine years after its composition, the Sonata in C minor, no. 20, was published with five more recent works, Nos. 35–9, by Artaria in Vienna. This marks the beginning of the important relationship between Haydn and his chief publisher. The Sonata in C sharp minor, no. 36, has a very fine first movement which, again, derives almost entirely from the two component parts of the main theme. It is full of pauses and silences of a kind that look both back to C. P. E. Bach and on to Beethoven. The minuet with which this work ends, though more unassuming, is of equally high quality; the central movement, however, is a comparatively trivial set of alternating variations, the first theme of which is used with greater resource in the rondo-like first movement of the Sonata in G, no. 39. The Sonatas in D and E flat, nos. 37 and 38, both have impressive slow movements in minor keys that lead without a break into the finales. The short Largo of the D major sonata has already been mentioned;[2] it contains some remarkable harmonies:

[1] Omitted in many editions.
[2] See p. 593.

Ex. 333 Largo e sostenuto

and is in the despairingly tragic mood which Beethoven expressed on a larger scale, as in the Largo of his Sonata in D, Op. 10, no. 3. The sense of the tragic in Haydn is no less deep, but with the possible exception of the 'Representation of Chaos' movement in *The Creation*, he never maintained it throughout a whole piece; some of his most sombre music is to be found in the slow introductions of otherwise cheerful symphonies.

The sonatas of 1780 were followed shortly by the six quartets, Op. 33, also published by Artaria; by this time Mozart, developing with meteoric brilliance, was shortly to write some of his greatest and most profound music. Haydn, proceeding with far more leisure, had reached a stage of maturity, thoroughly delightful, but less impulsive than his earlier and less profound than his latest work. The next three sonatas, nos. 40–2, which also exist as string trios, appeared in 1784; like the slightly later Quartet in D minor, Op. 42, they are deceptively relaxed in manner, but are far from being negligible. Each consists of only two movements and in only one of them, no. 41 in B flat, is there a fully developed allegro in sonata form. The finale of no. 40, in G major, is of considerable interest; basically it is in simple ternary form A–B–A', but the A section itself shows a miniature sonata-form construction, neatly demonstrating the way in which the 'sonata principle' was by this time penetrating into other spheres. The first movements of this sonata and of no. 42, in D, both consist of alternating variations, the latter set being in one of the composer's more thoughtful moods, while its finale offers an excellent sample of the famous Haydn gaiety and wit. In his two-movement sonatas there is usually a certain intimacy and informality which looks ahead to Beethoven's Sonatas in F sharp major, Op. 78, and E minor, Op. 90. In the opening Andante of the two-movement Sonata in C, no. 48, written *c.* 1789, the style has even more solemnity; it is a set of alternating variations in which both the major and the minor theme are variants of the same idea. By contrast the final movement is again in Haydn's most impish mood, and provides the first example in his keyboard sonatas of the use of sonata–rondo form. Composed about the same time was the Sonata in E flat, no. 49, dedicated to Marianne von Genzinger; here the sonata form of the first movement is handled with a strong sense of drama, which is intensified from time to time by a figure of four repeated notes, especially towards the end of the development:

Ex. 334 Allegro

Such moments, relying almost entirely on a masterly control of harmonic rhythm, show clearly Beethoven's debt to Haydn. The Adagio is in the A–B–A' form so often found in Haydn's late slow movements; there is a wealth of varied repetition, and a remarkably rich and sonorous middle section. To Haydn himself this Adagio had particular emotional significance and, perhaps for that reason, he followed it, not with the usual lively finale, but with a simple 'tempo di minuetto'.

After this work Haydn wrote only three more sonatas; they were composed in England in 1794 and written for Miss Therese Jansen, who was later to become Mrs. Gaetano Bartolozzi, a famous pianist and pupil of Clementi.[1] All three works are of exceptional quality. The Sonata in C, no. 50, has a particularly interesting first movement; it contains

[1] Cf. Oliver Strunk, 'Notes on a Haydn Autograph', *Musical Quarterly*, xx (1934), p. 192.

Haydn's only indications for the use of the pedal, and its seemingly trivial first theme:

Ex. 335
Allegro

is treated with astonishing imaginativeness and resource. The finale brings a singularly vivid foretaste of some of Beethoven's scherzi, with the rondo theme's continually frustrated attempts to modulate to unexpected keys. The Sonata in D, no. 51, returns for the last time to the two-movement form; the opening Andante is unusual, for it employs a mixture of sonata and rondo form, usually reserved for final movements, whilst the finale itself is a brief sonata-form movement, with the repeat of the development and recapitulation written out, though not varied in any way—perhaps to ensure that the performer did not omit it. Finest of all is the Sonata in E flat, no. 52, undoubtedly Haydn's greatest work for the piano. The first movement has a remarkable variety of material, the second subject being as light-hearted as the first is dignified. The descending passage beginning at bar 6 leads to some surprising chromatic developments and the range of modulation is unusually wide, the second subject appearing in the course of the development in the remote key of E major. This key is used again for the equally impressive slow movement, where it stands in a 'Neapolitan' relationship to the E flat of the first movement. Here, in contrast to the Allegro, everything seems to derive from the first three notes, and, as so often, the problem of developing a single theme stimulates Haydn to a particular emotional intensity that here finds vent sometimes in startling modulations and sometimes in cadenza-like outbursts. The finale provides a fine conclusion to the sonata, an almost flippant theme being treated with great power and imagination. The whole of this work is conceived on a larger scale than any of the previous sonatas and this is further emphasized by the heavy texture, especially in the first movement. The keyboard writing throughout is astonishingly rich and varied, and even the most brilliant passages always have real significance and life.

Apart from the sonatas there are several sets of variations, of which the finest is the work in F minor (Hob. XVII/6), where two alternating themes are treated with great sensitiveness, ending with a coda of exceptional length and containing some of the most extraordinary harmony in the whole of Haydn. This was written in 1793 for Barbara Ployer, to whom Mozart dedicated his Piano Concertos in E flat and G, K. 449 and 453, and was published by Artaria in 1799. Similar harmonic surprises are to be found in the Fantasia in C (Hob. XVII/4) of 1789, despite the simplicity of the main theme itself. The possibilities of modulation by semitonal movement seems to have attracted Haydn more and more at this time. This lengthy work is conceived in a free rondo form, handled with the utmost confidence.

Looking back on Haydn's keyboard music as a whole, it can be seen that as his style developed his treatment of the instrument became increasingly rich and inventive. But even at the end of his life he was obviously reluctant to entrust to it such broadly singing melodies as those of the slow movement of the Symphony no. 88, or of the Quartet in D, Op. 76, no. 5. It is interesting to see how, in the slow movement of the late Piano Trio in G, the delicately ornamented first theme is at one point transferred from the piano to the violin, but the broad and simple melody of the central section is never given to the piano. If we compare one of the less interesting movements from Haydn's sonatas with a similar movement from a Mozart sonata, it will usually be found that in the Mozart there are plenty of attractive melodic ideas that the composer has thrown off lightly and taken little trouble to develop, while with Haydn the themes may have little attraction in themselves, but the music may become far more vital and exciting with the process of development. A melodic gift as attractive and spontaneous as Mozart's will always find a willing audience, even in comparatively slight works; the intellectual curiosity and architectural imagination of Haydn's finest keyboard works may make a less quick and ready appeal but, once appreciated, they have a singularly enduring attraction. In all his works his capacity for imaginative thematic treatment added enormously to the range of sonata form; it was something that C. P. E. Bach, with all his gifts, could never achieve to anything like the same extent. Music for keyboard solo played a less important part in his output than in C. P. E. Bach's, but on the whole more than in Mozart's, who, in his last and finest years, wrote a comparatively small amount of it.

MOZART

The careers of Haydn and Mozart were perpetually reacting on each other, and to attempt to disentangle their mutual influences is a fascinating but difficult task. Mozart's early piano sonatas were to some extent influenced by Haydn; on the other hand Mozart's influence can be felt in one or two of Haydn's later sonatas, such as the 'Genzinger' E flat, but hardly at all in the last three. The first four sonatas Mozart is known to have written, (K. Anh. 199–202), dating from 1766, are lost, and the two short sonatas in C and F (K. 46d and e)[1] of 1768 are both very brief two-movement works, a binary Allegro being followed by a minuet and trio. Mozart's first full-scale sonatas were composed as a set of six (K. 279–84) in 1774–5, shortly after nos. 21–6 of Haydn; the slow movement of K. 280, in F, has a resemblance to the Larghetto of Haydn's twenty-third, in the same key, and the first movement of K. 279 and some of the finales have Haydnesque features. But there are other stronger influences; the lyrical passages are often reminiscent of J. C. Bach, though there is already more chromatic detail, both melodic and harmonic, and the general texture is often reminiscent of Johann Schobert, whom Mozart had met on his first visit to Paris in 1763–4. Several movements are notably more individual than their neighbours, especially perhaps the Adagio from K. 280, and the fiery and exhilarating finale of the otherwise placid work in G, K. 283. The slow first movement of the Sonata in E flat, K. 282, has a tantalizingly commonplace second theme, but it also contains much mature and beautiful music. The Sonata in D, K. 284, is on a larger, more ambitious scale than the first five, with strong suggestions of the concert symphony. The development section of the first movement is thematically quite irrelevant, but it has a powerful drive culminating in a fine and passionate outburst of a kind that is far from common in Mozart's music at this period:

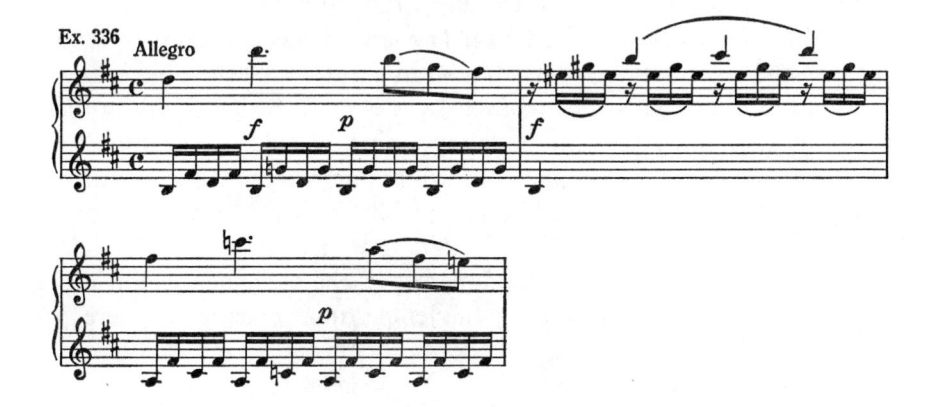

Ex. 336 Allegro

After the Rondeau en polonaise of the middle movement the sonata ends with an interesting set of variations. The theme has the unusual feature of a sudden silence near the end, which is filled in with unfailing

[1] J. Werner (ed.) (London, 1958).

appropriateness in each of the following twelve variations. There is an admirable variety of texture, a characteristic variation in the minor, and a certain amount of unobtrusive but effective counterpoint. As so often with Mozart, the penultimate variation is a floridly expressive Adagio, followed by a final Allegro variation, here in triple time. This sonata is the most forceful keyboard work that Mozart had yet written; something of the same urgency is found in the first movement of an unfinished Sonata in G minor, K. 312, which is usually thought to have been composed at this time, though Einstein eventually put it at a far later date.[1]

During the years 1777 and 1778 Mozart wrote seven piano sonatas, K. 309–11 and 330–3. The first two of these, K. 309 and 311, composed at Mannheim, are comparatively slight, but K. 309 has a slow movement, which is an ingenious mixture of variation and rondo form, apparently inspired by a passing love affair with Rosa Cannabich, and the rondo of K. 311 shows the wealth of melody so common in Mozart's later finales, and contains more than a hint of a concerto-like style. The first movement of this work has some interesting structural points; the development treats a short phrase from the exposition with almost Beethovenian persistence, and in the recapitulation the first theme does not appear until after the second, a feature significantly also to be found in many of the symphonies of Mannheim composers.[2] The Sonata in A minor, K. 310, which was composed in Paris in 1778, is, however, a work of very different calibre. Like the equally fine Violin Sonata in E minor, K. 304, it was probably written shortly after the death of his mother and both works seem to reflect the emotional shock that his bereavement must have caused him. The development sections of both the first and second movements abound in harmonic clashes, increasing the sombre spirit that is not relieved by the finale, which is still in the minor mode and whose continuous rhythmic drive adds to the intensity of the whole. The other sonatas of 1778 are more subdued in manner, but the best of them, K. 332, in F, has in all its three movements a strong undercurrent of agitation. That Mozart now had the ability to weld widely differing kinds of emotion together in one movement is attested by the finale of this sonata, where the tempestuous opening and serene end coexist quite happily; the single-*Affekt* theory of the Baroque is totally extinct. The Sonata in A, K. 331, opens with a well-known set of variations, which are more polished though less adventurous than the set in K. 284. After the fine minuet that follows, the Turkish finale is

---

[1] *Köchel's Verzeichnis sämtlicher Tonwerke W. A. Mozarts*, 3rd edition (Ann Arbor, 1947), p. 993.
[2] See p. 410.

something of an anticlimax, especially in the coda, though it may well have sounded exotic to contemporary hearers. The hand of a master, however, is evident in the Andante cantabile of the C major sonata, K. 330; it is in A–B–A form with a short coda added, in which, by referring back to the B section, not in its original minor mode, but transformed into the major, Mozart achieves an effect at once simple yet magical. The slow movement is again the most striking part of the Sonata in B flat, K. 333, especially in its development section, which relies almost entirely on the expressive effect of appoggiaturas.

After 1778 Mozart paid more attention to the piano concerto than to the piano sonata; the sonatas that he did write, however, are of the finest quality. K. 457, in C minor, the greatest of them all, was probably composed in 1784, and opens with a gesture of defiance similar to those that occur at the beginnings of the Wind Serenade, K. 388, and the Piano Concerto, K. 491, in the same key, a motif which is prominent throughout the movement and which is given additional emphasis at the beginning of the coda where it is used in stretto. The Adagio, like several other slow movements of the period, shows with what richness Mozart could handle the simpler A–B–A–C–A type of rondo; everything is laid out on the most ample scale, with a wealth of harmonic colour and melodic decoration. In its restlessness the finale displays an affinity with that of the A minor sonata, which likewise retains the minor mode of the opening movement. The remaining sonatas are less expansive emotionally, but several of them reflect the composer's increasing interest in counterpoint. This is particularly prominent in the first two movements of the Sonata in F, K. 533, written in 1788; they show that Mozart's skill in thematic development, though less frequently displayed, was no less than that of Haydn and Beethoven. This is most notable, because more unexpected, in the Andante, where a fragment of the opening theme:

Ex. 337 Andante

is transformed at the end of the development section into a strangely tortured sequential passage:

Ex. 338 Andante

In both movements the counterpoint is often harsher than anything in J. S. Bach. The Rondo in F, K. 494, of 1786 was published by Hoffmeister, with Mozart's consent, as the finale of this work; it is slighter and more relaxed in manner, but for its publication Mozart added to it a cadenza-like passage (bars 143–69) containing some striking polyphonic phrases that bring it admirably into line with the rest. The Sonatas in B flat, K. 570, and D, K. 576, both composed in 1789, show something of the same interest in polyphony in their outer movements; particularly fine is the opening Allegro of K. 576, which contains some of Mozart's most ingenious canonic writing and also one of the most sensuous of his lyrical tunes:

Ex. 339 Allegro
dolce

The beautiful Adagio from K. 570 is a near relation to the slow movement of the C minor piano concerto; it is in simple rondo form with a coda which looks back to both the episodes. In both of these subtle and highly polished masterpieces Mozart shows that, like Beethoven, he was quite willing, even in very late works, to make use of the simplest and most familiar accompaniments if the occasion demanded, and in the Andante of the little C major sonata, K. 545, he uses the Alberti bass with an almost super-Albertian persistence, but with no loss of individuality.

The separate sets of variations for piano solo[1] take more account of the virtuoso than most of the sonatas, and they are often rich and varied in their keyboard writing, though their musical content fluctuates greatly

[1] *Neue Mozart Ausgabe*, Ser. IX, Werkgruppe 26, ed. Fischer (Kassel, 1961).

in value. Of the early sets the most interesting is that on Salieri's 'Mio caro Adone', which apart from its rather perfunctory end sounds surprisingly mature. In many others, as in the early sonatas, there are individual things that stand out strikingly against less interesting backgrounds. The variations in minor keys often show an unusual degree of intensity, and in many of the sets the penultimate variation, in a slower tempo than the rest, is full of the floridly operatic type of melody so beloved by Mozart. Of the later sets the most noteworthy are those on Gluck's 'Unser dummer Pöbel', K. 455, of 1784 and on Schack's 'Ein Weib ist das herrlichste Ding', K. 613, written in the last year of his life. Here the themes are treated more freely with a more varied texture than in the earlier sets; the brilliant passages are far more organized, and by lengthening the finales Mozart brings the works to a more satisfactory conclusion.

The fantasias have some of the improvisatory manner of C. P. E. Bach, and although they are less wildly adventurous and more solid in their musical content, they all display the more overtly dramatic side of Mozart's personality. The very fine work in C minor, K. 475, composed in 1785 comes the nearest to Bach in the variety of its material and the wide range of key, but it makes a far more unified impression than any of Bach's works. It was published together with the C minor sonata, but each work is sufficiently great in its own right to be more effective when performed separately. In the Fantasia and Fugue in C major, K. 394, the Fantasia goes far beyond anything Mozart had attempted in the sonatas in the way of exploiting the resources of the piano; its extreme restlessness makes a suitable foil to the rather austere fugue, which is well endowed with learned devices and contrapuntal clashes. Of the other Fantasia in C minor, K. 396, only the first twenty-eight bars are by Mozart, the rest probably having been very ably written by Maximilian Stadler; Mozart had begun to add a part for violin, which Stadler integrated into the piano part when he completed the work. The Fantasia in D minor, K. 397, is a shorter work with strong suggestions of an operatic *scena*; here too, the last ten bars are probably not by Mozart, having apparently been added for the Breitkopf and Härtel edition of 1806.[1]

Two of the short mature dance movements are of excellent quality, the Gigue in G, K. 574, with its waspish contrapuntal energy, and the Minuet in D, a late work despite its Köchel number of 355, in which Mozart employs a degree of chromaticism quite alien to the *galant* style.

---

[1] Cf. Paul Hirsch, 'A Mozart Problem', *Music and Letters*, xxv (1944), p. 209; also Steglich, 'Über das melodische Motiv in der Musik Mozarts', *Mozart–Jahrbuch 1953*, p. 128.

In this piece there is an unusually direct suggestion of contrast between the polished musical idiom of the day and the intensity of Mozart's personal emotions. These find fuller expression in two larger works of exceptional beauty, the Rondo in A minor, K. 511, and the Adagio in B minor, K. 540. The Rondo, like the slow movements of the C minor and B flat (K. 570) sonatas, is of the simple A–B–A–C–A type, but is planned on a spacious scale, with great richness of detail, and a long and eventful coda. The wistful chromaticism and gently elegiac dance rhythm of the main theme have a strong foretaste of Chopin. The Adagio is in sonata form, with sharply contrasted themes; here again there is much poignantly expressive chromaticism, and in both the development and coda considerable dramatic tension is to be found. The fact that in his later years Mozart, like Haydn, wrote fewer and fewer slow movements in minor keys gives a particular significance to these masterpieces.

The keyboard works involving more than two hands[1] include the fiercest and harshest of all Mozart's contrapuntal movements, the Fugue in C minor for two pianos, K. 426, which was later arranged by the composer for string orchestra, K. 546, with an Adagio introduction added. In no other work does the polyphonic texture result in quite the same degree of tortured intensity, and it provides a startling contrast to the genial Sonata in D, K. 448, for the same medium. Of the works for two performers at one instrument the outstanding example is the Sonata in F, K. 497. It has the unusual feature of a slow introduction; the finale rivals those of the mature piano concertos in its wealth of ideas, and the Andante is of magnificent quality, the texture sometimes suggesting a kind of operatic ensemble—it was written in 1786, the year of *Figaro*. The other sonatas are of less value, though the slightly later work in C major, K. 521, is very effective, as is the delicate set of variations in G, K. 501. In all these later works for piano duet the melodic interest is well divided between the two parts, and, especially in the F major Sonata, the texture is often of a fascinating richness.

In his last years Mozart wrote three works for mechanical organ; of these the Adagio and Allegro, K. 594, and the Fantasia in F minor, K. 608, are in the composer's most mature style and are best known in their arrangements for organ solo or piano duet. The Fantasia is very original in design, combining in a single movement rhetorical, fugal, and lyrical elements. Mozart always had an innate sense of style that enabled him to alternate between harmonic and contrapuntal textures without any sense of incongruity. Sometimes the contrast is exploited lightly and humorously, as in the finale of the G major quartet, K. 387, but in

---

[1] *Neue Mozart Ausgabe*, ix, Gruppe 24, Abteilung 2, ed. Ernst F. Schmid, and Abteilung 1, ed. Wolfgang Rehm (Kassel, 1955).

such works as this fantasia and the late solo Sonata in F the intensity and continuity of the music leaves the listener hardly aware even of the suggestion of a contrast.

Although a fine executant, Mozart was not especially interested in exploiting the resources of the keyboard; far less so than Clementi,[1] who was his senior by a few years but who lived well into the nineteenth century. Nor had he much of the adventurousness that is found frequently in the music of C. P. E. Bach and Haydn, and occasionally in that of lesser men such as Johann Wilhelm Haessler (1747–1822) or Friedrich Wilhelm Rust (1739–96). Haessler's sonatas, and especially the curiously named *grande gigue* in D minor from his Op. 31, are sometimes remarkably original. His earlier sonatas reflect the conventional training he received from his uncle J. C. Kittel, himself a pupil of J. S. Bach, but throughout his long career he kept pace with formal and technical developments, and produced his most imaginative works after moving to Moscow in 1794. Mozart met Haessler in Dresden in 1789 but was disappointed by his playing on the organ and clavier.[2] The extravagant claims made on behalf of Rust by d'Indy were based on an edition of his sonatas which had been much modernized by his grandson in an attempt to convince posterity of his grandfather's influence on Beethoven. Ernst Neufeldt's discovery of the hoax in 1913[3] prompted d'Indy to attempt to justify his misguided enthusiasm by editing twelve Rust sonatas from the autographs and continuing to argue their position as precursors of Beethoven's sonatas. Such an argument is tenable from the point of view of their bold harmonic progressions, motivic development, and imaginative keyboard writing, but less convincing in view of Rust's uninspired melodic writing and retention, in some places, of the strict contrapuntal style belonging to the first half of the century.

The amount of piano music written during Mozart's last years is regrettably small, and it is perhaps significant that these latest works are on the whole less pianistic than their predecessors. The early sonatas, slight though they are, have interest for their periodic glimpses of the real Mozart, and the later works are of the greatest value as mature and consistent expressions of the uniquely fascinating and sensitive personality of the composer. And a brief backward glance will show at once how firmly integrated were the various elements of his style. Early in the eighteenth century J. S. Bach and Handel were both, in their different ways, successful eclectics and were able to absorb both Latin and Teutonic influences as essential features of

---

[1] For Clementi, see Vol. VIII.
[2] Emily Anderson, *The Letters of Mozart and his Family*, 2nd edition (New York, 1966), ii, p. 923.
[3] 'Der Fall Rust', *Die Musik*, xii (1912–13), Heft 6, p. 339.

their style. After them the two streams seemed to part for some time. W. F. Bach was influenced mainly by the more German side of his father's style, and was weakest when writing in the increasingly popular Italian idiom. The personality of C. P. E. Bach was more complex; sometimes, as in the *Sonaten mit veränderten Reprisen*, he showed a taste for melodic decoration of a decidedly Italian kind, but his rhetorical vigour and harmonic adventurousness came from Germany rather than Italy; also the homeliness and simplicity of some of his themes, especially in the rondos, is of a strongly Teutonic variety. The music of his younger brother, Johann Christian, on the other hand, is very Italian in its concentration on graceful lyric melody and its contentment with a very limited harmonic range. Haydn, like C. P. E. Bach, came to a limited extent under Italian influences, especially in his earlier slow movements, but his personality was predominantly non-Latin, particularly in his intellectual curiosity and the suggestion of folk-song, whether this was of Croatian or of purely German origin being in the long run a matter of minor importance. In Mozart's style the Italian element is of course far stronger, though it has sometimes been overstressed. As Dent so convincingly showed[1] we have only to put Mozart's work beside that of his Italian contemporaries and immediate predecessors to see to what an extent the Italian influence is modified by the instrumental German tradition. Even in a comparatively slight movement like the first movement of the Sonata in B flat, K. 333, which is very near to the Italianate idiom of J. C. Bach, there is a considerable amount of thoroughly Mozartian chromatic colour. And in the latest keyboard works the combination of sensitive and sometimes elaborately florid melody with an ever-increasing subtlety of harmony and polyphony brought about a supremely successful blend of the finest qualities of Germany and Italy.

[1] *Mozart's Operas* (2nd edn., London, 1947), pp. 26, 56 ff., 165, et passim.

XI
INSTRUMENTAL MASTERWORKS AND ASPECTS OF FORMAL DESIGN
By FREDERICK STERNFELD

INTRODUCTION

OF movements organized according to the sonata principle (as C. P. E. Bach and Haydn shaped the pattern) one part became crucial for the future of the symphony. This was the final section: the recapitulation with or without a coda. In the earlier binary forms of J. S. Bach and Domenico Scarlatti the opening sections often tended towards the formal and tonal designs of an exposition. True, there were important differences in rhythmic shape and melodic contour, and the contrast between 'first' and 'second' subjects was not one of character but rather of placement and dynamics. Yet the resemblance is so great that historians are tempted to discover sonata forms where, in truth, they do not exist. The development section, too, has close analogies in compositions of the generation born around 1685. Once the double bar is reached in the works of Bach and Scarlatti the course of the music is not far removed from that of countless symphonies in the second half of the century: there are the avoidance of the tonic, the rapid modulations, the occasional working out of the main theme, and the final, prominent return of the tonic. The character of the music, too, is not less serious than that of the later symphonies or overtures.

In contrast to these resemblances, the final section of the movement demonstrates the divergence between the practices of the High Baroque and the Enlightenment. Clearly, Bach and Scarlatti did not feel the need of a symmetrical restatement at the end of the movement of material first heard before the double bar. We may sympathize with this point of view, considering how many recapitulations become boring when they are not relieved by the tonal variations which a restatement in the tonic key of both the primary and the secondary material calls for. Beethoven himself was aware of the danger of monotony when he omitted this entire section in the second *Leonore* overture. (That he changed his mind in *Leonore* No. 3, and that in No. 2 his coda is as long as a recapitulation might have been, are circumstances whose significance belongs to a later volume.) At all events, composers of the time of Bach, Handel, and Domenico Scarlatti deemed it sufficient to restate merely a part of the opening section; complete restatements are rare, probably not more than once in every ten cases. So prevalent is this pattern that in discussions of Scarlatti and his contemporaries it is customary to speak of an A B::C B form where A and B, before the double bar, move away from the tonic; C, after the double bar, may or may not develop the opening material in foreign keys; and the final B restates the second part of the opening section transposed to the tonic.[1] Occasionally a composer would add a ritornello-like restatement of the opening theme at the very end of the movement, in the fashion of a concerto. But to relate such unchanging ritornelli to the codas of Haydn, not to mention Beethoven, would be false, for the very essence of these codas is thematic mutation. Whether in symphonies or operatic arias, Haydn and his successors seemed to favour a symmetrical restatement of the exposition. What was lost in dramatic cogency and interest would be gained in lucidity, intelligibility and recognition in the original sense of that word. To recognize in the recapitulation the return of the primary group as well as the secondary and closing groups produced the kind of delight cherished by the age of Enlightenment, for by this reprise one might understand more thoroughly the significance of the opening section. Following upon the sea-changes of the development this restatement furnished the coherence and symmetry of which the age was so fond. In excess, this spelled boredom, and to alleviate the ennui was still an artistic necessity – which brings us to one of the main glories of Haydn's symphonies. Tovey wrote that Haydn's recapitulations were Beethoven's codas, implying that the pleasure of the unexpected and the sense of depth in Beethoven's codas were to be found now and again in Haydn's considerably modified recapitulations. Like so many of Tovey's lapidary *mots*, this remark[2] has often been misunderstood. The truth is that Haydn uses both methods: on occasion he proceeds by 'varied' recapitulation; at other times he has the conventional recapitulation which is then followed by a coda (not a mere ritornello), and this latter method he bequeathed to both Mozart and Beethoven.

In Haydn's varied recapitulation we find that he produces variety by restating his material in an unexpected order. A link in the chain may not come in its proper place but, instead, be tagged on at the very end. (Such a postponed restatement is not to be confused with a genuine coda, that is to say, second or third or even fourth thoughts on a theme already restated.) At other times—and this is the pattern Haydn pre-

---

[1] Rita Benton, 'Form in the Sonatas of Domenico Scarlatti', *Music Review*, xiii (1952), p. 264; Ralph Kirkpatrick, *Domenico Scarlatti* (Princeton, 1953) pp. 251–79; Manfred Bukofzer, *Music in the Baroque Era* (New York, 1947), p. 237.

[2] *Essays in Musical Analysis*, i (London, 1935), pp. 145, 148, 157, 162, 165, 174; particularly p. 162.

ferred—he expanded the recapitulation at some point before the end. After this expansion (or insertion) the recapitulation proceeds to its final bars which are identical (save for transposition) with the final bars of the exposition. At the conclusion of both exposition and recapitulation there is the traditional double bar, and no final ritornello confuses the genres of sonata and concerto.

The concerto was clearly the leading genre in instrumental music in the first half of the eighteenth century. At its close, this role had been usurped by the symphony. Naturally, the historical development did not always proceed in a straight line. In the last quarter of the century, during his middle period, Mozart was more preoccupied with piano concertos. Moreover, the vast majority of extant symphonies conformed to the same pattern of movements as did the Vivaldi concertos and the Alessandro Scarlatti overtures. That is to say, they exhibit a fast tempo as well as an animated and pulsating rhythm in the outer movements. Still, the history of instrumental music in this period, whether pertaining to works of average or of exceptional merit, must be concerned primarily with the symphony.

C. P. E. BACH AND OTHER INFLUENCES ON HAYDN

The works of Emanuel Bach, Haydn's great predecessor, have been discussed in previous chapters. On pages 389–95 in particular the reader will find an account of how Emanuel developed the movement forms he inherited from the previous generation. The devices which he employed are not exclusive to him: composers of his own generation such as Stamitz (1717–57), and those born in the thirties such as Pugnani (1731–98), frequently varied or abbreviated the recapitulation, for instance, by severely reducing the primary subject group or omitting it altogether. But the majestic character and harmonic daring of Bach's music—in both symphonies and keyboard works—make it of inherent worth.

No two men could have had more dissimilar backgrounds than did Emanuel Bach and Joseph Haydn. Bach had many advantages: parental instruction at the highest level, a university education, and prolonged residence in large cities such as Leipzig, Berlin, and Hamburg. By contrast, the humble and ignorant Haydn seems to have had few early privileges, and on reaching maturity his attachment to the provincial court of the Princes Esterházy from 1761 to 1790 restricted his metropolitan musical activities. But his ceaseless experimentation, his astute assessment of the public's readiness for innovation and its tolerance of his more profound moods, led him to become in his old age the acknowledged grand master. At the time of his death his leadership in Mass and oratorio, in symphony and string quartet, was unchallenged. In effect, Haydn succeeded where Emanuel and Mozart had failed. Native talent alone cannot account for his success, though Haydn possessed it in abundance. He also commanded the shrewdness, tact, and sense of timing essential for success, qualities which were sadly lacking in Mozart. Even Emanuel Bach never gained the rapport with Frederick the Great which Haydn enjoyed with Prince Nicholas Esterházy. In the period of his rule from 1762 to 1790, Haydn established the string quartet and the symphony as the leading musical genres of the age.

But apart from personal considerations Haydn profited also from circumstances of time and place. Younger than Emanuel Bach, he was ready to experiment with a variety of patterns, such as the four-movement form with minuet, which Bach disdained. Then, as an Austrian, he was in closer proximity to Italy and the Italian tradition in opera, Catholic Church music, and symphony. It is true that Bach could have grafted the Italian tradition on to his German Protestant heritage, as did his younger brother Christian, for opera was, after all, a thoroughly Italian business, whether in Berlin, London, or Vienna. But as the son of Johann Sebastian, with his formative years passed in Leipzig, Emanuel remained aloof on the whole from the tunefulness, homophony, and widespread popular appeal of the Italian genre, restricting himself to a few ideas from the Italian aria and overture. Haydn, on the other hand, was constantly groping, primarily for self-fulfilment and for the right models, but also to meet his public, if not half-way certainly part of the way. Most of his achievements spring from his matchless invention. But there were also concrete influences from the south such as Sammartini and Boccherini as well as the north. This marriage of Italian tunefulness and lucidity with German counterpoint and profundity accounts for Haydn's world success in his own time, as well as his stature in posterity.

Amusingly enough, Haydn's recorded conversations deal with both influences. The Bohemian composer Mysliveček, upon hearing some of Sammartini's compositions, exclaimed, 'Ho trovato il padre dello stile d'Haydn.'[1] When Griesinger confronted Haydn with this statement he protested vehemently, admitting that he had known Sammartini's music but denying that he had ever esteemed it highly: Sammartini was a dauber, a scribbler (*ein Schmierer*). For Mysliveček's discernment he had only derision and insisted that he recognized only Emanuel Bach as his model (*nur den Emanuel Bach erkenne er als sein Vorbild*). Certainly Haydn, a world celebrity by the time he talked to Griesinger, was not

[1] Giuseppe Carpani, *Le Haydine*, (Milan, 1812), pp. 57–63; Georg August Griesinger, *Haydn* (Leipzig, 1810; new edn., Vienna, 1954), p. 12.

always either modest or accurate, yet a great deal may be learned from this outburst. Haydn was too shrewd to deny that he knew Sammartini's music. It was played in Milan (where Sammartini had taught Gluck) and in Vienna, and copies of it have been recorded in such scattered places as Esterház, Paris, and London. On the other hand, Haydn had no reason to 'esteem' his Italian predecessors and every right to consider Sammartini his inferior. To be sure, the Italians had provided him with several important elements of his craft—clarity of articulation, symmetrical length of the component sections of sonata form, hints of lucid thematic development and of pseudo-polyphony in a homophonic texture. Yet it remained for Haydn to refine these elements into a fully fledged obbligato homophony, as Guido Adler dubbed the Viennese style.[1] Patriotic pride, a craftsman's respect for solid counterpoint and expressive harmony, and a great artist's preference for the profound rather than the shallow, would induce Haydn to proclaim Emanuel as his model. Even so, it must be said that Haydn's immortality was nourished not only by the challenging stature of Emanuel but by the assured craftsmanship of Sammartini—and by an accurate assessment of the temper of his age.

HAYDN'S EARLY SYMPHONIES AND QUARTETS

In the symphonic works of Haydn one is struck first of all by their immense variety. The gamut stretches from magisterial seriousness to uninhibited playfulness, from melodies taken from Gregorian chant to quasi-folk-songs and quasi-dances. Haydn's restlessness and joy in experimentation extend equally to harmonic and formal procedures. Unexpected modulations and dissonances are set off by Alberti basses, and novel structures bearing the composer's own individual stamp are counterbalanced by works reminiscent of Lully, Corelli, and Sammartini. Symphony no. 15 in D major, for instance, opens with a French overture; the introductory adagio section ending on the dominant leads to a presto middle section, which also settles down on the dominant, after which the adagio of the opening is resumed. Then there are a number of early symphonies in which Haydn experiments with an opening slow movement followed by the usual allegro movement and foregoes the slow introductory section with which he begins his London symphonies. Obviously, the *sonata da chiesa* of Corelli and its countless Italian and German imitators have stood godfather here, and Haydn returns to this form again and again before he finally drops it (Symphonies nos. 5, 11, 18, 21, 22, 34, 49). Yet, it would be a mistake to discover

[1] Guido Adler, 'Die Wiener klassische Schule', *Handbuch der Musikwissenschaft* (Berlin, 1930), ii, pp. 768 ff., particularly p. 789.

in this formal scheme a dependence on the thematic or harmonic workmanship of Corelli or Handel. Within the framework of the *sonata da chiesa* Haydn employs the typical sonata form of the eighteenth century, like Sammartini and Boccherini. Modern writers frequently call it 'two-part' or 'binary' sonata form to indicate the division, by means of the double bar, into two unequal parts as well as that the second double bar—as in the binary dance movement of a suite—marks the end of the movement, there being no coda. Harmonically and melodically, too, the expression is highly individualistic and intense, pointing forward in the direction of Romanticism. Compare, for instance, the first four bars of the first movement of Haydn's Symphony no. 49 in F minor ('La Passione') (i) with those of the first variation from the slow movement of Schubert's Quartet in D minor ('Death and the Maiden') (ii). The pedal point, the expressive emphasis on the fifth degree of the scale (with its chromatic neighbouring note)—these and other features within the slow tempo make for a surprising similarity in two works more than half a century apart.

Ex. 340

Equally surprising and equally prophetic of Schubert's 'Death and the Maiden' quartet is the predominance of the minor mode, F minor being the tonality of the opening Adagio, the succeeding Allegro, the Minuet, and the Presto finale. Three of the four movements are in two-part sonata form (the minuet excepted) and each ends with the closing material from the exposition transposed to the tonic. The opening Adagio movement has a remarkably varied recapitulation: the first twenty-four bars are reduced to eight bars (62–9) while bars 34–43 are expanded to eighteen bars (79–96). The second movement has a long development which occupies more than a third of the entire movement, thus recalling Emanuel Bach.

It would be tempting to chronicle the achievement of Haydn exclusively in the genre of the symphony, a genre which commanded the widest public and affected taste on a much larger scale than chamber music did. Yet it was in the string quartet that the perfect blending of styles and epochs, so distinctive of Haydn's technique, took place. The very texture of four solo instruments without continuo was an auspicious basis for the development of obbligato homophony, and these pieces were held in the highest esteem by connoisseurs, witness Goethe's famous remark to Zelter: 'One listens to four intelligent people conversing with each other, one expects to gain from their discourse and to learn to know the peculiarities of the instruments.'[1] Indeed, these elements are important in the European fame of Haydn's quartets. The intelligent nature of the discourse and the improvement of the listener's mind were qualities dear to the Age of the Enlightenment. On the other hand, an awareness of the character of the instruments, the low range of the cello, the descant quality of the violin, anticipate to some extent the delight in sound for sound's sake in the century to come. By the 1800s the fame and esteem of Haydn's eighty-three quartets were so widespread that complete editions were published independently in Paris ('dediée au premier consul Bonaparte'), Leipzig, and Vienna. The house of Artaria, at Vienna, began its publication with no. 19 since Haydn had repeatedly voiced his opinion that the first eighteen works 'did not embody the true principle of the quartet form'. It is easy to see that these early divertimenti of five movements with two minuets, in the performance of which horns and other instruments were sometimes added, resembled serenades or suites for small orchestra more truly than quartets. Even so, if these early works are to be taken as genuine, real progress is observable in them. Gradually the four-movement form emerges, the time dimension increases, and even a miniature coda of sorts makes its appearance (no. 9—i.e. Op. 2, no. 3, first movement, bars 93–8). No. 16 (Op. 3, no. 4) is moderato, not presto, and its first movement (B flat major, 3/4) is of symphonic length (198 bars).[2] But in the short space of three years or so (1769–72) Haydn achieved a mastery that made all previous quartets, including his own, seem like apprentice pieces. Nos. 19–24 (Op. 9) introduce the thoughtful minor mode and nos. 25–30 (Op. 17) extend this and other achievements. Certainly, the

---

[1] *Goethe's Letters to Zelter*, tr. and ed. Arthur Duke Coleridge (London, 1892), p. 369 (9 November 1829).
[2] The authenticity of the six quartets published as Op. 3 has been questioned; cf. p. 554.

freedom with which the problem of symmetry versus asymmetry is handled in no. 28 in C minor is remarkable. Stretches of the exposition (bars 9–33) are never recapitulated, but the mezzoforte passage, changed in texture, and with imitation at the distance of two minims (bars 20 and 79), prepares for the contracted recapitulation (bars 92–120). At the end, there is a double bar with repeat sign which is then followed by a real coda (bars 120–30), in which the characteristic main motive appears in three different rhythmic guises (bars 120, 123, 125). With its pianissimo conclusion, the movement leaves the *galant* world of the divertimento completely behind.

Haydn's crowning achievement is, without a doubt, the Quartet in F minor, no. 35, of 1772. This tonality, as we have seen in Symphony no. 49, produced music in Haydn's most original vein. It has often been remarked that the finale is a double fugue; what matters is not the fact of fugal texture but the quality that is wholly novel in a homophonic tradition. Mozart was obviously influenced by Haydn's experiment: in the F minor movement of his Quartet in F major, K. 168, he used the same theme but at this early stage of his career Mozart could not command the mastery of his older colleague. Haydn himself had experimented with the insertion of fugal textures in sonata-form works for both orchestra and quartet. The finale of Symphony no. 40 in F major of 1763 is such an earlier effort. Priority matters little here, and one must agree with Tovey[1] that the Quartet no. 35 'is the most nearly tragic work Haydn ever wrote'. Its seriousness and high quality lead directly to the mature Mozart and to Beethoven.

The development of the first movement opens with a ninefold repetition of the first bar of the first theme, at different pitches, while the quaver figure of the accompaniment is subjected to even more extended repetition and fragmentation. After such an unusually intense development, we expect the recapitulation to be no more than a restatement, instead of which it provides Haydn with another opportunity for thematic development, revealing new potentialities in the material first heard in the exposition. Bars 5–10 are expanded to another ninefold development of the opening bar, bars 10–22 are entirely omitted (including the 'false' second subject at bar 20). A significant change occurs at bars 110–24. These fifteen bars correspond to a mere five bars earlier (31–7) and now offer development of the dotted quaver motive in bar 110. By the time we reach the double bar (136) we anticipate the end of the movement, but Haydn plunges us into a third development, a coda of twenty-three bars, with surprising enharmonic changes (B♭♭ and E♭♭), rising in a crescendo from pianissimo to fortissimo, and subsiding

---

[1] Tovey, *Essays and Lectures on Music* (London, 1949), p. 47.

again to pianissimo. Quartet no. 28 in C minor, discussed earlier, was obviously a precursor of this movement, but sheer length and intensity of expression together establish the slightly later work as a more lasting token of Haydn's genius.

The unrelieved gloom of the F minor tonality of this first movement also pervades the minuet to follow. The succeeding Adagio is interesting from two points of view: it combines the monism of Baroque variation form with the dualism of tonality in mid-eighteenth-century sonata form —in a remarkable way the main theme manages, in a movement without coda, to appear six times in the tonic (bars 1, 9, 17, 42, 57, 65; notice particularly the unusual F major at the beginning of the development). Secondly, there is the expressive manner in which the figuration of the first violin continues a step behind the chords in the three lower strings. Haydn proudly wrote in the score 'per figuram retardationis', implying a carefully rehearsed performance, 'dreamily and tenderly, not stiffly and coldly', as Joachim explained to Tovey.[1] The finale also bears several glosses wherein Haydn draws attention to his achievements. The title reads 'Fuga a due soggetti' and the inversion of the theme at bar 92 is labelled 'al rovescio'. Similarly the canon at the distance of a minim at bar 145, is marked 'in canone'. Other composers, following Fux's *Gradus ad Parnassum*, had continued the Baroque tradition of counterpoint, as in the quartets of Richter and Gassmann and the earlier efforts of Haydn. In the present fugue one can scarcely escape its connection with the Baroque, since the theme was used not only by Haydn and Mozart but also by Handel and J. S. Bach,[2] not to mention Pachelbel, Buxtehude, and Kuhnau.[3]

The terraced dynamics of the F minor quartet also hark back to the Baroque. Some crescendos and decrescendos do occur, as indeed they occur in the works of Emanuel Bach and Sammartini, but they are rare, most of the changes being dramatically sudden rather than graduated. Throughout the finale the strings play sotto or mezza voce until the coda is reached and the aforementioned canon is then pronounced fortissimo. Yet, even though so much of the method of statement is Baroque, the substance of the statement—as later in Beethoven's C sharp minor quartet, Op. 131—is very modern from the point of view of 1772: the amplitude of the entire movement, the length of the middle

---

[1] Tovey, *Essays and Lectures* (London, 1949), p. 47.

[2] 'And with his stripes' in *Messiah* and final chorus of *Joseph*; *Wohltemperiertes Klavier*, ii, no. 20, and 'Es ist der alte Bund' in the second movement of BWV. 106.

[3] Pachelbel, 'Magnificat Fugen', *Denkmäler der Tonkunst in Österreich*, viii (2), p. 15; Buxtehude, *Organ Works*, ed. J. Heder (Copenhagen and London, 1952), ii, pp. 73 and 123; Kuhnau, 'Neue Clavierübung', *Denkmäler der deutscher Tonkunst*, iv, p. 55.

section and coda, the scope of the modulations (reaching G flat major), and the lucidity with which the component parts balance each other. Particularly noteworthy are the extended pedals (bars 132–45, for instance); they function much like Stamitz's crescendos; their very length implies, and indeed, necessitates, that the matter to follow be substantial both in size and import.

At the age of forty Haydn had obviously achieved an equilibrium between his artistic purposes and the means of his craft that was altogether unprecedented. Quartets such as no. 35 in F minor, symphonies like nos. 44 in E minor and 45 in F sharp minor (nicknamed 'Mourning' and 'Farewell'), and the 'Missa St. Caecilia', established an eminence that explains Mozart's dedication of his own six quartets of the 1780s to the older composer as his mentor and the decision of the impatient and proud Beethoven to take lessons from Haydn. Yet in the two decades between 1772 and 1791 Haydn did not allow his inspiration unbridled rein. His biographers have had to record that the originality and audacity of the works just discussed were such that the compositions were considered too demanding, at least by some important contemporaries. The autograph of the slow movement of the Symphony no. 42 in D major, composed in 1771, bears a significant remark. At bar 45 (and at the corresponding place in the recapitulation, bar 143) Haydn originally had three additional bars, enlarging upon the chromaticism B♮—B♭. Later he excised these three bars, noting in the margin 'Dieses war vor gar zu gelehrte Ohren' (This was for much too learned ears). For some time Haydn was careful not to offend ordinary ears, attuned to the fashions of the day. The writing of string quartets ceased altogether between 1772 and 1781, and the symphonies written for Esterház in the later 1770s, and for Paris in the 1780s, delighted without straining conventional notions. It was not until Salomon arranged Haydn's visits to London in the 1790s that Haydn felt that Europe (or at least the wider public of Europe) had caught up with him, and that he was ready to offer the best he was capable of: the London symphonies, the last quartets, the final Masses and oratorios.

What circumstances caused the wonderful outburst of Haydn's compositions around 1770 is as unfathomable as the nature of genius. Some scholars have named it 'crise romantique', others 'Sturm und Drang' after the contemporary movement in German literature. The kinship with early Romanticism or proto-Romanticism implied by these terms is certainly to the point. Yet one cannot help feeling that local and personal factors must have played a role. The Court at Esterház had a predilection for the more easily approachable, while the Court at Vienna favoured a more learned style; and there was the European public at large, reluctant to accept music of an intense and exclusive character in place of more entertaining strains. Haydn steered a careful course until his departure for London, which he deemed the right moment to discard caution.

HAYDN'S LAST SYMPHONIES

If the qualities of the twelve London symphonies are to be summed up in a single work it must be one of the last three. The orchestral resources of metropolitan London and the adoration of both professionals and amateurs warmed Haydn's heart and mind. The special orchestra of sixty players, for the so-called Opera Concerts at the King's Theatre in the Haymarket, included some eminent composers and virtuosi, proud to play under the great Haydn. This orchestra more nearly approached the symphony orchestra of the nineteenth century, and the mere increase in size (about threefold) and consequent sonority, in contrast to the small band at Esterház, is indicative, on the one hand, of the stature Haydn had achieved and, on the other, of the rise of absolute instrumental music in general.

The Symphony no. 102 in B flat major was first performed in London on 2 February 1795. Thanks to extant sources (including the autograph) we have an exact knowledge of the composer's intentions. The dynamics are carefully and dramatically placed: crescendos and descrescendos on the single chord (bars 1 and 6) which dominate the slow introduction and sets off *p* and *pp* whispers in the strings. But, as previously observed, in spite of these (and other) crescendos and decrescendos both dynamics and textures are mainly of the terraced concertato kind as, for instance, the contrast between the tutti and flute-concertino statements of the main theme of the Vivace (bars 23 and 31) and the extraordinary antithesis between *ff* and *p* at the beginning of the subsidiary theme (bars 81–83). Imitative textures and motivic unity are other Baroque inheritances which Haydn put to novel and expressive use. The opening three bars of the Vivace, for example, supply three distinct quaver motives which appear frequently throughout the movement, particularly the second of them. Haydn uses this commonplace figure also in inversion and as a counterpoint:

Ex. 341

622 MASTERWORKS AND ASPECTS OF FORMAL DESIGN

(ii) bar 56   92

(iii) bar 198

The minim-crotchet figure to which the little motive serves as a counterpoint has, like every scale, its obvious polyphonic usefulness. It combines easily with its own melodic inversion, as seen above, and it adapts itself as well to stretto entries which give great pungency to the development – and, incidentally, recalls both melodically and in its polyphonic treatment the subsidiary theme of the overture to *Don Giovanni*.

Ex. 342

(i) bar 160

The development contributes much to the sense of spaciousness: it occupies more than four-tenths of the Vivace and gives the impression of even longer duration because Haydn indulges his fancy for the unexpected. This is largely due to the choice of tonalities and dynamics. The section starts in C minor (strings, concertino) and is followed by an entry of the main theme in E flat major. Among other keys touched upon are A flat major and, again, C minor. After thirty bars of tutti, the flutes pronounce the main theme in a concertino passage of C major. This takes us by surprise, and so does the development of motives y and z without the initial motive x (bars 192–217). It is this economy of thematic material, more than anything else, that demonstrates to what an extent the younger Mozart had influenced Haydn's method of composition, in a manner that later pointed the way to Beethoven. After this ambitious development there follows yet another one of the recapitulations Haydn so delights in. The movement is rounded off by the same closing material as the exposition, which precludes the addition of a coda. In this Vivace Haydn uses several means to inject variety, the most important of which is the transfer of the concertino statement of the main theme (flute) some fifty bars (bar 288) beyond the usual and expected place (bar 234). This deferred placement and new continuation (bars 295–302, with yet another development of the chromatic quaver motive) expand the movement to its utmost spaciousness. After this, the return of the closing material has the inevitability of a Baroque tutti conclusion or, perhaps the final return of a Romantic rondo.[1] In the slow movement to follow, the expressive use of decorated melodies is

---

[1] For a detailed discussion of the methods of recapitulation in Haydn's last symphonies, cf. Guy A. Marco, 'A Musical Task in the "Surprise Symphony"', *Journal of the American Musicological Society*, xi (1958), p. 41; and Eugene K. Wolf, 'The Recapitulations in Haydn's London Symphonies', *Musical Quarterly*, lii (1966), p. 71.

remindful of the Adagio of the F minor quartet of 1772 and the Andante of the F major quartet of 1799 (Op. 77, no. 1). The influence of Emanuel Bach is particularly pronounced in Haydn's slow movements, whether or not they are labelled 'Affetuoso'.

MOZART'S CHAMBER MUSIC

In the interim between Mozart's achievement of the early quartets of 1773 and Haydn's London symphonies, a matter of some twenty years, the younger composer progressed to a maturity that completely transformed his role in the musical scene of that period. With the three matchless symphonies of 1788 he became an important model for Haydn as well as for Beethoven. The group of six quartets numbered K. 168–173 was written after Mozart had experienced the challenge of Haydn's six quartets composed a year earlier, in 1772. The first of these, K. 168 in F major, has already been noted in relation to its slow movement which employs a fugato technique and the same theme as Haydn uses in the finale-fugue of his F minor quartet. The indifferent craftsmanship which this work by the seventeen-year-old composer reveals is compensated for by the promise of future greatness: a striking sense of drama in the slow movement, for instance, where a fugato for four voices in the tonic is set against a subsequent fugato, on another subject, for three voices, over a non-thematic, harmonic bass which moves to the dominant minor. By recapitulating both these passages in the tonic Mozart endowed his movement with a duality of both melody and harmony that passes beyond the Baroque, even though the imitatory devices were borrowed from that period. The first movement, too, is far from negligible. Its small motives are subject to ceaseless repetition and sequence until they become part of the thematic process: the dotted figure of the main theme (bars 3 and 12) develops into a miniature fugato of four entries in the exposition (13–16) and opens the development in another fugato of eight entries. In the recapitulation the four entries are expanded to six (75–80) and further prolonged by sequencing in a delightfully independent viola part. This is one of those varied recapitulations without coda which Mozart learned from Haydn (if not from Padre Martini and Sammartini as well).

All the same, even the young Mozart was fond of experimenting with an alternative pattern, namely, to provide yet further development at the end of the movement in a separate coda, and the opening movement of the last of the six quartets of 1773, in D minor, K. 173, offers a good example of this experimentation. A double bar separates the end of the recapitulation from a coda of eighteen bars which subjects both the primary and the subsidiary themes to a new development. Another interesting feature of this movement is the great importance of the second subject, in contrast to the monothematicism of Sebastian and Emanuel Bach and certain of Haydn's works (not to mention the preponderance of the opening subject in the dual sonata forms of Haydn and Beethoven). The second subject in this D minor movement not only dominates long stretches of the exposition and recapitulation, it also makes prolonged appearances in the development and coda. This emphasis seems to anticipate the Romanticism of Schubert.[1] The D minor fugue which functions as a finale employs the famous Baroque theme of the chromatically descending fourth which Mozart later put to such eloquent use in the second of the quartets dedicated to Haydn, K. 421, and in *Don Giovanni* (each also in D minor). It also manages to extract from a single theme—no duality in this movement—a surprising number of dissimilar expressions. Certainly, the answer at bar 4 to the first statement is unusual in that it is tonal, not real, and does not preserve the characteristic melodic shape. On the other hand, the final stretto, followed by an inner pedal in the second violin, winds up the whole work with dignity and a sense of drama and avoids the pitfalls of sentimentality, such as the conventional repetition of hackneyed cadences.

The promise of 1773 was, indeed, a rich one but, like Haydn, Mozart abstained from writing any more quartets for about a decade. When he resumed working in the medium the six quartets dedicated to Haydn left no doubt that the brilliant adolescent had gained his maturity. One has only to compare the D minor quartet of 1783 with that of 1773 to see this fact borne out. There is no denying that personal factors loomed large in the development of this elusive personality. Mozart's decision to seek professional freedom from employment in Salzburg and personal freedom from his father's guidance (however well founded and intended) led to the success of *Die Entführung* in July 1782, his wedding the following month, and to the birth of his first child in June 1783. The idea of death is universal enough to be independent of personal involvement, but it is more than likely that fear for the life of his dear ones was responsible for the sombre and tragic mien of this quartet. The traditional bass of grief, the chromatically descending fourth, is prominent in the first movement and may fairly be said to dominate the minuet and the coda-variation of the finale.[2]

[1] The comparisons made with Schubert in this chapter are efforts to demonstrate a similarity of temperament, of expressive devices, and of atmosphere; there is no attempt or need to prove direct influence.

[2] Concerning the relationship between the quartets of Haydn and Mozart and the particular assessment of the D minor quartet, cf. Jahn–Abert, *W. A. Mozart* (Leipzig, 1919–21), ii, pp. 168–180; Robert Haas, *Mozart* (Potsdam, 1933), pp. 78 and 117; Alfred Einstein, *Mozart* (New York, 1945), pp. 180–83; Arnold Schoenberg, *Style and Idea* (New York, 1950), pp. 96–7.

In his dedication to Haydn, Mozart states that the six quartets (composed 1782–85) were truly the result of long and arduous work ('è vero, il frutto di una lunga e laboriosa fatica'). One of the effects of these labours is the increasing deftness with which short fragments, rather than entire themes, are developed. The opening eight bars of the first movement of the D minor quartet appear, on the surface, to be typical of a symmetrical statement and restatement of a phrase of four bars. But the repetition is increased in intensity as the diatonic bass of the *sotto voce* beginning is replaced by the chromatic fourth of the forte repetition. More surprising is the fact that each of the motives of the opening three bars is separately developed: the trill of the second bar at the beginning of the development, the octave leap of the first bar immediately thereafter, and the rhythm of the third bar following that. In that curious order these motives are removed from their original thematic context and plunged into keys of utmost remoteness, such as A flat and A flat minor. The very beginning of the development with its unprepared switch from F major to E flat major betrays the hand of the dramatic composer; and eleven insistent repetitions of the trill motive, first on E flat, then on E natural, avoid boredom both by harmonic context and by the sharp awareness with which the listener experiences the reduction of the time dimension to a mere half-bar. A great deal has been written about the tragic overtones created in the minuet by the employment of the chromatically descending fourth and the octave leap, both so prominent in *Don Giovanni* of 1787.[1] What is even more remarkable is the dramatic unity imposed on the obbligato texture of the Minuet in D minor and the uncomplicated homophony of the Trio in D major. On the surface the trio belongs to the world of dance and entertainment music, but, like Schubert and Alban Berg in later centuries, Mozart manages to include both worlds in his universe and to do so without seeming effort or breach of style.

The finale is a set of variations on a siciliano theme and, again, its correspondence to similar movements of Haydn is obvious and perhaps even intended. What strikes the modern observer is that in this movement, too, Mozart frequently employs Baroque devices. (Throughout the six quartets fugatos and other imitatory passages are more prominent than in Haydn's quartets of 1781, Op. 33.) The concentration upon one theme and one key is closer to the expressive world of Sebastian Bach than to the dualistic variations of Haydn and Beethoven. Stylistic criticism sharpens our awareness of the debt Beethoven owed to Haydn, and Schubert to Mozart. The monistic variation technique of Sebastian Bach, Mozart, and Schubert is neither inferior nor superior to the dual-

[1] Haas, op. cit., p. 117.

istic variation movements of Haydn and Beethoven. Haydn's fondness for writing variations upon alternating themes or merely on themes alternately in the major and minor modes led directly to the slow movements of Beethoven's Fifth and Ninth Symphonies. (Beethoven's Trio, Op. 70, no. 2, also belongs here, though it is less widely known.) From the 1770s onward Haydn experimented with this novel technique in sonatas, trios, quartets, and symphonies. Mozart's variations make their impact by different means. Sometimes he introduces rhythmic complexity and even polyrhythms, as in the second variation of K. 421, justly praised by Schoenberg. Or he sets off the gloom of the minor mode by introducing a single variation in the tonic major. The crowning glory of the finale and, indeed, of the entire quartet in D minor is the coda variation in which the siciliano theme is combined with elements from the earlier movements, namely, the chromatic fourth and the octave leap. The thematic independence of the three lower parts, the eloquence of the second violin in the last four bars, the tension of chromaticism over pedals, all combine to produce an effect which defies verbal description. The result may be best defined in terms used in dramatic criticism: apotheosis and catharsis. Again, Mozart's universe is all-inclusive: the chirping of birds (the last four bars on the first violin) are as much a part of it as lofty grief. Only the tragi-comedian who created Don Giovanni and Leporello or, more strikingly, Sarastro and Papageno, could speak this language.

MOZART'S PIANO CONCERTOS

The extent of Mozart's influence on Beethoven and Schubert, and his relevance to the practices of our own century, give pride of place to the string quartet and the symphony, and it is these genres, therefore, that must be given primary consideration. Even within these species it is the dark, demoniac, and tragic aspect that has so affected posterity[1] that one is almost compelled to single out works in the minor mode: the String Quartet in D minor, the String Quintet in G minor, and the great G minor Symphony. These are masterworks, not only as specimens of the craft of composition but also as singularly concentrated documents of artistic expression. Yet one would paint a false picture of Mozart not to include mention of an entirely different species of instrumental works, usually in the major mode, and of a distinctly sunny mood and a less demanding nature. Mozart's piano concertos are, in the best sense of the words, *Gesellschaftsmusik* and *Gelegenheitsmusik,* that is to say, they

[1] See E. T. A. Hoffmann, whose 'Don Juan', half short story, half essay, first appeared in the *Allgemeine musikalische Zeitung* of 1813; English translation by Abram Loft in *Musical Quarterly*, xxxi (1945), pp. 504–16.

were written with a keen awareness of the expectations of society, and for a specific occasion, for the most part, benefit concerts (*Akademien*), in which the composer himself appeared as soloist. There are exceptions, the most prominent of which are the two concertos in the minor mode (K. 466 and K. 491). The marvellous chromaticism in the coda variation of the finale of the C minor concerto provoked Beethoven to exclaim to Cramer, in 1799, 'We shall never be able to do anything like that'.[1]

Still, the majority of the concertos, notably those published before Mozart's death and, therefore, in contemporary terms, the most successful specimens, are tuneful and frankly popular to a degree one could not reasonably expect to find among the quartets and symphonies. Between July 1782 (*Entführung*, Haffner Symphony) and May 1786 (*Figaro*) Mozart concentrated on the medium of the piano concerto expressly to conquer the Viennese public which favoured, above all, pianistic virtuosity, while the aristocracy offered lucrative opportunities of piano instruction. To woo this 'Clavierland', as he terms it in a letter, he composed no less than fourteen concertos (nos. 7–20) in those four years and but one symphony, the so-called 'Linz' of 1783. Obviously, the Viennese wanted to hear Mozart, the pianist, in his own concertos, and the mixture of virtuosity and musicianship proved attractive. The concerts (*Akademien*) that were so vital for Mozart's financial support were usually graced by a newly composed concerto, with the addition of an old symphony or overture and some arias to make up the balance. With the resumption of operatic commissions in the years between 1786 and 1791 (*Figaro, Don Giovanni, Così fan tutte, Tito, Die Zauberflöte*) the concerto as a genre lost its importance for Mozart. Whether the reasons for this were entirely practical is doubtful. The increased seriousness of the later concertos and the consequent decrease in opportunities for the display of virtuosity would seem to suggest that Mozart was turning away from the social exigencies of the eighteenth century, slowly moving instead in the direction later pursued by Beethoven. At the same time, no student of Mozart or the concerto can afford to ignore these works which, in their tunefulness, their Italianate melodies, their differentiation between virile primary and cantabile secondary themes, resemble Christian Bach more than they do Emanuel. This is also true as regards the formal patterns, for Mozart frames his sonata concerto movements by three ritornellos, omitting the fourth, that which precedes the recapitulation. Christian Bach, too, tended to slight or compress the tutti before the solo recapitulation or to integrate it with the development or recapitulation in a manner which robbed it of its distinctiveness.

[1] Alexander W. Thayer, *Ludwig van Beethovens Leben*, 3rd edition (Leipzig, 1922), ii, p. 78; English edition by Elliot Forbes (Princeton, 1964), i, p. 209.

Two compositions which display the happy side of Mozart's muse are the D major concerto of 1773, K. 175, and the G major concerto of 1784, K. 453. The latter work was written for Barbara Ployer for whom Haydn composed, in 1793, his exquisite F minor Variations for piano. Both works display a blend of substantial musicianship and charming entertainment ('*bedeutend und gefällig*' Goethe would have called it).

MOZART'S SYMPHONIES

To return to the symphonies of the mature Mozart: though few, their importance lies in their artistic stature and their influence on Beethoven. Few they certainly are, for the 'Linz' symphony of 1783 was followed by a mere four more: the so-called 'Prague' symphony of 1786 and the three last symphonies of 1788. The first aspect to claim attention in these compositions is the intense concentration on thematic work in the development sections. Whereas the concertos delight, as they should, by offering diversity and relief through their episodic developments which do not tax one's attention too heavily, the later symphonies pursue the lessons learned in the quartets that were dedicated to Haydn, to a point beyond Haydn. Nowhere is this more evident that in the opening movement of the great G minor symphony, completed 25 July 1788, a month after the E flat (26 June 1788) and a fortnight or so before the so-called 'Jupiter' (10 August 1788). The concentration upon the semitone motive of a mere half bar is as relentless as in Beethoven's terse developments, but complete as this concentration is, it seems to be arrived at without effort in true Mozartean fashion. In order to see the achievement of this work in perspective one must hark back to the 'little' Symphony in G minor of 1773, K. 183, which, along with the C major (K. 200, November 1773) and the A major (K. 201, April 1774) is known to the general public primarily as a precursor of the last three symphonies. Indeed, the use of counterpoint in the manner of Joseph Haydn, the coda-developments after the model of Michael Haydn, the general unity, individual as well as thematic, and the last three symphonies. Indeed, the use of counterpoint in the In the G minor it is remarkable how Mozart, not yet eighteen years of age, emancipates the chromaticism of the minor second and makes it speak by itself, devoid of melodic context:

Ex. 343
(i) bar 25   (ii) bar 109

The development section, too, in spite of its brevity, has weight as well as depth. In Mozart these penetrations from surface to bottom pass quickly but unmistakably. In eleven bars (87–97) the oboes play a modification of the main theme in semibreves, while violins and basses pronounce a new theme in crotchets, in free stretto imitation. But the return of this seemingly episodic crotchet theme as the primary material of the finale throws an entirely new retrospective light on it. In these early symphonies counterpoint provides one of the main excitements. Mozart's imitative passages are not lengthy but they are prominently placed. After the recapitulation, for instance, we find a double bar followed by the heading 'Coda'. The ensuing imitation, at intervals of two bars each (between violins, basses, and wind instruments), commands attention, even though it occupies a mere six bars. Then the rhythm of semibreves is reduced to minims, and the homophony of these minims is reminiscent of the atmosphere of the funeral march, on which note the movement concludes. All this is achieved in no time at all, and with the most modest scoring. In a movement of 214 bars the development measures 34, the coda 14 bars.[1] There are no flutes, no trumpets, not even clarinets. The orchestra is the standard Neapolitan band of Haydn and Mozart: strings plus oboes and horns (with implied bassoons to double the string basses). Even within this limitation greater amplitude of sonority is achieved in that four horns, instead of the customary single pair, are employed, the richer sound of the French horns in G being blended with that of the horns in B flat. Haydn's symphony in the same key (no. 39, *c.* 1768) also employs this blend harmonically and melodically. But in Mozart's 'great' G minor, two horns, one in G, one in B flat are given a more modest role, thereby throwing the effects of the woodwind into sharper relief.

It is altogether surprising that Mozart used his beloved clarinets so rarely in the orchestration of his symphonies, in contrast to his operas and piano concertos. External circumstances played a role, for the instrument was less readily available in Vienna and Salzburg than in Paris and Mannheim. Still, it is notable that while clarinets were called for in 1788 in the E flat symphony, K. 543, they were not considered equally indispensable for the last two works, the G minor and the C major. The case of the G minor is complicated, since it survives in two versions, the original scoring for oboes and the revised variant for clarinets and oboes. The C major or 'Jupiter' symphony (so nicknamed by Haydn's impresario Salomon) proceeds entirely without clarinets. Mozart obvi-

---

[1] The conciseness of Mozart's developments has been criticized by Théodore de Wyzewa and Georges de Saint-Foix, *W.-A. Mozart* (Paris, 1912–46), i, pp. 8–9, and defended by Einstein, op. cit., p. 155.

ously preferred, at times, the tone colour of the oboes with their pungent tang to the more mellow sonority of the clarinets. There is an example of this in the first movement of the G minor, where the second subject, in the exposition, has the melody alternately in violins and oboes, while in the recapitulation the alternation is between violins and oboes that are doubled by flutes at the higher octave. When Mozart revised the symphony to include clarinets he substituted these for oboes in the exposition, where the theme appears in the major mode; but in the recapitulation, where it is transposed (and transformed) from B flat major to G minor, the original scoring was maintained.

Ex. 344
(i) bar: 44 first version

*replaced by clarinet in second version

(ii) bar 227: first and second version

The presentation of the same melody alternately in the major and minor modes was a device wherein Mozart's individuality was pronounced. When the second subject appears in the relative major in the exposition the major mode could obviously be maintained in the recapitulation with the advantage of preserving the melodic contour and the contrast between primary and secondary material. Beethoven usually followed this plan. On the other hand, a tragic or pathetic or bitter-sweet mood is more consistently maintained if the subsidiary material is subjected to the minor modality and the consequent melodic changes as well. By and large, this was Mozart's method, as exemplified in the early and late G minor symphonies. (Haydn seems to have followed both methods at one time or another.) In this connection, the absence of clarinets in the revised version of Mozart's recapitulation is significant. The sharpness (or astringency) of the oboe is part of the original conception of this pathetic movement and in the careful revision and readjustment of sonorities the composer considered the effect his second subject would make on the occasion of its final, melodically altered, appearance. Parenthetically, it should be noted that the judicious alternation of major and minor is an important device to achieve poignancy and is best exemplified in the late works of Mozart. He seems to have influenced Schubert as well as countless lesser followers in whose hands this device quickly degenerated into mere sentimentality. Mozart usually avoided this pitfall by the rapidity with which his alternate versions succeed each other, as in the so-called 'Coronation' concerto, K. 537, where the second subject of the finale speaks with Schubertian eloquence (bars 89 and 240).

But the unique handling of the second subject must not overshadow the main theme of the G minor, which Mozart treated in a manner to command the admiration and, indeed, imitation of Beethoven. Among the methods of workmanship applied to this primary subject are concertato presentation, contrapuntal development. and thematic dismemberment. The contrast afforded by terraced dynamics is consistently employed in the last symphonies. The first eight bars of the C major alternate between forte and piano at intervals of two bars. The Allegro of the E flat, after an introductory Adagio of 25 bars, has 28 bars of concertino which are followed by 44 bars of tutti. The G minor has no slow introduction, its Allegro molto begins piano, in the strings alone, and only at bar 16 do we hear a short tutti forte which functions as a semicolon of sorts before the concertino resumes. It is reminiscent of the chromatic passage from the earlier G minor symphony (see Ex. 343). The quiet beginning of the Allegro molto is rather unusual; Mozart forces us to listen with concentration, as he does in some of the concertos.[1] Adagio introductions sometimes begin piano, but they are usually of little, if any, thematic importance, and they affect the audience more by their general mood. But when the opening bars of a quick symphonic movement are of thematic significance, they are apt to be preceded by some forte contrast, as in the opening two bars of the 'Eroica'. This method of building with blocks of noticeably different

---

[1] A similarly soft beginning of an opening movement that is also unusual will be found in Haydn's G minor Symphony, No. 39.

degrees of loudness harks back to the piano concertos of Mozart's middle period. With the exception of the non-thematic semicolon mentioned above (bars 16–20) the score remains piano until bar 28, when the tutti forte intervenes to modulate (bars 28–43) to another prolonged concertino passage, namely, the second subject. In the development section, too, dynamics as well as texture underline the contrast between the homophonic concertino treatment of the main theme at bar 103 and the contrapuntal tutti development at bar 114. This latter passage is, perhaps, the most conspicuous example of the many imitatory passages throughout the movement. The invertible counterpoint between the basses, which has the theme in quavers and crotchets, and the violins, which provide a quaver counterpoint, is maintained for a sufficiently long time (114–30) and the theme itself is long enough (four bars) to impinge forcibly upon the listener. Moreover, the quick figuration in the strings is brought into relief by the slowly moving chromaticism in the winds, which accentuates the basic notes of the counterpoint in the violins.

Ex. 345

In other imitatory passages the texture is simpler, for instance, in the latter portions of the exposition and recapitulation when the slow moving semitones of trebles and basses are heard in counterpoint against the first bar of the main theme in its original and rhythmic shape (bars 72 and 260). Equally lucid in texture is the imitation between flutes and oboes (flutes and clarinets in the revised version) which, over a dominant pedal in the bassoons, leads back to the recapitulation (bars 160–65). But in some ways the most striking imitatory passage comes near the very end of the movement because it occurs quite unexpectedly in a homophonic context. Between the scale run (276–81; exposition, 88–93) and the cadential theme (293–7; exposition, 95–9) which conclude both exposition and recapitulation, Mozart has placed one of those Haydnesque expansions which he had learned from the old master. First, the woodwind rise chromatically through the interval of a fifth (281–5) and then a miniature fugato with four entries is introduced (285–92). In spite of its brevity this fugato functions much in the manner of a coda, both by its surprising position and by the new aspects and capabilities of the main theme which it reveals.

If the imitatory passages (including fugatos) in the 'Eroica' are viewed as descendants of this movement, the same must be said about thematic dismemberment. The ruthless, yet miraculous way in which Beethoven reduces a long theme in the 'Eroica' to a single bar of two notes (bar 192)—and even to a single bar of a single note in the Fifth Symphony (bar 210)—may sound nonsensical on the surface. But to carry the process of thematic contraction to such a drastic degree that it approaches annihilation can be achieved only if the composer succeeds in conditioning his audience still to recognize the fragments no matter how pithy they may be. In other words, this achievement hinges on an infallible sense of timing on the part of the composer which succeeds in stimulating the memory of his listener to the point of recognition. It is precisely this sense of timing, developed in such earlier works as *Figaro* and *Don Giovanni*, with which Mozart carries out his thematic dismemberment effortlessly and elegantly. Everything takes place in the sixty-odd bars of the development. First, the theme is introduced in the strange key of F sharp minor (bar 103) and harmonic variation and sequence lead to the imitatory passage discussed above (bar 114). The four entries of that passage (bars 114, 118, 122, 126) present the theme in a shorter version of four bars, and this process of abbreviation forms an important stage in the gradual reduction of the theme. Further contraction takes place at bar 134, where the theme consists of only two bars and is modified melodically. It becomes merely a chromatic descending second and does not conclude with an ascending sixth.

Ex. 346

A great deal of repetition and sequencing ensues before the final, crucial, stages of dismemberment are reached. At bar 146 the strings play one and a half-bars of the theme, answered by half-bars in the woodwind, and at bar 152 the basses and upper strings answer each other antiphonally in a mere half-bar. These half-bars of a single interval, namely, the semitone, are the limit of Mozart's dismemberment. One ventures to say they must have strained the limits of tolerance of the average audience of the late eighteenth century.

BIBLIOGRAPHY

Compiled by PETER WARD JONES

A bibliography of books, articles, and modern editions of music for the period from 1740 to 1790 must of necessity be highly selective, and in compiling this list emphasis has been placed on the research and editions of the last twenty years. The literature on Haydn and Mozart has naturally been subject to the greatest degree of selection, but more comprehensive listings can be found in *Die Musik in Geschichte und Gegenwart*. For Haydn, Hoboken's thematic catalogue is also useful for references to the literature and modern editions, and for Mozart the sixth edition of Köchel's thematic catalogue lists the literature relevant to each work, while a full bibliography is to be found in the *Mozart-Handbuch*, edited by Otto Schneider and Anton Algatzy (Vienna, 1962), supplemented by the annual listings in the *Mozart-Jahrbuch*. Since there are numerous modern editions of the works of these composers only the standard collected editions and one or two collections of genres such as the symphonies and sonatas are listed here. For other composers the listings are fuller but again selective. General histories of music and encyclopedias have been omitted, but *Die Musik in Geschichte und Gegenwart* in particular should be noted as a standard source of information on most of the composers and topics mentioned in this volume. General books and articles on composers have been included in the general bibliography, unless discussion of a composer's works is virtually confined to a single chapter, when they will be found under that chapter. As the forms discussed in Chapter XI have already been the subjects of earlier chapters, no separate bibliography has been compiled for this chapter, and books and articles will therefore be found in the bibliography of the chapter relevant to the genre in question.

GENERAL

(i) *Modern Anthologies*

DAVISON, ARCHIBALD T. and APEL, WILLI, edd.: *Historical Anthology of Music*, ii (London, 1950).

GEIRINGER, KARL, ed.: *Music of the Bach Family* (Cambridge, Mass., 1955).

SCHERING, ARNOLD, ed.: *Geschichte der Musik in Beispielen* (Leipzig, 1931).

STEPHENSON, KURT, ed.: *Die musikalische Klassik* (*Das Musikwerk*, 6), (Cologne, 1953; English edition 1962).

(ii) *Books and Articles*
(a) *General Studies*

ABERT, HERMANN: 'Wort und Ton in der Musik des 18. Jahrhunderts', *Archiv für Musikwissenchaft*, v (1923), pp. 31–70. Reprinted in *Gesammelte Schriften und Vorträge* (Halle, 1929).

ADLER, GUIDO, ed.: *Handbuch der Musikgeschichte*, 2nd ed., ii (Berlin, 1930. Reprinted Tutzing, 1961).

——'Die Wiener klassische Schule', ibid., pp. 768–95.

ALBRECHT, JOHANN LORENZ: *Gründliche Einleitung in die Anfangslehren der Tonkunst* (Langensalza, 1761).

AVISON, CHARLES: *An Essay on Musical Expression* (London, 1752. 2nd edn., 1753. 3rd edn., 1775).

BECKING, GUSTAV: 'Klassik und Romantik', *Bericht über den I. musikwissenschaftlichen Kongress der Deutschen Musikgesellschaft in Leipzig . . . 1925* (Leipzig, 1926), pp. 292–6.

BLUME, FRIEDRICH: *Classic and Romantic Music: A Comprehensive Survey* (New York, 1970). A translation of the articles *Klassik* and *Romantik* in *Die Musik in Geschichte und Gegenwart*.
BOSSLER, HEINRICH P. C., ed.: *Musikalische Realzeitung* (Speyer, 1788-90; reprinted Hildesheim, 1971).
BREITKOPF, JOHANN G. I.: *The Breitkopf Thematic Catalogue. The Six Parts and Sixteen Supplements 1762-1787*. Facsimile edn., ed. Barry S. Brook (New York, 1966).
BROSSARD, YOLANDE DE: *Musiciens de Paris, 1535-1792; actes d'État civil d'après le Fichier Laborde de la Bibliothèque Nationale* (Paris, 1965).
BÜCKEN, ERNST: 'Der galante Stil. Eine Skizze einer Entwicklung', *Zeitschrift für Musikwissenschaft*, vi (1923/4), pp. 418-30.
—— *Die Musik des Rokokos und der Klassik* (Potsdam, 1927).
BURNEY, CHARLES: *A General History of Music from the Earliest Ages to the Present Period* 4 vols. (London, 1776-89). 2nd edn., 2 vols., ed. Frank Mercer (London, 1935; reprinted New York, 1957).
—— *Dr Burney's Musical Tours in Europe*, ed. Percy A. Scholes, 2 vols., (London 1959). Partly published by Burney as *The Present State of Music in France and Italy* (London, 1771. 2nd edn., 1773), and *The Present State of Music in Germany, the Netherlands, and United Provinces* (London, 1773, 2nd edn., 1775).
CHURGIN, BATHIA: 'Francesco Galeazzi's Description (1796) of Sonata Form', *Journal of the American Musicological Society*, xxi (1968), pp. 181-99.
COLE, MALCOLM S.: 'Sonata-Rondo, The Formulation of a Theoretical Concept in the 18th and 19th Centuries', *Musical Quarterly*, lv (1969), pp. 180-92.
CRAMER, CARL F.: *Magazin der Musik* (Hamburg, 1783-7; reprinted Hildesheim, 1971).
DAHMS, WALTER: 'The "Gallant" Style of Music', *Musical Quarterly*, xi (1925), pp. 356-72.
ELKIN, ROBERT: *The Old Concert Rooms of London* (London, 1955).
ENGEL, HANS: 'Die Quellen des klassischen Stiles', *International Musicological Society, Report of the Eighth Congress, New York 1961*, ed. Jan La Rue, i (Kassel, 1961), pp. 285-304.
FERAND, ERNST: *Die Improvisation in der Musik* (Zürich, 1938).
FINSCHER, LUDWIG: 'Zum Begriff der Klassik in der Musik', *Deutches Jahrbuch der Musikwissenschaft*, xi (1967), pp. 9-34.
FISCHER, WILHELM: 'Instrumentalmusik von 1750-1828', in *Handbuch der Musikgeschichte*, ed. G. Adler, ii, pp. 795-833.
—— 'Zur Entwicklungsgeschichte des Wiener klassischen Stils', *Studien zur Musikwissenschaft*, iii (1915), pp. 24-84.
FORKEL, JOHANN N.: *Musikalisch-kritische Bibliothek*, 3 vols. (Gotha, 1778-9; reprinted Hildesheim, 1964).
GEORGIADES, THRASYBULOS: 'Zur Musiksprache der Wiener Klassiker', *Mozart-Jahrbuch 1951*, pp. 50-59.
GERBER, ERNST LUDWIG: *Historisch-biographisches Lexikon der Tonkünstler*, 2 vols. (Leipzig, 1790-2).
—— *Neues historisch-biographisches Lexikon der Tonkünstler*, 4 vols. (Leipzig, 1812-14). Reprinted with a supplement of contemporary additions, corrections and reviews, ed. Othmar Wessely. 3 vols. (Graz, 1966-9).
GERICKE, HANNELORE: *Die Wiener Musikalienhandel von 1700 bis 1778* (Graz, 1960).
GOLDSCHMIDT, HUGO: *Die Musikästhetik des 18. Jahrhunderts und ihre Beziehungen zu seinem Kuntschaffen* (Zürich, 1915).
GRADENWITZ, PETER: 'Mid-Eighteenth-Century Transformations of Style', *Music and Letters*, xviii (1937), pp. 265-75.
GÜTTLER, HERMANN: *Königsbergs Musikkultur im 18. Jahrhundert* (Kassel, 1925).

HANSLICK, EDUARD: *Geschichte des Concertwesens in Wien*, 2 vols. (Vienna, 1869–70).
HAWKINS, SIR JOHN: *A General History of the Science and Practice of Music*, 5 vols. (London, 1776). 2nd edn., 2 vols. (London, 1853; reprinted New York, 1963).
HELFERT, VLADIMÍR: 'Zur Entwicklungsgeschichte der Sonatenform', *Archiv für Musikwissenschaft*, vii (1925), pp. 117–46.
HELM, ERNEST E.: *Music at the Court of Frederick the Great* (Norman, 1960).
HILLER, JOHANN A., ed.: *Wöchentliche Nachrichten und Anmerkungen die Musik betreffend* (Leipzig, 1766–70; reprinted Hildesheim, 1969).
JERGER, WILHELM: 'Zur Musikgeschichte der deutschsprachigen Schweiz im 18. Jahrhundert', *Musikforschung*, xiv (1961), pp. 303–12.
JOHANSSON, CARI: *French Music Publishers' Catalogues of the Second Half of the Eighteenth Century*, 2 vols. (Stockholm, 1955).
JUNKER, CARL LUDWIG: *Zwanzig Componisten* (Bern, 1776).
KAHL, WILLI: *Selbstbiographien deutscher Musiker des XVIII. Jahrhunderts* (Cologne 1948).
KAUL, OSKAR: *Geschichte der Würzburger Hofmusik im 18. Jahrhundert* (Würzburg, 1924).
KIRNBERGER, JOHANN PHILIPP: *Die Kunst des reinen Satzes in der Musik*, 2 vols. (Berlin, 1771–9; reprinted Hildesheim, 1968).
KOCH, HEINRICH C.: *Musikalisches Lexikon* (Frankfurt am Main, 1802; reprinted Hildesheim, 1964).
—— *Versuch einer Anleitung zur Composition*, 3 vols. (Leipzig, 1782–93).
KÖCHEL, LUDWIG: *Die Kaiserliche Hof-Musikkapelle in Wien von 1543 bis 1867* (Vienna, 1869).
KOMMA, KARL M.: *Johann Zach und die tschechischen Musiker im deutschen Umbruch des 18. Jahrhunderts* (Kassel, 1938).
LA BORDE, JEAN B. DE: *Essai sur la musique ancienne et moderne*, 4 vols. (Paris 1780).
LA LAURENCIE, LIONEL DE: *Inventaire critique du Fonds Blancheton de la Bibliothèque du Conservatoire de Paris*, 2 vols. (Paris, 1930–1).
LANDON, H. C. ROBBINS: *Essays on the Viennese Classical Style: Gluck, Haydn, Mozart, Beethoven* (London, 1970).
LARUE, JAN: 'Significant and Coincidental Resemblance between Classical Themes' *Journal of the American Musicological Society*, xiv (1961), pp. 224–34.
LIPOWSKY, FELIX J.: *Baierisches Musik-Lexicon* (Munich, 1811).
LONGYEAR, R. M.: 'The Minor Mode in the Classic Period', *Music Review*, xxxii (1971), pp. 27–35.
LONSDALE, ROGER H.: *Dr. Charles Burney: a Literary Biography* (Oxford, 1965).
MANFREDINI, VINCENZO: *Regole armoniche* (Venice, 1775).
MARPURG, FRIEDRICH W.: *Der critische Musicus an der Spree* (Berlin, 1749–50; reprinted Hildesheim, 1970).
—— *Historisch-kritische Beyträge zur Aufnahme der Musik*, 5 vols. (Berlin, 1754–78; reprinted Hildesheim, 1970).
—— *Kritische Briefe über die Tonkunst*, 3 vols. (Berlin, 1760–4).
MELLERS, WILFRID: *The Sonata Principle from c. 1750* (London, 1957), Vol. 3 of *Man and his Music* by A. Harman, A. Milner, and W. Mellers, also published in a single volume (London, 1962).
MEYER, KATHI: 'Early Breitkopf & Härtel Thematic Catalogues of Manuscript Music', *Musical Quarterly*, xxx (1944), pp. 163–73.
MITCHELL, WILLIAM J.: 'Chord and Context in 18th-Century Theory', *Journal of the American Musicological Society*, xvi (1963), pp. 221–39.
MIZLER VON KOLOF, LORENZ C.: *Neu eröffnete musikalische Bibliothek oder gründliche Nachricht nebst unpartheyischem Urtheil von musikalischen Schriften und Büchern*, 16 parts in 4 books (Leipzig, 1739–54; reprinted Hilversum, 1966).

NEWMAN, WILLIAM S.: 'The Recognition of Sonata Form by Theorists of the 18th and 19th Century', *Papers of the American Musicological Society 1941* (printed 1946), pp. 21–29.
OBERDÖRFFER, FRITZ: *Der Generalbass in der Instrumentalmusik des ausgehenden 18. Jahrhunderts* (Kassel, 1939).
OLIVER, ALFRED R.: *The Encyclopedists as Critics of Music* (New York, 1947).
PAULY, REINHARD G.: *Music in the Classic Period* (Englewood Cliffs N. J., 1965).
PROD'HOMME, JACQUES GABRIEL: 'Austro-German Musicians in France in the Eighteenth Century', *Musical Quarterly*, xv (1929), pp. 171–95.
QUANTZ, JOHANN J.: *Versuch einer Anweisung die Flute traversière zu spielen* (Berlin, 1752; facsimile of 3rd edn. (Berlin, 1789) Kassel, 1953). English translation, *On playing the flute*, transl. and ed. E. R. Reilly (London, 1966).
QUOIKA, RUDOLPH: *Die Musik der Deutschen in Böhmen und Mähren* (Berlin, 1956).
RACEK, JAN: 'Zur Frage des "Mozart-Stils" in der tschechischen vorklassischen Musik', *Bericht über den internationalen musikwissenschaftlichen Kongress Wien Mozartjahr 1956* (Graz, 1958), pp. 493–524.
RATNER, LEONARD G.: 'Eighteenth-Century Theories of Musical Period Structure', *Musical Quarterly*, xlii (1956), pp. 439–54.
—— 'Harmonic Aspects of Classic Form', *Journal of the American Musicological Society*, ii (1949), pp. 159–68.
REICHARDT, JOHANN F.: *Briefe eines aufmerksamen Reisenden die Musik betreffend*, 2 vols. (Frankfurt, 1774–6).
—— *Musikalisches Kunstmagazin*, 8 issues (Berlin, 1782–91; reprinted Hildesheim 1969).
REILLY, EDWARD R.: 'Further Musical Examples for Quantz's *Versuch*', *Journal of the American Musicological Society*, xvii (1964), pp. 157–69.
RETI, RUDOLPH: *The Thematic Process in Music* (New York, 1951).
RIEMANN, HUGO: *Handbuch der Musikgeschichte*, 2nd edn., vol. ii/3 (Leipzig, 1922).
RIEPEL, JOSEPH: *Anfangsgründe zur musikalischen Setzkunst*, 5 parts (Regensburg and Vienna, 1752–68).
RITZEL, FRED.: *Die Entwicklung der "Sonatenform" im musiktheoretischen Schrifttum des 18. und 19. Jahrhunderts* (Wiesbaden, 1968).
RONCAGLIA, GINO: *Il melodioso settecento italiano* (Milan, 1935).
ROSEN, CHARLES: *The Classical Style* (London, 1971).
ROUSSEAU, JEAN JACQUES: *Dictionnaire de Musique* (Paris, 1768; reprinted Hildesheim, 1969).
SADIE, STANLEY J.: 'Concert Life in Eighteenth-Century England', *Proceedings of the Royal Musical Association*, lxxxv (1958/9), pp. 17–30.
SCHEIBE, JOHANN A.: *Critischer Musicus*, revised edn. (Leipzig, 1745; reprinted Hildesheim, 1970).
SCHEURLEER, DANIEL F.: *Het Muziekleven in Nederland in de tweede helft der 18ᵉ eeuw* (The Hague, 1909).
SCHIEDERMAIR, LUDWIG: 'Die Blütezeit der Öttingen-Wallerstein'schen Hofkapelle', *Sammelbände der internationalen Musikgesellschaft*, ix (1907/8), pp. 83–130.
SCHNEIDER, CONSTANTIN: *Geschichte der Musik in Salzburg von der ältesten Zeit bis zur Gegenwart* (Salzburg, 1935).
SCHOLES, PERCY A.: *The Great Dr. Burney*, 2 vols. (London, 1948).
—— *The Life and Activities of Sir John Hawkins* (London, 1953).
SCHUBART, CHRISTIAN F. D.: *Ideen zu einer Ästhetik der Tonkunst*, ed. L. Schubart (Vienna, 1806; reprinted Hildesheim, 1969).
—— *Leben und Gesinnungen*, 2 vols. (Stuttgart, 1791–3).
SCHUELLER, HERBERT M.: 'The Quarrel of the Ancients and the Moderns', *Music and Letters*, xli (1960), pp. 313–30.
SITTARD, JOSEF: *Geschichte des Musik und Concertwesens in Hamburg vom 14. Jahrhundert bis auf die Gegenwart* (Altona, 1890).

—— *Zur Geschichte der Musik und des Theaters am Württembergischen Hofe 1458–1793*, 2 vols. (Stuttgart, 1890–91; reprinted Hildesheim, 1970).
STRUNK, OLIVER, ed.: *Source Readings in Music History* (New York, 1950). Also available in separate vols., of which vol. 4 is The Classical Era.
Studies in Eighteenth-Century Music. A Tribute to Karl Geiringer on his Seventieth Birthday, ed. H. C. Robbins Landon (London, 1970).
SULZER, JOHANN G.: *Allgemeine Theorie der schönen Künste*, 2 vols. (Leipzig, 1771–4) *Nachträge*, 8 vols. (Leipzig, 1782–1808).
SUPPAN, WOLFGANG: 'Moses Mendelssohn und die Musikästhetik des 18. Jahrhunderts', *Musikforschung*, xvii (1964), pp. 22–33.
TOBEL, RUDOLPH VON: *Die Formenwelt der klassischen Instrumentalmusik* (Bern, 1935).
TORCHI, LUIGI: *La musica instrumentale in Italia nei secoli XVI, XVII e XVIII* (Turin, 1901). Originally appeared in *Rivista musicale italiana*, iv–viii (1897–1901).
TORREFRANCA, FAUSTO: 'Intermezzo di date e documenti', continued as 'Le origini dello stile mozartiano', *Rivista musicale italiana*, xxvi (1919), pp. 140–67, 290–331; xxviii (1921), pp. 263–308; xxxiii (1926) pp. 321–42, 505–29; xxxiv (1927), pp. 1–33, 169–89, 493–511; xxxvi (1929), pp. 373–407.
WALTER, FRIEDRICH: *Geschichte des Theaters und der Musik am kurpfälzischen Hofe* (Leipzig, 1898; reprinted Hildesheim, 1968).
WERKMEISTER, WILHELM: *Der Stilwandel in deutscher Dichtung und Musik des 18. Jahrhunderts* (Berlin, 1936).
YORKE–LONG, ALAN: *Music at Court: Four Eighteenth-Century Studies* (London, 1954).

(b) *Individual Composers*
Albrechtsberger
OPPEL, REINHARD: 'Albrechtsberger als Bindeglied zwischen Bach und Beethoven' *Neue Zeitschrift für Musik*, lxxviii (1911), pp. 316–19.

T. A. Arne
CUDWORTH, CHARLES L.: 'Boyce and Arne: The Generation of 1710', *Music and Letters*, xli (1960), pp. 136–45.
—— 'Two Georgian Classics: Arne and Stevens', *Music and Letters*, xlv (1964), pp. 146–53.
CUMMINGS, WILLIAM H.: *Dr. Arne and " Rule Britannia"* (London, 1912).
HERBAGE, JULIAN: 'Arne: His Character and Environment', *Proceedings of the Royal Musical Association*, lxxxvii (1960/61), pp. 15–29.
LANGLEY, HUBERT: *Doctor Arne* (Cambridge, 1938).
PARKINSON, JOHN A.: *An Index to the Vocal Works of Thomas Augustine Arne and Michael Arne* (Detroit, 1972).

Bach Family
BITTER, CARL HERMANN: *Carl Philipp Emanuel und Wilhelm Friedemann Bach und deren Brüder*, 2 vols. (Berlin, 1868).
GEIRINGER, KARL: *The Bach Family* (London, 1954).
YOUNG, PERCY M.: *The Bachs, 1500–1850* (London, 1970).

C. P. E. Bach
HASE, HERMANN VON: 'Carl Philipp Emanuel Bach und Joh. Gottl. Im. Breitkopf', *Bach-Jahrbuch 1911*, pp. 86–104.
MIESNER, HEINRICH: 'Aus der Umwelt Philipp Emanuel Bachs', *Bach-Jahrbuch 1937*, pp. 132–43.
—— *Philipp Emanuel Bach in Hamburg* (Heide, 1929; reprinted Wiesbaden, 1969).
NEWMAN, WILLIAM S.: 'Emanuel Bach's Autobiography', *Musical Quarterly*, li (1965), pp. 363–72.

PLAMENAC, DRAGAN: 'New Light on the Last Years of Carl Philipp Emanuel Bach', *Musical Quarterly*, xxxv (1949), pp. 565–87.
SCHMID, ERNST F.: 'Joseph Haydn und Carl Philipp Emanuel Bach', *Zeitschrift für Musikwissenschaft*, xiv (1931/2), pp. 299–312.
STEGLICH, RUDOLPH: 'Karl Philipp Emanuel Bach und der Dresdner Kreuzkantor Gottfried August Homilius im Musikleben ihrer Zeit', *Bach–Jahrbuch 1915*, pp. 39–145.
VRIESLANDER, O.: *Carl Philipp Emanuel Bach* (Munich, 1923).
WOTQUENNE, ALFRED: *Thematisches Verzeichnis der Werke von Carl Philipp Emanuel Bach* (Leipzig, 1905).

J. C. Bach
SCHÖKEL, HEINRICH P.: *Johann Christian Bach und die Instrumentalmusik seiner Zeit* (Wolfenbüttel, 1926).
SCHWARZ, MAX: 'Johann Christian Bach', *Sammelbände der internationalen Musikgesellschaft*, ii (1900/1), pp. 401–54.
TERRY, CHARLES S.: *John Christian Bach*, 2nd edn. (London, 1967).

J. C. F. Bach
HEY, GOTTHOLD: 'Zur Biographie Johann Friedrich Bachs und seiner Familie', *Bach-Jahrbuch 1933*, pp. 77–85.
SCHÜNEMANN, GEORG: 'Johann Christoph Friedrich Bach', *Bach-Jahrbuch 1914*, pp. 45–165.
WOHLFARTH, HANNSDIETER: 'Neues Verzeichnis der Werke von Johann Christoph Friedrich Bach', *Musikforschung*, xiii (1960), pp. 404–17.

W. F. Bach
FALCK, MARTIN: *Wilhelm Friedemann Bach* (Leipzig, 1913).
ZEHLER, C.: 'W. Friedemann Bach und seine hallische Wirksamkeit', *Bach-Jahrbuch 1910*, pp. 103–32.

Benda Family
LORENZ, FRANZ: *Die Musikerfamilie Benda. I: Franz Benda und seine Nachkommen* (Berlin, 1967).

Boccherini
BARBLAN, GUGLIELMO: 'Boccheriniana', *Rassegna musicale*, xxix (1959), pp. 123–8 and 322–31; xxx (1960), pp. 33–44.
BONAVENTURA, ARNALDO: *Boccherini* (Milan, 1931).
GÉRARD, YVES: *Thematic, Bibliographical and Critical Catalogue of the Works of Luigi Boccherini* (London, 1969).
PICQUOT, LOUIS: *Notice sur la vie et les ouvrages de Luigi Boccherini* (Paris, 1851. 2nd edn., revised by G. de Saint-Foix, Paris, 1930).
ROTHSCHILD, GERMAINE DE: *Luigi Boccherini, sa vie, son oeuvre* (Paris, 1962). English translation (London, 1965).

Boyce
BEECHEY, GWILYM: 'Memoirs of Dr. William Boyce. With an Introduction and Notes', *Musical Quarterly*, lvii (1971), pp. 87–106.
CUDWORTH, CHARLES L.: 'Boyce and Arne: The Generation of 1710', *Music and Letters*, xli (1960), pp. 136–45.
DAWE, DONOVAN: 'New Light on William Boyce', *Musical Times*, cix (1968), pp. 802–7.

Camerloher
ZIEGLER, BENNO: *Placidus von Camerloher*. Munich Dissertation (Freising, 1919).

Cimarosa
CAMBIASI, POMPEO: *Notizie sulla vita e sulle opere di Domenico Cimarosa* (Milan, 1901).

TIBALDI CHIESA, MARY: *Cimarosa e il suo tempo* (Milan, 1939).
VITALE, ROBERTO: *Domenico Cimarosa* (Aversa, 1929).

Dittersdorf
DITTERSDORF, CARL DITTERS VON: *Karl von Dittersdorfs Lebensbeschreibung* (Leipzig, 1801). English translation by A. D. Coleridge (London, 1896).
KLOB, CARL MARIA: *Drei musikalische Biedermänner: Ignaz Holzbauer, Carl Ditters von Dittersdorf, Michael Haydn* (Ulm, 1911).
KREBS, CARL: *Dittersdorfiana* (Berlin, 1900).

Fasch
ZELTER, CARL F.: *Karl Friedrich Christian Fasch* (Berlin, 1801).

Fränzl
WÜRTZ, ROLAND: *Ignaz Fränzl. Ein Beitrag zur Musikgeschichte der Stadt Mannheim.* Mainz Dissertation 1969 (Mainz, 1970).

Galuppi
DELLA CORTE, ANDREA: *Baldassare Galuppi, profilo critico* (Siena, 1948).
PIOVANO, FRANCESCO: 'Baldassare Galuppi, note bio-bibliografiche', *Rivista musicale italiana*, xiii (1906), pp. 676–726; xiv (1907), pp. 333–65; xv (1908), pp. 233–74.
RAABE, FELIX: *Galuppi als Instrumentalkomponist.* Munich Dissertation (Frankfurt an der Oder, 1929).

Hasse
MENNICKE, CARL: 'Johann Adolph Hasse: eine biographische Skizze', *Sammelbände der internationalen Musikgesellschaft*, v (1903/4), pp. 230–44.

Joseph Haydn
ADLER, GUIDO: 'Haydn and the Viennese Classical School', *Musical Quarterly*, xviii (1932), pp. 191–207.
ARNOLD, J. F. C.: *Joseph Haydn, seine kurze Biographie und ästhetische Darstellung seiner Werke* (Erfurt, 1810, 2nd ed., 1825).
ARTARIA, FRANZ, and BOTSTIBER, HUGO: *Joseph Haydn und das Verlaghaus Artaria* (Vienna, 1909).
BARTHA, DÉNES, ed.: *Joseph Haydn: Gesammelte Briefe und Aufzeichnungen* (Kassel, 1965).
Beschreibung des hochfürstlichen Schlosses Esterhass in Königreiche Ungern (Pressburg, 1784).
CARPANI, GIUSEPPE: *Le Haydine* (Milan, 1812; reprinted Bologna, 1969).
DIES, A. C.: *Biographische Nachrichten von Joseph Haydn; nach mündlichen Erzählungen desselben entworfen* (Vienna, 1810); ed. H. Seeger (Berlin, 1962). See also G. A. Griesinger.
ENGEL, HANS: 'Haydn, Mozart und die Klassik', *Mozart-Jahrbuch 1959*, pp. 46–79.
FEDER, GEORG: 'Die Überlieferung und Verbreitung der handschriftlichen Quellen zu Haydns Werken (Erste Folge)', *Haydn-Studien*, i/1 (1965), pp. 3–42; English translation by Eugene Hartzell, 'Manuscript Sources of Haydn's Works and their Distribution', *Haydn Yearbook*, iv (1968), pp. 102–39.
FRAMÉRY, NICOLAS E.: *Notice sur Joseph Haydn* (Paris, 1810).
GEIRINGER, KARL: *Joseph Haydn* (Potsdam, 1932).
—— *Joseph Haydn. Der schöpferische Werdegang eines Meisters der Klassik.* Unter Mitarbeit von Irene Geiringer (Mainz, 1959).
—— *Haydn, A Creative Life in Music* (New York, 1946. 3rd edn., Berkeley and Los Angeles, 1968).
GOTWALS, VERNON: 'The Earliest Biographies of Haydn', *Musical Quarterly*, xlv (1959), pp. 439–59.

GRIESINGER, GEORG AUGUST: *Biographische Notizen über Joseph Haydn* (Leipzig, 1810; ed. Franz Grasberger, Vienna, 1954).
—— *Joseph Haydn: Eighteenth-century Gentleman and Genius. A Translation with Introduction and Notes by Vernon Gotwals of the Biographische Notizen über Joseph Haydn by G. A. Griesinger, and the Biographische Nachrichten von Joseph Haydn by A. C. Dies* (Madison, 1963). Reissued 1968 as *Haydn: Two Contemporary Portraits.*
HASE, HERMANN VON: *Joseph Haydn und Breitkopf & Härtel* (Leipzig, 1909).
Haydn-Studien. Veröffentlichungen des Joseph Haydn-Instituts, Köln. Band I, Heft 1 ff. (Munich, 1965 ff.).
The Haydn Yearbook, i ff. (Bryn Mawr, Penn., and Vienna, 1962 ff.)
HOBOKEN, ANTHONY VAN: *Joseph Haydn: Thematisch-bibliographisches Werkverzeichnis*, 2 vols. (Mainz, 1957–71).
HUGHES, ROSEMARY: *Haydn* (London, 1950. Revised eds. 1962 and 1970).
KOCH, LUDWIG: *Joseph Haydn* [Bibliography] (Budapest, 1932).
LANDON, H. C. ROBBINS, ed.: *The Collected Correspondence and London Notebooks of Joseph Haydn* (London, 1959).
LARSEN, JENS PETER: *Drei Haydn Kataloge in Faksimile* (Copenhagen, 1941).
—— *Die Haydn-Überlieferung* (Copenhagen, 1939).
NOWAK, LEOPOLD: *Joseph Haydn: Leben, Bedeutung und Werk*, 2nd ed. (Zürich, 1959).
POHL, CARL F.: *Mozart und Haydn in London*, 2 vols. (Vienna, 1867).
—— and BOTSTIBER, HUGO: *Joseph Haydn*, 3 vols. (Leipzig, 1875–1927; reprinted Wiesbaden, 1970).
REICH, WILLI: *Joseph Haydn* (Lucerne, 1946).
ROSCOE, CHRISTOPHER: 'Haydn and London in the 1780's', *Music and Letters*, xlix (1968), pp. 203–12.
RUTZ, HANS: *Joseph Haydn, Dokumente seines Lebens und Schaffens* (Munich, 1953).
SCHMID, ERNST F.: 'Joseph Haydn und Carl Philipp Emanuel Bach', *Zeitschrift für Musikwissenschaft*, xiv (1931/2), pp. 299–312.
—— 'Mozart and Haydn', *Musical Quarterly*, xlii (1956), pp. 145–61.
SCHNERICH, ALFRED: *Joseph Haydn und seine Sendung*. 2nd ed. (Zürich, 1926).
SCHWARTING, HEINO: 'Ungewöhnliche Repriseneintritte in Haydns späterer Instrumentalmusik', *Archiv für Musikwissenschaft*, xvii (1960), pp. 168–82.
SOMFAI, LÁSZLÓ, ed.: *Joseph Haydn, sein Leben in zeitgenössischen Bildern* (Budapest, 1966). English translation (London, 1969).
SZABOLCSI, BENCE and BARTHA, DÉNES, edd.: *Haydn emlékére* (Budapest, 1960).
UNVERRICHT, HUBERT: 'Die gesammelten Briefe und Tagebücher Joseph Haydns', *Musikforschung*, xvi (1963), pp. 53–62.
—— 'Unveröffentlichte und wenig bekannte Briefe Joseph Haydns', *Musikforschung* xviii (1963), pp. 40–5.

Michael Haydn
JANCIK, H.: *Michael Haydn, ein vergessener Meister* (Zürich, 1952).
KLOB, CARL MARIA: *Drei musikalische Biedermänner: Ignaz Holzbauer, Carl Ditters von Dittersdorf, Michael Haydn* (Ulm, 1911).
SCHINN, J. G., and OTTER, F. J.: *Biographische Skizze von M. H.* [*i.e. Michael Haydn*] (Salzburg, 1808). Published anonymously.

Hertel
HERTEL, JOHANN W.: *Autobiographie*, ed. E. Schenk (Graz, 1957).
MEYER, CLEMENS: *Geschichte der Mecklenburg-Schweriner Hofkapelle* (Schwerin, 1913).

Holzbauer
KLOB, CARL MARIA: *Drei musikalische Biedermänner: Ignaz Holzbauer, Carl Ditters von Dittersdorf, Michael Haydn* (Ulm, 1911).

Kraus

MEYER, KATHI: 'Ein Musiker des Göttinger Hainbundes Joseph Martin Kraus', *Zeitschrift für Musikwissenschaft*, ix (1926/7), pp. 468–86.
SCHREIBER, KARL F.: *Biographie über den Odenwälder Komponisten Joseph Martin Kraus* (Buchen, 1928).
—— 'Verzeichnis der musikalischen Werke von Jos. Kraus', *Archiv für Musikwissenschaft*, vii (1925), pp. 477–94.

L. Mozart

MOZART, LEOPOLD: *Versuch einer gründlichen Violinschule* (Augsburg, 1756. Facsimile ed., ed. B. Paumgartner, Vienna, 1922. 3rd ed., 1787. Facsimile ed., ed. H. J. Moser, Leipzig, 1956). English translation by E. Knocker, *A Treatise on the Fundamental Principles of Violin Playing* (London, 1948).

W. A. Mozart

ABERT, HERMANN: *W. A. Mozart*, 5th revised edition of Jahn's biography, 2 vols. (Leipzig, 1919–21. 6th ed., 1923–4. 7th ed., 3 vols. including index, 1955–66).
ANDERSON, EMILY, ed.: *The letters of Mozart and his family*, 3 vols. (London, 1938). 2nd ed., 2 vols. (London, 1966).
BAUER, WILHELM A. and DEUTSCH, OTTO E., edd.: *Mozart Briefe und Aufzeichnungen*, 6 vols. (Kassel, 1962–71).
BLOM, ERIC: *Mozart* (London, 1935).
BORY, ROBERT: *La vie et l'oeuvre de Wolfgang-Amadeus Mozart par l'image* (Geneva, 1948).
BURK, JOHN N.: *Mozart and his music* (New York, 1959).
DAVIS, SHELLEY: 'Harmonic Rhythm in Mozart's Sonata Form', *Music Review*, xxvii (1966), pp. 25–43.
DEUTSCH, OTTO E., ed.: *Mozart. Die Dokumente seines Lebens*, (Kassel, 1961). English translation, *Mozart, a Documentary Biography*, 2nd ed. (London, 1966).
EINSTEIN, ALFRED: *Mozart, his Character, his Work* (New York, 1945).
ENGEL, HANS: 'Haydn, Mozart und die Klassik', *Mozart-Jahrbuch 1959*, pp. 46–79.
HAAS, ROBERT: *Wolfgang Amadeus Mozart* (Potsdam, 1933; 2nd ed., 1950).
HERTZMANN, ERICH: 'Mozart's Creative Process', *Musical Quarterly*, xliii (1957), pp. 187–200.
HOLMES, EDWARD: *The Life of Mozart, Including his Correspondence* (London, 1845).
JAHN, OTTO: *W. A. Mozart*, 4 vols. (Leipzig, 1856–59). For 5th ed., see H. Abert; English translation by P. D. Townsend, *Life of Mozart*, 3 vols. (London, 1882).
KENYON, MAX: *Mozart in Salzburg* (London, 1952).
KING, A. HYATT: *Mozart in Retrospect* (London, 1955. 3rd impression revised, 1970).
KÖCHEL, LUDWIG RITTER VON: *Chronologisch-thematisches Verzeichnis sämtlicher Tonwerke Wolfgang Amadé Mozarts* (Leipzig, 1862. 6th ed., ed. Franz Giegling *et al.*, Wiesbaden, 1964).
LANDON, H. C. ROBBINS, and MITCHELL, DONALD, edd.: *The Mozart Companion* (London, 1956).
LOWINSKY, EDWARD E.: 'On Mozart's Rhythm', *Musical Quarterly*, xlii (1956), pp. 162–86.
MOZART, WOLFGANG AMADEUS: *Verzeichnis aller meiner Werke*. Facsimile ed., ed. O. E. Deutsch (Vienna, 1938). Modern ed., ed. Erich Müller von Asow (Vienna, 1943).
Mozart-Jahrbuch, ed. H. Abert, Erster (-dritter) Jahrgang (Munich, 1923–9); *Neues Mozart-Jahrbuch*, ed. E. Valentin, Erster (-dritter) Jahrgang (Salzburg, 1941–3); *Mozart-Jahrbuch 1950 ff.* ed. Internationale Stiftung Mozarteum (Salzburg, 1951 ff.)
NIEMETSCHEK, FRANZ X.: *Leben des k.k. Kapellmeisters Wolfgang Gottlieb Mozart nach Originalquellen beschrieben* (Prague, 1798. 2nd ed., 1808). English translation by H. Mautner (London, 1956).

NISSEN, GEORGE N. VON: *Biographie W. A. Mozarts* (Leipzig, 1828; reprinted Hildesheim, 1964).
OULIBICHEFF, ALEXANDRE: *Nouvelle biographie de Mozart*, 3 vols. (Moscow, 1843).
PAUMGARTNER, BERNHARD: *Mozart*, 6th ed. (Zurich, 1967).
POHL, CARL F.: *Mozart und Haydn in London*, 2 vols. (Vienna, 1867).
SCHENK, ERICH: *Wolfgang Amadeus Mozart: Eine Biographie* (Zürich, 1955). Translated as *Mozart and His Times* (London, 1960).
SCHLICHTEGROLL, F. V.: *Nekrolog auf das Jahr 1791* (Gotha, 1793). Modern ed., ed. L. Landshoff (Munich, 1924).
SCHMID, ERNST F.: 'Mozart and Haydn', *Musical Quarterly*, xlii (1956), pp. 145–61.
SCHNEIDER, OTTO and ALGATZY, ANTON: *Mozart-Handbuch* (Vienna, 1962).
SZABOLCSI, BENCE, and BARTHA, DÉNES, edd.: *Mozart emlékére* (Budapest, 1957).
TORREFRANCA, FAUSTO: 'Influenza di alcuni musicisti italiani vissuti a Londra su W. A. Mozart (1764–65)', *Bericht über den Musikwissenschaftlichen Kongress in Basel . . . 1924* (Leipzig, 1925), pp. 336–62.
VERCHALY, ANDRÉ, ed.: *Les influences étrangères dans l'oeuvre de W. A. Mozart* [1956 Colloquium] (Paris, 1958).
WYZEWA, THÉODORE DE, and SAINT-FOIX, GEORGES DE: *W.-A. Mozart*, 5 vols. (Paris, 1912–46).

Müthel
KEMMLER, ERWIN: *Johann Gottfried Müthel, 1728–1788, und das nordostdeutsche Musikleben seiner Zeit*. Saarbrücken Dissertation (Marburg, 1970).

Nardini
PFÄFFLIN, CLARA: *Pietro Nardini: seine Werke und sein Leben* (Stuttgart, 1935).

Neefe
LEUX, IRMGARD: *Christian Gottlob Neefe, 1748–1798* (Leipzig, 1925).

Pugnani
ZSCHINSKY-TROXLER, ELSA M. VON: *Gaetano Pugnani, 1731–1798* (Berlin, 1939).

Reichardt
SALMEN, WALTER: *Johann Friedrich Reichardt, Komponist, Schriftsteller, Kapellmeister und Verwaltungsbeamter der Goethezeit* (Freiburg im Breisgau, 1963).
SCHLETTERER, HANS M.: *Joh. Friedrich Reichardt, sein Leben und seine Werke* (Augsburg, 1865. 2nd ed., Leipzig, 1879).
SIEBER, PAUL: *Johann Friedrich Reichardt als Musikästhetiker* (Strasbourg, 1930).

Rosetti
FITZPATRICK, HORACE: 'Antonio Rosetti', *Music and Letters*, xliii (1962), pp. 234–47.

Rust
HOSÄUS, F. WILHELM: *Friedrich Wilhelm Rust und das Dessauer Musikleben 1766–1796* (Dessau, 1882).

Sacchini
SCHLITZER, FRANCO: *Antonio Sacchini* (Siena, 1955).

G. B. Sammartini
SARTORI, CLAUDIO: 'Giovanni Battista Sammartini e la sua corte', *Musica d'oggi*, iii (1960), pp. 106–21.
SONDHEIMER, ROBERT: 'Giovanni Battista Sammartini', *Zeitschrift für Musikwissenschaft*, iii (1920/21), pp. 83–110.

J. Stamitz
GRADENWITZ, PETER: *Johann Stamitz*, I [all published] (Brünn, 1936).

Stanley
FINZI, GERALD: 'John Stanley (1713–1786)', *Proceedings of the Royal Musical Association*, lxxvii (1950/1), pp. 63–75.

G. van Swieten
OLLESON, EDWARD: 'Gottfried van Swieten, Patron of Haydn and Mozart', *Proceedings of the Royal Musical Association*, lxxxix (1962/3), pp. 63–74.

Tartini
CAPRI, ANTONIO: *Giuseppi Tartini* (Milan, 1945).
PETROBELLI, PIERLUIGI: *Giuseppe Tartini. Le fonti biografiche* (Vienna, 1968).
PLANCHART, ALEJANDRO E.: 'A Study of the Theories of Giuseppe Tartini', *Journal of Music Theory*, iv (1960), pp. 32–61.
TARTINI, GIUSEPPE: *De' principj dell'armonia musicale contenuta nel diatonico genere* (Padua, 1767; reprinted Hildesheim, 1970).
—— *Traité des agrémens de la musique* (Paris, 1771).
—— *Trattato di musica secondo la vera scienza dell'armonia* (Padua, 1754).

Vogler
SCHAFHÄUTL, CARL E. VON: *Abt Georg Joseph Vogler* (Augsburg, 1888).
VOGLER, GEORG JOSEPH: *Betrachtungen der Mannheimer Tonschule*, 3 vols. (Mannheim, 1778–81; reprinted Hildesheim, 1969).

E. W. Wolf
BROCKT, JOHANNES: *Ernst Wilhelm Wolf. Leben und Werke*. Breslau Dissertation (Striegau, 1927, part only printed).

CHAPTER 1
OPERA IN ITALY AND THE EMPIRE

(i) *Modern Editions*
(a) *Anthologies*

ABERT, ANNA A.: *Die Oper: von den Anfängen bis zum Beginn des 19. Jahrhunderts* (*Das Musikwerk*, 5) (Cologne, 1953. English edition 1962). Includes excerpts from works by Dittersdorf, Gluck, Hasse, and Mozart.
ABERT, HERMANN, ed.: *Ausgewählte Ballette Stuttgarter Meister aus der 2. Hälfte des 18. Jahrhunderts (Florian Deller und Johann Joseph Rudolph)* (*Denkmäler deutscher Tonkunst*, 43–44) (Leipzig, 1913).
HAAS, ROBERT, ed.: *Deutsche Komödienarien, 1754–1758* (*Denkmäler der Tonkunst in Österreich*, Jg. 33/1, vol. 64) (Vienna, 1926).
LANDSHOFF, LUDWIG, ed.: *Alte Meister des Bel Canto*, vols. 1–2 (Frankfurt, 1912).
SCHOENBAUM, CAMILLO and ZEMAN, HERBERT, edd.: *Deutsche Komödienarien, 1754–1758. Zweiter Teil* (*Denkmäler der Tonkunst in Österreich*, vol. 121) (Graz, 1971).
WOLFF, HELLMUTH C., ed.: *Die Oper II: 18. Jahrhundert* (*Das Musikwerk*, 39) (Cologne, 1971). Includes excerpts from works by Gluck, C. H. Graun, Hasse, Hiller, Jommelli, La Borde, Leo, Piccinni, and Seedo.

(b) *Works by Individual Composers*
BACH, J. C.: *Temistocle*, vocal score ed. E. O. D. Downes and H. C. Robbins Landon (Vienna, 1965).
BENDA, G.: *Ariadne auf Naxos*, vocal score, ed. A. Einstein (Leipzig, 1920).
—— *Der Jahrmarkt*, ed. T. W. Werner (*Denkmäler deutscher Tonkunst*, 64) (Leipzig, 1930).
DITTERSDORF, C. DITTERS VON: *Doktor und Apotheker*, vocal score ed. R. Kleinmichel (Leipzig, 1890); ed. H. Burkard (Vienna, 1935).
—— *Hieronymous Knicker*, vocal score ed. R. Kleinmichel (Leipzig, 1890).
GALUPPI, B.: *Il filosofo di campagna*, vocal score ed. V. Mortari (Milan, 1938).
GASSMANN, F. L.: *La contessina*, ed. R. Haas (*Denkmäler der Tonkunst in Österreich*, Jg. 21, vols. 42–4) (Vienna, 1914).

GLUCK, C. W. VON: *Sämtliche Werke*, ed. R. Gerber (Kassel, 1951–).
—— *Don Juan*, ed. R. Haas (*Denkmäler der Tonkunst in Österreich*, Jg. 30/2, vol. 60) (Vienna, 1923).
—— *L'Innocenza giustificata*, ed. A. Einstein (*Denkmäler der Tonkunst in Österreich*, Jg. 44, vol. 82) (Vienna, 1937).
—— *Le Nozze d'Ercole e d'Ebe*, ed. H. Abert (*Denkmäler der Tonkunst in Bayern*, 14/2) (Leipzig, 1914).
—— *Orfeo ed Euridice*, ed. H. Abert (*Denkmäler der Tonkunst in Österreich*, Jg. 21/2, vol. 44a) (Vienna, 1914).
GRAUN, C. H.: *Montezuma*, ed. A. Mayer-Reinach (*Denkmäler deutscher Tonkunst*, 15) (Leipzig, 1904).
HASSE, J. A.: *Arminio*, ed. R. Gerber, 2 vols. (*Das Erbe deutscher Musik*, 27–28) (Mainz, 1957–66).
HAYDN, *Werke*, ed. Joseph Haydn-Institut, Cologne, series 24, *Marionetten-opern*; series 25, *Opern* (Munich, 1959–).
HOLZBAUER, I.: *Günther von Schwarzburg*, ed. H. Kretzschmar (*Denkmäler deutscher Tonkunst*, 8–9) (Leipzig, 1902).
JOMMELLI, N.: *Fetone*, ed. H. Abert (*Denkmäler deutscher Tonkunst*, 32–33) (Leipzig, 1907).
—— *L'Uccellatrice*, vocal score ed. M. Zanon (Milan, 1955).
MOZART, W. A.: Werke, ed. J. Brahms *et al.*, series 5, *Opern*; series 24, *Supplement* (Leipzig, 1879–86).
—— *Neue Ausgabe sämtlicher Werke*, ed. Internationale Stiftung Mozarteum, series 2, *Bühnenwerke* (Kassel, 1956–).
NEEFE, C. G.: *Amors Guckkasten*, ed. G. von Westermann (Munich, 1922).
PAISIELLO, G.: *La Molinara*, ed. A. Rocchi (Florence, 1962).
—— *Nina*, vocal score ed. C. Gatti (Milan, 1940).
PERGOLESI, G.: *Olimpiade*, vocal score ed. M. Zanon (Milan, 1915).
PICCINNI, N.: *La buona figliuola*, ed. G. Benvenuti (*I classici musicali italiani*, 7) (Milan, 1942).
TRAETTA, T.: *Ausgewählte Werke*, ed. H. Goldschmidt, 2 vols. (*Denkmäler der Tonkunst in Bayern*, 14/1, 17) (Leipzig, 1913–16).
—— *Antigona*, ed. A. Rocchi (Florence, 1962).
UMLAUF, J.: *Die Bergknappen*, ed. R. Haas (*Denkmäler der Tonkunst in Österreich*, Jg. 18/1, vol. 36) (Vienna, 1911).

(ii) *Books and Articles*
(a) *General*

ABERT, HERMANN: ' Die dramatische Musik' in *Herzog Karl Eugen von Württemberg und seine Zeit*, Heft 7 (Esslingen, 1905), pp. 555–611.
—— *Goethe und die Musik* (Stuttgart, 1922).
ALGAROTTI, FRANCESCO: *Saggio sopra l'opera in musica* (n. pl., 1755).
BACHER, OTTO: 'Frankfurts musikalische Bühnengeschichte im achtzehnten Jahrhundert. Teil I: Die Zeit der Wandertruppen (1700–1786)', *Archiv für Frankfurts Geschichte und Kunst*, fourth series, vol. 1 (Frankfurt, 1925), pp. 133–206.
—— *Die Geschicht eder Frankfurter Oper im achtzehnten Jahrhundert* (Frankfurt, 1926).
BAUR, UWE: 'Studien zur Arieneinleitung in der Oper des 18. Jahrhunderts', *Studien zur Musikwissenschaft*, xxvii (1966), pp. 125–50.
BLUME, FRIEDRICH: *Goethe und die Musik* (Kassel, 1948).
BONAVENTURA, ARNALDO: *Saggio storico sul teatro musicale italiano* (Livorno, 1913).
BROSSES, CHARLES DE: *Lettres familières sur l'Italie*, ed. Yvonne Bezard (Paris, 1931).
BROWN, JOHN: *Letters upon the Poetry and Music of the Italian Opera* (Edinburgh, 1789. 2nd ed., London, 1791).

DELLA CORTE, ANDREA: *L'Opera comica italiana nel '700*, 2 vols. (Bari, 1923).
DENT, EDWARD J.: 'Ensembles and Finales in 18th Century Italian Opera', *Sammelbände der internationalen Musikgesellschaft*, xi (1909/10), pp. 543–69; xii (1910/11), pp. 112–38.
—— 'Italian Opera in London', *Proceedings of the Royal Musical Association*, lxxi (1944/45), pp. 19–42.
—— 'Italian Opera in the Eighteenth Century, and its Influence on the Music of the Classical Period', *Sammelbände der internationalen Musikgesellschaft*, xiv (1912/13), pp. 500–9.
DEUTSCH, OTTO E.: *Das Freihaustheater auf der Wieden, 1787–1801* (Vienna, 1937).
DOWNES, EDWARD O. D.: 'The Neapolitan Tradition in Opera', *International Musicological Society, Report of the Eighth Congress, New York 1961*, ed. Jan LaRue, i (Kassel, 1961), pp. 277–84.
—— '*Secco* Recitative in Early Classical Opera Seria, 1720–80', *Journal of the American Musicological Society*, xiv (1961), pp. 50–69.
Enciclopedia della spettacolo (Rome, 1954–68).
ENGLÄNDER, RICHARD: 'Dresden und die deutsche Oper im letzten Drittel des 18. Jahrhunderts', *Zeitschrift für Musikwissenschaft*, iii (1920/1), pp. 1–21.
FLORIMO, FRANCESCO: *La scuola musicale di Napoli*, 4 vols. (Naples, 1880–1).
GIAZOTTO, REMO: *Poesia melodrammatica e pensiero critico nel Settecento* (Milan, 1952).
GROUT, DONALD J.: *A Short History of Opera*, 2nd ed. (New York and London, 1965).
HAAS, ROBERT: 'Die Musik in der Wiener deutschen Stegreifkomödie', *Studien zur Musikwissenschaft*, xii (1925), pp. 3–64.
—— 'Die Oper im 18. Jahrhundert', in *Handbuch der Musikgeschichte*, ed. G. Adler, ii, pp. 718–68.
HABÖCK, FRANZ: *Die Gesangskunst der Kastraten. Erster Notenband: A. Die Kunst des Cavaliere Carlo Broschi Farinelli. B. Farinellis berühmte Arien* (Vienna, 1923).
—— *Die Kastraten und ihre Gesangskunst* (Berlin, 1927).
HELFERT, VLADIMIR: 'Zur Geschichte des Wiener Singspiels', *Zeitschrift für Musikwissenschaft*, v (1922/3), pp. 194–209.
HERIOT, ANGUS: *The Castrati in Opera* (London, 1956).
HÖGG, MARGARETE: *Die Gesangskunst der Faustina Hasse und das Sängerinnenwesen ihrer Zeit in Deutschland*. Berlin Dissertation (Königsbrück, 1931).
HORÁNYI, MÁTYÁS: *The Magnificence of Eszterháza* (London, 1962).
HUCKE, HELMUTH: 'The Neapolitan Tradition in Opera', *International Musicological Society: Report of the Eighth Congress, New York 1961*, ed. Jan. LaRue, i (Kassel, 1961), pp. 253–77.
ISTEL, EDGAR: *Die Entstehung des deutschen Melodramas* (Berlin, 1906).
KERMAN, JOSEPH: *Opera as Drama* (New York, 1956).
KIRBY, F. E.: 'Herder and Opera', *Journal of the American Musicological Society*, xv (1962), pp. 316–29.
KRAUSS, RUDOLF: 'Das Theater', in *Herzog Karl Eugen von Württemberg und seine Zeit*, Heft 7 (Esslingen, 1905), pp. 481–554.
KUNZ, HARALD: 'Höfisches Theater in Wien zur Zeit der Maria Theresia', *Jahrbuch der Gesellschaft für Wiener Theaterforschung 1953/54* (Vienna, 1958), pp. 3–71.
LAZAREVICH, GORDONA: 'The Neapolitan Intermezzo and its Influence on the Symphonic Idiom', *Musical Quarterly*, lvii (1971), pp. 294–313.
LOEWENBERG, ALFRED: *Annals of Opera*, 2 vols. 2nd ed. (Geneva, 1955).
MARCELLO, BENEDETTO: *Il teatro alla moda* (Venice, 1720). English translation by Reinhard G. Pauly, *Musical Quarterly*, xxxiv (1948), pp. 371–403; xxxv (1949), pp. 85–105.

MUELLER VON ASOW, ERICH H.: *Angelo und Pietro Mingotti. Ein Beitrag zur Geschichte der Oper im XVIII. Jahrhundert* (Dresden, 1917).
PUTTMAN, MAX: 'Zur Geschichte der deutschen komischen Oper von ihren Anfängen bis Dittersdorf', *Die Musik*, iii/4 (1903/4), pp. 334–49, 416–28.
REICHARDT, JOHANN FRIEDRICH: *Über die deutsche comische Oper* (Hamburg, 1774).
ROBINSON, MICHAEL F.: 'The Aria in Opera Seria, 1725–1780', *Proceedings of the Royal Musical Association*, lxxxviii (1961/2), pp. 31–43.
—— *Opera before Mozart* (London, 1966).
ROLANDI, ULDERICO: *Il libretto per musica attraverso i tempi* (Rome, 1951).
RUBSAMEN, WALTER H.: 'Mr. Seedo, Ballad Opera, and the *Singspiel*', *Miscelánea en homenaje a Monseñor Higinio Anglés*, ii (Barcelona, 1958–61), pp. 775–809.
SCHERILLO, MICHELE: *Storia letteraria dell'opera buffa napolitana dalle origini al principio del secolo XIX* (Naples, 1883). 2nd ed. published as *L'opera buffa napoletana durante il Settecento: Storia letteraria* (Milan, 1917).
SCHNEIDER, MAX: 'Die Begleitung des Secco-Rezitativs um 1750', *Gluck-Jahrbuch*, iii (1917), pp. 88–107.
SCHWAN, WILHELM: *Die opernästhetischen Theorien der deutschen klassischen Dichter* (Bonn Dissertation, 1928).
STEINITZER, MAX: '*Zur Entwicklungsgeschichte des Melodrams und Mimodrams* (Leipzig, 1919).
TUTENBERG, FRITZ: 'Die Opera buffa-Sinfonie und ihre Beziehungen zur klassischen Sinfonie', *Archiv für Musikwissenschaft*, viii (1926), pp. 452–72.
VAN DER VEEN, J.: *Le mélodrame musical de Rousseau au Romantisme*. Dissertation (The Hague, 1955).
VETTER, WALTHER: 'Italienische Opernkomponisten um Georg Christoph Wagenseil; ein stilkundlicher Versuch', *Festschrift Friedrich Blume zum 70. Geburtstag*, ed. A. A. Abert and W. Pfannkuch (Kassel, 1963), pp. 363–74.
—— 'Zur Entwicklungsgeschichte der opera seria um 1750 in Wien', *Zeitschrift für Musikwissenschaft*, xiv (1931/2), pp. 2–28.
WELLESZ, EGON: 'Francesco Algarotti und seine Stellung zur Musik', *Sammelbände der internationalen Musikgesellschaft*, xv (1913/14), pp. 427–39.

(b) *Individual Composers and Librettists*
Adlgasser
SCHNEIDER, CONSTANTIN: 'Die Oratorien und Schuldramen Anton Cajetan Adlgassers', *Studien zur Musikwissenschaft*, xviii (1931), pp. 36–65.

André
STAUDER, WILHELM: 'Johann André. Ein Beitrag zur Geschichte des deutschen Singspiels', *Archiv für Musikforschung*, i (1936), pp. 318–60. Also published separately (Leipzig, 1936).

J. C. Bach
ABERT, HERMANN: 'Joh. Christian Bachs italienische Opern und ihr Einfluss auf Mozart', *Zeitschrift für Musikwissenschaft*, i (1918/19), pp. 313–28.
WARBURTON, ERNEST: 'J. C. Bach's Operas', *Proceedings of the Royal Musical Association*, xcii (1965/6), pp. 95–106.
WENK, ALEXANDER: *Beiträge zur Kenntnis des Opernschaffens von Johann Christian Bach*. (Frankfurt Dissertation, 1932).

G. Benda
BRÜCKNER, A. H. FRITZ: *Georg Benda und das deutsche Singspiel*. Rostock Dissertation, 1902 (Leipzig, 1904). Also published in *Sammelbände der internationalen Musikgesellschaft*, v (1903/4), pp. 571–621.
PILKOVÁ, ZDEŇKA: *Dramatická tvorba Jiřího Bendy* (Prague, 1960).

Bernasconi
WEISS, EDUARD J.: *Andrea Bernasconi als Opernkomponist*. (Munich Dissertation, 1923).

Bonno
WELLESZ, EGON: 'Giuseppe Bonno (1710–88). Sein Leben und seine dramatischen Werke', *Sammelbände der internationalen Musikgesellschaft*, xi (1909/10), pp. 395–442.

Da Ponte
BOAS, HANS: 'Lorenzo Da Ponte als Wiener Theaterdichter', *Sammelbände der internationalen Musikgesellschaft*, xv (1913/14), pp. 325–38.
DA PONTE, LORENZO: *Memorie*, 4 vols. (New York, 1823–7). English translations by L. A. Sheppard (London, 1929) and Elisabeth Abbott, ed. Arthur Livingston (Philadelphia, 1929; reprinted New York, 1967).
MARCHESAN, ANGELO: *Della vita e delle opere di Lorenzo da Ponte* (Treviso, 1900).
RUSSO, JOSEPH L.: *Lorenzo Da Ponte, Poet and Adventurer* (New York, 1922).

Dittersdorf
RIEDINGER, LOTHAR: 'Karl von Dittersdorf als Opernkomponist', *Studien zur Musikwissenschaft*, ii (1914), pp. 212–349.

Eberlin
HAAS, ROBERT: 'Eberlins Schuldramen und Oratorien', *Studien zur Musikwissenschaft*, viii (1921), pp. 9–44.

Galuppi
BOLLERT, WERNER: *Die Buffoopern Baldassare Galuppis*. Berlin Dissertation (Bottrop, 1935).

Gassmann
DONATH, GUSTAV: 'Florian Leopold Gassmann als Opernkomponist', *Studien zur Musikwissenschaft*, ii (1914), pp. 34–211.

Gluck
ABERT, ANNA A.: *Christoph Willibald Gluck* (Munich, 1959).
AREND, MAX: *Gluck, eine Biographie* (Berlin, 1921).
COOPER, MARTIN: *Gluck* (London, 1935).
CUCUEL, GEORGES: 'Les opéras de Gluck dans les parodies du XVIIIe siècle', *Revue musicale*, iii (1922), no. 5, pp. 201–21; no. 6, pp. 51–68.
EINSTEIN, ALFRED: *Gluck* (London, 1936. Revised ed., 1964).
ENGLÄNDER, RICHARD: 'Gluck-Pflege und Nachfolge Glucks in Schweden Gustavs III', *Musa-Mens-Musici, im Gedenken an Walther Vetter* (Leipzig, 1969), pp. 215–23.
—— 'Gluck und der Norden', *Acta Musicologica*, xxiv (1952), pp. 62–83.
GERBER, RUDOLF: *Christoph Willibald Ritter von Gluck* (Potsdam, 1942. 2nd ed., 1950).
Gluck-Jahrbuch, ed. H. Abert, Jahrgang I–IV (Leipzig, 1913–18).
HAAS, ROBERT: *Gluck und Durazzo im Burgtheater (Die Opéra Comique in Wien)* (Zürich, 1925).
HAMMELMANN, HANNS and ROSE, MICHAEL: 'New Light on Calzabigi and Gluck', *Musical Times*, cx (1969), pp. 609–11.
HOPKINSON, CECIL: *A Bibliography of the Printed Works of C. W. von Gluck 1714–1787*, 2nd ed. (New York, 1967).
HORTSCHANSKY, KLAUS: 'Doppelvertonungen in den italienischen Opern Glucks. Ein Beitrag zu Glucks Schaffensprozess', *Archiv für Musikwissenschaft*, xxiv (1967), pp. 54–63, 133–44.
—— 'Glucks Sendungsbewusstsein', *Musikforschung*, xxi (1968), pp. 30–5.
HOWARD, PATRICIA: *Gluck and the Birth of Modern Opera* (London, 1963).
KURTH, ERNST: 'Die Jugendopern Glucks bis Orfeo', *Studien zur Musikwissenschaft*, i (1913), pp. 193–277.
LARUE, JAN: 'Gluck oder Pseudo-Gluck', *Musikforschung*, xvii (1964), pp. 272–5.

MEYER, RALPH: *Die Behandlung des Rezitativs in Glucks italienischen Reformopern.* (Halle Dissertation, 1919). Published in *Gluck-Jahrbuch*, iv (1918), pp. 1–90.
MOSER, HANS: *Christoph Willibald Gluck* (Stuttgart, 1940).
MUELLER VON ASOW, H., and E. H., edd: *The Collected Correspondence and Papers of Christoph Willibald Gluck*, translated by S. Thomson (London, 1962).
STERNFELD, FREDERICK W.: 'Expression and Revision in Gluck's *Orfeo* and *Alceste*', *Essays presented to Egon Wellesz*, ed. J. Westrup (Oxford, 1966), pp. 114–29.
TENSCHERT, ROLAND: *Christoph Willibald Gluck, der grosse Reformator der Oper* (Olten, 1951).
VETTER, WALTHER: 'Gluck und seine italienischen Zeitgenossen', *Zeitschrift für Musikwissenschaft*, vii (1924/5), pp. 609–46.
—— 'Glucks Entwicklung zum Opernreformator', *Archiv für Musikwissenschaft*, vi (1924), pp. 165–212.
WOTQUENNE, ALFRED: *Thematisches Verzeichnis der Werke von Chr. W. v. Gluck* (Leipzig, 1904; reprinted Hildesheim, 1967).

Goldoni
CHATFIELD-TAYLOR, H. C.: *Goldoni: A Biography* (New York, 1913).
GOLDONI, CARLO: *Mémoires*, 3 vols. (Paris, 1787). English transl. by J. Black, ed. W. A. Drake (London, 1926).
HOLMES, WILLIAM C.: 'Pamela Transformed', *Musical Quarterly*, xxxviii (1952), pp. 581–94.
RABANY, CHARLES: *Carlo Goldoni: Le théâtre et la vie en Italie au XVIIIe siècle* (Paris, 1896).

C. H. Graun
MAYER-REINACH, ALBERT: 'Carl Heinrich Graun als Opernkomponist', *Sammelbände der internationalen Musikgesellschaft*, i (1899/1900), pp. 446–529.

Guglielmi
PIOVANO, FRANCESCO: 'Elenco cronologico delle opere (1757–1802) di Pietro Guglielmi', *Rivista musicale italiana*, xii (1905), pp. 407–46.

Hasse
ENGEL, HANS: 'Hasses Ruggiero und Mozarts Festspiel Ascanio', *Mozart-Jahrbuch 1960–61*, pp. 29–42.
GERBER, RUDOLF: *Der Operntypus Johann Adolf Hasses und seine textlichen Grundlagen* (Leipzig, 1925).
SONNECK, OSCAR G.: 'Die drei Fassungen der Hasse'schen "Artaserse"', *Sammelbände der internationalen Musikgesellschaft*, xiv (1912/13), pp. 226–42.

Haydn
BARTHA, DÉNES: 'Haydn's Italian Opera Repertory at Eszterháza Palace', *New Looks at Italian Opera: Essays in Honor of Donald J. Grout* (Ithaca, N.Y., 1968), pp. 172–219.
—— and Somfai, László, edd.: *Haydn als Opernkapellmeister; die Haydn-Dokumente der Esterházy-Opernsammlung* (Budapest, 1960).
HARICH, JÁNOS: 'Das Repertoire des Opernkapellmeisters Joseph Haydn in Eszterháza (1780–1790)', *Haydn Yearbook*, i (1962), pp. 9–110.
LANDON, H. C. ROBBINS: 'Haydn's Marionette Operas and the Repertoire of the Marionette Theatre at Esterház Castle', *Haydn Yearbook*, i (1962), pp. 111–97.
WENDSCHUH, LUDWIG: *Über Jos. Haydns Opern*. Rostock Dissertation (Halle, 1896).
WIRTH, HELMUT: *Joseph Haydn als Dramatiker* (Wolfenbüttel, 1940).
—— 'The Operas of Joseph Haydn before "Orfeo"', in *Analytical notes* to *Orfeo ed Euridice*, Haydn Society Recording (Vienna–Boston, 1951).

Hiller
CALMUS, GEORGY: *Die ersten deutschen Singspiele von Standfuss und Hiller* (Leipzig, 1908).

Jommelli
ABERT, HERMANN: *Niccolo Jommelli als Opernkomponist* (Halle, 1908).

Kraus
ANREP-NORDIN, B.: *Studier över Josef Martin Kraus* (Stockholm, 1924). Also in *Svensk tidskrift för musikforskning*, v (1923), pp. 15–20, 55–80, 117–38; vi (1924), pp. 16–41, 49–93.

ENGLÄNDER, RICHARD: *Joseph Martin Kraus and die Gustavianische Oper* (Upsala, 1943).

Logroscino
KRETZSCHMAR, HERMANN: 'Zwei Opern Nicolo Logroscinos', *Jahrbuch der Musikbibliothek Peters*, xv (1908), pp. 47–68. Reprinted in *Gesammelte Aufsätze*, ii (Leipzig, 1911).

PROTA-GIURLEO, ULISSE: *Nicola Logroscino, "il dio" dell'opera buffa* (Naples, 1927).

Metastasio
DELLA CORTE, ANDREA: 'Appunti sull' estetica musicale di Pietro Metastasio', *Rivista musicale italiana*, xxviii (1921), pp. 94–119.

GIAZOTTO, REMO: 'Apostolo Zeno, Pietro Metastasio, e la critica del Settecento', *Rivista musicale italiana*, xlviii (1946), pp. 324–60; xlix (1947), pp. 47–56; l (1948), pp. 248–58; li (1949), pp. 43–66, 130–61.

W. A. Mozart
ABRAHAM, GERALD: 'The Operas', *The Mozart Companion*, ed. H. C. Robbins Landon and Donald Mitchell (London, 1956), pp. 283–323.

ANHEISSER, SIEGFRIED: 'Die unbekannte Urfassung von Mozarts Figaro', *Zeitschrift für Musikwissenschaft*, xv (1932/3), pp. 301–17.

ARMITAGE-SMITH, J. N. A.: 'The plot of "The Magic Flute"', *Music and Letters* xxxv (1954), pp. 36–9.

BATLEY, EDWARD: *A Preface to the Magic Flute* (London, 1969).

—— 'Textual Unity in *Die Zauberflöte*', *Music Review*, xxvii (1966), pp. 81–92.

BENN, F. CHRISTOPHER: *Mozart on the Stage* (London, 1946).

BITTER, CHRISTOF: 'Don Giovanni in Wien, 1788', *Mozart-Jahrbuch 1959*, pp. 146–64.

BLOM, ERIC: 'The Literary Ancestry of Figaro', *Musical Quarterly*, xiii (1927), pp. 528–39.

BRANSCOMBE, PETER: 'Die Zauberflöte: Some Textual and Interpretative Problems', *Proceedings of the Royal Musical Association*, xcii (1965/6), pp. 45–63.

BROPHY, BRIGID: '*Figaro* and the Limitations of Music', *Music and Letters*, li (1970), pp. 26–36.

—— *Mozart the Dramatist* (London, 1964).

CHAILLEY, JACQUES: *La Flûte Enchantée. Opéra maçonnique* (Paris, 1968. English translation New York, 1971).

COHEN, HERMANN: *Die dramatische Idee in Mozarts Operntexten* (Berlin, 1915).

CONRAD, LEOPOLD: *Mozarts Dramaturgie der Oper*. Berlin Dissertation, 1942 (Würzburg, 1943).

DECKER, HERBERT: *Dramaturgie und Szene der Zauberflöte*. Munich Dissertation, 1946 (Regensburg, 1949).

DENT, EDWARD J.: *Mozart's Operas*, 2nd ed. (London, 1947).

—— 'The Plot of "The Magic Flute"', *Music and Letters*, xxxv (1954), pp. 175–81.

DEUTSCH, OTTO E.: 'Der ratselhäfte Gieseke', *Musikforschung*, v (1952), pp. 152–60.

EINSTEIN, ALFRED: 'Concerning some Recitatives in "Don Giovanni"', *Music and Letters*, xix (1938), pp. 417–25.

—— 'Die Text-Vorlage zu Mozarts "Zaide"', *Acta Musicologica*, viii (1936), pp. 30–37.

ENGEL, HANS: 'Hasses Ruggiero und Mozarts Festspiel Ascanio', *Mozart-Jahrbuch 1960–61*, pp. 29–42.

ENGLÄNDER, RICHARD: 'The Sketches for "The Magic Flute" at Upsala', *Musical Quarterly*, xxvii (1941), pp. 343–55.

FISCHER, WILHELM: '"Der welcher wandelt diese Strasse voll Beschwerden"', *Mozart-Jahrbuch 1950*, pp. 41–8.

GIEGLING, FRANZ: 'Zu den Rezitativen von Mozarts Oper "Titus"', *Mozart-Jahrbuch 1967*, pp. 121–26.

HAMMERSTEIN, REINHOLD: 'Der Gesang der geharnischten Männer. Eine Studie zu Mozarts Bachbild', *Archiv für Musikwissenschaft*, xiii (1956), pp. 1–24.

HEARTZ, DANIEL: 'The Genesis of Mozart's *Idomeneo*', *Mozart-Jahrbuch 1967*, pp. 150–64. Also printed in *Musical Quarterly*, lv (1969), pp. 1–19.

HEUSS, ALFRED: 'Mozarts "Idomeneo" als Quelle für "Don Giovanni" und "Die Zauberflöte"', *Zeitschrift für Musikwissenschaft*, xiii (1930/1), pp. 177–99.

KING, A. HYATT: 'The Melodic Sources and Affinities of *Die Zauberflöte*', *Musical Quarterly*, xxxvi (1950), pp. 241–58. Reprinted in *Mozart in Retrospect* (London 1955. 3rd impression revised, 1970).

KLEIN, HERBERT: 'Unbekannte Mozartiana von 1766/67', *Mozart-Jahrbuch 1957*, pp. 168–85.

KLOIBER, RUDOLF: *Die dramatischen Ballette von Christian Cannabich*. (Munich Dissertation, 1928).

KOMORZYNSKI, EGON: *Emanuel Schikaneder* (Vienna, 1951).

—— 'Ein Mädchen oder Weibchen wünscht Papageno sich', *Wiener Figaro*, x (August, 1940), pp. 10–12.

LERT, ERNST: *Mozart auf dem Theater* (Berlin, 1918; rev. ed. 1921).

LEVARIE, SIEGMUND: *Mozart's Le Nozze di Figaro. A Critical Analysis* (Chicago, 1952).

LIEBNER, JÁNOS: 'Le chant du cygne de Shakespeare et de Mozart', *Schweizerische Musikzeitung*, cii (1962), pp. 28–32.

—— 'Don Giovanni et ses ancêtres, ou La métamorphose d'une légende', *Schweizerische Musikzeitung*, civ (1964), pp. 237–43.

—— 'Encore Shakespeare et Mozart. La Tempête. La théorie de la "cassure" de la Flûte Enchantée', *Schweizerische Musikzeitung*, cii (1962), pp. 292–96.

LIVERMORE, ANN L.: 'Così fan tutte: A well-kept Secret', *Music and Letters*, xlvi (1965), pp. 316–21.

—— '*The Magic Flute* and Calderón', *Music and Letters*, xxxvi (1955), pp. 7–16.

—— 'The Origins of Don Juan', *Music and Letters*, xliv (1963), pp. 257–65.

—— 'Rousseau, Beaumarchais, and Figaro', *Musical Quarterly*, lvii (1971), pp. 466–90.

LOEWENBERG, ALFRED: '*Bastien und Bastienne* once more', *Music and Letters*, xxv (1944), pp. 176–81.

MÜLLER VON ASOW, ERICH H.: 'Mozarts "La Clemenza di Tito" im Spiegel des zeitgenössischen Schrifttums', *Wiener Figaro*, xi (August 1941), pp. 1–3.

MÜNSTER, ROBERT: '*Die verstellte Gärtnerin*. Neue Quellen zur authentischen Singspielfassung von W. A. Mozarts *La finta giardiniera*', *Musikforschung*, xviii (1965), pp. 138–60.

NETTL, PAUL: 'Prager Mozartiana', *Mitteilungen der Internationalen Stiftung Mozarteum*, ix (1960), nos. 3/4, pp. 2 ff.

—— 'Sethos und die freimaurerische Grundlage der "Zauberflöte"', *Bericht über die musikwissenschaftliche Tagung der Internationalen Stiftung Mozarteum in Salzburg . . . 1931*, ed. E. Schenk (Leipzig, 1932), pp. 142–9.

NOSKE, FRITS: 'Social Tensions in *Le Nozze di Figaro*', *Music and Letters*, 1 (1969), pp. 45–62.

OREL, ALFRED: 'Die Legende um Mozarts "Bastien und Bastienne"', *Schweizerische Musikzeitung*, xci (1951), pp. 137–43.

—— 'Mozarts Beitrag zum deutschen Sprechtheater. Die Musik zu Geblers "Thamos"', *Acta Mozartiana*, iv (1957), pp. 45–53, 74–81.

PAUMGARTNER, BERNHARD: 'Zur Dramaturgie der "Clemenza di Tito"', *Österreichische Musikzeitung*, iv (1949), pp. 172–6.
PIRKER, MAX: *Die Zauberflöte* (Vienna, 1920).
PREIBISCH, WALTER: 'Quellenstudien zu Mozarts "Entführung aus dem Serail": ein Beitrag zur Geschichte der Türkenoper', *Sammelbände der internationalen Musikgesellschaft*, x (1908/9), pp. 430–76.
RAEBURN, CHRISTOPHER: 'Mozarts Opern in Prag', *Musica*, xiii (1959), pp. 158–63.
ROSENBERG, ALFONS: *Die Zauberflöte, Geschichte und Deutung von Mozarts Oper* (Munich, 1964).
ROSENTHAL, AUGUST: 'Über Vokalformen bei Mozart', *Studien zur Musikwissenschaft*, xiv (1927), pp. 5–32.
SCHENK, ERICH: 'Zur Tonsymbolik in Mozarts "Figaro"', *Neues Mozart-Jahrbuch*, i (1941), pp. 114–34.
SCHNERICH, ALFRED: 'Wie sahen die ersten Vorstellungen von Mozart's Don Juan aus?', *Zeitschrift der internationalen Musikgesellschaft*, xii (1910/11), pp. 101–8.
SENN, WALTER: 'Mozarts Skizze der Ballettmusik zu "Le gelosie del serraglio" (KV Anh. 109/135a)', *Acta Musicologica*, xxxiii (1961), pp. 169–92.
—— 'Mozarts "Zaide" und der Verfasser der vermutlichen Textvorlage', *Festschrift Alfred Orel zum 70. Geburtstag* (Vienna, 1960), pp. 173–86.
STERNFELD, FREDERICK W.: 'The Melodic Sources of Mozart's Most Popular *Lied*', *Musical Quarterly*, xlii (1956), pp. 213–22.
TAGLIAVINI, LUIGI F.: 'Quirino Gasparini and Mozart', *New Looks at Italian Opera: Essays in Honor of Donald J. Grout* (Ithaca, N.Y., 1968), pp. 151–71.
TENSCHERT, ROLAND: 'Das Duett Nr. 8 aus Mozarts "Apollo et Hyacinthus" und das Andante aus der Sinfonie KV 43, *Mozart-Jahrbuch 1958*, pp. 59–65.
TIERSOT, JULIEN: *Don Juan de Mozart* (Paris, 1927).
VOLEK, TOMISLAV: 'Über den Ursprung von Mozarts Oper "La Clemenza di Tito"', *Mozart-Jahrbuch 1959*, pp. 274–86.
WALTERSHAUSEN, HERMANN W. VON: *Die Zauberflöte* (Munich, 1920).
WERNER, ERIC: 'Leading or Symbolic Formulas in *The Magic Flute*: a Hermeneutic Examination', *Music Review*, xviii (1957), pp. 286–93.
WESTRUP, JACK A.: 'Two first performances: Monteverdi's "Orfeo" and Mozart's "Clemenza di Tito"', *Music and Letters*, xxxix (1958), pp. 327–35.

Mysliveček
PEČMAN, RUDOLF: *Josef Mysliveček und sein Opernepilog* (Brno, 1970).

Naumann
ENGLÄNDER, RICHARD: *Johann Gottlieb Naumann als Opernkomponist, 1741–1801* (Leipzig, 1922).

Paisiello
ABERT, HERMANN: 'Paisiello's Buffokunst und ihre Beziehungen zu Mozart', *Archiv für Musikwissenschaft*, i (1918/19), pp. 402–21. Reprinted in *Gesammelte Schriften und Vorträge* (Halle, 1929).
DELLA CORTE, ANDREA: *Paisiello, con una tavola tematica* (Turin, 1922).

Piccinni
ABERT, HERMANN: 'Piccinni als Buffokomponist', *Jahrbuch der Musikbibliothek Peters*, xx (1913), pp. 29–42. Reprinted in *Gesammelte Schriften* (Halle, 1929).
BELLUCCI LA SALANDRA, MARIO: 'Opera teatrali serie e buffe di Niccolò Piccinni dal 1754 al 1794', *Note d'archivio*, xii (1935), pp. 43–54, 114–25, 234–48, and corrections etc. in xiii (1936), pp. 55–8.
DELLA CORTE, ANDREA: *Piccinni. Settecento italiano* (Bari, 1928).
GINGUENÉ, PIERRE L.: *Notice sur la vie et les ouvrages de Nicolas Piccini* (Paris, 1801).
HOLMES, WILLIAM C.: 'Pamela Transformed', *Musical Quarterly*, xxxviii (1952), pp. 581–94.

LA ROTELLA, PASQUALE: *Niccolò Piccinni* (Bari, 1928).
Porta
WESTERMAN, GERHART VON: *Giovanni Porta als Opernkomponist*. (Munich Dissertation, 1921).
Reichardt
PRÖPPER, ROLF: *Die Bühnenwerke Johann Friedrich Reichardts*, 2 vols. (Bonn, 1965).
Standfuss
CALMUS, GEORGY: *Die ersten deutschen Singspiele von Standfuss und Hiller* (Leipzig, 1908).
Traetta
BLOCH, HENRY: 'Tommaso Traetta's Reform of Italian Opera', *Collectanea Historiae Musicae*, iii (1963), pp. 5–13.
CASAVOLA, FRANCO: *Tommaso Traetta di Bitonto (1727–1779): La vita e le opera* (Bari, 1957).
DAMERINI, ADELMO: 'Un precursore italiano di Gluck: Tommaso Traetta', *Il pianoforte*, vii, no. 7 (July 1927).
NUOVO, ANTONIO: *Tommaso Traetta* (Bitonto, 1938).
SARACINO, EMANUELE: *Tommaso Traetta* (Bitonto, 1954).
Wagenseil
VETTER, WALTHER: 'Der Opernkomponist Georg Christoph Wagenseil und sein Verhältnis zu Mozart und Gluck', *Gedenkschrift für Hermann Abert von seinen Schülern*, ed. F. Blume (Halle, 1928), pp. 165–76.
—— 'Georg Christoph Wagenseil als Vorläufer Christoph Willibald Glucks', *Zeitschrift für Musikwissenschaft*, viii (1925/6), pp. 385–402.
Zeno
FEHR, MAX: *Apostolo Zeno und seine Reform des Operntextes. Ein Beitrag zur Geschichte des Librettos* (Zürich, 1912).
GIAZOTTO, REMO: 'Apostolo Zeno, Pietro Metatasio, e la critica del Settecento', *Rivista musicale italiana*, xlviii (1946), pp. 324–60; xlix (1947), pp. 47–56; l (1948), pp. 248–58; li (1949), pp. 43–66, 130–61.

CHAPTER II

OPERA IN FRANCE

(i) *Modern Editions*

BLAISE, A.: *Annette & Lubin*, ed. R. Montfort (Paris, 1910).
GLUCK, C. W. VON: *Sämtliche Werke*, ed. R. Gerber (Kassel, 1951–   ).
—— *Alceste*, ed. F. Pelletan and B. Damcke (Paris, 1874).
—— *Armide*, ed. F. Pelletan, C. Saint-Saëns and O. Thierry-Poux (Paris, 1890).
—— *Echo et Narcisse*, ed. F. Pelletan, C. Saint-Saëns and J. Tiersot (Paris, 1902).
—— *Iphigénie en Aulide*, ed. F. Pelletan and B. Damcke (Paris, 1873).
—— *Iphigénie en Tauride*, ed. F. Pelletan and B. Damcke (Paris, 1874).
—— *Orphée et Euridice*, ed. F. Pelletan, C. Saint-Saëns, and J. Tiersot (Paris, 1898).
GRÉTRY, A. E. M.: *Collection complète des oeuvres de Grétry*, ed. F. A. Gevaert *et al.* (Leipzig, 1884–1936).
PHILIDOR, F. A.: *Ernelinde*, vocal score ed. C. Franck (*Les Chefs-d'oeuvre de l'opéra français*) (Paris, 1883).
PICCINNI, N.: *Didon*, vocal score ed. G. Lefevre (*Les Chefs-d'oeuvre de l'opéra français*) (Paris, 1881).
—— *Roland*, vocal score ed. G. Lefevre (*Les Chefs-d'oeuvre de l'opéra français*) (Paris, 1882).

SACCHINI, A. M. G.: *Chimène*, vocal score ed. E. Gigout (*Les Chefs-d'oeuvre de l'opéra français*) (Paris, 1883).
—— *Renaud*, ed. E. Gigout (*Les Chefs-d'oeuvre de l'opéra français*) (Paris, 1883).
SALIERI, A.: *Les Danaïdes*, vocal score ed. G. Lefèvre (*Les Chefs-d'oeuvre de l'opéra française*) (Paris, 1881).
—— *Tarare*, vocal score ed. G. Lefèvre (*Les Chefs-d'oeuvre de l'opéra français*) (Paris, 1882).

(ii) *Books and Articles*
(a) *General*

ACHENWALL, J. MAX: *Studien über die komische Oper in Frankreich im 18. Jahrhundert und ihre Beziehungen zu Molière*. Leipzig Dissertation (Eilenburg, 1912).
ALBERT, MAURICE: *Les Théâtres de la Foire, 1660–1789* (Paris, 1900).
ARNOLDSON, L. PARKINSON: *Sedaine et les musiciens de son temps* (Paris, 1934).
BOYER, NOEL: *La guerre des Bouffons et la musique française 1752–54* (Paris, 1945).
CAMPARDON, EMILE: *Les spectacles de la foire—depuis 1595 jusqu'à 1791*, 2 vols. (Paris, 1877).
CAUX DE CAPPEVAL, N. DE: *Apologie du goût françois relativement à l'opéra* (Paris, 1754).
CUCUEL, GEORGES: *Les Créateurs de l'opéra-comique français* (Paris, 1914).
—— 'Sources et documents pour servir à l'histoire de l'opéra-comique en France', *L'Année musicale*, iii (1913), pp. 247–82.
GARLINGTON, AUBREY S.: '*Le merveilleux* and Operatic Reform in 18th-century French Opera', *Musical Quarterly*, xlix (1963), pp. 484–97.
GRIMM, FRIEDRICH MELCHIOR VON: *Lettre de M. Grimm sur Omphale* (Paris, 1752).
—— *Le Petit Prophète de Boemischbroda* (Paris, 1753).
HEARTZ, DANIEL: 'From Garrick to Gluck: the Reform of Theatre and Opera in the mid-Eighteenth Century', *Proceedings of the Royal Musical Association*, xciv (1967/8), pp. 111–27.
JULLIEN, ADOLPHE: *La cour et l'opéra sous Louis XVI* (Paris, 1878).
—— *L'opéra secret au XVIIIe siècle* (Paris, 1880).
KOCH, CHARLES E.: 'The Dramatic Ensemble Finale in the Opéra Comique of the Eighteenth Century', *Acta Musicologica*, xxxix (1967), pp. 72–83.
LECERF DE LA VIÉVILLE DE FRESNEUSE, JEAN L.: *Comparaison de la musique italienne et de la musique françoise*, 3 vols. (Brussels, 1704–6). This was reprinted as vols. 2–4 of the 1725 Amsterdam edition of Pierre Bonnet's *Histoire de la musique et de ses effets*.
MASSON, PAUL-MARIE: 'La *Lettre sur Omphale*', *Revue de musicologie*, xxvii (1945), pp. 1–19.
PROD'HOMME, JACQUES G.: 'La musique à Paris de 1753 à 1757, d'après un manuscrit de la Bibliothèque de Munich', *Sammelbände der internationalen Musikgesellschaft*, vi (1904/5), pp. 568–87.
TIERSOT, JULIEN: *Histoire de la chanson populaire en France* (Paris, 1889).

(b) *Individual Composers and Librettists*
Calzabigi
HAMMELMANN, HANNS and ROSE, MICHAEL: 'New Light on Calzabigi and Gluck', *Musical Times*, cx (1969), pp. 609–11.
MICHEL, HERTHA: 'Ranieri Calzabigi als Dichter von Musikdramen und als Kritiker', *Gluck-Jahrbuch*, iv (1918), pp. 99–171.

Gluck
ABERT, ANNA A.: *Christoph Willibald Gluck* (Munich, 1959).
AREND, MAX: *Gluck, eine Biographie* (Berlin, 1921).
COOPER, MARTIN: *Gluck* (London, 1935).
CUCUEL, GEORGES: 'Les opéras de Gluck dans les parodies du XVIIIe siècle', *Revue musicale*, iii (1922), no. 5, pp. 201–21; no. 6, pp. 51–68.

EINSTEIN, ALFRED: *Gluck* (London, 1936. Revised ed., 1964).
TIERSOT, JULIEN: 'Gluck and the Encyclopaedists', *Musical Quarterly*, xvi (1930), pp. 336–57.
VETTER, WALTHER: 'Glucks Stellung zur *tragédie lyrique* und *opéra comique*', *Zeitschrift für Musikwissenschaft*, vii (1924/5), pp. 321–55.

Grétry
BRENET, MICHEL: *Grétry, sa vie et ses oeuvres* (Paris, 1884).
BRUYR, JOSÉ: *Grétry* (Paris, 1931).
CLERCX, SUZANNE: *Grétry, 1741–1813* (Brussels, 1944).
CLOSSON, ERNEST: *André-Modeste Grétry* (Turnhout, 1920).
CURZON, HENRI DE: *Grétry (Paris*, 1907).
DEGEY, MAURICE: *André-Modeste Grétry* (Brussels, 1939).
FROIDCOURT, GEORGES DE, ed.: *La Correspondance générale de Grétry* (Brussels, 1962).
GRÉTRY, MODESTE: *Mémoires ou Essai sur la musique* (Paris, 1789).
LONG DES CLAVIÈRES, PAULINE: *La jeunesse de Grétry et ses débuts à Paris* (Besançon, 1921).
WICHMANN, HEINZ: *Grétry und das musikalische Theater in Frankreich* (Halle, 1929).

Monsigny
DRUILHE, PAULE: *Monsigny, sa vie, son oeuvre* (Paris, 1955).
POUGIN, ARTHUR: *Monsigny et son temps* (Paris, 1908).

Philidor
ALLEN, GEORGE: *The Life of Philidor, Musician and Chessplayer* (Philadelphia, 1858).

Rousseau
ARNHEIM, AMALIE: '*Le Devin du village* von Jean-Jacques Rousseau und die Parodie Les Amours de Bastien et Bastienne', *Sammelbände der internationalen Musikgesellschaft*, iv (1902/3), pp. 686–727.
ISTEL, EDGAR: *Jean-Jacques Rousseau als Komponist seiner lyrischen Szene "Pygmalion"* (Leipzig, 1901).
POUGIN, ARTHUR: *Jean-Jacques Rousseau, muscien* (Paris, 1901 [1900]).
ROUSSEAU, JEAN JACQUES: *Lettre sur la musique françoise* (Paris, 1753).
TIERSOT, JULIEN: 'La musique de J.-J. Rousseau', *Revue Musicale S.I.M.*, viii no. 6 (1912), pp. 34–56.
WHITTALL, ARNOLD: 'Rousseau and the Scope of Opera', *Music and Letters*, xlv (1964), pp. 369–76.

CHAPTER III
OPERA IN OTHER COUNTRIES

(a) *English Opera*
(i) *Modern Editions*

ARNE, T. A.: *Comus*, ed. J. Herbage (*Musica Britannica*, 3) (London, 1951).
STORACE, S.: *No Song, no Supper*, ed. R. Fiske (*Musica Britannica*, 16) (London, 1959).

(ii) *Books and Articles*

BEECHEY, GWILYM: 'Thomas Linley, junior, 1756–1778', *Musical Quarterly*, liv (1968), pp. 74–82.
BROWN, JOHN: *A Dissertation on the Rise, Union and Power . . . of Poetry and Music* (London, 1763).
DIBDIN, CHARLES: *The Musical Tour of Mr. Dibdin* (Sheffield, 1788).
DIBDIN, EDWARD R.: 'Charles Dibdin as a Writer', *Music and Letters*, xix (1938), pp. 149–70.

FISKE, ROGER: 'The Operas of Stephen Storace', *Proceedings of the Royal Musical Association*, lxxxvi (1959/60), pp. 29–44.
GRAVES, RICHARD: 'The Comic Operas of Stephen Storace', *Musical Times*, xcv (1954), pp. 530–2.
—— 'English Comic Opera, 1760–1800', *Monthly Musical Record*, lxxxvii (1957), pp. 208–15.
KELLY, MICHAEL: *Reminiscences of M.K. of the King's Theatre* (London, 1826).
LINCOLN, STODDARD: 'J. E. Galliard and *A Critical Discourse*', *Musical Quarterly*, liii (1967), pp. 347–64.
LOCKWOOD, ELISABETH M.: 'Charles Dibdin's Musical Tour', *Music and Letters*, xiii (1932), pp. 207–14.
PARKE, WILLIAM T.: *Musical Memoirs*, 2 vols. (London, 1830).
PARKINSON, JOHN A.: 'Garrick's Folly or, The Great Stratford Jubilee', *Musical Times*, cx (1969), pp. 922–6.
ROSCOE, P. C.: 'Arne and *The Guardian Outwitted*', *Music and Letters*, xxiv (1943), pp. 237–45.
SEAR, H. G.: 'Charles Dibdin: 1745–1814', *Music and Letters*, xxvi (1945), pp. 61–6.
TAYLOR, ERIC: 'William Boyce and the Theatre', *Music Review*, xiv (1953), pp. 275–87.
TREND, J. B.: 'Jonathan Battishill', *Music and Letters*, xiii (1932), pp. 264–71.
WINESANKER, MICHAEL: 'Musico-Dramatic Criticism of English Comic Opera, 1750–1800', *Journal of the American Musicological Society*, ii (1949), pp. 87–96.

(b) Russian Opera
(i) Modern Anthology
GINZBURG, SEMYON LVOVICH: *Istoriya russkoy muzïki v notnïkh obraztsakh*, i (Moscow, 1940; rev. ed. 1968).

(ii) Books and Articles
BERNANDT, GRIGORIY BORISOVICH: *Slovar' oper, vpervïe postavlennïkh ili izdannïkh v dorevolyutsionnoy Rossii i v SSSR, 1736–1959* (Moscow, 1962).
DOBROKHOTOV, B.: *D. S. Bortnyansky* (Moscow, 1950).
—— *E. I. Fomin* (Moscow, 1949).
FESECHKO, G. F.: 'Novïe materialy o kompozïtorakh P. A. Skokove i E. I. Fomine', *Muzïkal'noe nasledstvo*, ii, part 1 (Moscow, 1966), pp. 9–30.
FINAGIN, A. V.: 'Evst. Fomin. Zhizn i tvorchestvo', *Muzïka i muzïkal'nïy bït staroy Rossii*, ed. A. Finagin (Leningrad, 1927), pp. 70–116.
FINDEIZEN, NIKOLAY: *Ocherki po istorii muzïki v Rossii s drevneishikh vremen do kontsa XVIII veka*, 2 vols. (Moscow, 1928–29).
GINZBURG, SEMYON LVOVICH: *Russkiy muzïkal'nïy teatr 1700–1835* (Moscow, 1941).
KELDÏSH, YURY: *Russkaya muzïka XVIII veka* (Moscow, 1965).
LEHMANN, DIETER: *Russlands Oper und Singspiel in der zweiten Hälfte des 18. Jahrhunderts* (Leipzig, 1958).
LIVANOVA, TAMARA N.: *Russkaya muzïkal'naya kul'tura XVIII veka*, 2 vols. (Moscow, 1952–3).
MOOSER, ROBERT ALOYS: *Annales de la musique et des musiciens en Russie au XVIIIme siècle*, 3 vols. (Geneva, 1948–51).
—— *Opéras, intermezzos, ballets, cantates, oratorios joués en Russie durant le XVIIIe siècle*, 3rd ed. (Basle, 1964).
PROKOFYEV, V. A.: 'Mikhail Matinsky i evo opera "Sanktpeterburgskïy gostinïy dvor"', *Muzïka i muzïkal'nïy bït staroy Rossii*, ed. A. Finagin (Leningrad, 1927), p. 58.
RABINOVICH, ALEKSANDR S.: *Russkaya opera do Glinki* (Moscow, 1948).
SEAMAN, GERALD: 'The National Element in Early Russian Opera, 1779–1800', *Music and Letters*, xlii (1961), pp. 252–62.

VOLMAN, BORIS L.: *Russkie pechatnïe noty XVIII v* (Leningrad, 1957).
(c) *Spanish Opera*
(i) *Modern Editions*
   Anthologies
PEDRELL, FELIPE, ed.: *Teatro lírico español anterior al siglo XIX*, vols. 1–2 (Madrid, 1897).
SUBIRÁ, JOSE: *La tonadilla escénica*, iii (Madrid, 1930).
——, ed.: *Tonadillas teatrales inéditas: libretos y partituras* (Madrid, 1932).
   Works of Individual Composers
ROSALES, A.: *El recitado*, ed. J. Subirá (Madrid, 1930).
TERRADELLAS, D.: *La Merope*, ed. R. Gerhard (Barcelona, 1951).
(ii) *Books and Articles*
CHASE, GILBERT: *The Music of Spain*, 2nd ed. (New York, 1959).
COTARELO Y MORI, EMILIO: *Historia de la Zarzuela o sea El drama lírico en España, desde su origen a fines del siglo XIX* (Madrid, 1934).
——*Orígenes y establecimento de la ópera en España hasta 1800* (Madrid, 1917).
HAMILTON, MARY N.: *Music in Eighteenth Century Spain* (Urbana, 1937).
RUIZ CASAUX Y L. DE CARVAJAL, JUAN A.: *La música en la corte de Don Carlos IV y su influencia en la vida musical española* (Madrid, 1959).
SUBIRÁ, JOSÉ: *Historia de la música española e hispano-americana* (Barcelona, 1953).
—— *Historia de la música teatral en España* (Barcelona, 1945).
—— 'Les Influences françaises dans la tonadilla madrilène du XVIII siècle', *Mélanges de Musicologie offerts à M. Lionel de La Laurencie* (Paris, 1933), pp. 209–16.
—— 'Un manuscrito musical de principios del siglo XVIII: Contribución a la música teatral española', *Anuario musical*, iv (1949), pp. 181–91.
—— 'Le style dans la musique théâtrale espagnole', *Acta Musicologica*, iv (1932), pp. 67–75.
—— *Los maestros de la tonadilla escénica* (Barcelona, 1933).
—— *La tonadilla escénica*, 3 vols. (Madrid, 1928–30).

CHAPTER IV
CHURCH MUSIC

(i) *Modern Editions*
(a) *Anthology*
ROSENTHAL, KARL A. and SCHNEIDER, C., edd.: *Salzburger Kirchenkomponisten* (*Denkmäler der Tonkunst in Österreich*, Jg. 43/1, vol. 80) (Vienna, 1936). Includes works by Adlgasser and Eberlin.
(b) *Works of Individual Composers*
ALBRECHTSBERGER, J. G.: Mass in E flat major: Missa Sancti Josephi, ed. A. Weissenbäck (*Österreichische Kirchenmusik*, 8) (Vienna, 1951).
—— Mass in F major, ed. L. Dité (*Österreichische Kirchenmusik*, 1) (Vienna, 1946).
BACH, C. P. E.: *Die Israeliten in der Wüste*, vocal score ed. F. Steffin (Wiesbaden, 1955).
—— Magnificat, full score ed. G. Graulich (Neuhausen–Stuttgart, 1971); vocal score, ed. C. Deis (New York, 1950) and G. Graulich (Neuhausen–Stuttgart, 1969).
BACH, J. C.: Magnificat in C major, vocal score ed. F. van Amelsvoort (Hilversum, 1960).
BACH, J. C. F.: *Ausgewählte Werke*, ed. G. Schünemann, vol. 1, nos. 1 and 2, *Motetten für vierstimmigen a-cappella-Chor* (Bückeburg, 1921).

—— *Die Kindheit Jesu* and *Die Auferweckung Lazarus*, ed. G. Schünemann (*Denkmäler deutscher Tonkunst*, 56) (Leipzig, 1917).

BACH, JOHANN ERNST: *Passionsoratorium*, ed. J. Kromolicki (*Denkmäler deutscher Tonkunst*, 48) (Leipzig, 1914).

EBERLIN, J. E.: *Das blutschwitzende Jesus* and excerpts from other oratorios, ed. R. Haas (*Denkmäler der Tonkunst in Österreich*, Jg. 28/1, vol. 55) (Vienna, 1921).

GALUPPI, B.: Mass in C major, ed. H. Bäuerle (Leipzig, 1957).

GASSMANN, F. L.: *Kirchenwerke*, ed. F. Kosch (*Denkmäler der Tonkunst in Österreich*, Jg. 45, vol. 83) (Vienna, 1938).

HASSE, J. A.: *La Conversione di Sant' Agostino*, ed. A. Schering (*Denkmäler deutscher Tonkunst*, 20) (Leipzig, 1905).

HAYDN, JOSEPH: *Werke*, ed. E. Mandyczewski *et al.*, series 16, vol. 5, *Die Schöpfung*; vol. 6/7, *Die Jahreszeiten* (Leipzig, 1923–5).

—— *Kritische Gesamtausgabe*, general editor J. P. Larsen, series 23, vol. 1, Masses 1–4 (Boston, 1951).

—— *Werke*, ed. Joseph Haydn-Institut, Cologne, series 4, *Verschiedene Orchesterwerke: Die sieben letzten Worte*; series 23, *Messen*; series 28, *Oratorien* (Munich, 1958–).

HAYDN, MICHAEL: *Michael Haydn Choral Series*, ed. G. Pauly (New York, 1958 ff.).

—— *Kirchenwerke*, ed. A. M. Klafsky (*Denkmäler der Tonkunst in Österreich*, Jg. 32/1, vol. 62) (Vienna, 1925).

—— *Messen*, ed. A. M. Klafsky (*Denkmäler der Tonkunst in Österreich*, Jg. 22, vol. 45) (Vienna, 1915).

—— *Deutsche Messe*, ed. J. Haas (Mainz, 1961).

—— *Missa Sti. Aloysii*, ed. W. Reinhart (Leipzig, 1942).

—— *Missa Sanctae Crucis*, ed. E. Tittel (*Österreichische Kirchenmusik*, 7) (Vienna, 1949).

—— *Missa sub titulo Sti. Leopoldi in festo Innocentium*, ed. W. Reinhart (Zürich, 1952).

—— *Requiem solemne*, vocal score ed. O. Peter (Wiesbaden, 1962).

—— Te Deum in C major (1770), ed. R. G. Pauly (*Collegium Musicum, Yale University*, 3) (New Haven, Conn., 1961).

—— Te Deum in D major, vocal score ed. L. Dité (*Österreichische Kirchenmusik*, 2) (Vienna, 1946).

MOZART, L.: *Ausgewählte Werke*, ed. M. Seiffert (*Denkmäler der Tonkunst in Bayern*, 9/2) (Leipzig, 1909).

—— Mass in C major, vocal score ed. D. Townsend (New York, 1963).

MOZART, W. A.: *Werke*, ed. J. Brahms *et al.*, series 1, *Messen*; series 2, *Litanien und Vespern*; series 3, *Kleinere geistliche Gesangswerke mit Begleitung des Orchesters*; series 4, *Kantaten und Oratorien*; series 24, *Supplement* (Leipzig, 1877–85).

—— *Neue Ausgabe sämtlicher Werke*, ed. Internationale Stiftung Mozarteum, series 1, *Geistliche Gesangswerke* (Kassel, 1958–).

REUTTER, J. G. the younger: *Kirchenwerke*, ed. N. Hofer (*Denkmäler der Tonkunst in Österreich*, vol. 88) (Vienna, 1952).

SCARLATTI, A.: *Messa di Santa Cecilia*, ed. J. Steele (London, 1968).

TELEMANN, G. P.: *Der Tag des Gerichts* and *Ino*, ed. M. Schneider (*Denkmäler deutscher Tonkunst*, 28) (Leipzig, 1907).

(ii) *Books and Articles*
(a) *General*

ADLER, GUIDO: 'Zur Geschichte der Wiener Messkomposition in der zweiten Hälfte des XVII. Jahrhunderts', *Studien zur Musikwissenschaft*, iv (1916), pp. 5–45.

BLUME, FRIEDRICH: *Die evangelische Kirchenmusik* (Potsdam, 1931). 2nd ed., *Geschichte der evangelischen Kirchenmusik* (Kassel, 1965).

FELLERER, KARL G.: 'Die vokale Kirchenmusik des 17./18. Jahrhunderts und die altklassische Polyphonie', *Zeitschrift für Musikwissenschaft*, xi (1928/9), pp. 354–64.
FELLOWES, EDMUND H.: *English Cathedral Music*, 5th ed., revised by J. A. Westrup (London, 1969).
FUX, JOHANN J.: *Gradus ad Parnassum* (Vienna, 1725). Facsimile edn., ed. Alfred Mann, *Sämtliche Werke*, vii/1 (Kassel, 1967). English translation by Alfred Mann (London, 1944).
HANSELL, SVEN H.: 'Sacred Music at the *Incurabili* in Venice at the Time of J. A. Hasse', *Journal of the American Musicological Society*, xxiii (1970), pp. 282–301, 505–21.
OREL, ALFRED: 'Die katholische Kirchenmusik seit 1750', *Handbuch der Musikgeschichte*, ed. G. Adler, ii, pp. 833–63.
PAULY, REINHARD G.: 'The Reforms of Church Music under Joseph II', *Musical Quarterly*, xliii (1957), pp. 372–82.
SCHERING, ARNOLD: *Geschichte des Oratoriums* (Leipzig, 1911; reprinted Hildesheim, 1966).
SCHNERICH, ALFRED: *Messe und Requiem seit Haydn und Mozart* (Vienna, 1909).
SCHNOOR, HANS: 'Das Oratorium im 18. Jahrhunderts', *Handbuch der Musikgeschichte*, ed. G. Adler, ii, pp. 704–18.
URSPRUNG, OTTO: *Die katholische Kirchenmusik* (Potsdam, 1931).

(b) *Individual Composers*

Adlgasser
KELLER, P. SIGISMUND: 'Biographische Mittheilungen über Anton Cajetan Adlgasser', *Monatshefte für Musik-Geschichte*, v (1873), pp. 41–5.
SCHNEIDER, CONSTANTIN: 'Die Oratorien und Schuldramen Anton Cajetan Adlgassers', *Studien zur Musikwissenschaft*, xviii (1931), pp. 36–65.

Albrechtsberger
WEISSENBÄCK, ANDREAS: 'Johann Georg Albrechtsberger als Kirchenkomponist', *Studien zur Musikwissenschaft*, xiv (1927), pp. 143–59.

Bonno
SCHIENERL, ALFRED: 'Giuseppe Bonnos Kirchenkompositionen', *Studien zur Musikwissenschaft*, xv (1928), pp. 62–85.

Eberlin
HAAS, ROBERT: 'Eberlins Schuldramen und Oratorien', *Studien zur Musikwissenschaft*, viii (1921), pp. 9–44.
PAULY, REINHARD G.: 'Johann Ernst Eberlin's Concerted Liturgical Music', *Musik und Geschichte* (*Leo Schrade zum sechzigsten Geburtstag*) (Cologne, 1963), pp. 146–77.
—— 'Johann Ernst Eberlin's Motets for Lent', *Journal of the American Musicological Society*, xv (1962), pp. 182–92.

Gassmann
KOSCH, FRANZ: 'Florian Leopold Gassmann als Kirchenkomponist', *Studien zur Musikwissenschaft*, xiv (1927), pp. 213–40.

Hasse
KAMIEŃSKI, LUCJAN: *Die Oratorien von Johann Adolf Hasse* (Leipzig, 1912).
MÜLLER, WALTHER: *Johann Adolf Hasse als Kirchenkomponist* (Leipzig, 1911).

Joseph Haydn
BRAND, CARL M.: *Die Messen von Joseph Haydn*, Berlin Dissertation, 1939 (Würzburg, 1941).
FRIEDLÄNDER, MAX: 'Van Swieten und das Textbuch zu Haydns Jahreszeiten', *Jahrbuch der Musikbibliothek Peters*, xvi (1909), pp. 47–56.

GEIRINGER, KARL: 'Haydn's Sketches for "The Creation"', *Musical Quarterly*, xviii (1932), pp. 299–308.
GOTWALS, VERNON: 'Haydn's *Creation* Revisited: An Introductory Essay', *Studies in Music History: Essays for Oliver Strunk*, ed. H. Powers (Princeton, 1968), pp. 429–42.
MCCALDIN, DENIS: 'Haydn's first and last Work—the *Missa Brevis* in F major', *Music Review*, xxviii (1967), pp. 165–72.
OLLESON, EDWARD: 'Georg August Griesinger's Correspondence with Breitkopf and Härtel', *Haydn Yearbook*, iii (1965), pp. 5–53.
—— 'The Origin and Libretto of Haydn's "Creation"', *Haydn Yearbook*, iv (1968), pp. 148–68.
RIEDEL-MARTINY, ANKE: 'Das Verhältnis von Text und Musik in Haydns Oratorien', *Haydn-Studien*, i/4 (1967), pp. 205–40.
SCHENK, ERICH: 'Ist die Göttweiger Rorate-Messe ein Werk Joseph Haydns?', *Studien zur Musikwissenschaft*, xxiv (1960), pp. 87–105.
SCHMID, ERNST F.: 'Haydns Oratorium "Il ritorno di Tobia", seine Entstehung und seine Schicksale', *Archiv für Musikwissenschaft*, xvi (1959), pp. 292–313.
—— 'Joseph Haydn und die vocale Zierpraxis seiner Zeit, dargestellt an einer Arie seines Tobias-Oratoriums', *Bericht über die internationale Konferenz zum Andenken Joseph Haydns*, ed. B. Szabolcsi and D. Bartha (Budapest, 1961), pp. 117–29.

Michael Haydn
KLAFSKY, ANTON M.: 'Michael Haydn als Kirchenkomponist', *Studien zur Musikwissenschaft*, iii (1915), pp. 5–23.
PAULY, REINHARD G.: 'Some recently discovered Michael Haydn Manuscripts', *Journal of the American Musicological Society*, x (1957), pp. 97–103.
PFANNHAUSER, KARL: 'J. Michael Haydn und seine "Missa Sanctae Crucis"', *Chigiana*, xxiv (new series, iv) (1967), pp. 203–8.

W. A. Mozart
BAYER, FRIEDRICH: 'Über den Gebrauch der Instrumente in den Kirchen- und Instrumentalwerken von Wolfgang Amadeus Mozart', *Studien zur Musikwissenschaft*, xiv (1927), pp. 33–74.
BLUME, FRIEDRICH: 'Requiem but no Peace', *Musical Quarterly*, xlvii (1961), pp. 147–69.
CROLL, GERHARD: 'Briefe zum Requiem', *Mozart-Jahrbuch 1967*, pp. 12–17.
EINSTEIN, ALFRED: 'Mozart's Kyrie, K. 90', *Musical Quarterly*, xxxvii (1951), pp. 1–4.
FEDERHOFER-KÖNIGS, RENATE: 'Mozarts "Lauretanische Litaneien" KV 109 (74e) und 195 (186d)', *Mozart-Jahrbuch 1967*, pp. 111–20.
FISCHER, WILHELM: 'Das "Lacrimosa dies illa" in Mozarts Requiem', *Mozart-Jahrbuch 1951*, pp. 9–21.
GEIRINGER, KARL: 'The Church Music', *The Mozart Companion*, ed. H. C. Robbins Landon and Donald Mitchell (London, 1956), pp. 361–76.
HESS, ERNST: 'Zur Ergänzung des Requiems von Mozart durch F. X. Süssmayr', *Mozart-Jahrbuch 1959*, pp. 99–108.
KURTHEN, WILHELM: 'Studien zu W. A. Mozarts kirchenmusikalischen Jugendwerken', *Zeitschrift für Musikwissenschaft*, iii (1920/21), pp. 194–222.
LEWICKI, ERNST: 'Über Mozarts grosse C-moll-Messe und die Endgestalt ihrer Ergänzung', *Mozart-Jahrbuch*, i (1923), pp. 69–93.
—— 'Die Vervollständigung von Mozarts grosser C-Moll Messe durch Alois Schmitt', *Die Musik*, v/2 (1905/6), pp. 3–12, 168–75.
MARGUERRE, K.: 'Mozart and Süssmayr', *Mozart-Jahrbuch 1962/63*, pp. 172–7.
PFANNHAUSER, KARL: 'Zu Mozarts Kirchenwerken von 1768', *Mozart-Jahrbuch 1954*, pp. 150–68.

PLATH, WOLFGANG: 'Über Skizzen zu Mozarts "Requiem"', *Bericht über der internationalen musikwissenschaftlichen Kongress, Kassel, 1962*, ed. G. Reichert and M. Just (Kassel, 1963), pp. 184–7.
REICHERT, GEORG: 'Mozarts "Credo Messen" und ihre Vorläufer', *Mozart-Jahrbuch 1955*, pp. 117–44.
ROSENTHAL, KARL A.: 'Mozart's Sacramental Litanies and their Forerunners', *Musical Quarterly*, xxvii (1941), pp. 433–55.

Reutter
STOLLBROCK, L.: 'Leben und Wirken des K. K. Hofkapellmeisters und Hofkompositors Johann Georg Reutter jun.', *Vierteljahrsschrift für Musikwissenschaft*, viii (1892), pp. 161–203, 289–306.

Salieri
NÜTZLADER, RUDOLF: 'Salieri als Kirchenmusiker', *Studien zur Musikwissenschaft*, xiv (1927), pp. 160–78.

CHAPTER V
SOLO SONG

(i) *Modern Editions*
(a) *Anthologies*

ANSION, MARGARETE and SCHLAFFENBERG, IRENE, edd.: *Das Wiener Lied von 1778 bis Mozarts Tod* (*Denkmäler der Tonkunst in Österreich*, Jg. 27/2, vol. 54) (Vienna, 1920).
FRIEDLAENDER, MAX: *Das deutsche Lied im 18. Jahrhundert*, 2 vols. (Stuttgart, 1902; reprinted Hildesheim, 1962).
MOSER, HANS JOACHIM ed.: *Das deutsche Sololied und die Ballade* (*Das Musikwerk*, 14) (Cologne, 1957. English edition, 1958).
NOSKE, FRITS, ed.: *Das ausserdeutsche Sololied* (*Das Musikwerk*, 16) (Cologne, 1958. English edition, 1958).
POTTER, FRANK H., ed.: *Reliquary of English Song*, vol. 2, 1700–1800 (New York, 1916).
REIMANN, HEINRICH, ed.: *Das deutsche Lied*, 4 vols. (Berlin, 1892–3).

(b) *Works of Individual Composers*

ARNE, T. A.: 6 Songs, ed. G. E. P. Arkwright (*The Old English Edition*, 2) (London, 1890).
BACH, C. P. E.: Song selections ed. J. Dittberner (Leipzig, 1918), H. Roth (Leipzig, 1922) and O. Vrieslander (Munich, 1922).
HAYDN, F. J.: *Werke*, ed. E. Mandyczewski *et al.*, series 20, vol. 1, *Einstimmige Lieder und Gesänge* (Leipzig, 1933).
—— *Werke*, ed. Joseph Haydn-Institut, Cologne, series 29, *Einstimmige Lieder*; series 32, *Bearbeitungen von Volksliedern* (Munich, 1960–00).
MOZART, W. A.: *Werke*, ed. J. Brahms *et al.*, series 6, *Arien, Duette, Terzette und Quartette mit Begleitung des Orchesters*; series 7, part 1, *Ein- und mehrstimmige Lieder mit Klavierbegleitung*; series 24, *Supplement* (Leipzig, 1877–96).
—— *Neue Ausgabe sämtlicher Werke*, ed. Internationale Stiftung Mozarteum, series 3, *Lieder, mehrstimmige Gesänge, Kanons* (Kassel, 1963).
REICHARDT, J. F.: *Goethes Lieder, Oden, Balladen und Romanzen mit Musik*, ed. W. Salmen, 2 vols. (*Das Erbe deutscher Musik*, 58–9) (Munich, 1964–70).
SCHULZ, J. A. P.: Song selections, ed. B. Engelke (Leipzig, 1909), and F. Jöde (Wolfenbüttel, 1925).

(ii) *Books and Articles*
(a) *General*

FRIEDLAENDER, MAX: *Das deutsche Lied im 18. Jahrhundert*, 2 vols. (Stuttgart, 1902; reprinted Hildesheim, 1962).
JOHNSTONE, H. DIACK: 'English Solo Song, c. 1710–1760', *Proceedings of the Royal Musical Association*, xcv (1968/9), pp. 67–80.
KIDSON, FRANK: 'The Nurseries of English Song', *Musical Times*, lxiii (1922), pp. 394–5, 620–2.
—— 'Some Illustrated Music-Books of the Seventeenth and Eighteenth Centuries: English', *Musical Antiquary*, iii (1911/12), pp. 195–208.
KRABBE, WILHELM: 'Das deutsche Lied im 17. und 18. Jahrhundert', in *Handbuch der Musikgeschichte*, ed. G. Adler, vol. 2, pp. 691–703.
KRETZSCHMAR, HERMANN: *Geschichte der neuen deutschen Liedes. I Teil: Von Albert bis Zelter* (Leipzig, 1911).
MASSON, PAUL-MARIE: 'Les "Brunettes"', *Sammelbände der internationalen Musikgesellschaft*, xii (1910/11), pp. 347–68.
MÜLLER, GÜNTHER: *Geschichte des deutschen Liedes vom Zeitalter des Barock bis zur Gegenwart* (Munich, 1925).
POLLAK-SCHLAFFENBERG, IRENE: 'Die Wiener Liedmusik von 1778–1789', *Studien zur Musikwissenschaft*, v (1918), pp. 97–151.
SANDS, MOLLIE: *Invitation to Ranelagh* (London, 1946).
SEYFERT, BERNHARD: 'Das musikalisch-volksthümliche Lied von 1770–1800', *Vierteljahrsschrift für Musikwissenschaft*, x (1894), pp. 33–102.
SOUTHGATE, THOMAS L.: 'Music at the Public Pleasure Gardens of the Eighteenth Century', *Proceedings of the Musical Association*, xxxviii (1911/12), pp. 141–59.
STEVENS, DENIS, ed.: *A History of Song* (London, 1960).
WROTH, WARWICK: *The London Pleasure Gardens of the Eighteenth Century* (London, 1896).

(b) *Individual Composers*

André
PRETZSCH, OTTO: *Johann André und seine Stellung in der Berliner Liederschule*. (Leipzig Dissertation, 1925).

T. A. Arne
HERBAGE, JULIAN: 'The Vocal Style of Thomas Augustine Arne', *Proceedings of the Royal Musical Association*, lxxviii (1951/2), pp. 83–96.

C. P. E. Bach
BUSCH, GUDRUN: *C.P.E. Bach und seine Lieder*, 2 vols. (Regensburg, 1957).
WIEN-CLAUDI, HERTHA: *Zum Liedschaffen Carl Philipp Emanuel Bachs*. Prague Dissertation, 1926 (Reichenberg, 1928).

Haydn
EBERS, GERTRAUD: *Das Lied bei Haydn*. (Innsbruck Dissertation, 1943).
GEIRINGER, KARL: 'Haydn and the Folksong of the British Isles', *Musical Quarterly*, xxxv (1949), pp. 179–208.
SCOTT, MARION M.: 'Some English Affinities and Associations of Haydn's Songs', *Music and Letters*, xxv (1944), pp. 1–12.
STUBER, ROBERT: *Die Klavierbegleitung im Liede von Haydn, Mozart und Beethoven. Eine Stilstudie*. (Bern Dissertation, 1958).

Laruette
LETAILLEUR, PAULETTE: 'Jean-Louis Laruette, chanteur et compositeur', *Recherches sur la Musique française classique*, viii (1968), pp. 161–89; ix (1969), pp. 145–61; x (1970), pp. 57–86.

W. A. Mozart
HAMBURGER, PAUL: 'The Concert Arias', *The Mozart Companion*, ed. H. C. Robbins Landon and Donald Mitchell (London, 1956), pp. 324-60.

STUBER, ROBERT: *Die Klavierbegleitung im Liede von Haydn, Mozart und Beethoven. Eine Stilstudie.* (Bern Dissertation, 1958).

Reichardt
PAULI, W.: *J. F. Reichardt, sein Leben und seine Stellung in der Geschichte des deutschen Liedes* (Berlin, 1903).

Schulz
KLUNGER, CARL J.: *J. A. P. Schulz in seinen volkstümlichen Liedern.* (Leipzig Dissertation, 1909).

RIESS, OTTO: 'Johann Abraham Peter Schulz' Leben', *Sammelbände der internationalen Musikgesellschaft*, xv (1913/14), pp. 169-270.

CHAPTER VI
THE EARLY SYMPHONY

(i) *Modern Editions*
(a) *Anthologies*

BROOK, BARRY S.: *La symphonie française dans la seconde moitié du XVIIIe siècle*, iii (Paris, 1962).

HOFFMANN-ERBRECHT, LOTHAR, ed.: *Die Sinfonie* (*Das Musikwerk*, 29) (Cologne, 1967. English edition, 1967). Includes excerpts from works by Joseph Haydn, W. A. Mozart, G. B. Sammartini, and J. Stamitz.

HORWITZ, KARL and RIEDEL, KARL, edd.: *Wiener Instrumentalmusik vor und um 1750*, 2 vols. (*Denkmäler der Tonkunst in Österreich*, Jg. 15/2, vol. 31 and Jg. 19/2, vol. 39) (Vienna, 1908-12). Includes works by G. M. Monn, G. Reutter the younger, and G. C. Wagenseil.

RIEMANN, HUGO, ed.: *Sinfonien der pfalzbayerischen Schule* (*Denkmäler der Tonkunst in Bayern*, 3/1, 7/2, 8/2), (Leipzig, 1902-8). 24 symphonies were reprinted as *Mannheim Symphonists*, 2 vols. (New York, 1956), Contains works by F. Beck, C. Cannabich, E. Eichner, A. Filtz, I. Holzbauer, F. X. Richter, C. Stamitz, J. Stamitz, and C. J. Toeschi.

SENN, WALTER, ed.: *Tiroler Instrumentalmusik im 18. Jahrhundert* (*Denkmäler der Tonkunst in Österreich*, vol. 86) (Vienna, 1949). Includes works by F. S. Haindl, N. Madlseder, and J. E. de Sylva.

(b) *Works by Individual Composers*

ABEL, C. F.: *Kompositionen*, ed. W. Knape, vols. 1-8 (Cuxhaven, 1960-9).

ALBRECHTSBERGER, J. G.: *Instrumentalwerke*, ed. O. Kapp (*Denkmäler der Tonkunst in Österreich*, Jg. 16/2, vol. 33) (Vienna, 1909).

BACH, C. P. E.: Symphony in C major, Wq. 174, ed. F. Oberdörffer (*Gradus ad Symphoniam, Unterstufe*, 10) (Berlin, 1963).

—— Symphony in G major, Wq. 182 no. 1, ed. H. Riemann (Langensalza, 1897).

—— Symphony in B flat major, Wq. 182 no. 2, ed. E. F. Schmid (*Nagels Musik-Archiv*, 96) (Kassel, 1933).

—— Symphony in C major, Wq. 182 no. 3, ed. E. F. Schmid (*Nagels Musik-Archiv*, 73) (Kassel, 1931).

—— Symphony in A major, Wq. 182 no. 4, ed. E. Suchalla (Wiesbaden, 1965).

—— Symphony in B minor, Wq. 182 no. 5, ed. E. F. Schmid (*Nagels Musik-Archiv*, 130) (Kassel, 1937).

—— 4 Symphonies, Wq. 183, ed. R. Steglich (*Das Erbe deutscher Musik*, 18) (Leipzig, 1942).

BIBLIOGRAPHY

BACH, J. C.: 5 Symphonies, ed. F. Stein (*Das Erbe deutscher Musik*, 30) (Wiesbaden, 1956).
—— Symphony in B flat major, Op. 3 no. 4, ed. F. Kneusslin (Basle, 1953).
—— Symphony in E flat major, Op. 9 no. 2, ed. F. Stein (London, 1950).
—— Symphony in E flat major for double orchestra, Op. 18 no. 1, ed. F. Stein (Leipzig, 1932).
—— Symphony in B flat major, Op. 18 no. 2, ed. F. Stein (Leipzig, 1925).
—— Symphony in D major for double orchestra, Op. 18 no. 3, ed. F. Stein (Leipzig, 1930).
—— Symphony in D major, Op. 18 no. 4, ed. A. Einstein (London, 1949).
BACH, J. C. F.: 3 Symphonies, ed. F. Engel (*Schaumberger Faksimiledrucke*, 2) (Bückeburg, 1966).
BECK, F.: Symphony in D minor, ed. H. C. Robbins Landon (*Nagels Musik-Archiv*, 193) (Kassel, 1959).
BACH, W. F.: Symphony in D major, ed. W. Lebermann (Mainz, 1970).
BENDA, F.: Symphony, ed. H. Förster (Leipzig, 1961).
BENDA, G.: Symphonies, ed. J. Pohanka [later J. Sehnal] (*Musica Antiqua Bohemica*, 58, 62, 66, and 68) (Prague, 1962-6).
—— Symphony in F major, ed. M. Schneider (*Mittel-und Nord-deutsche Kammersinfonien*, 7) (Leipzig, 1954).
BOCCHERINI, L.: Symphony in D minor, Op. 12 no. 4, ed. P. Carmirelli (Milan, 1963).
—— Symphony in B flat major, Op. 21 no. 1, ed. W. Höckner (Frankfurt, 1957).
—— Symphony in E flat major, Op. 35 no. 4, ed. G. Guerrini (Milan, 1958); ed. N. Jenkins (New York, 1967).
—— Symphony in B flat major, Op. 35 no. 6, ed. E. Bonelli (Padua, 1957).
—— Symphonies, Op. 37 no. 3 in D minor and Op. 21 no. 3 in C major, ed. P. Carmirelli (*I classici italiani della musica*, 4) (Rome, 1962).
—— Symphony in A major, Op. 37 no. 4, ed. K. Geiringer (Vienna, 1937).
—— Symphony in D major (1767), ed. W. Lebermann (Mainz, 1968).
BOYCE, W.: *Overtures*, ed. G. Finzi (*Musica Britannica*, 13) (London, 1957).
—— Eight Symphonies, ed. M. Goberman (*Diletto Musicale*, 150-7) (Vienna, 1964).
BRUNETTI, G.: *Il Maniático* Symphony, no. 33, and Symphony in C minor, no. 22, ed. N. Jenkins (*I classici italiani della musica*, 3) (Rome, 1960).
—— Symphony no. 23 in F major, ed. N. Jenkins (New York, 1966).
CIMAROSA, D.: Symphony in D major, ed. U. Rapalo (Padua, 1966).
DITTERSDORF, C. DITTERS VON: *Ausgewählte Orchesterwerke*, ed. J. Liebeskind, 11 parts (Leipzig, 1899-1904).
—— Three Symphonies and a Serenata, ed. V. Luithlen (*Denkmäler der Tonkunst in Österreich*, Jg. 43/2, vol. 81) (Vienna, 1936).
—— Symphony in D major, ed. W. Lebermann (Mainz, 1970).
FILTZ, A.: 6 Symphonies, Op. 2, ed. J. Pohanka (*Musica Antiqua Bohemica*, 44) (Prague, 1960).
GALUPPI, B.: Symphony in D major, ed. E. Bonelli (Padua, 1956).
GASSMANN, F. L.: *Issipile*. Overture, ed. H. C. Robbins Landon (*Diletto Musicale*, 28) (Vienna, 1966).
—— Symphony in B minor, ed. K. Geiringer (Vienna, 1933).
HAYDN, JOSEPH: *Kritische Gesamtausgabe*, general editor J. P. Larsen, series 1, vols. 5, 9, and 10, *Symphonien* 50-7, 82-92 (Boston, 1950-1).
——*Werke*, ed. Joseph Haydn-Institut, Cologne, series 1, *Symphonien* (Munich, 1963–).
—— Symphonies, ed. H. C. Robbins Landon, miniature scores, 12 vols. (Vienna, 1963-8).
HAYDN, MICHAEL: *Instrumentalwerke I*, ed. L. H. Perger (*Denkmäler der Tonkunst in Österreich*, Jg. 14/2, vol. 29) (Vienna, 1907). Includes a thematic catalogue of his instrumental music.

—— Symphony in D minor (Perger, 20) ed. J. Vécsey (Budapest, 1960).
—— Symphony in D major (Perger, 42) ed. H. C. Robbins Landon (*Diletto Musicale*, 20) (Vienna, 1962). All the symphonies are planned for publication in this series, edited by C. Sherman and others. Thirteen have appeared up to 1971.
HOLZBAUER, I.: Symphony in D major, ed. F. Schroeder (*Diletto Musicale*, 166) (Vienna, 1968).
—— Symphony in E major, ed. E. Rabsch (Hamburg, 1960).
KRAUS, J. M.: Symphony in C minor, ed. R. Englander (*Monumenta Musicae Svecicae*, 2) (Stockholm, 1960).
LE DUC, S.: Symphony in D major, ed. F. Oubradous (Paris, 1957).
MOZART, LEOPOLD: *Ausgewählte Werke*, ed. M. Seiffert (*Denkmäler der Tonkunst in Bayern*, 9/2) (Leipzig, 1909).
—— Symphony in B flat major, ed. H. C. Robbins Landon (*Diletto Musicale*, 294) (Vienna, 1970).
—— Symphony in G major, ed. H. C. Robbins Landon (*Diletto Musicale*, 293) (Vienna, 1970).
MOZART, W. A.: *Werke*, ed. J. Brahms *et al.*, series 8, *Symphonien*; series 24, *Supplement* (Leipzig, 1879–88).
—— *Neue Ausgabe sämtlicher Werke*, ed. Internationale Stiftung Mozarteum, series 4, *Orchesterwerke*, group 11, *Symphonien* (Kassel, 1956–   ).
PAISIELLO, G.: *Il Barbiere di Siviglia*. Overture, ed. A. de Almeida (Paris, 1962).
PLEYEL, I.: Symphony in F major, ed. F. Oubradous (Paris, 1957).
REICHARDT, J. F.: Symphony in F major, ed. G. Ochs (Leipzig, 1939).
ROSETTI, F. A.: *Ausgewählte Sinfonien*, ed. O. Kaul (*Denkmäler der Tonkunst in Bayern*, 12/1) (Leipzig, 1912).
SACCHINI, A.: *Oedipe à Colonne*. Overture, ed. A. de Almeida (Paris, 1961).
SAMMARTINI, G. B.: *The Symphonies of G. B. Sammartini. Volume 1. The Early Symphonies*, ed. B. Churgin (*Harvard Publications in Music*, 2) (Cambridge, Mass., 1968).
—— Symphony in C major, ed. E. Bonelli (Padua, 1956).
—— Symphony in F major, ed. N. Jenkins (Frankfurt, 1953).
—— Symphony in G major, ed. F. Torrefranca (Milan, 1931).
—— Symphony in G major, ed. N. Jenkins (London, 1956).
STAMITZ, J.: Symphonies in A, G and B flat major, ed. A. Hoffmann (Wolfenbüttel, 1957).
—— Sinfonia Pastorale in D major, Op. 4 no. 2, ed. W. Upmeyer (Berlin, 1931).
TARTINI, G.: Symphony in A major, ed. H. Erdmann (*Hortus Musicus*, 53) (Kassel, 1950).
—— Symphony in D major, ed. H. Erdmann (Mainz, 1956).
VAŇHAL, J. B.: Symphony in A minor, ed. F. Kneusslin (Zürich, 1947).
—— Symphony in G minor, ed. H. C. Robbins Landon (*Diletto Musicale*, 38) (Vienna, 1966); ed. W. Hoffmann (Frankfurt, 1966).
WAGENSEIL, G. C.: Symphony in G major, no. 2. Facsimile of a manuscript (Munich, 1954).

(ii) *Books and Articles*
(a) *General*

ABRAHAM, GERALD: 'Some Eighteenth-Century Polish Symphonies', *Studies in Eighteenth-Century Music. A Tribute to Karl Geiringer on his Seventieth Birthday*, ed. H. C. Robbins Landon (London, 1970), pp. 13–22.
BARBOUR, J. MURRAY: *Trumpets, Horns and Music* (East Lancing, Mich., 1964).
BOSTIBER, HUGO: *Geschichte der Ouvertüre und der freien Orchesterformen* (Leipzig, 1913; reprinted Wiesbaden, 1969).
BRENET, MICHEL: *Les concerts en France sous l'ancien régime* (Paris, 1900).

BROOK, BARRY S.: *La symphonie française dans la seconde moitié du XVIIIe siècle*, 3 vols. (Paris, 1962).
BURTON, HUMPHREY: 'Les Académies de musique en France au XVIIIe siècle', *Revue de musicologie*, xxxvii (1955), pp. 122–47.
CAMPARDON, EMILE: *L'Académie royale de musique au XVIIIe siècle*, 2 vols. (Paris, 1884).
CARSE, ADAM: 'Early Classical Symphonies', *Proceedings of the Musical Association*, lxii (1935/36), pp. 39–55.
—— *18th Century Symphonies* (London, 1951).
—— *The History of Orchestration* (London, 1925; reprinted 1964).
—— *The Orchestra in the XVIIIth Century* (Cambridge, 1940).
CROLL, GERHARD: 'Zur Vorgeschichte der "Mannheimer"', *Bericht über den siebenten internationalen musikwissenschaftlichen Kongress Köln 1958* (Kassel, 1959), pp. 82–3.
CUCUEL, GEORGES: *Études sur un orchestre au XVIIIe siècle* (Paris, 1913).
—— 'La question des clarinettes dans l'instrumentation du XVIIIe siècle', *Zeitschrift der internationalen Musikgesellschaft*, xii (1910/11), pp. 280–4.
CUDWORTH, CHARLES L.: 'The English Symphonists of the Eighteenth Century', *Proceedings of the Royal Musical Association*, lxxviii (1951/52), pp. 31–51. Also *Thematic Index of English Eighteenth-Century Overtures and Symphonies* (London, 1953).
ENGLÄNDER, RICHARD: *Die Dresdner Instrumentalmusik in der Zeit der Wiener Klassik* (Upsala, 1956).
—— 'Dresdner Musikleben und Dresdner Instrumentalpflege in der Zeit zwischen Hasse und Weber', *Zeitschrift für Musikwissenschaft*, xiv (1931/32), pp. 410–20.
—— 'Zur Dresdner Instrumentalmusik in der Zeit der Wiener Klassik', *Zeitschrift für Musikwissenschaft*, xiii (1930/31), pp. 2–10.
FLUELER, MAX: *Die norddeutsche Sinfonie zur Zeit Friedrichs d. Gr. und besonders die Werke Ph. Em. Bachs* (Berlin, 1908).
HELL, HELMUTH: *Die neapolitanische Opernsinfonie in der ersten Hälfte des 18. Jahrhunderts* (Tutzing, 1971).
HEUSS, ALFRED: 'Über die Dynamik der Mannheimer Schule', *Riemann Festschrift ... Hugo Riemann zum sechzigsten Geburtstage* (Leipzig, 1909), pp. 433–55.
—— 'Die Dynamik der Mannheimer Schule; II. Die Detail-Dynamik, nebst einer dynamischen Analyse von Mozarts Andante aus der Mannheimer Sonate (Köchel-V. Nr. 309)', *Zeitschrift für Musikwissenschaft*, ii (1919/20), pp. 44–54
HILL, RALPH, ed.: *The Symphony* (Harmondsworth, 1949).
KAMIEŃSKI, LUCJAN: 'Mannheim und Italien', *Sammelbände der internationalen Musikgesellschaft*, x (1908/9), pp. 307–17.
KLAUWELL, OTTO: *Geschichte der Programmusik von ihren Anfängen bis zur Gegenwart* (Leipzig, 1910).
LA LAURENCIE, LIONEL DE, and SAINT-FOIX, GEORGES DE: 'Contribution à l'histoire de la symphonie française vers 1750', *L'Année musicale*, i (1911), pp. 1–123.
LARSEN, JENS PETER: 'Zur Bedeutung der "Mannheimer Schule"', *Festschrift Karl Gustav Fellerer zum sechzigsten Geburtstag*, ed. H. Hüschen (Regensburg, 1962), pp. 303–9.
LA RUE, JAN: 'Major and Minor Mysteries of Identification in the 18th-Century Symphony', *Journal of the American Musicological Society*, xiii (1960), pp. 181–96.
MECKLENBURG, PETER: *Die Sinfonie der Mannheimer Schule*. (Munich Dissertation, 1963).
NEF, CARL: *Geschichte der Sinfonie und Suite* (Leipzig, 1921).
OPIEŃSKI, HENRYK: 'La symphonie polonaise au XVIIIe siècle', *Revue de musicologie*, xviii (1934), pp. 193–6.

PROD'HOMME, JACQUES G.: 'A French Maecenas of the Time of Louis XV: M. de la Pouplinière', *Musical Quarterly*, x (1924), pp. 511-31.
REESE, WILLIAM H.: *Grundsätze und Entwicklung der Instrumentation in der vorklassischen und klassischen Sinfonie*. Berlin Dissertation (Gräfenhainichen, 1939).
SONDHEIMER, ROBERT: 'Die formale Entwicklung der vorklassischen Sinfonie', *Archiv für Musikwissenschaft*, iv (1922), pp. 85-99.
―― *Die Theorie der Sinfonie und die Beurteilung einzelner Sinfoniekomponisten bei den Musikschriftstellern des 18. Jahrhunderts* (Leipzig, 1925). See also: 'A Bibliographical Index to Robert Sondheimer's *Die Theorie der Sinfonie*', edited by Gene Wolf and Jan LaRue, *Acta Musicologica*, xxxvii (1965), pp. 79-86.
VALLAS, LÉON: *La Musique à l'Académie de Lyon au dix-huitième siècle* (Lyon, 1908).
VINTON, JOHN: 'The Development Section in Early Viennese Symphonies: a Revaluation', *Music Review*, xxiv (1963), pp. 13-22.
WALIN, STIG: *Beiträge zur Geschichte der schwedischen Sinfonik*. Upsala Dissertation (Stockholm, 1941).
WĘCOWSKI, JAN: 'La musique symphonique polonaise du XVIIIe siècle', *Musica Antiqua Europae Orientalis*, ed. Zofia Lissa (Warsaw, 1966), pp. 334-53.

(b) *Individual Composers*

Abel
BEECHEY, GWILYM: 'Carl Friedrich Abel's Six Symphonies, Op. 14', *Music and Letters*, li (1970), pp. 279-85.

J. C. Bach
TUTENBERG, FRITZ: *Die Sinfonik Johann Christian Bachs* (Wolfenbüttel, 1928).
SCHÖKEL, HEINRICH P.: *Johann Christian Bach und die Instrumentalmusik seiner Zeit* (Wolfenbüttel, 1926).

Beck
SONDHEIMER, ROBERT: 'Die Sinfonien Franz Becks', *Zeitschrift für Musikwissenschaft*, iv (1921/22), pp. 323-51, 449-69. Also published separately (Leipzig, 1922).

Cannabich
HOFER, HEINRICH: *Christian Cannabich* (Munich Dissertation, 1921).

Eichner
REISSINGER, MARIANNE: *Die Sinfonien Ernst Eichners (1740-1777)* (Wiesbaden, 1970).

C. H. & J. G. Graun
MENNICKE, CARL H.: *Hasse und die Brüder Graun als Symphoniker* (Leipzig, 1906).

Hasse
MENNICKE, CARL H.: *Hasse und die Brüder Graun als Symphoniker* (Leipzig, 1906).

Joseph Haydn
GERLACH, SONJA: 'Die chronologische Ordnung von Haydns Sinfonien zwischen 1774 und 1782', *Haydn-Studien*, ii/1 (1969), pp. 34-66.
KRETZSCHMAR, HERMANN: 'Die Jugendsinfonien Joseph Haydns', *Jahrbuch der Musikbibliothek Peters*, xv (1908), pp. 68-90. Reprinted in *Gesammelte Aufsätze*, vol. 2 (Leipzig, 1911).
LANDON, H. C. ROBBINS: *The Symphonies of Joseph Haydn* (London, 1955); *Supplement to The Symphonies of Joseph Haydn* (London, 1961).
―― *Haydn Symphonies* (London, 1966).
LARSEN, JENS PETER: 'Probleme der chronologischen Ordnung von Haydns Sinfonien', *Festschrift Otto Erich Deutsch zum 80. Geburtstag*, ed. W. Gerstenberg et al. (Kassel, 1963), pp. 90-104.
MARCO, GUY A.: 'A Musical Task in the "Surprise" Symphony', *Journal of the American Musicological Society*, xi (1958), pp. 41-4.

THERSTAPPEN, H. J.: *Joseph Haydns sinfonisches Vermächtnis* (*Die Londoner Sinfonien*) (Wolfenbüttel, 1941).
WOLF, EUGENE K.: 'The Recapitulations in Haydn's London Symphonies', *Musical Quarterly*, lii (1966), pp. 71–89.
WORBS, HANS C.: *Die Sinfonik Haydns* (Tutzing, 1956).

Holzbauer
WERNER, HILDGARD: *Die Sinfonien von Ignaz Holzbauer* (Munich Dissertation, 1942).

Le Duc
BROOK, BARRY S.: 'Simon le Duc l'ainé, A French Symphonist at the Time of Mozart', *Musical Quarterly*, xlviii (1962), pp. 498–513.

Mahaut
NOBLE, RICHARD D. C.: 'Antonio Mahaut—Forgotten Dutch Flautist', *The Consort* xvii (1960), pp. 32–46.

Maldere
CLERCX, SUZANNE: *Pierre Van Maldere* (Brussels, 1948).

G. B. Martini
BROFSKY, HOWARD: 'The Symphonies of Padre Martini', *Musical Quarterly*, li (1965), pp. 649–73.

Molter
O'LOUGHLIN, NIALL: 'Johann Melchior Molter', *Musical Times*, cvii (1966), pp. 110–13.

W. A. Mozart
BRODER, NATHAN: 'The Wind-Instruments in Mozart's Symphonies', *Musical Quarterly*, xix (1933), pp. 238–59.
DAVID, JOHANN N.: *Die Jupiter-Symphonie* (Göttingen, 1953).
DICKINSON, ALAN E. F.: *A Study of Mozart's Last Three Symphonies* (London, 1927. 2nd ed., 1939).
ENGEL, HANS: 'Über Mozarts Jugendsinfonien', *Mozart-Jahrbuch 1951*, pp. 22–33.
LA LAURENCIE, LIONEL DE, and SAINT-FOIX, GEORGES DE: 'Die Symphonien' in *Mozart-Aspekte*, ed. P. Schaller and H. Kühner (Olten, 1956), pp. 39–62.
LARSEN, JENS PETER: 'The Symphonies', *The Mozart Companion*, ed. H. C. Robbins Landon and Donald Mitchell (London, 1956), pp. 156–99.
SAINT-FOIX, GEORGES DE: *Les symphonies de Mozart* (Paris, 1932). English translation (London, 1947).
SCHULTZ, DETLEF: *Mozarts Jugendsinfonien*. (Leipzig Dissertation, 1900).
THIEME, CARL H. W.: *Der Klangstil des Mozartorchesters*. Leipzig Dissertation, 1935 (Borna–Leipzig, 1936).

Pokorny
BARBOUR, J. MURRAY: 'Pokorny Vindicated', *Musical Quarterly*, xlix (1963), pp. 38–58.

Richter
GÄSSLER, WILLI: *Die Sinfonien von Franz Xaver Richter und ihre Stellung in der vorklassischen Sinfonik*. (Munich Dissertation, 1941).

Rigel
SONDHEIMER, ROBERT: 'Henri Joseph Rigel', *Music Review*, xvii (1956), pp. 221–8.

Roman
BENGTSSON, INGMAR: *J. H. Roman och hans instrumentalmusik. Käll- och stilkritiska studier* (Upsala, 1955).

G. B. Sammartini

BARBLAN, GUGLIELMO: 'Sanmartini e la scuola sinfonica milanese', *Accademia musicale chigiana: Ente autonomo per le settimane musicale senesi*, xv (1958), pp. 21–40.

SAINT-FOIX, GEORGES DE: 'La chronologie de l'oeuvre instrumentale de Jean Baptiste Sammartini', *Sammelbände der internationalen Musikgesellschaft*, xv (1913/14), pp. 308–24.

TORREFRANCA, FAUSTO: 'Le origini della sinfonia. Le sinfonie dell'imbrattacarte (G. B. Sanmartini)', *Rivista musicale italiana*, xx (1913), pp. 291–346; xxi (1914), pp. 97–121, 278–312; xxii (1915), pp. 431–46.

C. Stamitz

KAISER, FRITZ: *Karl Stamitz (1745–1801). Biographische Beiträge. Das symphonische Werk.* (Marburg Dissertation, 1962).

J. Stamitz

DÜRRENMATT, HANS-RUDOLF: *Die Durchführung bei Johann Stamitz (1717–1757)* (Bern, 1969).

GRADENWITZ, PETER: 'Die Steinmetz-Manuskripte der Landes- und Hochschulbibliothek Darmstadt', *Musikforschung*, xiv (1961), p. 214. [A postscript to Noack's article].

—— 'The Symphonies of Johann Stamitz', *Music Review*, i (1940), pp. 354–63.

NOACK, FRIEDRICH: 'Die Steinmetz-Manuskripte der Landes- und Hochschulbibliothek Darmstadt', *Musikforschung*, xiii (1960), pp. 314–17.

Toeschi

MÜNSTER, ROBERT: *Die Sinfonien Toeschis.* (Munich Dissertation, 1956).

CHAPTER VII
THE CONCERTO

(i) *Modern Editions*

(a) *Anthologies*

BECKER, HEINZ, ed.: *Klarinetten-Konzerte des 18. Jahrhunderts* (*Das Erbe deutscher Musik*, 41) (Wiesbaden, 1957). Contains works by Molter and Pokorny.

ENGEL, HANS.: *Das Solokonzert* (*Das Musikwerk*, 25) (Cologne, 1964. English edition 1964).

LEBERMANN, WALTER, ed.: *Flöten-Konzerte der Mannheimer Schule* (*Das Erbe deutscher Musik*, 51) (Wiesbaden, 1964). Contains works by Filtz, Richter, A. Stamitz, C. Stamitz, J. Stamitz, and C. J. Toeschi.

SCHERING, ARNOLD, ed.: *Instrumentalkonzerte deutscher Meister* (*Denkmäler deutscher Tonkunst*, 29/30) (Leipzig, 1907). Includes works by C. P. E. Bach and Hasse.

(b) *Works by Individual Composers*

ABEL, C. F.: *Kompositionen*, ed. W. Knape, vols. 9, 10, 10 supplement, (Cuxhaven, 1960–9).

—— Cello Concerto in B flat major, ed. H. Lomnitzer (Wolfenbüttel, 1961).

—— Flute Concerto in C major, ed. G. E. Peters (Wilhelmshaven, 1965).

ALBRECHTSBERGER, J. G.: Concertino and Notturno for oboe and strings, ed. L. Kalmár (Mainz, 1967).

—— Concerto for alto trombone and strings, ed. G. Darvas (Budapest, 1966).

—— Harp Concerto, ed. O. Nagy (Budapest, 1964).

—— Organ Concerto, ed. L. Somfai (Budapest, 1964).

BACH, C. P. E.: Harpsichord Concerto in G minor, Wq. 6, ed. F. Oberdörffer (Kassel, 1952).

BIBLIOGRAPHY

—— Harpsichord Concerto in D minor, Wq. 23, ed. G. Wertheim (Wiesbaden, 1956); ed. G. Darvas (Budapest, 1968).
—— Harpsichord Concerto in D major, Wq. 27, ed. E. N. Kulukundis (*Collegium Musicum Yale University*, second series, 2) (Madison, 1970).
—— Harpsichord Concerto in F major, Wq. 33, ed. F. Oberdörffer (Kassel, 1952).
—— Harpsichord Concerto in D major, Wq. 43 no. 2, ed. L. Landshoff (Wilhelmshaven, 1967).
—— Concerto in E flat major for harpsichord, piano and orchestra, Wq. 47, ed. E. R. Jacobi (Kassel, 1958).
—— Oboe Concerto in B flat major, Wq. 164, ed. O. Kaul (Munich, 1965).
—— Oboe Concerto in E flat major, Wq. 165, ed. H. Töttcher and K. Grebe (Hamburg, 1959).
—— Organ Concerto in G major, Wq. 34, ed. H. Winter (Hamburg, 1964).
—— Organ Concerto in E flat major, Wq. 35, ed. H. Winter (Hamburg, 1964).
—— Concerto in A minor for cello or flute or harpsichord and strings, Wq. 170, 166 or 26 ed. W. Altmann (London, 1954).
—— Concerto in A major for cello, flute or harpsichord, Wq. 172, 178, or 29, ed. H. M. Kneihs (London, 1967).
—— Concerto in B flat major for cello or viola and strings, Wq. 171, ed. P. Klengel (Leipzig, 1931); ed. W. Schulz (Leipzig, 1938).
BACH, J. C.: Bassoon Concerto in E flat major, ed. J. Wojciechowski (Hamburg, 1953).
—— Flute Concerto in D major, ed. R. Meylan (Vienna, 1958).
—— Piano Concerto no. 2 in A major, ed. L. Stadelmann (Mainz, 1935).
—— Piano Concerto in B flat major, Op. 13 no. 4, ed. L. Landshoff (Frankfurt, 1955).
—— Piano Concerto in D major, Op. 13 no. 3, ed. L. Landshoff (Frankfurt, 1955).
—— Piano Concerto in E flat major, Op. 7 no. 5, ed. C. Döbereiner (Leipzig, 1927).
—— Piano Concerto in E flat major, ed. E. Praetorius (London, *c.* 1955).
—— Piano Concerto in F minor, ed. E. Martini (*Nagels Musik-Archiv*, 170) (Kassel, 1953).
—— *The Concerted Symphonies of John Christian Bach. Three symphonies in score*, ed. J. A. White, jr. (*Florida State University Studies*, 37) (Tallahassee, 1963).
—— Sinfonia Concertante in A major for violin and cello with orchestra, ed. A. Einstein (London, 1947).
—— Sinfonia Concertante in C major, for flute, oboe, violin, and cello, ed. C. R.F. Maunder (London, 1961).
—— Sinfonia Concertante in E flat major, for two violins and orchestra, ed. F. Stein (London, *c.* 1955).
BACH, J. C. F.: Concerto for piano and viola with orchestra, piano reduction, ed. E. Seiler (Wiesbaden, 1966).
—— Harpsichord Concerto in E major, ed. A. Hoffmann (Wolfenbüttel, 1966).
BACH, W. F.: Harpsichord Concerto in C minor, ed. W. Eickemeyer (Mainz, 1931).
—— Harpsichord Concerto in F minor, ed. W. Smigelski (Hamburg, 1959).
BENDA, F.: Flute Concerto in E minor, ed. W. Lebermann (Mainz, 1969).
BENDA, G.: 3 Harpsichord Concertos, ed. J. Racek and V. Bělský (*Musica Antiqua Bohemica*, 45) (Prague, 1960).
—— Harpsichord Concerto in G major, ed. M. Bethan (*Nagels Musik-Archiv*, 144) (Kassel, 1959).
—— Harpsichord Concerto in G minor, ed. J. Racek and V. Kaprál (*Musica Antiqua Bohemica*, 10) (Prague, 1950).
—— Viola Concerto in F major, ed. W. Lebermann (Mainz, 1968).
BOCCHERINI, L.: Cello Concerto in B flat major, ed. R. Sturzenegger (London, 1949).
—— Cello Concerto no. 1 in C major, ed. W. Lebermann (Mainz, 1968).
—— Cello Concerto no. 2 in D major, ed. W. Lebermann (Mainz, 1970).

BOCCHERINI, L.: Cello Concerto in G major, ed. M. DeRonde (*Smith College Music Archives*, 3) (Northampton, Mass., 1937).
BORGHI, L.: Cello Concerto, ed. E. Bonelli for cello & piano (Padua, 1961).
CAMBINI, G. G.: Piano Concerto in B flat major, Op. 15 no. 1, ed. G. Barblan (*Antica musica strumentale italiana*) (Milan, 1964).
—— Piano Concerto in G major, Op. 15 no. 3, ed. G. Barblan (*Antica musica strumentale italiana*) (Milan, 1959).
DANZI, F.: Sinfonia Concertante for flute, oboe, horn, and bassoon, ed. H. Zirnbauer (Mainz, 1939).
DITTERSDORF, C. DITTERS VON: Harpsichord Concerto in A major, ed. W. Upmeyer (*Nagels Musik-Archiv*, 41), (Hanover, 1929).
—— Oboe Concerto in G major, ed. G. Rhau (Wiesbaden, 1948).
—— Viola Concerto in F major, ed. W. Lebermann (Mainz, 1966).
—— Violin Concerto in C major, ed. W. Lebermann (Mainz, 1961).
FILTZ, A.: Cello Concerto in G major, ed. H. Klug (Wiesbaden, 1968).
—— Flute Concerto in D major, ed. H. Kašlík and F. Suchý (*Musica Antiqua Bohemica*, 18) (Prague, 1962).
FISCHER, J. C.: Oboe Concerto no. 2 in E flat major, ed. R. Meylan (Wiesbaden, 1963).
FREDERICK THE GREAT: *Musikalische Werke*, ed. P. Spitta, vol. 3, *Konzerte für Flöte, Streichorchester und Generalbass* (Leipzig, 1889).
GALUPPI, B.: Concerto in E minor for two flutes and strings, ed. F. Schroeder (Wilhelmshaven, 1962).
GIORDANI, T.: Harpsichord Concerto in C major, Op. 14 no. 3, ed. R. Castagnone (*Antica musica strumentale italiana*) (Milan, 1962).
—— Harpsichord Concerto in D major, Op. 14 no. 5, ed. R. Castagnone (*Antica musica strumentale italiana*) (Milan, 1962).
GIORNOVICHI, G. M.: Violin Concerto no. 1 in A major, ed. W. Lebermann (Mainz, 1962).
GRAUN, J. G.: Bassoon Concerto in B flat major, ed. H. Töttcher (Hamburg, 1955).
—— Harpsichord Concerto in F major, ed. H. Ruf (Heidelberg, 1959).
—— Oboe Concerto in C minor, ed. H. Töttcher (Hamburg, 1953).
HASSE, J. A.: Flute Concerto in D major, ed. R. Engländer (London, 1953).
HAYDN, JOSEPH: *Werke*, ed. Joseph Haydn-Institut, Cologne, series 3, *Konzerte für Streichinstrumente* (Munich, 1969–).
HAYDN, MICHAEL: Flute Concerto in D major, Perger 54, ed. J. Vécsey (Budapest, 1957).
—— Flute Concerto in D major, Perger 56, ed. H. C. Robbins Landon (Salzburg, 1959).
—— Violin Concerto in B flat major, ed. P. Angerer (*Diletto Musicale*, 3) (Vienna, 1960).
HOFFMEISTER, F. A.: Flute Concerto in D major, ed. J. Szebenyi (Budapest, 1966).
—— Piano Concerto in D major, Op. 24, ed. E. Hess (*Für Kenner und Liebhaber*, 27) (Basel, 1964).
HOLZBAUER, I.: Flute Concerto in D major, ed. I. Gronefeld (Munich, 1958).
KOŽELUH, L.: Piano Concerto in D major, ed. R. Meylan (Wiesbaden, 1964).
LE DUC, S.: Violin Concerto no. 2 in C major, ed. F. Oubradous (Paris, 1958).
MOZART, L.: *Ausgewählte Werke*, ed. M. Seiffert (*Denkmäler der Tonkunst in Bayern*, 9/2) (Leipzig, 1909).
MOZART, W. A.: *Werke*, ed. J. Brahms *et al.*, series 12, *Konzerte für ein Saiten- oder Blasinstrument und Orchester*; series 16, *Konzerte für ein, zwei oder drei Klaviere und Orchester*; series 24, *Supplement* (Leipzig, 1877–87).
—— *Neue Ausgabe sämtlicher Werke*, ed. Internationale Stiftung Mozarteum, series 5, *Konzerte* (Kassel, 1959–).

BIBLIOGRAPHY

MYSLIVEČEK, J.: Flute Concerto in D major, ed. M. Munclinger (*Musica Viva Historica*, 23) (Prague, 1969).
—— Harpsichord Concerto no. 2, ed. E. Fendler (London, 1964).
—— Violin Concerto, ed. K. Moor and L. Láska (Prague, 1948).
NARDINI, P.: Violin Concerto in F major, Op. 1 no. 3, ed. W. Lebermann (Mainz, 1968).
NICHELMANN, C.: Harpsichord Concerto in A major, ed. C. Bittner (*Nagels Musik-Archiv*, 145) (Kassel, 1928).
PLEYEL, I.: Viola Concerto in D major, Op. 31, ed. C. Herrmann (Frankfurt, 1951).
—— Sinfonia Concertante no. 5 in F major, for flute, oboe (or clarinet), horn, bassoon, ed. F. Oubradous (Paris, 1959).
REICHARDT, J. F.: Violin Concerto in E flat major, ed. H. Lungershausen (*Nagels Musik-Archiv*, 181) (Kassel, 1955).
RICHTER, F. X.: Harpsichord Concerto in E minor, ed. H. Höckner (Berlin, 1933).
—— Oboe Concerto in F major, ed. R.-J. Koch (Hamburg, 1965).
—— Trumpet Concerto in D major, ed. F. Schroeder (Cologne, 1968).
ROSETTI, F. A.: *Ausgewählte Kammermusik nebst einem Instrumentalkonzert*, ed. O. Kaul (*Denkmäler der Tonkunst in Bayern*, 25) (Augsburg, 1925).
—— Flute Concerto in G major, ed. J. Szebenyi (Mainz, 1963).
SAMMARTINI, G. B.: Concerto in C major for violoncello piccolo or violin and strings, ed. N. Jenkins (London, 1956).
SCHOBERT, J.: *Ausgewählte Werke*, ed. H. Riemann (*Denkmäler deutscher Tonkunst*, 39) (Leipzig, 1909).
SCHROETER, J. S.: Piano Concerto in C major, Op. 3 no. 3, ed. K. Schultz-Hauser (Mainz, 1964).
STAMITZ, C.: Bassoon Concerto in F major, ed. J. Wojciechowski (Hamburg, 1956).
—— Cello Concerto in A major, ed. W. Upmeyer (*Hortus Musicus*, 79) (Kassel, 1951).
—— Cello Concerto in C major, ed. W. Upmeyer (*Hortus Musicus*, 105) (Kassel, 1953).
—— Cello Concerto in G major, ed. W. Upmeyer (*Hortus Musicus*, 104) (Kassel, 1953).
—— Clarinet Concerto no. 3 in B flat major, ed. J. Wojciechowski (Frankfurt, 1957).
—— Clarinet Concerto no. 10 in B flat major, ed. J. Michaels (Hamburg, 1958).
—— Clarinet Concerto in E flat major, ed. J. Wojciechowski (Hamburg, 1953).
—— Flute Concerto in D major, ed. D. Sonntag (Hamburg, 1958).
—— Flute Concerto in G major, ed. W. Lebermann (Mainz, 1964).
—— Oboe Concerto in B flat major, ed. J. Wojciechowski (Hamburg, 1963).
—— Viola Concerto in D major, Op. 1, ed. K. Soldan (Leipzig, 1937).
—— Violin Concerto in G major, ed. M. Hochkofler (London, 1957).
—— Concerto in B flat major for clarinet, bassoon and orchestra, ed. J. Wojciechowski (Hamburg, 1954).
—— Concerto in B flat major for two clarinets, ed. W. Lebermann (Frankfurt, 1968).
—— Sinfonia Concertante in C major for two violins, ed. F. Kneusslin (Zürich, 1947).
—— Sinfonia Concertante in D major for two violins, ed. F. Schroeder (Hamburg, 1959).
STAMITZ, J.: Clarinet Concerto in B flat major, ed. P. Gradenwitz (New York, 1952); ed. W. Lebermann (Mainz, 1967).
—— Flute Concerto in C major, ed. H. Kölbel (Zürich, 1966).
—— Flute Concerto in D major, ed. W. Lebermann (London, 1961).
—— Oboe Concerto in C major, ed. H. Töttcher and H. F. Hartig (Hamburg, 1957).
STEFFAN, J. A.: Concerto in D major for harpsichord, flute, violin, horns, cello, and double bass, ed. V. Bělský (*Musica Antiqua Bohemica*, 39) (Prague, 1959).

TARTINI, G.: Violin Concerto in A major, ed. F. Schroeder (London, c. 1960).
—— Violin Concertos in A minor and F major, ed. G. Ross (*Smith College Music Archives*, 9) (Northampton, Mass., 1947).
—— Violin Concerto in D minor, ed. R. Baumgärtner (Zürich, 1958).
—— Violin Concerto in E major, ed. H. Scherchen (Zürich, 1942).
—— Violin Concerto in G minor, ed. M. Rostal (London, 1952).
TOESCHI, C. J.: Flute Concerto in G major, ed. R. Münster (Munich, 1962).
VAŇHAL, J. B.: Viola Concerto in C major, ed. V. Blažek (*Musica Viva Historica*, 10) (Prague, 1962).
VIOTTI, G. B.: Violin Concerto no. 22 in A minor, ed. A. Einstein (Zürich, 1929).
VOGLER, G. J.: Harpsichord Concerto in C major, Op. 2 no. 1, ed. G. Lenzewski (Berlin, 1927).
WAGENSEIL, G. C.: Cello Concerto in A major, ed. E. Mainardi and F. Racek (*Diletto Musicale*, 61) (Vienna, 1960).
—— Cello Concerto in C major, ed. F. Racek (*Diletto Musicale*, 121) (Vienna, 1963).
—— Harpsichord Concerto in D major (Leipzig, 1964).
—— Trombone Concerto, ed. K. Janetzky (Heidelberg, 1963).
WESLEY, C.: Concerto in C major, op. 2 no. 4 for pianoforte, harpsichord, or organ, ed. G. Finzi (New York and London, 1956).

(ii) *Books and Articles*
(a) *General*

BECK, HERMANN: 'Das Soloinstrument im Tutti des Konzerts der zweiten Hälfte des 18. Jahrhunderts', *Musikforschung*, xiv (1961), pp. 427–35.
BOESE, HELMUT: *Die Klarinette als Soloinstrument in der Musik der Mannheimer Schule*. Berlin Dissertation (Dresden, 1940).
BROOK, BARRY S.: 'The *Symphonie Concertante*: An Interim Report', *Musical Quarterly*, xlvii (1961), pp. 493–516.
COLE, MALCOLM S.: 'The Vogue of the Instrumental Rondo in the Late Eighteenth Century', *Journal of the American Musicological Society*, xxii (1969), pp. 425–55.
DAFFNER, HUGO VON: *Die Entwicklung des Klavierkonzerts bis Mozart* (Leipzig, 1906).
EDWARDS, OWAIN: 'English String Concertos before 1800', *Proceedings of the Royal Musical Association*, xcv (1968/9), pp. 1–13.
ENGEL, HANS: *Die Entwicklung des deutschen Klavierkonzertes von Mozart bis Liszt* (Leipzig, 1927; reprinted Hildesheim, 1971).
—— *Das Instrumentalkonzert* (Leipzig, 1932).
HILL, RALPH, ed.: *The Concerto* (London, 1952).
HUTCHINGS, ARTHUR J. B.: *The Baroque Concerto*, 2nd ed. (London, 1963).
KNÖDT, HEINRICH: 'Zur Entwicklungsgeschichte der Kadenzen im Instrumentalkonzert', *Sammelbände der internationalen Musikgesellschaft*, xv (1913/14), pp. 375–419.
LEBERMANN, WALTER: 'Zur Frage der Eliminierung des Soloparts aus den Tutti-Abschnitten in der Partitur des Solokonzerts', *Musikforschung*, xiv (1961), pp. 200–8.
MEYLAN, RAYMOND: 'Documents douteux dans le domaine des concertos pour instruments à vent au XVIIIe siècle', *Revue de musicologie*, xlix (1963), pp. 47–60.
NEURATH, HERBERT: 'Das Violinkonzert in der Wiener klassischen Schule', *Studien zur Musikwissenschaft*, xiv (1927), pp. 125–42.
SCHERING, ARNOLD: *Geschichte des Instrumentalkonzerts bis auf die Gegenwart*, 2nd edn. (Leipzig, 1927; reprinted Hildesheim, 1965).
SIMON, EDWIN J.: 'The Double Exposition in the Classic Concerto', *Journal of the American Musicological Society*, x (1957), pp. 111–18.

STEVENS, JANE R.: 'An 18th-Century Description of Concerto First-Movement Form', *Journal of the American Musicological Society*, xxiv (1971), pp. 85–95.
ULDALL, HANS: 'Beiträge zur Frühgeschichte des Klavierkonzerts', *Zeitschrift für Musikwissenschaft*, x (1927/28), pp. 139–52.
—— *Das Klavierkonzert der Berliner Schule* (Leipzig, 1928).
VEINUS, ABRAHAM: *The Concerto* (London, 1948; revised ed. New York, 1964).
WALDKIRCH, FRANZ: *Die konzertanten Sinfonien der Mannheimer im 18. Jahrhundert* Heidelberg Dissertation (Ludwigshafen, 1931).
WARD JONES, PETER: 'The Concerto at Mannheim c. 1740–1780', *Proceedings of the Royal Musical Association*, xcvi (1969/70), pp. 129–36.
WEBER, HANS: *Das Violoncellkonzert des 18. und beginnenden 19. Jahrhunderts*. (Tübingen Dissertation, 1932).

(b) Individual Composers

Albrechtsberger
RASMUSSEN, MARY: 'A Concertino for Chromatic Trumpet by Johann Georg Albrechtsberger', *Brass Quarterly*, v (1962), pp. 104–8.

Avison
CUDWORTH, CHARLES L.: 'Avison of Newcastle, 1709–1770', *Musical Times*, cxi (1970), pp. 480–3.

C. P. E. Bach
CRICKMORE, LEON: 'C. P. E. Bach's Harpsichord Concertos', *Music and Letters*, xxxix (1958), pp. 227–41.

F. Benda
BERTEN, FRANZI: *Franz Benda, sein Leben und seine Kompositionen*. Cologne Dissertation (Essen, 1928).

Binder
FLEISCHER, HEINRICH: *Christlieb Siegmund Binder* (Regensburg, 1942).

Croes
CLERCX, SUZANNE: *Henri-Jacques de Croes*, 2 vols. (Brussels, 1940).

Giornovichi
DJURIĆ-KLAJN, STANA: 'Un contemporain de Mozart, Ivan Mane Jarnović', *Bericht über den internationalen musikwissenschaftlichen Kongress, Wien, Mozartjahr 1956*, ed. E. Schenk (Graz, 1958), pp. 134–8.

F. J. Haydn
EDWALL, HARRY R.: 'Ferdinand IV and Haydn's Concertos for the *Lira Organizzata*', *Musical Quarterly*, xlviii (1962), pp. 190–203.
FEDER, GEORG: 'Wieviel Orgelkonzerte hat Haydn geschrieben?', *Musikforschung*, xxiii (1970), pp. 440–4.
HEUSSNER, HORST: 'Zwei neue Haydn-Funde', *Musikforschung*, xiii (1960), pp. 451–5.
NOWAK, LEOPOLD: 'Das Autograph von Joseph Haydns Cello-Konzert in D-dur, op. 101', *Österreichische Musikzeitschrift*, ix (1954), pp. 274–9.

Koželuh
POŠTOLKA, MILAN: *Leopold Koželuh* (Prague, 1964).

W. A. Mozart
BADURA-SKODA, EVA and PAUL: *Mozart-Interpretation* (Vienna, 1957). English translation, *Interpreting Mozart on the Keyboard* (London, 1962).
BLUME, FRIEDRICH: 'The Concertos: (1) Their Sources', *The Mozart Companion*, ed. H. C. Robbins Landon and Donald Mitchell (London, 1956), pp. 200–33.
DAZELEY, GEORGE: 'The Original Text of Mozart's Clarinet Concerto', *Music Review*, ix (1948), pp. 166–72.

GIRDLESTONE, CUTHBERT M.: *Mozart's Piano Concertos* (London, 1948; first published in French, Paris, 1939).
HESS, ERNST: 'Die ursprüngliche Gestalt des Klarinettenkonzertes KV 662', *Mozart-Jahrbuch 1967*, pp. 18–30.
HUTCHINGS, ARTHUR J. B.: *A Companion to Mozart's Piano Concertos* (London, 1948).
KELLER, HANS: 'K. 503: The Unity of Contrasting Themes and Movements', *Music Review*, xvii (1956), pp. 48–58, 120–9.
KRATOCHVÍL, JIŘÍ: 'Betrachtungen über die Urfassung des Konzerts für Klarinette und des Quintetts für Klarinette und Streicher von W. A. Mozart', *Internationale Konferenz über das Leben und Werk W. A. Mozarts, Praha . . . 1956: Bericht* (Prague, 1958), pp. 262–71.
—— 'Ist die heute gebräuchliche Fassung des Klarinettenkonzerts und des Klarinettenquintetts von Mozart authentisch?', *Beiträge zur Musikwissenschaft*, ii (1960), pp. 27–34.
LANDON, H. C. ROBBINS: 'The Concertos: (2) Their Musical Origin and Development', *The Mozart Companion*, ed. H. C. Robbins Landon and Donald Mitchell (London, 1956), pp. 234–82.
PAUMGARTNER, BERNHARD: 'Zu Mozarts Oboen-Concert C-Dur, KV 314 (285d)', *Mozart-Jahrbuch 1950*, pp. 24–40.
RUSSELL, JOHN F.: 'Mozart and the Pianoforte', *Music Review*, i (1940), pp. 226–44.
SCHROEDER, FELIX: 'Ist uns Mozarts Oboenkonzert für Ferlendi erhalten?', *Musikforschung*, v (1952), pp. 209–11.
SIMON, EDWIN J.: 'Sonata into Concerto. A Study of Mozart's First Seven Concertos', *Acta Musicologica*, xxxi (1959), pp. 170–85.
TISCHLER, HANS: *A Structural Analysis of Mozart's Piano Concertos* (Brooklyn, New York, 1966).
ZSCHINSKY-TROXLER, ELSA M. VON: 'Mozarts D dur-Violinkonzert und Boccherini', *Zeitschrift für Musikwissenschaft*, x (1927/8), pp. 415–22.

Nichelmann
DÖLLMANN, HEINZ: *Christoph Nichelmann, 1717–1762, ein Musiker am Hofe Friedrichs der Grossen*. Münster Dissertation (Löningen, 1938).
LEE, DOUGLAS A.: 'Christoph Nichelmann and the Early Clavier Concerto in Berlin', *Musical Quarterly*, lvii (1971), pp. 636–55.

Pugnani
MÜRY, ALBERT: *Die Instrumentalwerke Gaetano Pugnanis*. (Basel Dissertation, 1941).

Schmitt
DUNNING, ALBERT: *Joseph Schmitt* (Amsterdam, 1962).

Schroeter
WOLFF, KONRAD: 'Johann Samuel Schroeter', *Musical Quarterly*, xliv (1958), pp. 338–59.

J. Stamitz
GRADENWITZ, PETER: 'The Beginnings of Clarinet Literature: Notes on a Clarinet Concerto by Joh. Stamitz', *Music and Letters*, xvii (1936), pp. 145–50.

Tartini
DOUNIAS, MINOS: *Die Violinkonzerte Giuseppe Tartinis*. Berlin Dissertation, 1932. (Wolfenbüttel, 1935).

CHAPTER VIII
THE DIVERTIMENTO AND COGNATE FORMS

(i) *Modern Editions*

(*a*) *Anthologies*

HAUSSWALD, GÜNTER: *Die Orchesterserenade* (*Das Musikwerk*, 34) (Cologne, 1970). Includes excerpts from works by Dittersdorf, Gluck, Joseph Haydn, Michael Haydn, J. C. Monn, L. Mozart, W. A. Mozart, and G. Reutter, the younger.

HORWITZ, KARL and RIEDEL, KARL edd.: *Wiener Instrumentalmusik vor und um 1750*, 2 vols. (*Denkmäler der Tonkunst in Österreich*, Jg. 15/2, vol. 31 and Jg. 19/2, vol. 39) (Vienna, 1908–12). Includes works by J. C. Monn, M. Schlöger, and J. Starzer.

SENN, WALTER, ed.: *Tiroler Instrumentalmusik im 18. Jahrhundert* (*Denkmäler der Tonkunst in Österreich*, vol. 86) (Vienna, 1949). Includes works by G. P. Falk and Paluselli.

(*b*) *Works by Individual Composers*

ASPELMAYR, F.: Partita in D major for two oboes, two horns, and bassoon, ed. O. Pulkert (Munich, 1962).

—— Partita in F major for two oboes, two horns, and bassoon, ed. O. Pulkert (Munich, 1962).

HAYDN, JOSEPH: *Werke*, ed. Joseph Haydn-Institut, Cologne, series 7, *Notturni mit Orgelleiern* (Munich, 1971).

HAYDN, MICHAEL: *Instrumentalwerke I*, ed. L. H. Perger (*Denkmäler der Tonkunst in Österreich*, Jg. 14/2, vol. 29) (Vienna, 1907).

—— Divertimento in B flat major for oboe, bassoon, violin, viola, and double bass, Perger 92, ed. A. Strassl (*Diletto Musicale*, 24) (Vienna, 1962).

—— Divertimento in C major for violin, cello, and violone, ed. E. Rapp (Mainz, 1935).

—— Divertimento in D major, ed. W. Upmeyer (*Nagels Musik-Archiv*, 7) (Hanover, 1927).

—— Divertimento in D major (1764), ed. L. Kalmár (Budapest, 1965).

—— Divertimento in G major for flute, horn, violin, viola and cello, Perger 94, ed. A. Strassl (*Diletto Musicale*, 25) (Vienna, 1962).

—— Serenata in D major, Perger 85, ed. G. Darvas (Budapest, 1966).

MOZART, L.: *Ausgewählte Werke*, ed. M. Seiffert (*Denkmäler der Tonkunst in Bayern*, 9/2) (Leipzig, 1909).

—— 3 Divertimenti in G, C and D major for two violins and violoncello, ed. G. Lenzewski (Berlin, 1927); ed. M. Seiffert (*Organum*, series 3 no. 30) (Leipzig, 1930).

—— Divertimento I, for 2 violins and cello ed. W. Kolneder (Mainz, 1959).

MOZART, W. A.: *Werke*, ed. J. Brahms *et al.*, series 9, *Kassationen, Serenaden und Divertimenti für Orchester*; series 10, *Märsche, Sinfonie-Sätze u. kleinere Stücke für Orchester* (*auch für Harmonika u. Orgelwalze*); series 11, *Tänze für Orchester*; series 24, *Supplement* (Leipzig, 1878–89).

—— *Neue Ausgabe sämtlicher Werke*, ed. Internationale Stiftung Mozarteum, series 4, *Orchesterwerke*, group 12, *Kassationen, Serenaden und Divertimenti für Orchester*; group 13, *Tänze und Märsche* (Kassel, 1961–).

PAGANELLI, G. A.: *Divertissement de le beau sexe*, ed. G. Tagliapetra (Milan, 1936).

(ii) *Books and Articles*

ATTI, GAETANO: *Biografia di Bartolommeo Campagnoli da Cento* (Bologna, 1852).

BÄR, CARL: 'Zum Begriff des "Basso" in Mozarts Serenaden', *Mozart-Jahrbuch 1960/61*, pp. 133–55.

ENGEL, HANS: 'Der Tanz in Mozarts Kompositionen', *Mozart-Jahrbuch 1952*, pp. 29–39.
HAUSSWALD, GÜNTER: 'Der Divertimento-Begriff bei Georg Christoph Wagenseil', *Archiv für Musikwissenschaft*, ix (1952), pp. 45–50.
—— *Mozarts Serenaden* (Leipzig, 1951).
HESS, REIMUND: *Serenade, Cassation, Notturno und Divertimento bei Michael Haydn.* (Mainz Dissertation, 1963).
HOFFMANN, HANS: 'Über die Mozartschen Serenaden und Divertimenti', *Mozart-Jahrbuch*, iii (1929), pp. 59–79.
MEYER, EVE R.: 'The Viennese Divertimento', *Music Review*, xxix (1968), pp. 165–71.
MITCHELL, DONALD: 'The Serenades for Wind Band', *The Mozart Companion*, ed. H. C. Robbins Landon and Donald Mitchell (London, 1956), pp. 66–89.
NETTL, PAUL: 'Mozarts Prager Kontertänze', *Bericht über die musikwissenschaftliche Tagung der Internationalen Stiftung Mozarteum in Salzburg . . . 1931*, ed. Erich Schenk (Leipzig, 1932), pp. 133–5.
SCHENK, ERICH: *Giuseppe Antonio Paganelli*. Munich Dissertation (Salzburg, 1928)

CHAPTER IX
CHAMBER MUSIC

(i) *Modern Editions*
(a) *Anthologies*

BORMANN, PAUL, ed.: *Das Violinduett im 18. Jahrhundert*, 3 vols. (Hamburg, 1954–6).
RIEMANN, HUGO, ed.: *Mannheimer Kammermusik des 18. Jahrhunderts*, 2 vols. (*Denkmäler der Tonkunst in Bayern*, 15–16) (Leipzig, 1914–15). Contains works by Cannabich, W. Cramer, Edelmann, Eichner, Filtz, Holzbauer, A. Stamitz, C. Stamitz, J. Stamitz, Sterkel, C. J. Toeschi, Vogler, and Wendling.
SCHENK, ERICH, ed.: *Die ausseritalienische Triosonate* (*Das Musikwerk*, 35) (Cologne, 1970). Includes works by J. G. Graun and Wagenseil.
—— *Die italienische Triosonate* (*Das Musikwerk*, 7) (Cologne, 1954. English edition, 1955). Includes a sonata by Pugnani.

(b) *Works by Individual Composers*

ABEL, C. F.: *Kompositionen*, ed. W. Knape, vols. 11–14 (Cuxhaven, 1964–9).
—— Six Sonatas for viola da gamba and continuo, ed. J. Bacher, 2 vols. (*Nagels Musik-Archiv*, 39–40) (Kassel, 1937–42).
ALBRECHTSBERGER, J. G.: *Instrumentalwerke*, ed. O. Kapp (*Denkmäler der Tonkunst in Österreich*, Jg. 16/2, vol. 33) (Vienna, 1909).
ARNE, T. A.: Trio Sonatas, op. 3: no. 1, ed. M. Seiffert (*Collegium Musicum*, 57) (Leipzig, 1928); nos. 2, 4, 5, and 7, ed. H. Murrill (London, 1939–60).
ASPELMAYR, F.: Trio for two violins, cello, and continuo, Op. 1 no. 4, ed. E. Schenk (Vienna, 1954).
—— Trio, Op. 5 no. 1, ed. H. Riemann (*Collegium Musicum*, 39) (Leipzig, 1907).
BACH, C. P. E.: Quartet for piano, flute, viola and cello, Wq. 93–5, ed. E. F. Schmid (Kassel, 1952).
—— 6 Sonatas for clarinet, bassoon and piano, Wq. 92, ed. G. Piccioli (New York, 1955); ed. G. Balassa (Budapest, 1962).
—— 12 two- and three-part pieces for flute or violin and clavier, Wq. 82, ed. R. Hohenemser (Berlin, 1928).
—— 4 Sonatas for flute and piano, Wq. 83–6, ed. K. Walther, 2 vols. (Wiesbaden, 1955).
—— Sonatas for flute and continuo, Wq. 123, 124, 128 and 131, ed. K. Walther, 2 vols. (*Hortus Musicus*, 71, 72) (Kassel, 1968, 1967).

—— 6 Sonatas for flute and continuo, Wq. 125–7, 129, 130, and 134, ed. K. Walther, 6 vols. (Frankfurt, 1958).
—— Sonata in B minor for flute, violin and continuo, Wq. 143, ed. R. Ermeler (Leipzig, 1932).
—— Sonata in B flat major for flute, violin and continuo, Wq. 161 no. 2, ed. L. Landshoff (Leipzig, 1936).
—— Sonata in E major for two flutes and continuo, Wq. 162, ed. K. Walther (Leipzig, 1935).
—— Sonata in C major for harpsichord and flute, Wq. 87, ed. A. van Leeuwen (Leipzig, 1923).
—— Sonata in G minor for harpsichord and viola da gamba, Wq. 88, ed. F. Grützmacher (Leipzig, 1881).
—— 2 Sonatas in B minor and C minor for harpsichord and violin, Wq. 76 and 78, ed. H. Sitt (Leipzig, 1919).
—— Sonata in D major for harpsichord and violin, Wq. 71, ed. E. F. Schmid (Karlsbad, 1932).
—— Sonata in B flat major for harpsichord and violin, Wq. 77, ed. L. Landshoff (Leipzig, n.d.).
—— 2 Sonatas in F major and D minor for two violins and continuo. Wq. 154 & 160, ed. P. Klengel (Leipzig, 1933).
—— Sonata in G major for two violins and continuo, Wq. 157, ed. B. Hinze-Rheinhold (Leipzig, 1924).
—— Sonata in B flat major for two violins and continuo, Wq. 158, ed. G. Schumann (Leipzig, 1910).
—— 6 Trios for piano, violin and cello, Wq. 89, ed. E. F. Schmid, vol. 1, nos. 1–3 (Kassel, 1952).
BACH, J. C.: 4 Quartets for two flutes and strings, Op. 19, ed. L. Hoffmann-Erbrecht (*Organum*, series 3, nos. 63, 64, 66, 68) (Lippstadt, 1962–4).
—— 6 Quintets for flute, oboe, violin, viola, cello, and continuo, Op. 11, ed. R. Steglich (*Das Erbe deutscher Musik*, 3) (Hanover, 1935); nos. 1, 2, 3, and 5, ed. S. Sadie (London, 1962).
—— *Sei sinfonia pour deux clarinettes, deux cors de chasse et basson*, ed. F. Stein, 2 vols. (Leipzig, 1957–8).
—— Sonata in D major, Op. 2 no. 3, for harpsichord, violin or flute, and cello, ed. H. Riemann (*Collegium Musicum*, 19) (Leipzig, 1903).
—— Sonatas for violin and piano, Op. 10, ed. L. Landshoff, 2 vols. (London, 1938).
—— 6 *Sonate notturne* for two violins and viola or cello, ed. S. Beck (New York, 1937).
BACH, J. C. F.: *Ausgewählte Werke*, ed. G. Schünemann, vol. 7, nos. 1–4, *Kammermusik* (Bückeburg, 1920–6).
—— Cello Sonata in A major, ed. A. Wenzinger (Kassel, 1961).
—— Cello Sonata in D major, ed. J. Smith (Brunswick, 1905).
—— Cello Sonata in G major, ed. H. Ruf (Kassel, 1961).
—— Sonata in A major for flute, violin and continuo, ed. G. Frotscher (Hamburg, 1956).
—— 2 Sonatas for harpsichord and flute, ed. H. Ruf (Mainz, 1966).
—— Sonata in F major for harpsichord and flute or violin, ed. W. Hinnenthal (Wiesbaden, 1966).
—— Sonata in D major for harpsichord, flute and cello, ed. H. Ruf (*Nagels Musik-Archiv*, 192) (Kassel, 1957).
BACH, JOHANN ERNST: Violin Sonata in D major, ed. A. Küster (*Nagels Musik-Archiv*, 2) (Hanover, 1927).
BACH, W. F.: 6 Duets for two flutes, ed. K. Walther, 2 vols., 2nd edn. (Leipzig, 1954–7).

BACH, W. F.: 3 Trios for two flutes and continuo, ed. M. Seiffert (Leipzig, 1934).
BACH, W. F. E.: Sextet in E flat major for clarinet, two horns, violin, viola, and violoncello, ed. K. Janetzky (Halle, 1951).
—— Trio in G major for two flutes and viola, ed. R. Ermeler (*Hortus Musicus*, 57) (Kassel, 1951).
BARBELLA, E.: Sonata 1 for violin and piano, ed. F. Polnauer (Zürich, 1968).
BENDA, F.: 24 Caprices for violin, facsimile ed., ed. J. Müller-Blattau (Stuttgart, 1957).
—— 4 Violin Sonatas, ed. J. and B. Štědroň (*Musica Antiqua Bohemica*, 57) (Prague, 1962).
BOCCHERINI, L.: *Le opere complete*, ed. P. Carmirelli, vol. 1– (Rome, 1970–).
—— Cello Sonata in B flat major, ed. R. Ewerhart and K. Storck (Mainz, 1965).
—— 3 Oboe Quintets, Op. 45 nos. 1–3, ed. W. Lebermann (Frankfurt, 1967).
—— 4 Quintettini, Op. 30 and 6 Quartettini, Op. 33, ed. P. Carmirelli (*I classici italiani della musica*, 1) (Rome, 1960).
—— Sextets, Op. 42, nos. 1 and 2, ed. P. Bormann (Hamburg, 1954–6).
—— Sextet in B flat major, for oboe, bassoon, two violins, viola, and cello, ed. K. Janetzky (Leipzig, 1955).
—— 3 String Trios from Op. 38, ed. B. Päuler, 2 vols. (Wilhelmshaven, 1967).
—— 6 Trios, Op. 4, for two violins and cello, ed. B. Päuler (Wilhelmshaven, 1966).
—— Violin Sonatas, Op. 5, ed. E. Polo (*I classici musicali italiani*, 4) (Milan, 1941).
BOYCE, W.: Trio Sonatas, no. 2 in F major, ed. H. Murrill (London, 1951); no. 3 in A major, ed. G. Jensen (London, 1894); no. 5 in D major, ed. S. Sadie (London, 1969); no. 6 in B flat major, ed. S. Sadie (London, 1967); no. 7 in D minor, ed. A. Moffat (London, 1909); no. 8 in E flat major, ed. S. Sadie (London, 1961); no. 9 in C major, ed. S. Sadie (London, 1961); no. 11 in C minor, ed. A. Moffat (Berlin, 1902); no. 12 in G major, ed. S. Sadie (London, 1961).
CAMERLOHER, P. VON: 4 Sonatas for two violins and piano with cello ad. lib., ed. A. Hoffmann (Mainz, 1939).
CANNABICH, C.: 6 Duets for violin and viola, ed. W. Höckner and W. Twarz, 2 vols. (Hamburg, 1963).
COLLETT, J.: Violin Sonata in A major, ed. A. Moffat (London, 1907).
DITTERSDORF, C. DITTERS VON: String Quintet in C major, ed. W. Höckner (Leipzig, 1949).
—— 6 String Trios, Op. 1, ed. F. Noack (*Hortus Musicus*, 92) (Kassel, 1952).
FREDERICK THE GREAT: *Musikalische Werke*, ed. P. Spitta, vols. 1–2, *Sonaten für Flöte und Klavier* (Leipzig, 1889).
GASSMANN, F. L.: *Divertimento a tre* in C major, ed. E. Schenk (Vienna, 1953).
—— 6 Sonatas for flute, violin, and viola, ed. H. Albrecht (*Organum*, series 3, nos. 45, 48, 51, 53, 55, 58) (Lippstadt, 1950–7).
GIARDINI, F. DE: Quartet in D major, Op. 25 no. 3, for oboe, violin, viola and cello, ed. H. Steinbeck (Wiesbaden, 1961).
—— Sonatas for harpsichord and violin or flute, Op. 3, ed. E. Polo (*I classici musicali italiani*, 3) (Milan, 1941).
—— String quartets, Op. 23, nos. 3 and 4, ed. A. Poltronieri (*I classici musicali italiani*, 6) (Milan, 1941).
—— Violin Duet in D major, ed. K. Schultz-Hauser (Mainz, 1965).
GLUCK, C. W. VON: *Sämtliche Werke*, ed. R. Gerber, series 5, *Triosonaten* ed. F. H. Neumann (Kassel, 1961).
GRAZIANI, C.: 6 Sonatas for cello and continuo, Op. 3, ed. G. Benvenuti (*I classici musicali italiani*, 15) (Milan, 1943).
GUILLEMAIN, L.-G.: *Conversation galante et amusante*, Op. 12 no. 1, ed. P. Klengel (*Collegium Musicum*, 58) (Leipzig, 1930).
—— Sonata in G major for flute and continuo, ed. H. Ruf (Mainz, 1968).

HAYDN, JOSEPH: *Werke*, ed. Joseph Haydn-Institut, Cologne, series 12, *Streichquartette*; series 13, *Verschiedene Barytonwerke*; series 14, *Barytontrios*; series 17, *Klaviertrios* (Munich, 1958–).

HAYDN, MICHAEL: *Instrumentalwerke I*, ed. L. H. Perger (*Denkmäler der Tonkunst in Österreich*, Jg. 14/2, vol. 29) (Vienna, 1907).

—— 4 Duets for violin and viola, ed. J. Siderits (Vienna, 1950–2).

—— Flute Quartet in D major, Perger 117, ed. H. D. Sonntag (Berlin, 1959).

—— String Quartet in A major, ed. F. Beyer (Zürich, 1971).

—— String Quintet in C major, ed. H. Albrecht (*Organum*, series 3, no. 38) (Lippstadt, 1950).

—— String Quintet in F major, ed. H. Albrecht (*Organum*, series 3, no. 42) (Lippstadt, 1950).

—— String Quintet in G major, ed. H. Albrecht (*Organum*, series 3, no. 40) (Lippstadt, 1950).

—— Quintet for violin, viola, clarinet, horn and bassoon, Perger 111, ed. G. Balassa (Budapest, 1960).

HOFFMANN, L.: *Divertimento a tre* in C major, ed. E. Schenk (Vienna, 1953).

HOLZBAUER, I.: *Instrumentale Kammermusik*, ed. U. Lehmann (*Das Erbe deutscher Musik*, 24) (Kassel, 1953).

JANITSCH, J. G.: Sonata da camera in C major, Op. 4, for flute, violin, oboe, and continuo, ed. D. Lasocki (London, 1970).

—— Chamber Sonata 'Echo', Op. 8, for flute, oboe, viola and continuo, ed. H. C. Wolff (*Collegium Musicum*, 68) (Leipzig, 1938).

LAPSIS, S.: 3 Violin Sonatas from Op. 1, ed. H. Ruf (Mainz, 1956).

LATES, J.: Violin Sonata in G major, ed. A. Moffat (London, 1906).

LE DUC, S.: 4 Violin Sonatas, ed. E. Doflein, 2 vols. (Mainz, 1964).

MOZART, L.: *Ausgewählte Werke*, ed. M. Seiffert (*Denkmäler der Tonkunst in Bayern*, 9/2) (Leipzig, 1909).

MOZART, W. A.: *Werke*, ed. J. Brahms *et al.*, series 13, *Streich-Quintette*; series 14, *Streich-Quartette*; series 15, *Streich-Duos und Trio*; series 17, *Klavier-Quintett*, -*Quartette*, -*Trios*; series 18, *Sonaten und Variationen für Klavier und Violine*; series 24, *Supplement* (Leipzig, 1879–1905).

—— *Neue Ausgabe sämtlicher Werke*, ed. Internationale Stiftung Mozarteum, series 8, *Kammermusik* (Kassel, 1957–).

MYSLIVEČEK, J.: 3 String Quintets, ed. J. Racek and V. Bělský (*Musica Antiqua Bohemica*, 31) (Prague, 1957).

—— Trio in B flat major, Op. 1 no. 4, for flute, violin and cello, ed. H. Riemann (*Collegium Musicum*, 20) (Leipzig, 1906).

NARDINI, P.: Six String Quartets, ed. W. Altmann (*Collegium Musicum*, 63–5) (Leipzig, 1937).

NAUMANN, J. G.: Duet for oboe and bassoon, ed. P. Bormann (Hamburg, 1954).

—— *Six duos faciles pour deux violons à l'usage des commençants*, ed. P. Bormann (*Hortus Musicus*, 90) (Kassel, 1951).

NEUBAUR, F. C.: Trio in C major, Op. 3, no. 3, for flute, violin or second flute, and viola, ed. P. Bormann (Hamburg, 1954).

PLEYEL, I.: 6 Duos, Op. 8, for two violins, ed. F. David and C. Herrmann (Leipzig, 1951); ed. H. Mlynarczyk (Leipzig, 1952).

—— 3 Duos, Op. 61, for two violins, ed. F. Hermann (Leipzig, 1891); ed. E. Polo (Milan, 1929).

—— Flute Quartets, op. 20 nos. 1–3, ed. H. Albrecht (*Organum*, series 3, nos. 39, 44, 47) (Lippstadt, 1951).

PORPORA, N. A.: *Sinfonia da camera*, Op. 2 no. 4, ed. H. Riemann (*Collegium musicum*, 23) (Leipzig, 1906).

PUGNANI, G.: Violin Sonata in C major, Op. 3 no. 1, ed. C. Arrieu (Paris, 1957).

PUGNANI, G.: Violin Sonata in E major, Op. 7 no. 4, ed. G. Jensen (*Classische Violin Musik*, 4) (Mainz, 1911).
RICHTER, F. X.: 6 Sonatas, Op. 2, for flute or violin, cello, and harpsichord, ed. W. Upmeyer, vol. 1 (*Hortus Musicus*, 86) (Kassel, 1951).
ROSETTI, F. A.: *Ausgewählte Kammermusik nebst einem Instrumentalkonzert*, ed. O. Kaul (*Denkmäler der Tonkunst in Bayern*, 25) (Augsburg, 1925).
RUST, F. W.: *Werke für Klavier und Streichinstrumente*, ed. R. Czach (*Das Erbe deutscher Musik*, 2nd series, Landschaftsdenkmale, Mitteldeutschland, 1) (Wolfenbüttel, 1939).
SAMMARTINI, G. B.: *Sonate Notturne*, Op. 7 nos. 1–6, for two violins and continuo, ed. C. Perinello (*Raccolta nazionale delle musiche italiane, prima serie, quaderno 114–19 = I classici della musica italiana*, 28) (Milan, 1919).
—— Trio Sonata in A minor, Op. 3 no. 9, ed. H. Riemann (*Collegium Musicum*, 28) (Leipzig, 1907).
SCARLATTI, A.: *Sonate a quattro* in D minor and G minor, ed. H. David (New York, 1940).
SCHOBERT, J.: *Ausgewählte Werke*, ed. H. Riemann (*Denkmäler deutscher Tonkunst*, 39) (Leipzig, 1909).
—— *Sechs Sinfonien für Cembalo mit Begleitung von Violine und Hörnen ad libitum*, Op. 9 and 10, ed. G. Becking and W. Kramolisch (*Das Erbe deutscher Musik*, Sonderreihe, 4) (Kassel, 1960).
SOLER, A.: 6 Quintets for organ and strings, ed. R. Gerhard (Barcelona, 1933).
STAMITZ, C.: 6 Duos, Op. 18, for viola and viola, ed. A. Ott, 2 vols. (Munich, 1958–60).
—— Clarinet Quartet in F major, Op. 8 no. 3, ed. H. Winschermann (Hamburg, 1962).
—— Quartet in D major, Op. 8 no. 1 for flute or oboe, violin, viola or horn, and cello, ed. W. Upmeyer (*Hortus Musicus*, 109) (Kassel, 1954).
—— Trio in G major, Op. 14 no. 1, for flute, violin and continuo, ed. W. Upmeyer (*Nagels Musik-Archiv*, 33) (Hanover, 1928).
STAMITZ, J.: Trios for two violins, cello and continuo, ed. H. Riemann (*Collegium Musicum*, 1–7 and 48–49) (Leipzig, 1903–11); Op. 1, nos. 1 and 5 also ed. C. Döbereiner (Mainz, 1936–7).
STANLEY, J.: Violin Sonata in G minor, ed. A. Moffat (London, 1907).
STEFFAN, J. A.: Concerto in D major for harpsichord, flute, violin, horn, and double bass, ed. V. Bělský (*Musica Antiqua Bohemica*, 39) (Prague, 1959).
VAŇHAL, J. B.: Easy Trios for two violins and cello, ed. F. Vohanka (Prague, 1960).
WAGENSEIL, G. C.: Trio Sonata in B flat major, Op. 1 no. 3, ed. E. Schenk (Vienna, 1953).
—— Trio Sonata in F major, ed. K. Geiringer (Vienna, 1934).

(ii) *Books and Articles*
(a) *General*

BECKER, CARL F.: *Die Hausmusik in Deutschland in dem 16. 17. und 18. Jahrhunderte* (Leipzig, 1840).
COBBETT, WILLIAM W.: *Cobbett's Cyclopedic Survey of Chamber Music*, 2nd ed., 2 vols. (London, 1963).
CUCUEL, GEORGES: *La Pouplinière et la musique de chambre au XVIIIe siècle* (Paris, 1913).
DENT, EDWARD J.: 'The Earliest String Quartets', *Monthly Musical Record*, xxxiii (1903), pp. 202–4.
FUHRMANN, RODERICH: *Mannheimer Klavier-Kammermusik*, 2 vols. (Marburg Dissertation, 1963).
HERING, HANS: 'Das Klavier in der Kammermusik des 18. Jahrhunderts', *Musikforschung*, xxiii (1970), pp. 22–37.

HOFFMANN, HANS J. K.: *Die norddeutsche Triosonate des Kreises um Johann Gottlieb Graun und Carl Philipp Emanuel Bach* (Kiel Dissertation, 1924).
KIRKENDALE, WARREN: *Fuge und Fugato in der Kammermusik des Rokoko und der Klassik* (Tutzing, 1966).
LA LAURENCIE, LIONEL DE: *L'École française de violon de Lully à Viotti*, 3 vols. (Paris, 1922–4).
LEHMANN, URSULA: *Deutsches und italienisches Wesen in der Vorgeschichte des klassischen Streichquartetts*. Berlin Dissertation 1938 (Würzburg, 1939).
MERSMANN, HANS: 'Beiträge zur Aufführungspraxis der vorklassischen Kammermusik in Deutschland', *Archiv für Musikwissenschaft*, ii (1919–20), pp. 99–143.
MOSER, ANDREAS: *Geschichte des Violinspiels* (Berlin, 1923).
NEWMAN, WILLIAM S.: 'Concerning the Accompanied Clavier Sonata', *Musical Quarterly*, xxxiii (1947), pp. 327–49.
—— *The Sonata in the Baroque Era* (Chapel Hill, 1959).
—— *The Sonata in the Classic Era* (Chapel Hill, 1963).
REESER, EDUARD: *De Klaviersonate met vioolbegeleiding in het Parijsche Musiekleven ten tijde van Mozart* (Rotterdam, 1939).
SCHMITT, EDUARD: *Die kurpfälzische Kammermusik im 18. Jahrhundert.* (Heidelberg Dissertation, 1958).
STRAETEN, EDMUND S. J. VAN DER: *History of the Violoncello, the Viola da Gamba, Their Precursors and Collateral Instruments, with Biographies of All the Most Eminent Players of Every Country* (London, 1915).
STUDENY, BRUNO: *Beiträge zur Geschichte der Violinsonate im 18. Jahrhundert* (Munich, 1911).
TORREFRANCA, FAUSTO: 'Avviamento alla Storia del Quartetto Italiano', *L'Approdo musicale*, no. 23 (1966), pp. 5–181.
—— *Le Origini italiane del romanticismo musicale: i primitivi della sonata moderna* (Turin, 1930).
UNVERRICHT, HUBERT: *Geschichte des Streichtrios* (Tutzing, 1969).
WASIELEWSKI, JOSEPH W. VON: *Die Violine und ihre Meister*, 5th ed., revised and enlarged by Waldemar von Wasielewski (Leipzig, 1910).

(b) *Individual Composers*

Arne
SADIE, STANLEY: 'The Chamber Music of Boyce and Arne', *Musical Quarterly*, xlvi (1960), pp. 425–36.

C. P. E. Bach
MERSMANN, HANS: 'Ein Programmtrio Karl Philipp Emanuel Bachs', *Bach-Jahrbuch 1917*, pp. 137–70.
SCHMID, ERNST F.: *Carl Philipp Emanuel Bach und seine Kammermusik* (Kassel, 1931).

Boccherini
BARSHAM, EVE: 'Six new Boccherini Cello Sonatas', *Musical Times*, cv (1964), pp. 18–19.
KELLER, HANS: 'Mozart and Boccherini', *Music Review*, viii (1947), pp. 241–7.

Boyce
SADIE, STANLEY: 'The Chamber Music of Boyce and Arne', *Musical Quarterly*, xlvi (1960), pp. 425–36.

Cambini
TRIMPERT, DIETER L.: *Die Quatuors concertants von Giuseppe Cambini* (Tutzing, 1967).

Dittersdorf
RIGLER, GERTRUDE: 'Die Kammermusik Dittersdorfs', *Studien zur Musikwissenschaft*, xiv (1927), pp. 179–212.

Förster
WEIGL, KARL: 'Emanuel Aloys Förster', *Sammelbände der Internationalen Musikgesellschaft*, vi (1904/5), pp. 274–314.

Haydn
BELL, A. CRAIG: 'An Introduction to Haydn's Piano Trios', *Music Review*, xvi (1955), pp. 191–7.

BLUME, FRIEDRICH: 'Josef Haydns künstlerische Persönlichkeit in seinen Streichquartetten', *Jahrbuch der Musikbibliothek Peters*, xxxviii (1931), pp. 24–48; reprinted in Blume, *Syntagma Musicologicum: Gesammelte Reden und Schriften*, ed. M. Ruhnke (Kassel, 1963), pp. 526–51.

FINSCHER, LUDWIG: 'Joseph Haydn und das italienische Streichquartett', *Analecta Musicologica*, iv (1967), pp. 13–37.

HUGHES, ROSEMARY: *Haydn String Quartets* (London, 1966).

SANDBERGER, ADOLF: *Zur Geschichte des Haydn'schen Streichquartette* (Munich, 1899). Originally appeared in *Altbayerische Monatshefte*. Reprinted in *Ausgewählte Aufsätze zur Musikgeschichte*, i (Munich, 1921).

SCHWARTING, HEINO: 'Über die Echtheit dreier Haydn-Trios', *Archiv für Musikwissenschaft*, xxii (1965), pp. 169–82.

SONDHEIMER, ROBERT: *Haydn, a Historical and Psychological Study based on his Quartets* (London, 1951).

STRUNK, OLIVER: 'Haydn's Divertimenti for Baryton, Viola, and Bass (After Manuscripts in the Library of Congress)', *Musical Quarterly*, xviii (1932), pp. 216–51.

TYSON, ALAN: 'Haydn and two stolen Trios', *Music Review*, xxii (1961), pp. 21–5.

—— and LANDON, H. C. ROBBINS: 'Who composed Haydn's Op. 3?', *Musical Times*, cv (1964), pp. 506–7.

Mozart
CROLL, GERHARD: 'Eine neuentdeckte Bach-Fuge für Streichquartett von Mozart', *Österreichische Musikzeitschrift*, xxi (1966), pp. 508–14.

DANCKERT, WERNER: 'Mozarts Menuettypen', *Bericht über die musikwissenschaftliche Tagung der Internationalen Stiftung Mozarteum in Salzburg . . . 1931*, ed. Erich Schenk (Leipzig, 1932), pp. 129–32.

DUNHILL, THOMAS F.: *Mozart's String Quartets*, 2 vols. (London, 1927).

FISCHER, WILHELM: 'Mozarts Weg von der begleiteten Klaviersonate zur Kammermusik mit Klavier', *Mozart-Jahrbuch 1956*, pp. 16–34.

HOLSCHNEIDER, ANDREAS: 'Zu Mozarts Bearbeitungen Bachscher Fugen', *Musikforschung*, xvii (1964), pp. 51–6, 463–4.

KELLER, HANS: 'Mozart and Boccherini', *Music Review*, viii (1947), pp. 241–7.

—— 'The Chamber Music', *The Mozart Companion*, ed. H. C. Robbins Landon and Donald Mitchell (London, 1956), pp. 90–137.

KING, A. HYATT: *Mozart Chamber Music* (London, 1968).

KIRKENDALE, WARREN: 'More Slow Introductions by Mozart to Fugues of J. S. Bach?', *Journal of the American Musicological Society*, xvii (1964), pp. 43–65.

LEAVIS, RALPH: 'Mozart's Flute Quartet in C, K. App. 171', *Music and Letters*, xliii (1962), pp. 48–52.

MARGUERRE, K.: 'Mozarts Klaviertrios', *Mozart-Jahrbuch 1960/61*, pp. 182–94.

SIEGMUND-SCHULTZE, WALTHER: 'Mozarts "Haydn-Quartette"', *Bericht über die internationale Konferenz zum Andenken Joseph Haydns*, ed. B. Szabolcsi and D. Bartha (Budapest, 1961), pp. 137–46.

TANGEMAN, ROBERT S.: 'Mozart's Seventeen Epistle Sonatas', *Musical Quarterly*, xxxii (1946), pp. 588–601.

G. B. Sammartini
CHURGIN, BATHIA: 'New Facts in Sammartini Biography: The Authentic Print of the String Trios, Op. 7', *Journal of the American Musicological Society*, xx (1967) pp. 107–12.

MISHKIN, HENRY G.: 'The Published Instrumental Works of Giovanni Battista Sammartini: A Bibliographical Reappraisal', *Musical Quarterly*, xlv (1959), pp. 361–74.
—— 'Five Autograph String Quartets by Giovanni Battista Sammartini', *Journal of the American Musicological Society*, vi (1953), pp. 136–45.

Soler
NIN, JOAQUÍN: 'The Bi-Centenary of Antonio Soler', *The Chesterian*, xi (1929-30), pp. 97–103.

Tartini
BOYDEN, DAVID D.: 'The missing Italian Manuscript of Tartini's *Traité des Agrémens*', *Musical Quarterly*, xlvi (1960), pp. 315–28.
BRAINARD, PAUL: 'Tartini and the Sonata for Unaccompanied Violin', *Journal of the American Musicological Society*, xiv (1961), pp. 383–93.
—— *Die Violinsonaten Giuseppe Tartinis*. (Göttingen Dissertation, 1960).

CHAPTER X

KEYBOARD MUSIC

(i) *Modern Editions*
(a) *Anthologies*

BELLARDI, R., ed.: *Deutsche Klaviermusik des Rococo* (Stuttgart, 1926).
BENVENUTI, GIACOMO, ed.: *Cembalisti italini del settecento* (Milan, 1926).
ESPOSITO, MICHELE, ed.: *Early Italian Piano Music* (Boston, Mass., 1906).
FARRENC, J. H. ARISTIDE and FARRENC, J. LOUISE, edd.: *Le Trésor des pianistes*, 20 vols. (Paris, 1861–72). Also issued differently grouped in 23 vols.
FISCHER, HANS: *Die Sonate* (*Musikalische Formen in historischen Reihen*, 18) (Berlin, 1937).
—— and OBERDOERFFER, FRITZ, edd.: *Deutsche Klaviermusik des 17. und 18. Jahrhunderts*, vols. 1, 3, 6–9, 2nd ed., (Berlin, 1960).
FISCHER, KURT VON, ed.: *Die Variation* (*Das Musikwerk*, 11), (Cologne, 1956. English edition, Cologne, 1962).
GEIRINGER, KARL, ed.: *Wiener Meister um Mozart und Beethoven* (Vienna, 1935).
GEORGII, WALTER, ed.: *Keyboard Music of the Baroque and Rococo*, vol. 3, *Music after Bach and Handel* (Cologne, 1960).
GIEGLING, FRANZ, ed.: *Die Solosonate* (*Das Musikwerk*, 15) (Cologne, 1959. English edition Cologne, 1960).
KANN, HANS, ed.: *Klavier-Musik aus Österreich* (Vienna, 1965).
MALIPIERO, GIAN FRANCESCO, ed.: *18th Century Italian Keyboard Music* (Bryn Mawr, 1952).
NEWMAN, WILLIAM S., ed.: *Thirteen Keyboard Sonatas of the 18th and 19th Centuries* (Chapel Hill, 1947).
—— *Six Keyboard Sonatas from the Classic Era* (Evanston, Ill., 1965).
PAUER, ERNST, ed.: *Alte Meister, Sammlung werthvoller Klavierstücke des 17. und 18. Jahrhunderts*, 6 vols. (Leipzig, 1868–85).
RACEK, JAN, EMINGEROVÁ, K. and KREDBA, O., edd.: *České Sonatiny* (*Musica Antiqua Bohemica*, 17) (Prague, 1954).
SCHLEUNING, PETER: *Die Fantasie*, 2 vols. (*Das Musikwerk*, 42–3) (Cologne, 1971).
TAGLIAPIETRA, GINO, ed.: *Antologia di musica antica e moderna per pianoforte*, vols. 12–13, (Milan, 1931).

(b) *Works by Individual Composers*

ALBRECHTSBERGER, J. G.: *Instrumentalwerke*, ed. O. Kapp (*Denkmäler der Tonkunst in Österreich*, Jg. 16/2, vol. 33) (Vienna, 1909).

ARNE, T. A.: 8 Sonatas, facsimile edn. by G. Beechey and T. Dart (London, 1969).
BACH, C. P. E.: *Abschied vom Silbermannischen Clavier in einem Rondeaux*, ed. A. Kreutz (Mainz, 1950).
—— *Kurze und leichte Klavierstücke mit veränderten Reprisen*, ed. O. Jonas, 2 vols. (Vienna, 1962).
—— *Neues C. Ph. E. Bach Album*, ed. E. Caland (Münster, 1929).
—— 18 *Probe-Stücke*, Wq. 63, ed. E. Doflein (Mainz, 1935).
—— The "Prussian" Sonatas, Wq. 48, ed. R. Steglich, 2 vols. (*Nagels Musik-Archiv*, 6, 15) (Hanover, 1927).
—— The "Würtemberg" Sonatas, Wq. 49, ed. R. Steglich, 2 vols. (*Nagels Musik-Archiv*, 21, 22) (Hanover, 1928).
—— *Die sechs Sammlungen von Sonaten, freien Fantasien und Rondos für Kenner und Liebhaber*, Wq. 55–9, 61, ed. C. Krebs and L. Hoffmann-Erbrecht, 6 vols. (Leipzig, 1954).
—— *Sonaten und Stücke*, ed. K. Herrmann (Leipzig, 1938).
BACH, J. C.: 10 Sonatas, ed. L. Landshoff (Leipzig, 1925).
BACH, J. C. F.: *Ausgewählte Werke*, ed. G. Schünemann, vol. 5, Klaviersonaten Nr. 1–4 (Bückeburg, 1920).
—— 6 Easy Sonatas, ed. H. Ruf and H. Bemmann (Mainz, 1968).
BACH, W. F.: Concerto in E flat major for two harpsichords, ed. H. Riemann (Leipzig, 1894).
—— Concerto in F major for two harpsichords, ed. H. Brandt Buys (London, 1953).
—— *Concerto per il cembalo solo* in G major, ed. L. Hoffmann-Erbrecht (*Organum*, series 5 no. 27) (Lippstadt, 1960).
—— Fantasias, ed. P. Schleuning (Mainz, 1970).
—— 6 Fantasias, ed. C. Banck (Lippstadt, 1881).
—— Fantasia in C major, ed. L. Hoffmann-Erbrecht (*Organum*, series 5, no. 31) (Lippstadt, 1963).
—— Fugues and Polonaises for keyboard, ed. Walter Niemann (Leipzig, 1914); Fugues only, ed. C. de Nys (Paris, 1961).
—— Polonaises, ed. F. Wührer (Vienna, 1949–53).
—— Sonatas, ed. F. Blume, 3 vols. (*Nagels Musik-Archiv*, 63, 78, 156) (Hanover, 1930–40).
BENDA, G.: Sonatas, 1–16, ed. J. Racek and V. J. Sýkora (*Musica Antiqua Bohemica* 24) (Prague, 1957).
—— Sonatinas 1–34, from *Sammlung vermischter Clavier- und Gesangstücke*, ed. V. J. Sýkora (*Musica Antiqua Bohemica*, 37) (Prague, 1958).
CIMAROSA, D.: 32 Sonatas, ed. F. Boghen, 3 vols. (Paris, 1925–6).
DURANTE, F.: *Sei studi e sei divertimenti per cembalo*, ed. B. Paumgartner (Kassel, 1949).
ECKARD, J. G.: *Oeuvres complètes pour le clavecin ou le piano forte*, ed. E. Reeser (Amsterdam, 1956).
GALUPPI, B.: *Passatempo al Cembalo*, ed. F. Piva (Venice, 1964).
—— 12 Sonatas, ed. G. Benvenuti (Bologna, 1920).
GRAZIOLI, G.: 12 Sonatas, ed. R. Gerlin (*I classici musicali italiani*, 12) (Milan, 1943).
HÄSSLER, J. W.: 6 Easy Piano Sonatas, ed. L. Hoffmann-Erbrecht, 3 vols. (*Organum*, series 5, nos. 26, 28, 30) (Lippstadt, 1960–1).
HAYDN: *Werke*, ed. Joseph Haydn-Institut, Cologne, series 18, *Klaviersonaten* (Munich, 1966–70).
—— Sonatas, ed. C. Landon, 3 vols. (Vienna, 1964–6).
MARTINI, G. B.: Sonatas, 1742 set, ed. M. Vitali (Milan, n.d.).
—— Sonatas, 1747 set, ed. L. Hoffmann-Erbrecht (*Mitteldeutsches Musikarchiv*, series 1 no. 5) (Leipzig, 1954).
—— 6 Sonatas, ed. D. Cipollini (*I classici della musica italiana*, 18), (Milan, 1920).

MOZART: *Werke*, ed. J. Brahms *et al.*, series 19, *Für Klavier zu 4 Händen* (*und für 2 Klaviere*); series 20, *Sonaten und Fantasien für Klavier*; series 21, *Variationen für Klavier*; series 22, *Kleinere Stücke für Klavier*; series 24, *Supplement* (Leipzig, 1878–92).
—— *Neue Ausgabe sämtlicher Werke*, ed. Internationale Stiftung Mozarteum, series 9, *Klaviermusik* (Kassel, 1955–   ).
—— Sonatas and Fantasies, ed. N. Broder (Bryn Mawr, Penn., 1956).
—— Sonatas, ed. W. Lampe, 2 vols. (Munich, 1957).
PARADIES, D.: *Sonate di gravicembalo*, ed. H. Ruf and H. Bemmann, 2 vols. (Mainz, 1971).
PLATTI, G. B.: 12 sonatas, ed. L. Hoffmann-Erbrecht (*Mitteldeutsches Musikarchiv*, series 1 vols. 3–4) (Leipzig, 1954).
—— 18 sonatas in Fausto Torrefranca, *Giovanni Benedetto Platti e la sonata moderna* (Milan, 1963).
RUST, F. W.: *Werke für Klavier und Streichinstrumente*, ed. R. Czach (*Das Erbe deutscher Musik*, 2nd series, Landschaftsdenkmale, Mitteldeutschland, 1) (Wolfenbüttel, 1939).
SOLER, A.: Sonatas, ed. S. Rubio, 6 vols. (Madrid, 1957–62).
—— 34 Sonatas, ed. F. Marvin, 3 vols. (London, 1957–61).
WAGENSEIL, G. C.: 4 Divertimenti, ed. F. Blume (*Nagels Musik-Archiv*, 36) (Hanover, 1929).

(ii) *Books and Articles*
(a) *General*

AUERBACH, CORNELIA: *Die deutsche Clavichordkunst des 18. Jahrhunderts* (Kassel, 1930).
GEORGII, WALTER: *Klaviermusik*, 2nd ed. (Zürich, 1950).
HEUSCHNEIDER, KARIN: *The Piano Sonata of the Eighteenth Century in Italy* (Cape Town, 1967).
HOFFMANN-ERBRECHT, LOTHAR: *Deutsche und italienische Klaviermusik zur Bachzeit* (Leipzig, 1954).
—— 'Sturm und Drang in der deutschen Klaviermusik von 1753–1763', *Musikforschung*, x (1957), pp. 466–79.
KAMIEN, ROGER: 'Style Change in the Mid-18th-Century Keyboard Sonata', *Journal of the American Musicological Society*, xix (1966), pp. 37–58.
KLAUWELL, OTTO: *Geschichte der Sonate* (Leipzig, 1899).
LANGE, MARTIN F. W.: *Beiträge zur Entstehung der südwestdeutschen Klaviersonate im 18. Jahrhundert*. (Giessen Dissertation, 1930).
NEWMAN, WILLIAM S.: *The Sonata in the Baroque Era* (Chapel Hill, 1959).
—— *The Sonata in the Classic Era* (Chapel Hill, 1963).
PARRISH, CARL: 'Criticisms of the Piano When It was New', *Musical Quarterly*, xxx (1944), pp. 428–40.
SCHLEUNING, PETER: 'Die Fantasiermaschine. Ein Beitrag zur Geschichte der Stilwende um 1750', *Archiv für Musikwissenschaft*, xxvii (1970), pp. 192–213.
SEIFFERT, MAX: *Geschichte der Klaviermusik* (Leipzig, 1899; reprinted Hildesheim, 1966). This is the 3rd completely revised edition of C. F. Weitzmann's *Geschichte des Clavierspiels*.
SHEDLOCK, JOHN S.: *The Pianoforte Sonata* (London, 1895).
STILZ, ERNST: *Die Berliner Klaviersonate zur Zeit Friedrichs der Grossen*. Berlin Dissertation (Saarbrücken, 1930).

(b) *Individual Composers*

Alberti
WÖRMANN, WILHELM: 'Die Klaviersonaten Domenico Albertis', *Acta Musicologica*, xxvii (1955), pp. 84–112.

T. A. Arne
DICKINSON, A. E. F.: 'Arne and the Keyboard Sonata', *Monthly Musical Record*, lxxxv (1955), pp. 88–95.

C. P. E. Bach
BACH, CARL PHILIPP EMANUEL: *Versuch über die wahre Art das Clavier zu spielen*, 2 vols. (Berlin, 1753–62). Facsimile ed., ed. L. Hoffmann-Erbrecht (Leipzig, 1957). English translation by William J. Mitchell, 2nd ed. (London, 1951).
BARFORD, PHILIP: *The Keyboard Music of C. P. E. Bach* (London, 1965).
BEURMANN, ERICH H.: *Die Klaviersonaten Carl Philipp Emanuel Bachs*. (Göttingen Dissertation, 1953).
—— 'Die Reprisensonaten Carl Philipp Emanuel Bachs', *Archiv für Musikwissenschaft*, xiii (1956), pp. 168–79.
FISCHER, KURT VON: 'C. Ph. E. Bachs Variationwerke', *Revue belge de Musicologie*, vi (1952), pp. 190–218.
WYLER, ROBERT: *Form- und Stiluntersuchungen zum ersten Satz der Klaviersonaten Carl Philipp Emanuel Bachs*. Zürich Dissertation (Bern, 1960).

Eckard
PAAP, WOUTER: 'De Klaviersonates van Joh. G. Eckard', *Mens en Melodie*, xii (1957), pp. 109–12.
REESER, EDUARD: 'Johann Gottfried Eckard, 1735–1809', *Tijdschrift voor muziekwetenschap*, xvii/2 (1949), pp. 89–127.

Galuppi
TORREFRANCA, FAUSTO: 'Per un catalogo tematico delle sonate per cembalo di B. Galuppi detto il Buranello', *Rivista musicale italiana*, xvi (1909), pp. 872–81.

Haydn
ABERT, HERMANN: 'Joseph Haydns Klavierwerke', *Zeitschrift für Musikwissenschaft*, ii (1919/20), pp. 553–73; iii (1920/1), pp. 535–52.
PARRISH, CARL: 'Haydn and the Piano', *Journal of the American Musicological Society*, i no. 3 (1948), pp. 27–34.
STRUNK, OLIVER: 'Notes on a Haydn Autograph', *Musical Quarterly*, xx (1934), pp. 192–205.
VIGNAL, MARC: 'L'Oeuvre pour piano seul de Joseph Haydn', *Revue Musicale*, xxx (1961), Carnet critique no. 249, pp. 5–20.

Kirnberger
BORRIS, SIEGFRIED: *Kirnbergers Leben und Werk und seine Bedeutung im Berliner Musikkreis um 1750* (Kassel, 1933).
KIRNBERGER, JOHANN PHILIPP: *Methode Sonaten aus'm Ermel zu schüddeln* (Berlin, 1783).
NEWMAN, WILLIAM S.: 'Kirnberger's Method for Tossing Off Sonatas', *Musical Quarterly*, xlvii (1961), pp. 517–25.

Krebs
LÖFFLER, HANS: 'Johann Ludwig Krebs: Mitteilungen über sein Leben und Wirken', *Bach-Jahrbuch 1930*, pp. 100–29.

Mozart
BRODER, NATHAN: 'Mozart and the "Clavier"', *Musical Quarterly*, xxvii (1941), pp. 422–32.
DENNERLEIN, HANNS: *Der unbekannte Mozart: die Welt seiner Klavierwerke*, 2nd ed. (Leipzig, 1955).
HIRSCH, PAUL: 'A Mozart Problem', *Music and Letters*, xxv (1944), pp. 209–12.
HUTCHINGS, ARTHUR: 'The Keyboard Music', *The Mozart Companion*, ed. H. C. Robbins Landon and Donald Mitchell (London, 1956), pp. 32–65.
KING, A. HYATT: 'Mozart's Piano Music', *Music Review*, v (1944), pp. 163–91.

MERIAN, WILHELM: 'Mozarts Klaviersonaten und die Sonatenform', *Festschrift Karl Nef zum 60. Geburtstag* (Zürich, 1933), pp. 174–201.
STEGLICH, RUDOLF: 'Studien an Mozarts Hammerflügel', *Neues Mozart-Jahrbuch*, i (1941), pp. 181–210.
―― 'Über das melodische Motiv in der Musik Mozarts', *Mozart-Jahrbuch 1953*, pp. 128–42.

Platti
TORREFRANCA, FAUSTO: *Giovanni Benedetto Platti e la sonata moderna* (Milan, 1963).

Reichardt
DENNERLEIN, HANNS: *Johann Friedrich Reichardt und seine Klavierwerke* (Münster, 1930).

Rolle
KAESTNER, RUDOLF: *Johann Heinrich Rolle* (Kassel, 1932).

Rutini
TORREFRANCA, FAUSTO: 'Il primo maestro di W. A. Mozart (Giovanni Maria Rutini)', *Rivista musicale italiana*, xl (1936), pp. 239–53.

Schobert
DAVID, HANS T.: *Johann Schobert als Sonatenkomponist*. Berlin Dissertation 1927 (Leipzig, 1928).

Vaňhal
DEWITZ, MARGARETHE VON: *Jean Baptiste Vanhal, Leben und Klavierwerke* (Munich Dissertation, 1933).

LIST OF CONTENTS OF
THE HISTORY OF MUSIC IN SOUND
VOLUME VII

The History of Music in Sound is a series of volumes of gramophone records, with explanatory booklets, designed as a companion series to the *New Oxford History of Music*. Each volume covers the same ground as the corresponding volume in the *New Oxford History of Music* and is designed as far as possible to illustrate the music discussed therein. The records are issued in England by E.M.I. Records Ltd. (H.M.V.) and in the United States by R.C.A. Victor, and the booklets are published by the Oxford University Press. The editor of Volume VII of *The History of Music in Sound* is Egon Wellesz.

The History of Music in Sound is available on LP records, and the side numbers are given below.

FRENCH OPERA
Side I   Band 1   Scene from *Iphigénie en Aulide* (Gluck)
SINGSPIEL
         Band 2   Quartet: *Ach Belmonte!* from *Die Entführung aus dem Serail* (Mozart)
         Band 3   Aria: *Verliebte brauchen keine Zeugen* from *Doktor und Apotheker* (Dittersdorf)
OPÉRA COMIQUE
Side II Band 1   Air: *Si l'univers entier m'oublie* from *Richard Cœur-de-Lion* (Grétry)
OPERA SERIA
         Band 2   Aria: *Se all'impero* from *La clemenza di Tito* (Mozart)
OPERA BUFFA
         Band 3   Duet: *Io ti lascio* from *Il matrimonio segreto* (Cimarosa)
CHURCH MUSIC
         Band 4   *Prope est* (Michael Haydn)
         Band 5   *Agnus Dei* from *Litaniae Lauretanae* (K. 195) (Mozart)
SYMPHONY
Side III Bands 1–2 Symphony No. 8 in D minor (Boyce)
         Bands 3–4 Allegro assai and Andante from *Symphony in E flat* (*La melodia Germanica*, No. 3) (Stamitz)
Side IV Bands 1–2 Allegro and Finale from *Symphony No. 31 in D* (Horn Signal) (Haydn)
         Band 3   *Symphony No. 3 in F* (C. P. E. Bach)
CONCERTO (I)
Side V   Band 1   Allegro from *Cello Concerto in G minor* (M. G. Monn)
DANCE MUSIC
         Bands 2, 3, Nos. 1, 6, and 7 of *12 Deutsche Tänze* (Haydn)
         & 4

CONCERTO (II)
>   Band 5   Allegro from *Piano Concerto in A* (J. C. Bach)

CHAMBER MUSIC
Side VI Bands 1-2 Minuet and Adagio from *Divertimento in E flat* (K. 289) (Mozart)
>   Band 3   Fuga con 3 soggetti from *String Quartet in A* (Op. 20, no. 6) (Haydn)
>   Band 4   Adagio from *Piano Trio in F sharp minor* (Haydn)

KEYBOARD MUSIC: CLAVICHORD
>   Band 5   *Fantasia in C minor* (C. P. E. Bach)

INDEX

Compiled by Frederick Smyth

Page numbers in *italic type* indicate the more important references. Operas and other stage works, and oratorios, are indexed under composers and librettists, the latter being identified as such.

Abaco, Felice dall', 519.
Abaco, Giuseppe dall', 519.
  Trios for three cellos, 550.
Abel, Carl Friedrich, 324, *426–7*, 431, *482–3*, 484, 486, 491.
  Cello Concerto in C, 482 (Ex. 266).
  Cello Concerto in B flat, 482–3 (Ex. 267).
  Piano Concerto in F, Op. 11, no. 1, 482 (Ex. 265 (i)).
  Piano Concerto in G, Op. 11, no. 5, 482 (Ex. 265 (ii)).
  Sonatas, 518.
  Symphonie concertante, 483.
  Symphony in E flat, Op. 10, no. 3, 427 (Ex. 206).
Abert, Anna Amalie, 119 n[3].
Abert, Hermann, 36 n[2], 46 n[1], 59 n[1], 89 n[2], 143 n[4], 205 n[3], 541, 564.
  Goethe und die Musik, 85 n[2].
  Niccolò Jommelli als Opernkomponist, 24 n[2], 34 nn[1–3], 35 n[1], 36 n[1].
  W. A. Mozart, 293. 625 n[1].
  ibid. (7th edn.), 97 n[2], 154 n[3], 159 n[1], 163 n[1], 167 n[1], 169 n[1], 171 n[1], 316 n[1], 317 nn[2, 3], 318 n[3].
Ablesimov, Aleksandr (librettist), *The Miller-magician*, 273.
Abraham, Gerald, 431 n[1].
Adamberger, Valentin, 141, 144, 149 n[2].
Adler, Guido, 294 n[1], 395 n[1], 615.
Adlgasser, Anton Cajetan, 296 *bis*, 309, 326.
Agrell, Johan, 423, *431–2*, 452.
Air de cour, 344.
Alba, Duke of, 382.
Albertarelli, Francesco, 159.
Alberti, Domenico
  harpsichord sonatas, 577.
  'Alberti bass', 340, 532, 576–7, 606, 615.
Albinoni, Tomaso, 378 n[1], 434.
Albrecht, Hans, 563 n[1], 569 n[4].
Albrecht, Otto, 358 n[2].
Albrechtsberger, Johann Georg, 467–8.
  Concertos, 467–8 (Exx. 246–7).
  Quartets, 560.
Albrekht, Konstantin, 273.
Alembert, Jeanle Rond d', xvi, xx, 226.
Algarotti, Francesco, 230.
  Saggio sopra l'opera in musica, xviii, 229.

Almeida, Antonio de, 372 n[1], 373 n[1].
Altmann, Wilhelm, 453 n[3].
Anderson, Emily
  The Letters of Mozart and his Family, 106 n[1], 118 n[1], 126 n[2], 127 n[1], 133–44 nn *passim*, 148 n[2], 159 n[2], 250 n[1], 299 n[1], 310 n[1], 313 n[1], 315 n[4].
  ibid. (2nd edn.), 412 n[1], 609 n[2].
André, Johann, 6 n[1], 86, 88–9, 351.
  Barbier von Bagdad, Der, 88.
  Entführung aus dem Serail, Die, 88–9, 141, 146 (Ex. 90).
  Laura Rosetti, 89.
  Songs
    'Bekränzt mit Laub den freudenvollen Becher', 351.
    'Lenore', 349.
    Musikalischer Blumenstrauss für das Jahr 1776, 351 n[2].
  and Mozart's K. 537, 501.
  as a publisher, 128, 349, 481, 483, 490, 501, 547 n[5].
Anfossi, Pasquale, 8, 32, 45, 58, 63, 371.
  Curioso indiscreto, Il, 149 n[2].
Angerer, P., 472 n[1].
Angiolini, Gasparo, 43.
Anglès, Higini, 532 n[4].
Anna, Empress of Russia, 270.
Anna Amalie, Grand Duchess of Saxe-Weimar, 85.
Ansion, Margarete, *see* Pollak-Schlaffenberg, Irene.
Anyuta (composer unknown), 272.
Apel, Willi, *see* Davison, Archibald T.
Araja, Francesco, 8, 270.
  Artaserse, 270.
  Finto Nino overo la Semiramide reconosciuta, Il, 270.
  Forza dell'amore e dell'odio, La, 270.
  Tsefal i Prokris, 271.
Aria cantabile, 21, 22, 55 (Ex. 30), 135.
Aria di bravura, 21, 22–3 (Ex. 10), 54–5 (Ex. 29), 74, 114–15, 137, 145, 161, 232.
Aria di mezzo carattere, 21.
Aria di portamento, 21.
Aria finale, 56.
Aria parlante, 21, *135* (Ex. 86).
Armitage-Smith, J. N. A., 167 n[2].

INDEX

Arne, Michael (with Jonathan Battishill), *Almena*, 260.
Arne, Thomas, 258, 261, 263 n[1], 269, 325, 339–40, *429*.
   Artaxerxes, *258–60* (Ex. 127), 264, 267, 269.
   Comus, 258.
   Eliza, 258, 260.
   Guardian Outwitted, The, 429, 430.
   Judith, 325.
   Love in a Village, 258, 260–1, 264, 269.
   Thomas and Sally, 339.
   Concertos, 434.
   'Rule, Britannia', 487.
   Sonatas for harpsichord, *580* (Ex. 318), 581.
   Songs, 339–40.
      Lyric Harmony . . ., 339 n[1], 340.
      Vocal Melody . . ., 339 n[2].
   Trios, Op. 3, *529*.
Arnold, Samuel, 263–5 *passim*, 269, 325, 581.
   Castle of Andalusia, The, 264.
   Children of the Wood, The, 264.
   Maid of the Mill, The, 261.
   Prodigal Son, The, 325.
   Siege of Curzolo, The, 265.
   (ed.) *Cathedral Music*, 324.
Arrieu, Claude, 519 n[1].
Artaria (publishers), 172, 181, 349 n[5], 402, 563, 598–9, 602, 617.
Aspelmayr, Franz, 24, 91 n[3], 94, 509.
   trio sonatas, 526.
Astaritta, Gennaro, *Mondo della luna, Il*, 192.
Auersperg, Prince Karl, 140.
Auletta, Pietro (*et al.*), *Maestro di musica, Il*, 255.
Avison, Charles, 434.

Bach, Carl Philipp Emanuel, xvi, xvii, 383, 448, 594–5, 610–11, 619, 625.
   influences on
      J. C. Bach, 484.
      Beethoven, 626.
      Benda, 594.
      J. Haydn, 553–5 *passim*, 562, 566, 593, 596–8, *613–15*, 617, 624.
      Mozart, 359, 540.
   Thematic catalogue, *see* Wotquenne.
   Chamber music without continuo, 534–5.
   Church music
      'Heilig', 330, *331–2* (Ex. 148).
      Magnificat, 330.
   Concertos, 435, *453–5*, 471, 489, 628.
      Cello, in B flat (Wq. 171), 450, *454* (Exx. 227–8).
      Cembalo, in A minor (Wq. 26), 453 (Ex. 226).
      Cembalo, in D minor (Wq. 23), 454 (Ex. 229).
      Piano, in D minor (Wq. 43/2), 455 (Ex. 230).
   Keyboard works, xix, *583–93*, 597, 602, 607, 609.
      Probestücke (Wq. 63), *585–6*, 591.
   Sonatas
      Wq. 48, 389 n[2], *584* (Ex. 323), 585.
      Wq. 49, *585* (Ex. 324), 586, 587.
      Wq. 50 (*Sonaten mit veränderten Reprisen*), 387, *586–7* (Ex. 325), 589, 591, 610.
      Wq. 51, *587–8* (Ex. 326).
      Wq. 52, 587, *588*.
      Wq. 53, 588.
      Wq. 54, 588.
   Sonatas, Rondos and Fantasias (*für Kenner und Liebhaber*)
      Wq. 55, *588–90* (Exx. 327–8), 591, 592 (Ex. 330), 593.
      Wq. 56–8, *590–1*.
      Wq. 59, 590 (Ex. 329), 591.
      Wq. 61, 591.
   Sonatinas (Wq. 63), 592.
   Titled pieces, 592.
   Oratorios
      Auferstehung und Himmelfahrt Jesu, Die, 331 (Ex. 147).
      Israeliten in der Wüste, Die, 330–1.
   Orchester-Sinfonien (Wq. 183), 387, *393–4*.
   Sonatas for flute, 518, 520.
   Songs, 347–8 (Ex. 153).
   Symphonies, 375, *385–95*, 412.
      Van Swieten, No. 3 in C, *386–8* (Exx. 174–6), 392–3.
      Van Swieten, No. 4 in A, 391–2 (Ex. 177).
      Van Swieten, No. 5 in B minor, 392 n[1], *393*.
   Trios, 527–8.
Bach, Johann Ernst, 535–6.
Bach, Johann Christian, xvi, 32, 431, 522, 610, 614.
   influence on Mozart, 487, 491, 570, 594–6 *passim*, 603, 628.
   in London, 8, 324, 426, 486, 581.
   Mozart and, 97, 102, 110–11.
   Aria, 'Dolci aurette', 539.
   Chamber music with clavier, 538–9.
   Concertos, *483–5* (Exx. 268–70), 494, 594.
   Keyboard sonatas, 594–6 (Ex. 332).
   Operas, 46–7.
      Alessandro nell'Indie, 46–7 (Ex. 24 (ii)).
      Catone in Utico, 46 (Ex. 24 (i)).
      Orione (ov.), 427, 428.
      Temistocle (ov.), 428–9.
   Quartet (attr.), 544 and n[2].
   Quintets, Op. 11, 569–70.

INDEX

Sonate notturne (string trios), 549.
Symphonies, *427–9* (Exx. 207–8), 432.
Violin sonata, Op. 10, no. 1, 538–9 (Ex. 302).
Bach, Johann Christoph Friedrich, 67 n[1], 329 n[1], 594.
  Oratorios
    Auferweckung Lazarus, Die, 329.
    Kindheit Jesu, Die, 329.
  Sextet in C, 563 (Ex. 300).
  Sonata in A for cello and clavier, 536.
  Trios, 536.
Bach, Johann Sebastian, xv, 330, 390, 392, 435, 520, 574, 582–4 *passim*, 609–11 *passim*, 619, 625–6.
  Graun's work compared with, 329.
  influence on Mozart, 315, 316, 552.
  his pupils, 455, 593, 609.
  Brandenburg Concertos, 172.
  Chromatic Fantasia, 592.
  English Suite in D minor, 593.
  Fugues, Mozart's arrangements of, 552 and n[3].
  Goldberg Variations, 389 n[2].
  Italian Concerto, 583.
  Mass in B minor, 291, 316, 330.
  Motet, 'Singet dem Herrn', 317.
  Organ Fantasia in G minor, 592.
  Partita no. 1 (*Clavierübung*), 539.
  Prelude in F minor (2nd Book), 592.
Bach, Wilhelm Friedemann, 448, *452–3*, 527, 534, *581–3*, 610.
  Concerto for 2 cembali in E flat, 452 (Ex. 225).
  'Concerto' for 2 harpsichords in F, 583.
  Instrumental duets, 546.
  Keyboard works, 581–3 (Exx. 320–2).
  Sonata for 2 flutes in F, 546 (Ex. 306).
  Trio in A minor, 527.
Bach, Wilhelm Friedrich Ernst
  Trio in G for 2 Flutes and Viola, 550.
Bacher, J., 518 n[4].
Bacher, Otto, 80 n[1], 126 n[1].
Baden, Margrave of, 433.
Bader, Philipp Georg (librettist)
  Bestrafte Rachbegierde, Die (Haydn), 177, 179.
  Dido (Haydn), 177.
Badini, Carlo Francesco (librettist)
  Orfeo ed Euridice (Haydn), 196.
Badura-Skoda, Paul and Eva
  Interpreting Mozart on the Keyboard, 440 n[2].
Bailleux (publisher), 405 n[1], 463, 547.
Balet, L., 552 n[1].
Ballad opera, 257–8.
Ballard, Christophe (publ.)
  Brunettes ou Petits airs tendres, 342 n[1].
Balsam, Artur, 494 n[1].
Banck, C., 583 n[2].

Banti, Brigitta, 199.
Barbella, Emanuele, Duet in G, 547.
Barbour, J. M., *Trumpets, Horns, and Music*, 432 n[4].
Barford, Philip, 586 nn[2, 3]
  The Keyboard Music of C. P. E. Bach, 584 n[1], 586 n[2].
Barmherzige Brüder, Eisenstadt, 304.
Barrington, Daines, 97 n[3].
Bartha, Dénes, 404 n[2].
  (with László Somfai), *Josef Haydn als Opernkapellmeister*, 173 n[1], 198.
Barthélemon, François, 487.
Bartolozzi, Mrs. Therese (*née* Jansen), 600.
Baryton, 551.
Bates, William, *Pharnaces*, 260.
Batley, E. M., 167 n[2].
Battishill, Jonathan
  'O Lord, look down from heaven', 324–5.
  (with Michael Arne) *Almena*, 260.
Bauer, Wilhelm A., and O. E. Deutsch (eds.), *Mozart: Briefe und Aufzeichnungen*, 98 n[4], 318 n[2], 445 n[2], 486 n[1].
Baur, Uwe, 14 n[1].
Beard, John, *258*, 269.
Beaumarchais, Caron de (playwright and librettist)
  Barbier de Séville, Le, 150, 151.
  Mariage de Figaro, Le, 150, 151, 241, 250.
  Tarare (Salieri), 244, 246.
Bebung, 589, 592.
Beck, Franz, 414, *416–18*, 423, 509.
  Symphony in G minor, Op. 3, no. 3, 417–18 (Ex. 198).
Beck, Sydney, 549 n[1].
Becker, H., 432 n[2].
Bedini, Domenico, 165 n[1].
Beechey, Gwilym, 426 n[1], 580 n[1].
Beethoven, Ludwig van, xvi, 386–7, 390, 398, 405, 461, 532, 566, 628, 629, 631.
  and Albrechtsberger, 467, 560.
  his cadenzas, 488.
  his codas, 612.
  compared with
    Haydn, 598.
    Mozart, 436, 570, 605, 606.
    Salieri, 246.
  dramatic style, 244.
  and Frederick the Great, 394.
  influenced by
    C. P. E. Bach, 392, 455.
    Haydn, 555, 562, 600, 601, 620, 626–7.
    Mozart, 624, 627.
  on Mozart's K. 491, 628.
  and Rust, 609.
  Schobert and, 534.
  Aria, 'Ah, perfido', 199.
  Christus am Oelberge, 333.
  Egmont, 221.

Beethoven, Ludwig van (*cont.*):
  Fidelio, 152, 209, 221, 238.
  Leonora (overtures), 611.
  Masses
    in C major, 319.
    in D ('Missa Solemnis'), 303.
  Piano sonatas, 589, 599.
  Quartets, 278, 619-20.
  Quintet in E flat (piano and wind), 545.
  Symphonies
    no. 1, 411.
    no. 2, 502.
    no. 3 ('Eroica'), 428, 632, 634.
    no. 5, 627, 634.
    no. 9 ('Choral'), 627.
  Trio, Op. 70, no. 2, 627.
  Variations on 'Une fièvre brulante', 221.
Beggar's Opera, The, 257-8.
Bělský, Vratislav, 450 n[2], 566 n[1].
Bemetzrieder, Anton, xvii.
Benda, Franz, 448, 449.
Benda, Friedrich Ludwig, 450-1.
  Violin Concerto in C, 450-1 (Ex. 222).
Benda, Georg, 76-9, 86, 128, 448, *449-50*, 458.
  Concertos for cembalo, 450 (Ex. 220-1).
  Keyboard works, 594.
  Operas
    Ariadne auf Naxos, 76-9 (Ex. 45).
    Dorfjahrmarkt, Der, 86-8 (Exx. 52-4).
    Holzhauer, Der, 88.
    Julie und Romeo, 88.
    Medea, 76, 127.
    Walder, 88.
Bengtsson, Ingmar, *J. H. Roman*, 431 n[2].
Benti-Bulgarelli, Marianna, 4.
Benton, Rita, 612 n[1].
Benvenuto, Giacomo, 372 n[3], 519 n[5], 576 nn[1, 2].
Berezovsky, Maksim Sozontovich, 278.
Berg, Alban, 626.
Berlioz, Hector, 240, 244.
  Damnation de Faust, La, 236.
  Troyens, Les, 234, 240-1.
Bernacchi, Antonio, 4.
Bernandt, Grigory, *Slovar' oper . . . 1736-1959*, 272 n[2].
Bernardi, Francesco (Senesino), 4.
Bernardon, *see* Kurz.
Bernasconi, Andrea, 2.
Berquin, Arnaud, *Romances*, 343 n[2].
Bertati, Giovanni (librettist), *Don Giovanni* (Gazzaniga), 154, 155.
Berton, Pierre, 225.
  Adèle de Ponthieu, 225.
  Rigueurs du cloître, Les, 256.
Bertoni, Ferdinando, 282.
Bianchi, Francesco, *Villanella rapita, La*, 149 n[2].

Bickerstaffe, Isaac (librettist), 263.
  Ephesian Matron, The (Dibdin), 262.
  Lionel and Clarissa (Dibdin), 261.
  Love in a Village (Arne), 260.
  Padlock, The (Dibdin), 261.
  Sultan, The, 142.
Bicknell, Alexander (playwright), *Patriot King, The*, 183.
Billington, Mrs. Elizabeth, 265, 269 *bis*.
Binder, Christlieb Siegmund, 456.
Birchall and Andrews (publishers), 470, 579 n[1].
Bitter, Christof, 158 n[2].
Bittner, C., 456 n[1].
Blaise, Benoît
  Annette et Lubin, 208 *bis*.
  Isabelle et Gertrude, 229.
Bloch, Henry, 38 n[1].
Blom, Eric, 150 n[2].
Blume, Friedrich, 490 n[1], 509 n[1], 555 n[1], 582 nn[1-5].
  his theory on Mozart's *Requiem*, 316 n[1], *318-19*.
  Goethe und die Musik, 85 n[2].
Boccherini, Luigi, *379-81*, 382, *445-6*, 614, 616.
  Cello Concertos, 380, *445-7* (Exx. 214-15).
  Divertimenti, Op. 11, 506.
  Flute Quintets, 569.
  Oboe Quintet, Op. 55, 569.
  Piano Quintets, Opp. 56-7, *532*.
  Sextets, 572 and n[1].
  Sinfonia funebre, 380.
  Sonates pour clavecin et violon, Op. 5, *532* (Ex. 298).
  String Quartets, 558-9 (Ex. 310).
  String Quintets, *567-9*, 570.
  String Trios, 550-1.
  Symphonies, 379-80 (Ex. 168).
  Violin Duets, Op. 3, 547.
Boghen, Felice, 577 n[2].
Böhm theatrical company, the, 6, 126, 128.
Boismortier, Joseph, 204 n[1], 223-5 *passim*.
  Daphnis et Chloé, 223.
Bollert, Werner, 58 n[1].
Bonaparte, Lucien, 569.
Bonaventura, Arnaldo, 4 nn[2, 3].
Bonelli, E., 376.
Bonin (publisher), 594.
Bonno, Giuseppe, 2, 295-6.
  Isaaco, 327.
Bordoni-Hasse, Faustina, 4, 25.
Borghi, Luigi, 486.
Bormann, Paul, 545 n[1], 547 nn[1, 2], 548 n[4], 550 n[1], 572 n[1].
Bortnyansky, Dmitry, 279.
  Alcide, 281.
  Creonte, 281.
  Faucon, Le, 281.
  Fils rival, Le, 281.

INDEX

Quinto Fabio, 281.
Botstiber, Hugo, *Geschichte der Ouvertüre*, 395 n[1].
 (with Carl F. Pohl)
  Joseph Haydn, 182 and n[2], 334 n[2].
Bouffons, *see* 'Querelle des Bouffons'.
Bouilly, Jean Nicolas (dramatist), *Léonore ou l'Amour conjugal*, 221.
Boutmy, Josse, 481.
Boyce, William, 257, 324–5.
 Harlequin's Invasion, The, 339 n[3].
 Solomon (ov.), 429.
 Songs
  'Hearts of Oak', 339 and n[3].
  'Orpheus and Euridice', 338 (Ex. 149 (i)).
 Trio sonatas, 529.
 (ed.) *Cathedral Music*, 324.
 Eight Symphonys in Eight Parts (1760), 430.
Brahms, Johannes, 392, 571, 583 n[3].
 (*et al.*, eds.) *Gesamtausgabe der Werke Mozarts*, 308 n[1], 494 n[1].
Brand, Carl M.
 (ed.) *Joseph Haydn, The Complete Works*, 300 n[1].
 Die Messen von Joseph Haydn, 301 n[1], 302 n[1], 322 n[3].
Breitkopf and Härtel, 182, 301 n[2], 322 n[1], 445 n[3], 607.
 the Breitkopf catalogues (pre-1795), 378, 383–4, 395, 400, 403–4, 406, 430, 439 and n[1], 444 n[2], 445 n[1], 457 n[3], 471, 486.
Bremner, Robert, 403, 427, 430.
 (pub.) *Periodical Overtures*, 403, 426.
Brent, Charlotte (Mrs. Pinto), 258 *bis*.
Brescianello, Giuseppe Antonio, 441.
Bretzner, Christoph Friedrich (librettist), *Belmont und Constanze oder Die Entführung aus dem Serail*, 89, 141, 142.
Bréval, Jean-Baptiste, 478, *479–80*.
 Cello Concerto in C, Op. 26, no. 6, 479.
 Cello Concerto in F, Op. 20, no. 3, 480 (Ex. 262).
Brioschi, Antonio, *378*, 383 n[1], 530 n[3].
British Union Catalogue of Early Music, 529 n[6], 560 n[3], 575 n[4].
Brook, Barry S., 424 n[2], 441 n[1], 477 n[1].
 La Symphonie française . . ., 419, 422 n[1], 423 nn[1,2], 477 n[1].
Broschi, Carlo (Farinelli), 4, 281.
 his vocal embellishments, 15–16 (Ex. 3).
Brosses, Charles de, 12 n[3].
Brown, John,
 A Dissertation on . . . poetry and music, 269 n[3].
 Letters on the Italian Opera, 21 n[1].
Brückner, Fritz, 76 n[4], 86 n[1].
Brunette (= pastoral love-song), 342 nn[1,2].
Brunetti, Antonio, 490.

Brunetti, Gaetano, *382*.
 Symphony in C minor, 382 (Ex. 170).
Bukofzer, Manfred, *Music in the Baroque Era*, 612 n[1].
Bullandt, A., *Sbiten-seller, The* (*Sbitenshchik*), 276.
Bureau d'Abonnement Musical (publishers), 445.
Bürger, Gottfried August (poet)
 'Gegenliebe' (Haydn), 355.
 'Lenore' (anon.), 343.
  (André, Reichardt, and Zumsteeg), 349.
Burgoyne, General John (librettist), *The, Lord of the Manor* (Jackson), *269*, 270.
Burney, Dr. Charles, xvi, xviii, 4 n[1], 172, 225, 243, 257, 288–9, 294, 325, 401, 430.
 General History of Music, A, xx, 527 n[5], 529.
 Present State of Music in France and Italy, The, 225.
 Present State of Music in Germany, The, 25 and n[2], 288.
Busby, Thomas, 269.
Busch, Gudrun, *C. P. E. Bach und seine Lieder*, 347 n[1].
Buxtehude, Dietrich, 619.

Cadenza, in the concerto, 437, *440*, 488.
Caffarelli, *see* Majorano.
Caland, Elizabeth, 587 n[1].
Caldara, Antonio, 294, 326, 395.
Calderón de la Barca, Pedro (poet and dramatist), *El purgatorio de San Patricio*, 168 n[2].
Calmus, Georgy, 80 nn[2,3].
Calzabigi, Ranieri (librettist), 42, 121, 327.
 Alceste (Gluck), 44, 127.
 Ipermestra (*Les Danaïdes*) (Salieri), 241.
 Opera seria, L' (Gassmann), 48.
 Orfeo ed Euridice (Gluck), 43, 229.
Cambini, Giovanni Giuseppe, 423, 425, 478, *480*.
 Symphonie concertante in F, 480 (Ex. 264).
Camerloher, Placidus von, *432*, 509, *525*.
Campagnoli, Bartolommeo, 507.
Campra, André, 223, 224.
 Idoménée, 133.
Cannabich, Christian, 414, *415–16*, *460*, 482.
 Flute concerto in D, 460 (Ex. 236).
 Symphonie périodique no. 5, 415 (Ex. 196).
 Symphony in B flat, 415–16.
Cannabich, Rosa, 604.
Canobbio, Carlo (with Sarti and Pashkevich), *Nachal'noe upravlenie Olega*, 272 n[1], *277–8*.

Cantata, solo, 361, *363–5*.
Cantatille, 364.
Cappelletti, Theresa Poggi, 181.
Cappeval, Caux de, *Apologie du goût français . . .*, 226.
Capri, Antonio, *Giuseppe Tartini*, 442 n[1].
Carmirelli, P., 380 n[3].
Carolan, Turlough, *A Favourite Collection . . .*, 264.
Carpani, Giuseppe, *Le Haydine*, 614 n[1].
Carse, Adam, 371 n[1].
Eighteenth Century Symphonies, 366.
Cartier, J. B., 443.
Carvalho, Joãs, 282.
Cassation (*cassazione*), *505*, 517.
Casti, Giovanni Battista (librettist), 49.
Prima la musica . . . (Salieri), 48, 149.
Castrati, 4–5.
Catherine II (the Great), Empress of Russia, xv, 2, 206, *270*.
as librettist
Fevey (Pashkevich), 276.
Gore-bogatïr' Kosometovich (Soler), 277.
Ivan Tsarevich (Vančura), 276.
Nachal'noe upravlenie Olega (Pashkevich et al.), 272 n[1], 277.
Novgorodoskïy bogatïr' Boeslavich (Fomin), 279.
Cavalieri, Katharina, 141, 145.
Cavatina, 33, 52.
Cerlone, Francesco (librettist), 48, 49.
Cervetto, Giacomo, 507.
'C'étoit l'hiver' (composer unknown), 343 (Ex. 151).
Chailley, Jacques, *La Flute Enchantée, Opéra maçonnique*, 167 n[2].
Champein, Stanislas
Mélomanie, La, 255.
Nouveau Don Quichotte, Le, 208, *256*.
Charles III, King of Naples and Spain, 281.
Charles VI, Emperor, 117, 294, 326.
Charles Theodore, Elector of Bavaria, 2.
Charpentier, Marc-Antoine, 324.
Cherubini, Luigi, 226, 244, 324.
Démophoon, 244.
Médée, 234, 236.
Chevardière, de La (publisher), 364 n[4], 394, 412, 415.
Journal Hebdomadaire . . ., 344 n[5].
Chiesa, Melchior, 378.
Chilcot, Thomas, *Suites of Lessons*, 579.
Church music, 289–325.
in England and France, 323–5.
Joseph II's restrictions on, 305–6.
Neapolitan School of, *289–93*, *295–6*, 300, 316.
in Salzburg, 296–8.

symphonic influences on, 298–300.
in Vienna, 293–7.
Churgin, Bathia, *The Symphonies of G. B. Sammartini*, 374 n[2].
Ciampi, Vincenzo, 202.
Bertoldo in corte, 204.
Diable à quatre, Le, 205 (Ex. 103).
Cimarosa, Domenico, 8, 32, 45, 58, 64, 183, 271, 371–2.
Due baroni di Rocco Azzura, I, 64 (Ex. 37).
Giannina e Bernardone, 64
Impresario, L', 371.
Infedeltà fedele, L', 180.
Matrimonio segreto, Il, 64, 371.
keyboard sonatas, 577.
Cipollini, D., 575 n[1], 576 n[2].
Clairval, Jean-Baptiste Guignard, called, 207.
Clarinets, earliest use of, 410–11, 411 n[1].
Clementi, Muzio, 574, 578, 600, 609.
Clercx, S., *P. Van Maldere*, 432 n[3].
Coffey, Charles
Devil to Pay, The, 80.
Merry Cobbler, The, 80.
Cogan, Philip, 487.
Colasse, Pascal, *Enée et Lavinie*, 225.
Coleridge, Arthur Duke, 617 n[1].
Colleredo, Hieronymus, Archbishop of Salzburg, 298, 310, 314, 547.
Collett, John, *430*, 521.
Coltellini, Marco (librettist), 42, 102, 121, 195.
Ifigenia in Tauride (Traetta), 230.
Infedeltà delusa, L' (Haydn), 176.
'Comedians, War of the', *see* 'Querelle des Bouffons'.
Comédie larmoyante bourgeoise, 48, 209, 234.
Comédie mêlée d'ariettes, 204.
Commedia dell'arte, 47, 184–5, 192, 194.
Commedia musicale, 47.
Concert Spirituel, 172, 243, 324, 419, 446, 477, 479.
Concerto, 434–502.
in Austria, 465–77.
in England, 481–7.
evolution of, 434–7.
in Italy, 440–8.
in Mannheim, 456–65.
and Mozart, 487–502.
in North Germany, 448–56.
in Paris, 477–81.
patterns and clichés in, 437–9.
performance, 439–40.
Constantin, Titus Charles, *Oie du Caire, L'*, 148 n[5].
Conti, Francesco, 326.
Cooke, Benjamin, 553 n[2].
Corelli, Arcangelo, 389, 421, 435, 440, 448, 529.
Sonate da chiesa, 615–16.

INDEX

Corneille, Pierre (poet), 227.
Corrette, Michel, 506.
Corri, Domenico, *Select Collection* (of Songs), 269.
Corte, Andrea della, 9 n[1], 59 n[1].
Cotarelo y Mori, Emilio, *Don Ramón de la Cruz*, 282 n[1].
Couperin, François, 574.
Cramer, K. F., 628.
  Magazin der Musik, 540 n[1].
Cramer, Wilhelm, 551.
Crescentini, Girolamo, 363.
Crickmore, Leon, 453 n[1].
Croes, H. J. de, 481.
Croll, Gerhard, 552 n[3].
Cruz, Ramón de la (librettist), 282–4.
  Briseida, La (Hita), 282–3.
  Cazadores, Los (Gassmann), 282.
  Espigadera, La (Esteve), 284.
  Espigadera y la vendimia, La (Esteve), 284.
  Foncarraleras, Las (Galván), 284.
  Labradoras de Murcia, Las (Hita), 283–4.
  Licenciado Farfulla, El (Rosales), 284.
  Quien complace a la deidad (Pla), 282.
  Segadoras de Vallecas, Las (Hita), 283.
  Zagales de Genil, Los (Esteve), 283.
Cucuel, Georges
  Études sur un orchestre . . ., 411 n[1], 530 n[1].
  La Pouplinière et la musique de chambre . . ., 225 n[1].
Cudworth, Charles, 429 n[2], 430 n[1].
Cuzzoni, Francesca, 4, 6.
Czach, R., 563 n[2].

Da capo arias, 14, 23, 33, 52, 363.
  in French opera, 227.
  Gluck and, 232.
  Mozart and, 105, 111, 131, 133, 137, 359.
Daffner, Hugo, *Die Entwicklung des Klavierkonzerts bis Mozart*, 452 n[1], 455 n[1], 456 n[1], 466 n[4].
Dalayrac, Nicolas, 250.
  Deux petits Savoyards, Les, 250, 253.
  Nina, ou la Folle par amour, 250.
  Raoul, Sire de Créqui, 253.
  Renaud d'Ast (Georg von Asten), 254–5 (Ex. 126).
Dalberg, Heribert von, 127.
Damerini, Adelmo, 38 n[2].
Danchet, Antoine (playwright), *Idoménée*, 133.
Dante, Alighieri, 243.
Danzi, Franz, 463.
Da Ponte, Lorenzo (librettist), 49, 57, 158–60 *passim*, 170.
  Axur re d'Ormus (Salieri), 244.
  Cosa rara, Una (Soler), 154.
  Così fan tutte (Mozart), 159.
  Don Giovanni (Mozart), 154, 155 n[1].

Equivoci, Gli (Storace), 266.
  Nozze di Figaro, Le (Mozart), 150–4 *passim*.
  Sposo deluso, Lo (Mozart), 148, 150.
  Memorie di Lorenzo da Ponte . . ., 49 n[2], 57 n[2], 150 n[1].
Dart, R. Thurston, 580 n[1].
Darvas, Gábor, 468 n[1].
Dauvergne, Antoine, 230.
  Enée et Lavinie, 225.
  Troqueurs, Les, 203–4.
Davaux, Jean-Baptiste, 425, 478, *479*.
David, Ferdinand, 518 n[1], 545 n[4].
David, Hans, 553 n[1].
Davidde, Giacomo, 181.
Davison, Archibald T., and W. Apel, *Historical Anthology of Music*, 33 n[1], 85 n[1], 95 n[3], 203 n[1], 219 n[5], 328 nn[1,2], 396 n[3], 559 n[1].
Dazeley, George, 493 n[1].
De Brosses, Charles, *Lettres familières écrites d'Italie*, 407–8.
Debussy, Claude, 228.
  Pelléas et Mélisande, 232 n[4].
De Jean, 492.
Deller, Florian, 24.
Denis, Michael ('Sined') (poet), 353.
  'Ode on the Defence of Gibraltar' (Mozart), 353 n[1].
Dent, Edward J., 56 nn[1,2], 167 n[2], 553 n[1], 610.
  Alessandro Scarlatti, 291 n[1].
  Mozart's Operas, 97 n[2], 163 n[1], 167 n[3], 610 n[1].
Deutsch, Otto Erich, 167 n[3], 496 n[1].
  Mozart, Die Dokumente seines Lebens, 97 n[3], 107 n[1], 109 n[2], 111 n[1], 119 n[1], 121 n[1], 122 n[1], 128 n[2], 136 n[1], 142 n[1], 160 n[1], 315 n[1].
  Das Wiener Freihaustheater . . ., 167 n[3].
  (ed., with Bauer), *Mozart: Briefe* . . ., 98 n[4], 318 n[2], 445 n[2], 486 n[1].
Devienne, François, *480*, 481.
  Flute Concerto No. 3, 480 (Ex. 263).
  Les Visitandines, 256.
Dezède, Nicolas ('de Z'), 207.
  Blaise et Babet, 209.
Dibdin, Charles, *261–3*, 265, 269, 339–40.
  Operas, 261–3.
    Ephesian Matron, The, 262–3 (Ex. 128).
    Lionel and Clarissa, 261, 262.
    Padlock, The, 261.
    Poor Vulcan, 262.
    Recruiting Sergeant, The, 262.
    Wedding Ring, The, 262.
    'Dialogues', 262.
  Songs, 339–40.
  Musical Tour (1788), 263 n[1].
Dibdin, Edward R., 263 n[1].
Dickens, Charles, 253.

Diderot, Denis, xvi, xvii, xviii, xx, 209, 230.
Dies, Albert C., *Biographische Nachrichten von Joseph Haydn*, 178, 182 n[1], 191.
Dieter, Christian Ludwig, 89.
  Belmont und Konstanze, 143.
Dittberner, Johannes, 347 n[1].
Dittersdorf, Karl Ditters von, 95–6, 178, 394, *402–4*, 413.
  Concertos, 469–70 (Exx. 249–50).
  Divertimenti, etc., 509.
  Operas
    Betrug durch Aberglauben, 95.
    Doktor und Apotheker, 95–6 (Ex. 61).
    Liebe im Narrenhaus, Die, 95.
  String quartets, 563.
  Symphonies, *402–4*.
Divertimenti, *503–14*, 517.
  French and Italian, 506–7.
  the Haydns', 509–11.
  Mozart's, 505, *512–14*.
  Vienna and Mannheim, 507–9.
Djurič-Klajn, Stana, 444 n[3].
Döbereiner, Christian, 485 n[1], 523 n[2].
Dobiáš, Václav, 404 n[2].
Dobrokhotov, B.
  D. S. Bortnyansky, 281 n[2].
  E. I. Fomin, 279 n[1].
Doebbelin ensemble, 6.
Doflein, Erich, 585 n[1].
Donath, Gustav, 64 n[2].
Donnias, Minos, *Die Violinkonzerte Giuseppe Tartinis*, 442 and nn[1–3], 443 nn[1–3].
Downes, Edward O. D., 9 n[1], 12 n[2].
Dubreuil, Alphonse du Congé (librettist)
  Iphigénie en Tauride (Piccinni), 240.
  Dictionnaire lyrique portatif, 344 n[4].
Duets for strings or wind, *545–8*.
Duni, Egidio Romoaldo, 204 and n[1], 206.
  Bertoldo in corte, 204.
  Buona figliuola, La, 48.
  Fée Urgèle, La, 208.
  Peintre amoureux de son modèle, Le, 204.
Dunning, Albert, *Joseph Schmitt*, 464 n[1].
Dupuis, Thomas, 581.
Durán, José, *Antigone*, 282.
Durante, Francesco, 291.
  Divertimenti, 506.
Durazzo, Count, 42, 228–9.
Durchkomponiertes Lied, 361.
Duschek, Josepha, 160.

Eberlin, Johann Ernst, 296, 309, 326.
Eckard, Johann Gottfried, xvii, 578.
Edelmann, Johann Friedrich, 509.
Eichner, Ernest, 414, *416* (Ex. 197).
  Cembalo Concerto in C, Op. 6, 462–3 (Ex. 241).

'Einladung zum Tanz' (anon.) (dance song), 346.
Einstein, Alfred, 128 n[4], 148 n[1], 158 n[1], 309 n[1], 312, 446 n[3].
  Gluck, 205.
  Köchel's Verzeichnis . . ., 3rd edn., 604, 625, 630 n[1].
Elizabeth, Empress of Russia, 270.
Elssler, Johann, 181 n[1].
Engel, Hans, 1 n[1], 118 n[2], 504, 515 n[1], 525 n[1].
  Das Instrumentalkonzert, 466 n[2].
Engelke, Bernhard, 352 n[1].
Engländer, Richard, 3 n[3], 45 n[2], 76 n[1], 167 n[1].
Epstein, Julius, 583 n[1].
Ermeler, Rolf, 527 n[3], 550 n[2].
Esterházy, Prince Anton, 181, 319.
  Prince Nicolaus I, 172–81, *passim*, 195, 304, 319, 551, 614.
  Prince Nicolaus II (Count Nicolaus), 179, 183, 319, 323.
  Prince Paul Anton, 174, 176.
  Princess (Dowager) Maria Anna Louise, 176.
  Princess Maria Hermengilde, 319.
Esteve, Pablo, 285, 287.
  Espigadera, La, 284.
  Espigadera y la vendimia, La, 284.
  Jardineros de Aranjuez, Los, 283.
  Signos del año, Los, 287.
  Zagales de Genil, Los, 283.
  additional numbers for *La buena hija* (Piccinni), 281.
Euripides, *Alcestis*, 278.

Falck, Martin, *W. F. Bach*, 546 n[1], 583 n[4].
Farinelli, *see* Broschi.
Farrenc, Louise, 575 n[1], 576 n[2].
Fauner, Adalbert, 91 n[3].
Favart, Charles Simon (librettist), 200, 205, *207–8*, 228–9.
  Chercheuse d'esprit, La, 200–1.
  Fée Urgèle, La (Duni), 208.
  Ninette à la cour, 204.
  Rose et Colas (Monsigny), 208.
  Solimann II, 175.
  (with Justine Favart and Harny)
    Amours de Bastien et Bastienne, Les, 107, 203, 207.
Favart, Marie, 207, 208.
Feder, Georg, 596 n[1].
Federhofer-Königs, Renate, 310 n[2].
Fehr, Max, 8 n[1], 11 n[2].
Fel, Marie, 207.
Fellerer, Karl Gustav, 289 n[1], 432 n[1].
Felton, William, 579.
Fendler, Edvard, 572 n[4].
Feo, Francesco, 233.

INDEX

Ferdinand, Archduke of Austria, 110, 117, 118, 178.
Ferrandini, Giovanni, 2, 506.
  Catone in Utica, 2.
Ferrarese del Bene, Adriana, 154.
Fesechko, G. F., 279 n[1].
Festa teatrale, 24, 26, 239.
Fétis, François, 216 nn[1, 2], 569.
Feyer, ? 438 (Ex. 211 (i)).
Fiala, Joseph, 476.
Fielding, Henry, *Tom Jones*, 209.
Filtz, Anton, 404 (Ex. 185), 408, *458–60*, *524*.
  Cello Concertos, 459 (Exx. 233–5).
  Symphonies périodiques, 412–14 (Exx. 193–4).
Finagin, A., (ed.) *Muzïka i muzïkal'nïy byt staroy Rossii*, 274 n[6], 279 n[1].
Finzi, Gerald, 429 n[3].
Fioravanti, Valentino, 363.
Fischer, Hans, 606 n[1].
  Musikalische Formen . . ., 586 n[2].
Fischer, Johann Christian, xvi, *485*, 487.
Fischer, J. M., xviii.
Fischer, Kurt von, 575 n[2].
Fischer, Ludwig, 142 *bis*, 149 n[2].
Fischer, Wilhelm, 171 n[1], 318 n[1], 396 n[2], 465 n[1], 466 n[3], 507 n[2], 515 n[1], 525 n[6].
Fisher, John Abraham, 430.
Floquet, Étienne Joseph, *Le Seigneur bienfaisant*, 250.
Fomin, Evstigney Ipat'evich, 276, *278–81*.
  Americans, The (Amerikantsy), 280.
  Boeslavich, the Novgorod Bogatyr (Novgorodoskïy bogatïr' Boeslavich), 279.
  Golden Apple, The (Zolotoe yabloko), 280.
  Orpheus and Euridice (Orfey i Evredika), 280–1.
  Post-drivers at the Post-station, The (Yamshchiki na podstave), 279–80 (Ex. 134).
  reviser of *The Miller-magician* (arr. Sokolovsky), 273–4.
Fontenelle, Bernard le Bouvier de (author), *Enée et Lavinie*, 225.
Forbes, Elliot, 628 n[1].
Forkel, Johann Nicolaus, xx.
Fortepiano, introduction of the, 516.
Francis II, Emperor of Austria, 322.
Francoeur, François, 202.
Fränzl, Ignaz, 438 (Ex. 211 (i)), 463.
Frederick II (the Great), King of Prussia, xv, xviii, 2, 383, 394, 448, 458 n[1].
  and C. P. E. Bach, 330, 453, 584, 614.
  and Graun, 33, 453.
  and Hasse, 33, 448.
  and Quantz, 448.
  and Rolle, 594.
  Sonatas for Flute and Bass, 520 (Ex. 292).
Frederick William II, King of Prussia, 562, 565.
  as Crown Prince, 394.
Freeman, Robert S., 8 n[1].
Freemasonry, 168, 306.
  Recueil de Chansons des Franc-Maçons, 344 n[1].
Friberth, Carl, 354.
  with L. Hoffmann
  Sammlung deutscher Lieder, 353.
Fridzeri, Alessandro Maria Antonio, 206.
  Les Souliers mordorés, 207, *247–50* (Ex. 123).
Friedlaender, Max, 334 n[2].
  Das deutsche Lied im 18. Jahrhundert, 81 n[2].
Fry, Christopher (playwright), *A Phoenix too Frequent*, 262.
Fux, Johann Joseph, 294, 326, 395, 412.
  Gradus ad Parnassum, 290 n[1], 294, 412, 619.

Gabrielli, Catterina, 4.
Galliard, Johann Ernst, 257.
Gallini, Sir John, 181–2.
Galuppi, Baldassare, 8, 32, 45, 58, 271, 282.
  Antigono, 368–9.
  Cantarina, La, 48.
  Filosofo di campagna, Il, 58 n[1], 262, 368.
  Siroe, 369.
  Keyboard sonatas, *575–6* (Ex. 314).
  Overtures and Symphonies, *368–9*, 383.
Galván, Ventura, 285.
  Las Foncarraleras, 284.
Garrick, David, 64, 257, 258, 260, 263, 339 n[3].
Gassmann, Florian Leopold, 2, 63, 105, 295, 395, *399–400*, 404
  Amor e Psiche (ov.), 399.
  Contessina, La, 47, 63 (Ex. 36), 399, 400 (Ex. 182 (ii)).
  Filosofo innamorato, Il (ov.), 400.
  Issipile, 399.
  Rovinati, I, 400.
  Uccellatori, Gli (Los cazadores), 282.
  Viaggiatore ridicolo, Il (ov.), 400 (Ex. 182 (i)).
  Divertimento a tre in C, 526.
  Quartets, *560*, 619.
  Symphonies, 399.
Gatti, Luigi, 147.
Gaviniès, Pierre, 243, *477*.
  24 Matinées, 517.
Gazzaniga, Giuseppe, 58, 173, 183.
  Don Giovanni . . ., 154.
Gebler, Tobias Philipp, Freiherr von (playwright), *Thamos, König in Ägypten*, 119, 168.
Geiringer, Karl, 334 n[1], 379 n[2], 399 n[3], 525 n[3], 553 n[3], 560 n[2], 572 nn[3, 4].

Geiringer, Karl (*cont.*):
Bach Family, The, 515 n[1], 527 nn[1,4].
Haydn (1946), 176 n[3], 182 and n[2].
Haydn, A Creative Life in Music (1968), 526 n[5].
Joseph Haydn (1959), 515 n[1].
Musical Instruments, 563 n[3].
(ed.) *Music of the Bach Family*, 389 n[2], 535 n[5].
Geistliches Lied, 345, 346 and n[3], 347 nn[1,2], 355.
Gellert, Christian Fürchtegott (poet), *Geistliche Oden und Lieder* (C. P. E. Bach), 347 and n[1].
Gemmingen, Otto, Freiherr von, 127.
Genzinger, Marianne von, 196, 600.
George III, King, 182.
George, Prince of Wales (King George IV), 182.
Gérard, Yves, *Thematic . . . Catalogue of the Works of Luigi Boccherini*, 379 nn[1,2], 380 nn[2,3], 445 n[4], 446 nn[1,2], 532 nn[1,2], 547 nn[2,3], 550 n[4], 558 n[1], 567 n[2], 572 n[1].
Gerber, Ernst Ludwig, *Historisches-biographisches Lexicon . . .*, 84 n[3], 226 n[1].
Gerber, Rudolf, 9 nn[1,2], 11 n[1], 13 n[1], 25 n[1], 26 n[1], 42 n[1], 205 n[1], 385 n[2].
Gerhard, Roberto, 532 n[4].
Gerlin, R., 578 n[1].
Gerstenberg, Henrik von, 364.
Gerstenberg, Walter, 274.
Gevaert, François A., 216 nn[1,2].
Giardini, Felice de, 531, 533, *557*.
Giazotto, Remo, 8 n[1], 9 n[1], 12 n[1].
Tomaso Albinoni, 377 n[1].
Giegling, Franz, 166 n[1], 577 n[1].
Giesecke, Carl Ludwig (librettist), *Oberon, König der Elfen*, 167.
Gilbert, William Schwenk, 269.
Ginzburg, S. L., 278 n[1], 280 n[2], 281 n[1].
Istoriya russkoy muzïki . . ., 273 n[2], 274 nn[2,3,5], 276 nn[1,3,5], 280 nn[1,3].
Russkïy muzykal'nïy teatr 1700–1835, 272 n[2].
Giordani, Giuseppe, 444.
Giordani, Tommaso, 261, *486*.
Giornovichi, Giovanni Mane, 444.
Girdlestone, Cuthbert M.
Jean Philippe Rameau, 227 n[1].
Mozart and his Piano Concertos, 490 n[2].
Giržik, 180, 181 n[1].
Giulini, Count Giorgio, 378–9.
Glinka, Mikhail, 276.
Ruslan i Lyudmila, 280–1.
Gluck, Christoph Willibald, xvi, xviii, 6, 8, 394.
'contest' with Piccinni, 126, 231, 235, *239–41*, 255, 342, 372.

contributions to others' operas, *205–6* (Ex. 103), 231.
influence on Haydn, 183–4.
and the *opéra comique*, *204–6*, 250, 256, 344.
remarks on Mozart, 147.
and Salieri's *Les Danaïdes*, 241.
and Sammartini, 615.
Operas/Ballets, 33, *42–5*, 66–7, 111, 138–9, 216, 222–3, *226–36*, 243–4.
Alceste, 42, 44, 127, 227, 228, 231, 232.
Antigone, 238.
Armide, 231, 232, 235, 236.
Cinesi, Le, 505.
Clemenza di Tito, La, 235, 237.
Cythère assiégée, La, 228, 231, 235.
Don Juan, 43, 235.
Echo et Narcisse, 232, *239*.
Feste d'Apollo, Le, 235.
Festin de pierre, Le, 154.
Iphigénie en Aulide, 223, 228, *230–1*, *233–5* (Exx. 114, 116, 117), 236, 237.
Iphigénie en Tauride, 226, 231–2, *236–9* (Ex. 119), 243.
Ippolito, 235.
Isle de Merlin, L', 228.
Orfeo ed Euridice, *42–4*, 173, 194, 196, 205, 228–35 *passim*, 239, 280.
Paride ed Elena, 44, 235, 239.
Rencontre imprévue, La, 229.
Roland (sketches for), 231, 235.
Semiramide, 237.
Telemacco, 233–4 (Ex. 115), 235, 238.
Songs (Klopstock settings), *349–50* (Ex. 154).
Trio sonatas, 528–9 (Ex. 297).
Gobermann, Max, 429 n[3].
Goethe, Johann Wolfgang von, xx, *85–6*, 617, 629.
'An die Einzige', 351.
Egmont, 221.
Götter, Helden und Wieland, 71.
Götz von Berlichingen, xv.
Letters to Zelter, 617 n[1].
Singspiel texts, *79, 85*.
Stella, 175.
'Veilchen, Das', 355.
Werther, 349.
Wilhelm Meister, 350–1.
Goldoni, Carlo (playwright, librettist), *48–9*, 58, 154, 155 n[1].
Bella verità, La (Piccinni), 48.
Cantarina, La (Galuppi), 48.
Cecchina ossia La buona figliuola (Duni, Piccinni), 48.
Finta semplice, La (Mozart), 102.
Mondo della luna, Il (Haydn), 179, 192.
Pescatrici, Le (Haydn), 176, 187.
Servitore di due padroni, Il, 147–8.

Speziale, Lo (Haydn), 175, 185–6.
Statira, La, 49 n[1].
Uccellatori, Gli (Gassmann), 282.
Mémoires, 49 n[1].
Goldschmidt, Hugo, 38 n[2].
  Die Musikästhetik des 18. Jahrhunderts, 8 n[1], 12 n[1], 66 nn[1,2], 228 n[2].
Gossec, François Joseph, 225, 230, 243, 323–4, 423, 477.
  Scythes enchaînés, Les, 239.
  Nativité, La, 324.
  Symphonies, *421–2* (Ex. 202), 425.
  Trios, 529–30.
  Violin Duets, 547.
Gothaer Theater-Kalendar, 179.
Göttinger Musenalmanach, 349 n[5].
Gottsched, Johann Christoph, 66, 80.
Göttweig Abbey (Monastery), 300, 401, 402, 431.
Gotwals, Vernon, 554 n[1].
Götz (publisher), 463.
Gräfe, Friedrich, 345.
Grasberger, Franz, 554 n[1].
Graun, Carl Heinrich, xviii, 2, 32–3, *383*, 384, 448–9, 453.
  Artaserse, 2.
  Cleopatra e Cesare, 2.
  Der Tod Jesu, xviii, *329–30* (Ex. 146), 331, 383.
  Overtures, 383 and n[1].
  Songs, 346–7 (Ex. 152).
Graun, Johann Gottlieb, 527.
  Concertos, 448–9 (Exx. 218–19).
  Symphonies, 383–4 (Ex. 171).
Gray, Thomas, 'Elegy written in a Country Churchyard' (Storace), 341.
Graziani, Carlo, 519–20.
Grazioli, Giambattista, 578 (Ex. 316).
Greene, Maurice, 324.
Grétry, André Ernest Modeste, xvi, 206, 213, *216–23*, 256, 323.
  Aucassin et Nicolette, 253–4 (Ex. 125).
  Caravane du Caire, La, 207, 250.
  Colinette à la Cour, 219.
  Épreuve villageoise, L', 219, 222.
  Guillaume Tell, *219–20* (Ex. 111), *221–2* (Ex. 112).
  Huron, Le, 216, 225.
  Lucile, 209 (Ex. 104), 216.
  Pierre le Grand, 219.
  Raoul Barbe-Bleu, 223, 256.
  Richard Coeur de Lion, 219–21 *passim*, 250, 253.
  Rosière de Salency, La, 219, 222.
  Tableau parlant, Le, 216, *217–19* (Ex. 110).
  Zémire et Azor, 208, 222.
  Mémoires ou Essai sur la musique, 216.
Griesinger, Georg August, 306, 322 nn[1,2], 614.

Biographische Notizen über Joseph Haydn, 554, 614 n[1].
Grimm, Melchior, 207, 226.
  Lettre sur Omphale, 201, 202.
  Le Petit Prophète de Boehmisch-Broda, 201.
Groll, Gerhard, 318 n[3].
Grossmann, G. F. W. (librettist), *Adelheit von Veltheim*, 142.
Grothius, Dietrich Ewald von, 592.
Grout, Donald Jay, 33 n[1].
Grünwald, 'Die tote Nachtigall', 354.
Grützmacher, Friedrich, 445 n[3], 535 n[1].
Guadagni, Gaetani, 4.
Guardasoni, Domenico, 163.
Guénin, Marie-Alexandre, 479.
Guglielmi, Pietro, 8, 32, 45, 58, 63–4.
  Overtures, 371.
Guillard, Nicolas-François (librettist)
  Iphigénie en Tauride (Gluck), 236, 240.
  Oedipe à Colone (Sacchini), 243.
Guillemain, Louis-Gabriel, *420–1*, 477 n[1].
  Conversation galante et amusante, Op. 12, no. 1, 530.
  Symphony, Op. 6, no. 2, *420–1* (Exx. 200–1).
  Trios, 529.
Guines, Duc de, 492.

Haas, Robert, 6 n[2], 89 nn[3,4], 91 n[4], 94 nn[1,2], 95 n[1], 98 n[3], 174 n[2], 326 n[2], 400 n[1].
  Mozart, 625 n[2], 626 n[1].
  Musik des Barocks, Die, 368 n[1].
Haböck, Franz, 4 n[4], 15 n[1].
Haessler, Johann Wilhelm, 609.
Haffner, Elizabeth, 504.
Haffner, Ulrich (publisher), 533, 581.
Hagenauer, Cajetan (Fr. Dominicus), 308.
Hagenauer, Lorenz, 106 n[1].
Hammerstein, Reinhold, 171 n[1].
Handel, George Frideric, xvi, 226, 324, 325, 339, 389, 426, 431, 481, 581, 609, 616, 619.
  and the concerto, 434, 435.
  influence on others, 216, 243, 244, 315, 316, 333.
  Mozart's arrangements of his works, 315.
  Oratorios, 325, 326.
    Messiah, 265, 315, 330, 333, 435.
Harich, János, 173 n[1], 179 n[5], 180 n[1].
Härting, Michael, 551 n[4].
Hase, Hermann von, 331 n[1].
Hasse, Johann Adolf, 2, 8, 42, 389, 448.
  Church music, *291–3*, 307.
    Mass in D, 291, 292 (Ex. 137 (i)).
    Requiem in C minor, 293 n[1].
    'Salve Regina' in G, 291, 292–3 (Ex. 137 (ii)).

Hasse, Johann Adolf (*cont.*):
  Operas, *25–31*, 31–4 *passim*, 36, 45, 81, 110–11.
    Arminio, 13 (Ex. 1), 14 (Ex. 2), 17 (Ex. 4), 19–21 (Exx. 6–8), 385 (Ex. 173).
    Clemenza di Tito, La, 270.
    Re pastore, Il, 17–18 (Ex. 5), 22–3 (Ex. 10), 28–9 (Exx. 12–13).
    Ruggiero, 21–2 (Ex. 9), 26–8 (Ex. 11), 29–32 (Exx. 14–16), 118.
  Opera-symphonies, 383, *384–5* (Exx. 172–3).
  Oratorio, *Conversione di Sant' Agostino, La*, 328.
Hausswald, Günter
  Mozarts Serenaden, 504 nn[1, 3].
Hawkins, Sir John, xx.
Haydn, (Franz) Joseph, xvi, xix, 189, 299, 401, 402, 614, 630.
  birthplace, 509.
  codas and recapitulations, *612–13*.
  Collected Correspondence, *see* Landon, H. C. R.
  his *Entwurfkatalog*, 547.
  his form, 375, 389–93 *passim*, 491, 625–7 *passim*.
  and Fux, 396.
  influenced by
    C. P. E. Bach, 553–5 *passim*, 562, 566, 593, 596–8 *passim*, *613–15*, 624.
  influences on
    Beethoven, 600, 601, 620.
    Mozart, 500, 563–5 *passim*, 602–3, 612, 618, 624, 625 and n[2].
    Pleyel, 563.
  and London, 325, 481–2.
  Mozart's quartets dedicated to, 563, 629.
  and Pleyel, 425, 481, 563.
  in relation to
    C. P. E. Bach, 389–93 *passim*, 535, 585.
    J. C. Bach, 427, 594.
    J. C. F. Bach, 594.
    Beck, 418.
    Cannabich, 415.
    M. Haydn, 297.
    others, 377, 382, 399, 403–5 *passim*, 413.
  and Reutter, 294.
  Salieri on, 296.
  on Sammartini, *614–15*.
  thematic catalogue, *see* Hoboken.
  Arias, etc., 198–9.
  Arianna a Naxos, 365.
  'Misera noi, misera patria', 199.
    Scena di Berenice, 199.
  Chamber Music
    Baryton trios, 551–2 (Ex. 307).
    with Clavier, 536–8.
    Duets for violin and viola, 547.
    Piano trios, *537–8* (Ex. 301), 602.
    Sextets, 572 and nn[3, 4].
    String quartets, *see post*.
    String quintet, 567.
    Trio sonatas, 526.
    Trios for flutes and cello, 552.
  Church Music, 289, *300–6*, *319–23*.
    Emperor's Hymn, 359.
    Masses, *see post*.
    Motet, 'Insanae et vanae curae', 327.
    Die sieben Worte, 333.
    Stabat Mater, 172, 173, 304.
    Te Deum in C, 322.
  Concertos, 453, 455, *472–6*, 487.
    Cello in C (Hob. VIIb), 474 (Ex. 256–7).
    Cello in D, 475 (Exx. 258–9).
    Cembalo in C (concertino), 473 (Ex. 255).
    Cembalo in D, 440 n[2], 474.
    Horn in D, 474.
    Organ in C, 301, 473.
    Trumpet in E flat, 468, *476*.
    Symphonie concertante in B flat, 475–6.
  Keyboard works, 585, 587, 591, *596–602*, 603, 608–10 *passim*.
    Fantasia in C, 602.
    Sonatas, *596–602*, 603.
      no. 19 in D, 596–7.
      nos. 21–6, *597*, 603.
      no. 30, 597–8.
      no. 31, 598.
      no. 36, 598.
      no. 37, 593, *598–9* (Ex. 333).
      nos. 40–2, *599*.
      no. 49, *600* (Ex. 334), 603.
      no. 50, *600–1* (Ex. 335).
      nos. 51–2, *601*.
    Variations in F minor, *601–2*, 629.
  Masses, 288, 294, 295, 298, *300–6*, *319–23*, 620.
    'Harmoniemesse', 300, 323.
    'Missa in Angustiis' ('Nelson' Mass), *321–2*.
    'Missa Brevis', 300.
    'Missa brevis Sancti Johannis de Deo' ('Little Organ Mass'), *304–5*, 312–13 (Ex. 142).
    'Missa Cellensis' ('Mariazell' Mass), *305*, 306, 312, 319, 321.
    'Missa in honorem Beatissimae Virginis Mariae' ('Great Organ Mass'), 301–2 (Ex. 141).
    'Missa Rorate coeli desuper', 300 and n[2].
    'Missa Sancti Bernardi de Offida' ('Heiligenmesse'), 321.
    'Missa Sanctae Caeciliae' ('Cecilia' Mass), 190, *301–3*, 311, 327, 620.
    'Missa Sancti Nicolai', 304–5.

INDEX

'Missa in Tempore Belli' ('Paukenmesse'), *320–1* (Ex. 145).
'Schöpfungsmesse', 322–3.
'Theresienmesse', 322.
Miscellaneous works
  Divertimenti, 505, 509, 510–11 (Exx. 286–7).
  Incidental Music, *Alfred*, 183.
  Notturni for lira organizzata, etc., 572 and n[4], 573.
Operas, *172–99*.
  Acide e Galatea, 174, 176, 179, 183–4.
  Anima del filosofo, L' (*Orfeo ed Euridice*), 181–3, *196–8* (Ex. 101).
  Armida, 180–1, 191, *195–6*.
  Canterina, La, 175, *184–5* (Ex. 94), 192.
  Fedeltà premiata, La (*L'infedeltà fidele*), 173, 180.
  Incontro improvviso, L', 172, 178, 190–1.
  Infedeltà delusa, L', 172, 174, 176, *187–90* (Exx. 96–8), 191, 195.
  Infedeltà fedele, L', see *La fedeltà premiata*.
  Isola disabitata, L', 179–80, 183, 194–5.
  Krumme Teufel, Der, 89, 174.
  List und Liebe, see *La vera costanza*.
  Marchesa Nespola, La, 174.
  Mondo della luna, Il (*Die Welt auf dem Monde*), 179, 186, *192–4* (Ex. 100), 305.
  Orlando Paladino (*Ritter Roland*), 180, 183, 194.
  Pescatrici, Le, 172, 176, *187*, 195.
  Ritter Roland, see *Orlando Paladino*.
  Speziale, Lo, 175–6, *185–6* (Ex. 95).
  Vera costanza, La (*List und Liebe* or *Die wahre Beständigkeit*), 178, 180, *191–2* (Ex. 99).
Operas, Marionette, *174–80*.
  Abgebrannte Haus, Das (*Die Feuersbrunst*), 174, 177, *194–5*.
  Bestrafte Rachbegierde, Die, 177, 179.
  Dido, 177, 178, 179.
  Götterrath, Der, 177.
  Hexen-Schabbas, 177, 179.
  Philemon und Baucis, 177, 183.
Oratorios
  Jahreszeiten, Die, 323, 332–3, *334–5*.
  Ritorno di Tobia, Il, 172, *327*.
  Schöpfung, Die, 322–3, 325, 328–9, *332–4*, 402, 403, 599.
Songs, 340, *353–9*.
  'Spirit's Song, The', 358–9 (Ex. 158).
  'Trost unglücklicher Liebe', 356–7 (Ex. 157).
String Quartets, 226, 526, *553–5, 560–2, 565–6*, 614, *617–20*.
  Opp. 1–2, *553–4*, 617.
  Op. 3, 554, 617 and n[2].
  Op. 9, *554*, 617.

Op. 17, *554–5*, 559, 617–19.
Op. 20 ('Sun'), 190, 303, *555*, 559–60, 568, 597, *618–19*, 620, 624.
Op. 33 ('Russian'), xx, *560–2* (Ex. 311), 563–5, 597, 626.
Op. 42, *562*, 599.
Op. 50, *562*, 565.
Op. 54, 562.
Op. 55, 562.
Op. 64, 562.
Op. 71, 565.
Op. 74, 565–6.
Opp. 76–7, 565–6, 602, 624.
Op. 103, 565.
Symphonies, 319, 322, 376, 396, 397, 405, 431–2, *614–21 passim*, 632.
  Nos. 5, 11, 15, 18, 21, 22, 615.
  No. 26 (*Lamentatione*), 321.
  No. 31, 474.
  No. 34, 615.
  No. 39, 630, 632 n[1].
  No. 40, 618.
  No. 42, 620.
  No. 44 ('Mourning'), 620.
  No. 45 ('Farewell'), 620.
  No. 46, 396.
  No. 49 (*La Passione*), 615, 616 (Ex. 340), 618.
  Nos. 60, 63, 175.
  No. 73 (*La Chasse*), 355 n[1].
  No. 85, 480.
  No. 88, 602.
  No. 94 ('Surprise'), 335.
  No. 102, 538, *621–4* (Exx. 341–2).
  No. 104, 426.
  the 'London' Symphonies, 615, 620, 621, 624.
Haydn, (Johann) Michael, *297–8*, 299, 326, *405–7*, 543, 629.
  Church music, xix, *297–8* (Ex. 140).
  Concertos, 472 (Ex. 254).
  Divertimenti, 509–10 (Ex. 285).
  Duets for violin and viola, 547–8.
  Overture, *Andromeda e Perseo*, 406.
  Quintets, *569*, 570.
  Symphonies, 406–7 (Ex. 187).
Hayes, Philip, 486.
Heartz, Daniel, 133 n[1].
Heckmann, 128 nn[1, 2].
Heder, J., 619 n[2].
Helfert, Vladimir, 89 n[3].
Hell, Helmuth, 24 n[1].
Hensler, Karl Friedrich (librettist), *Das Sonnenfest der Brahminen* (Müller), 168.
Herder, Johann Gottfried von (poet and librettist), xv.
  Auferweckung Lazarus, Die (J. C. F. Bach), 329.
  Brutus, 67.
  Kindheit Jesu, Die (J. C. F. Bach), 329.

Heriot, Angus, 4 n⁴.
Hermann, Friedrich, 432 n², 545 n⁴.
Herrmann, K., 586 n², 587 n¹.
Hertel, Johann Wilhelm, 383, *384, 451*.
  Violin Concerto in G minor, 451 (Exx. 223–4).
Hess, Ernst, 316 n¹, 493 n¹.
Hess, R., *Serenade, Cassation, . . . bei Michael Haydn*, 504 n¹.
Heuss, Alfred, 119 n³, 172 n¹.
Hiller, Johann Adam, 80 n², *81–5*, 86, 89, 94, 95, 349, 401.
  Jagd, Die, 82, 84 (Ex. 51).
  Liebe auf dem Lande, Die, 82.
  Lisuart und Dariolette, 85 n¹.
  Löttchen am Hofe, 82–4 (Exx. 48–50).
  Lustige Schuster, Der, 81.
  Verwandelten Weiber, Die, 81–2 (Ex. 47), 349.
  Lieder für Kinder, preface quoted, 353 n³.
Hinze-Rheinhold, B., 527 n³.
Hirsch, Paul, 607 n¹.
Hita, Antonio Rodriguez de
  Briseida, La, 282–3.
  Labradores de Murcia, Las, 283–4 (Ex. 135), 285.
  Scipion en Cartagena, 284.
  Segadoras de Vallecas, Las, 283.
  Diapason instructivo, 282.
Hoboken, Anthony Van, *Joseph Haydn: Thematisch-bibliographisches Werkverzeichnis*, 402 n², 440 n², 473 *n²*, 526 n⁷, 537 nn¹,², 547 n⁵, 596 n¹.
Höckner, Walter, 567 n¹.
Hofer, Josefa, 159–60.
Hofer, Norbert, 294 n³.
Hoffmann, A., 525 n⁵.
Hoffmann, E. T. A., 627 n¹.
Hoffmann-Erbrecht, Lothar, 575 n¹, 583 n², 588 n³.
Hoffmann, Leopold, *401–2*, 403, 415, 421, *468–9*, 471.
  Cembalo concertos, *468–9* (Ex. 248), 473.
  Symphony (4 movements), 401–2.
  Trio in C, 526.
  (with Carl Friberth)
    Sammlung deutscher Lieder, 353.
Hoffmeister, Franz Anton, 476, 544, 606.
Hofstetter, Romanus
  and Haydn's Op. 3 Quartets, 554.
Högg, Margarete, 4 n⁵.
Hohenemser, Richard, 535 n⁴.
Holbach, Paul Heinrich Dietrich d', 226.
Holmes, William C., 48 n¹.
Holschneider, Andreas, 552 n³.
Holzbauer, Ignaz, 2, *72–6*, 84, 408, *412*, *458*.
  Divertimenti (quintets), 567.
  Opera, *Günther von Schwarzburg, 72–5* (Exx. 42–4), 127.
  Quartets, 556–7 (Ex. 309).

Quintets, 533.
Symphonies, 412.
Trios (*sinfonie*), 524–5 (Exx. 295–6).
Holzer, Johann
  Songs, 354–5.
Honauer, Leontzi, xvii, 578.
Hook, James
  Concertos, 486.
  Songs, 338–40 (Ex. 149 (ii)).
Horwitz, Karl, 508 n¹, 525 nn²,⁴, 556 n¹.
Huberty (publisher), 398, 526.
Hucke, Helmuth, 9 n¹.
Hummel, J. J. (publisher), 403 and n¹, 404 n¹, 439 n¹, 464 n³, 470, 486, 518, 519, 555 n², 560.
Hunter, Anne (poet)
  'O Tuneful Voice' (Haydn), 357.

Imbault (publisher), 425.
Impresarios, leasing of court opera to, 3.
Indy, Vincent d', 609.
Intermezzi, 24, 47.
Istel, Edgar, 76 nn³,⁴.
Ivanschiz, Amandus, 431.

Jackson, William, *The Lord of the Manor*, 264, 269.
Jahn, Otto, 490; *see also* Abert, Hermann.
Jancik, Hans, 405 n².
Janet and Cotelle (publishers), 567 n⁵.
Janetzki, Kurt, 572 n¹.
Janitsch, J. Gottlieb, 530.
Jélyotte, Pierre de, 202, 207.
Jenkins, Newell, 374 n², 382 n².
Jensen, Gustav, 519 n¹, 529 n².
Jeunehomme, Mlle., 494.
Joachim, Joseph, 619.
Jöde, Fritz, 352 n¹.
Johansson, Carl, *French Music Publishers' Catalogues . . .*, 367 n¹.
Johnson, John (publisher), 576, 580
Jolivet (publisher), 404 n¹.
Jommelli, Niccolò, xviii, 2, 8, 24, 32, 41, 43, 45, 89, 585.
  Divertimenti, 506.
  Operas *33–8*, 45, 58.
    Achille in Sciro, 35, (Ex. 18 (i)).
    Critica, La, 48.
    Demofoonte, 35 (Ex. 18 (ii)).
    Fetonte, 36–8 (Exx. 19–20).
    Olimpiade, L', 36.
    Semiramide, 34 (Ex. 17).
    Vologeso, 36.
  Overtures/Symphonies, *368–70*, 383, 409, 422, 429, 431.
    Ciro riconosciuto, Il, 369–70 (Ex. 161).
Jones, John, 581.
Jordan, Mrs. Dorothea, 265, 269.

Joseph II, Emperor, xv, 2, 353.
and Haydn, 178.
and Mozart, 102, 150, 158–9.
and the 'National Singspiel', 6, 91, 95, 353 n².
his restrictions on Church music, 305–6.
and Sacchini, 243.
Jurgenson, Pyotr Ivanovich (publisher), 273–4.

Kamieński, Lucian, 408 n¹.
Kammel, Anton (Antonìn), 429.
Kant, Immanuel, xv, xix.
'Kapitanskaya doch' (folk melody), 279 (Ex. 134).
Kaul, Oskar, 464 n⁴.
Kayser, Johann, 270.
Kayser, Philipp Christoph, 85.
Keats, John, 349.
Keldïsh, Yury, *Russkaya muzïka XVIII veka*, 274, 278, 279 n³, 280 n³.
Keller, Hans, 500 n¹.
Kelly, Michael, 266, 269.
Reminiscences, 264 n².
Kelly, Thomas Erskine, Earl of, *430*.
Symphony No. 5, 430 (Ex. 209).
Kelway, Joseph, keyboard sonatas, 580.
Kerzelli, M. F.
Derevenskoy vorozheya, 272 n¹.
Lyubovnik-koldun (The Lover-magician), 273.
Kidson, Frank, 337, 338 n¹.
King, Alexander Hyatt, 119 n³, 172 n¹, 494 n¹.
Kirby, F. E., 67 n¹.
Kirkendale, Warren, 552 n³.
Kirkpatrick, Ralph, *Domenico Scarlatti*, 612 n¹.
Kirnberger, J. P., 593.
Methode Sonaten aus'm Ermel zu schüddeln, 593.
Kittel, J. C., 609.
Klafsky, Anton M., 297 n¹, 298 nn²,³.
Klauwell, Otto, *Geschichte der Programmmusik*, 402 n⁵.
Klein, Anton (librettist), 149.
Günther von Schwarzburg (Holzbauer), 71–2.
Klein, Herbert, 98 n².
Kleinmichel, Richard, 95 n³.
Klengel, Paul, 454 n¹, 527 n³, 530 n⁵.
Klinger, Maximilian, xv.
Klopstock, Friedrich Gottlieb, 353.
Settings by C. P. E. Bach, 349.
Gluck, 67, 349–50.
Neefe, 349.
Steffan, 355.
Knape, W., 482 n².
Knyazhnin, Y. B. (librettist).

Misfortune of having a Carriage, The (Pashkevich), 275.
Orpheus and Euridice (Fomin, Torelli), 280.
Koch (Opera) Company, the, 6, 80, 81
Köchel, Ludwig von
Verzeichnis . . . Mozarts Werke.
3rd. edn. (1937), 148 n¹, 604 n¹.
6th. edn. (1964), 98 n¹, 145 n¹, 148 n⁶, 154 n¹, 158 n¹, 307 n², 308 n², 313 n¹.
Kohout, Joseph, 206.
Komorzynski, Egon, 169 n¹.
Emanuel Schikaneder, 168 n².
Kosch, Franz, 295 n².
Kotzwara, Franz, *The Battle of Prague*, 581.
Kozeluch (Koželuh), Leopold, 476.
'Der Langmut Lohn', 354.
Kraft, Anton, 476.
Kratochvíl, Jiří, 493 n¹.
Kraus, Joseph, 432.
Krause, Christoph Gottfried, *see* Ramler, K. W.
Krauss, Rudolf, 1 n², 2 n², 3 n¹.
Krebs, Carl, 588 n³.
Dittersdorfiana (thematic catalogue), 402 n⁴, 403.
Krebs, Johann Ludwig, 593.
Kremsmünster, 431.
Kretzschmar, Hermann, 56 n²,³.
Kreutz, Alfred, 592 n².
Kroměříž, 467, 468, 471 n¹.
Krumpholtz, Johann Baptist, 438 (Ex. 211(ii)).
Kuhnau, Johann, 619
Biblical Sonatas, 407.
Kunz, Harold, 3 n².
Kurthen, Wilhelm, 307 n³.
Kurz, Josef Felix von (Bernardon), *89–91*, 174.
Der aufs neue begeisterte und belebte Bernardon, 90–1 (Exx. 55–6).
Küster, Albert, 535 n⁵.

Laborde, Jean Benjamin de, *Essai sur la musique ancienne et moderne*, xx, 424.
La Bruère, Charles Antoine Leclerc de (librettist), *Dardanus* (Rameau & Sacchini), 243.
Lafermière, F. H. (librettist)
Faucon, Le (Bortnyansky), 281.
Fils rival, Le (Bortnyansky), 281.
La Fontaine, Jean de, 204.
La Guimard, Madeleine, 239.
La Harpe, Jean François de, 231.
Lalande, Michel Richard de, 243.
La Laurencie, Lionel de, 420 n¹.
Inventaire critique du Fonds Blancheton, 374 and n².

La Laurencie, Lionel de (*cont.*):
L'École française de violon, 517 n[2], 529 n[7].
(and Albert Lavignac), *Encyclopédie de la musique*, 282 n[6].
Lamberg, Countess, 176.
Lambert, Constant, 429 n[3].
Lampugnani, Giovanni Battista, 8, 32.
Landon, Christa, 475 n[2], 596 n[1].
Landon, H. C. Robbins, 300 n[1], 315 n[2], 358 n[2], 399 n[2], 401 n[1], 431 n[1], 472 n[2], 473 n[2], 552 n[1], 554 n[3].
The Collected Correspondence and Notebooks of Joseph Haydn, 172 nn[1,2], 181 n[2], 323 n[2], 401 n[2].
The Symphonies of Joseph Haydn, 175 n[2], 355 n[1], 401 n[1], 551 n[5], 554 n[2].
(with D. Mitchell, eds.) *The Mozart Companion*, 490 n[1].
Landshoff, Ludwig, 527 n[3], 535 n[1], 538 n[3], 539 n[2], 594 n[3].
Lange, Aloysia, 127, 149 n[2], 160, 362.
'Lango Lee', British tune, 485, 487.
Lapis, Santo, 519.
La Pouplinière, Le Riche de, 225, 228, 230, 423.
Larsen, Jens Peter, *Drei Haydn Kataloge in Faksimile*, 547 n[4].
LaRue, Jan, 366 n[1], 396 n[1], 434 n[1], 436 n[1], 439 n[2], 460 n[1].
Láska, Ladislav, 445 n[1].
Lates, James, 521.
Latilla, Gaetans, 58, 202.
Leavis, Ralph, 565 n[2].
Lebermann, Walter, 457 n[2], 460 n[3], 462 n[2], 469 nn[1,2].
Lebrun, Ludwig A., 463.
Lecerf de la Viéville, 227.
Comparaison de la musique italienne et . . . française, 342 n[2].
Leclair, Jean-Marie, 477, 479, 520.
Sonata for Flute or Violin, Op. 9, no. 7, 518–19 (Ex. 291).
Le Clerc (publisher), 378 n[3], 530.
Le Duc, Pierre, *Journal Hebdomadaire* . . . (1784–1808), 344 n[5].
Le Duc, Simon ('l'Aîné'), *423–4, 479*.
Symphonie concertante, 479 (Ex. 261).
Symphony in E flat, 423–4 (Ex. 203), 479.
Leemans, H., 423.
Leeuwen, Arij van, 535 n[1].
Le Febvre, Louis Antoine (André), 364.
Cantatilles, 364.
Le Gros, Joseph, 172, 243.
Lehmann, Dieter, *Russlands Oper und Singspiel* . . ., 280 n[1].
Lehmann, Ursula, 524 n[3].
Leibniz, Gottfried, xix.

Leo, Leonardo, 291, 368, 374.
Concertos, 441.
Leopold II, Emperor, 163, 501.
as Leopold of Tuscany, 281.
Lessing, Gotthold Ephraim, 'Lob der Faulheit' (Haydn), 356.
Lesueur, Jean François, 323–4.
Leutgeb, Ignaz, 492, 571.
Levarie, Siegmund, *Mozart's 'Le Nozze di Figaro'*, 151 n[1].
Lewicki, Ernst, 315 n[3].
Ley, Henry G., 581 n[1].
Liber, Joseph Anton, 509.
Licenza, 98, 361.
Liebeskind, Joseph, 402 n[4].
Liebner, Anton (Edler von Kreutzner), 305.
Liebner, János, 154 n[2], 167 n[2], 168 n[2].
Linley, Elizabeth (Mrs. Sheridan), 265.
Linley, Thomas (the elder), 258, 263–6 *passim*.
Linley, Thomas (the younger), 261, 266
The Duenna, 261, 264, 269.
Linley, William, *Harlequin Captive or the Magic Fire* (pantomime), 269.
Lira organizzata, 572 and n[4], 573.
Livanova, Tamara, *Russkaya muzïkal'naya kul'tura XVIII veka*, 273 n[1], 280 n[1].
Livermore, Ann, 154 n[2], 160 n[2], 168 n[2].
Locatelli, Giovanni Battista, 5.
Locatelli, Pietro, *441*, 443.
Lockwood, Elizabeth M., 263 n[1].
Lodovica, Alessandro, 507.
Loewenberg, Alfred, 107 n[2].
Annals of Opera, 107 n[1], 121 n[3], 126 n[1], 148 n[5].
Loft, Abram, 627 n[1].
Logroscino, Nicola, 56 n[2], 58 and n[1].
Il governatore, 56 n[3].
Lolli, Antonio, 444.
Lombardini-Sirmen, Maddalena, 444.
Longman (Lukey) & Co. (publishers), 428, 531.
Lops, Rosa, 181.
Lorenzi, Giambattista (librettist), 47.
L'infedeltà fedele (Cimarosa and Haydn), 180.
Lotti, Antonio, 289.
Louis XIV, King of France, 223, 226, 336.
Louis XV, King of France, 231.
Lully, Jean-Baptiste, 200, 223, 224, 227–8, 232 n[4], 389, 615.
Amadis, 200, 225.
Armide, 43.
Bellérophon, 225.
Lusse, Mathis de, *Recueil de Romances* . . ., 343 n[3].
Lvov, N. A. (librettist), *The Post-drivers at the Post-station* (Fomin), 279.

INDEX

Madonis, Luigi, 270.
Mahaut, Antoine, 423.
Majo, Francesco di, 32, 45.
Majorano, Gaetano (Caffarelli), 4.
Maldere, Pierre Van, 432.
Malherbe, Charles Théodore, 489.
Manfredini, Vincenzo, 271.
Mangean, Etienne, 383 n[1].
Mann, J. C., see Monn, J. C.
Manzuoli, Giovanni, 97.
Marcello, Benedetto, 16 n[1].
Marchand (Opera) Company, 6.
Marchandt (publisher), 428.
Marco, Guy A., 623 n[1].
Marguerre, K., 316 n[1].
Maria Christine, Archduchess of Austria, 175.
Maria Ludovica, Empress, 166.
Maria Luisa, Infanta of Spain, 281.
Maria Ricciarda Beatrice, Princess of Modena, 117.
Maria Theresa, Empress (1717–80), 2, 172, 174, 176–7, 179, 294, 353, 593.
Maria Theresa, Empress (consort of Francis II), 322.
Marie Antoinette, Queen of France, 226, 229, 230, 243.
Marmontel, Jean François (librettist), 230, 231.
  Atys (Piccinni), 239.
  Didon (Piccinni), 239.
  Huron, Le (Grétry), 216.
  Roland (Piccinni), 239.
  Zémire et Azore (Grétry), 208.
Marpurg, Friedrich Wilhelm, *Berlinische Oden und Lieder*, 346 and nn[4,5].
Marsh, John, 430–1.
  Conversation Symphony, 430–1 (Ex. 210).
Marsollier, J. B. (librettist)
  Deux petits Savoyards, Les (Dalayrac), 253.
  Nina (Dalayrac), 250.
Martin, François, *421*, 422.
Martín y Soler, Vincente, 58.
  Ballet, *Didon abandonnée*, 272 n[1].
  Operas
    Cosa rara, Una, 154, 158, 267, 282.
    Gorebogatïr' Kosometovich, 272 n[1], 277.
    Mélomanie, La (Pesnolyubie), 255, 272 n[1].
Martinelli, Gaetano (librettist)
  Critica, La (Jommelli), 46.
  Schiava liberata, La, 142.
Martini, E., 483 n[2].
Martini, (Padre) Giovanni Battista, xx, 293–4, 299, 307, 309, 311, 400, 587, 624.
  Concertos, 441.
  Keyboard sonatas, *574–5* (Ex. 313), 576.
Martini (Schwarzendorf), Johann (il Tedesco), 206, 221.

Droit de seigneur, Le, 250–3 (Ex. 124).
  Henry IV, 221.
Martinotti, Sergio, 8 n[1].
Marvin, F., 579 n[1].
Marylebone Gardens, 266, 337 and n[1], 338 n[1], 339 n[2].
Masses, styles of
  'cantata mass', 290, 291 298, 299, 301, 303, 307, 315.
  missa brevis, 298, 300, 308, 310, 312, 313.
  missa a cappella, 289.
  missa solemnis, 288, 290, 291, 307.
Masson, Paul-Marie, 342 nn[1,2].
Matinsky, Mikhail, 278.
  The St. Petersburg Bazaar, 272–3, *274–6* (Ex. 131).
Mattheson, Johann, 328.
Maunder, R., 484 n[2].
Maximilian, Archduke of Austria, 119.
Maximilian Joseph III, Elector of Bavaria, 2, 126.
Mayer-Reinach, Albert, 2 n[1], 33 n[1].
Mazzolà, Caterino, 2, 163, 165.
Mederitsch, Johann, 94.
Méhul, Étienne Nicolas, 373, 425.
Melk Monastery, 402.
Mel'nik-koldun, see *Miller-magician, The*.
Mendelssohn-Bartholdy, Ernst von, 145 n[1].
Mennicke, Carl, 25 n[1], 26 n[1], 383 and n[1].
  Hasse und die Brüder Graun als Sinfoniker, 383 n[2], 384 n[1], 385 n[1].
Mersmann, Hans, 527 n[5].
Mesmer, Dr. Franz Anton, 107, 109.
Metastasio, Pietro, 2, 4, 8, 42, 49, 110, 134, 267, 325, 326.
  and Hasse, 25–6, 45.
  and Jommelli, 34, 36.
  and Klein, 72.
  his libretti, *8–12*.
    Alessandro nell'Indie, 10.
    Antigono (Durán), 199, 282.
    Artaserses (Araja, Arne, Storace), 110, 259, 267, 270.
    Betulia liberata, La (Mozart), 326.
    Clemenza di Tito, La (Mozart), 163, 165.
    Demetrio, 10, 110.
    Demofoonte, 110, 126.
    Ezio, 11.
    Isola disabitata, L' (Haydn), 179.
    Olimpiade, 10-11.
    Re pastore, Il (Mozart), 119.
    Ruggiero (Hasse), 25.
    Semiramide (Araja), 270.
    Sogno di Scipione, Il (Mozart), 117.
    Zenobia, 11.
Meyer, Ernst H., 45 n[2].
Meyerbeer, Giacomo, 236.
Meylan, Raymond, 439 n[1].

Miča, František Adam, 433.
Miča, František Václav, 433.
Michaels, Jost, 462 n[1].
Michu, 207.
Miesner, Heinrich, *Philipp Emanuel Bach in Hamburg*, 330 n[1].
Migliavacca, Giovanni Battista, 174.
Mille et une bagatelles, Les (song collection), 344.
Miller-magician, The (*Mel'nik-koldun, obmanshchik i svat*), 272, *273–4, 275, 276*.
Millico, Giuseppe, 45.
Milton, John, 258, 325, 334.
Mingotti, Pietro and Angelo, 5, 6.
Mingotti, Regina, 4, 181.
Misón, Luis, *Los ciegos, 285–6* (Ex. 136).
Mitchell, Donald, *see* Landon, H. C. R.
Mitjana, Rafaël, 282 n[6], 283 n[1], 284 n[1].
Moffat, Alfred, 521 nn[1-3], 529 nn[2,5].
Molière (Jean Baptiste Poquelin), 272.
Le Festin de pierre, 155 n[1].
Molter, Johann M., 402 and n[3], *432*.
Mondonville, Jean Joseph de, *224*, 225, 229, 520.
Pièces de Clavecin avec voix ou violon, 531.
Operas
Daphnis et Alcimadaure, 224.
Titan et l'Aurore, 224 (Ex. 113).
Monn, Georg Matthias, 295, *395–7* (Ex. 178), 398.
Concertos, *465–6* (Ex. 244), 469.
Cello in G minor, 466 (Ex. 245).
Cembalo, 466, 468.
Divertimento in G, 508.
Sonata in A, 525.
Symphony in B, 397.
Symphony in D, 294, 378, *395–7* (Ex. 179), 401, 411, 466.
Monn (Mann), Johann Christoph, *507–8*.
Divertimento in D, 507–8 (Exx. 281–3).
Divertimento a tre, 525–6.
Monnet, Jean, 206.
Anthologie française ou Chansons choisies, 342 n[1].
Monsigny, Pierre Alexandre, 207, 216, 250, 256
Aveux indiscrèts, Les, 204.
Déserteur, Le, 209–11 (Exx. 105–6).
Félix ou l'Enfant trouvé, 216.
On ne s'avise jamais de tout, 234–5 (Ex. 118).
Rose et Colas, 208.
Monteverdi, Claudio, 43, 44.
Moor, Karel, 445 n[1].
Mooser, Robert-Aloys, 5 n[2-3], 38 n[2], 45 n[3].
Annales de la musique . . . en Russie, 270 n[1], 273 n[1], 274 n[6].
Opéras . . . en Russie, 271 n[1], 272 n[2], 273 n[3].

Moser, Andreas, *Geschichte des Violinspiels*, 518 n[1].
Moser, Hans Joachim, *Das deutsche Sololied*, 346 n[4], 347 n[1], 349 nn[3,4], 352 nn[1,2], 356 n[1], 359 n[2].
Mouret, Jean Joseph, 223, 224.
Mozart, Constanze, 143, 314–15, 316, 490.
Mozart, Leopold, 98, 102, 106, 107 n[2], 109, 118 n[1], 150, 489.
Divertimento militaire, 511–12 (Ex. 288).
'Litaniae Venerabili', 296.
Mozart, Wolfgang Amadeus, xvi, 44, 176, 196, 266, 296, 353 n[3], 463, 599, 619.
characteristics (musical), 189, 379, 480, 561, 595.
compared with
Hasse, 293.
Monn, 294.
others, 461, 619.
influenced by
Abel, 427.
C. P. E. Bach, 359, 540.
J. C. Bach, 484–5, 570, 594, 595–6, 603, 628.
J. S. Bach, 315, 316.
J. Haydn, 500, 563–5 *passim, 602–3*, 612, 618, 624, 625 and n[2].
M. Haydn, 406, 569.
Schobert, 534, 603.
Wagenseil, 593–4.
see also 404 n[2].
influences on
Beethoven, 624, 627.
Dittersdorf, 96.
J. Haydn, 623.
Pleyel, 563.
Schubert, 626, 632.
Letters of . . ., *see* Anderson.
thematic catalogue, *Verzeichnis aller meiner Werke*, 496.
views on
Adlgasser and M. Haydn, 296–7.
Gluck, 138.
Gossec, 530.
Holzbauer, 73, 412.
length of Masses, 298–9, 310.
Mysliveček, 445.
Schweitzer, 71.
Arias and vocal ensembles, *98, 126–7*, 140, 148 n[1], *149* n[2], 154, *159–60*, *361–3* (Ex. 160), 487.
Chamber music, 522, 532.
Clarinet Quintet, K. 581, in A, *571–2*.
Duet for Bassoon and Cello, K. 292, 548 n[3].
Duos for Violin and Viola, 548.
Flute Quartets, 565.
Horn Quintet, K. 407, in E flat, 571.
Piano Quartets, 544–5 (Ex. 305).
Piano Trios, 541–4 (Exx. 303–4).

INDEX

Piano/Wind Quintet, K. 452, in E flat, 545.
Sextets, 572.
String Quartets, 394, *559–60*, *563–5*.
  K. 80, 155–60, *559*,
  K. 168–73, 118, *559–60*, 624.
    K. 168 in F, 618, *624*.
    K. 173 in D minor, 624–5.
  K. 387, 421, 428, 458, 464–5 ('Haydn' Quartets), 303, *563–4*, 620, *625–7*.
    K. 387 in G, 303, 608.
    K. 421 in D minor, 497, 625, *626–7*.
  K. 499, 564.
  K. 575, 564–5.
  K. 589–90, 565.
String Quintets, *569–71* (Ex. 312), 627.
String Trio (Divertimento) K. 563, *552*.
Violin Sonatas, *539–41*, 604.
Church music, 288, 289, *306–19*.
  Cantata, K. 469, *Davidde penitente*, 316, 327.
  'Epistle' sonatas, 298, *526–7*, 533.
  Kyries
    K. 90 in D Minor, 309.
    K. 341 in D minor, 314.
  Litanies
    K. 125, 'de venerabili altaris sacramento', 309.
    K. 195, 'Lauretanae', 310.
    K. 243, 'de venerabili altaris sacramento', 311.
  Masses
    K. 49 in G, *308–9* (Ex. 143).
    K. 65 in D minor, *308–9*.
    K. 66 in C ('Dominicus'), 308.
    K. 115 in C ('brevis'), 310.
    K. 116 in F ('brevis'), 310.
    K. 139 in C minor, 307, 308.
    K. 167 in C ('Trinity'), *310*.
    K. 192 in F, 310–11, 312.
    K. 194 in D, 310.
    K. 220 in C ('Sparrow'), 311.
    K. 257 in C ('Credo'), 311, 312.
    K. 258 in C ('Spaur'), 312.
    K. 259 in C ('Organ Solo'), 312–13.
    K. 262 in C ('longa'), *311–12*.
    K. 275 in B flat ('brevis'), 311, 313 (Ex. 144).
    K. 317 in C ('Coronation'), 313, *314*.
    K. 337 in C, 313, *314*.
    K. 427 in C minor, 291, 306, *314–16*.
    K. 626 in D minor (Requiem), 306, *316–19*.
    K. 296 a–c (fragments), 313 n[1].
  Motets, etc.
    K. 108, *Regina coeli* in C, 309.
    K. 127, *Regina coeli* in B flat, 309.
    K. 165, 'Exsultate, jubilate', 309.
  K. 618, 'Ave verum corpus', 306, 316.
  Offertories
    K. 72, 'Inter natos', 310.
    K. 222, 'Misericordias Domini', 311.
  Vespers
    K. 321 ('de Dominica'), 313.
    K. 339 ('solennes de confessore'), 313, 314.
Concertos, 465, 470, *487–502*.
  Baroque aspects, 434.
  cadenzas, 488.
  Classical development, 436, 437.
  continuo in, 440.
  melodic fluency, 459.
  openings, 415.
  related to other composers', 446, 461, 464, 471, 475.
  Bassoon
    K. 191 in B flat, *492*.
    K. 196d, 489.
  Cello
    K. 206a in F, 489.
  Clarinet
    K. 622 in A, 476, *492–3* (Ex. 273), 498.
  Flute
    K. 313 in G, 492.
    K. 314 in D, 492.
  Flute and Harp
    K. 299 in C, *492*.
  Horn
    K. 412/514 in D, 489.
    K. 417 in E flat, 492.
    K. 447 in E flat, 492.
    K. 495 in E flat, 492.
    K. 371 (Rondo) in E flat, 489.
  Oboe
    K. 271k in C, 492.
  Piano, *494–502*, 613, *627–9*, 633.
    K. 37, 39, 40–1, 107 (arrangements), 494 n[1], 578, 595.
    K. 175 in D, 118, 490, *494*, 629.
    K. 238 in B flat, 494.
    K. 242 in F (3 pianos), 494.
    K. 246 in C, 494.
    K. 271 in E flat, *494–5* (Ex. 274), 496.
    K. 365 in E flat (2 pianos), 496.
    K. 413 in F, 496.
    K. 414 in F, 496.
    K. 415 in C, 496.
    K. 449 in E flat, *496*, 602.
    K. 450 in B flat, *496*, 498.
    K. 451 in D, *496–7*, 498.
    K. 453 in G, *497*, 602, 629.
    K. 456 in B flat, 497.
    K. 459 in F, 497.
    K. 466 in D minor, *497–8*, 628.
    K. 467 in C, 487, *498*.
    K. 482 in E flat, 498.

Mozart, W. A., Piano Concertos (*cont.*):
    K. 488 in A, 498–9 (Ex. 275).
    K. 491 in C minor, 387, *499–500* (Exx. 276–8), 501, 605, 606, 628.
    K. 503 in C, 500–1 (Ex. 279).
    K. 537 in D ('Coronation'), *501*, 632.
    K. 595 in B flat, 501–2 (Ex. 280).
  Sinfonie concertanti
    K. 297b (Wind) in E flat, 490.
    K. 364 (Violin & Viola) in E flat, *491–2* (Ex. 272), 495, 548, 570.
  Triple (fragment), K. 320e, 489.
  Trumpet, 498.
  Violin
    K. 207 in B flat, 490.
    K. 211 in D, 490.
    K. 216 in G, 490.
    K. 218 in D, 490–1.
    K. 219 in A, *491*, 494–5.
    K. 268 in E flat, 491 n[1].
    K. 271i in D, 491 n[1].
    K. Anh. 294a, 491 n[1].
  Violin and Piano (fragment), K. 315f, 489, 490.
  Keyboard works, 597–8, *602–10*.
  Adagio, K. 540 in B minor, xix, *608*.
  Adagio and Allegro, K. 594, 608.
  Cadenzas, K. 626a, 486.
  Fantasias
    K. 396 in C minor, 607.
    K. 397 in D minor, 607.
    K. 475 in C minor, 607.
    K. 608 in F minor, 608–9.
  Fantasia and Fugue, K. 394 in C, 315, 607.
  Fugue, K. 426 in C minor (2 pianos), 608.
  Gigue, K. 574 in G, 607.
  Minuet, K. 355 in D, 607.
  Rondos, 591.
    K. 485 in D, 544.
    K. 494 in F, 606.
    K. 511 in A minor, 608.
  Sonatas
    K. Anh. 199–202, 603.
    K. 46d–e, 603.
    K. 279–80, 282–3, 603.
    K. 284 in D, 603–4 (Ex. 336).
    K. 309 in C, 604.
    K. 310 in A minor, 597, *604*, 605.
    K. 311–12, 604.
    K. 330–2, 604–5.
    K. 333 in B flat, 595, 605, 610.
    K. 448 in D (2 pianos), 608.
    K. 457 in C minor, *605*, 607, 608.
    K. 497 in F (4 hands), 608.
    K. 521 in C (4 hands), 608.
    K. 533 in F, *605–6* (Exx. 337–8), 609.
    K. 545 in C, 606.
    K. 570 in B flat, 606, 608.
    K. 576 in D, 606 (Ex. 339).
  Suite, K. 399, in C (in style of Handel), 315.
  Variations
    K. 179 on Minuet by Fischer, 485.
    K. 180 on Salieri's 'Mio caro Adone', 607.
    K. 455 on Gluck's 'Unser dummer Pöbel', 607.
    K. 501 in G (4 hands), 608.
    K. 613 on Schack's 'Ein Weib ist das herrlichste Ding', 607.
  Lieder, 354, *359–60* (Ex. 159).
  Miscellaneous works
    Adagio and Fugue in C minor (K. 546), 608.
    Arrangements of J. S. Bach's Fugues (K. 404a), 552.
    of Handel's choral works, 315.
    Ballets
      Le gelosie del serraglio (K. Anh. 109), 118 n[1].
      Les petits riens (K. Anh. 10), 127.
    (Canonic study) (K. 73x), 309.
    Movements for Symphonies (K. 102, 120–1), 121 n[1].
    'Ode on the defence of Gibraltar' (K. 386d), 353 n[1].
    Sonate di chiesa ('Epistle' sonatas), 298, *526–7*, 533.
    Thamos, König von Ägypten (Gebler), incidental music (K. 345), *119*, 127, *128*.
  Occasional music
    Cassation (K. 99), 505.
    Divertimenti, 509, *512–14*, 552, 559.
      K. 289 in E flat, *513–14* (Exx. 289–90).
    Notturno for 4 orchs. (K. 286), 505, 573.
    Serenades, *504–6*, 572 n[2], 573.
      K. 388 (Octet), 570, 605.
    Serenata notturna (K. 239), 505, 573.
  Operas 33, *97–172*, 244.
    Apollo et Hyacinthus (K. 38), 97, *98–101* (Exx. 62–4), 109.
    Ascanio in Alba (K. 111), 110, *117–18* (Ex. 75), 119, 121, 505.
    Bastien und Bastienne (K. 50), 97, *107–9* (Exx. 68–70), 203.
    Clemenza di Tito, La (K. 621), 134, 159, *163–6* (Ex. 93), 168, 183, 196, 226, 317.
    Così fan tutte (K. 588), 158, *159–63*, 168, 196, 204.
    Don Giovanni (K. 527), 65, 149, *154–9*, 159–60, 163, 165, 171, 249, 497, 622, 625–6, 634.
    Entführung aus dem Serail, Die (K. 384), 89, 124, 128–9, 133–4, 140, *141–7* (Ex. 89), 149, 151, 162, 186, 219, 246, 266, 625.

INDEX

Finta giardiniera, La (K. 196), 119, 121, 122–6 (Exx. 77–81), 127, 133, 140, 311.
   Die verstellte Gärtnerin (*Singspiel* version), 126.
Finta semplice, La (K. 51), 97, *102–6* (Exx. 65–7), 109, 121.
Idomeneo, re di Creta (K. 366–7), 24, 119, *133–40* (Exx. 86–8), 147, 164, 166, 172, 183, 196, 314.
Lucio Silla (K. 135), 110, *111–17* (Exx. 71, 73–4), 118, 309.
Mitridate, re di Ponto (K. 87), 97, 110, *111–17* (Ex. 72).
Nozze di Figaro, Le (K. 492), 96, 130, 148, *149–54*, 155, 158–60 *passim*, 163, 165, 192, 196, 212, 249, 266, 314, 372, 634.
Oca del Cairo, L' (fragments) (K. 422), 148 (Ex. 91).
Re pastore, Il (K. 208), *119–21* (Ex. 76).
Schauspieldirektor, Der (K. 486), *149*, 255.
Semiramis (projected), 127.
Sogno di Scipione, Il (K. 126), 110, 117, 121.
Sposo deluso, Lo (K. 430), *148–9* (Ex. 92), 150.
Zaïde (K. 344), 119, 127, *128–33* (Exx. 82–5), 139, 141.
Zauberflöte, Die (K. 620), xviii, 97, 119 n³, 139, 145, 159, 163–4, *166–72*, 195, 245–6, 254, 317, 319, 390.
Oratorios
  Betulia liberata, La (K. 118), 326.
  Schuldigkeit des ersten Gebotes, Die (K. 35) (with Anton Weiser), 98, 105, 326.
Symphonies, 387, 407, *629–35*.
  related to other composers', 389–90, 405, 416, 423–4, 427, 432.
  K. 45 in D, 106.
  K. 161/163 in D, 121 n¹.
  K. 183 in G minor, 118, *629–30* (Ex. 343), 632.
  K. 200 in C, 629.
  K. 201 in A, 118, 629.
  K. 385 in D ('Haffner'), 573.
  K. 425 in C ('Linz'), 628, 629.
  K. 504 in D ('Prague'), 629.
  K. 543 in E flat, 629, 630, 632.
  K. 550 in G minor, 498, 627, 629–30, *631–5* (Exx. 344–6).
  K. 551 in C ('Jupiter'), 311, 376, 406, 541, 629–30, 632.
Mueller, Erich H., 5 n⁴.
Müller, W., *Johann Adolf Hasse als Kirchenkomponist*, 291 n².
Müller, Wenzel
  Kaspar der Fagottist, 97.

Sonnenfest der Brahminen, Das, 97, 168.
Müller von Asow, Eric H., 166 n², 496 n¹.
Münster, Robert, 126 n¹, 414 n¹, 460 n³.
Murrill, Herbert, 529 nn²,⁵.
Müry, Albert, *Die Instrumentalwerke Gaetano Pugnanis*, 444 n².
Mussorgsky, Modest, *Boris Godunov*, 278.
Müthel, Johann Gottfried, 455.
Mysliveček, Josef, 423, 444, 614.
  Concertos, 444–5.
  Quintets, 566–7.

Nail violin (*Nagelgeige*), 563 and n³.
Nares, James, 579.
  Il Principio, 581 and n².
  Keyboard Lessons, Opp. 1–2, 580–1 (Ex. 319).
Naumann, Johann Gottlieb, 3 n³, 33, 76.
  Duets for violin, 545 n³.
  Duets for wind, 548.
  Operas
    Amphion, 45.
    Cora och Alonzo, 45, 76.
    Gustaf Wasa, 45.
    Osiris, 168 n¹.
Neapolitan School, church music of the, *289–93*, 295–6, 300, 316, 327, 333.
Neefe, Christian Gottlob, 79, 86, 88–9.
  Adelheit von Weltheim, 88–9.
  Songs
    'Hermann und Thusnelda', 349 n³.
    'Vaterlandslied', 349.
Nef, Karl, 374 n¹.
Neruda, Johann Baptist Georg, 452.
Nettl, Paul, 165 n¹, 168 n¹.
Neubaur, Franz Christoph, Trio in C for Flute, Violin, and Viola Op. 3, no. 3, 549–50.
Neuber, Karoline, 80, 270.
Neufeldt, Ernst, 609.
Neumann, Friedrich-Heinrich, 128 nn²,⁴, 528 n¹.
Newman, William S., 577 n¹, 581 n³.
  The Sonata in the Baroque Era, 529 n⁶.
  The Sonata in the Classic Era, 593 n¹.
Nichelmann, Christoph, 456.
Niecks, Frederick, *Programme Music*, 402 n⁵.
Niemann, Walter, 582 n⁶, 583 n¹.
Nikolev, N. P. (librettist), *The Lovermagician* (Kerzelli), 273.
Nissen, Georg Nicolaus von, *Mozart*, 107 n², 544.
Noske, Frits, 150 n³.
  Das ausserdeutsche Sololied, 343 n¹.
Notturno, *505–6*.
Noverre, Jean Georges (choreographer), 24, 43, 44, 126, 585.

716 INDEX

Noverre, Jean Georges (*cont.*):
  Echo et Narcisse (Gluck), 239.
  Petits riens, Les (Mozart), 127.
  Scythes enchaînés, Les (Gossec), 239.
Nowak, Leopold, 475 n[1] *bis*.
Nuovo, Antonio, 38 n[2].
Nützlader, Rudolf, 295 n[4].
Nys, Carl de, 582 n[6].

Oberdörffer, Fritz, 453 n[4].
Offenbach, Jacques, 201, 256.
Oglio, Domenico dall', 270.
O'Keeffe, John, 264.
Olleson, Edward, 306 n[2], 315 n[4], 322 nn[1,2], 323 n[1], 333 n[1].
Opera buffa, xviii, 3, *4–5*, 8, 45, 91, 94, 327.
  composers of, *58–66*.
  French craze for, 201–2.
  Haydn and, 172–99 *passim*.
  Mozart and, 97–172 *passim*.
  styles and forms of, *47–57*.
  translations of, in Vienna, 95.
Opéra comique, xvi, xviii, 3, 64, 79–97 *passim*, 144, 150, 152, 341.
  in France, 200–56 *passim*.
  introduced to Russia, 206.
  outside France, *204–6*.
  translations of, in Vienna, 95.
Opera seria, xviii, 2, *4–5*, 93, 169, 288, 328.
  in Germany, *66–79, 87–8* (Ex. 54).
  in Italy, *8–25, 26–45* passim, *45–7*.
  and the Metastasian libretto, *8–12*.
  prime rule of, 166.
  related to *opera buffa*, 47–58 *passim*, 108.
  see also Haydn, 172–99 *passim*; Mozart, 95–172 *passim*.
Oratorio, 288, *323–35*.
  in Catholic Europe, 325–8.
  in England, 325.
  in France, 324.
  in Protestant Germany, 328–32.
Ordoñez, Carlos d', *401*.
  Alceste, 178–9.
  Symphonies, 401.
Orel, Alfred, 98 n[4], 107 n[2], 109 n[1], 128 nn[2,4].
Orléans, Louis Philippe Joseph, Duke of, 207.
Ossian, 349.
Oswald, James, *The Dust Cart*, 364.

Pachelbel, Johann, 619.
Paër, Ferdinando, 363–4.
Paganelli, Giuseppe Antonio, 506.
Paganini, Niccolo, 546 n[1].
Paisiello, Giovanni, 8, 9 n[2], 32, 45, 58, 59 n[1], 63, 183, 189, 271.

Operas
  Barbiere di Siviglia, Il, 47, 57 (Ex. 31), *61–3* (Exx. 34–5), 271, 372.
  Pirro, 182.
  Overtures, 371–2.
  Passione, 326.
  Symphonies, 366.
Palestrina, Giovanni Pierluigi, 289.
Paradeiser, Marian Carl, 431.
Paradies (Paradisi), Domenico, Keyboard sonatas, *576–7* (Ex. 315).
Paradisi, Count Agostino, 229.
Parini, Giuseppe, 117.
Parke, W. T., 265.
  Musical Memoirs, 265 n[1].
Pashkevich, Vassily Alexeyevich, 275.
  Fevey, 272 n[1], 276.
  (with Canobbio and Sarti). *Misfortune of having a Carriage, The* (*Neschastie ot karetï*), 272, 273, 275–6.
  First Government of Oleg, The (*Nachal'noe upravlenie Olega*), 272 n[1], *277–8* (Ex. 133).
Pasquini, Claudio, 2.
Pasticcio, 24–5.
Pasterwitz, Georg, 431.
Pastorale héroïque, 224.
Pauer, Ernst, 580 n[2], 594 n[1].
Pauersbach, Karl Joseph von, 177, 179, 180.
Paul Petrovich, Grand Duke, 561.
Pauly, Reinhard, G., 306 n[1], 515 n[1].
Paumgartner, Bernhard, 163 n[1], 506 n[1].
Pauselli, Stefan, 507.
Perez, Davide, 7, 32, 45, 58.
  Alessandro nelle Indie, 45.
  Solimano, 45.
Perger, Lothar H., 405 n[2], 509 n[2].
Pergolesi, Giovanni Battista, 202, 386, 521, 523.
  La serva padrona, 5, 47, 175, 184, 201, 202.
Perinello, Carlo, 506 n[3], 522 n[1].
Persuis, Louis, 568.
Peters (publishers), 518 n[1].
Petronius, Gaius, 262.
Pfäfflin, Clara, *Pietro Nardini: seine Werke und sein Leben*, 443 n[4].
Pfannhauser, Karl, 307 n[3].
Philidor, André Danican, 216, 225, 229, 243, 244, 250, 256.
  Blaise le Savetier, 204, 208.
  Diable à quatre, Le, 204.
  Jardinier et son seigneur, Le, 208.
  Maréchal ferrant, Le, *211–13* (Exx. 107–8).
  Tom Jones, 209, *213–16* (Ex. 109).
Piccinni, Nicola (Niccolò), 32, 45, *58–63 passim*, 126, 183, 243.
  and the 'contest' with Gluck, 231, 235, *239–41*, 255, 342, 372.

Operas
Atys, 239, 240.
Bella verità, La, 48.
Buona figliuola, La, 48, *49–55* (Exx. 25–30), 57 n[1], 59–61 (Exx. 32–3), 281.
Didon, 239, 240–1.
Iphigénie en Tauride, 240.
Roland, 231, 239, *240*, 373.
Overtures, 371, *372–3* (Exx. 162–3).
Pichl, Wenzel (Václav), 476, 509.
Picquot *Notice sur . . . L. Boccherini*, 568.
Pindar, *Odes*, 278.
Piovano, Francesco, 64 n[1].
Piva, F., 576 n[1].
Pla, Manuel, *Quien complace a la deidad . . .*, 282.
Plath, Wolfgang, 318 n[3].
Platti, Giovanni Benedetto.
Concertos, 441–2.
Keyboard sonatas, 581.
Pleyel, Ignaz Joseph, 438 (Ex. 211 (ii)).
Concertos, 481.
Duets for strings, 545.
Flute Quartets, *563*.
Symphonies, 425–6 (Ex. 205).
Ployer, Barbara von, 496, 497, 602, 629.
Plümicke, K. M. (playwright), *Lanassa*, 128 n[2].
Pohl, Carl F., *see* Botstiber, Hugo.
Pohl, Wilhelm, Songs, 354.
Pokorný, Franz Xaver, 396 n[1], 402, 432, 445 n[4].
Pollak-Schlaffenberg, Irene, 354 n[1].
Polo, Enrico, 522 n[1], 531 n[2].
Poltronieri Alberto, 557 n[1].
Polzelli, Luigia, 182, 198.
Pompadour, Madame de (Jeanne Poisson), 203, 207, 224, 229.
Popov, M. V. (librettist), *Anyuta* (composer unknown), 272–3.
Porpora, Niccolò, 25, 368.
Porta, Giovanni, 2.
Porta, Nunziato (librettist), *Orlando Paladino* (Haydn), 180.
Post-horn, in ensembles, 572 and n[2].
Poštolka, Milan, *Leopold Koželuh*, 476 n[3].
Prač, Ivan, 274–80 *passim*.
Praetorius, Ernst, 484 n[1].
Prato, Vincenzo dal, 135.
Preibisch, Walter, 89 n[1], 142 nn[1, 2], 143 n[3], 146 n[1].
Pressburg (Bratislava), Prince Archbishop of, 175.
Pressburger Zeitung, Die, 175, 177.
'Pri dolinushke' (folk-song), 278.
Prokofiev, V. A., 274 n[6].
Pröpper, Rolf, 76 n[2].
Provence, Comte de (Louis XVIII), 207, 250.
Puccini, Giacomo, 577.
Puchberg, Michael, 160, 196.

Pugnani, Gaetano, 486, 613.
Concertos, 444.
Overtures and Symphonies, 381–2 (Ex. 169).
Sonatas, 519.
Trios, 522.
Pulkert, Oldřich, 474 n[1].
Puttini, Francesco, and Pietro Travaglia (librettists), *La vera constanza* (Haydn), 178.

Quantz, Johann, xvi, 448.
Quartets
for nail violin and strings, 563.
for strings, *552–66*.
for wind and strings, 557, 563, 565.
'Querelle des Bouffons', 5, *201–2*, 224, 342.
Quinault, Philippe (librettist), 229.
Armide (Gluck, Lully), 231, 235.
Atys (Piccinni), 239.
Roland (Piccinni), 231, 239.
Quintets
for strings, *566–71*.
for wind and strings, *571–2*.

Raabe, F., *Galuppi als Instrumentalkomponist*, 575 n[3].
Raaff, Anton, 127, 134.
Rabinovich, Alexander S., *Russkaya opera do Glinki*, 273 n[1], 274 n[5], 279 nn[1, 5].
Racek, Jan, 566 n[1], 594 n[2].
Racine, Jean, xviii, 227, 230, 233.
Raeburn, Christopher, 165 n[1].
Rameau, Jean Philippe, 43, 200–4 *passim*, 223–5 *passim*, 227–30 *passim*, 364.
Castor et Pollux, 225, 229.
Dardanus, 223, 225, 243.
Hippolyte et Aricie, 229.
Platée, 200.
Zoroastre, 223, 225, 411 n[1].
Ramler, Karl Wilhelm (poet and librettist), 364.
Auferstehung und Himmelfahrt Jesu (C. P. E. Bach), 331.
Tod Jesu, Der (Graun), 329, 333.
(with C. G. Krause)
Lieder der Deutschen, 346 nn[1, 2].
Oden mit Melodien, 346.
Ramsay, Allan, *Tea Table Miscellany*, 340.
Ranelagh Gardens, music at, 337 and n[1], 339 n[2].
Rasmussen, Mary, 468 n[2].
Rationalism, 8.
Raupach, Hermann Friedrich, 578.
Rauzzini, Venanzio, 261, 309.
Recitativo accompagnato (examples), 13–14 (Ex. 2), *26–8* (Ex. 11), *34–5* (Exx. 17–18),

Recitativo accompagnato (cont.):
37–8 (Ex. 20), *39–41* (Ex. 21), *50–1* (Ex. 26), *72–3* (Ex. 42), *115–16* (Ex. 74), *122–3* (Ex. 77).
Recitativo secco (examples), 13 (Ex. 1), 67–8 (Ex. 39).
Redlich, Hans, 476 n[1].
Reeser, Eduard, 578 n[5].
Regnard, Jean François, 175.
Rehm, Wolfgang, 608 n[1].
Reicha, Joseph, 464.
Reichardt, Johann Friedrich, 84, 86, 351, 390–1.
  Ariadne, 364–5.
  Concertos, *455–6*.
  Singspiele and Opera, 76, 77, 85.
  Solo Sonatas, 517.
  Songs, etc., 349, *350–1*, 365.
Reichert, Georg, 311 n[1].
Reutter, Johann Georg (the younger), 2, 294–5, 298, 300 and n[2], 395, 467 n[2].
Rhau, G., 469 n[1].
Rheineck, Christoph, 352.
Rich, John, 257, 258.
Richardson, Samuel, 48.
Richter, Franz Xaver, 424, 425.
  Concertos, 457, *458*.
  Divertimenti, 509.
  Quartets, *555–6*, 619.
  Sonate da camera, *533*.
  Symphonies, 408 (Ex. 188), *411–12* (Ex. 192).
  Trio sonatas, 523.
Riedel, Karl, 508 n[1], 525 nn[2, 4], 556 n[1].
Riedinger, Lothar, 95 n[2].
Riemann, Hugo.
  as editor, 392 n[1], 452 n[2], 521 n[5], 523 nn[1, 2], 526 n[1], 528 n[2], 531 n[1], 534 n[1], 538 n[2], 578 nn[3, 4].
  and the Mannheim School, 379, 407, 412, 418, 457, 463.
Riepel, Joseph, 509.
Rigel, Henri-Joseph, Symphonies, 424 (Ex. 204).
Rinaldo di Capua, 202, 368.
Ringmacher (publisher), 439 n[1].
Ristori, Giovanni, 270.
  Calandro, 270.
Ritter, Peter, 463.
Roeser, Valentin, 423.
Rolandi, Ulderico, 49 n[1].
Rolla, Alessandro, 444, 546 n[1].
Rolland, Romain, *Musiciens d'autrefois*, 232.
Rolle, Johann Heinrich, 328.
  Lazarus, 328.
  Sonata in E flat, 594 (Ex. 331).
  Tod Abels, Der, 328.
Roman, Johan, 431.
Romance, the, xvi, *342–4* (Ex. 151).

Rosales, Antonio, 285.
  El licenciado Farfulla, 284.
Rosen, Charles, 515 n[1].
Rosenberg, Alfons, *Die Zauberflöte, Geschichte und Deutung* . . ., 167 n[2].
Rosenberg, Count, 147.
Rosenthal, Karl A., 296, 309 n[2].
Rossini, Gioacchino Antonio, 226, 374.
Rösler (Rossetti), Franz Anton, *432*, 438 (Ex. 211 (iii)).
  Concertos, 464–5.
  Flute in D, 464 (Ex. 242).
  Horn in E flat, 464 (Ex. 243).
Roth, Herman, 347 n[1].
Roullet, François du (librettist), 230, 231, 236, 241.
  Iphigénie en Aulide (Gluck), xviii, 228, 230, 233, 236.
Rousseau, Jean-Jacques, xv, xvi, xx, 226, 230.
  on French opera, *227–8*.
  his naturalism, 85, 522.
  and opéra comique, 202–3, 206–8 *passim*.
  and the 'Querelle des Bouffons', 201–2.
  Consolations des misères de ma vie, 343 and n[1].
  Dictionnaire de musique, xvi, xx, 342, 343.
  Lettre sur la musique française, 201–2, 232 n[4].
  Devin du village, Le, 107, 202–3 (Ex. 102), 207, 273.
  Pygmalion, 76.
Royer, Joseph, *Zaïde*, 225.
Rubsamen, Walter H., 80 n[2].
Rubio, S. (publisher), 579 and n[1].
Rudolph, Johann Joseph, 24.
Ruf, Hugo, 519 n[2].
Ruge, Filippo, 423.
Ruprecht, Joseph, 94.
Rush, George.
  The Royal Shepherd, 260.
  Piano Concerto, 486.
Rust, Friedrich Wilhelm, 517–18, 518 n[1], 609.
  Quartet for nail violin and strings, 563.

Sacchini, Antonio, 8, 32, 45, *243–4*, 246, 261, 374, 522–3.
  Operas, *243–4*.
  Cidde, Il, 243.
  Dardanus, 243.
  Oedipe à Colone, 243–4, *373* (Ex. 164).
  Rinaldo, 243.
  Semiramide, 373.
  Overtures, 371, *373*.
Sachsen-Teschen, Duke Albert von, 175.
Sadie, Stanley, 529 nn[1, 2, 6].
Sadler's Wells, 338 n[1].

INDEX

Sainete, 283, 285.
Saint-Aman, Louis Joseph, *Alvar et Mincia*, 225.
St. Florian Monastery, 431.
Saint-Foix, Georges de, 374 n^1, 420 n^1, 568 n^1.
  (with T. de Wyzewa)
    W. A. Mozart, 119 n^2, 548 n^1, 569 n^4, 630 n^1.
Saint-Georges, Chevalier Joseph de, 425.
  Concertos, 478–9 (Ex. 260).
Saint-Huberty, Antoinette de, 240, 241.
Salieri, Antonio, 8, 32, 243, *295–6*.
  Mass in D minor, 296 (Ex. 139).
  Operas
    Danaïdes, Les, 241–3 (Ex. 120).
    Prima la musica e poi le parole, 48, 149.
    Tarare (Axur, re d'Ormus), 244–7 (Exx. 121–2).
Salmen, Walter, 365 n^1.
Salomon, Johann Peter, 181, 487, 620, 630.
Salzburg, Prince Archbishop of, 118, 140.
Sammartini, Giovanni Battista, 519, 614–16 *passim*, 619, 624.
  Haydn's opinion of, *614–15*.
  Concertos, 435, 441.
  Divertimenti, 506.
  Sonatas, 374 and n^1, *522* (Ex. 293), 528, *530*.
  Symphonies, *374–8* (Exx. 165–7), 378–9, 383 n^1, 408, 422.
Sammartini, Giuseppe, 374, 530.
  Trio in A minor, Op. 3, no. 9, *521–2*.
Sandberger, Adolf, 333 n^2, 572 n^4.
Sands, Mollie
  Gardens of Hampton Court, The, 337 n^1.
  Invitation to Ranelagh, 337 n^1.
Sarjent (trumpeter), 265.
Sarti, Giuseppe, 8, 32, 45, 271.
  Giulio Sabino, 45.
  Overtures, 371, *374*.
  see also Canobbio.
Scarlatti, Alessandro, 25, 367–8.
  Masses, 291.
  Overtures, 368, 613.
  String quartets, *553*.
Scarlatti, Domenico, 390, 533, 574, 579, 611–12.
  Keyboard music, 574, 576–7, 584.
Scarlatti, Giuseppe, 282.
Schachtner, Andreas, 128 and n^1.
Schaffrath, Christoph, 456.
Schale, Christian Friedrich, 456.
Scheibe, Johann Adolf, *64*.
  Critische Musicus, Der, 64.
  Thusnelde, 64.
  Tragische Kantaten, 364.
Schemelli, Georg Christian, *Musicalisches Gesang-Buch*, 347.

Schenk, Erich, 300 n^2, 444 n^3, 525 n^3, 526 nn$^{1, 2, 4}$.
  The Italian Trio Sonata, 522 n^2.
Schenk, Johann, 94.
Scherillo, Michele, *Storia letteraria . . .*, 47 n^1.
Schering, Arnold, 328 n^1, 454 n^2.
  Geschichte der Musik in Beispielen, 80 n^3, 85 n^1, 293 n^1, 347 n^1, 432 n^1, 520 n^1, 592 n^1.
  Geschichte des Oratoriums, 326 n^1.
Schiebeler, Daniel, 85 n^1.
Schiedenhofen, Joachim Ferdinand von, 128 n^2.
Schiernerl, Alfred, 295 n^3.
Schikaneder, Emanuel Johann
  as librettist, *Die Zauberflöte* (Mozart), 166–8 *passim*.
  as manager, 6, 128 n^3, 180, 183.
Schiller, Johann Christoph Friedrich von, xv, 71.
Schlegel, Johann Elias, 364.
Schloeger, Matthaeus, 395.
Schmid, Balthasar, 389 n^1.
Schmid, Ernst F., 307 n^3, 327 n^2, 392 n^1, 535 nn$^{1-3}$, 572 n^4, 608 n^1.
  C. P. E. Bach und seine Kammermusik, 518 nn$^{2, 3}$, 520 n^2.
Schmitt, Eduard, 307 n^1.
Schmitt, J. (publisher), 563.
Schmitt, (Father) Joseph, 464.
Schneider, Constantin, 98 n^3, 296.
Schneider, Max, 328 n^2, 473 n^1.
Schnerich, Alfred (publisher), 317 n^1.
Schobert, Johann, xvii, 97.
  Chamber music with clavier, *534* (Ex. 299).
  Concertos, 464.
  Keyboard sonatas, *578*, 603.
Schoenberg, Arnold, *Style and Idea*, 625 n^2, 627.
Schökel, Heinrich Peter, *J. C. Bach und die Instrumentalmusik seiner Zeit*, 483 n^1, 595 n^1.
Scholes, Percy A., 4 n^1.
Schönemann (Opera) Company, 6, 80.
Schroeter, Johann Samuel, Concertos, *485–6* (Ex. 271).
Schröter, Corona, 85.
Schubart, Christian Friedrich Daniel (poet and composer), 352, 414.
  Deutsche Chronik, on Mozart, 122.
  'Die Forelle' (Schubert), 352 n^2.
Schubert, Franz Peter
  comparisons with, 305, 365, 392, 398, 424, 566, 570, 625 and n^1, 626.
  Mozart's influence on, 626, 627, 632.
  'Gretchen am Spinnrade', 352.
  Quartet in D minor (Death and the Maiden), 616 (Ex. 340).

Schulz (Schultz), Johann Abraham Peter, *Lieder im Volkston*, *351–2* (Ex. 155).
Schumann, Georg, 527 n[3].
Schumann, Robert, 356.
Schünemann, Georg, 329 n[1], 536 nn[2, 3].
Schwann, W. B. S., 66 n[4].
Schweitzer, Anton, 67–72 *passim*, 74, 76, 84, 86.
  Alceste, *67–71* (Exx. 39–41), 127.
  Rosemunde, 71, 127.
Schwickert, 450.
Schwindl, Friedrich, *429*, 464.
Scott, Marion, 357, 358 n[1], 553 n[3].
Sebastiani, Franz Joseph (librettist), *Das Serail, oder die unvermuthete Zusammenkunft . . .*, 128.
Seckendorff, Freiherr von, 85.
Sedaine, Michel Jean (librettist)
  Blaise le Savetier (Philidor), 208.
  Déserteur, Le (Monsigny), 209–11.
  Félix, ou l'Enfant trouvé (Monsigny), 216.
  Jardinier et son seigneur, Le (Philidor), 208.
  Richard Coeur de Lion (Grétry), 220–1.
Seiffert, Max, 296 n[3], 511 n[1], 527 n[2], 529 n[5].
Senesino, *see* Bernandi.
Senn, Walter, 118 n[1], 128 nn[3, 4], 507 n[1].
Serenade (cf. Divertimento), *504–6*.
Serenata (festa teatrale), 24, 505.
Serpent, in ensembles, 572 and n[3].
Šetková, Dana, 471 n[1].
Seufzer, 379, 408, 457.
Seyler, Friederike Sophie (librettist), *Hüon und Amanda*, 167 n[3].
Shadwell, Thomas, 154.
Shakespeare, William, 358.
  Comedy of Errors, The, 266.
  Hamlet, 175.
  Midsummer Night's Dream, A, 258.
Sharp, Cecil, 264.
Sheridan, Richard Brinsley, 265–7 *passim*.
  The Duenna (Linley), 261.
Shield, William, 263–4, *265*, 268–9.
  Operas
    Farmer, The, 265.
    Fontainebleau, 265.
    Poor Soldier, The, 265.
    Robin Hood, 265.
    Rosina, 265.
    Travellers in Switzerland, The, 265.
    Woodman, The, 265.
  Songs, 340, 341 n[1].
Siderits, J., 547 n[6].
Sieber (publisher), 447 n[1].
Siege of Gibraltar, The (marionette spectacle), 179–80.
Siegmund-Schultze, Walther, 564 n[1].
Sievers, Gerd, 98 n[1].
Simon, Edwin J., 494 n[1], 578 n[2].
Simpson, John (publisher), 378, 528.

Singende Muse an der Pleisse, Die, 345.
Singspiele, xvi, xviii, 3, *6–7*.
  German, 67, 76, *79–89*, 353.
  Haydn's, 195.
  Mozart's, 126–8 *passim*, 159, *see also Die Zauberflöte*.
  Viennese, 80, 89–97, 129, 147, 149, 168, 169.
Sitt, Hans, 535 n[1].
Smethergell, William, 430.
Smith, John, 536 n[1].
Smith, John Christopher (father), *Paradise Lost*, 325.
Smith, John Christopher (son), 260.
  Fairies, The, 258.
  Tempest, The, 258.
Sokolovsky, 273; *see also Miller-magician*.
Soldan, Kurt, 474 n[3].
Soler, Antonio
  Keyboard sonatas, 579 (Ex. 317).
  Quintets for organ and strings, 532–3.
Somfai, László, 467 n[3], 554, 560 n[4]; *see also* Bartha, Dénes.
Sondheimer, Robert, 419 n[1].
Song
  Austria, 352–7.
  England, 337–41, 357–9.
  France, 341–4.
  Germany, 344–52.
  Haydn's, 355–9.
  Mozart's, 359–63.
Spaeth, Anton, 504.
Spitta, Philipp, 520 n[1].
Spontini, Gasparo Luigi Pacifico, 226.
Stadelmann, L., 484 n[1].
Stadler, Anton, 165, 493 n[1], 571–2.
Stadler, Maximilian, 540 n[2], 542 n[1], 607.
Stählin, Jakob von, 270.
Stamitz, Anton, 438 (Ex. 211 (iii)), 509.
  Concertos, 462 (Ex. 240).
  Duets, 545.
  Trio in E flat, Op. 4, no. 1, 551.
Stamitz, Carl, 546 n[1].
  Concertos, *461–2* (Exx. 238–9), 464, 465, 475.
  Divertimenti, 509.
  Symphonies, 414, *418–19* (Ex. 199).
  Trios, Op. 14, *524*.
Stamitz, Johann, 370, 394, *407–8*, 412, 414, 423, 430, 456, 613, 620.
  and La Pouplinière, 224–5, 230, 423.
  Concertos, *457–8*, 460, 464.
    Flute in D, *457* (Ex. 231).
    Oboe in C, 457–8 (Ex. 232).
  Divertimenti, 509.
  Symphonies, *408–11* (Exx. 188–91), 417, 419, 422, 429, 430.
  Trio sonatas, *523–4* (Ex. 294).
Standfuss, J. C., 85 n[1].
  Der lustige Schuster, 80–1 (Ex. 46).

INDEX

Stanislas, King of Poland, 221.
Stanley, John, 325.
   Cantatas, 364.
   Concertos, 434.
   Sonatas, 520–1.
Starhemberg, Count, 204.
Starzer, Josef, 24, 91 n[3], 561.
   Divertimenti, 508 (Ex. 284), 556 (Ex. 308).
Stauder, Wilhelm, 6 n[1], 88 n[1].
Steffan, Josef Anton
   Concertos, *471–2*, 473.
   Songs, *354–5* (Ex. 156).
   Sammlung deutscher Lieder, 353 and n[2].
Steglich, Rudolf, 393 n[1], 394 n[1], 570 n[1], 584 n[2], 585 n[1], 607 n[1].
Stein, Fritz, 429 n[1], 484 n[3].
Stein, Johann Andreas, 353 n[3], 578.
Stephanie, Gottlieb, 141–3 *passim*.
   as librettist, *Der Schauspieldirektor* (Mozart), 149.
Stephenson, Kurt, *Die musikalische Klassik*, 395 n[3].
Sternfeld, Frederick W., xix, xx, 169 n[1], 475 n[1].
Steves, H. H., 474 n[2].
Stierle, Franz Xaver, 126.
Stile antico, in church music, 289, 291.
Stoll, Anton, 316.
Stollbrock, L., 294 n[4].
Storace, Nancy, 65, 266, 269.
Storace (Sorace), Stefano, 265–6.
Storace, Stephen, 260–4 *passim*, *265–8*, 270.
   Operas and After-pieces
      Cherokee, The, 267.
      Dido, Queen of Carthage, 267.
      Equivoci, Gli, 266.
      Haunted Tower, The, 266.
      No Song, No Supper, 267–8, 269.
      Pirates, The, *266–7* (Ex. 129).
      Siege of Belgrade, The, 267, *268* (Ex. 130).
      Sposi malcontenti, Gli, 266, 267 n[1].
   Songs, 341 (Ex. 150).
      Eight Canzonetts . . ., 341 n[1].
   Storace's Collection of Original Harpsichord Music, 470.
Strauss, Richard
   Salome, 241.
Strinasacchi, Regina, 541.
Strunk, Oliver, 600 n[1].
   Source Readings in Music History, 201 n[3], 202 n[1], 230 n[1].
Sturm, Christoph Christian (poet), C. P. E. Bach's settings, 347–8.
Sturm und Drang, xv, 345, 515, 556, 595, 620.
Sturzenegger, Richard, 445 n[3], 446 n[1].
Subirá, José, 285 nn[1, 3], 287 n[1].
   Historia de la música teatral . . ., 282, 284.
Suchalla, Ernest, 392 n[1].

Sullivan, Arthur Seymour, 269.
Sumarokov, Alexander Petrovich (librettist), *Tsefal i Prokris* (Araja), 271.
Sumerau, Freiherr von, 175.
Süssmayr, Franz Xaver, 316 n[1], *317–19*.
Swedenborg, Emanuel, xix.
Swieten, Baron Gottfried von, 333–4.
   and C. P. E. Bach, 386, 390–2 *passim*.
   and Mozart, *315*, *540*.
   as librettist
      Schöpfung, Die (Haydn), *334*.
      Sieben Worte, Die (Haydn), 333.
Sychra, Antonín, 404 n[2].
Sykora, Václav Jan, 594 n[2].
Symphonie concertante, 366, 419, 420, *425*, 439, 441 and n[1], *477–81*, 482, 484.
Symphonie périodique, 425–6.

Tagliapetra, Giovanni, 506 n[2].
Tagliarini, Luigi F., 110 n[1], 118 n[2].
Tagliazucchi, Giovanni Pietro, 2, 33.
Tartini, Giuseppe
   Concertos, 441, *442–3*, 444, 446, 489.
      Violin in E, 442 (Ex. 212).
      Violin in G, 443 (Ex. 213).
   Solo sonatas, 519.
   Symphonies, 378.
   Arte dell' arco, L', 444.
   De' prinzipi dell' armonia, 442 n[4].
   Trattato di musica . . ., 442 n[4].
Tasso, Torquato, *Gerusalemme liberata*, 181.
Tchaikovsky, Peter
   on Mozart, 570–1.
   Queen of Spades, 211.
   Symphony No. 4, 277.
Telemann, Georg Philipp, 330, 389 and n[2].
   Tag des Gerichts, Der, 328.
   Songs, 345.
Tenducci, G. F., 127.
Tenschert, Roland, 100 n[1].
Terradellas, Domenico, 32.
Terrasson, Abbé Jean, *Sethos . . .*, 168.
Terry, Charles Sanford, *J. C. Bach*, 46 n[1], 544 n[2].
Teyber, Franz, 94.
Thayer, Alexander W., *Ludwig van Beethovens Leben*, 628 n[1].
Theatres
   Aranjuez
      Court, 281.
   Esterház
      Marionette, 177, 179.
      Schloss, 172–3.
   London
      Covent Garden, 257–67 *passim*, 325.
      Drury Lane, 257–69 *passim*, 325.
      Haymarket (King's), 265–6, 621.
      Haymarket (Little), 257, 263.
      Ranelagh Gardens, 262.

Theatres (*cont.*):
  Sadler's Wells, 262.
  Madrid
    del Principe, 283 *bis*.
  Milan
    Regio Ducale, 110.
  Moscow, 273.
  Naples, 4.
  Palermo, 4.
  Paris
    Comédie Française, 206.
    Comédie Italienne, 206–8 *passim*.
    Opéra (Académie Royale), 203, 224–5, 231, 244.
    Opéra Comique (de la Foire St. G.), 206.
  Pressburg (Bratislava)
    Erdödy, 180, 181 n[1].
  St. Petersburg, 270–5 *passim*.
  Venice
    S. Benedetto, 109 n[2].
  Vienna
    Burg, 91, 173, 229.
    Kärntnertor, 95.
    Leopoldstadt, 96.
    National, 353 n[2].
    auf der Wieden, 96, 163, 166–7, 254.
Theodor, Johann, Prince Bishop of Freising, 432.
Thomson, James, *The Seasons* (Haydn), 334–5.
Thomson, William, *Orpheus Caledonius*, 340.
Tiersot, Julien, *Histoire de la chanson populaire en France*, 200–1.
Tillet, du, 229.
Tirso da Molina, Gabriel Tellez (dramatist), 160.
  El burlador de Sevilla, 154, 155 n[1], 158 n[3].
Toeschi, Carl Joseph (Carlo Giuseppe)
  Divertimenti, 509.
  Flute Concerto in F, 460 (Ex. 237).
  Quintet in F, Op. 3, no. 6, 567.
  Symphonies, *414–15*, 416, 417, 423.
    in G, 408 (Ex. 188).
    Symphonie périodique no. 26, 415 (Ex. 195).
Tonadilla escénica, 282, *284–7*.
Tonkünstler-Societät, Vienna, 327.
Torelli, Federico, *Orfey i Evredika*, 280.
Torelli, Giuseppe, 434, 435.
Torrefranca, Fausto, 375–6, 575 n[3], 581.
  G. B. Platti e la sonata moderna, 441 n[3], 581 n[3].
Tost, Johann, 562.
Töttcher, H., 457 n[3].
Tovey, Donald Francis
  Essays and Lectures on Music, 618, 619.
  Essays in Musical Analysis, 393, 444, 475, 612.

Traetta, Tommaso, xviii, 8, 32, 33, 43, 45, 173, 271.
  Operas, 33, *38–42*, 58, *229–30*.
    Antigona, 38, 42 (Ex. 23).
    Armida, 42, 229.
    Ifigenia in Tauride, 38, 40–2 (Exx. 21 (ii)–22), 199, 230.
    Sofonisba, La, 38, 39–40 (Ex. 21 (i)).
Tragédie lyrique, xviii, 97, *223–6*, 227–30 *passim*.
Travaglia, Pietro and Francesco Puttini (librettists), *La vera costanza* (Haydn), 178–9.
Trediakovsky, Vasily Kirillovich, 270.
Tricklir, Johann Balthasar, 456.
Trio sonatas, 521–31.
Trios for strings or wind, 548–52.
Trutovsky, Vasily Fedorovich, 274.
Tschoudi, Baron de (librettist), 241.
  Echo et Narcisse (Gluck), 239.
Tutenberg, Fritz, 57 n[4].
  Die Sinfonik Johann Christian Bachs, 393 n[1], 427 n[1].
Tyson, Alan, 554 n[3].

Ulbrich, Maximilian, 94.
Uldall, Hans, *Das Klavierkonzert der Berliner Schule*, 452 n[1], 455 n[2], 456 n[1], 466 n[4].
Umlauf, Ignaz
  Bergknappen, Die, *91–4* (Exx. 57–60), 353 n[2].
  Souliers mordorés, Les, 250.
Unverricht, Hubert, 551 nn[4,5].
Upmeyer, W., 524 n[2], 533 n[1].
Uttini, Francesco, 8.

Vadé, Jean Joseph (librettist), *Les Troqueurs* (Dauvergne), 203–4.
Vančura, Ernest, 274 and n[3].
  Ivan Tsarevich, *276–7* (Ex. 132).
Van den Borren, Charles, 575 n[3].
Van den Bosch, Pieter, 481.
Van der Straeten, Edmond, *History of the Violoncello*, 519 n[4].
van der Veen, J., 76 n[3].
Vaňhal, Jan (Johann Baptist Wanhal), 425, 426, 502.
  Concertos, 470–1 (Exx. 251–3).
  Sonatas, 531.
  Symphonies, 403–5 (Exx. 183–4, 186).
Varesco, Abbate Giambattista (librettist)
  Idomeneo (Mozart), 133, 134.
  Oca del Cairo, L' (Mozart), 148.
Vauxhall Gardens, 337 and n[1], 338 nn[1,3], 339 n[2].
Vélez de Guevara, Luis, 65.

INDEX

Venier (publisher), 381, 394, 417 n[1], 558 n[2].
  Sinfonie da vari autori, 368–9, 379, 398–9.
Verazi, Mattia, 2.
Verchaly, André, 404 n[2].
Verdi, Giuseppe
  Aida, 234.
  Rigoletto, 157.
Vestris, Maria Caterina, 239.
Village Opera, The, 260.
Villati, Leopoldo de, 2.
Villeneuve, Louise, 159.
Vinci, Leonardo, 291, 368, 374.
Viotti, Giovanni Battista, Violin Concertos, *446–7* (Exx. 216–17), 489.
Vitali, M., 575 n[1].
Vivaldi, Antonio, 389, 392, 420, 453.
  Concertos, 378, 390, 434–6 *passim*, 440–2 *passim*, 448, 451, 613.
'Vo pole bereza stoyala' (folk-song), 277, 280.
Vogler, Abbé Georg Joseph, *463*.
  Pièces de musique, Op. 4, 531.
Volek, Tomislav, 163.
Voltaire, François Marie Arouet de, xv, 207, 208, 216, 230, 324.
Vrieslander, Otto, 347 n[1].

Wagenseil, Georg Christoph, xvi, 2, 471, 504 n[1].
  Concertos, *466–7*, 468, 469, 471, 473, 491.
  Divertimenti, 509.
  Keyboard sonatas, *593–4*.
  Mass in G, *295* (Ex. 138).
  Oratorio, *Redenzione*, 327.
  Symphonies and Overtures, 395, *397–99* (Exx. 180–1), 400–1, 403, 412, 525.
Wagner, Richard, 44, 227.
  Götterdämmerung, Die, 243.
  Lohengrin, 234.
  Meistersinger, Die, 195.
  Parsifal, 236.
  Tristan und Isolde, 196, 564.
Wahr, Karl, 175.
Waisenhauskirche, Vienna, 307.
Walsegg, Count Franz von, 317.
Walsh (publisher), 521 n[5], 529 and n[4], 575–6.
Walter, Friedrich, 71 n[5].
Walter, Horst, 551 n[4].
Walther, Johann Gottfried, *Musicalisches Lexicon*, 441.
Walther, Kurt, 527 n[3], 546 n[3].
Weber, Aloysia *see* Lange, Aloysia.
Weber, Carl Maria von, *Der Freischütz*, 219.
Weber, Constanze, *see* Mozart, Constanze.
Weber, Hans, *Das Violoncellkonzert . . .*, 459 n[2].
Weber, Josefa, *see* Hofer, Josefa.

Weckler (publisher), 581 n[2].
Węcowski, Jan, 431 n[1].
Weidinger, Anton, 476.
Weigl, Joseph, 94.
Weinmann, Alexander, 98 n[1].
Weiser, Anton, *Die Schuldigkeit des ersten Gebotes* (with Mozart), 98.
Weiskern, Friedrich Wilhelm, 107, 203.
Weisse, Christian Felix, 80, 81, 85, 86, 94.
Weissenwolf, Countess Maria Anna von (Countess Nicolaus Esterházy), 179.
Welcker (publisher), 381 and n[2], 403 n[1], 429, 457, 484, 485 n[1].
Wellesz, Egon, 295 n[3].
Wendling, Dorothea, 127, 136.
Wendling, Elisabeth, 136.
Wendling, Johan B., 463.
Wendschuh, Ludwig, *Über Joseph Haydns Opern*, 180 n[4].
Werner, Eric, 172 n[1].
Werner, Franz Gregor, 301.
Werner, J., 603 n[1].
Werner, Theodor W., 86 n[1].
Wertheim, G., 454 n[2].
Wesley, Charles, 487.
Westrup, Jack A., 165 n[1].
Wieland, Christoph Martin, 67, 71, 72.
  Dschinnistan . . ., 168.
  Oberon, 167 n[3].
  as librettist,
    Alceste (Schweitzer), 67, 71.
    Rosemunde (Schweitzer), 71, 127.
Wien-Claudi, Hertha, 347 n[1].
Wiener Diarium, 175, 176.
Wilder, Victor (librettist), *L'Oie de Caire* (Constantin), 148 n[5].
Winckelmann, Johann Joachim, xv, xix, 43, 226.
Winter (publisher), 586.
Winter, Peter, 509.
Wirth, Helmut, 195.
Witvogel (publisher), 443.
Wojciechowski, J., 461 n[1].
Wolf, Eugene K., 623 n[1].
Wolff, Hellmuth Christian, 530 n[4].
Wollheim, Heinrich, 494 n[1].
Worgan, John, 581.
Wotquenne, Alfred, *Thematisches Verzeichnis der Werke von C. P. E. Bach*, 453, 518 n[2].
Wranitzky, Paul, *Oberon, König der Elfen*, 97, 167.
Württemberg, Charles Eugene, Duke of, 1, 2, 585.
Wyzewa, Théodore de, and Georges de Saint-Foix, *W. A. Mozart*, 119 n[2], 569 n[3], 630 n[1].

Yaguzhinsky, Count, 274.

Zarzuela, *282–4*, 285.
Zchinsky-Troxler, E., *Gaetano Pugnani*, 381 nn[2, 3], 444 n[2].
Zeno, Apostolo, 8, 11, 325.
Ziegler, B., *P. von Camerloher*, 432 n[1].
Zimmermann, Anton, 476.
Zimmermann, Dominikus, xviii.
Zingarelli, Nicolò Antonio, 363.
   Armida, 364.

Zinzendorf, Count, 160.
Zirnbauer, H., 524 n[4].
Zorin, Dementy Alekseyevich, *Pererozhdenie* (The Rebirth), 273.
Zumsteeg, Johann Rudolf, 79, 89, 349.
   Armida, 89.
   Zalaor, 89.